To be modern may mean many different things,
Europeans "modernity" suggested a new form c
activities, people, attitudes, and values all playe(
panoramic new history offers a magisterial and
the ties between modernity and bourgeois life, arguing that they can be best
understood not in terms of the rise and fall of social classes, but as features of
a common participation in expanding and thickening "networks of means"
that linked together distant energies and resources across economic, political,
and cultural life. Exploring the different configurations of these networks
in England, France, and Germany, he shows how their patterns gave rise to
distinctive forms of modernity in each country and shaped the rhythm and
nature of change across spheres as diverse as politics, money and finance, gender
relations, morality, and literary, artistic, and musical life.

JERROLD SEIGEL is Kenan Professor of History Emeritus, New York
University. His previous publications include *The Idea of the Self* (Cambridge,
2005), *Bohemian Paris* (1986), and *Marx's Fate* (1978).

Modernity and Bourgeois Life

Society, Politics, and Culture in England, France, and Germany since 1750

Jerrold Seigel

CAMBRIDGE
UNIVERSITY PRESS

CAMBRIDGE UNIVERSITY PRESS
Cambridge, New York, Melbourne, Madrid, Cape Town,
Singapore, São Paulo, Delhi, Mexico City

Cambridge University Press
The Edinburgh Building, Cambridge CB2 8RU, UK

Published in the United States of America by Cambridge University Press,
New York

www.cambridge.org
Information on this title: www.cambridge.org/9781107666788

© Jerrold Seigel 2012

First published 2012

Printed in the United Kingdom at the University Press, Cambridge

A catalogue record for this publication is available from the British Library

Library of Congress Cataloguing in Publication data
Seigel, Jerrold E.
  Modernity and bourgeois life : society, politics, and culture in England, France and
  Germany since 1750 / Jerrold Seigel.
    pages cm
  Includes bibliographical references and index.
  ISBN 978-1-107-01810-5 (hardback) – ISBN 978-1-107-66678-8 (paperback)
    1. Middle class–Europe, Western–History.   2. Social classes–Political aspects–Europe,
  Western–History.   3. Civilization, Modern.   I. Title.
  HT690.E73S57   2012
  305.5'5094–dc23
  2011049200

ISBN 978-1-107-01810-5 Hardback
ISBN 978-1-107-66678-8 Paperback

CONTENTS

ILLUSTRATIONS

PREFACE

In my second semester of graduate school, the professor who soon became my main advisor – a deeply serious man with a broad streak of playful irony – assigned me the boggling task of regaling the following week's seminar with ten minutes of reflection on the question: "What is the bourgeoisie?" How I sought to meet his challenge is not worth recalling, but in many ways I have been trying to face up to it ever since. Among the disparate subjects I have attempted to teach and write about over the years, a number turn out to have been linked together by a not-always-evident effort to chisel out bits and pieces of an answer: Karl Marx, French bohemianism, the history of modern thinking about the self, even the career of Marcel Duchamp. Except that I have come to think that we do better to recast the question, replacing its traditional nominative formulation with ones that are more adjectival and historical: why does the modifier "bourgeois" bear a range of meanings that often apply to people, things, actions, and ideas outside the social group it is supposed to designate? What does this array of meanings tell us about the link often posited between bourgeois life and modernity? How does this relationship between the things we call bourgeois and those we call modern alter as both of its components change over time? These questions are not always explicitly addressed in *Modernity and Bourgeois Life* – the Introduction sets out the ones that are – but they outline the historical and analytical space the book attempts to explore.

I am pretty sure my teacher would not have anticipated that a project with such an agenda would have operated, as this one does, with the notion of networks – more specifically "networks of means" – at its center. I admit to a certain unhappiness with what may seem to be close ties between my use of the term "network" and its ubiquity in contemporary discussions of all kinds, but my discomfort is lightened by the conviction that historians like everyone else are bound to have their thinking shaped by the world around them; and I accept, even welcome, Max Weber's demonstration that the necessity to operate from within some distinct perspective is a source of illumination as well as of limitation, since we are creatures who can make sense of our vast and complex world only by approaching it (responsibly, to be sure) from some particular point of view. Had I been able to substantiate the basic intuitions on which this book rests ten years ago, when I first spoke about "networks of means" in public (more accurately in a small invitational seminar), I might be able to argue a stronger case for my independence from its current omnipresence, but there is little to be gained by making much of this now. I hope, all the same, that readers may find in my way of giving substance to what can be a highly malleable and banal notion a capacity to illuminate some worthwhile matters and issues.

Over the years of working on this book I have been aided by the help and support, and sometimes by the strictures and skepticism, friends and colleagues have offered in regard to it. Among those who have listened and questioned, or who have read proposals or chapters in earlier versions, I need particularly to thank Carl Schorske, Philip Nord, Isser Woloch, Theodore Koditschek, Laura Lee Downs, John Gillis, Suzanne Marchand, Robert Seltzer, Mitchell Cohen, Jacques Revel, Gilles Pecout, Edward Berenson, Herrick Chapman, Samuel Moyn, Andrew Sartori, and (his words all the more resonant in my head because he is, alas, no longer here to add to them) Tony Judt. I owe debts of both a similar and a different kind to three anonymous readers for Cambridge University Press and to Thomas Laqueur, all of whom firmly and rightly insisted that an earlier and much longer text had to be subjected to major surgery before it could see the light, and to Louis Sass, who not only read some early chapter drafts but helped me through the difficulties of recognizing the path I had to take at that moment. My attempt to follow that path has been much aided by the patient good sense and critical attention of my Cambridge editor, Michael Watson. Alison Walker's careful and attentive copy-editing added clarity and accuracy to both the text and the notes. Some of my work was carried out while I was supported by a Gugggenheim Fellowship in 2004–05, and during the months I very happily spent at the Luguria Study Center, Bogliasco, in 2006. As with all my books, I do not see how I could have completed this one without my wife Jayn Rosenfeld's wonderful ability to provide sympathy and sustenance of all kinds while never letting me take myself too seriously.

1 INTRODUCTION: ENDS AND MEANS

Modernity, money, networks of means

Toward the middle of the nineteenth century many people agreed – not always happily – that Western Europe was giving birth to a new form of life, often called modern, in which bourgeois activities, people, attitudes, and values all played a large role. How should we understand the relations between this European modernity and the bourgeois life that was so important an element in it? The question is a thorny one for many reasons, first because what people meant by the two terms is far from clear.

"Modern" was an uncertain notion partly because it was not a new one, in use to describe present or recent times at least from the sixteenth century, and partly because the things to which it was applied differed from place to place, not least in the three large countries whose nineteenth-century transformations were most striking: England, France, and Germany. A similar uncertainty surrounded the range of phenomena designated by "bourgeois," or rather by the French term and its German and English counterparts, *bürgerlich* and middle class. The social formations called up by the three were kindred but also distinct, and each term reflected a particular historical experience. A bourgeois was originally a town-dweller, especially one who possessed some special status or privileges; a *Bürger* was a townsperson too but the German word also meant a citizen, a difference that would be of some moment in the history of both; as for "middle class," it was the least specific of the set, and unlike the others never designated a legally defined group. The shifting and uncertain meanings of both "modern" and "bourgeois," combined with the generations of controversy that have accumulated around each, make attempting to start out with a precise definition of either a bootless task. But the links often posited between them suggest that we may be able to move toward a better understanding by considering them together.

For reasons I will come to later it was "bourgeois" rather than its cousins in other languages that gained currency as the nineteenth century went on; as it did its original reference yielded to a broader range of meanings, calling up a species of society or a form of life not limited to well-off urbanites, however prominent they remained within it. Marx was an early proponent of this usage, and he would be partly responsible for its spread, but it was already in the air when he began to develop it in the 1840s. That the regime set up following the brief revolution of July, 1830, in Paris acquired the label "Bourgeois Monarchy" encouraged people to couple the adjective to other nouns as well; in addition, the term's broadening sense owed much to the common German employment of *bürgerliche Gesellschaft* to translate the Latin phrase *societas civilis*, civil society, meaning an organized form of social life governed by laws. Marx's great predecessor G. W. F. Hegel had given the German term greater range and substance in his political lectures and writings, especially *The Philosophy of Right* elaborated in the 1820s; here *bürgerliche Gesellschaft* designated the specifically modern form of social existence in which individuals satisfy many of their needs through market exchanges, at once enjoying the opportunities and suffering from the limitations such relations entail. Hegel's *bürgerliche Gesellschaft* was not ruled by bourgeois, however. His work reflected the situation of Prussia, where he lived and taught, and where landed aristocrats long retained far better access to political authority than *Bürger*. Marx, however, convinced that the latter's needs and interests determined the form and direction of existence in the present, and taking advantage of the term's ambiguity in German, shifted its meaning toward "bourgeois society," making class power the determining element of modern social life. To him "bourgeois society" was a deeply significant but temporary historical configuration, powered by commodity exchange and wage labor, and ruled by the capitalist owners of the means of production, whose actions had the unintended effect of preparing the way for a more just and egalitarian form of life to come, grounded in worker-based socialism. This better world would fully inherit the advances humanity owed to bourgeois efforts, however: the development of new and more powerful productive forces, the liberation of human energies, the elaboration of global interchange in every sphere, the revelation of previously hidden truths about individual and social life, and the possibility of fulfilling both material and more broadly human needs.

The residue of Marx's powerful analysis of nineteenth-century modernity, combined with the failure of his most cherished predictions, continues both to inspire and to weigh on attempts to understand the historical role of bourgeois people, activities, and values. Many features of the world we inhabit in the twenty-first century are ones he and other nineteenth-century observers rightly associated with bourgeois doings and aspirations: the urbanization and globalization of life, the ascendancy of market relations, the opening of new paths and opportunities for individuals, the expansion of education, the extension of political rights; all of them, now as then, combined with a litany of associated discontents, chief among them persisting social inequality. When we look back on the ways this world has come about, however, we find much that Marx and many of his contemporaries did not grasp or foresee.

First, historical research in the past half-century has cast much doubt on earlier convictions about the political role once assigned to bourgeois people as a class. Individual bourgeois exercised certain kinds of power to be sure (as they still do), but attempts to identify particular regimes with some generalized middle-class interest separate from others have become increasingly difficult to maintain, and the governments that did most to foster economic advance, expand education, and secure property rights often had a markedly non-bourgeois character. Formerly it was common even for non-Marxists to regard the great French Revolution that began in 1789 as in some way the work of the bourgeoisie. A well-known French book bore the title *Les Bourgeois conquerants*, "the conquering bourgeois"; the textbook most widely used in European history courses in the United States in the 1950s (when this writer first studied the subject) confidently summed up the results of reforms and regime changes in the early 1830s as "The Triumph of the West-European Bourgeoisie." These certainties are much diminished now. Writers have emphasized that the Revolution of 1789 took place in a country whose economy was still largely untouched by modern industry and remained in many ways closer to what it had been in 1650 than to what it would be in 1914, that many bourgeois were among the privileged groups the Revolution displaced ("pillars of the regime," as Pierre Goubert put it, and – with exceptions – quite "at home inside it"), and that the Revolution probably did as much to retard French economic development as to further it. Even at the next revolution in 1830 the country's economic life still went on almost wholly inside structures already in place a century earlier. The main bourgeois supporters of the government set up then were bankers, financiers, office holders, and landowners much like those who had flourished in a cozy relationship to the old monarchy, and recent historians have offered good reasons to understand the regime as one dominated by what people in the time called "notables" (a term to which I will return below) rather than bourgeois. Restrictive electoral laws denied many (even most) merchants, manufacturers, and professionals the right to vote or hold office, and some among them were important contributors to the opposition and agitation that helped produce the return of revolution in 1848, out of which emerged not a more broadly bourgeois government but the authoritarian Bonapartist Second Empire. During its two decades of life the Empire fostered railroad building, urban reconstruction, and industrial investment, but bourgeois groups often opposed these measures, fearful that their own vested interests would be damaged or that the state would gain too much power.[1]

Were political revolution a response to the needs of a developing modern bourgeoisie, then it "should" have occurred in England, the most highly developed commercial society and first home of machine industry, rather than in France; none ever did. The putative British counterpart to the establishment of the French "Bourgeois Monarchy," the Reform Bill of 1832 that extended suffrage to many middle-class men in the ballooning northern industrial cities, was largely arranged and managed by Whig grandees, and it shored up the ground on which aristocratic dominance in British politics persisted through most of the nineteenth century. Save for the few months following March, 1848, no German territorial state before 1918 enjoyed (or suffered) a government that can persuasively be said to have been put in place or managed by people from the *Bürgertum* (to be sure independent cities were still controlled by their burgher inhabitants, although they had less autonomy than during the Middle Ages, middle-class influence was greater in some regions – notably the southwest – than in others, and between

1860 and 1873 Austria was in part an exception, shaken up by a series of military defeats). The regime that oversaw the most powerful wave of German economic expansion and provided the legal framework for a modern civil society was the Bismarckian *Reich* that crumbled in World War I. It had been established by force of arms and as part of the Prussian minister's campaign to defeat liberal *Bürger* politicians between 1862 and 1871, and it gave much support to aristocratic *Junker* interests and values, particularly after 1878, when Bismarck jettisoned the policies that had partially reconciled him with liberals in the new state's first years. Later on I will give reasons for rejecting claims by certain historians that, all the same, the Bismarckian regime should be seen as a kind of substitute bourgeois revolution.

In all three countries the importance of such older and non-bourgeois forces eventually receded, but in situations that simultaneously fostered the growth of working-class and peasant political influence; as before, what power middle-class people could command depended on compromise with individuals and groups who bore other social identities. Those who persist in attributing effective hegemony over European politics during the nineteenth century to the bourgeoisie often do so by assuming, explicitly or implicitly, what they need to prove, namely that political power must always be the power of some distinct social class: since the long-assumed preeminence of aristocrats was being called into question, and since workers and peasants clearly did not rule, the bourgeoisie must have been at the helm. Logicians call this kind of fallacious reasoning *petitio principi*, injecting an assumed conclusion into the terms that formulate a question.[2]

Moreover, the bourgeoisie Marx and others sought to identify toward the middle of the nineteenth century subsequently lost many of its distinguishing features. Over time many and perhaps most middle-class people have moved toward ways of dressing, speaking, and interacting, and toward attitudes and beliefs in morality, politics, gender relations, and culture that contrast with the ones that marked their predecessors as recognizably bourgeois. All through the nineteenth century the staid, careful, formal behavior displayed by some bourgeois groups, intent on maintaining separate roles for men and women and fearful of moral deviations, was challenged by people no less middle-class than the others. By the time of World War I (and especially in the years just after it) signs were already widespread that "Victorian" attitudes and mores were on the way to being replaced by the more informal and open style of self-presentation and interaction, the more candid discussion of once-veiled topics, and the altered relations between the middle classes and various forms of culture, that would transform social life from the 1960s.

These observations can be summed up in a few sentences. First, modernity has some of its essential roots in the efforts and activities of a category of people we call bourgeois, but these developments have taken place under political regimes in which bourgeois power was at best sporadic and limited; only at passing moments was anything it makes sense to call the bourgeois class dominant in society and politics. Second, bourgeois were exemplary contributors to making the world modern but so were people with contrary social identities, some of whom acted as opponents of bourgeois power and interests and in the face of resistance from middle-class individuals and groups. And third, as the form of life we call modern has evolved and unfolded, the bourgeois people who contributed to it have increasingly adopted behaviors, attitudes, and beliefs that contrast with those that once seemed to define them. We need a perspective that can put all the parts of this picture into a comprehensible relationship with each other.

In what follows I seek to develop such a perspective by considering the relationship between modernity and the range of phenomena to which we attach the adjective "bourgeois" not in terms of the rise of a class, but as the emergence and elaboration of a certain "form of life." Ludwig Wittgenstein used this term (in German, *Lebensform*) to refer to a complex of social and cultural practices that develop inside some set of practical and productive activities (one example was a construction site and the people who work and interact on it), a sense broader than what the French sociologist Edmond Goblot was probably the first to call a "style of life," made up of everyday features of behavior and interaction such as dress, language, forms of politeness, and domestic arrangements. I take the term in Wittgenstein's broader sense, but the content I give it owes most to the sociologist Georg Simmel, especially his inquiries (pursued in the years around 1900) into what he called *The Philosophy of Money*. Simmel sought to grasp the significance of money as a social phenomenon, to comprehend what the predominance of money in social relations tells about human beings, and to elucidate the kinds of relations between people, things, values, and cultural practices that become paramount in a society in which connections and interactions based on money are widely diffused.

Simmel called money a "social tool," meaning that it gives people power to extend and multiply the capacities they can bring to bear in pursuing their goals or ends. It does this by providing a medium with which to compare, exchange, and combine disparate goods (in the broadest sense), often far removed from each other, and thus to establish long chains of connection through which individuals can gather together objects, resources, assets, or energies, and concentrate them at a given point. Although money is the paradigmatic instance of such a means or instrument, Simmel also regarded other social institutions as tools in this same sense, including bureaucracies, armies, legal systems, academies, and scientific societies. All of them, he observed, "become the junction of countless individual teleological sequences and provide an efficient tool for otherwise unattainable purposes"; they create or extend "chains of purposive action." An individual who is able to employ and in some degree direct any one of such instruments "possesses a collectively established tool that multiples his own powers, extends their effectiveness and secures their ends." However diverse the "content" such tools support, that is the goals or purposes people pursue through them, they resemble each other in what Simmel called their "form," their common ability to assemble and make available diffused and distant resources and assets, generating powers people would not otherwise possess. A society in which many individuals are able to call upon such tools, and through them collect and focus social resources, will possess capacities not available, and characteristics not developed, where such practices are absent or limited; when they are present many aspects of life will be shaped and colored by them. *The Philosophy of Money* is really a book about what life and social relations in such societies are like.[3]

I think considerable light can be cast on the relations between modernity and bourgeois life by thinking about both in terms of the forms and histories of such tools or implements. In order to do so we need a term that allows us to describe and specify their features more clearly (and resolve a certain confusion in Simmel's usage, to which I will come in a moment). I propose to call them "networks of means." A network of means is a chain or web of people and instruments that links distant energies and resources to each other, allowing individuals and groups to draw them together, create synergies between them, and employ the capacity they generate for some particular purpose or goal. Networks of means generate social power both for society as a whole, and for particular individuals and groupings within it. To society at large they impart an ability to accomplish otherwise unattainable things. But the power thus released flows differentially to particular individuals and groups, altering the relations among them.

It seems reasonable to distinguish three species of such networks on a large scale: 1. markets; 2. states and other administrative structures; and 3. webs of information and communication. The place of each in the development of modernity has often been recognized, but considering them all as networks of means puts their relationship in a different light. Despite the ways they differ from each other, and which will demand our attention soon enough, all are structures through which scattered people, objects, and implements can be linked together by way of "chains of purposive action," allowing the diverse elements of social power to be exchanged and gathered at some chosen point. Markets do this by tying together ways of collecting materials or resources, ways of turning them into useful or valuable commodities, and ways of exchanging and distributing the products. Modern states are complex linkages of agencies for gathering (as well as expanding) a population's assets or resources, deciding about the uses to which they should be put, and then directing them toward these ends. Networks of communication allow information, knowledge, or skills based on them to be transmitted from place to place, making them available to people who would otherwise not have access to them. Sometimes they do this by diffusing physical objects, such as newspapers or books, and sometimes simply by spreading data, for instance in the form of travelers' reports or radio broadcasts. The relations into which people are drawn by states are often more geographically limited than are markets or communicative networks, reminding us that not all distant ties involve people and resources equally remote from each other, but states have often appeared and still appear to many as foreign to everyday local experience; as a result they exemplify very well the ability of extended connections to generate social power, benefitting those who are able to share in it and threatening or hindering those who are not.

The three large-scale networks are all made up of a wide range of smaller and more contained ones. Present-day examples of these more specific formations include corporations, political parties, and professional or scientific societies. One example of such a smaller structure that was important in the emergence of modern society, and modern bourgeois life, is the putting-out system (sometimes called "proto-industry") that linked together scattered workers (most often in textiles) and their implements of work under the direction of merchants who (sometimes owning the tools, sometimes not) distributed and collected materials, providing opportunities for part-time employment and selling the products in some market. A second instance, not usually linked to the first, is what early modern people called the Republic of Letters, which bound writers and thinkers to each other and to publishers, periodicals, academies, and libraries, giving its members access to both resources and audiences not otherwise at hand.

Thinking simultaneously about these two early networks helps to point up the common features imparted to such connections by their form, despite their different kinds of content. First, such linkages allow scattered productive resources and implements to be joined together or aggregated, effecting over long distances what large-scale farms, cities, and (later) factories do inside more limited and defined spaces; by bringing people and the materials they employ effectively closer, such chains of connection generate powers to produce objects and to call up and direct energies to which more isolated individuals and groups have no access. Second, by spreading knowledge about materials available and conditions obtaining in one place to others, they enhance possibilities for comparison, competition, and improvement. Third, by providing access to materials not available locally and opportunities to engage in activities oriented toward a wider public (whether for books or thread or cloth) they offer rewards to those willing to make use of otherwise idle stretches of time, allowing for the realization of undeveloped productive potentials and offering satisfactions both material and personal that would not be available inside strictly local contexts. And fourth, they allow individuals to enter into relations with others at a distance, ties that supplement and in some degree supplant their connections with close-by people who may have greater immediate power to direct their lives. To be sure, each of these effects could be described in different and more negative terms; living and acting through extended and distant relationships brings losses as well as gains, and we will have occasion to recognize their harms as well as benefits.

The idea of a network has a certain easy appeal in the age of the Internet, when media of all kinds are viewed as being at the center of life.[4] The connection between the notion of "networks of means" and these often-observed phenomena and images needs to be acknowledged, and it will prove to be neither irrelevant nor trivial. Most of the effects of networks listed just above can be seen in the World Wide Web no less than in the putting-out system or the Republic of Letters. But the current popularity of the idea of networks requires that we distinguish the species of them being considered here from some others. The first of these are the tissues of family, kinship, friendship, and patronage to which anthropologists, sociologists, and historians all give attention. Neighborhoods or villages were the first homes of such social networks, but they have been set up in larger settings such as cities or corporations too. Some of the work that centers on these networks can offer us important methodological guidance (as I will suggest briefly later in this chapter), but in contrast to networks of means, these are personal networks, established directly between individuals or families. By contrast, the connections people establish in and through networks of means have a more impersonal quality, imparted by the role that objects, whether books or tools or raw materials and products, play in them, as the examples of the putting-out system and the Republic of Letters already suggest. Ties of kinship or patronage may become part of these more complex kinds of chains, or support people's ability to connect to them, but the resources to which such ties in and by themselves give access are much more limited. In addition, as I will try to explain in a moment, they are differently mediated, so that they do not constitute such networks by themselves. Understanding the ways connections are established and mediated within networks of means will also provide us with a basis for distinguishing them from the kinds of structures posited by advocates of action network theory, about which I will have a word to say later.

By recognizing that the frames networks of means provide to support human interactions at a distance bring similar advantages despite the different ends to which they contribute, we adopt Simmel's view that the "form" of human interactions can be no less important than their content. Physical labor and its products, resources managed through administrative structures, and knowledge and skill communicated from one social location to another, are all instances of the realized human potential that networks of means stimulate or amplify.

Perhaps it is no longer necessary to insist that information constitutes a source of power no less than material wealth and effective organization, but the long career of belief in the superiority of "hard" to "soft" resources still leaves its residue, making it worthwhile to recall the recent case made by Mary Douglas and Baron Isherwood to the effect that a chief ground of poverty is an inability to participate in the networks through which information is diffused and shared.[5] Grasping all these species of connections as sources of potency in social relations will, I think, prove to be one significant benefit of such an approach. But the most basic way in which rethinking social and cultural history around the category of networks of means introduces a new perspective is by highlighting the extent and form of distant connections as a major element in the emergence of modernity, perhaps even the central one, so that market relations, political and administrative organization, and modes of communication all constitute instances of the mediation through which such distant linkages are established, giving access to the potential they contain.

In what follows, I will try to show how focusing on the history of such networks and the particular mix of them that evolved in different places provides a basis for better understanding the chronology of modernity's emergence, the separate paths taken by individual countries (at least by the ones considered in some detail here), the peculiar physiognomy of the bourgeois or middle-class groups that developed in each, and the rhythm and direction through which crucial political, social, and cultural phenomena developed. Because networks of means have exhibited a persisting tendency to become more extended and thicker over time, partly as a result of projects undertaken by people who recognize their benefits, and partly in response to new material and technological resources (often developed in order to capitalize on those same advantages), the modernity they ground is constantly evolving, taking different forms at successive moments. We can reasonably refer both to the eighteenth century and to the period after 1850 as "modern," but the term points to different features of life in the two moments; a chief source of what made the modernity of the second one more thoroughgoing and complete, as I will argue in numerous connections in the chapters that follow, was the far more pervasive diffusion of distant relationships into every aspect of life.

Before considering these questions, I need to say something more about how networks of means are structured, about the roles played in them by people it makes sense to call bourgeois, and about the historical forms they have taken.

First, networks of means function by virtue of some "medium," an abstract criterion of interaction and exchange which can be given concrete form through some kind of institution, that is, an agreed social practice. The medium regulates access to the network, and allows flows along it to proceed; it is the role played by such abstract media that distinguishes these structures from the more directly personal networks mentioned above.[6] Such media need to be abstract because they must establish an equivalence between objects, people, or circumstances that differ in their concrete qualities and characteristics; but they must also be able to take on some concrete form or character, so that they can be possessed by or assigned to particular persons. The medium that most clearly and directly fulfills these conditions is money, the exemplary constituting element of a network of means. Money acquires this capacity not through any quality of the particular substances employed to embody it – shells, crops, particular animals or parts of them, coin, paper – but by virtue of a power human groups attribute to it, implicitly or explicitly, namely generalized exchangeability. As the universal equivalent, money allows exchanges of goods to transcend the limitations of direct barter, by providing a common standard against which all commodities can be valued. It thus allows local and distant exchanges to take place on a common basis, at once enlarging the scope of market relations and providing a means to regulate the circulation of goods. Strictly speaking, however, it is the network and not the medium that is the "tool" in the sense of being able to multiply the effective power of those who use it; otherwise Simmel could not have included bureaucracies, academies, and other instruments of collective action in his list of social tools, since none of them are media. Distinguishing between networks of means and the media that regulate them clears up this confusion, and it is for this reason that "network" is preferable to Simmel's "social tool." But it also requires the identification of the media that correspond to money in the other networks, which Simmel did not seek to do.

Specifying them is not a simple task, however, because the qualities that correspond to universal exchangeability in the other cases are less easily embodied in material forms, and less universally designated by material tokens than is the case with markets and money. All the same there is a political counterpart to the value money represents in

economic relations, namely legitimacy or legitimate authority, the criterion that regulates access to political resources, and which people
seek to attach to themselves through the relations they have with
others. Legitimacy takes a concrete form (without ceasing to be an
abstraction) when certain powers are assigned to organs of a state or
government, or when specific people or groups are accorded the right
to exercise control over them.[7] This concreteness is typically achieved
in modern states by constitutions (most often written out), which at
various times have accorded the powers just mentioned to princes
and nobles, corporate groups often called estates (in French *états*, in
German *Stände*), taxpayers at a certain level, and more recently the
whole body of citizens, originally limited to males. Although tokens
are not always required as signs of possessing this capacity, they may
be, and have appeared in such varied forms as inclusion in a register of privileged persons (for instance the "Golden Book" of medieval Venice), lists of eligible office holders or voters, birth records, tax
receipts, identity cards, or passports.

Almost universally, however, the power individuals exercise is
presumed to derive from the political entity as a whole, so that political legitimacy is the medium that warrants particular individuals to
exercise some influence over the resources that a state or population
draws from itself (as well as from others, through conquest or some
other means) by way of whatever network of relations joins it together.
In traditional monarchies kings were regarded as the embodiment of
the nation or community, and the chief source of lawful authority
(even the only one, which made possible Louis XIV's famous declaration, *L'État, c'est moi*). Rousseau made the rootedness of legitimate
state power in the whole body of people over which it is exercised still
more explicit by tracing it to the act by which a community or nation
constitutes itself as a political unit, the "social contract"; the body
of citizens then exercises power over itself by establishing the rule of
law, made effective through some particular form of government. Such
forms may be princely or aristocratic as well as democratic, depending
on circumstances, but in every case they derive their legitimacy from
the political nation as a whole. Governments or power holders may
claim legitimacy on other, less ostensibly democratic bases, notably
(as Weber listed them) tradition, which assigns authority in accord
with arrangements handed down from the past, rationality, which
purports to effect a proper management of a state and its resources,

and "charisma," the personal quality that identifies certain people as worthy of being followed by others. In each of these cases, however, the principle that establishes power as legitimate regulates access to the resources generated by the interactions of some recognizable community or body of people.[8]

As in the case of politics, identifying the vehicle that allows for and regulates flows inside communicative networks is less simple than with money and market relations. In general, however, this medium can be specified as (the term has been employed by Jürgen Habermas) "communicative competence," the ability to send and receive particular kinds of messages. Exercising this competence may require some material implement as a precondition, such as a telegraph key and sounding device, a radio, or a computer with some kind of connection to others. But in operative networks such technical means are never sufficient without some cultural attainment: spoken or written proficiency in a language; understanding less common signs such as codes or ciphers (semaphoric signals or Morse dots and dashes); or the ability to use a specialized idiom, such as Latin, legalese, mathematics, or the terms of some learned or scientific discipline. Like legitimacy, the possession of these general means is not always signaled by a concrete token, but often it is, namely a license or certificate obtained through some test or other means of demonstrating competence at a certain level, and designating their possessors as proper or legitimate participants in and operators of the networks (as a teenager I acquired a license to be an amateur radio operator; now my colleagues and I have PhDs.). That these requirements are less substantive and less easily enforced or policed than in the other cases is one circumstance that distinguishes this species of networks from the others, with significant consequences to which I will give attention later on.

The important role that such networks play in modern life has a particular relevance to the place bourgeois people and activities have occupied in its emergence. Just as we have identified three distinct sorts of networks, so do historians and sociologists recognize three kinds of bourgeois occupations, three basic divisions that constitute the modern bourgeoisie. Of these the one most people are likely to bring to mind first consists of business people of various sorts, merchants, manufacturers, bankers, salespeople, some of them owners of their own enterprises, others managers or employees at various levels. The second category is that of administrators, including office holders, state servants, or bureaucrats, whether national or local. Officials in some private or semi-public organizations come under this rubric too. Historically these functions have sometimes been carried out by people whose aristocratic status and self-identification marked them as non-bourgeois, but even in pre-modern situations state officials were often non-noble, and government service has been a major sphere of bourgeois activity since the eighteenth century; indeed the ideal of "careers open to talent" often invoked in the era of the French Revolution and after applied especially to such occupations (as well as to military ones). The third section is made up of professionals – lawyers, notaries, doctors, architects, engineers, academics, and teachers, a group that shades off toward artists and writers, despite the resistance of some among the latter to being considered bourgeois at all.[9] These categories are not sealed containers, since certain occupations may straddle them, and individuals may move between them during their lifetimes. Some people whose activities put them in one or another of these groupings may not be bourgeois according to certain criteria, based on their level of income or wealth for instance, or aristocratic lineage, or their eventual turn to living "nobly," without working. But categorization always makes divisions sharper than they are in actual life; the aim of this one is not to distinguish bourgeois people rigidly from each other or from non-bourgeois, but to identify the range and the chief modes of bourgeois activity.

The three bourgeois categories correspond to the three species of networks, business people belonging primarily to the market, administrators to entities that organize and direct resources within a given political formation or territory, and professionals to webs of connection that transmit and regulate information, knowledge, or skill. To be sure, professionals sometimes produce and exchange material objects, but the basic qualification or competence that identifies them as practitioners can be transmitted to others without any loss to those who already possess it; indeed passing it on may heighten or amplify their status or their ability to exercise the activity in question, which persists as long as they retain the requisite physical and mental attributes. All these occupations involve participation in networks, more or less extended in space depending on surrounding conditions. The work performed in them is done in, or at least with reference to, some identifiable location, a factory or warehouse or office, a store or shop or studio, but it is mediated through some extended structure that provides a common frame of action or reference. These linkages often set limits to what individuals can do within and through them: markets impose competition and discipline, bureaucracies subject people to regulations, professions set up obligatory standards and procedures, or minimum levels of competence. But each network also makes it possible for people associated by way of it to accomplish things they could not do in separation, giving them access to connections and resources made available through it. Manual workers and other less privileged people also labor inside such configurations, but they less often draw (and before the late nineteenth century almost never drew) the same kinds of benefits from them as do people commonly characterized as bourgeois or middle class. I will return to this difference later on.

In their functions as constituents of social life, the three networks are at once mutually interdependent and independent. The interdependence takes multiple forms. Each of the media of access proper to one or another particular network operates to some degree in the others. Money is of course at work in all of them, but so in a way are considerations of legitimacy and standards of competence or skill operative in the market. Markets rely on states for the social and legal stability that allows economic interchange to proceed regularly, as well as for defense or conquest in the interest of trade, and on communicative or professional networks both for services to productive enterprises and individuals, and for the development of media of presentation and representation that help create various sorts of links to consumers (product design, displays, advertising, etc.). States rely on market exchanges (not always free of control, to be sure) to sustain their population and develop the wealth from which tax revenues come, as well as to provide other goods that governments require, such as weapons for armies; and they depend on communicative networks to diffuse information, to educate or influence citizens and officials, and to provide relevant scientific knowledge. Similarly, professional organizations rely on the market to mediate between their members and those who use their services or acquire their products, and (at least in some important cases) on states for legal enforcement of the standards set up to exclude outsiders from membership.

Thus the three networks of means fit together into an organized structure of social life, so that those who operate by way of one of them share orientations and expectations with those who function inside another that belong much less to people whose lives unfold largely outside them, such as local chiefs, artisans who make and sell goods inside a relatively closed community, or subsistence farmers. Simmel described one effect of living inside what he called "long chains of purposive action" as an "intellectualization of the will," a more mediated and abstract style of conceiving of the relations between means and ends than is fostered by an orientation to immediate circumstances, relations, and satisfactions. (What impact this intensified rationalization has on emotional life is an intricate question that will reappear in later discussions.) Although such people retain many important ties to persons and things physically close to them (families, neighbors, lands, towns), their lives do not unfold wholly inside the kinds of communities where all or most significant relations – economic, social, political familial – take place within a bounded and mutually known population.

The ground that bourgeois people in different occupations share through being both limited and empowered by their participation in such networks owes much to the formal similarities between their modes of work. By contrast, the content of what such people do in their daily lives is often diverse and sometimes in conflict. Each network generates a different and self-defining form of social power, and people even quite well furnished with one may be relatively or absolutely deprived of the others (to be sure, the opposite case often obtains too). The continued operation of the whole depends on each network fulfilling its primary function, and thus on each occupational group carrying out its particular tasks and roles, with their diverse orientations and goals. The overlapping of functions that often obtains in practice testifies to the need that every sphere of modern life has for material goods, for organized management of resources, and for knowledge and skill. But each group predominates in the office that corresponds to it, businesspeople in production and exchange, administrators in organizing and managing collective resources, professionals in developing and employing specialized understandings and abilities. The mix of separation and porousness in relations between the groups corresponds to the blend of dependence and interdependence between the functions. Given these connections, it seems reasonable to think that any satisfactory history of "the bourgeoisie" and its role in developing and preserving modern life must simultaneously be a history of the emergence and development of the complex of networks through which all these activities take place. To separate out one species of bourgeois from the others and regard it as the independent foundation on which the whole category rests, or to envision a history of "the bourgeois class" abstracted or removed from the overall configuration of the networks that constitute its frame of existence in particular times and places, is to invite misunderstanding and confusion.

From teleocracy to autonomy

So far I have considered networks of means as structures identifiable inside modern settings, and in relation to a developed form of bourgeois life. But such linkages have a much longer history. Markets, state structures, and webs of cultural interchange were already extensive, if less thickly developed, in the ancient and medieval worlds, and outside of Europe. These older networks, however, commonly had a different form, both in actuality and in the way people imagined them. I propose to designate them as "teleocratic" or "ordained," to indicate that flows through them were directed by some end outside themselves. They were characteristic of an age or a culture in which social life was thought to be ordered by a transcendent or inherited hierarchy of values and functions. By contrast modern networks may be labeled "autonomous" or "self-constituting": they operate according to rules, but ones generated – sometimes actually, sometimes only ideally or in imagination – by the interactions that take place within them. They embody the expectation Immanuel Kant famously associated with Enlightenment, that people in the present ought to be their own lawgivers.

Ordained or teleocratic networks possess a real or imagined center that directs the resources that flow through them along some predetermined path; they are regarded as disordered if the power they generate is turned toward goals or purposes that claim independence from their externally given end. If represented visually, such networks would resemble the nineteenth-century French railroad system, with all (or most all) the lines radiating out from Paris. (I shall consider later what it was about French history that stamped such a pattern on its version of what nineteenth-century people saw as a quintessentially modern phenomenon.) By contrast, self-constituting or autonomous networks contain many centers, whose relations are established and regulated by the media that connect them, and which I identified above as money, political legitimacy, and recognized forms of competence or skill. They can be likened visually to the British or German railway systems, with lines running between points of interchange in unpredictable and seemingly chaotic (but hardly ever reasonless) directions. What disorders them is the imposition of some exterior aim or purpose that restricts the uses to which their means can be put. As networks assume a more autonomous character, one of the chief goals of people who operate within them becomes to liberate those means from restrictions so that they can develop unhindered by external constraints.

The medieval Church is an example of a teleocratic network, while the early modern Republic of Letters sought to be an autonomous one. The Church was a far-flung web linking together the religious and intellectual goals and resources of people separated by great distances. Both society and individuals, particularly the clergy whose special *professio* made them its exemplary members, were able to draw power from it, but on the condition that they remained within the bounds of orthodoxy and agreed to reserve the resources brought together by the network and the energies it generated for its foreordained purpose. Groups deemed to be heretical might make use of means that were part of the official Church, for instance texts or monasteries, pilgrimage sites or bodies of clergy or teachers, but the disorder this was perceived to engender was a candidate for suppression. The Republic of Letters, by contrast, proclaimed the principle of equal access for all those who had some degree of literary or intellectual competence, rejecting (as irrelevant, restrictive, or divisive) religious and ideological criteria both for membership and for judging the uses people made of the assets to which it gave access. The means were valued for whatever contributions to knowledge and understanding they fostered; hence their use was not supposed to be constrained by some set of predetermined ends.[10] Given the persisting weight of patronage relations and the ability of prominent individuals to exercise power over cultural production, this description needs to be recognized as an ideal rather than an actual one, but the principle proved capable of maintaining itself against the exceptions.[11]

A similar contrast differentiated the economy regulated by guild or mercantilist principles from the one for which Adam Smith argued. The first was organized so as to give special protection to the position of certain individuals or groups, such as guild masters or participants in chartered companies; the second justified itself by its ability to contribute to wealth in general, an end product whose sum depended on allowing the network to operate according to principles that arose inside it. A parallel line of division exists between a polity organized so that the ends to which its combined means are devoted are supposed to be determined by tradition or the independent will of some transcendent being or power, and one where the interactions members themselves develop provide the grounds and principles for giving direction to their common life. In his *Persian Letters* Montesquieu has one of his characters say that after long seeking to "decide which government was most in conformity with reason, I have come to think that the most perfect is one that attains its purpose with the least trouble."[12] Where such a political association sets ends for itself, they are likely to be ones that support its independence and its ability to develop principles it comes to recognize as its own. One might list the goals of such a polity as "to form a more perfect union, establish justice, insure domestic tranquility, provide for the common defense, and secure the blessings of liberty to ourselves and our posterity," that is to advance mutual interchange in a legally established framework, protect the association from external threats, and assure its continued ability to determine its own direction. To be sure ancient city-states and medieval communes posited similar ends for themselves, but seldom outside a transcendent order thought to contain them, and in whose service they were expected to operate.

The passage from a form of life primarily characterized by ordained or teleocratic networks to one in which autonomous ones become increasingly prominent brought changes that it makes a certain sense to see in terms of gains and losses, however subjective and contested such judgments may be. The strength of ordained or teleocratic networks is that they infuse social interaction with a set of common values and (in theory at least) subordinate individual ambitions and desires to the fulfillment of what are commonly regarded as "higher" purposes. They impart lofty meaning to various spheres of life, and may restrict the resources invested in "base" ones. But they impede the release of productive energies that originate in unauthorized places or that cannot be harnessed to reinforce whatever system of already specified goals they are expected to serve. The strength of autonomous or self-constituting networks is that they give free rein to such activities as producing wealth, developing the organized life of a political community, or furthering the growth and elaboration of media of expression and communication that allow professions and other activities in the sphere of culture to flourish and evolve. But were they to exist in a pure form, such networks would offer no guidance either about the use to which wealth is to be put or about the modes in which it is produced, about the purposes to which political power is devoted, or the ends and consequences of intellectual, artistic, or scientific activity. The means themselves become ends: money, power, recognition. The litany of laments that arises out of such situations (which Max Weber described in terms of a shift from substantive to instrumental rationality) has long been painfully familiar to modern people: life becomes empty of worthwhile goals, individuals grow selfish, unable to recognize ends higher than their own personal interests, and feel alienated from the life around them. Marx praised the bourgeoisie as showing for the first time "what man's activity can bring about." But the other side of this release of human energy was highlighted by Dickens as the philosophy of Mr. Pancks in *Little Dorrit*: "Keep always at it, and I'll keep you always at it, and you keep somebody else always at it. There you are with the Whole Duty of Man in a commercial country."[13]

In practice, of course, such transformations are never complete. Teleocratic networks did not wholly rule over pre-modern life, nor have purely autonomous ones acquired full dominion in modern times. There are reasons for being glad that this is the case, since pre-modern societies would have been deprived of significant quantities of vitality and creativity and remained largely stagnant had all their activities been directed toward preordained goals, while the ills of modern life would be deeper and less tractable were people unable to set other ends for their activities than the mere development of the means they employ to achieve them. (At the same time, this persistence of pre-modern values and orientations also needs to be recognized, as I will argue below, as one source of some of the rigidity and narrow-mindedness for which nineteenth-century life has often been taken to task.) Indeed it remains difficult in contemporary society, as it already was earlier, to distinguish means unfailingly from ends and to privilege one over the other, since, as Simmel noted in considerable detail, there is no means employed by human beings that cannot become an end in itself, and no end that cannot become a means to some other one. Money is the most striking example of a means that easily becomes an end for many people, but power is close behind, and the history of religion is shot through with moments of recognition that the faith that ought to be an end in itself has in fact served as a means for a wide range of self-interested aims, from achieving power over others in purely secular, sometimes highly suspect ways to gaining bliss or avoiding torment (as opposed to the purer religious goal of union between individuals and God).[14] It remains true all the same that much of the history of bourgeois life and culture is a story of attempts to liberate means from ends that imposed external restrictions on them. I will argue below that pressures to eliminate such constraints increased from around the middle of the eighteenth century, generated in good part inside networks of means originally set up under teleocratic assumptions, but whose expansion and thickening offered those with access to them opportunities to use their resources in new ways, and that similar changes on a much larger scale gave a new quality to life after 1850. Bourgeois were prominent among those who seized or benefitted from such opportunities in both periods, but they were not alone.

Networks, classes, individuals

It would not be wrong to describe the overall goal of this book as to provide a new perspective on the history of the European bourgeoisie, but it is a perspective in which the bourgeoisie as a class is not the main character in the story. The history of bourgeois life is first of all the history of the evolving networks of means that provide its frames of action and development, as well as the basis of its special relationship to modernity, the kernel of its larger historical significance. This shift in perspective rests partly on the ideas sketched out so far in this Introduction, but partly too on some considerations about the role of social classes and especially of the bourgeois class in history. The topic is too large to receive adequate treatment here, but I need to say certain things about it. The first is that class remains a significant category in the discussions that follow. I have already emphasized that the power networks of means generate is social power, and that such power, however much it may benefit society as a whole, does not flow equally to everyone. Instead it often accrues chiefly to those who possess resources that facilitate access to it: money, property, connections, talents. In principle access to such social power is open and democratic in ways that the inherited or legally conveyed social position or privilege characteristic of Old Regime societies was not, but in practice it often perpetuates and even amplifies social differences.

Both the process whereby class became an important category of social thinking and some of the difficulties it created will appear in the historical accounts that follow, but I need to say a preliminary word about both these matters here. The idea of class began to replace older notions such as "rank" or "order" from late in the eighteenth century; for this shift there were a number of reasons, but for now we can content ourselves with two. First, administrators and state officials sought to divide people into categories, chiefly in order to count, oversee, or act on them in some way, reckoning up resources, trying to guide behavior, recruiting soldiers or collecting taxes. Second, politicians in search of support sought to build up a following by appealing to sections of the public on the basis of shared interests or situations, at once distinguishing those they sought to enlist from others and giving a broad reach to the category they claimed to represent. Both ways of constituting classes drew on concrete similarities between people, but both were also abstract and – willfully or not – ignored certain differences, so that those who relied on them sometimes miscalculated the effects of their actions or experienced frustration and disappointment at the results.

Among these was Marx, even though his views about classes were more subtle and complex than some of his famous formulas may suggest. Even as he declared all history to be the history of class conflict he recognized that every large social category consisted of many sub-groups with diverse and competing orientations and interests, economic, geographic, occupational, and cultural; conflicts existed within as well as between classes. But he argued that these internal dissensions would be overcome as struggles with people in other classes pushed workers or bourgeois to join together in order to act effectively against their enemies. Class conflict turned otherwise divided and fragmented classes into unified agents able to pursue common goals and participate in the drama of history's unfolding. When revolution came in 1848, however, Marx was disappointed to find that this expected fusion did not take place, at least not for the bourgeoisie, which grew increasingly fragmented as its various sections proved unable to resolve their differences; it was this failure to unite that allowed the upstart

Louis Bonaparte to triumph over his bourgeois enemies, dissolving the Assembly where bourgeois politicians sought power and proclaiming himself emperor – independent of class and party – as Napoleon III. Marx responded to this unexpected and distressing outcome, as I tried to show some years ago, with a marked inversion of his historical theory: accounting for historical events required showing how revolutionary struggle dissolved class unity instead of consummating it. Had the revolution not had this effect, bourgeois and proletarians would have confronted each other as singular agents, preparing the final struggle that would transform society. Marx continued to believe that this conflict would come someday, but he had to project it into a more distant (and as it turned out ever-receding) future.[15]

Marx failed to predict the future history of class relations but he defined the terms in which many later writers would seek to consider them: do classes possess a real or potential unity that allows them to act for themselves and against others or are they assemblages of diverse parts that never effectively cohere? With regard to the bourgeoisie in particular, three separate answers have been given. Some historians and theorists have taken positions close to Marx's, attributing an essential unity to the bourgeoisie on the ground that all its members depend somehow on those who own and run the means of production and must eventually act in accord with them; others have denied such unity altogether, pointing to multiple instances of division and opposition between, say, French bureaucrats and industrialists, German *Bildungsbürger* and *Wirtschaftsbürger* (respectively people who were bourgeois by virtue of education, or of economic position), London financiers and provincial manufacturers, urban and rural property owners, or "old" and "new" bourgeois in the same city; a third group has acknowledged many differences between various kinds of bourgeois while still arguing that class unity of a kind exists or can come about by way of participation in a common "spirit," culture, or "style of life."[16]

Although each of these positions may have something to recommend it, the objections that arise against all of them are weighty enough to require that we look beyond them. The kind of unity posited by Marx's theory is at best ephemeral or momentary and at worst merely imagined. There is no instance in modern history of a bourgeois class on a more than local scale ever acting as a unified and independent agent against other social groupings over a significant span of time; even inside particular towns and cities a variety of groups all in their way bourgeois often contended against each other. Appeals to such a unity have often served as rhetorical screens behind which some particular sub-group or self-constituted body of representatives or leaders claims a particular political goal – commercial freedom or protection, support for or opposition to a given political regime, an expanded or limited suffrage – as embodying the bourgeoisie's presumed shared interest, or its historical role or destiny. What the recurrence of such visions attests is that the bourgeoisie, like other social classes, fits the description Benedict Anderson famously gave of nations: they are "imagined communities." Classes like nations are contested categories, so that even if some particular version of how one or another might be unified succeeds temporarily in representing it, such attempts are signs of an ongoing and in the end unresolvable debate about what it is or ought to be.

To think about the bourgeoisie as essentially constituted by capitalist industry and to see those bourgeois not directly involved in business or finance as accessories or servants of capitalists made perfect sense as part of Marx's larger political and intellectual project: because he conceived the socialist future in terms of working-class control over the means of industrial production, it made sense in his schema to define the bourgeoisie in the same way. But such a perspective creates a false parallel between the two classes, radically narrowing both the social basis of bourgeois existence and (as I have been arguing) the nature of the means by which bourgeois activities generate power in social relations: political and cultural action each bring forth independent forms of social power. Failure to recognize this was one reason (together with similar impediments to the reality of working-class unity) why faith in Marx's predictions led many of his disciples along the dark and sometimes tragic paths they followed.

The opposite perspective, from which the bourgeoisie appears as a mere assemblage of groups with only accidental connections to each other, is equally unsatisfactory. It often takes the negative form of labeling as "middle class" all those who are neither peasants or workers on the one side, nor aristocrats by birth on the other. Such a notion of bourgeois identity as being neither one thing nor another seems to make a certain sense when applied to the conditions of the Old Regime, where the aristocratic power of the few and the peasant status of the great majority strongly marked social life. There is no doubt that bourgeois activities (not by themselves, however, as I will have occasion to insist) did much to put an end to this situation. But viewing social relations in this way obscures the crucial point that many people thereby categorized as middle class or bourgeois were deeply inserted into Old Regime practices and attitudes and loyal to the authorities and values that sustained them. In the singular, "middle class" implies a kind of unity that those who are named by it never possessed, whereas in the plural "middle classes" crumbles into a heap of interpretive dust. The notion of being-in-the-middle, whatever its relationship to Aristotle's claims about the moral superiority of those who incarnate the golden mean over those who embody one or the other extreme, provides no clue to what makes bourgeois life especially relevant to modernity.

The third strategy, recognizing the manifold differences between various species of bourgeois but positing a generic unity that overcomes the divisions through the development of a common culture, based on values, beliefs, or learned behavior, seems much more attractive on the surface, and it has drawn the loyalty of some distinguished historians of bourgeois life, including Adeline Daumard in France and Jürgen Kocka in Germany. But its validity is very limited. One reason is that it remains too much rooted in the Marxist assumption that real or potential unity is an essential condition of class as a social category. In the Marxist schema, where history's meaning resides in the successive replacement of one dominant class by another, culminating in the end of class differences, achieving such unity is essential since without it history cannot be driven forward. But historical development has left this scenario in tatters, and taking it off the table allows us to see that the real but less portentous power bourgeois possess does not require class unity to sustain it. To be a banker, a state official, a lawyer or doctor is sufficient in itself to be able to influence the outcome of social interactions in ways that factory workers, lower-level service employees or day laborers cannot; no process of "class formation" is required. To be sure, sharing values and attitudes, forms of dress, and preferences in leisure and culture, all provide people with grounds for mutual recognition and identification. But such commonalities do not overcome the divisions of occupation, interest, or conviction that persist inside the bourgeoisie, they merely coexist with them.[17]

In place of the debate about whether what predominates in bourgeois existence is unity or division, these considerations suggest that we need to develop an understanding that makes the modern bourgeoisie's simultaneous and enduring mix of singularity and diversity constitutive of its existence. Between the various forms of bourgeois activity there exists not any overarching unity *in potentia*, but – to adopt another famous phrase from Ludwig Wittgenstein – a "family resemblance," a kinship that ties individuals together without eliminating the tensions and conflicts that arise between them. It is such a family resemblance that constitutes what identity the bourgeoisie possesses as a social class. Its history is not the story of its development toward unity and collective agency, but of its evolution inside the three networks of means that provide the ground for its activities, and of the shifting relations that obtain both among its segments, and between them and people whose social being is constituted on a different basis.

Among recent writers who have considered social action from a similar point of view are the Italian "microhistorians," who also make networks essential elements in social relations, although they chiefly have in mind the smaller-scale webs people construct in local contexts and that do not require the abstract mediations of money or legitimacy. All the same their conclusions are close to ours. As Maurizio Gribaudi sums up the perspective that emerges from his attempt to account for the disconcerting appeal fascist ideas exercised for some Turin workers after World War I:

> One thing at least social history has finally clarified: the bases of collective existence remain incomprehensible if we do not take account of the dynamics that flow together within them as the result of the interaction of individual motives ... Only by starting from the individual level does it seem to us possible to grasp the contradictory quality and the richness of the social warp and woof, and together with it the mechanisms that generate its dynamic ... [constituted by] the interaction of all the variables of the social panorama within which the relations of individuals and groups take place.[18]

Such a perspective discloses individuals as living within their social conditions by constantly making and remaking them, giving substance and life to boundaries and rules partly by transgressing them, and

thereby revealing themselves to be at once the sources and the sub-
verters of the social limits within which they think and act. The paradoxical situation this suggests has been captured by Edoardo Grendi's
perhaps initially jarring but highly suggestive and in the end unsurpris-
ing notion of the "normal exception."[19]

To focus on networks of means as frameworks for social interchange locates human action in a space that is both constricted and
open, because networks possess both a material and an intellectual
dimension. The material dimension consists of the implements of work
and communication and the physical objects that link the points on
the web to each other, together with the constraints that develop in
and through them; the intellectual one arises because of the element
of abstraction that such interweavings require. I noted earlier in this
chapter that networks of means require some abstract medium capable of being given concrete form in order to regulate access to the
resources they develop, and provide a standard of comparison for the
diverse objects and energies that flow between points within them.
Networks of means could not exist if humans did not have the capacity to operate by way of such abstractions, and they provide scope to
develop it, contributing to what Simmel called "the intellectualization
of the will" that takes place when people act by way of "long chains
of connection." Such relations thus give scope to the peculiarly human
power to stand back from whatever conditions or relations shape the
lives of individuals in a given moment and to submit them to reflection, at once limiting their force and finding within them possibilities
that had not appeared before. To be sure the freedom gained in these
ways is never complete and abstraction and reflection can undermine
it even as they make space for it. But it is from within this space that
people put their own stamp on the world they inhabit. It was the powers humans derive from their capacity for abstraction, together with
money's status as its most widely diffused embodiment, that led the
eighteenth-century writer Bernard Mandeville to regard money, for
all the evil that may be done by way of it, as perhaps the greatest
and most typically human of all humanity's inventions, "a thing more
skillfully adapted to the whole Bent of our Nature, than any other
of human Contrivance."[20] Networks extend, amplify, and invigorate
human activity, but they are not themselves the source of the subjective agency that sets this activity in motion; that source lies in human
desire, will, and reason. Whether it be a market, a state, a profession,

a large corporation, the Republic of Letters, NBC, or the Internet, networks of means only exist in practice through the actions of the individuals who animate them.

To understand networks in this way is to reject out of hand the claims recently made on behalf of action network theory to the effect that networks themselves are sources of agency (or, in some versions, that no identifiable source of agency can be distinguished in network relations). To be sure human doings and fates are often affected by non-human powers, including earthquakes, floods, tornadoes, and the geographical features of particular settings such as rivers, lakes, coastlines and mountains (I place considerable emphasis on such factors below). In addition, the structures humans create to pursue their ends – markets, states, instruments of communication – all sometimes impede or distort the goals they are expected to serve, leading to unintended consequences including wars, economic depressions, and the degradation of social relations. But if people often fail to achieve the aims they pursue through these means, the reasons lie in the complex mix of motives and strategies that interact and clash within them, making their outcomes difficult to control or predict. None of these results justify giving both beings that possess and exercise will and reason and entities that are devoid of them the same status as agents.[21]

Many characteristic qualities of modern bourgeois life testify to its kinship with this human faculty of abstract reflection, liberated from the leading-strings by which people in many times and places have sought to constrain it, and applied to the concrete situations where action takes place. That bourgeois life rests on a mix of concrete and abstract dimensions is one reason why (as I will suggest below) the first great theorist of bourgeois society could be the idealist philosopher Hegel, whose way of comprehending every phenomenon of existence was to analyze the interaction of abstract and concrete determinations within it. Marx would adopt this analytic in a different way when he sought the key to capitalism and its history through dissecting the commodity and the social relations it represented into concrete and abstract dimensions, each the product of a corresponding form of labor, one producing coats or shoes, the second exchangeable value. Simmel drew on these Hegelian and Marxist themes in writing *The Philosophy of Money*, making them less metaphysical than in Hegel, and less teleological than in Marx. In keeping with his title he sought to address certain speculative questions about human nature that I leave aside here, but we remain close to him in not considering "capitalism" as a system or organism with an internal logic or dynamic that underlies its various appearances and sets it on some internally generated developmental trajectory. Viewing modern history as if capitalism had such a nature has fostered many failed efforts to grasp and direct historical evolution, foreshadowed in Marx's own attempt to predict the future collapse of bourgeois society in the great book he could never finish, *Capital*, at whose historical position and theoretical dilemmas we will look more closely later on. Not capital, but money, conceived in the broad manner Simmel proposed, provides the best optic through which to examine the emergence and development of both bourgeois life and modernity.

Such an approach does, I acknowledge, seek to recognize the evolution of bourgeois life as the development of innate and in some degree universal human powers, and it may point toward some reasons why its basic structures, as opposed to the particular attitudes and assumptions characteristic of its agents in given times and places, have never been superseded. But it also opens a window on many of the tensions and contradictions that such a form of life entails. How the resulting pressures and strains have been confronted, developed, and worked out over time is a large part of the history of the subject to which this book is dedicated.

An outline of what follows

Before closing this Introduction I owe prospective readers a brief preliminary outline of the chapters that will follow it, together with some of the ways they seek to carry on the interpretive project just sketched out. Part I aims to develop a comparison of the historical trajectories of Britain (chiefly England), France, and Germany, plotted in relation to the differing configurations assumed by the three major types of networks in each place, and the distinct character of bourgeois existence that developed in relation to them. In general Chapters 2, 3, and 4, focus on the period before 1850 and Chapters 5, 6, and 7 on forms of economic and political modernity that emerged after that date, but the distinctive shape of the three histories requires that each be treated in chapters with somewhat different chronological frames. The book's overall temporal boundaries are roughly 1750 and World War I, but these are often transgressed: the patterns exhibited by the comparisons have many earlier roots that cannot be ignored, nor can the later unfolding of the developments I consider. That a book focused on the "long nineteenth century" ends with some observations involving the place of the Internet in the history of networks may raise some historians' eyebrows but its aim is to suggest the continuing significance of the story I seek to tell.

Britain here emerges as the place where geography and history combined to afford all three kinds of networks early and extensive development, giving it a precocious modernity and putting a special stamp on both its middle classes and its aristocracy, no less conscious of their social difference than elsewhere, but all the same sharing many more orientations and attitudes than did their counterparts in other places. That the category of "bourgeois" had to be imported from France in the nineteenth century is one sign that the common participation of town and country people in national networks made social identities more permeable and destinies less sharply divergent there; the shift from teleocracy to autonomy in network relations occurred earlier and more spontaneously than anywhere else. The state was no less important than in other places, in some ways it was even more so, but state power was shared with people outside official institutions much more than in France or Germany, and many initiatives that required government sponsorship elsewhere grew out of private actions and relations. Both England's role as the pioneer of industrial innovation and its later overshadowing by the continental countries, especially Germany, were rooted in the conditions that made all these special features of its history possible.

Differently situated, France followed a path where the royal project of political integration had to confront far greater resistance from already established local powers, and where economic geography combined with this political opposition to retard the establishment of a national market until well into the nineteenth century. Only the coming of railroads after 1850 brought France's regions into the kind of effective proximity that England exhibited much earlier. The compromises into which the monarchy was forced by this situation generated a baroque structure whose inner contradictions no reform program could ever overcome. Much of the reason why France was the only country to erupt in nationwide revolution at the end of the eighteenth century lay in this situation, not in the "rise" of its bourgeoisie. The latter would long bear the marks of its formation inside an

Old Regime where the politics of privilege generated deep and lasting social antagonisms, and where the state felt called on to foster economic innovations because most private individuals had little incentive to undertake them.

In the German-speaking lands both economic and political integration were long absent, producing a situation where local independence reached heights attained nowhere else, and where the absence of an effective central authority opened up unique opportunities for territorial states to seek expansion of their reach and power against their rivals. The rulers sought support for these projects in various ways, of which one of the most significant was developing a body of literate officials to bring administrative unity to their domains; set free of many local connections through their work and the education it demanded, the bureaucrats became in many ways the first modern bourgeois in the German lands, providing the core of the group later called *Bildungsbürger*. Everywhere dependent for their positions at once on culture and on state power, the group as a whole was tinged by the involvement of its Prussian section in the Hohenzollern recognition that the German situation offered special rewards to a state able to develop a powerful army, providing the ground on which the country developed the characteristic Janus-faced orientation toward *Geist* and *Macht* that long marked its history. Paradoxically it was in Germany, the least "developed" of the three major European nations, that members of the *Bürgertum* – these same administrators and intellectuals more than businessmen – most self-consciously pursued a process of social transformation, becoming the pioneers of a new form of *bürgerliche Gesellschaft* that was not yet modern bourgeois life but that tended toward it in visible ways. It was in Germany that the bourgeois character of modern society was most self-consciously asserted and theorized, but it was there too that the *bürgerliche* legal and political order proved to be the least stable, the most vulnerable to tensions and conflicts generated by the growing weight of relations at a distance in everyday life.

These contrasts in the three countries' histories must not be allowed to hide some significant similarities between them, however, and in particular the shared rhythm of transformation that made the decades following the abortive revolutions of 1848 the moment when newly powerful networks greatly heightened the importance of distant and mediated relationships in society as a whole. As I will try to show below, the developing connections between people at a distance effected earlier by such linkages as international trade, the putting-out system, urban growth, improved transport, "public opinion," and Enlightenment criticism encouraged the emergence of "autonomous" principles in opposition to the ordained or teleocratic ones supposed to regulate economic, political, and cultural interchanges. But traditional structures, practices, and beliefs still retained much of their power, reasserting themselves even in the face of revolutionary crises and the beginnings of industrial innovation, so that overall the decades between 1750 and 1850 were an age of instability but not of lasting reorganization; only the age of railroads and telegraphs that began after the mid century brought the main lines of a new and more distinctly modern form of life. Like other features of the general interpretation offered here, this one is not radically new, but I hope to show that the effects of spreading and thickening networks in the decades after 1850 were more pervasive than has usually been recognized, encompassing Britain as well as the continent, and extending to a whole series of crucial modern phenomena, all of which followed a similar drumbeat of change.

Some of these phenomena are the subjects of the chapters that make up Part II, "Calculations and Lifeworlds." The topics assembled under this rubric are varied to be sure: changes in time measurement and in the forms of money and banking, Marx's attempt to subsume modern economic relations within a particular theorization of capitalism, relations between men and women, the emergence and decline of the strict moral regime often dubbed "Victorian," and the special but unstable prominence of Jews in European life. What links them together, I will try to show, is that each displays a pattern of development orchestrated by the evolution of networks of means and in particular by their marked expansion and thickening after 1850. The most powerful force in establishing modern ways of reckoning time was the advent of the railroads, but it was not technological change in itself that made the difference, since the deepening importance of distant relations had been creating pressures to standardize the length of days and hours for over a century before. What makes the history of money so significant in our overall story is its demonstration of how incompletely modern forms of economic exchange remained in the period before 1850, given that most of the money in circulation was still private in nature and widely varying in its value.

Marx's economic theory was ingenious and brilliant, but its deep coloration by the regime of manufacture still dominant in the first half of the nineteenth century gave it a peculiar and limited perspective on the relations between capitalism and modern mechanized industry. Despite the emancipatory hopes fostered by Enlightenment and political reform, traditional forms of both gender relations and morality took on a more rigid cast from late in the eighteenth century, fed by the expansion of markets, state functions, and public discussion; but the changed conditions brought by the further evolution of these same extended connections in the age of railroads, telegraphs, and the large-scale political organizations they enabled, allowed the liberalizing potential bottled up earlier to find increasing realization. For Jews the story was reversed as in a mirror: long practiced in acting through distant ties and linkages, Jews achieved remarkable degrees of both prominence and advancement in the era when most sections of society were only beginning to become involved in such relations, but their comparative advantage became a liability once people formerly focused chiefly on local contexts and relations were drawn into more extended connections and became able to draw social and political power from them.

The same perspective underlies the accounts offered in Part III, devoted to culture as a separate realm of intellectual and artistic activity, the guise it took on from late in the eighteenth century. In Chapter 12 I argue that a main reason for culture's acquiring this status as a sphere apart was that literature, painting, and music came to occupy a larger position in public consciousness as a consequence of the remarkable expansion in the implements and institutions that supported them – publishing, museums and galleries, public concerts. The new forms and institutions of culture had a number of consequences, one of which was to contribute to the exaltation of art and artists that developed in the age of romanticism; at the same time, the more public and anonymous relations between cultural producers and their audiences opened up new spaces for private and ungoverned encounters between individuals and cultural materials, creating both new opportunities for individuals to draw on culture for personal development and perceived dangers for society in the reduced power of oversight these changes entailed. The altered situation of culture simultaneously contributed to giving prominence to the distinction and even opposition between "high" and "popular" culture that developed from around 1800, in good part because only elite cultural forms participated in the expanding cultural networks at first, giving their producers and distributors new connections to their audience and a heightened position in public life. Here too however the second half of the century brought a turn in a different direction, the subject of Chapter 13: as the continued extension and thickening of networks of culture and communication began to have an impact on popular cultural forms too, these began to exhibit powers and energies they had lacked before, weakening the separation between levels this expansion had at first encouraged. In this way the stage was set for the ongoing transformation of culture and its relations to other regions of life that has continued down to our own day. Modern culture at every level has become a culture of means, inseparable from the large-scale media within which it is created and diffused. In some ways it has become the most open and democratic of the spheres of modern existence, alas not always with effects that deserve to be cheered.

Within this sphere of culture, bourgeois activities generated powerful currents of self-criticism and pressures for transformation, releasing energies drawn on by the avant-garde movements that emerged in the *fin-de-siècle*. Although numerous vanguard figures would have bristled to be told so, many of the most determined avant-garde efforts to oppose and transcend bourgeois ideas and practices drew much of their energy and inspiration from the very endeavors and achievements they aimed to controvert and supercede. Marx understood this particular dialectic of bourgeois life very well, but some of those who sought to develop his legacy in the realm of culture have not followed his lead, perhaps unnerved by the surprising persistence of the bourgeois form of life they hoped to see replaced by a "higher" one. I seek to restore this connection in Chapter 14.

I need to make two last observations before closing this Introduction. The first is that this is a book which owes many and large debts to other scholars, on whose work it repeatedly draws to assemble materials for its discussions and arguments. Little of the information provided here is new or based on original research (except for the readings of literary and philosophical texts and visual images, which are my own and may offer some surprises); throughout it is the general argument outlined above that ties the material together and gives the discussion whatever power of illumination it may bear. One reason why I have been able to draw on other people's work so extensively is that seeds and springs of the interpretation I offer have been developing for some time, if largely unawares, in much of it, so that taken together earlier studies provide more nourishment for the perspective developed here than their authors might have supposed (or in some cases wished). At the same time, giving substance to the ideas developed here entails arguing against some widely accepted notions and the writers who propound them (a task already begun in this Introduction). The need to draw on much earlier work while disputing the claims advanced in some of it shapes my engagement with the existing historical literature; even were it possible to have read all the studies relevant to the large questions I deal with, my aim would not have been to provide up-to-date general accounts of these topics, and I hope readers will not expect to find such accounts here. I follow Max Weber in believing that historians have an obligation to seek objectivity in the sense of dealing responsibly with their materials and taking account of evidence that may call their own views into question, but also that these commitments have to be honored while recognizing that no god's-eye vision of the past is possible, and that knowledge is only obtainable from some developed point of view.[22]

At the same time (this is the second observation) certain prominent trends in current historical writing make little or no appearance here. Chief among these is a widespread enthusiasm for dissolving European developments in a larger world-historical narrative so as to develop one or another strategy for "provincializing Europe." The reasons for such enthusiasm are evident enough in a time when Europe's once-vaunted supremacy over other regions has collapsed and the justifications offered for it have lost whatever persuasive power they may have possessed, and it deserves to be welcomed to whatever degree it serves to further equality and mutual recognition between different human groups. But the special role played in world history by Europe, and especially by the Western European countries on which I concentrate here cannot be gainsaid. Against those who reject the comparative history of countries and states with national identities on the grounds that it encourages a false or outdated sense of the substantiality and importance of national differences, and that other political forms, notably empires, have been the major frames of experience in the largest part of the world, the history told here reaffirms the importance of the special kind of competition between distinct cities, regions, and states that Europe developed and on which its early and still exemplary emergence into modernity rested. This rivalry was regrettable in many ways to be sure, breeding violence, cruelty, and deception, but it had the crucial effect of visiting failure on every attempt to establish an imperial hegemony in Western Europe itself, whether that of the Habsburgs in the age of Reformation, of Louis XIV in the seventeenth century, or of the French Republic and Empire a century later, giving the continent a character that contrasted with the unitary empires achieved by Seljuks and Ottomans in the Near East and by the series of dynasties that ruled the enormous expanse of China. To be sure wonderful things were achieved in those regions, but the persistence in Europe of competing centers of power, their rivalries exacerbated by religious disunity, undermined attempts to give a unitary direction to the region as a whole, maintained the existence of multiple centers in search of innovation and improvement both in the arts of war and those of peace, endowed the continent with borderlands where competition between authorities weakened the possibility of stable control and gave heterodox people and practices of all kinds – religious, political, and even industrial – better chances to survive, and eventually encouraged rulers, however reluctantly, to tolerate unorthodox ideas and practices in their own lands. Like others I no longer feel comfortable labeling this dynamism and ferment with the title given to the best attempt I know to identify its geographical and historical foundations, E. L. Jones's *The European Miracle*, but I freely admit that the current book too is about things that make Europe significant to world history because of its differences from other parts of the globe, and that made it the original home of processes and experiences that increasingly make themselves felt elsewhere.[23]

Part I

Contours of modernity

2 PRECOCIOUS INTEGRATION: ENGLAND

The most bourgeois country and the least

From the perspective just proposed modernity appears both as a singular thing, "everywhere the same," as Hegel said of spirit, and as a plurality of diverse things, markedly different from place to place. Among the most significant differences were the contributions bourgeois people and activities made to the evolving life around them and the ways this larger context shaped bourgeois or middle-class existence. These contrasts were firmly rooted in earlier history.

National feeling in the sense some nineteenth-century people would celebrate (and others decry) was at best embryonic before 1750, but some explicit consciousness of national identity existed in all three of the countries on which I focus here (and in others too), grounded in various mixes of political, economic, or cultural (including religious) relations. To be sure, some of these ties connected people to inhabitants of other countries as well, but this is a point we must leave aside for now. If we were simply to rank the three in terms of the level of consolidation each had achieved by around 1750, there would be good reason to put England at the top, Germany at the bottom, and France between them. But such a quantitative ranking is less informative than a more qualitative comparison, based on the differing modes of integration each territory had developed. An illuminating way to highlight these differences is to note that each one displayed some characteristic paradox, a distinctive, and in some way surprising, set of relations between elements of society and culture; these paradoxes gave a specific

Paris never became a major ocean port, and had no easy communication with Bordeaux or Marseilles. Germany's situation (we will come to details later on), was still worse in this regard.[4] In addition the successful conquest of England by William of Normandy and his band of some six or seven thousand landless knights in 1066 laid the basis for a unified political elite whose most powerful figures had good reason to cooperate with the monarch, generating a more positive and mutually supportive relationship between central and local power than existed where kings had to extend their sway by competing with already-established lesser lords and princes. Even efforts by ambitious or unscrupulous rulers to impose their will on dukes and earls did not lead to attempts to dismantle central authority (as would occur in France during the Hundred Years War); the barons who forced King John to issue Magna Carta in 1215 combined their insistence on limiting royal power with a determination to preserve it. They and their dependents retained leadership in their areas, providing the Justices of the Peace who long served as local agents of the central power; in contrast, the succession of French bureaucrats (of whom the *intendants* of the seventeenth century are perhaps the most famous) appeared as foreign intruders in many regions of that country. Serious divisions and conflicts existed to be sure, but the underlying sense of unity in the upper reaches of society re-asserted itself when they were settled, after the Wars of the Roses in the fifteenth century and again following the expulsion of the Stuarts in 1688. The early and continuing development of Parliament owed much to this history.[5]

Geography and politics also favored the development of perhaps the main vehicle of English national integration in practically every sphere, namely the city of London, at once the generator of vital energies that spread through the country and the nodal point of connection between its regions and classes. London's growth and its role in national life rested on the unique mix of activities that made it at once a commercial city, reaching out from the wharves and docks of the Thames to every accessible region of the world, a center of manufacturing both for the supply of its own population and for the refinishing and export of imported goods, and a political and administrative capital, the seat of power. The multiform nature of the city's distant connections would make it a locus of imperial power unique in its range and continuity. Medieval London was smaller than Paris, reaching only around 200,000 people by 1600, when the French capital had twice that many, but a century later it had surpassed the city on the Seine, boasting well over half a million people compared with something under that for its rival. During the eighteenth century Paris remained at around 500,000, whereas London continued to grow rapidly, to 900,000 at the first reliable census in 1801 (a figure Paris would reach in the 1840s, but by then London was growing much faster, to 4.5 million by 1881). London's pre-1800 growth was largely responsible for the British Isles being the only European area that underwent continuous and accelerating urbanization through the whole of the early modern period, when other regions displayed seesaw patterns of alternating expansion and stagnation.[6] What made its size especially significant, however, was the proportion of the overall English population it contained, already around 7% in 1650, and 10% in 1750 (compared with the roughly 2.5% of French who lived in Paris at both those dates). Given the high mortality rates prevalent in early modern cities, London's expansion could only be fed by immigration, its newcomers arriving from both nearby and distant British points (along with smaller groups of Jews from Spain and Eastern Europe, French Protestants, and Irish). The Thames city's ability to draw people from counties both close and far away gave it a role in national life and a familiarity to people throughout the country that Paris would acquire only in the later nineteenth century; many big London merchants were immigrants in the sixteenth century, and three-quarters of the city's Elizabethan mayors had not been born there.

So striking was London's growth in relation to the rest of England that many early modern Britons feared the city was parasitically draining resources from the provinces, a judgment in which recent historians find some merit, but only for the period up to the mid or late seventeenth century; after this point the stimulation of the London market and the funds the city furnished to finance improvements elsewhere gave it a positive influence on the national economy as a whole. Only in the eighteenth century would Daniel Defoe write of the "general dependence of the whole country upon the city of London … for the consumption of its produce," but the synergy through which the city's expansion fostered economic activity elsewhere was already operative a hundred years before, and even earlier in nearby areas. By 1681 London had road links to eighty-eight other towns, a number that rose to 180 by 1705, even before the great age of turnpike-building. A similar level of geographic and economic integration came to continental countries only in the era of the railroads.[7] The draw of the London market encouraged agricultural and commercial improvements elsewhere, more productive farming techniques (the use of animal fertilizer and the enclosure of commons) to increase supply, and industrial advances too: by 1650 London was consuming over 300,000 tons of Newcastle coal each year (the smoke from which added to the city's health problems), and twice that a century later. This early development of coal mining would later be important in making England the first home of modern industry by virtue of the cheaper fuel prices that obtained there.[8]

England's political and geographic integration, reinforced by the role London played in it, gave a compactness and concentration to its national life matched nowhere else. France lacked the myriad interurban and interregional connections Britain possessed by 1700. Its road network followed the paths and needs of royal administration: maritime commercial centers like Marseilles and Bordeaux were better connected to distant regions outside the country than to other French cities; most places that housed provincial *parlements* engaged in little or no long-distance trade, so that the networks in which they participated were largely limited to those associated with state activity (a difference still evident enough in the 1770s for Adam Smith to remark on it in *The Wealth of Nations*).[9] In Germany the still greater depth and power of both political and economic division meant that the same kinds of relations stood out in even sharper relief. Hamburg, the preeminent German commercial city, had closer ties to London and even to regions outside Europe than to other German places, a situation that would continue to mark its history – with certain dangerous consequences, as we shall be reminded below – to the end of the nineteenth century. No English city, certainly none of the provincial centers such as Bristol, York, Norwich, Exeter, or Newcastle, had so remote or weak a relationship to the national life around it (even though the trade of sixteenth-century Exeter, for instance, was largely with France). This exceptional integration of the country provided the foundation for a precocious modernity that was not merely anticipatory, in the manner of Renaissance Italy or Golden Age Holland, but bore an unbroken continuity with defining features of nineteenth-century life.

Markets, principles, and forms of production

This modernity made itself felt in all three of the chief spheres of national life, the economy, politics, and culture, giving impetus to the transition from "ordained" or "teleocratic" principles to ones that were "autonomous" in the sense I proposed in Chapter 1. In the rest of the current chapter I look at some of the ways these effects were made evident in each realm.

To speak of economic institutions and practices as "ordained" or "teleocratic" means two things in concrete terms: first that production and exchange were supposed to be directed and limited by moral considerations, and second that the wealth produced was expected to preserve and maintain inherited positions, the differences of status inscribed in the social order through both custom and law. In England each of these principles exhibited clear signs of weakening from at least the seventeenth century. By then what Keith Wrightson describes as "an emergent national economy which was increasingly influenced by participation in a nascent world economy" was creating situations (however locally distinct) "in which the livelihoods of individual households had become increasingly dependent on the markets for their products, skills and labor." A persistent sense of moral obligation limited the impact of this market dependency on behavior, but the conflicts spawned by the Reformation made moral questions subject to dispute. In this situation, as Richard Grassby puts it, increasing numbers of people found it necessary or convenient "to accept and follow those interpretations of the normative order which best suited their purposes," and thus to adjust their behavior to the demands and opportunities they confronted. This was especially true where traditional inhibitions were diminished by geographical and social distance, allowing the "norms of a more competitive economic environment" to gain power through the "daily accretion ... of decisions taken and transactions concluded in the course of simply earning a living."[10] In other words, activities once directed by goals set outside the domain of economic interactions were coming to be regulated by principles that developed out of those exchanges themselves.

Such shifting attitudes did not find expression without provoking public controversy. The original premises that provided the background for such discussions were simultaneously religious and economic, restricting the degree to which individuals were supposed to pursue private interest at once in terms of biblical injunctions to act with charity and protect the poor and weak, and on grounds that assumed the existence of pre-existing limits to what both nature and labor could provide. The world of what E. P. Thompson famously called the "moral economy" was a pessimistic one, structured around the conviction that the product to be divided in a given community could not expand beyond already-known limitations – although it might well contract in bad times. In such a situation it could seem only just to make communal survival the first priority, and to stand against attempts by those with holdings big enough to yield a surplus to sell their produce in the market instead of adding it to the common store, especially when reduced harvests led at once to shortages and to higher prices. But as expanding urban markets for agricultural products encouraged farmers to clear and improve land, and to find ways to increase yields, evidence mounted that these limits could be stretched, allowing more and better food to be produced. In the debate that ensued some quickly argued, in terms that would later come to be widely diffused, that the larger product, even if brought forth in conditions that heightened inequality, could provide better for the community as a whole, including its poorer members, than the traditional arrangements. In this way they justified the "enclosures" that aristocratic and gentry landowners sought to practice on their holdings, fencing off and taking over formerly common lands in ways that threatened the livelihoods of poor villagers by excluding them from the arable fields previously farmed in scattered strips, and from less easily cultivated ground where they had been able to pasture a few animals.

As Joyce Appleby's work makes clear, the argument was joined in quite modern terms in mid seventeenth-century pamphlets. "The advancement of private persons will be the advantage of the publick," a landowner and minister wrote, "if men by good husbandry, trenching, manuring their Land &c do better their Land, is not the Common wealth inriched thereby?" The author of these words did not make clear how he thought those without work would survive, but he argued that with an expanded product, greater resources would be available than before to relieve the plight of the poor. And he specifically rejected custom and tradition as guides to economic behavior: "Suppose it ... hath heretofore been so, is it therefore necessary that it be so alwayes?"[11]

Other seventeenth-century writers agreed, considering economic questions from a utilitarian viewpoint that made moral considerations dependent on practical ones, and justifying the pursuit of self-interest as a path to greater well-being for society as a whole, even if a community's more vulnerable members had to suffer in the short run. To a number of observers in the 1690s, "it was the pervasive and universal capacity of demand to grow from the desires of ordinary men and women that made it a natural and powerful stimulant to productivity." Some of these writers drew the conclusion that restrictions on trade with other countries should be eliminated in order to allow market pressures to do their bracing work, but most who argued this way were merchants who could profit from expanding imports and exports; by contrast both manufacturers and landowners feared foreign competition and favored protection (similar line-ups in debates about free trade and protection would long persist). These latter were able to put their stamp on British commercial policy in the eighteenth and early nineteenth century, contributing to the preservation of both commercial monopolies by powerful groups of organized traders (deplored by Adam Smith in *The Wealth of Nations*) and of the import duties that would draw the fire of liberals in the anti-Corn Law movement after 1815.[12] All the same, it is clear that the thickening web of distant relations within which production and exchange were carried on, and the expanding horizons this brought, were drawing people to question the subordination of economic behavior to ends rooted outside it, and to offer new principles derived from the operation of market networks themselves. Whether people subscribed to these principles did not depend on whether they were aristocrats or bourgeois, but on the particular relationship they had to such networks.

Many traditional restrictions on economic activity remained in pre-industrial Britain, but one declined markedly, namely the power of guilds to determine who could practice a given occupation and offer its products in the market. Often religious in their origins (a connection preserved in ceremonies and rituals), guilds of artisans and merchants were primarily economic institutions by the sixteenth century. As "the principal weapons of economic restriction and regulation," they controlled apprenticeships, production standards, and competition among the masters, while working to keep outside competitors at bay. The tone in which they defended the monopolies of their members was often highly moralistic, as illustrated by the tailors' guild of Leicester, who protested publicly against non-members "who like drone bees to the hive, paying neither scot nor lot [i.e. town taxes], lie lurking in the suburbs and other secret places in and about this town, and rob your suppliants of the work which they should do, to their great disgrace and utter undoing." Such complaints echoed both the language of the moral economy and the assumption that markets ought to be regulated so as to preserve acquired position and privilege. Many who made them deserve to be called middle class. But the power of guilds was waning by late in the seventeenth century for a number of reasons: sometimes because competition from producers located outside the reach of urban authorities could not be blocked; sometimes because town magistracies influenced by manufacturers with ties to unregulated rural industry turned a deaf ear to more traditional producers; and sometimes because competition between guilds over which of them had the right to produce or sell certain products could not be resolved. In London, artisans had long been able to escape guild regulations by taking up residence outside the area where having the "freedom" of the town was a requirement for offering goods in the market. By 1700 suburban expansion had reached a point where London craft companies lost any real ability to regulate production, and in 1712 the city abandoned the attempt to enforce the "freedom" in regard to merchants trading overseas in joint-stock companies. Although the weakness of some guilds at certain moments may have been a consequence of economic difficulties, overall (as two recent historians conclude) the guilds' decline "indicates the discrediting of the kind of commercial protectionism which they had exemplified. Whether out of choice or necessity civic policy was becoming less restrictive," and guilds that had once jealously protected the economic interests of their members were turning into mere social clubs.[13]

This English story was not matched elsewhere. To be sure, ambitious people had long sought to escape the restrictions guilds imposed on them, and some of these, for instance a German wool producer active in late seventeenth-century Nordlingen, argued (like the landowners encountered just above) that by avoiding guild regulations they could expand production and thus provide a livelihood for larger numbers of people than the regulated economy allowed. Against such practices town officials upheld the duty of citizens, "who should stand by one another through thick and thin, and must partake of each other's joys and sorrows," to resist innovations that might "cause any further diminution of each other's livelihoods, which are already far too difficult to obtain."[14] Such debates continued, but guild power survived in German towns and regions at least until early in the nineteenth century, when Napoleon abolished it (temporarily, as it turned out) in the areas that came under his control, an example followed by German reformers convinced that freeing up economic activity would enrich subjects and expand tax revenues. In France a distinction existed in theory between *villes libres* and *villes jurées*, but the "free" quality of the first merely meant that guilds did not have the legal status of sworn associations (*jurandes*), and that regulation was in the hands of the city government, as opposed to the syndics of the guilds themselves; in practice, entry into occupations was subject to rigid restrictions throughout the country. Both journeymen and outsiders objected to the power this conferred on an often self-perpetuating group of masters in the name of tradition and equity, and sometimes both urban magistrates and royal officials were on the side of liberalization. In 1614 the last Estates General to meet before the one called in 1789 even abolished *jurandes*. But the howl of protest sent up by aggrieved master artisans caused the government to reverse itself. The scenario was replayed in 1776 when Louis XV's minister Turgot, acting in accord with the physiocratic theory I will consider later, again did away with the *corporations de métiers*, but had to retreat in the face of guild supporters who did not hesitate to depict the hierarchical organization of industry as essential to social cohesion, so that its abolition would destroy the "primal links that gather men together," turning each one into "nothing more than a gnawing individual."[15]

Consumption, industry, and the economy of manufacture

By the middle of the eighteenth century the combined effects of the London market in fostering productive energies throughout the country and of the transportation system set up to make it accessible had created a network of economic connections sufficient to constitute a national market for both agricultural and manufactured goods in England. Regions retained much autonomy to be sure, and specialized in particular kinds of products (a circumstance that would be brought into higher relief with the beginnings of mechanized industry), but many types of goods circulated readily through the country as a whole. A century before it could be called "the workshop of the world," Britain had become what Neil McKendrick and his colleagues dubbed "the first modern consumer society." Contemporaries were struck by the rate at which people at many social levels bought up household goods such as furniture, rugs, pottery, cooking implements, cutlery, soap, and beer, as well as clothing and accessories of all kinds – coats, dresses, stockings, ribbons, buttons. Statistics drawn from records of the excise tax suggest that consumption was growing twice as fast as the population. Merchants traveled widely in search of raw materials and customers, and advertising occupied much space in newspapers. An enthusiasm for fashion spread outward from London and down the social scale, not always meeting with approval to be sure. In 1781 an observer groaned that he wished "with all my heart that half the turnpike roads of the kingdom were plough'd up," since they had "depopulated the country" and spread London manners too widely: "I meet milkmaids on every road, with the dress and looks of Strand misses." Descriptions of shop-window displays with goods arranged to attract buyers already sound much like later department stores. As McKendrick concludes, "a mass consumer market awaited those products of the industrial revolution which skillful sales promotion could make fashionably desirable, heavy advertisement could make widely known, and whole batteries of salesmen could make easily accessible."[16]

That these developments predated the era of industrial innovation that began in the second half of the eighteenth century has been one reason why many historians have come to stress the gradual nature of economic change, casting doubt on the classic image of an "industrial revolution." It is necessary to avoid getting too deeply drawn into the debates that rage around this question, but they cannot be avoided entirely. That the textile industry was rapidly transformed in the decades just before and after 1800, with the mechanization first of spinning and later of weaving, seems undeniable, just as does the sharp impact railroad building had on metals and machine making a few decades after. But neither the reality of those transformations nor the strong consciousness of change they fostered in contemporaries should lead us to think that the story ought to begin or end with them. If, as a recent analysis argues, British manufacturers were spurred to invest in machine technology earlier than their counterparts elsewhere because labor costs were relatively high in Britain, while the price of coal to drive engines was comparatively low, this situation owed much to the precocious integration of markets there, and the role played by London in bringing it about: the demand for labor fed by expanding consumption put upward pressure on wages, while the early development of the coal industry to supply the city's need for fuel spurred developments in mining that cheapened production costs. Colonial markets and supply sources were crucial to London's growth and its role in national life, to be sure, but the expanding domestic market kept pace with international trade and spurred industrial innovation.[17] In an illuminating essay, Samuel Lilley plotted the major inventions that transformed cotton spinning in the last decades of the eighteenth century along a line showing the consumption of thread at the same time; in each case (the spinning jenny, the water frame, the "mule") a spurt in demand preceded the new machine. Moreover, each of these innovations was technically quite simple, involving the combination or multiplication of common tools and techniques, so that the encouragement provided by growing demand could have been enough to incite clever artisans to imagine them, and then to try them out.[18] Other important innovations had roots in the special qualities of English society to which I pointed earlier. The large proportion of people at higher social levels drawn into market relations contributed to making class barriers more fluid and permeable than elsewhere, helping to purge British life of the haughty disdain for practical activities, and the knowledge connected to them, visible in upper classes elsewhere, especially in France. A number of historians assign this difference considerable weight in Britain's earlier turn to industrial innovation, since it fostered easier communication between the holders of theoretical and practical knowledge, and a more widespread interest in how things worked.[19]

Support for an account that gives domestic market relations a central role in driving economic change comes also from Jan de Vries, who suggests that the industrial revolution was preceded by an "industrious revolution," that is by a decision on the part of many ordinary people to devote more of their time and effort to productive activity for the market, in order to increase their income and thus their ability to consume available goods. Such a strategy required becoming more diligent and efficient in work (although it was not necessarily incompatible with binge-type consumption by men in taverns), as well as increasing the time devoted to market-oriented work on the part of women. "A shift from relative self-sufficiency toward market-oriented production by all or most household members necessarily involves a reduction of typically female-supplied home-produced goods and their replacement by commercially produced goods. At the same time the wife was likely to become an autonomous earner." De Vries suggests that such strategies allowed some working-class families to maintain a certain level of consumption even in times of falling real wages, as was the case between around 1815 and 1850; but in England between 1760 and 1790 wage rates were rising, and McKendrick observes a somewhat similar pattern of behavior in working-class families in those years, with wives working in order to add to family money income and thus to buying power. Both writers suggest that there were untapped productive energies available to be drawn on by changes in work patterns in pre-industrial Europe, and that attractive and available consumer goods could push people to produce more in order to buy more, thus furthering the development of market relations and the innovations they encouraged.[20]

How much weight such an analysis deserves in accounting for industrial change is difficult to decide; much depends on just what we are trying to understand or explain. If the object of inquiry is the world of modern industry and mass consumption that came into being in the course of the nineteenth century, then earlier changes like those just noticed do not belong at the center of the story. Only a rise in productivity on the scale accomplished by the substitution of fossil fuels for human and animal energy could bring national income to a level able to support the kind of long-term growth in both output and demand evident in the quarter-century before 1900. Not industriousness but inventiveness was the basis for change of that type and magnitude, and the story of the application of steam and later electrical power to industry had only barely begun to unfold by 1800.[21] But that is just what needs to be highlighted: the English economy, not only in the last three decades of the eighteenth century, but even until the last three decades of the nineteenth, remained traditional in ways its famous innovations often obscure.

Among recent writers the one who has made this point in the clearest and most suggestive way is Richard Price. In the helpful terms he provides, what existed in England before around 1870 was not an "industrial economy" in which machine production and non-human sources of energy were the central determinants but an "economy of manufacture," a structure in which producing goods for the market gave the tone to economic activity as a whole, but whose chief features still reflected the etymology of manufacture as hand-work. To be sure, the roots of the later economic regime were already at work in the earlier one, and many lines of continuity crossed the boundaries between them. I think the best way to reconcile the distinction Price puts in place with the features of economic history that seem to undermine it is to recognize that the history of what has long been called the industrial revolution needs to be recounted not from one but from two perspectives. The first puts in relief England's role as the pioneer industrial nation, the forerunner whose path other countries would seek to follow, but at a distance. This story can be read off from the statistical record: between 1800 and 1852 annual pig iron output in Britain increased nearly tenfold, to 2.7 million tons; in the same period the capacity of steam engines went from around 10,000 horsepower to well over a million, three-quarters of it in locomotives on the railways whose future impact was already evident; by 1870 engine capacity had doubled again, and mechanization had become dominant in nearly every branch and stage of the textile industry. Other similar figures could be cited; no other country exhibited advances on this scale.[22]

But from the second perspective England itself would not become a modern industrial economy before the last decades of the nineteenth century either. Before 1850 people who stood open-mouthed before the radically new conditions had their eyes on a very few places, the exploding northern cities such as Manchester (the locale of Engels's *Condition of the Working-Class in England*) or Oldham (Dickens's Coketown of *Hard Times*). Manchester was, as Asa Briggs puts it, the "shock city" of the 1840s, disrupted by mushroom-like growth (its population of around 140,000 in 1831 was roughly six times what it had been in 1770), and buffeted about by cycles of boom and bust in the aftermath of the Napoleonic wars. But these places, revelatory as they were, bore little resemblance to life in the rest of the country; indeed the heightened local and regional differences to which they testified were themselves a distinctive feature of the period, one that would recede later (in ways I will consider below). In his classic study of *Victorian Cities*, Briggs contrasted Manchester with Birmingham, also a center of manufacture, but based on small workshops, a more skilled labor force, closer relations between owners and workers, and a political life marked by greater cooperation between middle-class and working-class groups. Lest it be thought that such emphasis on the limited applicability of the factory model to England in this period is a tack taken by defenders out to show that conditions were not so bad as critics claimed, it should be noted that one of the most powerful accounts of the persistence of traditional methods of work before 1850 comes from a distinguished socialist historian, Raphael Samuel. In colorful and often wrenching detail, Samuel makes clear that it was human muscle, male and female, not machine power, that did the work on which society depended in this period, making goods, building cities, roads, and railroads, and providing food. The toil of miners, construction workers, and iron workers was often painfully hard, particularly the "puddlers" who had to employ great strength and withstand extreme heat in order to produce cast iron free of the ore's impurities (steel only became practical much later). In many trades the chief difference between nineteenth century labor and its earlier forms lay not in any use of machines, but in the higher degree of organization required to utilize the larger numbers of workers involved, and the more demanding oversight and discipline to which they were subjected. Many writers have pointed out that the largest categories of workers enumerated in the census of 1851 were still agricultural laborers and domestic servants. Retailing in particular remained as it had been for centuries, based on small-scale units, limited demand, and a predominance of craftspeople with special knowledge about the things they sold.[23]

All these conditions support Price's characterization of the British economy before 1870 as an "economy of manufacture" rather than a modern "industrial economy." What distinguished this economy from other countries' was not mechanization but the much greater weight that market relations exerted within it, and the mix of pressures and opportunities that access to markets, both foreign and domestic, provided. The advantage large firms enjoyed over smaller ones in this period did not come from investments in machines, but from their ability to organize access to markets, gathering information and using agents and salesmen to establish connections to supplier and buyers. "The key to economic survival in an increasingly complex domestic market structure was access to distribution networks both for the raw material and the product ... There was an inexorable tendency for small producers to be separated from their markets and for middlemen and merchants to control the channels of distribution," leaving the lesser players in an increasingly unfavorable position. Independent artisans who felt pressured and endangered by these conditions between around 1790 and 1840 were thus right to blame middlemen for their plight, not factory owners; indeed Price observes that the chief reference for the term capitalist in this period was to middlemen, not industrialists.[24]

Factory production, sometimes involving hundreds of workers, was surely part of this "economy of manufacture," but in the form it would still largely retain through most of the nineteenth century: that is, most "factories" were assemblages of workers using traditional methods in a single place, where their work could be more closely overseen and better organized. Factories could operate, employ large numbers of workers and begin to apply machine technology to production only because they were tied to suppliers and consumers by less easily discernible webs of connection. They were and are (the description fits cities as well and helps to account for their growth) aggregations of means inside networks of means, and it made sense to assemble the first only because they could be inserted into the second. The conditions in which such factories operated have been well described by Price:

> Factory and workshop were locked in a relationship of close interdependence. Mechanization and larger-scale units complemented rather than displaced small-scale production. Many of the machines were ancillary to hand labor, rather than its substitute ... At the heart of manufacturing lay a combination of small and large units of production bound together by many layers of subcontracting with labor processes that were highly subdivided and dominated by hand technology.

Water power remained the chief non-animal source of energy until the steam turbine became widely available in the 1880s, and gains in productivity came much less through technical innovations than through more intensive use of traditional methods. The proportion of men working in industries that relied significantly on machine technology was still only 1 in 10 in 1831, and even in 1851 only 27 percent of male and female laborers as a whole were employed in such branches. One reason factories by themselves have often been portrayed as the chief source of change is simply that they were concrete and visible, striking in their size, their noise, the changes they made in the land-scape, the disruptions they brought to people's lives. The emphasis on factories sometimes causes historians to forget that (especially in the period before the railroad network was completed) their expansion depended on the simultaneous growth of another kind of business that did not generate quite the drama they did, namely warehouses. Even in Manchester, as Briggs pointed out, the warehouses were more impressive than the factories; some of them operated by foreign firms with connections to Europe and beyond, such as the family enterprise in which Friedrich Engels was active for many years.[25]

By the middle of the eighteenth century, however, these methods were being employed on a scale and with a dynamism that marked a new stage, distinct from the productive regime operative earlier in England, and still dominant on the continent. The fact that the economy drew a much higher proportion of the population into manufacture than elsewhere was largely responsible for a marked rise in national income and well-being. By 1700 British per capita income had already reached a level that Sweden would achieve only in 1870. (How different conditions would be by the later date becomes evident when we note that Swedish national income did not begin to rise from traditional levels until around 1850, after which point it took only twenty years to accomplish the rise that required the whole of the seventeenth century for Britain in pre-modern conditions. Other countries exhibited similar rhythms in the nineteenth century.) The number of households with middle-class income levels (defined as those having revenues between £50 and £400 per year) rose significantly, from around 15 percent in 1750 to some 25 percent in 1780. Release from the subsistence economy that tied population growth to agricultural conditions and thus to the cycle of harvests meant that England was no longer subjected to the traditional "scissors" pattern of demographic increase followed by painful contraction still evident elsewhere. Many people still lived in wretched and precarious conditions, to be sure, especially in small villages and towns, but the overall improvement was sufficient for British population (and British cities in particular) to grow steadily through the eighteenth century, a period when other areas still exhibited the old pattern of alternating rise and fall.[26]

All the same, the dominant productive methods were not yet those that would more fully transform life later on. This was reflected in the conviction shared by almost all observers and theorists, even in the face of relative prosperity, that natural conditions set strict limits to economic development. It was this widespread and pessimistic sense of limits that earned economics its sobriquet, "the dismal science." David Ricardo and Robert Malthus agreed in regarding land as the ultimate determinant of well-being: the first on the ground that its extent and quality determined the level of rents and thus the flow of revenues and investment; and the second because the supply of land set limits to the food supply. On this basis both believed that growth would soon reach its endpoint. These views grounded Malthus's conviction that the poor were responsible for their own plight, given that they brought children into the world who could not be supported by the labor available to working-class families, as well as his conclusion that only a reduction in the number of births could alleviate the problem. It made no sense to expect manufacturers to provide for the needs of the burgeoning numbers of poor, he maintained, because there was no way to expand production and incomes beyond their natural bounds. Since the rich did "not in reality possess the *power* of finding employment and maintenance for the poor," the latter could not "in the nature of things possess the *right* to demand them."[27] We will see later that such views waned from around 1870.

Despite this pessimism, however, it is crucial for understanding the place of this period in the broader history of modernity to recognize that it was on this basis that the British economy achieved the increased productivity and vitality on which the remarkable rise in national income rested, providing greater well-being for many people, and creating the conditions within which later and still larger changes would take place. Not fossil-fuel technology but the effect of long-developing networks that drew increasing numbers of people into distant relationships provided the foundation on which the distinctive features of English live rested. Much the same can be said of the special quality of British political relations.

State power, national integration, and public opinion

Historians were long wont to regard the eighteenth-century British state as weak, especially in comparison to France, but this view was largely demolished by John Brewer's demonstration that British naval might rested on well-developed state institutions, including an efficient corps of tax collectors. The older position was not mere Whiggish fantasy, however, since the English state before the nineteenth century never directed local affairs through a body of provincial administrators comparable to the French *intendants*; local government remained in the hands of Justices of the Peace, holders of royal commissions but only nominally servants of the crown, since they were people with independent standing in their areas, and their appointments were under the control of county aristocrats and upper gentry. The strength Brewer rightly attributes to the British state did not derive from an imposition of royal power on resistant subjects, which had always constituted one important dimension in the growth of the French monarchy, but precisely on the precocious national integration described above, and on the cooperative and synergistic relation between central and local power that found its paradigmatic expression in Parliament. However paradoxical it may sound, the enabling key to the British state's impressive strength in the eighteenth century was the defeat of Stuart absolutism and the establishment of Parliamentary supremacy from the 1680s. In one crucial regard Brewer's revision makes no significant departure from the traditional Whiggish view: if British rural and urban people paid taxes more willingly and at a higher rate based on their national income than the French did, they did so because royal policy was responsive both to the interests represented at Westminster and to the demands for accountability often voiced there.[28]

All the same, as the state's fabric grew stronger and its threads wove themselves more thickly into national life, relations between its means and ends began to reveal new patterns. One of these involved a move away from traditional aristocratic forms of office-holding toward more rationalized bureaucratic procedures. In the seventeenth century government departments were often run by officials who obtained their posts by patronage, and who then staffed the office with a body of clients who performed lesser tasks under their direction and whose salaries they paid out of their income. Government offices in such a system were the personal preserve of those who obtained them, so that state resources were channeled toward shoring up established social hierarchies, just as the position of master artisans and merchants was perpetuated in the guild economy. After the 1690s these practices became much less common. Agencies increasingly hired their personnel individually and paid their salaries directly; managers, clerks, and tax collectors were subject to standard rules and given advancement according to how their work was evaluated. To be sure, neither personal influence nor poor performance disappeared from the system, and they would later provoke outcries for reform, especially as higher government expenditures occasioned by the renewed outbreak of warfare after 1790 opened up new opportunities for enrichment to individuals both responsible and unscrupulous; but in the mid eighteenth century Parliamentary oversight kept abuses in check and bodies such as the Admiralty and Navy Boards were "too vital to the national interest to be held hostage by the forces of graft and corruption."[29] We shall see below that comparable developments were taking place in both France and Germany by the end of the eighteenth century: in all three places state activities formerly organized so as to benefit people whose claims rested on inherited social standing were coming to be directed by principles generated out of the evolving structure of government operations themselves. In France, however, these changes were not sufficient to rescue the state from the crushing burden of its obligation to social powers whose goals were often in conflict with its own, and with which it had been forced into damaging compromises over the centuries. In Germany they operated inside territorial states whose mutual competition preserved the country's traditional fragmentation.

The importance of England's early integration in making possible the features that distinguished it from France is evident in the famously unique system of government finance it set up. The keystone of the structure was the Bank of England, established in 1694 to provide credit for government operations through bonds sold to the public. Because the bonds were backed by tax revenues, they were highly successful in mobilizing economic resources and creating an identity of interest between well-off people and the state. The taxes in turn were collected more readily and easily, and at a higher per-capita level than anywhere else in Europe, largely because Parliamentary government generated a measure of trust and allowed for a degree of oversight no other state achieved. The chief levies were three: a land tax, customs duties, and an excise tax. It was the third of these that became the most important during the eighteenth century, collected on a wide range of consumer goods by a body of centrally appointed officials who manned local offices, and whose manner of recruitment and employment have just been noted. Parliament was able to enforce a considerable degree of oversight on the taxation system, subjecting it to a degree of public scrutiny that contrasted with the veil of secrecy the French monarchy cast over its finances.[30] All these features of the British taxation system – its efficiency, its uniformity, its relative openness to view – heightened the confidence in government that Parliamentary supremacy bred in wide segments of the upper-classes, strengthening the state's ability to borrow money from those who had it to lend. The state's ability to borrow directly from the public allowed the government to meet needs for more funds when they arose and reduce its obligations at other times, thus tapping the resources of the country far more efficiently than other countries were able to do. As Niall Ferguson has recently argued, it was this ability to marshal resources effectively that accounted for British military success through much of the modern period, since overall the country was less wealthy than its larger rival, France.[31]

The relationship between such a system and the general features of English society and politics highlighted here was close. What stood in the way of a uniform mode of revenue collection elsewhere was the system of venal offices, making state service a source of investment and profit for those with sufficient capital to buy into it, and of tax privileges too, creating both inequality and inefficiency in state finance. In France many kinds of taxes (and attempts to bypass exemptions led to repeated creation of new ones, most of them quickly assimilated to the same baroque system) were farmed out to people who often became visibly (and to many suspiciously) rich, profiting from the difference between the purchase price of their "farm" and the revenue they could squeeze out of it. Venal offices were not unknown in Britain, but they receded during the seventeenth century just when they were expanding in France, partly through the lucky circumstance that expenses for war were less crushing. But the whole system put down much shallower roots in Britain also because monarchical power there did not have to expand by buying off nobles with privileges in exchange for allowing the royal administration to take over local functions; here we see what Brewer recognizes as the "strength of a national system of provincial governance which relied for its implementation on local dignitaries," people whose willingness to accept central power did not depend on gaining special privileges and immunities for themselves. This does not mean that British aristocrats were unable to manipulate the system to their advantage:

one reason why the excise tax became the chief levy was that large holders preferred it to the land tax, whose burden fell largely on them. But they were not exempt, and taxation did not shine a powerful spotlight on social privilege and inequality as it did across the Channel.

All the same, considerable criticism of this system developed almost as soon as it was set up, and the terms in which it was couched bear a revealing relationship to the ones I am employing here. The critics were, in general, "country" rather than "court" people, that is, ones who had not been part of the Whig coalition of landed and commercial interests that brought William and Mary to replace the Stuarts in 1688. Still tied to an older and more exclusively agrarian ideal of life, they were fearful that the powerful resources mobilized in the new fiscal system would raise the state too high and open the way to corruption, giving the government resources with which to manipulate individuals in return for favors; but a second and more insidious malignity in their eyes was the public market in government bonds spawned by the system of funded debt. The prices of these securities rose and fell in response to both domestic and international affairs, creating unprecedented possibilities for venturesome investors to gain or lose large sums. Critics often condemned the resulting situation in terms drawn from classical republican theory, contrasting the menace the new system posed with an idea of virtue in which devotion to public good excluded the pursuit of private, individual interest. The votaries of such virtue often compared it to that displayed by citizens of ancient city-states, but they recognized that it could only be maintained by those with sufficient means to rise above the temptations fostered by opportunities for speculative gains. The vocabulary these "country" critics employed sometimes seemed to make commerce and money responsible for the evils they bewailed, but as J. G. A. Pocock has argued, it was the system of state finance, not commercial expansion, that they most feared:

> It was not the merchant trading upon his own stock who
> transformed and corrupted the relation of property to
> government ... The danger lay with the owner of capital,
> great or small, who invested it in systems of public credit
> and so transformed the relations between government and
> citizens, and by implication those between all citizens and

all subjects, into relations between debtors and creditors. It was not the market, but the financial market, which pre- cipitated an English awareness, about 1700, that political relations were on the verge of becoming capitalist rela- tions ... The merchant became involved in the indictment of capitalism, and the credit society became known as the "commercial society," because it was observed that there was a fairly obvious relation between trade and credit.[32]

Some might regard such an account as one-sided, giving too little weight to fears engendered by market agriculture and the atti- tudes it was nurturing (as in the defense of enclosures already con- sidered). But the significance of the opposition Pocock identifies does not depend on his being wholly correct about the primacy of political relations over commercial ones (although I believe he largely is). What matters is the way that the new system of state finance, and its connec- tion to markets more generally, moved people to contrast the situation they saw developing around them, in which personal and social fates were caught up in extended networks of relations that threatened to impose their own patterns everywhere, with an opposite one where virtue had been guaranteed by people's insertion in local relations and contexts whose patterns remained under their more immediate con- trol. Such a view of the past was only partly accurate, since it left out of the account the degree to which institutions such as the state, the Church, and commerce had long fostered and relied on distant net- works. But because the earlier ones were still in principle teleocratic, structured in obedience to norms rooted outside them, they had not bred the same kind of anxieties; the relations fostered by the new and more autonomous web of financial connections appeared problematic because the flow of resources it facilitated had a more abstract charac- ter and was no longer under the control of identifiable superiors.

The new power the British state was able to gain from its system of funding and taxation did not lead only to a centraliza- tion of power, however. It was accompanied by a simultaneous and remarkable diffusion of power, one that provided a further testi- mony to the way that the thickening of the web of political inter- action altered the principles under which it operated. Recognizing both the power of Parliament and its need for cooperation from citizens, people worked to influence the state on behalf of their interests, creating an extensive system of lobbies. The interests such organizations served were sometimes religious, sometimes commercial or fiscal (makers of certain goods called for reductions of the excise imposed on them), sometimes local (there were many pleas for aid in constructing turnpikes), but all aimed to influence members of Parliament and government officials to pass legislation they favored. Some sent representatives to London to meet with political figures, others employed solicitors, some of whom began to specialize in representing such groups. Many of them were well organized and operated in more than one region, or cooperated with people in other areas in presenting petitions; as Brewer notes, "The levying of indirect taxes which imposed *nationally* uniform rates on commodities, encouraged the emergence of organizations which transcended local and regional boundaries." One common tactic of such groups was to present their cases in either local or national newspapers (the latter printed in London and distributed to other places, their circulation unimpeded after Parliament's decision in 1694 not to renew the Licensing Act that regulated publication before), arguing that their own interest was also the public interest, especially if their first appeals to Parliament did not succeed. "The emergence of special interest groups willing to lay their case before the public was in part a *consequence* of Parliament's claim to be the sole body to adjudicate what was *pro bono publico*. When lobbies failed in Parliament they transferred their appeal to a more public court."

Thus there developed a regular debate on the nature of the public interest and its relationship to various private ones. To be sure many participants had no compunction about seeking their own advantage under the cloak of high-sounding rhetoric (the same was true of the seventeenth-century debates considered earlier), and critics like Adam Smith sought to unmask their self-centered claims. But one consequence of these debates was that individuals began to see the defense of their own interests and rights, in the face of Parliamentary power that might be used against them, in a way that echoed and extended the claims of the 1688 revolutionaries to safeguard the rights of the nation against the king. The political redirection of governmental power effected in the seventeenth century was now replayed on a broader social plane, so that "government intervention helped to create new social forms in civil society."[33]

In this way the expansion of the web of governmental institutions controlled from the center gave birth to further networks of means, whose operation both implicitly and explicitly introduced other principles into the system of gathering and directing resources. As the network of connections between Parliament and the public developed, their extent and thickness opened up possibilities for using the resources they provided not only from the center, but from a growing number of points outside it. The relatively democratic character of British politics – Parliamentary supremacy and a degree of local independence – was partly responsible for this but not wholly, since, as we shall see, certain rather similar things were taking place in France, where attempts by the monarchy to expand its power, but on a basis that did not involve representative institutions, also called forth strategies for turning an administrative and communicative network set up by the monarchy to purposes it had not envisioned. We shall see, however, that the language in which the appeal to public opinion and principle was carried out would be significantly different there, reflecting the contrasting nature of the connections on which national integration rested.

Divisions and linkages

The close ties between the various forms of integration that marked eighteenth-century England – economic, political, and cultural – are evident in a number of phenomena characteristic of the time. One was the energetic and multifaceted campaign mounted in favor of the anti-monarchical critic and Parliamentary reformer John Wilkes in the 1760s. Wilkes (who was jailed for attacking George III and prevented from taking the seat in Commons to which he was elected) was supported by a widespread network of clubs, some of which had ties to existing voluntary organizations partly devoted to furthering trade, and to self-help for their members. The activities in his favor involved not just pamphlets, speeches, and meetings (often held at taverns, whose owners profited from the agitation), but the sale of a wide variety of artefacts and souvenirs, including ceramics, clothing, pipes, pots, cakes, and candlesticks. Newspapers were central to the movement, so that there is reason to believe that by 1770 the public appetite for political news was so great that editors who refused to provide it would have faced failure as a result.[34]

Not everyone welcomed these changes to be sure; many people felt challenged or weakened by them. The divisions apparent in the criticism of the post-1688 fiscal system studied by John Pocock, between a form of existence in which an elite rooted in local independence gave the tone to social life and one reshaped by the power of more remote and abstract relationships, made itself felt in other respects too. In his study of the culture of British towns and urban building in this period, Peter Borsay noted how the spread of literacy and reading led to a split between those still oriented toward locally based attitudes and pursuits and those whose preferences were growing more cosmopolitan. "Traditional culture focused *inwards* on local customs and practices, whereas ... its polite counterpart looked *outwards* towards London and the continent." One expression of this difference took form in the contrast between older vernacular architecture and the international Palladian classicism that inspired many urban rebuilding projects; another appeared in the awareness that newspapers drew people into a world outside the local one. A satirical poem described the scene in a Bath coffee-house:

> CHREMES sits scheming on affairs of state,
> And on his shoulders bears all Europe's weight;
> He cannot drink his coffee with a goût,
> 'Till he has read the papers thro and thro ...
> RATTLE, joined by a whole unthinking crowd,
> At least once ev'ry day calls out, aloud,
> Boy, does the London post set out? I pray:

Papers were read and discussed in local clubs and associations (some of them of the kind that would provide support for the Wilksite movement), and a sort of informal or invisible society grew up, joining local readers of papers to their counterparts elsewhere in the county; editors encouraged this connection by running competitions, giving public replies to readers' questions, and printing their letters and contributions, tactics that would still seem novel and strikingly modern when taken up by much later publications.[35]

Dror Wahrman has drawn on this and similar descriptions of eighteenth-century life to argue that a series of social and political conflicts and controversies in which the sides do not correspond to the often-invoked opposition between landed and commercial classes turn out to pit people with largely local orientations against others more involved in national networks. Thus a study of Justices of the Peace finds a division between one group whose members rested their position largely on private ties that bound them to the communities they inhabited, and another that sought prestige through cultural and institutional connections to their counterparts elsewhere in the country. Sometimes local political struggles (in places as distant from each other as Middlesex and Wales, for instance) seem to have involved a clash between people of similar social position, ranging some with interests and connections in London against others who sought support through their more immediate ties to neighbors. Borsay notes that a significant current of gentry culture drew those involved in it away from local customs and practices in favor of amusements and manners learned from connections to London or other outside centers; for example, literate Welsh landowners abandoned the local language still spoken by most of their countrymen in favor of English. Such people contrasted with others in the same places, and at the same social level, who remained committed to traditional sports and pastimes.[36] Thus the growth of national networks in politics and culture led to divisions between those who found opportunities in them and others who for whatever reason sought to ward off their influence, giving a new form to the old split between "court" and "country."

Well before industrial innovations provided means to generate new forms of social power, and before government was formally democratized, the effects of living in a situation permeated by distant linkages spread a precocious modernity through English life. It was because networks of all kinds drew people at different social levels into similar kinds of social relationships that commercial and industrial activities and the people involved in them assumed an ever-larger place in English life, not in opposition to aristocrats and landowners but in ways that provided power and resources to both groups. This was the situation that makes understandable the mix of what otherwise might seem paradoxical qualities I highlighted at the start, making England at once the most bourgeois country and the least.

A digression: empire and nation

Before leaving this discussion of England's precocious integration I
need to say a word about the relationship between the developments
I have highlighted and a phenomenon of great importance to them,
namely the rise of Britain as an imperial power. England's empire
(British after the unification with Scotland in 1707) had been growing from early in the sixteenth century, but its economic and political
importance swelled in the eighteenth with the expansion of the East
India Company's operations in one direction and the bourgeoning trade
with an increasingly populous and prosperous North America in the
other. Although continental Europe remained Britain's most important foreign market through most of the eighteenth century, the value
of trade there grew only very slowly after 1700, whereas commerce
with foreign and colonial areas expanded dramatically; the value of
tea imported by the East India Company multiplied some forty times
by 1760, imports from North America rose fourfold and those with
the West Indies doubled in the same period. By the mid century nearly
40 percent of the goods Britain sold on the continent were colonial in
origin, and the expanding domestic market absorbed large quantities
of them too, in the process instilling new tastes and habits – tea-drink-
ing prominent among them – in consumers. The energy and riches
pumped into the British economy by these connections and the need
to defend them against jealous foreigners were the chief reasons that
made the Admiralty and Navy Boards (in the words of John Brewer
quoted a moment ago) "too vital to the national interest to be held hostage by the forces of graft and corruption."[37]

Historians have long been aware that imperial connections
were central to English history over centuries but this awareness has
recently assumed different forms as historical understanding has been
reshaped by a series of connected factors: the collapse of European
empires during the twentieth century, the sense evolved and propa-
gated by formerly colonized peoples and writers seeking to speak on
their behalf that Europe's chief importance in global history lies in
the rise and decline of its world domination, the heightened attention
to the suffering and disruption brought on by the violent and inhu-
mane practices put in place to enforce colonial control, and resolute
critiques of the pretentious and self-righteous claims developed to justify it. Much new and valuable awareness has been gained by these

developments, but they have also generated more questionable claims, in particular through attempts to assign empire a place so central in historical understanding that forms of national experience become radically dependent on it. The editor of a recent volume propounding this kind of interpretation chides those who stand outside the enterprise she and her colleagues pursue for their unwillingness to embrace "the notion that the nation is not only *not* antecedent to empire, but that as both a symbolic and material site the nation – as Judith Butler has argued for identity and Joan Scott for gender and experience – has no originary moment, no fixity outside of the various discourses of which it is itself an effect."[38]

Such a view (present in more nuanced form in other writings) makes sense if it is taken to mean that the particular features attributed to a nation by those who seek to define its character to itself and others are produced through assertion, discussion, and debate, and that these interchanges involve spoken or unspoken comparisons with outsiders. But the claim such a formula puts forward reaches beyond this to include "nation" in a second sense, the "material" one that I presuppose here when I take the term "nation" to refer to a definable population whose mutual interactions, economic, political, and cultural, establish characteristic and distinctive patterns of relations between its components that persist in some degree over time. Even before coming to our substantive treatments of other countries, the comparisons we have begun to make with them suggest how deeply rooted in geography and history the defining qualities of the English national community were. Empire was to be sure far from irrelevant to the precocious integration that gave a special shape to so many features of the country's life, and by the middle of the eighteenth century imperial connections had become important factors in strengthening it. But the account I have been developing makes clear that the special shape of English history had many other roots. France had an empire in the eighteenth century too, but its impact on national life as a whole was much weaker, in good part because the country was more fragmented and the state far less interwoven with the varied social forces who could make their voices heard in Parliament; it was the form given to English national life by the webs of interaction constituting it that determined the role empire played, not the other way around.

One point often urged by those who give empire priority over the nation is that pride in imperial power infused English people's self-understanding (and later that of other Europeans). Indeed a "cult of commerce" had become part of British national identity by the mid eighteenth century, and both the far-flung reach of trade and its role in spreading English ideas and institutions throughout the world heightened the value attached to it. Here too, however, empire fit inside a larger and older national frame, largely constructed out of other elements. The first and core component of national self-esteem was the celebration of "English liberty" and the laws and institutions that protected it, to which defense of the "true," that is Protestant, Christianity was added after the Reformation (and especially after the union with Scotland). The moral worth ascribed to trade and empire rested on their supposed ability to spread these advantages elsewhere, and the recognition that instead imperial domination often led those it empowered to behave in ways unworthy of the civilization they claimed to represent – by profiting from the horrors of the slave trade or exploiting and corrupting natives in India (a cause taken up with force by Edmund Burke) and elsewhere – soon became a reason for critics to see imperial relations in a much more negative light.[39]

These nay-sayers never became a majority, although the successful revolt of the American colonies put more wind in their sails for a time, so that during the early nineteenth century the ability to manage relations with non-European areas by economic rather than political means – dubbed "the imperialism of free trade" by some historians – was often preferred to formal control. What underlay the opposite turn to a "new imperialism" after 1860 was less popular support for empire (although there was much of that) than competition with other countries, a rivalry that became sharper as France and Germany, their national spaces remade through new networks of transport and communication, were able to achieve the tighter kind of integration England had exhibited more than a century earlier, and on that basis move to new and more modern forms of industry and politics. I will argue later that it was the creation of these more closely structured national frames that made the era of heightened imperial competition also the moment when England lost the advantages her precocious integration had yielded before: at this point as earlier the relationship between empire and nation was part of the broader evolution of networks of means within which both developed. In the later period as in the earlier one the various purported elements of national identity could conflict with each other, and when they did the imperial one did not always win out.[40] These are sketchy observations perhaps, but hopefully they suffice to indicate why I think we should agree with the eminent imperial historian P. J. Marshall that "The Empire … reflected and reinforced trends in British history, but rarely seems to have pushed it into radically new directions."[41] We need now to recognize a similar power in the longstanding historical patterns that defined national life in other countries.

3 MONARCHICAL CENTRALIZATION, PRIVILEGE, AND CONFLICT: FRANCE

The mosaic of privilege

If England was at once the most bourgeois country and the least, a correspondingly revealing paradox for France was that the country which became the homeland of modern revolution was also the one whose transformation between the eighteenth century and the twentieth was the slowest and least complete. The nation that provided the exemplary instance of large-scale social and political upheaval and gave the term "bourgeois" to the world might be expected to be a trailblazer in modernity and an exemplary case of fundamental and sweeping social change, but it was neither. The Revolution changed much to be sure but it left many features of French life intact, as Alexis de Toqueville famously argued. No major European economy grew as slowly and with so little transformative impact on daily life, at least until the last years of the nineteenth century, as did the French.

A few statistics tell the story. In 1880 approximately half of the active population of France was still working in agriculture. In England that number had declined to 25% by 1840, forty years earlier, a level that France would not reach until the 1950s. In 1861 only 11% of French people lived outside the *Département* where they had been born; in 1881 the number was still only 15%. Save for Paris and a few other cities, it was only after 1850 that urban population grew faster than that of the country as a whole; until then cities expanded at a rate equal to or below that of France overall. Even at the end of the nineteenth century the country's urban fabric exhibited a pattern remarkably continuous with the Old Regime. Of the fifteen French cities with a population greater than a hundred thousand in 1906, only two, Roubaix and Saint-Étienne, had what Jean-Pierre Daviet calls "a character broadly determined by the industrial urbanism we associate with the nineteenth century." All the others had already figured among the country's biggest cities before the Revolution, continuing to grow largely on their earlier foundations, so that "the nineteenth century gave clearer shape to a pre-existing urban hierarchy, without really creating its own."[1] The contrast between the gradual, unhurried pace of French economic change and the country's agitated political history, punctuated by revolutionary moments in 1830, 1848, and 1871, should caution us against believing that the two spheres of the economy and politics must necessarily develop in tandem (that economic conditions often have a powerful impact on politics is a different matter), and historians have been too slow to take the lessons of this rhythmic discord. We will see that both the French version of modernity and the French bourgeoisie was deeply marked by this two-sided quality of the country's life.

As in the English case, we can best understand this paradox by considering the configuration of networks through which France achieved its particular mode of unification over the centuries. Monarchy was a main vehicle of integration for both, but two features of the French instance gave it a distinctive character. First, in contrast to its rival, geography offered little support for creating links between cities, towns, or regions. Distances were significantly greater than in England, rivers (as noted in the previous chapter) provided less favorable arteries for travel, and it was far more difficult to connect major cities by coastal shipping. The factors that favored the spontaneous growth of trade between distant areas in England and contributed to the early rise of a national market there worked instead to impede such a development in France. This meant that royal attempts to draw regions into a web of political ties could not rest on an underlying weave of economic connections; sometimes they had to substitute willful policy for unplanned growth. Second, unlike the Normans in England, the French kings had to confront feudal competitors often no less and at some moments more powerful than they, so that their centuries-long efforts to draw together the territories that eventually became the French nation had to be carried out against strong resistance. The need to make various compromises with these rivals led them to create what Joseph Strayer revealingly called a "mosaic state," a collection of variously shaped and colored pieces whose setting into a single frame left the differences between them an important determinant of the overall pattern. As Robert Darnton observed some time ago, if any single word can characterize the structure and spirit of the Old Regime it is "privilege," a term that literally means private law. The French monarchy was a public entity, but one based on relations that often had the character of private transactions, dealing with both regions and categories of people by offering them exemptions from principles and arrangements it aspired to make general. Individuals and groups in all three of the estates of the realm (clergy, nobility, and the Third Estate that included everyone else) had relations to the government based on complex and often baroque combinations of obligations and exemptions. Nobles were the most famously privileged group, but we will see that numerous bourgeois acquired privileges of various kinds too, and they were no less committed to maintaining them. The tissue of threads that wove the country together was strewn with a variety of messy knots.

Central to this peculiarly French pattern of integration was the issue of taxation, especially thorny because it was the juncture where the two main species of privilege, social and regional, came together; the Revolution could not abolish the first without also targeting the second. Despite the national status of certain taxes, they were differently levied and collected in different parts of the kingdom; some regions were exempt from certain levies, or paid them at a lower level, and the exemptions enjoyed by social groups were woven into these geographical distinctions. The regions that paid less were determined to maintain this favorable treatment, creating a barrier against reformers' attempts to institute a more uniform and efficient system. Since, in addition, customs barriers separated some of these same regions from the rest of the country, efforts to eliminate internal duties on goods were resisted too, for fear that the tax privileges would disappear with the tariffs.[2]

It was widely recognized that barriers to the flow of goods detracted from prosperity, making commodities more expensive and putting a rein on both trade and manufacturing. Even some figures whose policies are usually seen in terms of regulation and restriction, such as Louis XIV's famous minister Jean-Baptiste Colbert, argued that French well-being could be furthered by simplifying and lowering internal tariffs, and to the very end of the Old Regime royal officers sought to inject more regularity into the system, aiming to foster what one recent historian calls "greater efficacy of government policy in economic matters."³ But these efforts were constantly stymied by the architecture of regional privilege through which the kings had built up political unity. The monarchy that was the chief vehicle of national integration was saddled with a contradictory logic, pitting its efforts to give the country a more coherent and workable structure against the compromises with privileged groups it had found it necessary to adopt in order to pursue its goal.

The Old Regime and the limits of reform

We can see these patterns at work in the decades between the death of Louis XIV in 1715 and the outbreak of the Revolution by looking at a series of attempts by the government to improve the economy and rationalize political life, and at the underlying economic situation these efforts sought to manage and reshape. This survey will show both that people in the Old Regime were well aware of the need to extend and develop distant connections inside the country, and that the difficulties of doing so made the transition from the kinds of regulative principles we have called teleocratic to ones that can be seen as autonomous much slower in France than in England.

A good place to start is with the theoretical grounds offered for economic integration, not because these ideas determined the outcome of reform efforts, but because they revealed much about the character of the country. By the eighteenth century the voices long raised on behalf of eliminating barriers to internal commerce had swelled to a chorus. Because those who made it up called for freer trade, they have often been linked to their contemporary Adam Smith, and to later liberal writers, who advocated reduced regulation as a spur to more efficient production. But many of these French figures shared a view at odds with Smith's belief that the key to heightened productivity and thus to national well-being lay in the more efficient organization of industry; in their eyes only one productive activity possessed the power to create new wealth: agriculture.

The best-known proponents of these views, and the origina-
tors of the oft-repeated slogan *laisser-faire, laisser passer,* were the
group called the physiocrats, among them François Quesnay and
Pierre Samuel du Pont de Nemours, whose influence on officials such
as Anne-Robert Jacques Turgot and Daniel-Charles Trudaine gave
them considerable practical importance. The reason they saw farming
as the only enterprise able to yield a product greater than the materials
and labor invested in it was that land alone benefitted from the vital
powers lodged in nature that made seed grow into crops. By contrast,
manufacturing merely turned raw materials into finished goods without adding any new value to the product, trade only moved existing
values from one place to another, and labor merely transferred the
value of wages to the things workers produced. In such a perspective
the purpose of reducing trade barriers was not to encourage the division of industrial labor but to allow the surplus product that could
not be consumed where it was produced to flow to places that could
not meet their own needs by themselves, at once shoring up well-being in these less-favored locales and further stimulating production
by sending the realized surplus, in the form of payments, back to a
region where it could be profitably invested in renewed agricultural
production.[4]

Along with the elimination of trade restrictions, the physiocrats advocated agricultural improvements in line with those practiced
in England, land-clearing, fertilization, and the removal of traditional
and communal restrictions on how farms were organized, seeing them
as an important lever of prosperity. The advantages to such a policy
in their eyes were not only economic: as production expanded on this
basis, the higher incomes generated would allow the state to institute
a more uniform tax system (based on the rising net product of agriculture), and with it a national bank something like the English one.
These notions led the physiocrats to posit a close connection between
the greater economic freedom they called for and vigorous government
action to effect and manage it. They were thus supporters at once of
liberal policy and of central control, a position less paradoxical than
it may seem, once we remember that the state was the chief creator
of national space in France, and that state officials were among the
main proponents of economic integration, often desiring it at a higher
level than their own unavoidable compromises with privileged interests allowed. The economic thinking behind such proposed reforms

focused on freeing up natural forces by a kind of governmental fiat, since fearful private people were often resistant to change, rather than looking to the power of demand to stimulate investment and raise productivity. Policies along these lines were actually adopted in the 1760s, when Louis XV's minister Choiseul introduced reforms aimed at freeing up the grain trade and ending other economic restraints. But the measures could hardly have been enacted at a worse moment, since a series of poor harvests put the ability of many rural people to survive in jeopardy, breeding pressures to provide grain at cheap prices, rather than giving market forces a freer rein. The government quickly abandoned its experiment. Historians have argued about how much improvement took place in French agriculture before the Revolution (as indeed for some decades after); there was surely some, but innovations of the kind associated with the spread of enclosures in England were largely limited to the area around Paris, where the pull of so large an urban market made itself directly felt. In many ways French agriculture remained traditional and locally oriented until after the middle of the nineteenth century. Other reform proposals, such as various attempts to abolish guilds, called forth even greater protests (as noted in Chapter 2), so that they too had to be given up.[5]

Both the kinds of visions that inspired attempts to integrate and develop national life and the barriers they encountered are well illustrated by a project to which the state devoted great resources, cheered on by writers and reformers outside the government, namely the efforts to improve transport and communication set in motion by the government department responsible for bridges and roads, the *ponts et chaussées*.

One reason why the projects conceived there deserve special notice is that, as François Caron has shown, they created the terms in which French railroad construction would be debated, planned, and carried out after 1830. French observers in the early nineteenth century still echoed the plaints of their mid eighteenth-century predecessors, that the country's development was impeded by its lack of commercial integration, and railroad construction would be seen as realizing, finally, "the national unity that road-building had only begun."[6] Their forerunners had been similarly inspired by a "coherent and centralizing vision of the organization of the national territory," to be realized in the earlier case by means of a "national network of roads and canals." To this end they set up construction sites in various parts of the country, building more than 20,000 kilometers (over 12,000 miles) of land and water routes (far more in roads than in canals). Behind their efforts were economic notions like those voiced for instance by the Marquis de Condorcet when he wrote that good roads capable of rapidly moving a surplus not needed in the region where it was produced to another where it could be sold were implements for making "something of nothing," letting an otherwise stunted potential for wealth blossom, as well as providing new capital for agricultural improvement and encouraging other forms of production. In a similar vein Charles-Joseph Panckoucke wrote in his well-known *Encyclopédie méthodique* published in the 1780s that improved roads had the ability to "double riches."

At the same time, however, the officials of the *ponts et chaussées* had other, less specifically economic goals in mind, namely furthering the cultural unity of a country where the languages and customs of some regions remained strange and foreign to people from others (a concern that would still inspire the proponents of railroads in the following century), and above all serving the political and military aims of the state. To these ends, connections between Paris and other cites were favored over direct links between provincial places, and roads between major locales were laid out on lines intended to be as straight as possible, often bypassing lesser towns, which had to be served by secondary branches. (Needless to say, such measures were not intended to spare urban centers from excess traffic in the manner of more modern ring roads.) Trade and commerce were sometimes served by these projects, but the planners had little interest in giving merchants or producers better connections to their suppliers or consumers; the stimulus to national life the administrators hoped to provide was to come from the center, letting information and activity flow outward to the distant reaches of the kingdom. Impressive as the results were, they still left France with what later observers and planners would recognize to be a limited and fragmentary system of communication. Bernard Lepetit emphasizes the difference between the relatively well-developed road network that came to characterize the northern part of the country and the much inferior one in the south. Caron prefers to speak of "a structure split up into regional networks, between which relations remained difficult." Both agree that the cities favored by the administrators were those that occupied prominent places in an already established urban hierarchy, based on their importance in administration, and whose non-state revenues came chiefly from agriculture and land rent.[7]

The limits to what the French state achieved in improving internal communication stand out especially when compared to English developments. The much greater improvement in British road travel was brought about by turnpike trusts, private companies licensed by Parliament but set up through local initiative, that collected tolls from users and invested part of the revenues in maintaining and bettering the roads, a system made possible by the greater development and importance of distant markets there. By 1750 there was hardly an English town without a good connection to this system. The dominance of state action in France was premised on an understanding that too few private individuals had either the desire or the resources to effect a similar improvement in social infrastructure. The state's assets were limited too, given the growing budgetary difficulties with which warfare and the inefficient tax system saddled the monarchy, and the recourse to forced peasant labor, the royal *corvée*, to maintain the roads, was both inefficient and a source of resentment. In the 1770s Turgot set out to speed up road travel by instituting a service with faster coaches called *diligences* that reduced the travel time between Paris and other cities (at least for customers able and willing to pay their higher fares), and his efforts were widely praised. But here too government policy was intended largely to serve ends that grew out of its own operations, rather than ones that emerged independently outside it; connections involving Paris were of primary importance, and overall the service remained spotty and irregular. English travelers remarked on the lack of traffic on French roads, and Arthur Young (whose reports on his travels in France provided much information about the country as a whole that few French observers possessed themselves) observed that the "universal circulation of intelligence, which in England transmits the least vibration of feeling or alarm, with electric sensibility, from one end of the kingdom to another, and which unites in bands of connection men of similar interests and situations, has no existence in France."[8] His comment testifies to the developed awareness people had of how important travel and communication networks were to national life, and how differently they functioned in the two places.

None of this should be taken to indicate that the French economy was in general backward in the eighteenth century; in many ways it was just as dynamic as the British one. Much of the energy driving it forward came from an impressive expansion of foreign trade (some numbers suggest it quadrupled during the eighteenth century), partly with France's own colonies, especially in the Caribbean, and partly with Italy, Spain, northern Europe, and the Levant. One result of this expansion was a boost to the commerce of port cities, notably Bordeaux, Marseilles, and Nantes, and a consequent building boom that made the construction industry one of the success stories of the pre-Revolutionary economy, producing new streets and squares in a manner much like the "urban Renaissance" that began after 1660 in England. The rebuilding of Bordeaux was particularly impressive, and Arthur Young opined that no city of similar size in his own country could stand comparison with it. All the same, the conditions of communication in France set limits to the impact these developments could have in many parts of the country, and one historian has recently remarked that anyone who journeyed from Bordeaux to the Massif Central at this time "would have found himself moving from a maritime to a mule-pack economy in the space of a few days." At the same time, however, the advance of international trade drew some distant places into new networks in beneficial ways; for instance, the grain exported through Bordeaux to America from Montauban, some 200 kilometers to the southeast, tripled during the first half of the eighteenth century.[9]

Mushrooming trade opportunities also stimulated manufacturing, especially of textiles and of iron, giving a strong boost to French industry, whose output may have been expanding at a faster rate than Britain's, probably producing a larger per capita product, at least during most of the century.[10] Although much manufacturing (especially of the more skilled variety) was located in urban places, the work was increasingly done in the countryside, usually organized by merchants from nearby towns who put the materials out to part-time workers unable to support themselves fully through agriculture. Some of these merchants took the next step toward something more recognizable as modern industry, gathering workers together in factories, at first on the basis of traditional techniques, but sometimes adopting new tools from England, such as the spinning jenny, soon after they were introduced across the channel.[11] Even where older methods still prevailed, the effect of distant connections on local life could be profound. A study of peasants who doubled as textile workers in the northern village of Montigny, near Cambrai, describes the way some rural people engaged in linen-weaving used the income they derived to set themselves up as little entrepreneurs, organizing the work of their neighbors. The lives of such people were marked by their connection to distant markets no less than in England: "Montigny's peasants saw further than the farm gates and the village boundaries. Their connections to the world beyond were dynamic, born out of a mixture of necessity and response to opportunity," and some of them "actively sought such contacts and inserted themselves within far-flung networks." With their partners in urban markets they often formed connections based on "mutual recognition and potential trust and respect" (like those between urban traders in different cities). Their activities weakened certain traditional communal solidarities, and some around them resented their greater affluence (although we need to remember that differences of wealth and status were a common feature of rural and village life), but such people were not bourgeois; they remained villagers engaged in an essentially peasant form of existence. Similar situations probably obtained in other, less-closely studied villages.[12]

Despite all these achievements, however, France's economy never developed the self-generated dynamism that England's did. One testimony to this was the large role played by state action in introducing new techniques. The mid century minister Daniel Trudaine, a friend of the economist Vincent de Gournay from whom the physiocrats and Turgot derived some of their chief ideas, and a force behind the push to build roads and canals mentioned above, set up industrial projects in order both to bring prosperity to declining agricultural regions and to assure a demand in France for cotton grown in the colonies. His enterprises were freed from guild and other restrictions, producing a situation where, as Paul Butel puts it, "monarchical interventionism and liberal policy were closely allied," a connection whose necessity physiocratic theory took for granted, and that would long remain important in France (as in Germany). His son and successor carried on his work, setting up a cotton-spinning factory under the direction of an English businessman, John Holker, who introduced the recently invented spinning jenny. The government also initiated efforts to modernize cast iron production, recognizing its possible military importance, and bringing in another prominent Englishman, John Wilkinson, to oversee a coke-fired foundry at Le Creusot in 1785. The town would later be an important site of the French metal industry, but in this period activity languished there, "too dependent on the subventions of an impecunious state, and suffering from the lack of skilled workers and above all from the narrowness of the market."[13]

That the state was drawn into such activities was partly a continuation of its longstanding attempt to develop the economy and bring the country's regions more closely together, but these initiatives also reflected an explicit or tacit recognition that the fragmentation which the officials of the *ponts et chaussées* sought manfully to overcome left many areas without sufficient incentive to pursue innovation and expansion on their own. By the 1780s, when France faced a series of poor harvests that put a sharp dent in the prosperity brought by the earlier part of the century, certain structural weaknesses in the economy, especially in comparison to Britain, came to the fore, contributing to the Revolutionary crisis. As a recent French writer puts it, the "essential difference" between the two economies "were those having to do with the structures of production and of the market, more than the rhythms of growth."

> The proportion of the active population employed in industrial production in Great Britain was more than double the French, 43 percent against only 19 percent, and the relatively weak productivity of French agriculture, joined to the conjunctural difficulties of the period, depressed the level of life of the majority of the peasant population, and thus the demand for manufactured articles. In the English cities, by contrast, growing and with a unified national market, general demand was rising and demand for manufactured articles stayed at a higher level.[14]

Those contrasts rested on the differing degrees of integration in the two cases, and they would persist well past the end of the eighteenth century.

To round out this picture of the continuing hold Old Regime conditions retained over French life and the ways they limited reform efforts, we look for a moment at attempts to improve the royal financial administration. As in England, the government department in charge of tax collection in France, the *Contrôle générale des finances*, was long organized as a complex structure of patron–client relations. The people appointed to head its various *bureaux* gained their places through royal favor or purchase, appointing their own favorites in turn to the lower positions under their sway, and paying them out of the income they received from their offices. John Bosher, in a classic study, described the system as "a combination of aristocracy and private business," well aware that the "business" in question had nothing to do with industrial production. Each head ran his section in the way he chose, and social hierarchy always took precedence over efficient operation. If the minister at the top happened to be a commoner, as was the reforming banker Jacques Necker, some fictional veil had to be fabricated to make it seem that no aristocratic official received his salary from him, lest he suffer an insult to his dignity. The whole configuration perfectly exemplified the way that "the aristocratic society of the *ancien régime* inevitably undermined all general laws and regulations because privileges, *grâces*, favors and marks of distinction consisted in personal exemptions and exceptions." Similar arrangements had prevailed in England until after 1688, when they were replaced by the modernized bureaucracy we encountered in the previous chapter.

In France, efforts to effect a change along the same lines appeared almost a century later than in Britain, under Necker's first ministry (1776–81). Necker sought to introduce a uniform system in which the principle of efficient service to the government replaced the maintenance of patronage and hierarchy, abolishing venal offices and special gifts, and establishing a chain of authority based on administrative rather than social criteria. But Necker's opponents accused him of putting France under the rule of a *bureaucratie*, by which they meant not government by royal councils (as in earlier usage) but rule by unworthy officials whose abstract methods subverted the "natural" hierarchy on which social order rested, much in the way Turgot's critics of 1776 viewed his attack on guilds. His successor Calonne restored the old system. The failure to reform it came partly from resistance on the part of influential aristocratic groups and individuals who profited from it, and partly from the size and weight of the administration itself. By the end of the *ancien régime* the *ferme générale* (the agency charged with harvesting the excise taxes on salt, wine, soap and oil, in the provinces where it could be levied, as well as the customs duties on goods entering from regions outside this so-called *grande ferme*) had become what one recent historian calls "a state within a state" with 58 offices in Paris employing 685 people, and 228 *bureaux* in the provinces employing over 28,000. Not surprisingly, its officials did not welcome reforms that would have reduced or eliminated their functions.

Only under the Revolution would administrative reform measures in the spirit of Necker's be permanently put in place. The changes focused at first on organization rather than personnel: salaries were paid directly to employees, who were made responsible to the managers of their departments instead of to aristocratic patrons, offices were reorganized so as to bring related tasks into a single section. Under the Directory (after 1795) large-scale replacements of staff were undertaken as well, so that by the end of the century the old system of favoritism and clientage had been superseded by what Bosher calls a national civil service. Personal influence did not disappear, to be sure, but it was no longer accepted as a basis for organization: a network long subjected to teleocratic purposes defined outside it had been reshaped in accord with principles formulated in accord with its own operations.[15]

The monarchy and the bourgeoisie

All these elements of the pre-Revolutionary economy and state contributed to forming the Old Regime bourgeoisie. Despite dissatisfactions that found expression in the famous criticisms of society and the state mounted by writers such as Voltaire and others, most French bourgeois were, in the words of Pierre Goubert cited in Chapter 1, "pillars of the régime and felt at home inside it." Merchants, traders, and manufacturers were part of this group, and I will come to them in a moment. But in order to grasp the overall conditions of bourgeois existence the best starting point lies with those whose activities Goubert describes as "perhaps the essential functions of the old bourgeoisie," namely "collection, taxation, conversion, and circulation of money."[16]

The wealthiest and most influential of these *bourgeois d'ancien régime* were the *financiers* who performed this family of tasks in the higher reaches of the royal bureaucracy. That they were only partly bourgeois, or bourgeois only from a certain point of view, is one thing that makes their existence so revealing, since it was they who succeeded best in the ambition they shared with many other upwardly mobile commoners, namely to become ennobled through holding a state office. Such changes in status had gone on since the sixteenth century, producing the species of nobility called the *noblesse de robe*, in distinction from the "sword nobility" that constituted the original second estate. The *financiers* both did and did not belong to the category of robe nobles. As a group they were, in Guy Chaussinand-Nogaret's account, "common in origin, noble by recent elevation, whose wealth was based on the manipulation of public funds and on various banking and commercial operations ... they belonged both to the Third Estate, where some of their families were still stuck, and to the upper nobility, with whom they intermarried and shared sinecures and positions of power." These were the very people who ran the unreformed financial administration, and it was their presence within it that made evident to many in the country how beholden the state was to both privilege and money. Indeed it was to them, more than anyone else, that the label "capitalist" was applied in the eighteenth century (the word was used in much the same way in Britain). People of this stripe were responsible for building or renovating many of the great chateaux in the Loire valley and elsewhere that remain jewels of the French tourist industry. In eighteenth-century Paris all the richest members of the *parlements* (sovereign courts) were descended from them. What made them so representative of the Old Regime was that, as Gwynne Lewis puts it,

> they formed the elite of that financial group of intermediaries who controlled the economic communication lines between power and the people: the *fermier*, who collected rents and dues for absentee seigneurs; the *receveur des biens du clergé*, who collected tithes for absentee abbots; the customs official, responsible for the collection of local taxes. They were the essential cogs that activated the complicated, often corrupt, machinery of government at Versailles, machinery geared to ensuring the passage of money from the pockets of the poorest to the coffers of the richest subjects of the king.[17]

That such intermediaries were so common and important a feature of pre-Revolutionary life reminds us that during the Old Regime activities and structures dedicated to drawing resources out of separate localities, often from people whose other connections to the world outside remained very limited, were means of mobilizing wealth no less important, and in many respects more fruitful, than were market connections to distant producers and consumers. The networks set up to collect the revenues of landlords and church officials were not political in the sense of pertaining to the state and its powers, but like the conduits of taxation, they were dedicated to drawing wealth (whether in money or in kind) from people, mostly peasants, who would otherwise have consumed it somehow themselves. Exactions set up by both church and state added to the grinding poverty that afflicted many country people (and against which numbers of them revolted in moments of unusual hardship; during the Revolution the *financiers* would be raucously denounced as "bloodsuckers of the people"), but if there was a surplus it was often swallowed up at special moments of celebration such as holidays and carnival time.

To be sure, many French bourgeois devoted themselves to commerce of a more productive sort, seeking to generate wealth rather than simply gathering and mobilizing it. Chief among these were the *négociants*, traders and big wholesale merchants such as those who ran the commerce between Bordeaux and France's Caribbean colonies, people with far-flung connections, often savvy, well informed, with direct knowledge of other countries, at once willing to take risks and careful in their account-keeping. Many lent money to other traders, and sometimes to the state as well. A level below them stood smaller merchants and *fabricants*, their operations as sellers, makers, or finishers of goods more locally based, although traffic in such goods as coffee, sugar, spices, or silks often linked their towns or regions to more distant places. Both these categories contained people who felt oppressed by government policies that reserved access to certain markets to the members of chartered trading companies, especially under Louis XIV and Colbert, and some of them fit a traditional Marxist description of "rising bourgeois" seeking liberation from "feudal" restrictions. Yet numerous sons of such people sought entry into the state's system by buying offices, many of which imposed few duties and amounted to loans or investments, entered into for the sake of a safer return than the ups and downs of commerce provided, as well as for the tax exemptions and noble status they afforded (although usually it was only conveyed after two or more generations). Arrived at this point they commonly espoused views about the social world close to those voiced by the guild masters who denounced Turgot's attempt to dissolve *corporations* in 1776 as turning people into mere "gnawing individuals"; indeed many of the protesting guild masters were hardly distinguishable from merchants and *fabricants*, and among their allies were members of the *parlement de Paris*, some of whose ancestors were bourgeois of this stripe.[18]

In order to appreciate the nature and extent of bourgeois insertion into the Old Regime system of privilege, we need to keep in mind the circumstance, so difficult to grasp from a perspective that equates bourgeois existence with a coming modernity against an aristocracy identified with resistance to it, that bourgeois status could itself be a form of nobility before the Revolution. French kings beginning in the thirteenth century had granted certain inhabitants of chartered towns privileges and exemptions similar to those enjoyed by nobles (if never quite so extensive), based on the assumption that such *bourgeois du roi* in Paris and elsewhere, lived "nobly" off rents and government investments. They could engage in certain economic activities such as money-lending without losing their status, but not in retail trade. This line between bourgeois and noble existence was blurred also from the other side, through noble participation in manufacturing and commerce, especially (but not uniquely) in such activities as mining and metals, that used resources derived from rural land. Guy Chaussinand-Nogaret may exaggerate the progressive character of this aristocratic activity, but his general point is surely correct: the line between those who resisted change and those who furthered it in the eighteenth century seldom ran clearly between nobles and commoners, but there was a marked distinction between those who sought to preserve existing forms of local life both rural and urban from wider economic or cultural connections that might undermine them, and those willing to see the first evolve along with the second.[19]

All the same, there were limits to how comfortable and satisfied bourgeois people could feel in the Old Regime. It was after all a society dominated by aristocratic activities and values (and in which religion fostered an other-worldly orientation that could question bourgeois doings and motives), and strongly hierarchical in its spirit. At least from the twelfth century, bourgeois had been the objects of satire and sarcasm in literature, sermons, and festivals, partly from jealousy perhaps, but partly from distaste for what they did. People who made money through trade and commerce but who sought to imitate aristocratic forms of behavior could easily be made to look silly, as Molière showed in his *bourgeois gentilhomme*, Monsieur Jourdain. Anti-bourgeois sentiment seems to have been at its height under Louis XIV's reign, and it may be that it receded somewhat as Enlightened ideas with their respect for practical accomplishment and material progress gained more influence. Figures like Voltaire and Diderot did not hesitate to voice sharp criticism of aristocrats. All the same, the old disdain for money-grubbing bourgeois never disappeared and it could be easily mobilized (as was still the case even in the nineteenth century) in personal relations. Right down to 1789 it seems that significant numbers of bourgeois felt themselves to be the objects of the "cascade of disdain" that was at least one possible description of social relations under the Old Regime.[20]

Sara Maza has these features of Old Regime life partly in mind when she maintains that few French in the eighteenth century (apart from Anglophiles such as Voltaire) "made a case for the intrinsic value of commercial activity," and those who did defended it "as a means to higher ends, such as the glory of the state or the pursuit of honor in war." She may exaggerate the point somewhat, since there were bourgeois perfectly capable of asserting the greater usefulness of economic and professional work over the leisured luxury of nobles. The anonymous citizen whose long description of his town Montpellier in the 1760s has been highlighted by Robert Darnton had no hesitation in referring to those like himself who belonged to the "bourgeois estate" (including professionals, *financiers*, merchants, tradespeople, and *rentiers* who lived off investments) as "the most useful, the most important, and the wealthiest in all kinds of countries," noting that through their resources they supported the nobles above them and could "manipulate" those below them as they liked. He seemed unworried, perhaps even proud, that in his city people "were known exclusively by the extent of their fortune." But he did not regard all bourgeois activity with the same favor, since he expressed particular doubt about the value of manufacturing, whose products he described as superfluous, in contrast to agriculture, and perhaps morally harmful, since they tempted people to live luxuriously. As John Shovlin has shown, many eighteenth-century French recipes for economic improvement relied less on competition, the motor identified by Smith, than on "emulation," a striving for betterment that involved imitation and the desire for social recognition, encouraged through the prizes offered by various local organizations; for many, it was only when reconfigured as emulation

that economic activity acquired moral value. The role assigned to emulation would persist into the nineteenth century, when many local societies continued to offer prizes for new techniques intended to improve
both economic and moral well-being in their areas.[21]

The palpable but limited degree to which bourgeois might
preserve an existence outside the Old Regime system of favor and
patronage is suggested by a recent study of Paris. Mathieu Marraud
distinguishes two largely separate groups of well-off bourgeois in the
capital during the seventeenth and eighteenth centuries. Both accorded
with aristocrats in valuing family continuity and status above individuality, in their concern for honor, and in their attempts to gain it
by occupying public offices; but those involved chiefly in commerce
sought this affirmation inside the city's own corporate institutions of
administration and government, rather than through becoming part
of the royal system of venal office-holding. Their lives were more
strictly bourgeois than were those whose families sought to clothe
themselves in quasi-noble forms of privilege, a difference heightened
by the Jansenist religious identifications many of them shared, which
encouraged a stricter kind of morality than did the casuistical reasoning of the Jesuits, often criticized as offering excuses for the lax
moral demeanor of some courtly aristocrats. But the border between
the two groups was permeable. Certain members of the more "bourgeois" group did seek a path to ennoblement: some as a next step after
achieving high urban positions, while others looked to royal offices as
a means of advancement when other paths failed to work out for them.
Overall the more "bourgeois" group surely constituted no challenge to
the hierarchical system of which the king was the head. Only the monarchy's collapse and the failed attempt of the Restoration government
to use royal patronage as a political vehicle to restore the fortunes of
Old Regime nobles during the 1820s would remove the system of privilege as a major pole of attraction for ambitious French bourgeois.[22]

The incontrovertible role played by the state in the evolution
of French bourgeois existence, even where other factors were at work
in shaping it, appears also in David Garrioch's study of the increasing
integration he finds in the Parisian bourgeoisie from late in the eighteenth century. Garrioch observes that it makes little sense to speak
of a unified bourgeoisie before then, since the manner of life of well-
off Parisians splintered them almost into separate little worlds. Their
wealth and status might derive from connections to distant markets

or state agencies, but medieval and early modern bourgeois organized their existence through participation in the local life of their neighborhoods. Families (the very ones studied more recently by Marraud) remained in the same *quartier* over generations, participating in parish life, marrying neighbors, gaining their power and status from local office-holding, and finding both patrons and clients in their own section of the city. Over the course of the eighteenth century these separate aggregates began to interact more and fuse, as well-off individuals became increasingly involved in the city as a whole, moving about in their carriages, shopping for special articles in more distant parts of town (aided by street signs and house numbers that now appeared for the first time), and finding marriage partners outside their neighborhoods. One reason for this change was the expansion of commerce and consumption that accompanied the growth in international trade and the improvement in interior communication, drawing people from different areas of the city into similar activities beyond it, and into the more cosmopolitan and secular culture of the Enlightenment. But a still stronger factor in this heightened unity was the expansion of the royal bureaucracy, creating more positions, deepening the common interests and concerns of those who occupied them, and widening the gap between officials and the lesser people around them.

Already visible in the eighteenth century, this process was greatly accelerated during the Revolution. The number of office holders reached 670 in 1780, but by 1795 the number of employees in state service had exploded to around 13,000 (this included many in relatively modest employments, however, of a sort that may not have been counted in the earlier statistics). Many of these people participated in the Revolution, serving as leaders in its early phases and supporting the more moderate regimes that succeeded the radical Jacobin and sans-culotte phase of 1792–94. The challenges of those years, although chiefly directed against aristocracy and privilege and seldom targeting bourgeois as a class or group, nonetheless encouraged a defensive unity among property-owners anxious to protect themselves against egalitarian claims. Later the measures taken by the Restoration government in favor of Old Regime aristocrats would give non-nobles cause to defend themselves against a different danger, preparing for the moment when "bourgeois" could emerge as a political identity. Just what this meant and how far it should be taken as testimony to greater class unity are questions to which I will return in a moment.[23]

Public opinion, state action, and commerce

An important indicator of the special stamp that all these conditions put on bourgeois life in France was the way that "public opinion" emerged during the eighteenth century. Recent historians and theorists have agreed in recognizing the importance of public opinion, and of what Jürgen Habermas famously called the "public sphere," both in preparing the ground for the Revolution, and in regard to the culture and politics of modernity more generally. For Habermas, this public sphere was unquestionably bourgeois, growing up in the spaces created by an increasingly commercialized society and given life by the institutions of communication and discussion – newspapers, reading societies, coffee houses – it brought forth.[24] Although there are good reasons to accept much of this picture (I will specify some of these in a moment), certain of Habermas's critics have made a persuasive case that, at least in France, the emergence of public opinion owed more to actions of the monarchy than to economic or social changes independent of it.

What makes the process these critics describe particularly relevant here is that it exemplifies very well the movement through which "teleocratic" networks, originally established to serve goals defined outside themselves, evolve into "autonomous" ones that generate their principles of operation from within. The starting point was the monarchy's need, from late in the seventeenth century, to gain support for attempts to extend its power in ways that infringed on established positions, or that required higher levels of support from its subjects. Louis XIV first directed his propaganda campaign of pamphlets and diplomatic connections outside of France, since it was intended to justify his conquests and annexations, but meeting the rising expenses of war soon required that he employ similar techniques at home. Faced with a need "to secure the legitimacy of claims that could no longer be made binding in the terms (and within the traditional institutional circuit) of an absolutist political order," the state seemed to have no choice (as Keith Baker writes) but to

> address its claims to a domestic 'public,' deploying pamphlets and other devices of political contestation in internal affairs with as much energy as it had previously done in the international arena. It also required that the

government tolerate (and attempt to use to its advantage) the circulation within French borders of relatively independent newspapers such as the *Gazette de Leyde*, which in turn advanced their own competing claims to define the nature and content of public opinion. But by accepting the logic of a politics of contestation in this way, the royal government unwittingly conspired with its opposition to foster the transfer of ultimate authority from the public person of the sovereign to the sovereign person of the public.[25]

The argument has been extended in a slightly altered form by David Bell:

> Over the course of the seventeenth and eighteenth centuries, the crown did much to build up national lines of communication. Its new administrative officers, even if they often served principally as conduits of information rather than as governors, nonetheless brought vast numbers of Frenchmen into direct contact with the central government … The monarchy itself – rather than the capitalist interests described by Habermas – first sponsored a national press in France … the *Gazette de France*, followed by the *Mercure* and the *Journal des savants*.[26]

Once this tissue of newspapers and contacts had been set up and employed by the king to propound his case, others quickly seized the opportunity to use the same means against him. Among the first to do this were the lawyers who held offices in the *parlements* where the king had to seek approval for legal changes (although if they refused he could force them to register his edicts in the famous *lits de justice*), and it was largely in the debates this occasioned that the new phenomenon of public opinion emerged. Public opinion became independent of the king by virtue of a transformation of the network by means of which he and his ministers had sought to constitute it.

> As long as the king had remained theoretically absolute, any attempt by the French to press claims upon each other (which is what politics is ultimately about) could proceed

licitly only in the form of appeals to the king himself, or
to bodies that acted in his name ... After the middle of the
eighteenth century, however, as royal authority declined,
political claims increasingly took the form of appeals to
the judgment of the 'public' ... [The king now became]
simply another litigant before this new 'tribunal.'[27]

In other words, by extending and thickening a web of relations intended
to further the goals of the higher power on whose behalf it was organized, the government unwittingly provided means by which those
connected to the network could discover and employ lines of communication that bypassed its putatively central and directing point. As
its operations expanded, the volume of communications the network
generated overwhelmed the principle according to which only those
flows directed by royal authority should be regarded as legitimate; the
new standard validated any communication, regardless of where it
originated or to whom it was directed, as long as it contributed to the
public interchange the network afforded.

French observers maintained both that public opinion was a
force emerging all over Europe and that it exhibited certain special
features in their country. On the one hand, as one publicist wrote,
through the agency of public opinion "an entire sect, an entire nation,
the whole of Europe, is called to pronounce judgment upon a host of
objects regarding which, previously, only despotism or the interest of
particular individuals had the right to make themselves heard. From
this gathering of ideas, from this concentration of enlightenment, a
new power has formed that, in the hands of public opinion, governs
the world and gives laws to the civilized nations." On the other hand,
French public opinion was seen as differing from other cases, in particular from the English one, first because, in a country without effective representative institutions, it had to be more powerful in order to
restrain sovereign authority without the aid of an institution such as
Parliament. At the same time, it was less individualistic, because in
contrast to England, where "liberty ... inspires in men more confidence in their own judgments, and one could even say that, jealous of
every kind of empire, they cherish their own opinions to the point of
independence and take a secret pleasure in diverging from the opinions
of others," French public opinion sought a rational consensus as a basis
for national unity. In practice particular, groups sought to improve

their position by appealing to public opinion, but public discussion was expected to give rise to general principles of government, not to compromises of the sort effected by the clash of parties and lobbies.[28] Pierre Rosanvallon points out that many critics of absolutism in eighteenth-century France judged the legitimacy of laws not according to who made them, as they saw to be the case in Parliamentary England, but based on a belief in their rationality. The sovereign nation was imagined as the embodiment of this rationality rather than as a body assembled to represent the totality of groups and interests that composed it.[29] Much of the later contrast between the roles the two countries would assign to intellect in politics seems already foreshadowed here. Despite this difference, however, both cases testified to a shift in the nature of the principles expected to regulate political and discursive interactions, from ones set out in advance and embodied in external and higher powers, toward ones generated out of those interactions themselves, giving autonomy to the expanding networks of communication through which they took place.

This is not quite the whole story of eighteenth-century public opinion, however, since more strictly commercial developments also played a role in its emergence; chief among them was the expansion in publishing. "The production of books in France tripled between 1701 and 1770, the newspaper press went from three titles to several hundred, and the volume of pamphlet literature grew by leaps and bounds after mid century."[30] Much of this journalistic activity served mercantile purposes, and its marked growth in the later eighteenth century has inspired one historian to propose that we recognize a different ground for the development of a sphere of public discourse and discussion in France, namely advertising. The medium of this publicity was a network of papers established throughout the country called *Affiches*, literally public announcements. Much space in them was given over to offering a wide range of things for sale, including articles of everyday use, remedies for various ailments (often touted by people condemned as quacks or charlatans by established physicians, although they also feared their competition), urban and rural property, and venal offices, the latter sometimes recommended to buyers on the ground that they demanded little work. Services were advertised too, including legal and medical help, courses of instruction (some by well-known figures), and genealogical research. Employers and job-seekers advertised too, especially for domestic service at various levels. Alongside these *annonces* the papers printed articles and information, some commercial, listing arrivals of goods or grain prices, some literary, including poetry and observations about life (marriage and family were lauded, and women expected to devote themselves to domesticity), and some in praise of progress and improvement, including road-building, the Republic of Letters, and the *Affiches* themselves. The reach of these papers was local to begin with, but they were also drawn into more distant connections. Colin Jones, who argues strongly for their significance, observes that their animating spirit was that of "the parish pump," but notes too that their localism was far from closed or introverted, opening out onto a wider world.[31] The papers understood their role in just this way, seeing themselves not as the organs of any social group, but of public communication itself. "Men owe their enlightenment to communication and literary correspondence," one paper wrote, "and it is by means of this priceless good of which the barbaric centuries of ignorance knew nothing that uncultivated man began to feel what he could be, and know his value." Speaking of the progress of sciences and arts since the days of the Greeks and Romans, another paper declared that "communication has done everything," and attributed the lesser progress of non-Europeans to "the small amount of communication they have with other peoples."[32]

Here was a public sphere with many of the features Habermas emphasizes, but it too came with a particularly French inflection. Unlike the eighteenth-century English press, which became national in scope as printers and publishers in London and elsewhere took advantage of Parliament's decision to let the Licensing Act lapse in 1694, thus freeing journalism from censorship and restriction, the *Affiches* were indebted to government stimulus for their blossoming. They began in 1753 when the Paris-based proprietors of the *Gazette de France* conceived a plan to develop provincial journals by selling local printers the right to publish public notices in 35 French cities. The papers showed little life, however, until 1771, when they became the instruments for carrying out a government edict requiring that all contracts for land sales be published, in order to protect mortgage holders. It was government action too that opened the papers up to things outside their localities, namely a provision requiring each paper to send a copy of every issue to all the others, in order to give the local *intendants*, who were responsible for censorship, easy access to what was being published.[33] Not surprisingly, considering that the papers were censored, they contained poems and articles glorifying the monarchy. It may be that some readers took the praise of "nature" and the condemnation of luxury as veiled attacks on a social and political order in need of radical reform, as both Colin Jones and Jack Censer suggest, but it is well established by now that such criticisms were neither exclusively nor even characteristically "bourgeois" – how could they be, given what we have seen above about the Old Regime bourgeoisie? Support for Enlightened ideas, as Didier Masseau has noted, was not located on one or another side of a dividing line between classes or indeed of institutions, but ran "through the Church itself as well as through the elites that held the reins of political power."[34] Important as commercial activity was in giving substance to the segment of the French public sphere occupied by the *Affiches*, the papers' history closely parallels the conclusion we have drawn from Keith Baker's and David Bell's accounts of the more strictly political realm: past a certain point of development, networks of communication fostered by the state in order to serve its own purposes could no longer be strictly controlled by it. As the means they offered were seized by individuals with no traditional claim to legitimate authority, it was their mutual connections and interactions that generated a new meaning for the term "public."

This conclusion can be reinforced by looking for a moment at the world of consumption to which the advertisements in the *Affiches* were tied, and comparing it to the English case considered earlier. The two were alike in important ways. In France as in England people at all social levels were buying and using more items of daily living, from plates, knives, forks, and furniture to textiles of all kinds, including curtains, rugs, underwear, shirts, and skirts. Especially in cities, life was becoming more comfortable, more varied in diet and dress, brighter, more civil and elegant, better provided with amusements, and for some more luxurious. In Paris the value of the clothing owned by people at their death mushroomed spectacularly during the century, tripling in the middle classes, quadrupling for domestic servants (whose wardrobe often included their employers' cast-offs). The most attentive and insightful student of these changes, Daniel Roche, notes that they brought members of the urban working classes into the world of regular commercial consumption. In France as in England these developments were decried for creating breaches in the walls of social distinction, and in particular for the way they eliminated the visible signs of class and status cherished and even legislated in a frankly and self-consciously hierarchical social order. The Montpellier citizen referred to earlier bemoaned the way "the most vile artisans" in his city tried to live as the equals of people superior to them, spending and clothing themselves above their station. Like others, he saw such behavior as morally, not just socially, dangerous. It is this "increasingly materialistic, consumerist world" that Colin Jones sees represented in the *Affiches*, which therefore reveal "close links between the practices of commercial capitalism and the formation of the bourgeois public sphere."[35]

All the same, the French world of consumption had features that distinguished it from the British one. One was its greater fragmentation. Fashions, tastes, and desires for goods spread from Paris to the provinces and from cities to the countryside, but often very slowly. Daniel Roche notes that a place such as Limoges was fifty years behind Paris both in turning to more colorful clothing and in adopting underwear, and that Brittany and Alsace trailed still farther in the rear. Given the lack of connection between regional road networks, this is not surprising. In some places the spread of the new consumption patterns followed on the work of the *ponts et chaussées* officials mentioned above; in Le Mans the opening of a new *grande route* made upper-class women customers for Paris fashions, followed later by more ordinary people.[36] Certain considerations suggest that active marketing was less important than social imitation in diffusing demand for goods in France. Neil McKendrick points out that in England by late in the century the "fashion dolls" used to advertise new styles of clothing and solicit orders were being made cheaply and printed by the thousands, at a time when the French equivalents remained life-size and expensive.[37]

It is not wrong to associate the rising French interest in consumption goods with a society becoming more commercial and materialistic – more "bourgeois" in the ordinary sense – but the elites who led the way owed their wealth, much more than in England, to state employment. Administrative functions often contributed as much or more to urban growth than did economic ones: the expansion of Caen owed less to lace-making than to state officers and bureaucrats, and the quite rapid development of Dijon and Montpellier before the Revolution depended primarily on the increase in royal officials who worked there.[38] In his invaluable book on cities and towns in the Old Regime, Bernard Lepetit pointed out that political economy before the nineteenth century regarded towns as economically important largely because of the mix of population they contained, and in particular because spending by their wealthiest inhabitants provided a stimulus to all forms of production and exchange; only after 1800 did writers such as Jean-Baptiste Say begin to theorize economic advance as a function of productive innovations, rather than attributing prosperity to the social emulation that town life promoted.[39] "As the [eighteenth] century advanced," Gwynne Lewis notes, "the increase in wealth of the top 5 percent of the population provided work for a legion of merchants, artisans and shopkeepers, all devoted to the task of gilding the lives and properties of the rich and the super-rich." The persisting French orientation toward luxury production, in contrast to England, was grounded here. Paris was the great magnet for French consumption and fashion, and Daniel Roche points out that only a third of the city's income, as calculated by Lavoisier in 1791, came from mercantile and agriculture activities; 20 percent derived from urban rents, and the rest, fully half, from the salaries, interest, and other payments that flowed out of the royal treasury.[40] The expansion of French consumption was fed in good part by the very form of wealth mobilization that made financial intermediaries so important an element in the *ancien régime* bourgeoisie, and that made government employment a central feature in the more integrated quality of Parisian bourgeois existence visible by the end of the century.

Revolution, state, and Third Estate

All the same, the new attention given to public opinion and the relations out of which it arose testified to the way that autonomous principles were coming to challenge teleocratic ones in French life. This challenge would take a new and more practical form in 1789, as those elected to the Estates General called to aid the monarchy in reforming its institutions took them over on behalf of new grounds of legitimacy. We cannot enter very far into the thorny question of assigning causes to the Revolution, but near the top of any list would have to be the collapse of the royal financial system in the face of mounting debt, spurred on by the state's inability to replace its complex and corrupt system of overlapping taxes and exemptions with one that mobilized the country's resources efficiently. The inner contradictions to which we have pointed, surfacing in sometimes desperate attempts to push through reform measures, and the struggle they set off between the monarchy and the *parlements* that had to approve them, gave the regime a vulnerability to the decades-long critique of absolutism and privilege mounted by *philosophes* and popular writers far deeper than in any other country.

Once in session, the Estates General found itself drawn away from regulative principles of government long claimed to reside in a sphere of values prior to political life and superior to it, and toward ones like those that critics such as Montesquieu and Rousseau had been seeking to draw forth out of the structures of political interaction itself. Rousseau's concept of sovereignty specifically reconceived the state on such a basis, making it arise out of the mutual interaction of a body of citizens, who simultaneously constitute themselves as the source of legitimate authority and agree to be subject to the laws they collectively sanction. The core of what Rousseau called the "General Will" was precisely the collective will to establish and maintain political life on this basis; the sole ground of legitimacy in civil society was the recognition that all who belonged to it, despite their many differences, were equal both as constituting members of the sovereign authority and as subject to its laws. Thus the principles of any state's existence arose out of the interaction of its members, not from some prior or higher authority or end. It was just this elimination of any aim thought to be more exalted than the will citizens developed out of their mutual relations that made the new notion of legitimate sovereignty so worrisome to conservatives such as Joseph de Maistre. For them, only an "ordained" polity, one ruled by a goal or principle independent of its members wills, could have either legitimacy or the power to endure.

The turn from a teleocratic to an autonomous organization of the French state was announced at the Revolution's very beginning, in the famous "Tennis Court Oath" of June 20, 1789, through which the delegates of the Third Estate constituted themselves as the National Assembly and swore not to disband until they had provided France with a constitution. Giving authority to such a body implied the existence of a nation without division into Estates and founded on its own act of self-creation. This nodal point, marking the formal dissolution of the Old Regime, would be given substance in the succession of later moments of which the famous night of August 4, in which nobles renounced their special privileges, was the first; the successive Revolutionary assemblies would seek to establish institutions for the new regime in the following years. But the end of the Old Regime was also a culmination of certain tendencies within it, expressions of the logic that led the monarchy and its officials to give the country a more uniform and effective organization by reducing internal tariffs, freeing up the grain trade, reforming the taxation system, reorganizing the financial administration, and doing away with guilds. Reconstituting the nation on a basis that eliminated the regional and corporate divisions into which it had been divided was a more fundamental measure than any of these, but it shared with them the impulse to restructure society on a ground not mapped by privilege.[41]

The Tennis Court Oath has sometimes been regarded as a defining moment in the drama whereby classes play their successive roles on the stage of world history, for the reason that the social group most closely associated with privilege was the Second Estate, the nobility, while most bourgeois belonged to the Third. But the deep insertion of the eighteenth-century bourgeoisie into the Old Regime system, and the role of the monarchy itself in undermining it, provide reasons to understand things differently. There is no better prism through which to pursue such an understanding than the famous pamphlet that the Abbé Emmanuel Joseph Sieyès published in the spring of 1789, *What Is the Third Estate?* and the interpretations that historians persist in giving to it. It was Sieyès who proposed the motion that transformed the representatives of the Third Estate into the National Assembly, and his pamphlet was the most important and influential of the many writings justifying the Third's claims that hit the streets at this moment. The famous answer he gave to his title's question argued that the estate of commoners was not simply one part of the nation but "the whole" of it, since it included all those whose productive efforts made it "subsist and prosper." The privileges and exemptions that defined the nobility (but that extended beyond it to non-nobles) contributed nothing to the survival and development of national life, they simply set the Second Estate apart as a foreign body within the country. Thus it was perfectly in order to regard the Third as embracing everything that made French national existence possible, and capable by itself of setting up the body of laws under which it should live. At the root of these claims was a conception of national life that was fundamentally productivist and economic: even in the Middle Ages the Third was the Estate of the *laboratores*, those who worked; by the eighteenth century the work such people did both in towns and on the land was coming to be seen as "industry" – not in the meaning the word would later acquire, but in the more general sense of industriousness, productive activity.

This vision of the country as an entity that produced itself out of its own labor and the devaluation of nobility that accompanied it made Sieyès the major spokesman for the Revolution in its early, liberal phase, before the onset of more radical actions and demands in 1792–93, a role he would partly fill again in the later period of renewed moderation that followed the dismantling of the Terror in 1794–95. His prominence at these moments is one reason some historians have looked on his pamphlet as part of a program to replace aristocratic with bourgeois leadership. The case has recently been restated by William Sewell, who characterizes Sieyès's famous pamphlet as "a rhetoric of bourgeois revolution." Sewell is too savvy a historian not to recognize that such an assertion needs to be carefully qualified. If Sieyès had some bourgeoisie in mind as a revolutionary agent, it cannot have been one in whose existence modern industrialists and entrepreneurs had a significant part, since they were simply too few, as well as too scattered and fragmented, to constitute a political class. If he was seeking to make such an appeal, its objects could only have been those to whom the term bourgeois applied in the variety of meanings it bore in the eighteenth century, some urban and some not, some active outside government and some inside, referring sometimes to all those who did not benefit from the system of privilege and sometimes only those who had acquired a certain position within it (such as the *bourgeois du roi*). What Sewell believes made so varied a group a candidate for the role he thinks Sieyès had in mind for them was the hierarchical culture and ideology that cast them into an inferior status, making them objects of the "cascade of disdain" that people higher up in the Old Regime social scale regularly directed toward those below them.

There can be no doubt that many bourgeois resented the position in which this put them, but even Sewell admits that this did not dispose them to give heed to Sieyès's supposed call: "He was unable, in the end, to convince them that they were a bourgeoisie in the sense that their nineteenth-century successors or twentieth-century historians would have recognized. That the eighteenth-century bourgeoisie failed to recognize itself in Sieyès's political-economic mirror reveals the depth of the gulf – economic, social, cultural, and political – separating it from the bourgeoisie of the nineteenth century."[42] Why then should we even think of him as aiming for such a result, especially since he never expressed himself in these terms, and since most of those who composed the Third Estate, and whose work sustained the country, were not bourgeois at all? Both resentments against the Old Regime and desires for fundamental political change were widely diffused in French society, animated much less by class differences than by the divisive effects of privilege and corruption. Indeed Sieyès wrote a slightly earlier companion piece to *What Is the Third Estate?*, an *Essay on Privilege*, in which he blamed the regime of favors, exclusions, and exemptions – not social difference as such – for dividing France into separate nations and making the nobility into a parasite on the true nation of productive citizens.[43]

To be sure, once the crisis came, the Revolution would be carried on largely by urban-based people, many of them bourgeois by formation and occupation, with some experience in local government or administration. Where else could sufficient numbers of people be found to carry on the reconstruction of the political system on a basis that would be free of the debilitating contradictions and shackles that brought it down? They were not alone in taking up the responsibilities and opportunities the new situation offered, however; despite the emphasis historians have given to the nobles who emigrated, some 40 percent of noble army officers remained in their posts, and participation by former nobles remained significant in all the Revolutionary assemblies, even the radical National Convention of 1792–94.[44] Nor did contemporary observers use the term "bourgeois" to describe the Revolution's supporters. Many labels were applied to them – members of the Third Estate, patriots, democrats, Girondins, Jacobins, sans-culottes – but not bourgeois. As for its enemies, they were almost never labeled "bourgeois" either, save by radicals who attached it as an adjective to the noun aristocrat, creating a typically Old Regime configuration that precisely elided the opposition between the two categories; for most people it was the idle, the selfish, and above all the privileged who were identified with the old order.[45] These reasons for abandoning the scenario that makes classes the agents of historical change in the Revolution have been accepted by many (though not all) historians, but I hope broader and stronger grounds for putting it to rest have emerged here. The shadow still cast by the longstanding association between the Revolution and the bourgeoisie obscures what really underlay the crisis of the Old Regime. It was not the rise of a bourgeois class that made France revolutionary at the end of the eighteenth century, but the truncated form of national integration that had evolved over time, in which all kinds of internal divisions were as much solidified as weakened by the monarchy's attempts to overcome them. The country's persisting fragmentation made it necessary for the government to take a large part in fostering industrial advance and innovation, since the absence of a national market reduced the incentives for private individuals to engage in it, leaving them to cling to the very order of privilege that stood against efforts at reform, as responses to the state's attempts to abolish internal tariffs and guilds in the 1760s and 1770s revealed.

Reading Sieyès's pamphlet as an appeal to the bourgeoisie as a class not only attributes to him a purpose there is no reason to think he harbored, it also stands in the way of recognizing how deeply his thinking was marked by the special features of the Old Regime. Sieyès was a student of economics and a reader of Adam Smith, whose emphasis on the importance of labor division he shared and developed, but in quite a different way. His starting point seems to echo Smith, making labor an important productive force alongside the creative energies inherent in nature, and seeing labor division as essential to what made it so. But Sieyès maintained that his appreciation and understanding of the division of labor predated his reading of Smith (who, to be sure, did not invent the notion), and the account he gave of it testifies to the divergence in their viewpoints. Whereas Smith began *The Wealth of Nations* with an analysis of industrial labor division, showing how the output of goods (in the famous case of making pins) could be increased by dividing production into delimited and easily repeatable tasks, Sieyès was chiefly concerned about the social division of labor that allowed people to devote themselves to a single occupation (such as baking), and to exchange their products with others similarly focused. Smith had recognized the importance of this form of labor division too, and like him Sieyès regarded its advance as productive both of freedom, since it replaced direct dependency on one or a few powerful superiors with reciprocal ties to a wide variety of differently situated individuals, and of greater wealth, since people became more efficient when they concentrated on a limited line of work. But the champion of the Third Estate was little concerned about the power of market relations to push the makers of goods toward higher productivity under the pressure of competition. Instead he located the source of well-being in the necessity that "society, independently of the power of nature which produces goods, must have a *living force* coproductive of wealth, and it is necessary that the elements of that force, united by society, produce more than they would if they remained isolated. The sum of the labors of all citizens forms the living force."[46]

What allowed society to combine the efforts of its members in this way was the presence within it of "co-productive" workers, people whose endeavors created connections between isolated producers and made exchanges between them more efficient and fruitful. This group included merchants and haulers, as well as scientists and educators, who added to the social product by improving ways of making it. But particularly important within it were those who did the work of the state, taking on a special role in giving society its vital unity just as bakers and butchers did in supplying food. Their work included providing improved means of communication, roads, canals, and ports that "assuredly make a nation richer than if it were deprived of them."[47] The importance of these means and networks was not quite what it was in Smith's scenario, however, since when goods were exchanged in the market, their commerce was regulated not by the abstract mechanisms that gave things market prices, but by the "representations" people made of their own and each other's work. Sewell recognizes that this put a special stamp on Sieyès's thinking: "His basic paradigm for the economy is a network of voluntary, rational, contractual relations – a network of mutual 'representations.'" Social existence and the increase in wealth it generates arise not out of the competition that pushes workers to become more efficient and productive, but "from intentional agreements about mutual advantage; economic progress is a consequence of reason, intentionality, and mutual trust."[48] State officials were particularly important in making these exchanges possible, because their work was "representation" in the most emphatic sense, aiding people to see others as workers like themselves with particular needs and interests, and thus making it possible for society to exist as the "network of representations" that gave stability and order to exchanges and made the product of social labor greater than the sum of its individual parts. Sieyès "never fully grasped the significance of Smith's discovery that the economy could be understood as a self-sufficient system, governed by laws of its own, distinct from those of political science." His principle was not *laisser-faire* but its near-opposite *faire faire*, "cause to be done."[49] Although Sewell maintains that Sieyès's putting state action in the frame of labor division means that he saw politics in economic terms, it makes better sense to conclude the opposite: that viewing the economy as a "network of representations" in whose construction state officials played a crucial role testifies to the central place that governmental action occupied in shaping his understanding of what made the economy work. Such an account puts him in the line of reformers such as Trudaine and the *ponts et chaussées* planners and reformers, for whom state action was an essential tool of economic advance. No more than they did he appeal to some bourgeois class as an independent agent of the changes all of them sought.

The bourgeois monarchy and its meanings

This persistence of these older patterns needs to be remembered in order to understand what it meant – and did not mean – that the term "bourgeois" became an important part of the French political vocabulary during the 1820s and 1830s, and that the regime set up in July of 1830, acquired the name "Bourgeois Monarchy." The term *bourgeois* was largely absent from public discussion in the early years of the Restoration, when Louis XVIII and his ministers sought to rule France harmoniously, preserving the principles of constitutional government and legal equality introduced after 1789, and avoiding policies that would offend or frighten those who had been active in the Revolution and profited from it. The government was friendly and helpful to nobles who had either fled or withdrawn from public life between 1792 and 1815, but it did not question the property transfers that had taken place through the sale of church and *emigré* lands. From around 1820, however, the regime began a marked tilt to the right, pressured by a party of "ultras" seeking more one-sided favoritism for aristocrats, and frightened by what seemed to be a resurgence of radical activity, brought home by the assassination of the king's nephew (and only male heir) the Duke of Berry in 1820. This shift became more marked after Charles X ascended the throne in 1824, instituting defensive and reactionary policies that generated increasing opposition.

It was this turn away from the early Restoration policy of conciliation and social peace on the part of the monarchy, not bourgeois efforts to gain new powers at the expense of aristocrats, that set in motion the developments that would issue in renewed revolution six years later. The critical moment came with the government's decisions to shut down liberal newspapers and put in place a new electoral law, giving greater weight to rural districts and according a "double vote" to their richest inhabitants, many of them large landowners with aristocratic pedigrees. Liberal political figures organized opposition, supported by writers who now urged the claims of "middle class" and "bourgeois" people in a new way. In earlier debates the liberals (dubbed "doctrinaires" because of their fondness for general principles) had sometimes invoked "middle-class" virtues, but in terms still redolent of Aristotle's praise of "middling" people as neither powerful enough to oppress others nor weak enough to be easily corrupted. Rather than put forward claims on behalf of any class, they had offered support for what Sara Maza notes was "the Charter's transcendent, timeless synthesis of the French nation's different components." But faced with a government no longer interested in upholding this synthesis, the liberal writers and politicos moved toward presenting themselves as representatives of the non-noble groups the regime was squeezing out of it.[50]

The case they made for these groups' importance was based on an account or rather a series of accounts of French history which rooted the opposition between bourgeoisie and aristocracy deep in the past, and presented the bourgeois as having always in some way been champions of national unity and well-being. Like the liberal response to Bourbon politics after 1820, these histories were defensive to begin with, conceived in response to aristocratic writers such as the Count of Montlosier, who (writing in 1814) blamed the Revolution and its violence on the medieval communes that, in alliance with the monarchs, had undermined and eventually destroyed the country's original aristocratic constitution. Using language inherited from eighteenth-century writers, Montlosier depicted French history as a struggle not just between principles but between different "races," descendants of the original Franks and Gauls. It was this model that liberal writers, notably Augustin Thierry and François Guizot, took over and inverted, viewing French history as a struggle in which heroic "bourgeois" defenders of freedom and order stood up against violent aristocrats out to consolidate and extend their destructive privileges. The two historians made important contributions to the idea of history as a continuing struggle between classes that Marx would take over a few years later (he acknowledged his debt to them), but they told somewhat different stories. Thierry, a former disciple of Saint-Simon (about whom more in a moment), attributed both political and economic virtues to the Third Estate and the "bourgeois" heroes of his story, using terms that resonated both with Sieyès's portrayal of the unprivileged as sustainers and promoters of material well-being, and with Saint-Simon's celebration of *l'industrie*. Guizot, however, largely saw the Old Regime bourgeoisie through the prism of a different component of it, namely the judges, lawyers, and office holders who, in alliance with the monarchy, had brought order and justice to the country, providing the foundation for national unity. Thierry sometimes gave a place in the story to artisans and poorer town-dwellers, especially where he thought they had joined to resist attacks on civic freedom by bishops and nobles, but Guizot did not hesitate to label such people a "rabble," regretting that their presence inside towns helped to keep educated and stable bourgeois from achieving the position in national life their virtues merited. Taken together, the two accounts show that from the start the bourgeoisie as a historical actor was a construction, not an actual entity, differing in its composition according to who was appealing to it, and invoked in order to give social and moral justification to a particular political program.[51]

The point holds even more clearly for the appearance in these same years of the term bourgeoisie used in a more critical and pejorative sense, as a kind of new aristocracy separate from the mass of French people, and either standing in the way of further progress or exploiting the work of others for their own profit. The most influential source of this usage was Saint-Simon, who arrived at it only by stages. Casting about during the early Restoration for an explanation of the Revolution's failure to establish a regime devoted to developing *l'industrie* and ending privilege and domination, he found it in a conception of social division based on a distinction between idle and productive classes (*oisifs* and *industriels*) much as had Sièyes. Saint-Simon assigned the great majority of his countrymen to the category of producers, at one point estimating it at 96 percent of the population. What had prevented the Revolution from establishing an order in accord with their activities and principles was that the political leaders of the 1790s had not been *industriels* but Old Regime office holders and hangers-on, people he characterized variously as *légistes*, *avocats*, *métaphysiciens*, all of them linked to the monarchy and aristocracy, and infused with their spirit of domination. That he did not label such people bourgeois was partly due to the close ties he still maintained to liberal economists and publicists, particularly Thierry, who portrayed the bourgeoisie he championed as similarly encompassing the great majority of Frenchmen, making it more or less equivalent to Saint-Simon's *industriels.*

But Saint-Simon's ties to liberals weakened as he saw how willing were Guizot and those close to him to work with the restored Bourbon regime. Put off by such cozying up to the aristocracy, Saint-Simon now began to equate the *bourgeois* the liberals were claiming to represent with those he blamed for the failure of the Revolution. The *bourgeois* he targeted included "soldiers who were not noble, lawyers who were commoners, and *rentiers* who were not privileged," all people whose roots lay outside the dominant groups of the Old Regime, but who did well in it and thus became its supporters. It was a motley assemblage, but one he saw as unified by failure to stand on the side of social and political progress. Such bourgeois had little or no connection to the new "industrious" society Saint-Simon identified with the future, and it was this separation that accounted for the narrow results of the Revolution. Saint-Simon's followers picked up on this usage in the years after 1830, picturing bourgeois not just as idlers but as exploiters of the great mass of productive people, a narrow class that sought to grow rich on the work of others, and whose power blocked the coming of the new society where the fruits of heightened productivity would include not just general well-being but also social justice as well. Many elements of later critical views of the bourgeois as a class had their roots here, and the story of Saint-Simon's evolving thinking and vocabulary highlights just how fluid and uncertain the term bourgeois was in the moment when it was becoming part of the political vocabulary.[52]

Once the new regime was established in 1830, its ruling groups turned out to resemble Saint-Simon's narrow and restricted image of the bourgeoisie more than the expansive and inclusive one proposed by liberals such as Thierry. Guizot had propounded a similarly limited but more positively toned image of the group even before 1830, and the qualifications established for voting and office-holding in the July Monarchy hewed close to it. Under the Restoration perhaps 100,000 people, or around one percent of the population had the right to vote; the number was increased by about two-thirds in 1830, and probably reached something between 200,00 and 300,000 (in a population of between 30 million and 40 million) by 1848. England, with a much smaller population, had something over 400,000 voters after 1832. Although it makes little sense to say that the middle class or bourgeoisie as a whole held power in either country, the French "Bourgeois Monarchy" was clearly a much narrower regime than the one across the Channel; many people whose bourgeois status was incontestable could not vote (much less run for office, since requirements for doing so were still higher). And since the government (of which Guizot was the prime minister through most of the 1840s) determinedly resisted calls to extend the suffrage, many of its opponents were no less bourgeois than those it placed in power. The campaigns that eventually led to the crisis of February, 1848, were organized mostly by middle-class politicians and writers. By dividing France into the "legal country" (*pays legal*) that was enfranchised and the remainder (the *pays réel*) that was not, the regime drew a line through the general category of "bourgeois" much like the one set up by the contrast between ordinary town-dwellers and the privileged among them before the Revolution.

Guizot became notorious for rejecting one demand for suffrage extension with the retort "*enrichissez-vous,*" easily taken as a motto of bourgeois materialism. Like his historical work, however, Guizot's political notions focused less on the bourgeoisie as an economic force than on the professional and administrative groups who still predominated within it. His recommendation that those in search of political rights should earn them by enriching themselves included the proviso "by work and saving," and it was the moral qualities made possible by economic independence he valued, not mere material power. With his "doctrinaire" associates, Guizot justified suffrage restrictions on more sophisticated and revealing grounds, marshaling two closely linked arguments noteworthy for the continuities they displayed with pre-Revolutionary ideas and attitudes. One was that it was "reason" not interest that should govern society, as well as constitute public opinion; the second was that the realization of freedom required the intervention of political power: society needed to have the state operate inside it in order to become free.

Like other French liberals at the time, Guizot regarded France as a particularly divided and contentious place, as both the outbreak of the Revolution and its continued influence in French life showed. Whereas English politics proceeded through compromise, with parties willing to make and accept concessions to and from each other, France needed a stronger and more coercive mode of government because it was divided by quarrels between "the most hostile interests, the most violent passions, the most contrary intentions." In such a place, the restricted franchise was necessary in order to assure that power rested with those whose work did not tie them to everyday needs and the passions they aroused, and who had sufficient leisure and intelligence to exercise self-control and cultivate rationality. Included in this group were both upper bourgeois and aristocrats, and the regime Guizot served drew on both: although the contentious spirit that dominated public life for a few years following the upheaval of July, 1830, frightened many aristocratic supporters of the Bourbons out of politics, the government welcomed many of them back as time went on, reestablishing something like the social synthesis sought by the early Restoration (which Guizot himself had served until he was forced out after 1820). The "Bourgeois Monarchy" was dominated by the Old Regime's elite of privilege, reconstituted in the name of the bourgeois element that the second phase of the Restoration had sought to exclude from it.[53]

An important constituent of the political system Guizot believed the July Monarchy represented, and an essential vehicle for the rationality and liberty he thought it made possible, was public opinion. Like earlier liberals, Guizot described the press as the means by which citizens communicate freely with each other and become aware of their common concerns, in the process enlightening authority about the nation's condition and beliefs. But he also approved of the government's using the press to form and lead opinion, drawing people away from their particular interests toward what the state knew to be the general interest. Public opinion was partly a product of discussion and exchange, but it was also, and essentially, a means by which government knit an otherwise scattered and contentious society together, bringing it toward a unity of rational understanding. And since unity and rationality were the grounds of freedom, the state's ability to shape the public opinion it required was essential to the country's enjoyment of liberty.[54]

What made it possible for the state to nurture freedom at the same time it imposed direction was its quality of lying at once outside society and within it. At certain moments in his writings and speeches, Guizot seems to describe society in terms that suggest its autonomy from political power: society is capable of existing independently of any exterior force, many kinds of human relations go on without any reference to outside authority, and the range of these kinds of interactions grows wider as civilization advances. But it turns out that Guizot all along premises this autonomy of social life on the presence of a species of government within society itself, which comprised an essential component of social interaction. Society contains its own system of regulative powers in which "heads" give guidance to "members": in the family, in communities, in formal and informal activities of all kinds. Thus government is able to serve as a kind of mirror of social existence, reflecting it, summing it up, making its common features manifest. Pierre Rosanvallon sees a kind of Hegelian substrate to Guizot's thinking: for both thinkers the state constituted at once the underlying presupposition of social life and the higher form to which it tends. In contrast to Hegel, however, Guizot did not locate the unity the state imparts to society in the monarch (although he assumed that there would and should be one) or in any institutional locus, but in what he called "an abstract unity that can only produce and realize itself through the concourse of all the intelligences and forces within which its elements are scattered."[55]

Such an image of the relations between state and nation recalls Sieyès, who rested the ability of the Third Estate to sustain national life on the presence within it of a class of officials whose task in the division of labor is to represent the whole, thus both framing and animating the "network of representations" through which social and economic exchanges take place. Guizot's theory establishes a similar synergy between government and society, the first giving stability and energy to the second by realizing its potential unity in a self-representation that reflects its own life back in a more developed form. In modern life social power is decentralized, spread throughout society, but a common spirit of civilization and progress animates all these separate points, preparing them to be drawn together by the active political force that realizes their unity. Because the spirit that the state diffuses into the separate regions of local life is the synthesis of all the nation's potential sources of unity, state power does not dampen local energies, it liberates them, and "a large administrative organization, general, regular, and centralized" will serve to establish "a regime of political liberty." As Rosanvallon puts it, what we find in Guizot's liberalism is no "invisible hand" in the manner of Smith, but an "irresistible hand" that, by bringing society to unity and reason, makes political liberty possible.[56]

Thus both the regime that established "bourgeois" as a term in the European political vocabulary and the political theory that justified it testify to the continuing weight that the forms of integration characteristic of the *ancien régime* maintained in nineteenth-century France. Paul Butel's observation that in eighteenth-century political practice (as in physiocratic theory) "monarchical interventionism and liberal policy were closely allied" applies just as well to Guizot's theory of society and government: without the state's nurture and direction of public opinion and its ability to draw society's scattered bits and pieces of rationality together in one central place, the country's potential to advance and to rule itself would remain unrealized. It was just this equation of liberty with centralized authority that Tocqueville deplored as the chief barrier to the development of effective institutions of self-government in his country, the consequence of the bourgeoisie's having learned politics in the same school of monarchical interventionism as the aristocracy. France would eventually evolve other institutions and forms of political practice, making Tocqueville's pessimism less applicable. Like the country's economic transformation, however, they would emerge in the space created by the more extended and thicker networks made possible by railroad building and telegraphy, providing an effective basis for national integration of a kind about which Guizot, like the *ponts et chaussées* officials of the Old Regime, could only dream. We shall see later on how this space allowed France to confront the complex fabric of its past in new ways.

4 LOCALISM, STATE-BUILDING, AND *BÜRGERLICHE GESELLSCHAFT*: GERMANY

Fragmentation, consolidation, and the *Bürgertum*

No less paradoxical than the status of England as both the most bourgeois country and the least, or the case of France as at once the homeland of modern revolution and the country whose transformation during the nineteenth century was most gradual and the least complete, is the case of Germany. By many measures the country of the three where bourgeois groups retained their pre-modern features for the longest time, and where middle-class influence over the direction of government policy was weakest, it was nonetheless the place where the characterization of modern society and politics as "bourgeois" first found clear expression.

In its fully fledged form the notion only emerged during the 1840s, in the writings of Marx and Engels, and soon after, rather differently, in their contemporary W. H. Riehl (whom we will meet later in this chapter). But all of them relied greatly on Hegel's theorization of *bürgerliche Gesellschaft* in his *Philosophy of Right* of 1821. In Hegel as in his German predecessors, *bürgerliche Gesellschaft* had a meaning best rendered in English as "civil society" rather than "bourgeois society" (*Bürger* also means a citizen in German), and their use of the term owed much to earlier discussions about it in other countries, notably eighteenth-century Scotland. But Hegel's theorization differed from these others in a way that revealed its peculiarly German lineage. As will be seen when we consider his analysis in a bit more detail later on, he made a clearer distinction between civil society and the state than earlier thinkers did. The general notion of civil society as an organized form of social life governed by laws made it seem natural to consider political authority as part of it; but rulers and administrators in Germany sowed the seeds of their separation by taking *bürgerliche Gesellschaft* as an object of state action and policy, focusing on social relations and private behavior as targets of their efforts to improve and develop their territories. Hegel's clear distinction between society and the state gave more explicit theoretical form to this division. In doing so he provided the starting point from which Marx, in a dialectical reversal of a kind he first learned from Hegel, would turn the notion of bourgeois society as a formation whose development and elaboration served the aims of state policy into the idea that state power had to be subservient to the needs of society's dominant forces. That Germany provided the ground where this development could take place had much to do with the particular relations that obtained between politics, economics, and culture in the German lands, which is to say with the unusual configuration that developed there between the three major species of networks.

Whereas the French monarchy during the Old Regime drew the country's diverse and economically fragmented regions into a powerful – albeit conflicted and tangled – web of ties to a political center, the German lands remained without effective threads of unity in either sphere to the end of the eighteenth century and beyond. There were many reasons for this persisting disunity, some of them rooted in geography. As Hans-Ulrich Wehler points out, early modern Germans inhabited a wide range of landscapes and conditions. Rural life in the west, where small independent farms were common, contrasted with the big Junker estates worked by unfree peasants in the east; some cities survived mostly from trade or manufacturing (usually for local markets, although places like Hamburg and Cologne were important exceptions) while others, including some of the most prosperous, were *Residenzstädte*, housing princely courts and living chiefly off their revenues and expenditures. The country was religiously divided into sizable Protestant and Catholic areas (the first chiefly in the north, the second in the south), and linguistic variations were so great that well into the nineteenth century people speaking only a single regional dialect could not converse with those who spoke a different one (many dialects still survive today). The underdeveloped state of transport helped maintain these divisions. As David Blackbourn observes, "it was not until the 1820s and 1830s that the course of major rivers, including the Rhine, Neckar, Mosel and Danube, was straightened to make season-round river traffic easier (and to reduce flooding)." Good roads were rare everywhere, even more in the north of the country than in the south.[1]

Many of these conditions existed in France before the nineteenth century too, but in Germany they were both solidified and amplified by political division. The region's nominal rulers, the heads of the Holy Roman Empire, never pursued the territorial consolidation that came to England with the Norman Conquest, and that the French kings undertook over a long period. Already in the thirteenth century the unpromising prospect offered by Germany as a field for establishing power contributed to the decision of the brilliant Hohenstaufen ruler Frederick II to seek resources for his ambitions by establishing power in Italy, and in particular in the then-prosperous region of Sicily, rather than Germany (his intervention in the fierce partisan struggles of the peninsula was welcomed by those such as Dante who hoped he could give victory to their imperial or "Ghibelline" party in local politics), and in order to facilitate his efforts there he left German princes and cities relatively free to develop their domains on their own. Later the Habsburgs exhibited a similar willingness to allow independent centers of power to flourish inside Germany in order to pursue goals outside it, a stance that contributed to their famous preference for expanding their imperial pretensions through dynastic marriages rather than by warfare.[2]

The situation these policies helped promote by the time of the Reformation was one reason why the emperor Charles V found himself incapable of imposing unity against Protestant rebels, as he acknowledged in accepting the Treaty of Augsburg in 1555, and a century later the same mix of religions and political disunity was confirmed by the Treaty of Westphalia's formula of *cuius regio eius religio*, recognizing the country's divisions and giving each ruler the right to determine the official religion of the state. After 1648 many lesser princes, secular and ecclesiastical, seized on this situation to shore up their independence. The more than 300 separate political entities that made up the German lands in the eighteenth century were mostly small in size, some even minuscule, such as the the inward-looking and self-protective "hometowns" studied by Mack Walker, their residents devoted to the communal autonomy they enjoyed inside their walls, and determined to preserve local life as they knew it against outsiders. Like other Germans, they benefitted from the emperors' policy of protecting smaller states against larger ones in order to prevent rivals from emerging, thus making the Empire into what Walker calls "the incubator of German localism." In David Blackbourn's formulation, the Empire "protected the particular in the name of the universal." There were no German officials in a position to espouse unifying visions in the way French ones did, no *ponts et chaussées* department to invest imagination, money, and effort in better communication and transport. And of course, "[t]he relative isolation of these self-sufficient worlds was reinforced by a luxuriant structure of tariffs and excises both between and within the individual German territories."[3]

These geographical and political divisions also heightened social distinctions, especially between many *Bürger* and nobles. Social mixing took place in the *Residenzstädte*, where a certain number of middle-class people drew close to princes and courts through the goods or services they provided, some of them receiving titles and privileges in return. But both in the small towns studied by Mack Walker and in larger independent commercial cities such as Cologne or Hamburg, territorial autonomy (still marked by the presence of urban walls) greatly narrowed the space for such contacts. This would be one important reason why consciousness of *Bürger* independence was especially strong in Germany. The overall effects of German fragmentation were summarized by Adolf von Knigge, author of a well-known eighteenth-century advice book on manners and proper behavior: "Perhaps in no country of Europe is it so hard to gain general approval, when interacting with people from different classes, regions, and estates … as in our German fatherland; for perhaps nowhere does there reign at once such a great multiplicity of conversations, of modes of education, of religious and other opinions, or such a great diversity in the objects that engage the attention of particular classes of people."[4]

Even in the face of this fragmentation, however, Germany still appeared to people as a distinct cultural and social field (as Knigge's comment testifies), and its division into so large a number of units, many of them small and weak, offered opportunities for reshaping society and politics from within that were available nowhere else. After 1648 a number of territorial states, both threatened and encouraged by the growing power of the French monarchy, would seek to take advantage of the openings this situation provided. In part, state construction in Germany followed lines common to other places; like the French kingdom, German states grew by uniting previously independent territories. But by this time Britain and France were long-established entities, the identity of the first grounded in geography and by now distant conquest, that of the second built up in a process stretching back into the Middle Ages. The expanding German princely states had roots in the distant past, but their modern manner of existence arose out of the post-Reformation settlement formalized in the Treaty of Westphalia, which gave Protestant sovereigns control over the former lands of the Church (and all rulers considerable influence in religious affairs), while creating the conditions for expansion through marriage and inheritance, diplomacy, or warfare. Saxony, Württemberg, Bavaria, Baden, Hanover and Hesse all grew in these ways, but the most remarkable and successful creation was of course Prussia, like its imperial rival Austria an agglomeration of territories put together through marriage and diplomacy, and later by conquest. The former elector of Brandenburg, who acquired the duchy of Prussia by inheritance in the late seventeenth century, proclaimed himself king there only in 1701, adding to his territories another duchy, two counties and several bishoprics. It was a meteoric rise, famously supported by the newly created, highly organized and disciplined Prussian army.

To bring unity to such agglomerations, and to draw sufficient resources from them, the rulers needed servants and officials, and they set about assuring that they would be loyal and effective. In Prussia as in other states the originally separate territories had long possessed bodies of officials and administrators, but the Hohenzollern rulers' determination to squeeze more resources out of them to bolster their military ambitions led them to absorb these earlier corps into a single one organized in order to support and supply the army, a pattern echoed in less militaristic fashion elsewhere.[5] Good state servants had to be literate and educated, qualities the sovereigns sought to assure through establishing, maintaining, and regulating universities. In Protestant regions new faculties had been founded first of all to provide alternatives to Catholic religious institutions, but state officials were trained in them as well as pastors. The original Prussian one, opened in Königsberg in 1544, served both groups from the beginning, providing training for officials in the faculties of law and philosophy that were set up alongside the theological one. In the eighteenth century Immanuel Kant would spend his whole career there, teaching students who would mostly become clergy or state officials. By then other states had begun to set up universities to train their civil servants as well; in the century after 1694, new ones were established all across Germany, at Halle, Göttingen, Erlangen, Münster, and Bonn.[6] There future state officials were trained in the administrative disciplines called *Cameralistik*, but in addition the state governments fostered the spread of Roman law, in part because princes could use its statist principles "to assert their authority *vis-à-vis* both local rivals and the imperial authorities."[7]

Out of these developments there would emerge a social phenomenon unique to Germany, a distinct grouping of high-status non-nobles called the *Bildungsbürgertum*. The term would become common only in the twentieth century, but the phenomenon was already emerging in the developments just mentioned. As the name indicates, the members of this group owed their position first of all to education; their occupations were primarily state service and professional work (chiefly law, medicine, teaching, and the ministry), categories that would long be more closely linked in Germany than elsewhere. Hans-Ulrich Wehler maintains (perhaps with a small amount of pardonable hyperbole) that no comparable group in modern European and North American history has had "such lasting influence and such an astounding impact down into the twentieth century."[8] To be sure, non-noble state officials operated elsewhere, collecting the excise and manning government agencies in England, and sometimes achieving high position and riches in France. But English excise tax collectors did not have university educations, and French *intendants*, although mostly graduates of a law faculty, often owed their positions to personal connections. Many had noble origins and those who did not acquired some species of noble status through their work: they were part of the Old Regime system of privilege, not members of a separate *Stand*; as a group they never developed the same close relationship to *Bildung*.[9] These features of the *Bildungsbürgertum* were one source of the characteristically German orientation toward the two seemingly opposite poles of *Macht* and *Geist*, power and the things of the mind.

The role governments envisaged for these officials was not merely administrative; they were to be the agents of the states' efforts to give a new emphasis and coloration to the notion of *bürgerliche Gesellschaft*. In the seventeenth century the idea included an expectation that the state would act as overseer of social life in both its economic and moral dimensions, working to improve well-being and assuring that behavior reflected religious and communal standards. After around 1700 it acquired a heightened association with developing economic resources in order to add to wealth and the tax base, with establishing uniform legal procedures and obligations throughout previously independent and differently governed territories, and with a more positive view of individual citizens (especially men as heads of households) as bearing both the ability and the responsibility to contribute to social advance through their own efforts. Isabel Hull rightly emphasizes that this idea of civil society was largely future oriented: it rested on a sense of human potential yet to be realized, a vision that inspired its departures both from the prevailing belief that production and consumption had to be limited to traditional levels and from the longstanding assumption that it was the responsibility of authorities to provide moral discipline for their subjects. But the writers and officials who gave voice to this vision easily underestimated the power of the forces whose development they encouraged; they wanted "to open the floodgates of production, consumption, population, and wealth," but expected the flow of new energy to strengthen society as they knew it, preserving its hierarchical structures.[10]

In order to grasp the importance of the officials whose lives were devoted to these policies for the development of a modern form of bourgeois life we need to view them against the background of existing ways for defining bourgeois status in pre-modern Germany. The fragmentation of the country meant that the local forms taken by membership in urban society varied greatly in their details, but the spirit was broadly similar everywhere. *Bürgerrecht* or urban citizenship was articulated in accord with the assumptions of the *ständisch* order; it was not a single category, but a congeries of greater and lesser rights to participate in urban affairs. As one recent historian puts it, "The early modern state and early modern cities were tangles of legal distinctions, special provisions for special groups, stratified levels of rights, privileges, and duties that classified individuals into specified relationships with the governing authority." The complexity of such arrangements is well illustrated by the case of Bremen, where four different kinds of *Bürgerrecht* co-existed at the end of the eighteenth century, two of them associated with residence in the *Altstadt*, the original and most prestigious part of the city, of which only one, requiring a higher payment, gave the right to guild mastership and thus to sell goods (*Handelsfreiheit*); the others (neither of which conveyed these commercial privileges) were associated with residence in newer sections, the *Neustadt* and the *Vorstadt* whose inhabitants had less status and power. Some places such as Hamburg (the subject of the study from which the general statement quoted just above comes) were relatively open to outsiders, even Jews, who could sometimes make their way into the urban elite on the basis of success in business, but even there governing arrangements were strictly hierarchical and set up to preserve the position of families with deep roots. Much more exclusive were locales like the "hometowns" studied by Mack Walker, where *Bürger* spoke of themselves in terms of equality and democracy, but in a manner that limited participation to those whose rights derived from an inherited place in a bounded collectivity determined to protect itself against outsiders.[11]

As the social identity of the fledgling *Bildungsbürger* developed, it exhibited a clear contrast to all these situations. Earlier the graduates of university faculties had been inserted into local society as members of what was called the *Gelehrtenstand* (sometimes referred to as the *Gebildete* or educated), a category that like other estates varied from place to place but which everywhere carried certain privileges, involving dress, forms of respect, and a place in both ceremonial processions and council meetings. Like other modes of urban status, this one was often inherited or acquired chiefly through family connections. In the early eighteenth century positions in the Prussian judiciary were largely of this sort, requiring some education to be sure, but depending less on demonstrated qualifications than on patronage; judges were more concerned about status and precedence than personal formation, an easily understandable preference given that their income came more from fees, gifts, and bribes than from regular salaries. Administrative bureaucrats were even less likely to put a high value on learning or training; they have been described as "a hodge-podge of social types and backgrounds," including "adventurers, favorites, and coat-tail riders." Neither the loyalty nor the efficiency of such people could be firmly relied on.

It was to free itself from this situation that the Prussian state began to institute its system of professional qualification through university attendance and testing, beginning with judicial officials and spreading to administrative ones. The system evolved in stages, but had achieved considerable regularity by 1760. Similar requirements were applied to clergy at this time, and by the end of the century they had been extended to other professionals and copied in other states. Although nobles continued to occupy posts at the highest level in administration and the judiciary, all these groups took on a character that reflected the states' demands that their members complete a certain level of schooling, either in a university or an upper secondary institution such as a *Gymnasium*, and that they be able to pass one of the increasingly rigorous examinations. In this way the old *Gelehrtenstand* gave way to a new professional intelligentsia, defined by its demonstrated qualifications, and deeply connected to the state that regulated its training and certified its suitability.[12]

By the middle of the eighteenth century "the core of academically trained professionals and bureaucrats stood under the direct jurisdiction of the central state," the effect of monarchical campaigns to "detach these groups from their municipal bonds." They could be judged only in state courts, not local ones, they were exempt from military service as well as from many taxes, and affronts to their honor were considered offenses against the state itself. These privileges and exemptions testified to their condition as *staatsunmittelbar*, directly connected to the state. Anthony La Vopa suggests that they understood and appreciated their situation in just these terms: even those who stood relatively low in the ranks of eighteenth-century *Bildungsbürger* saw themselves as liberated from the constricted and often merely private relations in which local institutions (such as schools) operated; as state servants they were "perched above local society and invulnerable to its pressures," and they valued their state office for its "promised disentanglement from local dependencies." This sense of independence was nurtured too by the increasing prominence in German universities of the neo-humanist classicism of Christian Wolff and Wilhelm von Humboldt, with its aspirations to represent universal *Kultur*. Conceiving their identity in terms of this education may have been especially attractive to the state officials in face of the disappointment some voiced about the often dreary and mechanical specialization their actual work imposed. Isabel Hull's observation that they had "literally fallen out of the *ständisch* order" highlights their situation very well, except that it would be more accurate to say that they had been drawn out of that order through insertion into the network of institutions through which the territorial states pursued their goals. As a result, "they pointed to a new conception of *Bürgertum*, in the sense of *Staatsbürger*, or active, participating citizen-members of the new civil society."[13] They were in an important sense the first modern German bourgeois, independent of the old and complex order of locally based *ständische* society more than even big merchants and manufacturers in Hamburg or Bremen, who still belonged to it.

Important as we should recognize this move away from the old order to be however, it was by no means complete. The Prussian constitutional law of 1794, the *Allgemeine Landrecht*, designated state officials as a separate *Stand*, thus making them part of a society still structured as a graded hierarchy. Hegel called up this mix of qualities by naming them the "*allgemeine* [general or universal] *Stand*," an oxymoronic construction (since each *Stand* was by definition particular to some function) that attached modern features to an older social vision. Moreover their status as citizens was rendered uncertain in the eyes of some by the oath of loyalty they had to swear to the monarch, depriving them of the personal independence that citizenship was taken to presuppose. Assertions that such people were too dependent on authority to be genuine *Bürger* were voiced well into the nineteenth century.[14] These features stood in contrast to the more modern ones etched by their independence from traditional local status hierarchies and their work in infusing social relations with the general principles of civil society. Their situation reveals both that powerful modernizing visions were generated out of the web of institutions and people the states wove, but also how incompletely those visions were realized.

Bürgerlichkeit and the networks of *Aufklärung*

The new notion of citizenship that developed in connection with the reforming activities of states gained an additional dimension from a specifically cultural network in which the early *Bildungsbürger* played an important role, namely the chain of people and instruments dedicated to spreading Enlightenment. This network was particularly significant in German history because it constituted the first vehicle through which activity of any kind on a national scale was fostered. Like much else in Germany at the time, the *Aufklärung* belonged largely to a world of scattered localities. Whereas the French Enlightenment had an undoubted center in Paris, from which it spread to provincial academies and readers, and London had a similar status in England, in Germany the *Aufklärung* had no single focal point, or rather it developed simultaneously in a variety of separate but connected places.[15] In them, interested people formed local associations, some called reading societies, some patriotic societies, some masonic lodges, all devoted to general improvement through individual and collective self-cultivation. Newspapers, travel accounts, reports of scientific discoveries and experiments, and foreign and domestic fiction were all among the materials around which people came together in these groups. Wilhelm Ruppert discerns in this phenomenon a felt "need for an expansion of the *Lebenswelt*," a phenomenon that mirrored, in reverse, the fragmentation and localism that characterized so much of German life. Answering the question to which Kant also gave a more famous reply, Moses Mendelssohn said that *Aufklärung*, *Bildung* and *Kultur* were all "modifications of social life, effects of people's efforts and strivings to improve their social existence." James Sheehan notes that a central part of this program was to "set free human talents and productive powers" by doing away with restrictions that enclosed people within local condition and the limits they imposed.[16]

The project bore some of the same contradictory features we have just seen in the condition of the early *Bildungsbürger*, because in most ways German society gave little evidence of spontaneous activity by individuals. John Brewer and Eckhardt Hellmuth note that many activities and projects carried out by private initiative in Britain remained the province of the state in Germany. "The spectrum ranges from schools and theaters to hospitals, which were frequently maintained by private subscriptions."[17] In cultural matters, however, Germans proved perfectly capable of spontaneous action; the very absence of good means of communication encouraged people (partly inspired by the contrast they knew to exist with other countries) to create or foster them. From the 1720s a number of writers and publicists devoted themselves to developing a single literary language for all of Germany, so as to overcome the many linguistic divisions that hindered cultural interchange. Some of the same people advocated improvements in roads and in the postal service, without which, as one put it, "our knowledge of the world remains full of defects, all commercial and literary commerce nearly impossible, and the circle of friendship, humanity's greatest good fortune, limited to the narrow region of our physical surroundings."[18] The patriotic and literary societies and masonic lodges that sprang up in the next decades gave further expression to this sense that Germany both needed such efforts and offered a particularly favorable field for them. Just as the territorial states took advantage of the relative political vacuum created by German fragmentation to expand their power by developing new administrative networks and the cultural institutions to support them inside their borders, so did the promoters of Enlightenment seize the chance to create webs of their own so as to gain contact with distant resources through which to develop the potential capacities that they believed awaited realization in themselves.

The promoters of this expanded culture were a varied lot; no more than in France can they be identified with a single social class. James Sheehan likens them to a vein of ore running through German society at many levels, rather than a delimited stratum, and Isabel Hull rejects the label "new *Bürgertum*" proposed by other scholars in favor of the more sociologically neutral description "practitioners of civil society." Both (along with other writers) emphasize the presence of nobles, most of them office holders, in the group, casting doubt on older views of the Enlightenment as a "bourgeois" movement.[19] This does not mean that the social identities of these people were not significant, however. The largest component of the literary and patriotic societies, and of the masonic lodges, were fledgling *Bildungsbürger* – state officials, academics, lawyers, judges, schoolteachers, pastors, booksellers, journalists, and estate administrators. Merchants, manufacturers and other *Wirtschaftsbürger* belonged to the associations too (and I will have something more to say about them in a moment), but in markedly smaller numbers. Between 1783 and 1796 some eighty professors, sixty state functionaries, and thirty pastors published articles in periodicals seeking to foster Enlightenment, alongside only five businessmen. Around 60 percent of the subscribers to such journals were *Bildungsbürger*, compared with 7 percent who were merchants and traders (the remainder were a mix of types, including the already-mentioned nobles).[20] What distinguished the advocates of *Aufklärung* and *Bildung* from others around them, however, was not their social position (which, all the same, continued to define them locally, and to provide resources for their activities), but their insertion into the networks created by the publications, communications, and correspondence that tied the local societies together. One contemporary writer, Christoph Wieland, described those active in the various associations as "in a certain sense the actual *men of the nation*, because their immediate circle of activity is all of Germany," a description hardly applicable to anyone else at the time.[21]

Given both Wieland's description and what was noted above about the relationship of incipient *Bildungsbürger* to the old *ständisch* order, it should not be surprising that among the ideas fostered inside these groups was a new notion of citizenship, closely related to the one nurtured by the states. In order to replace traditional *Stadtbürgertum* (urban citizenship) with *Staatsbürgertum* (state citizenship), individuals had to exhibit *Bürgerlichkeit*, the attribute or disposition that made individuals able to become independent participants in civil society. Although every person bore the potential to develop this quality, achieving it required a certain level of personal and moral development. Bringing people to this level was precisely the aim of the associations devoted to *Bildung* and *Aufklärung*, whose goal of collective self-cultivation and mutually beneficial exchange with others provided a model of the kind of social relations *bürgerliche Gesellschaft* aimed to establish. In the smaller associations as in the larger one membership was often declared to be independent of the old *Stände*, and people of different social conditions were expected to treat each other as equals. "Character" began to acquire a new meaning, no longer referring to a social and occupational identity but to a cluster of personal qualities that represented "individual responsibility and self-improvement." Local communities were still the chief places where *Bürgerlichkeit* operated, but belonging to them took on new dimensions, involving personal development best nurtured by cultural resources diffused through a range of distant locations.[22]

The new notion of citizenship seemed full of promise to many, but it was seen to harbor two fundamental problems, both of which would recur in the subsequent history of bourgeois life and culture. The first arose from its claim to inclusiveness, even to a kind of democratic universality. Every (male) person who developed himself to a certain level could be a *Bürger* and a patriot (that is, a person devoted to civic improvement), and many of the new associations formed for the purpose declared themselves to be independent of traditional social distinctions. In Hamburg Jews were allowed to join the Patriotic Society, and there was discussion about extending citizenship rights to them (like the actual abolition of the older requirements for citizenship, and of the guilds tied up with them, this proposal was only realized in the mid nineteenth century). But older forms of exclusiveness were replaced by a new one, since only those with the personal resources to engage in self-cultivation could advance themselves in this way. Groups that declared themselves open to "the public" still set membership dues that only well-off people could afford, and one quality many of them required was "independence," a condition that excluded those who had to work for wages.[23]

Immanuel Kant recognized this difficulty when he wrote that "everybody is born as a potential citizen [*möglicher Staatsbürger*], but in order to become such, he must possess some means [*Vermögen*], whether it be in merits [*Verdiensten*] or in things [*Sachen*]." Without such "means," individuals could not sustain the independence citizenship required.[24] Kant's formulation already recognized both the connection and the difference between the later categories of *Wirtschaftsbürger* and *Bildungsbürger*, since the latter did indeed claim their "merits," that is their qualifications not their wealth, as the basis for their position. Perhaps his formulation somewhat obscured the attempt by those *Wirtschaftsbürger* who participated in patriotic and literary societies to pursue *Bürgerlichkeit* through "merits" too, joining their more intellectual cousins in the pursuit of self-cultivation. The main point, however, is that he recognized that the ideal of universal citizenship could not do away with significant differences between individuals. In this he was joined by other advocates of the new kind of citizenship, who like him hoped that the interaction promoted by the various kinds of cultural and moral associations could lessen the impact of these differences. One of these was the writer and critic Gottfried Ephraim Lessing, who was troubled by the way that masonic lodges, in the very act of seeking to transcend the old divisions between *Stände*, made people aware of other inequalities, some of which emerged in the meetings themselves. Thus he wrote in 1780 that *bürgerliche Gesellschaft* "wholly against its own intention," cannot unite people "without dividing them, without bolstering the gaps between them, without raising up walls of division between them." Instead of the hoped-for relations between "just plain men and just plain men" what surfaced were ones that ranged "certain kinds of men against certain others." Lessing did not say what kinds of distinctions he had in mind, and wealth was doubtless one of them. But he was aware of rifts produced by contrasts in occupation and education as well. He still hoped that organizations such as masonic lodges could work to "narrow as much as possible those divisions through which men become so foreign to each other."[25] It seems unlikely, however, that he thought the activities of such associations could overcome the difference between those people who had one or another of the kinds of "means" Kant pointed to and those who did not, since very few people on the lower side of that line belonged to the lodges.

The second dilemma of the new *Bürgerlichkeit* had to do with the tension it created between traditional forms of participation in local communities and the external involvements that self-development was seen to require. The problem was especially acute in Germany, because the web of connections made up of clubs and associations and the materials (publications and letters) they shared and exchanged was the only national network the country possessed, as Wieland recognized when he referred to those people who animated it as the sole "men of the nation." Intellectually nourishing as participation in such activities might be, it could also feel thin and insubstantial to those accustomed to more compact kinds of communal life. In 1797 Christian Garve revealed the obverse side of Wieland's image when he bemoaned the separation and isolation that attachment to such distant relations could bring: because those who developed viewpoints grounded in a cosmopolitan culture cut themselves off from the people around them, the new kind of *Gesellschaft* was stalked by *Einsamkeit*, loneliness.[26]

One person who felt just this kind of separation as a consequence of his attempt to make a career in the developing *Bildungsbürgertum* was Johann Gottfried Herder, who developed the age's most substantial defense of cultural difference and of what the later anthropologist Clifford Geertz would call "local knowledge." After attending the grammar school in the small town where his father was a schoolteacher, Herder took a degree at the University at Königsberg, where he attended Kant's lectures during the 1760s, after which he accepted a post as a teacher in the prestigious cathedral school at Riga. But his discomfort with the distance this put him from his origins led him to voice nostalgia for "the true commerce of hearts and minds" obtainable in traditional communities, and he resigned his place, beginning the turn that would make him a pioneer of ethnographic description and an opponent of the cosmopolitan rationality of which his one-time teacher Kant was a prime exemplar.[27]

Very similar tensions appeared in other instances where the ideas and values spread by the new cultural networks made an impact, and notably in the cities that became important entry points for it. Hamburg provides the exemplary case. The largest and most prosperous German commercial city, it was also one of the most independent, remaining an autonomous republic until it was absorbed into Bismarck's North German Confederation in 1867, and the Reich in 1871 (even then it remained exempt from certain customs duties until the late 1880s). Hamburg's power depended largely on its economy, centered on foreign trade (England and South America were major partners), and on refinishing imported goods such as sugar and textiles. But the city's position was also grounded in Germany's peculiar constitution: like other places, it was able to preserve its independence because it could play off various more powerful states against each other, aided by diplomatic connections made through the Imperial Court. In this way the city protected itself especially against the nearby Danish monarchy's attempts to absorb or dominate it.[28] The city's independence was one reason it was able to develop strong ties with distant places, especially England; for many these were closer than its links to other parts of Germany. Its already-mentioned openness to outsiders meant that by the eighteenth century a number of its leading families had foreign backgrounds. Some were said to know more about South America or Britain than about Germany, having traveled to London and Peru but never to Berlin. Merchant sons were often sent to England to apprentice and learn business methods, (a practice not limited to Hamburg, to be sure), sometimes marrying women they met there, adopting British dress and customs, and giving their children English names.

These circumstances contributed to making Hamburg a favorable point of entry for Enlightenment ideas. A visiting schoolmaster from Thuringia found himself bowled over by the variety of publications from all over the world available in the city's bookstores (as well as by the constant movement and noise of the streets), making him feel the "narrow limits" of his own town. The *Aufklärung* in Hamburg proceeded in the same way as in other cities, through the founding and activity of literary and patriotic societies, as well as masonic lodges, and the periodicals and communications they published or exchanged. But it had a special role as the place where the first of the numerous "moral weeklies" that circulated in Germany in the 1730s and 1740s was founded. Called *Der Patriot*, and modeled on such English publications as the *Spectator* and the *Tatler*, the magazine appeared between

1724 and 1726. It aimed to improve the moral behavior of *Bürger* families and individuals, through criticizing indulgence, laxity, and excess of all kinds, and recommending such qualities as earnestness, hard work, and moderation. These are good bourgeois virtues, but many Hamburg citizens bridled against the new vehicle through which they were being recommended; some may have felt they were the targets of the critiques, or that their position in town life was being challenged. A lively pamphlet war developed, and the excitement generated by the controversy helped the paper to achieve wide circulation, some issues selling as many as 5,000 copies. But many townspeople would have been happy to see the paper banned; it survived because the group sponsoring it contained a number of substantial citizens who, as members of the city Senate, were able to afford it protection. A similar paper founded ten years earlier but without such defenders had been forced to close down in the face of the same kind of opposition.[29]

Although material that would allow for a social analysis of who made up the two sides of this dispute may never be available, the debate seems to have pitted people who saw distant connections and relationships as pertinent to issues of moral criticism and personal improvement against others who preferred to refer such matters to traditional local authorities. The earlier weekly had been edited by a musician and writer who was the secretary of the English consul in the city, and the group around *Der Patriot* contained a nucleus of scholars and intellectuals who had encountered Enlightenment ideas in the Netherlands, or who had contacts with people in places that were early centers of new thinking such as Halle; a common recommendation in the paper's articles was that readers expand their knowledge of foreign places, and some writings attempted to correct misinformation about them. Imitators of the Hamburg journal in other places took names such as Göttingen's *Der Bürger,* Danzig's *Der Freydenker* ("Freethinker") and Berlin's *Der Weltbürger* ("World Citizen").[30] Neither *Der Patriot* nor these other publications were wholly secular; all accepted the need to retain a close tie between religion and morality. But theirs was a religion neither dogmatic nor defined by local institutions and practices, creating a contrast with their opponents, who preferred to vest moral authority in their pastors and other members of the traditional *Gelehrtenstand.*[31] Clearly both sides were *Bürger,* and each was represented in the Senate, so that what chiefly divided them seems to have been no clear social difference but their contrasting attitudes toward local and distant involvements (along with whatever personal circumstances and relationships helped to determine them). The situation was reproduced in other German towns, and it recalls ones we encountered earlier. In England, as Dror Wahrman noted, quarrels and conflicts of various kinds sometimes attributed to class differences actually set people whose positions derived largely from local relationships against socially similar others who were inserted into national networks. And in France, Guy Chaussinand-Nogaret concludes that class position seldom accounts for the difference between those who supported reform and those who resisted it; what set the two groups apart was a contrast between those who, for whatever reason, wanted to open up local life to broader national currents and influences and those who strove to shield it from them.[32]

Rulers, *Bürger*, "movers and doers"

The German lands could not escape being profoundly affected by the convulsions that rocked France at the end of the eighteenth century. Although many people were horrified by what seemed mere chaotic violence, others sought to bring the French example home. But the very different conditions of German life, its fragmentation and lack of a political center, and the absence in the German states of the crisis conditions that brought the French monarchy toward collapse, kept the country free of any similar upheaval. France made its strongest impact on Germany not through the Revolution itself, but through the wars it set off and in particular the domination Napoleon established over much of the country in the decade before his fall. So powerful was the effect of the French supremacy that one distinguished historian begins his account of nineteenth-century developments with the declaration: "In the beginning was Napoleon."[33]

There is something to be said for this claim, but it also contains considerable hyperbole. The French occupation itself had a deep impact, and both during and after it German states sought to respond to the French challenge by reforms, intended at once to stir up political energies, improve military organization, and remove restraints that had hindered economic development. Supporters of these initiatives described their purpose as to arouse "sleeping forces," and there can be no doubt that they helped to infuse new vitality into what many regarded as a dormant country. But many of the reforms proceeded along lines already traced out by the vision of *bürgerliche Gesellschaft* that inspired similar efforts in the eighteenth century, some novel proposals were never carried out (in particular those for giving more power to representative institutions), and in many ways the new measures fell short of their hoped-for effects. The decades after 1850, and especially after 1870, would bring far more profound changes than the previous half-century, radically and rapidly transforming every level of life.

All the same it was through these early nineteenth-century reforms that such elements of civil society as legal equality, uniform administration, and protection of property rights were furthered in post-Napoleonic Germany; even though they are well known, we need to give attention to them for a moment because the measures undertaken reveal much about the ways the interests and aims of states on the one hand and bourgeois on the other both came together and diverged. What especially spurred the changes was the demonstration that state power could be hugely enhanced by the kinds of restructuring the Revolution brought: putting an end to Old Regime social and corporate divisions, increasing the efficiency of financial administration, and drawing a population of formally equal citizens into national life and especially military service. Echoes of the Revolutionary slogans of universal citizenship and careers open to talents sounded in all the German reforms. Under the occupation both territorial states and independent cities responded to the need to meet French fiscal exactions with measures to reform tax structures, abolish guilds, and establish uniform conditions of citizenship. Once the foreign troops were gone some independent cities reverted to their old regimes, restoring both guilds and the older forms of unequal citizen rights, but the demonstrated effects of French-style reconstruction inspired an era of state-led reform intended to profit from the foreign example.[34]

The Prussian instance was the most famous; its measures included eliminating guilds, establishing more participatory forms of municipal government, giving a more uniform organization to the army (with expanded opportunities for non-noble officers), an end to serfdom (but on terms that turned out to benefit large landowners far more than the legally liberated peasants), greater access by commoners to ownership of estates formerly reserved to nobles, and the promise (not kept) of a new constitution. Despite its limitations the program helped give people a sense that things were moving in Germany. Prussia became an object of admiration to many liberal supporters of progress (including Hegel and his more left-wing followers, a group that included the young Marx), and in people's minds "this period established the state as the motor of modernization." At the same time however some states did not hesitate to regulate such minor matters as where people could smoke and when property owners had to remove snow from their roofs, so that the measures amounted to a "growing penetration of the state into many spheres of life."[35]

Within the *Bürgertum*, people reacted differently to these policies, according to their particular situations. Those most opposed to the reforms were people such as the "hometownsmen" studied by Mack Walker, chiefly craftsmen and small traders still devoted to the independence their towns had developed over the centuries, even though many of them lost it in 1815. They were, as Walker notes, "middle-class and even *bürgerlich*," but in a special way, more concerned about the position they held inside the world shielded by their walls than about the possibility of achieving something in the wider one outside. They saw their own milieu as egalitarian and democratic, but in a way that rejected the value liberals bestowed on "the individual capacity to move, to change, to differ." In their eyes the outsiders who threatened them were all "movers and doers," a term Walker sees as equally applicable to the officials who carried out state policies and to merchants and traders who sought to expand production and evade economic regulation by setting up their operations where traditional guild controls were weak; the category also included university students moving about in search of general education, and even pastors, since their profession was sometimes a vehicle of social mobility and they were members of "a mobile institution hierarchically organized like a bureaucracy." Recognizing them all as "movers and doers" takes on special significance here because it points to the way that all the people whose activities took place through participation in extended and distant networks, economic, political, or cultural, constituted the same kind of threat to a way of life that defined itself in local and traditional terms.[36]

For other kinds of *Bürger*, however, the reforms provoked more complex reactions. David Blackbourn notes that "businessmen welcomed the promotion of commerce and communications, but chafed at bureaucratic regulation. The more class-conscious merchants and entrepreneurs wondered why, if economic restrictions could be loosened, political controls could not also be relaxed. ... But the official mind was convinced that true liberty was founded on administration, not constitutions." Overall, and despite the benefits some *Wirtschaftsbürger* received through the reform programs, the social group most favored by them were the bureaucrats themselves; their status as both an independent power in state and society and a group dependent on princely favor now became more marked.[37]

Only after 1850 (as Jürgen Kocka has observed) did *Wirtschaftsbürger* begin to replace *Bildungsbürger* as the dominant section of the *Bürgertum* as a whole. One reason this did not occur earlier was that change in the economy was slow to take off. As in other places before the mid century – including England – new techniques were confined to certain regions, in Germany chiefly those with favorable access to raw materials or markets, leaving most of the economic landscape untouched. The most dramatic advance was in cotton textiles, the only branch in which mechanized spinning and weaving could be employed, but even there growth occurred chiefly in areas where the old putting-out system had expanded during the eighteenth century, and many "factories" were simply assemblages of workers using traditional techniques in a single place, not sites for large-scale machine production. Iron output rose significantly from around 1830, driven by the beginnings of railroad construction, but the scale was still far smaller than would be the case from the 1850s. Some rural workers produced goods for outside markets, but snails or dried fruit and cherry juice (the staple exports of two villages in Württemberg) were neither novel products nor vehicles of economic expansion, and most rural energies still went into subsistence farming or items for local exchange. Hunger and food shortages were recurring problems. Meanwhile particular cities largely continued to focus on the activities that had sustained them earlier. The old urban economy predicated on a stable hierarchy of social groups and values was showing many strains, but it was far from clear what would replace it.[38]

A longstanding commonplace about the period, put forward by enthusiasts at the time and developed by a number of modern historians, portrays the Prussian customs union, to which other states could adhere after 1834, as an important engine of economic change, but recent writers have cast considerable doubt on this claim, arguing that its impact was much smaller. To be sure some businesses were helped by access to new bodies of consumers, but the *Zollverein* was far from giving Germany a national market of the kind England already possessed a century earlier, and many barriers to trade between states and regions remained until political unification and the advent of large-scale rail transport removed them in the 1860s and 1870s. Because members of the customs union remained at odds over how to tax goods that individual states treated as government monopolies such as tobacco and wine, some commodities could not move across political boundaries, and local and regional variations in weights, measures, and currencies reduced the ease with which other products could travel too. Roads in many places still left much to be desired. As James Sheehan concludes, the *Zollverein* "was created by bureaucrats, who were interested in fiscal reform and administrative consolidation rather than nation-building"; it was an event in the history of state construction much more than in the coming of modern industry.[39]

These limits affected both the lives of middle-class Germans and their relations with people in other social groups. People at the lower reaches of the scale were still threatened with hunger and unemployment whenever bad weather reduced harvests, driving up food prices and draining away the demand for manufactured goods. Such situations had long obtained, but they were now made worse by population growth, evident in the cities but even more marked in the countryside, where improvements in public health, the abolition of earlier legal restrictions on marriage, and expanded opportunities for part-time work in rural industry when times were good, led to a marked increase in numbers, especially among landless peasants, who made up around half the population everywhere and as much as 80 percent in some areas. The proportion was particularly high in the Prussian East, where many "emancipated" peasants were unable to pay the fees required in order to acquire property, leaving them shorn of their earlier rights to glean harvested fields, gather fallen branches, or pasture animals, so that they had only their labor to sustain themselves. Such people provided an opportunity eagerly exploited by the more unscrupulous among the entrepreneurs who organized the putting-out system in the countryside, a group epitomized by the Zwanziger family in Silesia whose notoriously heartless treatment sparked the revolt of weavers there in 1844, later dramatized by Gerhard Hauptmann. There was much discussion in newspapers and pamphlets of what people called *Pauperismus*, and Hegel described the existence of a "rabble of paupers" as an inescapable consequence of civil society's inability to provide for all its members on the basis of the limited productive resources it could command (a view in close accord with the pessimism of contemporaries such as Ricardo and Malthus). Although some of the people these writers had in view were traditional craft workers unable to survive in the face of falling prices for their goods, what brought them to this pass was not competition from machine industry but the expansion of traditional rural production and the spread of "factories" that were in fact assemblages of workers using longstanding techniques in a single place. In some parts of Germany the term *Fabrikant* was used to describe the proprietors of these sorts of *Fabriken* through most of the century.[40]

Such conditions were far from universal in the country, however. In the southwest, at the opposite corner from Prussia, there were few landless peasants and a high proportion of small but independent artisans, conditions that, as Manfred Heitling argues, made the liberal vision of a *bürgerliche Gesellschaft* as a highly inclusive body of independent citizens far from illusory there. Politics had a different character than in Prussia too, particularly in Württemberg, where relations between the king and both urban and rural citizens (many of whom had the right to vote) were based on considerable cooperation and compromise. The new constitution established in 1819 was not the product of a royal decree, like the Prussian *Allgemeine Landrecht* of 1794, but a contract between the king and the representative assembly. In Prussia the monarchy's accelerating retreat from the reform program of the century's first years in the 1830s and 1840s, and the widening gulf it opened up between advocates of reform and the militaristic, authoritarian state, made Berlin fertile soil for revolutionary agitation when rising food prices, unemployment, and the news of the July Monarch's collapse in Paris touched off the crisis of March, 1848. By contrast neither Württemberg nor most of the other southwestern states saw violent clashes during the revolutionary year (although disputes over reform measures broke out once agitation for them spread through the country), leading Heitling to conclude that "what was revolutionary in 1848 was not *bürgerlich* and what was *bürgerlich* was not revolutionary."[41] Even in places where social divisions were sharper than in cities such as Mannheim or Stuttgart, the sense that *Bürgerlichkeit* could encompass very large proportions of the population had considerable resonance. In Cologne (officially part of Prussia, but a very different kind of place from the garrison city Berlin) as Pierre Ayçoberry notes, *Bürgertum* still served as a broadly inclusive term, retaining the possibility that it could refer to all the city's residents; thus master carpenters referred to themselves and their colleagues elsewhere as *Bürger Arbeiter*, "citizen-workers." As Wilhelm Heinrich Riehl recognized (we will look more closely at him in a moment), Germans in the 1830s and 1840s who wanted a term to designate the bourgeoisie as a distinct and exclusive group (such as did Marx) took up the French one, first because it had largely lost the original sense of *citoyen* that still clung to the German equivalent, and second because it was by then colored by the repeated resistance of the "Bourgeois Monarchy" to extending voting rights, and the conflicts it provoked (even though, as noted above, bourgeois were prominent on both sides of these struggles).[42] In Germany *bürgerliche Gesellschaft* did not mean the rise of bourgeois to political dominance (Bürger rule of independent cities was an old story, and diminished in the Napoleonic period and after, with the territorial changes effected in 1815); it was precisely by attaching the French adjective to what was a distinctively German notion that Marx gave the idea of "bourgeois society" a new sense.

Bürgerliche Gesellschaft probed and mirrored: Hegel, Riehl, Freytag

To sound out the resonances of *bürgerliche Gesellschaft* in Germany before the unification I end this chapter with three prominent writers who focused on it: the philosopher G. W. F. Hegel, the journalist, folklorist, musician, and critic W. H. Riehl, and the novelist Gustav Freytag.

Hegel spent most of his career in Prussia, but he was a native of Württemberg, and his work bears the marks of both environments, emphasizing at once the separation between society and the state and the continuity between them.[43] As noted above, his major work of social and political theory, *The Philosophy of Right*, contrasted society and the state more sharply than earlier writers had. Departing from the old notion of a *societas civilis* that was at once political and social, Hegel portrayed *bürgerliche Gesellschaft* as resting on a basis diametrically opposite to that of the state. Drawing at once on his observation of contemporary conditions, on his reading in British economists and social theorists, notably Smith, Ricardo, and Adam Ferguson, and on the characteristically German manner of taking civil society as an object of state policy, Hegel portrayed society as the sphere in which individuals act to meet their needs and pursue their interests through work and exchange. As a form of life it had many positive features to which we will come in a moment, but in principle little restrained this quest for personal satisfaction from becoming mere selfishness; by putting their own aims and interests first and making others means to these ends, society's inhabitants created "a spectacle of extravagance and want as well as the physical and ethical degeneration common to them both."[44] In contrast the state was the realm of universality, "the actuality of the ethical idea," where the same individuals are drawn to seek the higher kind of freedom that results from affirming and obeying laws that rein in selfish desires, rest on general principles of understanding, and give a definite and rational shape to their common life. The divergence between the sometimes arbitrary and willful "particularity" exhibited by individuals as denizens of society and the "rational universality" to which all were called as members of the state made the two levels of existence polar opposites.

Despite this contrast, an inner unity joined society and the state together. One root of this reconciliation lay in social relations. By encouraging exchanges of goods and services and extending them over an ever-wider range, society draws individuals to recognize both their dependence on others and the need to treat them as bearers of rights who like themselves were deserving of legal protection; thus exchange relations prepare the transition from the first level to the second. The passage between the two was also smoothed by the existence of guilds and other corporate groups where individual interest was moderated through being pursued in concert with others, and through education and culture, which drew people toward universally valid ideas and moral principles.

The same unification had a different, and in Hegel's view more profound, basis on the side of the state. The major agent of the harmonization of the two realms was the class of government officials, the *allgemeine Stand*, whose task was to develop "the universal interests of the community," and in whose activity alone "private interest finds its satisfaction in its work for the universal." In contrast to the two other classes or estates (*Stände*, not *Klassen*) that made up civil society, the business class of the towns and the agricultural class of the countryside, the officials had their origins not in the needs and activities of private individuals, but in the state policies that brought the special *Stand* into being. This was a difference of great importance to Hegel because it provided support for the conclusion to which his whole argument was directed: in one of the dialectical reversals that characterized his thinking, Hegel argued that even his own account of the way that the state seemed to emerge out of the needs of social life was a matter of mere appearance. The true and right relationship was that the state is "not so much the result as the beginning," the "true ground" in which are rooted all those aspects of civil society through which individual existence is drawn away from itself and toward some kind of "universality." This was true not only of the extension of exchange relations that brought individuals into contact with increasing numbers of others, and of education, since it was state action that fostered both, but also of the family, whose limited, private orientation toward a collective ethical existence remained unable to infuse life as a whole without the presence of the state.[45] To present the state in this way as the very ground out of which civil society developed marked Hegel as the German thinker he was, calling up the unique history followed in this chapter.

Hegel's account of both civil society and the state was replete with details, many of them drawn from Prussia where he taught, and especially from the *Allgemeine Landrecht* of 1794 that served as its constitution. But the whole schema was also highly abstract. This combination was typical of all his writing and thinking, and is responsible for some of the famous difficulty of reading him. One reason he did not shy away from abstraction was that he believed it to be a defining quality of the world no less than of thought. His whole intellectual project was devoted on one level to showing that behind all the concrete phenomena of existence as we encounter them there stand abstract ideas and relationships without which we could not bring them to mind (I cannot know the book in my hand as particular thing without simultaneously conceiving the "thing" as a general notion applicable to many other ones); this is one ground out of which Hegel developed the "idealism" that was the essence of his philosophy. As we act in the world we employ our capacity of abstracting from the particular things and circumstances in which we find ourselves in order to alter them and make them more amenable to our goals. An essential instance of this is the human manner of fulfilling needs in civil society. Unlike animals who satisfy their wants with what nature provides, humans construct a "system of needs," a structure of action and market exchange that effects both "the multiplications of needs and [of the] means of satisfying them." Abstraction is the necessary ground of this multiplication, since only by means of it can diverse goods be seen as exchangeable and techniques developed in one context be extended to others. The whole of life takes on an altered character as a result: "When needs and means become abstract in quality ... abstraction is also a character of the reciprocal relation of individuals to one another." Such a result had negative dimensions to be sure, but it is abstraction that makes it possible to bring the diverse totality of needs, means, and relations together into a single whole, an overall system of relations that is "concrete, i.e. social."[46]

Hegel did not use the term "network" to describe this system of needs and means, but he found particular interest in the writings of economists whose analysis of exchange relations showed the mass of apparently unrelated actions through which people exchange objects and services to be a series of "chains of activity all leading back to the same point," and he described the "mutual interlocking of particulars" that subjects individuals to laws operative throughout the system, as a sign that the rationality which found higher expression in the state was already at work on some level here.[47] Hegel gave little direct attention to money as the instrument through which all these connections are established, but he did note that it provided the universal criterion of value, making it a basis for the abstraction that makes an integrated social life on a large scale possible. Simmel would draw greatly on Hegel in his later elaboration of the "philosophy of money." There is reason to regard Hegel as having achieved an important insight into the nature of modernity precisely through his attention to the simultaneously abstract and concrete qualities of modern social relations. As noted in Chapter 1, the media that make the structures we are calling networks of means possible, and regulate flows along them, must be at once abstract and concrete, in order to permit comparisons and exchanges of disparate goods while also allowing specific persons to possess and employ the tokens that represent them. Despite the abstract considerations that operate when people establish relations through such networks, the objects the media represent are concrete ones, involving specific articles of trade, taxes or government operations, or books and newspapers. Using Hegelian language one might call networks of means "concretized abstractions," in which the first term takes on a higher valence as the networks expand and thicken. One way to characterize the comparisons we have been making here between English, French, and German conditions, is in terms of the particular mix of concreteness and abstraction that obtained in each place. That Germany was the most abstract was what Christoph Wieland recognized in characterizing writers active in spreading Enlightenment as the "sole men of the nation," the only ones whose sphere of activity was the country as a whole, and Christian Garve in diagnosing their condition as one of *Einsamkeit*, loneliness.

Hegel recognized the abstract quality of his analysis in a second way, namely in connection with his presentation of the state as able to bring people toward the higher and "universal" principles of reason and humanity, even as their lives in civil society draw them toward self-centeredness and the immorality of using others as means for their ends. That the very same individuals appear to themselves and others in both guises seemed to him a sign that the modern state (including the civil society that was a part of it) had a special importance for humanity: "The principle of modern states has prodigious strength and depth because it allows the principle of subjectivity to progress to its culmination in the extreme of self-subsistent personal particularity, and yet, at the same time brings it back to the substantive unity and so maintains this unity in the principle of subjectivity itself."[48] Marx, who would at first be drawn to Hegel precisely because he offered a way to root these abstract human qualities in actual life, would later reject Hegel's kind of abstract analysis as the root of the delusions idealism generated, seeking to replace them through a concrete and materialist understanding of history.

But Hegel was not so naive about his portrayal of the state's ability to resolve the dilemmas of everyday social existence as some of his formulations may suggest. Because he recognized that society was a realm of egotism where class division and poverty created misery and conflict, he saw the attempt to show that there was something essentially rational in the state as a challenge he could not decline, since it was his philosophic task to show that the whole world was subject to being understood in the terms reason provided. But it was the hardest of the challenges that faced him, as he declared by famously invoking the classical tag "Hic Rhodus, hic saltus" – here is Rhodes, jump here, now is the time to show that you can do what you boast you can – in the preface to his book. The treatise was "nothing other than the *endeavor* [italics added, but the emphasis is already there] to apprehend and portray the state as something inherently rational." Philosophy could reconcile the contradictory principles of society and the state, but only in thought, not in reality: by comparison with what Goethe called the green of "life's golden tree," philosophy's theory is "gray in gray"; it provides reconciliation "in the ideal, not the actual world." The consequence, as he recognized elsewhere, was that the typical condition of moderns like himself, drawn to ideal resolutions that could not be brought to realization, was not satisfaction, but "vexation."[49] Hegel knew full well that the resolution he proposed to effect between the categories of individuality and universality, egotism and devotion to the social whole, self-centeredness and moral uprightness, was only an abstract one.

To take such a position, at once attributing to thought and thinkers great power in the world and recognizing that in fact their means were abstract and thus very limited, marked Hegel as the early *Bildungsbürger* he was, given an important position as part of a state apparatus that needed such people as he to do its work, but in the end dependent on its power and threatened with unhappiness and frustration at moments when it failed to live up to the hopes they invested in it. It is clear that this discord between everyday existence and the aspirations for it embodied in *Kultur* and *Bürgerlichkeit* affected other educated state servants too, since, as noted above, they complained about the dreary and "mechanical" quality of their actual work. Hegel insisted that those who, unlike himself, preferred to measure the state against some ideal vision of what it should be, opened themselves up to deeper disappointments even than his own. But the advantage brought by "the peace with the world which knowledge [that is, his own kind of philosophical understanding] supplies" was only "less chill" – not even more warmth.[50] Hegel's project of reconciling himself to the world by way of philosophical abstractions that even he recognized as cold and existentially unsatisfying was responsible for some of the elements in his thinking that seem least persuasive to us today, as they already did to others in his time, but it was this same intellectual enterprise that provided him with a perspective from which to grasp the important – and by no means wholly positive – role played by abstract and distant relations in both modernity and bourgeois life.

Many similar themes, but organized to quite a different end, can be found in the second German writer who demands our attention now, the publicist and critic W. H. Riehl, whose book *Die bürgerliche Gesellschaft*, published in 1851, was often reprinted. Riehl drew on Hegel, but unlike the philosopher he was a self-conscious conservative, a defender of the old order of *Stände*, and an advocate of trying to preserve its character under modern conditions. This made him an enemy of some of the things Hegel regarded as most positive in modern life, notably the bureaucracy that the latter made the vehicle of reconciliation between society and the state. But Riehl also recognized that powerful and in some ways positive forces of change were at work in his time, and that the urban middle classes were the source of some of them. The most-often quoted sentences from his book declare that in his age the *Bürgertum* possessed "prevailing material and moral power," and that "the whole age bears a *bürgerliche* character." Many readers have taken *bürgerlich* to mean simply bourgeois, and we will see that such a rendering conveys a part of what Riehl had in mind. But in 1851 the French word had not yet acquired the general applicability it later came to possess, and Riehl himself specifically distinguished between it and the German variant when he pointed out (as noted above) that revolutionaries in his own country named their enemies "bourgeois," not *Bürger*, because the history of the July Monarchy gave the French word an association with reaction or resistance to change. The German term had (as yet) no such connotation, and could not be used in the same way, since those it named had no political power on a national scale.[51]

Although well aware that much middle-class activity was economic, Riehl identified what marked *Bürger* off from other social groups in quite different terms; what distinguished them was that they "strive for the general or universal" [*dem Allgemeinen*], for things whose value transcended local and limited conditions and could be recognized anywhere. The contrast was especially sharp with country people, devoted to concrete and particular things such as homegrown food, dress, and language. And whereas "the particular" was usually something that already existed, "universality has first to be created." This led him to the second distinctive quality of *Bürger*, their penchant for reaching and striving, an orientation that made them value movement itself, even above the goal that drew it forth. Riehl found the quintessential expression of this stance in Lessing's declaration that he preferred seeking the truth to having it, a position echoed in a different connection by Friedrich List (the advocate of tariffs to protect German manufactures from English competition) that "the power to create riches is infinitely more important than riches themselves." It was this spirit that made taking pride in becoming something through one's own efforts "genuinely *bürgerlich*." And it was because modernity shared with bourgeois existence an orientation that transcended local situations, and a persisting impulse to push beyond given conditions, that contemporary life had a *bürgerliche* character. The *Bürger* were the part of society with the ability "to give most decisive expression to the universality of modern social life." One testimony to this was the role Riehl believed the bourgeoisie played in the French Revolution. He did not say that they became the ruling group then but that it was in the Revolution's universal principles that the *Bürgertum* "found its voice." Testimony that it was the voice of modernity and not just of a part of it was provided by the way people used the term *bürgerlich* to mean social or civil, as when they spoke of *bürgerliche* honor or a *bürgerliche* death, applying it to things outside the middle classes.[52]

All the same, *Bürger* were not oriented only to movement and fluidity (as the increasingly dissatisfied fourth estate of workers was), but also to stability and calm. They wanted not to dissolve or explode society but to "bridge over its sharp distinctions"; their paradigmatic exemplar was Luther, the model German *Bürger* because he was at once radical and conservative.[53] One reason for the *Bürgertum*'s multiple orientation, and for its ability to represent modernity as a whole, was that it contained parts corresponding to other social strata: there existed "an aristocratic, a specifically *bürgerlich*, and a proletarian *Bürgertum*." (Engels, as we saw, said a similar thing about England, but to quite different effect.) Riehl gave particular emphasis to the middle class's quality of mediating or transcending oppositions, both between itself and other parts of society, and between the present and the past; its ability to do so provided him with evidence that society could become, as he hoped it would, at once more *bürgerlich* and more *ständisch*, continuing to progress beyond any given point while still preserving the sense of stable integration it possessed in the past. Evidence that the *Bürgertum* could be the bearer of these hopes came from the attachment many of its members maintained to associations of producers, not just the old guilds but also (he believed) new forms that would emerge as the traditional ones waned. Even as industry expanded along the lines List and others projected, these associations would impart to their members a sense of unity, loyalty, and moral commitment, qualities that society was in danger of losing by virtue of the purely individualistic attitudes that threatened to fragment and weaken it in the present.[54]

These dangerous attitudes derived in Riehl's view from two quarters. The first was a certain segment of the *Bürgertum* itself, those who favored unbridled industrial expansion, seeking to produce ever more goods and profit without concern for the effects on either workers or the quality of their wares. Here he had in mind people such as those who had provoked the Silesian revolt of 1844; he may have included advocates of mechanical methods on a large scale too, but it should be remembered that there were still few of these on the German scene at the time he wrote. Whoever they were, such people had no care for society's unity, and their actions would end up reducing it to a stark opposition between rich and poor. Their stance did not represent contemporary *bürgerliche Gesellschaft* as a whole, however, since to generate social solidarities was equally characteristic of it. Society's defining characteristic was that it "naturally" generates divisions between people based on the kind of work they do, large distinctions as between peasants and town-dwellers, and smaller ones between tailors and shoemakers, but these collective identities had always been and could still be sources of the solidarities and moral commitments that generated the principles of civilized life.[55]

For this reason it was the second source of atomistic and dangerous individualism that was the most threatening. It was rooted not in society but in the state. Riehl considered the division between the two to be a defining characteristic of his age, drawing here as elsewhere on Hegel. But he placed this separation in a wholly different light, because in his eyes what made it both powerful and perilous was the work of the very bureaucrats whom the author of *The Philosophy of Right* saw as the vehicle of its overcoming. Devoted to the notion that all the inhabitants of a state belonged to a single category, that of *Staatsbürger*, the bureaucrats (among whom the Prussians were the preeminent, that is the worst, example) did away with every traditional distinction between people, weakening or destroying the guilds and kindred associations through which individuals could develop other and independent identities. The officials may have seen their aim as raising productivity and increasing well-being, but the effect of their policies was to deprive society of its own more varied form of existence, and thus to foster a tyrannical kind of state authority, meanwhile giving free rein to shoddy work and shady dealing, and spreading impoverishment among worthy craftsmen. Riehl thus presented what he called his "social politics" as a defense of society against the state, a plea to limit bureaucratic incursions into the social realm in order to return to an order that could preserve social coherence and well being.[56]

Riehl's way of identifying the essence of what was *bürgerlich*, and what it shared with modernity, had much in common with Hegel's emphasis on the abstractness of needs and means that made social life on a large scale possible, but where Hegel saw the apparent opposition between society and the state as reconciled on a higher level, Riehl regarded the contrast between the two as more permanent and dangerous. To him, bureaucrats were not really part of society, they were too one-sided and abstract to be genuinely *bürgerlich*. He was not alone in taking such a view; as we have seen, others regarded the dependency of officials on states and sovereigns as disqualifying them from *Bürger* status too. But there can be no doubt that the *Bildungsbürgertum* of which they formed the core was an essential, and at the moment Riehl wrote his book was still the preeminent component of the German bourgeoisie.

Riehl's understanding of *bürgerliche Gesellschaft*, like Hegel's, fits well with the perspective I am trying to develop here, which regards involvement in distant connections and the kinds of abstract and mediated relationships they foster as characteristic of all three main species of bourgeois: merchants and traders, administrators and officials, and professionals and intellectuals. It was just this orientation that made all of them appear to the traditional townspeople Mack Walker studied as "movers and doers." But the particular role of each group was different in different countries, and Riehl was also correct to see state action as more wholeheartedly devoted to principles that undermined the traditional place of local and particularistic forms of existence in Germany than were *Bürger* as a general category. Merchants and traders were drawn into distant relationships to be sure, but many of them remained more attached to the traditional forms of communal life than were state officials or the intellectual supporters of *Aufklärung* Wieland described as the sole "men of the nation." Like Hegel, but in a different way, Riehl's analysis of *bürgerliche Gesellschaft* could not fail to highlight the features of it that made it different from bourgeois existence elsewhere.

The limits within which the participation of merchants and traders in distant networks drew them away from traditional middle-class values and attitudes are also a feature of a third revealing portrait of bourgeois existence, Gustav Freytag's novel *Debit and Credit* (*Soll und Haben*), published first in 1855, four years after *Die bürgerliche Gesellschaft*. Freytag's fictional account of the life of a young merchant does not make easy reading today, partly because it is both militaristic and anti-Semitic (one of its characters, Veitel Itzig, became a stock figure of anti-Jewish polemic and satire); it depicts the relations between bourgeois and aristocratic characters in ways intended to show the first as both morally and intellectually superior to the second, despite the persisting power of the latter to surround themselves with an alluring but deceptive aura of quality. But Freytag's several invocations of the way bourgeois endeavors created distant connections able to awaken and sustain human powers that lie dormant or shrivel in their absence deserve to be highlighted.

The life course of Anton Wohlfahrt, the novel's hero, took its rise from a good turn his father, a village accountant, once did for a merchant house in his province's capital. In response, the firm sent him a gift of sugar and coffee each year, leading him to take an interest in the prices of these commodities, keeping track of them in a local newspaper. "A strange, invisible, filmy thread it was, this which connected Wohlfart's quiet household with the activity of the great mercantile world, and yet it was by this that little Anton's whole life was swayed." The connection stimulated the boy's imagination, making him see his own future by way of a "kaleidoscope picture" that mixed up images of exotic wares with his father's pleasure in the gift, and "the mysterious daylight which the arrival of the box always occasioned him." Later on, after Anton has begun to work for the same firm, he makes the nature of this illumination more explicit:

> I know nothing so interesting as business. We live amid a
> many-colored web of countless threads, stretching across
> land and sea, and connecting man with man. When I place
> a sack of coffee in the scales, I am weaving an invisible
> link between the colonist's daughter in Brazil, who has
> plucked the beans, and the young mechanic who drinks

it for his breakfast; and if I take up a stick of cinnamon, I seem to see, on the one side, the Malay who has rolled it up, and, on the other, the old woman of our suburb who grates it over her pudding.

To be sure the image is much idealized, and we should not pass over the unlikely claim that the coffee beans had been gathered by "the colonist's daughter" without calling to mind the actual realities of coffee-growing in a slave society. All the same, the connections Freytag idealizes had some of the power he attributes to them, as did the effects of their dissolution in moments of commercial crisis, the one in question brought on by the Polish wars of the 1830s. The breakdown of civic order at that moment meant that products could not be safely transported and that the sums invested in them would be lost. As people drew back out of anxiety, "Hundreds of ties, woven out of mutual interest, and having endured for years, were snapped at once. Each individual existence became more insecure, isolated, and poor … the country was out of health."[57] Freytag makes clear that the market ties that give way in such moments are material, even self-interested ones, but he sees them all the same as operating on other levels too, establishing contacts that involve more than profit and loss. We cannot pause here to attend to the novel's romantic themes, but they too make clear that the world of debit and credit is also a world of human feelings, some ugly and destructive, but others (among some of the Jewish characters too) capable of fostering commitment and devotion.

In Freytag's story, these ties have the character of a particular time, the one before German life began to be altered by the revolution in transport that made the world of his readers in 1855 already different from Anton Wohlfahrt's. "The business was one of a kind becoming rare nowadays, when railroads and telegraphs unite remotest districts, and every merchant sends from the heart of the country to bid his agents purchase goods almost before they reach the shore." In those older and slower-moving times, business had both a certain dignity, since undermined by modern pressures, and a higher element of risk, because "the sea was far off, facilities of communication were rare, so that the merchants' speculations were necessarily more independent, and involved greater hazard." Factories have no significant presence in this world, the only one that appears in the novel being a failed attempt to manufacture bricks by a noble fated to lose his estate to the machinations of Jewish speculators, but whose family Anton saves by careful management of the much poorer lands where they are constrained to live, in Poland.

Freytag's account of *bürgerliche Gesellschaft* shared much with his contemporary Riehl's: the bourgeois penchant for establishing distant and generalizing connections was a source of strength and change for both, cut across by a commitment to social and moral stability, and a determination to distinguish between the genuine spirit of bourgeois enterprise, always connected to real objects of use, and the dangerous abstraction from it constituted by pure speculation. Freytag gave the state no place in his story, nor did he seek to account for the changes that separated Anton Wohlfart's world from the one coming into being after 1850. Whether or not he recognized state action as an important contributor to the changes he described, there is no doubt that it played a part, as we shall see when we come to German industrialization later on. Well into the twentieth century, the special function of the state as an engine of modernization, and the ability of state power sharply to alter social relations, would be a defining characteristic of German history. In the period considered here, it was the opportunities a still fragmented and undeveloped country offered interventionist states to take *bürgerliche Gesellschaft* as an object of action, and the linked encouragement to make it an object of contemplation fostered in members of a developing stratum of *Bildungsbürger* by their close but often uncomfortable ties to those same states, that made Germany the site where bourgeois society as a form of life received its most elaborate and in some ways most insightful theorizations, albeit ones that could not escape being abstract and one-sided.

5 MODERN INDUSTRY, CLASS, AND PARTY POLITICS IN NINETEENTH-CENTURY ENGLAND

By the last decades of the nineteenth century the three countries on which we are focusing, England, France, and Germany, all possessed more tightly integrated national spaces, linking together regions and their components – towns, cities, countrysides, people, resources – through networks structured in remarkably similar ways. Everywhere railroads and telegraphs were creating conditions for the rapid spread of modern industry, and a new species of nationally organized parties gave a changed character to politics. Sharing common institutions and frames of action (in culture too, as will be seen later on), all three places seemed in many ways to be traversing a shared path to modernity. Yet the diverse earlier patterns of development generated by the differing configuration of networks we have sought to describe still made themselves felt, giving a distinct quality to life in each place, and in particular to the relations between bourgeois or middle-class people and those with other social identities. In this and the next two chapters we consider the particular path each country followed as it achieved this tighter mode of integration, the distinct kinds of industrial modernity and party politics each evolved, and the forms and limits of bourgeois power that ensued.

Industrial growth and the limits of precocious integration

The two-sided story in which England appears at once as the pioneer industrial nation and the model for others from late in the eighteenth century, and as following a rhythm more like that of France and Germany than has often been recognized, achieving a modern industrial economy only from around 1870, is well exemplified in the crucial topic of railroad building. Railroads were a key element of modern industry because of their importance first as a means for improving the speed and reducing the cost of transport for both people and goods, and second as a powerful stimulus to metal production and manufacturing more generally. Britain embarked on building railroads markedly earlier than any other country, and by 1850 the United Kingdom had almost 10,000 kilometers of track, nearly twice the German number and three times that of France at the same date – especially remarkable given her smaller size. Beginning from their lower bases, the latter two countries chalked up striking gains in the next two decades, Germany multiplying its mileage by a factor of around four and France by five. But Britain's growth in the same period continued at an impressive pace too, giving her nearly two and a half times the 1850 figure by the early 1870s, so that only at that point can the rail network be described as providing a unified web of connection for the country as a whole.[1]

The numbers in themselves are significant, but still more was the impact this completion now had on the British economy. To be sure the difference it made was less sharp than on the continent, since there (as will be seen in detail later) the railroads brought sudden and radical change, linking distant producers and consumers together for the first time and giving an economic viability to significant investment in machine production that England already exhibited a century before. But the island nation's market was transformed too. Before 1870 goods circulated easily between regions, but transport costs still gave local conditions power to determine what it made economic sense to produce in particular places; not only were regional specializations not undermined by the kind of integration Britain exhibited until around 1870, they were amplified and expanded. As Lynn Lees notes, "the pattern of industrial expansion that dominated Britain during the industrial era was a regional one," concentrating "all the stages of production of a commodity within one area, [and] mixing management, production and exporting." In textiles, as Richard Price points out, the kinds of cloth produced in parts of the country depended on each region's earlier history: manufacturers in Yorkshire specialized in cheaper worsteds, while weavers in the southwest continued to devote themselves to higher-quality woolens. In general, before the mid century "it is not possible to speak of a nationally integrated economy whose imperatives dictated regional development." This changed in the next decades: from the 1870s "the industrial revolution arrived in the East Midlands in the wagons of the railways," whose ability to reduce the price of both raw materials and finished goods "transformed the potential of the region beyond the local market." The same conditions encouraged the development of industry on a larger scale: it was at this point that "the workshop basis of the manufacturing sector gave way to larger industrial structures as heavy industry made its appearance." William Langer provides evidence of similar transformations: between 1850 and 1880 there occurred a marked expansion in the average number of spindles in British cotton factories (although the pace, like that of railroad building, was less rapid than in France or Germany), and the larger capital requirements led to an expansion in corporate as opposed to family organization of firms.[2] Further technical advances such as the "second industrial revolution" techniques in chemistry, metallurgy, and electricity, now combined to carry Britain, like the major continental countries, into the era of "large-scale industry, integrated production, scientific management, reconfigured social relations, and the fusion of science and technology." We should not neglect the role played in creating the foundation for these results by the steady growth of railroad construction, iron production, textile mechanization, and steam engine capacity throughout the century, but Price seems justified in insisting that in Britain no less than across the Channel the era in which the railroad network approached its completion ushered in a new and more markedly modern phase in industrial history.[3]

The history of steam power and its effect on what the term "factory" called up in people's minds provides one revealing index of this change. The first steam engines in factories made a strong impression on observers from late in the eighteenth century, but only in the 1870s did steam replace water as the most common source of manufacturing power, and only with the widespread turn to the steam turbine from the 1880s (it was invented in 1884) did mechanized power come fully to dominate industrial production, allowing the term "factory" to take on its modern connotation as a locale of machine production rather than an assemblage of workers using various techniques. Because the turbine directly produces rotary motion it is far more efficient than the piston-driven Newcomen-Watt engine, and especially well suited to generating electricity; as with other new technologies, however, investing in it became economically viable only because market conditions made it so. The general validity of this point has been emphasized by Samuel Lilley in connection with his demonstration that steam power did not replace wind and sails in ocean shipping until well after the change had become technically possible, because the cost of taking away cargo space for engines and of setting up fueling stations only became worth paying when the volume and distance of trade reached a certain level. Many-masted sailing ships dominated international sea routes all the way to the 1880s because only then did the volume of international trade (aided by the opening of the Suez Canal in 1869) give enough value to greater speed and regularity to overcome the price that had to be paid for them. Here, as in other instances, Lilley concludes, "it was the general movement of the economy and not the technical innovations as such, that dictated the pace of change."[4]

The same understanding provides us with a necessary perspective from which to grasp an otherwise puzzling feature of economic history, namely that the moment when modern industry spread through Europe as a whole was also the one when Britain, the pioneer innovator, could no longer keep up with the rivals she had outdistanced earlier. Various explanations have been offered for this reversal, including the one I noted earlier, that the persistence of aristocratic values and preferences gave English businessmen a "gentlemanly" orientation (fostered for instance in the public schools where offspring of middle-class and aristocratic families intermingled) that discouraged cutthroat competition and encouraged retirement from business in favor of more refined pursuits.[5] Such an account is hard to credit given that aristocratic values survived everywhere at the end of the nineteenth century and that of all European aristocracies, the English was the one with the deepest history of involvement in commerce, so much so that the contrast between French elite disdain for practical knowledge and upper-class British interest in it has been suggested as a reason for the slow pace of French industrial change. A much more cogent explanation is simply that the conditions that made the international spread of modern industry possible turned the advantages England had enjoyed earlier into limitations. The economic regime that put her markedly ahead of other countries before 1850 rested on the geographical conditions – smaller size, navigable rivers – that allowed for a precocious integration and therefore a more consolidated national market on the basis of a pre-industrial technology of roads, canals, and costal shipping, invigorated by the special role London played in national life. France and Germany could not achieve such integration before modern means of transport brought their more distant and varied regions into closer effective connection, but once they did they were able to draw on bigger populations and greater endowments of resources than Britain possessed. Their larger, and in Germany's case much faster-growing, populations gave them bigger internal markets, expanded supplies of labor, and greater potential tax revenues; in addition, they possessed more highly developed educational institutions, originally instituted to support pre-industrial programs of military and administrative expansion, but able to aid economic advance as science and technology assumed greater importance in it (I will return to this question in the German context in Chapter 7).[6] Once these resources could be effectively mobilized, Britain's relative position was bound to reveal limitations hidden before.

In a certain way the higher level of national integration England achieved in the last decades of the nineteenth century was part of what worked against her. In the first half of the nineteenth century, the relations between London and the rest of the country that had been so important in its early economic advance continued to be favorable to it. More than any other country England as a whole could profit from the economic development of certain regions – notably the burgeoning cities of the north – because of the way they were tied into the national economy as a whole. Could any similar development have somehow taken place in Toulouse, say, or Frankfurt, it would not have had the same kind of impact on France or Germany that Manchester and Birmingham had in England, if only because regional connections were simply too weak (in the German case Hamburg developed important industries based on refinishing imported goods well before 1850, but with little direct impact on other German areas).

One illustration of the peculiar English synergy between regional and national development appears in the development of local banking. Although capital requirements for manufacture were generally low during the eighteenth century, they began to grow even before the need to invest in machines made its impact, as market opportunities encouraged merchants to expand their reach and their ambitions; in response, the number of banks grew too. In 1750 there seem to have been fewer than a dozen regularly constituted banks outside London; twenty-five years later the number was closer to a hundred, and growing. Many of these new banks developed out of other businesses (a common occurrence in financial history), and they played a large role in underwriting industrial expansion and innovation during the eighteenth and early nineteenth centuries. Although local in their character and scope, a number of them developed connections with London money men, augmenting the resources they could provide in their areas. Self-finance through reinvesting profits (once thought to be the more or less exclusive source of capital in this period) was important too, but the ability of businessmen to use their profits to add to their long-term fixed capital depended on their being able to rely on banks to meet their shifting needs for shorter-term working funds.[7] By contrast, there was little reason for French regions to evolve similar structures, and the big Parisian bankers, the so-called Haute Banque, operated largely as organizers of state finance; some, such as the Rothschilds (whose history we will consider later on), had branches in other capitals, but no significant connections in French provincial cities. In contrast to their British counterparts, French banks remained famously reluctant to lend money to new business enterprises until well into the nineteenth century and in some cases even beyond.

After 1870, however, British banks no longer served industrial development in the same way. What made them less favorable partners for industry than they had been in the first phase of innovation was the increasing centralization of banking in London, just at the time when commercial agents there were becoming more involved in the international transactions (bill discounting and payment settlements) that were making the City the world's financial capital. These operations depended on the maintenance of the gold standard that gave unquestioned stability to the pound sterling, but which also kept interest rates relatively high (by limiting the money supply), to the detriment of industrialists in search of capital. Combined with a fear of industrial investment on the part of some bankers, stemming from business failures in crises of the 1860s and 1870s, and the difficult conditions many faced as competition grew fiercer in the next decades, these changes deprived Britain of the benefits of the nurturing symbiosis between central and regional development that had aided its industrial development before. British industry did not cease to grow, to be sure, but it expanded at a slower pace than its rivals, presaging the post-World War I situation in which the country's economic weaknesses would be increasingly on display.

Statistical support for this view is provided by the figures Simon Kuznets generated some time ago, indicating that whereas the proportion of British national product devoted to capital formation hovered around 12 percent in the last decades of the nineteenth century, the German figure was well over 20 percent in every decade between 1870 and 1900. As world markets became more closely integrated in the age of the "second industrial revolution" and heightened imperial competition, London was drawn into tighter connections with places outside Britain, at the same time that its financial supremacy over other domestic regions was growing. The city's changing relations to the rest of the country and the world at once magnified England's position as a financial center and contributed to the passing of its industrial leadership.[8] It should be noted that the British empire in these years entered into a phase of tighter integration that paralleled the transformation of the mother country itself: whereas earlier the various colonial regions had generally been regarded as too separate from each other and from England to be part of an integrated political space, from around 1870 "the profound transformation in political consciousness generated by the revolution in communication technology" led a number of observers to argue "that the colonial empire formed part of a single political field, that it constituted a unified community stretching across the globe."[9] The same transformation was part of what made it possible for other countries to challenge Britain's imperial supremacy, just as they were overtaking it economically. The evolving relations between banking and manufacture in Britain thus form part of a broader history that testifies to the way the country's singular rhythm of development gave her advantages in the period before the railroad age that she lost as the more powerful networks that now developed spread through Europe and the world.

Class and middle class

The creation of more fully integrated national spaces that altered the conditions of industrial development had an impact in the political realm too, most visibly in the prominence assumed in the nineteenth century by two phenomena of little moment before: the recognition of class as a social identity and an instrument of action, and the appearance of modern nationally organized political parties. As with industry, these features of modern politics emerged in two distinct phases, with modern political parties taking the stage only from the 1860s, while the class-based feeling and rhetoric whose proper place in their activity was often debated already bulked large in the decades just after 1815, drawing on a vocabulary that had begun to develop during the eighteenth century. But the two phenomena were closely related in that authority relations in a society ordered along a hierarchy of ranks or degrees rested on vertical connections between individuals whose personal status determined their place in both local and national life, whereas class as a category projected a more anonymous and generalized form of identification, appropriate to the more impersonal and more abstractly mediated political space where nationally organized parties would act and compete. We have already considered aspects of the early use of class language in France and Germany, but the English case casts additional light on the whole topic, particularly in showing how both the spread of class as a category and of parties as instruments of action were tied up with the growing weight of abstract relations and the networks that fostered them. In all these respects, the English case will become a point of comparison to the French and German ones in the two chapters that follow.

Although people in the nineteenth century believed that the practice of dividing society into distinct and separate classes was a novelty of their time (and Asa Briggs, in a famous and still valuable article, took them pretty much at their word), Penelope Corfield has shown that the term "class" was regularly used before 1800, first alongside the older vocabulary of "ranks" and "orders," then in its stead. The earlier vocabulary reflected a notion of society as a stable configuration of parts whose relations to each other were widely presumed to be rooted in some divine or natural principle independent of human will; it made little sense to speak of a struggle between "orders" or "ranks." Class, by contrast, referred not to an ordained division but either to one in which particular human action played some part, for instance that of officials who put people into some category for administrative purposes, or one marked by an awareness of large and more anonymous changes in people's conditions, as when economic improvement or decline led people to alter their behavior. Unlike ranks or orders, such classifications allowed for the possibility of change, "whether by cooperation, competition, or conflict," so that class presupposed more fluidity in social relations; it also encouraged "a much more conscious scrutiny" of social arrangements, including questions about the worldly sources of wealth and poverty.

This focus gave what has been called "the language of class" a certain concreteness, but from the start it also exhibited a tendency to be vague and abstract. The number of classes spoken about varied from one observer to another. Those who counted as many as seven divisions could distinguish (as did Daniel Defoe) between "the great," "the rich," and "the middling sort," adding in townspeople and country folk before arriving at one or more species of laborers (some impoverished, some reasonably well-off), but there was already a tendency to simplify the categories, reducing them to "upper," "middle," and "lower" or even to starker oppositions between the few and the many, the useful and the useless, or the rich and the poor. From the start many ways of naming classes involved people's economic condition, but sometimes this concerned relative wealth and sometimes function or source of income (these latter would be developed by economists), and certain descriptions, such as "industrious" or "respectable" carried moral overtones as well. Some categories cut across others, creating a complex social field in which particular individuals might belong to more than one group at the same time, a situation which some would seek to avoid by employing highly general and inclusive categories. The language of class thus at once fostered a recognition that actual social relations are intricate and unpredictable, and offered opportunities and temptations to reduce them to some simpler state.[10]

The motives for such simplification might sometimes be disinterestedly analytical, seeking to impose order on an complex and fluid reality, but sometimes they were pointedly rhetorical, giving prominence to class identities in pursuit of particular ends. The latter purpose is particularly evident in the growing prominence of appeals to the middle class, both as an actual group and as a reference point for policy, during the early nineteenth century. The idea of a middle class had been part of the new idiom from the start, but not yet in the way it would appear after around 1815. Some people emphasized the special virtues of middling people, but along lines laid down long before by Aristotle, naming stability, moderation, and relative independence as the qualities of those who were neither powerful enough to oppress others nor needy enough to be easily corrupted by poverty and temptation. In particular there was still no talk of a "rising middle class" whose ascension altered the substance of social relations. This notion, as Dror Wahrman has shown in an exhaustive study, arose in connection with the agitation for suffrage extension that led to the landmark Parliamentary Reform Bill of 1832. The foreign and still unfamiliar term bourgeois was not part of this discussion; for this reason we will mostly employ "middle class" in the rest of this chapter too.

Before the reform campaign got under way English commentators often described the middle class or classes as essential to the country's well-being, but in terms that equated social health with stability, not change, and identified the middle as a chief guarantor of it. Although it was sometimes associated with commerce and industry, its size or social role were seldom described as expanded by virtue of economic advance. From around 1815, however, the middle section of society came to be seen as dynamic, both a motor and an index of social transformation. As a writer in the *Edinburgh Review* put it in 1820, comparing the present with the mid eighteenth century: "Villages have since sprung up into immense cities; great manufactures have spread over wastes and mountains; ease, comfort and leisure, have introduced, among the middle classes of society, their natural companions, curiosity, intelligence, boldness, and activity of mind. A greater proportion of the collective knowledge and wealth of the nation has thus fallen to their lot." What chiefly drew observers to call attention to such developments was the perceived destabilization of the British political system, which had failed to respond to changes in the society around it; thus the need arose to reform Parliament, so as to give middle class people the "political rights" that their "social importance" demanded. Among the events that helped to spread such views was the famous "Peterloo Massacre" of 1819 when eleven people were killed (and many more injured) by troops dispersing a giant demonstration on behalf of reform in Manchester. Middle-class radicals as well as workers were among the organizers of the meeting, and the violence to which it led drove some of the former to more conservative positions, while moving others to insist that reform was all the more necessary in order for stability to return. The moment led to a spreading recognition of the need to satisfy middle-class demands, and encouraged people to emphasize social change as the reason why new political measures were required. Without them the danger remained

that a discontented middle class would spread its penchant for disorder downward to more dangerous groups below; given satisfaction,
however, they would use their resources and influence to calm society
as a whole.[11]

These discussions, along with the debates about the historical
role played by bourgeois or middle-class people in France in the same
years, provided much of the vocabulary of class conflict that would
be developed in Marxism and used to different effect by others. The
English discussions shared much with the French ones, but they had a
different inflection, discernible in a famous speech the Whig politician
and historian Thomas Babington Macaulay gave in 1831. Marx would
later find it easy to acknowledge his debt to such a view as this:

> All history is full of revolutions, produced by causes
> similar to those which are now operating in England. A
> portion of the community which had been of no account
> expands and becomes strong. It demands a place in the
> system, suited, not to its former weakness, but to it pre-
> sent power. If this is granted, all is well. If this is refused,
> then comes the struggle between the young energy of
> one class and the ancient privileges of another. Such was
> the struggle between the Plebeians and the Patricians
> of Rome. Such was the struggle of the Italian allies for
> admission to the full rights of Roman citizens. Such was
> the struggle of our North American colonies against the
> mother country. Such was the struggle which the Third
> Estate of France maintained against the aristocracy of
> birth. Such was the struggle which the Roman Catholics
> of Ireland maintained against the aristocracy of creed.
> Such is the struggle which the free people of color in
> Jamaica are now maintaining against the aristocracy of
> skin. Such, finally, is the struggle which the middle classes
> in England are maintaining against an aristocracy of mere
> locality.[12]

Here is a whole theory of history as class conflict, but we must
not miss the broad and indiscriminate sense Macaulay gives to the
term "class," which simply designates a distinguishable "portion of
the community." (*The Communist Manifesto* would not abandon this

usage altogether, since its authors too invoked a wide variety of class conflicts; their contention was that under modern conditions all were being absorbed into the struggle between bourgeoisie and proletariat.) The only example of an urban middle class cited is the one to which Macaulay himself belonged (the French Third Estate contained far more peasants than bourgeois), but there are several different species of aristocracies (of "creed," of "color," "of skin"), of which only one, the French, was defined by birth. That Macaulay did not view the English aristocracy in the same light should not be overemphasized, but it should not go unnoticed either; the Whig circles in which he moved were ones in which the longstanding commercial and political connections between English aristocrats and middle-class people were well represented. This makes Macaulay's characterization of the English aristocracy as one "of mere locality" all the more worthy of being underlined. The term seems to refer in part to the degree to which the new middle class belonged especially to the north of the country, but also to the historical circumstance that those cities with no representation in Parliament were ones which for whatever reason had not been incorporated as boroughs (each of which had the right to send two representatives to Westminister), so that the "class" opposition that produced the crisis was one rooted at least as much in the happenstance of political history as in the general frame provided by social change. For Macaulay to characterize the English middle class in earlier times as "a portion of the community which had been of no account," and its right to "a place in the system" as only recently asserted, really applied only to places such as Manchester and Birmingham, rather than to the broader category he invoked, which had long been a recognized part of British society and of Parliament. By giving a general significance to "class" conflicts that made the term refer to a variety of different kinds of exclusions, Macaulay made it easy to apply his words to broader changes than the one about which he was speaking, and taking them in that sense has become a more powerful temptation as the social transformations associated with modernity have proceeded. But the Reform debates of these years, although surely rooted in economic change, had just as much to do with the issue Richard Price locates at the center of British political debate in the whole period from 1688, when Parliamentary supremacy was established, to 1867, when votes were first given to a large number of workers: who would be included in the political nation and who excluded from it? (The same issue was present when suffrage requirements were set in other countries too, but as we shall see it was overshadowed by more basic constitutional questions.) Macaulay's reference to excluded portions of a national community demanding a place in the political system shows that he understood the situation of 1832 very much in these terms. [13]

The connection between the appeals to class in the agitation for the Reform Bill and the changing nature of the political system to which we pointed a moment ago can be seen if we pause to note some things the rightly famous Act did and did not accomplish. The suffrage it established was much broader than the one set up in France by the revolution of July, 1830, but it was far from democratic, leaving out most artisans and workers and making the exclusion of women explicit for the first time. In some ways, recent historians have argued, the new system was less democratic than the old, since the latter's lack of uniformity left room for arrangements in some districts that gave the vote to modest middle- and even working-class people whom the 1832 settlement excluded. As noted earlier, historians by now largely agree that it did not – as was long asserted – transfer political power from the aristocracy to the middle classes; promoted by Whig magnates such as Earl Grey, it re-established the cross-class alliance that made figures such as Macaulay largely dependent on aristocratic patrons (Gladstone first entered politics on the same basis), helping to preserve its power through most of the century. The Bill went a certain distance toward bringing representation into line with population, depriving some of the hundred or so "pocket" or "rotten" boroughs whose few inhabitants voted in accord with the wishes of some local notable of their seats and assigning them to places recently grown much larger. But it left intact over forty of these tiny jurisdictions, and with them the power of some local bigwig to march voters to the poll, often entertaining them lavishly in the old and typically raucous style. What made it the first step toward a modern form of politics was less these specific provisions than the fact that it replaced a system based on historical precedent and local custom, and that made no provision for adjustments in response to population changes, with a much more uniform and (I need to risk the word) rational electoral system. Qualifications for voting in urban areas were made the same throughout the country, granting the franchise to any male householder who occupied premises worth £10 or more in yearly rent. The requirements in county districts were more diverse, reflecting different modes of landholding in different places, but they too were given greater uniformity.[14]

It was this homogeneity that allowed the 1832 Bill to serve as the basis for later extensions of voting rights in 1867 and 1884. None of the three reforms cut to the quick in the way demanded by the Chartist movement of the 1830s and 1840s, which would simply have rendered all adult males equal as voters. But the latter two developed the democratizing implications of the first Bill's impersonal logic. The 1867 Bill kept the urban household as the basis for voting, but eliminated the distinction based on property value or rent, thus enfranchising large sections of the working class. The 1884 Bill applied the same standard to rural heads of households; at this point few adult males were left out (although the full principle of complete manhood suffrage was not given legislative embodiment until 1918). Meanwhile the secret ballot had been adopted in 1868. This had been a Chartist demand too, but a stronger reason for its success was that it fit in with what Richard Price calls the "more formal machinery of politics" that the first Reform Bill began to put in place, and to which we now need to attend.

Here too it was the rationalization introduced in 1832 that pointed to the political future more than the specific changes in Parliamentary representation. Along with the Bill's turn to uniform qualifications went measures to make elections more regular and orderly, beginning with standard procedures for registering voters and confirming their eligibility: none had existed before. Getting potential voters to register now became a concern of national leaders and their local supporters. Partisan struggles broke out immediately over who had the right to be on the roll, sometimes carried out in ways that replaced "old corruption" with newer kinds. But the lists provided the foundation on which national party organizations would later establish ongoing links to supporters in the districts, undermining the traditional position of local notables. The Ballot Act was seen in much the same light, intended less to protect voters' privacy than to undercut bribery and "treating" by local bigwigs, practices which first came under the purview of the courts at the same time (earlier only Parliament itself had the authority to deal with these abuses).

The overall effect of such measures was progressively to weaken the old political culture in which local and vertical social relations were dominant, in favor of one shaped by the horizontal ties that drew all voters into the national political system. Whether this structure made people more free or independent may be debated, but it lessened the personal influence of powerful superiors (Adam Smith had made a similar point about the development of distant markets). Outlines of this new political culture were already visible in the eighteenth century, for instance in the Wilksite movement, whose national network of clubs and other informal organizations of presumed equals, tied together by newspapers and "public opinion," provided alternatives to the homegrown and personal hierarchies that dominated traditional politics. Such extended connections continued to develop in the 1820s and 1830s, notably in the "political unions" that served as mediating points through which local groups participated in the national campaign for reform. As these linkages underwent further development (we shall have more to say about them later on), they contributed to the situation whereby (as Price writes) "by the 1880s the world of politics was no longer bounded by the practices of social reciprocity and deference."[15] Because "class" politics implied the use of uniform and quantifiable criteria of participation in the political nation, it was part of the same logic that replaced local and directly personal relations of authority with the abstract and mediated ones that would be the ground for nationally organized parties.

Class, nation, and the divine economy

The way in which appeals to class were shaped at once by the need to operate in the widening political space where local identities were giving way to national ones, and by the opportunity such language offered to forge solidarities in the name of class for political purposes, can be seen in the cause with which middle-class identity was most closely involved in the period after the passage of the Reform Bill, the movement to repeal the Corn Laws (the duties on grain imposed at the end of the Napoleonic Wars) during the 1840s. The anti-Corn Law agitation carries an additional interest from the perspective I am seeking to develop here because some of the people involved in it exhibited a remarkable sense for the central place of distant connections in bourgeois life, a connection they understood in terms of great importance to people in their time, namely the tie between worldly activity and a religious understanding of the world.

One reason why the anti-Corn Law campaign is revealing is that it came to the language of class after first employing the related but separate idiom of "interest," turning to "class" instead in order to broaden its appeal. The notion of an "interest" was commonly employed in the eighteenth century in connection with attempts to influence Parliamentary action. An "interest" was both something of concern or importance to some person or persons, and a group organized on behalf of it (Adam Smith used the term in both senses). Some of these groups were "classes," but chiefly in the fluid sense that allowed any social grouping to be one. There was a manufacturing interest, a trading interest, a "monied" interest, a landed interest, as well as many smaller ones. Because these interests were in some degree self-serving, a certain pejorative aura hung over the term, although efforts were made to dispel it by insisting that separate interests could live in harmony, or that they all shared a higher concern for social order and stability.[16] The same was true of classes (which also had their "interests" to be sure), but the broader nature of class, and perhaps a certain link the term retained to ranks or orders, allowed classes to serve as the bearers of moral qualities thought to be beneficial to the nation as a whole. This had long been true of the aristocracy, often portrayed as the essential component of the nation on the grounds that its ownership of land gave it a permanent attachment to the country that holders of mere movable property lacked.[17] As for the middle class, it too had sometimes been ascribed the virtue of stability, as we saw, to which the debates over Parliamentary reform added qualities of initiative, knowledge, and even cultivation.

These features of the vocabulary of class and interest help us to understand the way the terms were employed by members of the Anti-Corn Law League, whose leaders in Manchester Asa Briggs describes as "perhaps the first men to think of themselves as a 'class.'"[18] It took them some time to come to this view, however. As one active member of the League who later wrote its history noted, when the group first organized in 1839 he and his fellows advocated eliminating the duties on grain on "the untenable and unpopular ground that it was necessary to have cheap bread in order to reduce the English rate of wages to the continental level." This was the language of interest, narrowly conceived, and, as the same observer went on, "so long as they persisted in this blunder, the cause of free trade made but little progress." Things changed as the Leaguers, seeking to appeal to a wide public, came to see and present their project in more broadly social and moral terms. The image of the middle class developed in the debates over Parliamentary reform, as representing both the dynamism of the modern nation and its best hope for achieving harmony and stability, became part of the case. In the rhetoric of the campaign that began at the end of the 1830s, the Corn Laws were portrayed as a barrier to progress, and damaging not just to manufacturers but to all who suffered from the high price of bread. The duties were an example of "class legislation" in a negative sense, shifting wealth to an unproductive oligarchy of landowners. Free trade, by contrast would benefit not just a "manufacturing interest," but the nation as a whole. As Briggs puts it, "the promptings of a commercial shrewdness were gradually enlarged into enthusiasm for a far-reaching principle." Class here had both a negative and a positive connotation, depending on the social group to which it applied, just as it later would for Marx.[19]

It is simple enough to see this as an example of the emergence of a "class ideology," and surely it was one: a policy originally pressed for the sake of personal advantage was now recommended on general principles claimed to be beneficial to everyone. But the language of class was just as equivocal here as it had been in the reform campaign. The League's claim to represent the middle class as a whole was simply false, since many people who clearly belonged to it were either lukewarm or cold toward the repealers' goals and activities. This was notably true of businessmen and professionals in London, among whom the Leaguers found as much indifference or opposition as support. As a contemporary biographer of Richard Cobden, one of the League's leaders, wrote, "In London there is no effective unity; interests are too varied and discursive; zeal loses its direction and edge amid the distracting play of so many miscellaneous social and intellectual elements." In an election of 1843 a free trade candidate won in London, but only by a narrow margin and against much opposition. (Similar divisions had kept London from providing wholehearted support for Parliamentary reform in the previous decade.) That some of these features of London society and politics reflected the closer relations of bourgeois elements in the capital to the aristocracy was one thing that made it such a different place from Manchester, but even there the League hardly enjoyed general middle-class support. As Sidney Pollard reminds us, many cotton manufacturers were skeptical of free trade because they feared that exporting machinery would subject them to tougher foreign competition. The *Manchester Guardian*, already emerging as the organ of liberal opinion it has remained, was never friendly to the League; it objected to the group's "dogmatic" adherence to its principle, and denied that its position represented "the community at large." The paper supported anti-League candidates in local elections.[20] Similar divisions existed in other towns throughout the country. For activists such as Cobden to present themselves as spokesmen both for the middle class as a whole and for the needs of the nation more broadly was indeed ideological, but their rhetoric was just as much aimed at gaining support in the section of society the League claimed to represent as in those that lay outside it. The close association between class analysis and a supposedly materialist and hard-nosed understanding of history makes it easy to miss the function of "class" as an "imagined community": to propose some policy as essential or vital to it as a whole was to stamp all its members with a particular character or shape, constituting it mentally in a way that privileged certain claims to direct or lead it. What brought these claims to the fore, and with it the rhetoric of class through which they were urged, was precisely the attempt to make the campaign national, to project it outside the local context where the language of interest at first seemed so natural, and appeal to a wider range of middle-class people. That the appeal was never wholly successful underscores the very internal division inside the middle class that made it necessary in the first place.

There was a second aspect to this rhetoric that made it characteristic of its time and place, and that could sometimes invoke the power of distant relationships in a different way, namely its easy turn to religious language. The Anti-Corn Law League often made its case in religious terms, sometimes presenting the tax on bread as an affront to "the revealed law of God." As one minister wrote, the English as a "nation of Bible Christians ... ought to realize that trade should be as free as the winds of Heaven." Although disappointment with the narrowness of the franchise extension in 1832 fostered suspicion of bourgeois political projects among those left out, such notions (combined with the fact that cheaper bread was indeed desired by many) helped to draw numbers of nonconformist workers into alliance with the middle classes in a common agitation for reform.[21] In this way religion served an ideological function too, encouraging people below the middle classes to accept bourgeois leadership. But religion was too important in the lives of many nineteenth-century people, of whatever social identity, to warrant viewing the appeals people made to it as primarily calculated or self-interested. We need to pause for a moment to consider some indications of how religious consciousness helped to develop a sense of identity in the middle classes.

Whatever one thinks about Max Weber's famous and much-debated thesis that a "Protestant ethic" of worldly activity and self-denial played a crucial role in injecting an entrepreneurial spirit into early modern society, there seems no doubt that the attitude he described was visible in the lives of many early nineteenth-century British entre-preneurs. As two eminent feminist historians have observed, non-conformist and evangelical varieties of religion fostered an image of manliness in which old codes of honor based on qualities useful in war or sport gave way to an emphasis on virtues such as diligence, honesty, and devotion to everyday duty.[22] Such an ethic had many uses. An illu-minating (and in many ways justifiably critical) study of entrepreneurs in the important wool-manufacturing center of Bradford reveals that the generation of people who fostered and managed the new indus-trial techniques there (as in other places) were largely newcomers, often small-town folk whose first experiences of the city might be exciting, but were also disorienting and confusing. What rescued them from anxiety and helped put them on the road toward success was "the pur-itan moral and religious legacy … inherited from their families." They and their pastors were comforted by the notion that moral behavior and steady application to the task at hand could be taken as fruits of the "indwelling" of the spirit, evidences of being among God's chosen.[23]

But an even closer tie linked their relation to God with their place in the economy. As one Bradford minister put it, not even his own vocation was as conducive to virtuous living as was work that involved constant transactions with other people and with things exchanged in the market. Business "accustoms us to subordination," because it imposes the need for a methodical attention to details and the external condi-tions that shape them; it makes us recognize our responsibility for our own fates, but also fosters awareness of the much more powerful forces that finally determine them: "It places our earthly lot so far within our own reach as to hold out an almost certain reward for diligence and fru-gality – and yet its issues are so far beyond our individual control … as to throw us most sensibly upon the over ruling providence of God." The minister, Edward Miall, was here describing what it was like to confront opportunities and dangers created by market forces so extensive and intricate that their mysterious operations could be compared to divine providence. The analogy worked both ways: finding one's way through worldly situations too broad and powerful for anyone to master the whole of them was good preparation for recognizing human dependency on the Almighty; at the same time religion's insistence on personal responsibility within a world governed by transcendent and ultimately invisible forces provided a training ground for acting inside the vast network of connections where modern enterprise operated.

Miall did not see this network only in economic terms. Like Gustav Freytag's young hero in his near-contemporary novel *Debit and Credit*, whom we met in Chapter 4, the minister viewed market relations as part of the larger web of culture that links people to each other across great distances, creating a wide range of bonds and attachments: "Trade multiplies our relations with our fellow men ... It creates countless grades of mutual dependence and necessitates mutual trust in all its stages ... I can scarcely conceive of a high cultivation of spiritual life in this world ... save by means and arrangements partaking very closely of the nature of trade."[24] Like Weber half a century later, Miall saw both the divine economy and the worldly one as objective frames that set limits to human action, even as they provided it with powers individuals could never possess on their own (a characteristic, as noted in Chapter 1, of networks of mean of all kinds). Unlike Weber, however, Miall did not see the web of connections humans created for their mutual interchange as having become so colossal and ponderous that it became an "iron cage," threatening to stifle the energies whose release had promoted its construction. We noted earlier that a different species of economic pessimism was present in this period, the inherited conviction that nature imposed strict limits on what could be produced, reworked in their separate ways by Malthus and Ricardo, and which earned for economics the label "the dismal science." In the expanding northern cities, however, and among those who saw them in a positive light, the growing and partially mechanized economy encouraged a new kind of optimism, a vision of a productive system that would improve life by multiplying wealth and goods, and with them the kinds of connections Miall highlighted.

Miall's language reminds us that many businessmen viewed their activity not as taking place in an independent sphere of pure economic relations, but as continuous with morality and religion. An older scholarship that emphasized the unalloyed individualism of economic enterprise in this period has given way to accounts that recognize entrepreneurship as closely woven into social and communal relations (I will have more to say about this in connection with the importance of family to individual well-being below).[25] If we ask what class identity such relations imparted, "bourgeois" or "middle class" is one possible reply, but alongside it we need to keep in view the now mostly forgotten but once widespread categories of "industrious" or "producing" classes. The terms appeared in England from the 1760s; in the nineteenth century they bore a kinship to the French word *industriels*, dear to the Saint-Simonians: both comprised all those engaged in productive work. Because such terms located entrepreneurs and workers in a single category, they have often been rejected as ideological constructions, and indeed they could be employed to serve a particular interest, as can any social categories. But both the vocabulary and the values it expressed drew people together across class lines, just as religious values did. As one thoughtful historian of working-class culture and politics concludes,

> Honesty, orderliness, punctuality, hard work and the refinement of manners and morals may all have been congruent with the industrial system and thus in the interest of the bourgeoisie but they were not therefore middle-class values. The great divisions in early nineteenth century society were not between the middle and the working classes but between the idle and the non-idle classes, between the rough and the respectable, between the religious and the non-religious ... The Puritan ethic was ... the ideology of those who worked as against those who did not.[26]

As we will now see, many of these same themes and relations reemerged in a different context once new-style political parties – and especially the liberals – appeared from the 1860s.

The advent of modern parties

The advent of modern political parties provided one of the grounds on which European countries came to resemble each other at the end of the nineteenth century. Resting on the suffrage extensions that vastly expanded electorates everywhere, the new parties took the form that has come to seem so natural since, in which some central organ oversees and is supported by a permanent network of local offices and committees set up to organize members, appeal to voters, and obtain financial support. The novelty of these organizations has sometimes been obscured, as Geoffrey Barraclough pointed out in some illuminating pages, by the usage that calls both older-style groupings and these more modern organizations by the same name.[27] Earlier "parties," such as British Whigs and Tories, or the Girondins and Jacobins of the French Revolution, were factions inside an assembly. A "party" might also consist of people who shared ideas and opinions and worked in concert for their spread or realization, but connections between such individuals were usually limited to correspondence or shared periodicals.[28] Factions inside assemblies might have links to like-minded circles outside, but (with temporary exceptions such as the nexus of Jacobin clubs in 1790s France) not through an organized structure, and never to one with the ability to endure. Nationwide movements such as the Anti-Corn Law League, Chartism, and earlier the supporters of Wilkes in England, or the National Society that campaigned for unification in Germany during the 1850s and 1860s (like its Italian model) were single-issue pressure groups, disappearing with the victory or collapse of the cause they championed. Chartism's absence of permanent structures was one reason why the movement could fade so quickly from the English political scene after 1848.

During the revolutionary upheavals of the mid century political groupings intended to influence elections were organized in both France and Germany, and might have become permanent had the hopes of those years that governments responsible to voters and citizens would become regular features of politics been fulfilled; but they melted away with the revolutionary excitement that spawned them. The fall of the Bonapartist Empire in France, and Bismarck's decision to introduce universal male suffrage in elections for the North German Confederation of 1867, and then for the Empire founded in 1871, reestablished conditions for the growth of nationally organized parties on the continent; by then such groupings were already developing in England. All exhibited the more closely knit organization and the greater capacity for long survival provided by the more powerful networks of transportation and communication coming into prominence in the same years. Parties were not the only such organizations that now proliferated; alongside them emerged interest groups of many kinds, representing economic (agrarian, mercantile, manufacturing), professional, occupational, gender, cultural, or religious identities. But it was large-scale political associations that had the greatest impact.

It is a particular and defining feature of this period that it created the conditions under which working-class and socialist organizations grew large and powerful – without, however, bringing about the transformation for which many within them called. By the 1890s the German Social Democrats had become the country's largest party (measured by votes in elections) and in 1912 they would achieve a plurality in the Reichstag; at the same time British workers were well on the way to setting up the independent forms of organization that freed them from earlier dependence on the liberals (the Labour Representation Committee, forerunner of the Labour Party, put its first representatives into Parliament in 1906), putting in motion the developments that would make Labour and not the liberals the chief alternative to the Conservatives after World War I; in France suspicion of electoral politics among socialists remained stronger than elsewhere, in accord with the country's history of violent social conflict and presaging the later role of the Communist Left, but by the 1890s the socialists were obtaining considerable electoral success, aided by left-leaning bourgeois republicans, from whose ranks some of the main socialist leaders emerged.

These groupings gave expression to a widespread sense of exclusion and injustice on the part of workers in the period before 1914, and their prominence gave class divisions and antagonisms an unmistakable place in politics. But these conflicts no longer took the form they commonly assumed before 1850, and especially in the European-wide revolutions of 1848. Then it had appeared to many people, in every camp and social stratum, that workers could not become part of the existing political system without challenging and destabilizing it; now the evidence increasingly pointed in the opposite direction. Despite the continued presence within socialist parties of many who cherished visions of an imminent social transformation, and the continued appeal to revolution in official doctrine, the practice of party organizations became overwhelmingly reformist. These were the developments (amplified by the patriotic loyalty evinced by most socialists once the Great War broke out) that led Lenin to conclude in

1917 that "A democratic republic is the best possible political shell for capitalism," and Eric Hobsbawm – the most distinguished contemporary Marxist historian writing in English – to note more recently that "in the years between 1880 and 1914 ruling classes discovered that parliamentary democracy, in spite of their fears, proved itself to be quite compatible with the political and economic stability of capitalist regimes." This revelation, he adds, was both "disappointing to revolutionaries" and quite at odds with what "either supporters or opponents" of bourgeois society mostly believed earlier in the century.[29]

So it was. All the same, these developments showed the capacity of bourgeois life to provide openings through which forces outside the middle classes could gain a share of social and political power. Together with national working class parties supranational labor organization gained stature and force too. The Second International, founded in 1889 and flourishing until the outbreak of World War I, represented the height of working-class internationalism, nurturing the hope that a new kind of society was in the offing. Both national and international socialist organizations relied on the railroad networks and national newspaper press that facilitated the movement of leaders and ideas, overcoming (as Eugen Weber and Gérard Noiriel have noted) the isolation that had earlier separated workers in different regions. Newspapers printed in capital cities were quickly disseminated to other places, and some, notably the German Social-Democratic organ *Die Neue Zeit*, obtained an international readership; information about conflicts, strikes, meetings, and candidates for election was rapidly spread about, and the European-wide reputations acquired by leaders such as Karl Kautsky, Keir Hardie, and Jean Jaurès contributed to their ability to give direction to their own parties. Thus there existed a close "relationship between technological progress and the methods of communication and propaganda open to socialist theorists and leaders."[30] The same could be said in regard to their liberal and conservative rivals; indeed, as James Sheehan notes, these conditions were hardly less important in fostering the new kind of party organization than was suffrage extension itself. Before democratic politics could draw in people who had no prior experience of it, "large sections of the population had to become convinced that participation in electoral politics had some connection with their lives," an evolution already underway in England but that on the continent (and especially in Germany) depended on new networks of communication and the messages passed along them.[31]

The reasons why the advent of modern parties had these effects were many. The influence that reformist ideas and practices gained within organized working-class groups owed much to the expanding economy's ability to provide a larger quantity and a wider range of consumer goods, together with the generally rising curve of real wages that marked the period from 1850 until nearly the outbreak of the War. But two other more strictly political circumstances were at play too. The conditions under which "parties" operated before the 1860s were ones that favored groupings of people who could bring significant personal resources to them: sufficient wealth to be able to devote time and funds (for travel or correspondence) to participation, status in local communities and connections to similar people outside, literacy and some knowledge of people and conditions beyond their localities. We will see below that under these circumstances liberal parties in particular were chiefly collections of "notables," people with reputation and standing in some particular place; the dependence of political participation on such standing was one reason why political positions were fairly often passed down from fathers to sons. Modern parties by contrast were able to link together and empower people who had few personal resources to bring to them, since the generally available means of communication and transport allowed them to disseminate information and draw people into common activities whether these members possessed the kinds of assets that were important earlier or not. Given the much larger numbers to which workers' organizations could appeal, even quite small individual contributions could provide sufficient funds to meet expenses. Some workers made careers inside party organizations; for them as for others these conditions meant, as Hobsbawm puts it, that "it was the party that made the notable," rather than the other way round.[32]

To this we need to add a second political advantage of working-class parties in this period, namely the depth of the divisions within the middle classes that efforts to establish modern parties revealed. In every country the projects advanced by some liberals to represent middle-class or bourgeois interests found barriers in the impossibility of giving unity to a part of society that remained especially fragmented and splintered. Liberals were not alone in experiencing a "crisis" in this period; the split between reformists and revolutionaries was recognized as one for socialists too. But working-class groupings were better able to forge a common basis for action than their bourgeois counterparts, who in addition were divided between those who saw politics in terms of class and those for whom liberalism was a vehicle for transcending it. These factors will be examined in different national contexts in this and the next two chapters.

Party organization, middle-class politics, and the coming of the "new liberalism"

As the only country where a central representative body with real power was an ongoing feature of politics, England developed the earliest effective party organizations. Their growth was fostered by the provisions of the 1832 Reform Bill noted earlier, in particular the listings of qualified voters created in order to administer the broader and more uniform suffrage; these provided local party committees with a basis on which to identify people over whom to seek influence. Before the second franchise extension in 1867, however, party loyalties were not grounded in organization of the later sort; in particular the great mid century leaders Gladstone and Disraeli first achieved their preeminence on the basis of their direct personal appeal to newly enfranchised voters. As John Vincent observes in his classic study of the Liberal Party and its voters, the followings acquired by the famous politicians of the era "were all achievements in the realm of sentiment." The Party was less a formal organization than "a habit of cooperation and a community of sentiment"; the enthusiasm and loyalty of its voters owed more to "the novelty of participation in politics" than to "attachment to programme or doctrine." Social conflicts had as yet little impact on national politics, in part because they were still largely "absorbed within a local situation" (the same was true in France) and in part because Gladstone, drawing on a rhetoric rooted in religious Dissent, was able to represent both moral seriousness and (especially as modern industry advanced after 1850) material progress. This combination had much to do with the appeal the Liberal Party made to working-class voters; from the onset of Gladstone's leadership in the 1850s and 1860s to near the end of the century, most workers gave their support in elections to liberals. "The massive development of party loyalties throughout the country preceded any corresponding full development of party organization by almost a generation."[33]

This later turn began in the 1870s, the decade when both liberals and conservatives constructed elaborate electoral machines, with local committees and chapters integrated into centrally controlled party structures. In both cases, but especially the liberal one, the more formal and mediated kind of organization was favored as a way to provide a substitute for the old politics of deference. The liberal efforts began in Birmingham, where Joseph Chamberlain (a manufacturer who was the town's mayor and later became an important figure in national politics, eventually becoming a conservative) and his associates set up a committee soon copied elsewhere, and which took the American name "Caucus." Its activities included choosing candidates and working for their election through meetings, pamphlets, and canvassing. From the start both a strength and a problem of the Caucus was that it represented a radical faction inside the Liberal Party, consisting of people opposed both to the old gentlemanly style of the Whigs and to their moderation in policy. The Caucus played a role (how important has been disputed) in one of the first truly national election campaigns, Gladstone's "Midlothian Campaign" of 1879. But its radical spirit made for tense relations with the National Party, leading to a crisis when Gladstone announced his conversion to Home Rule (that is autonomy) for Ireland in 1886, a policy that many in the radical wing, Chamberlain among them, opposed for reasons to which we will come in a moment. Gladstone's influence and prestige was sufficient to carry the majority in the Caucus along with him, however, and this allowed it to draw closer to the official Party, from which many prominent radicals who shared Chamberlain's views on Ireland now withdrew (becoming "Liberal Unionists," that is, supporters of keeping Ireland united to Britain). At this point the Caucus organization moved its headquarters from Birmingham to London, and merged with the National Liberal Federation, making clear its role as an agency of the Party.

On the conservative side, local associations in support of candidates had grown up from the mid 1830s, but the impetus to central organization came from national Party figures. Sir Robert Peel had urged Tories to organize in the 1840s, and after 1867 Disraeli, convinced that conservatives had the power to compete with liberals for working-class votes (it was he who put through the "leap in the dark" of the Second Reform Bill), assigned the task of encouraging and uniting local associations to one of his lieutenants. But it was younger figures acting after Disraeli's death in 1881, notably Randolph Churchill, who created the structures through which the Party sought to give practical substance to Disraeli's vision of "popular Toryism," through a network of local chapters of the "Primrose League," at once a political and social organization (named after Disraeli's favorite flower). As with the liberals, tensions surfaced between an older, more strictly aristocratic vision of the Party and a more populist one that sometimes inspired sharp criticism of its traditional orientation and leaders, but these were resolved with less conflict than in the liberals' case. By the late 1880s the Primrose League had become an important presence in many localities, spreading an image of Conservatism as open to the needs of ordinary people and able to enter into their concerns, and providing an efficient engine of electoral organization and fund-raising.[34] In certain ways its manner of generating support went beyond its liberal rivals; through its social events and use of symbols such as the Primrose itself, it provided the elements of a culture of conservatism infused into daily life by threads of activity in which sentiment and political calculation were deeply entwined.[35]

Since there was no separate Labour party until the 1890s, these developments would appear to have had no clear parallels further to the left. But English workers had already produced impressive, albeit impermanent, national organizations with clear political goals before 1850, in the forms of Chartism and Owenite socialism, phenomena on a scale that none of their continental counterparts could match, and like the distinguishing features of English economic and political life in general, testimony to the existence of networks that gave the country a more effective integration. In the decades when liberals and conservatives were evolving the rudiments of national party organizations, working-class activists made significant moves in the direction of formal organization too. Perhaps the chief of these, the formation of a Labour Representation League in 1869, occurred in the context of the continuing ties between liberals and workers; some of the latter to be sure would have preferred their own organizations, but their efforts to foster them, for instance in keeping the heritage of Chartism alive, produced meager results, in part because they were able to raise little money. The League was founded by workers disappointed at the failure of any working-class candidates to win seats in Parliament in the first election after the Second Reform Bill, but willing to take advantage of the greater resources possessed by liberals to

The history of the Liberal Party shows these relationships in action. Both Whiggism and radicalism sought to unify at least a large swath of the broad spectrum of the middle classes, but the efforts of both ended up giving new relief to the divisions they sought to overcome. The most revelatory moment came with the crisis provoked when Gladstone endorsed Home Rule for Ireland in 1886, which exposed oppositions within both radicalism and the Party as a whole. One current within radicalism favored a wholehearted and largely class-based attack on the remnants of aristocratic power everywhere, often dubbed "feudalism," and this impulse fed support for Home Rule, since aristocratic landowners were among the chief beneficiaries (and to many the villains) of the existing regime in Ireland. But other radicals were among the strongest opponents of Home Rule, since for them the sphere in which traditional and hierarchical power was most objectionable was religion. Some of these were Dissenters and some secularists, but both saw in Irish self-rule the specter of Catholic ascendancy, especially in education. (Many radicals in England also fought the official recognition given to Anglican schools by the 1870 Act that established universal primary education.) These were the chief grounds on which Chamberlain and his faction deserted the Gladstonian official Party for Unionism, allying themselves on this issue with conservatives (and beginning an association that would lead some of them to join the Tories later on). There was both irony and confusion in this move to the right, since the strength of the Chamberlain radicals inside the Party, and in particular their advocacy of social reform measures, was already driving some more moderate liberals in the same conservative direction, impelled by the linked fears of greater government interference in private life and higher taxes. This exodus was enlarged by the Irish issue too, since moderate liberals, and especially landowners, had their own reasons to draw back from what seemed to many a radical turn. At the same time, the new Irish policy pushed some workers previously attracted to Gladstone away from the liberals as well, moved by anxiety that an independent Ireland would lead to higher levels of immigration and thus competition for jobs; some of these people, however, were already being drawn toward specifically working-class and socialist organizations, whose growth was nurtured by the economic difficulties that spread through Europe in the 1880s. All these divisions inside the Party were brought to a boil by Gladstone's conversion of 1886, but they had long simmered inside it.[40]

These disengagements and defections would weaken the liberals in the next decades, but the Party's later fate had most to do with its relations to workers, since it was the Independent Labour Party that would become the chief alternative to the conservatives after 1914. The path toward this outcome, however, was one that sought to strengthen the longstanding alliance between workers and liberals, and it ended with the Party's adoption of the "New Liberalism" exemplified by the measures enacted under the government led by Herbert Asquith and David Lloyd George in their "People's Budget" of 1909 – most famously the beginnings of a graduated income tax, government-sponsored old-age pensions, and unemployment insurance. Moves in this direction were already visible in the 1860s and 1870s, in the cooperation radical liberals sought to establish with groups of working-class democrats who favored suffrage extension rather than direct action as the most promising route to social reform. Some liberals sought to establish closer relations with such workers by rejecting the principles of *laisser-faire* advocated by leaders of the Anti-Corn Law League, and to which many workers were opposed. Middle-class and working-class radicals were also brought closer in the same years by continental issues, moved by a common enthusiasm for nationalist movements in Italy and Hungary and by shared opposition to authoritarian regimes such as the Bonapartist Second Empire.[41]

Parallel to these moves in another realm were the economic and social analyses provided by L. T. Hobhouse and John A. Hobson. Both argued that the liberal vision of a society able to nurture the independence and self-development of individuals could only be fulfilled through social reforms that reduced inequality, opened up opportunities to those denied them, and lessened the power of the rich. Their economic justification for this program involved significant departures from classical liberal theory; in particular "the two Hobs" sought to show that the economy could be made more efficient and more productive if consumption levels were boosted through raising the level of wages, thus enlarging the market for goods. This went directly against the classical economists' notion that workers had to be paid out of a limited "wages fund," so that any increase in pay meant a decline in the number of people who could be employed. (It should be noted, however, that such views were not unheard of among earlier liberals. One reform-minded businessman wrote in the Chartist paper *The Northern Star* in 1838 that "it is the undoubted interest of all the middle classes to support the interest of and promote the prosperity of the working class. My experience goes to prove that the more the working classes receive in wages, the more I receive in the way of business and that my profits are in ratio to the remuneration of labour.")[42] Here economics ceased to be "the dismal science" of ineluctable limitations on life and well-being exemplified by Ricardo and Malthus. Like such earlier schools as mercantilism and physiocracy, these writers still regarded nature as the source of limits to what work and exchange could provide, a view that marked them as belonging to the phase in economic history Richard Price calls the "economy of manufacture." By contrast Hobson and Hobhouse reflected the new conditions of the emerging modern industrial economy, which they recognized as capable – despite its limits and potential for harm – of expanding its output to provide much greater well-being, provided it be regulated by principles in accord with the possibilities it generated.[43]

All these currents in the Party were tied up with the cooperation the leadership undertook with workers determined to organize politically on their own, and who formed the Labour Representation Committee (LRC) in 1900. Liberal and LRC candidates worked together in local elections in 1903, a strategy that helped to achieve a liberal victory, the Party's first since 1885, and that brought twenty-nine "Lib–Lab" candidates to Westminster. The collaboration continued at the next election in 1910, when the liberal victory probably owed still more to LRC support. That liberal leaders such as Gladstone's son Herbert believed the Party could be strengthened by its cooperation with the LRC may have been based partly on idealism and partly on a false expectation that the elder Gladstone's appeal to workers (which partook of old-style notability while shading off into what Weber saw as a modern form of charsima) could be preserved in the changed conditions of the end of the century.

Such visions proved illusory, however, for several reasons. One was that the Party found itself caught between its traditional attempt to support workers and gain their loyalty, and the conviction cherished by many of its members that it stood above class. Liberals enacted legislation aimed at improving the situation of workers, and they gave support to unions, but high-minded Party figures insisted that workers' interests be pursued in ways that gave equal weight to those of other groups and classes. A separate Labour Party, as one Liberal leader declared, was "wrong in principle." In moments of considerable economic difficulty, when conflicts between employers and workers could turn sharp and bitter, claims to preserve a balance among diverse interests could easily appear to laborers as too favorable to business owners, and the support liberals offered unions usually fell short of what workers hoped for and expected. After unions were declared liable for damages to employers caused by strikes in the (in)famous Taff Vale decision of 1901, liberals worked to have the verdict reversed; but they rejected union demands for complete immunity from responsibility for actions by their agents, on the grounds that such protection would be unfair to other kinds of organizations, since they did not enjoy it. Similarly, even those liberals who favored certain forms of public ownership for public works (the policies that gave birth to what was called "municipal socialism" in Birmingham and other places) refused to accept the construal of such departures as inroads against capitalism, in the way some labour activists did. In addition (and most damaging of all, in G. R. Searle's view), the Party failed to put up workers as liberal candidates in places where they had a good likelihood of being elected, in general underestimating the degree to which workers, excited by their new capacity to vote and organize, wanted to be represented by people who spoke and dressed as they did. Whether these limits should be attributed to the Liberals' status as a "governing party," as one writer has suggested, or to their rejection of class politics, is perhaps not resolvable; either way of understanding the situation points at once to the Party's aspiration to represent workers, and to its limits.[44]

In any case, it was the new conditions of organized politics at the end of the century, more than any deep ideological gap between liberals and workers, that produced the dilemmas of liberal politics and led to the foundation of a separate Labour Party. That Party's later history would show that liberal and Parliamentary principles remained powerful within it, especially those embodied in the People's Budget of 1909, the program of consumption-based growth proposed by "the two Hobs," and the kinds of cooperation that developed between radical middle-class liberals and working-class democrats in the 1860s and 1870s. Class hostility was surely one element in the support workers gave to the new organizations, but class conflict by itself cannot provide an explanation for the turn to a separate Party because its intensity at the end of the century was surely much lower than it had been in the 1840s, when even England seemed close to revolution.

The decline of the Liberal Party testifies to the difficulty of keeping an organization whose chief social base lay in the broad middle classes united in the conditions of the *fin-de-siècle*, and to the way that liberals were almost fated to contribute to their Party's decline by at once encouraging and resisting the independent working-class organization that worked against them. The many uncertainties about what a middle-class politics could amount to in practice meant that the vague "community of sentiment" of the mid century was a better basis for liberal integration and loyalty than the more abstract and mediated politics that replaced it. We shall see that the same was largely true for France and Germany, in their different ways, as well.

6 FRANCE AND BOURGEOIS FRANCE: FROM TELEOCRACY TO AUTONOMY

In French history one theme has often dominated discussions of both the structure of national life and the coming of modernity, namely the centralizing role of the state. The state's importance in creating a unified territory and nation cannot be gainsaid; it occupies a major part in the account developed in Chapter 3 and it will continue to do so here. But recent writers have made it clear that one reason why centralization has so often taken center stage in France, both in actual life and in the way historians have portrayed it, is that regional and local contrasts and the independence to which they testify have persisted too, providing the continuing material on which centralizing efforts have worked. François Guizot, as we saw above, justified the role he assigned to the state in creating national unity in part on grounds that the new monarchy still faced many of the internal divisions confronted by the old one, and a number of recent historians have emphasized the enduring power of local differences in French history; a short list would have to include Eugen Weber, Pierre Rosanvallon, Stéphane Gerson, Susan Carol Rogers, and Gérard Noiriel.[1] Here we draw on their work in order to sharpen our focus on the ways people whose lives were often dominated by their local situations came to be drawn into the expanding and thickening networks that opened the way to new forms of modernity and of bourgeois life during the nineteenth century.

Keeping distance at a distance

In England, industrial development took place in a still regionally divided country, but it was one in which a functioning national market made an impact in many places, encouraging investment in new forms of production. French economic regionalism was of a more pronounced kind, leaving local economies relatively unaffected by changing market conditions, so that traditional techniques remained dominant practically everywhere. As Gérard Noiriel notes, until late in the nineteenth century French industry expanded primarily inside long-established structures, resting "on the dispersal of industrial work in the countryside, accentuating forms of production and a type of working class born under the Old Regime." For most French workers before the advent of the Third Republic "industrial work was seen above all as a kind of rural work."[2] When people spoke of a French city's *fabrique* they had in mind not a place but a system, well established before the Revolution, in which merchant entrepreneurs organized production carried out chiefly by part-time workers in the countryside, with only the stage of final finishing assigned to skilled urban craftspeople.[3] Even in such famous manufacturing centers as the silk capital Lyons, rural work expanded through most of the nineteenth century, and production continued to be organized by merchant masters who both provided the raw materials and sold the products, as the city's historian Yves Lequin has shown.[4] This mix in which workshop production remained more important than factory labor had much in common with the structure we noted in Britain, but with the difference that for most French workers manufacturing continued to be a seasonal activity. Inhabitants of little-changed rural communities, they devoted most of their time to agriculture, turning to mining or weaving or metal work only when the rhythm imposed by planting and harvest cycles allowed. In some places this pluriform economy was compatible with production of goods for export, and it certainly made working for money wages part of some workers' lives. But such activities were carried out inside a loosely linked assemblage of largely unconnected local economies, each producing most of the goods its inhabitants consumed.

Both Noiriel and Eugen Weber, in his classic account of the transformation of French rural life during the Third Republic, emphasize that most French regions retained these characteristics at least into the 1870s. Agricultural rhythms determined the season for other kinds of work in the coal-mining region near Aix-en-Provence (where operations began only after the olive harvest was completed), and in the cases of silk spinning in the southeast and sugar manufacture in Picardy. Some rural people who engaged in manufacturing or construction as secondary activities traveled great distances to find such work, but they went back to their places of origin every year, where they often used the income they brought home to shore up or improve their local positions. People from the Massif Central who labored in the Paris construction industry when the city was undergoing its transformation in the 1850s and 1860s devoted their urban earnings to purchasing a piece of village land, or paying off a local debt, for instance to a brother who renounced his portion of the family inheritance in exchange for a money payment, thus maintaining the family property intact (those who gave up their shares often used the compensation paid by siblings to establish themselves nearby, or to improve a position acquired by a local marriage). These part-time Parisians were typical in believing that whatever work they took on outside their community had the purpose of assuring or improving their position within it, and thus maintaining social ties across generations. Weber observes that such doings were typical of a world in which people moved about a great deal physically, but "mentally they stayed at home," traveling with their neighbors and living among them, birds of passage inside cities where they kept to themselves. Their migrations "did not break up the solidarity of the village, but on the contrary reinforced it, staving off deterioration." Noiriel details some of the activities on which such people lavished resources in order "to preserve their traditional ways of life," spending their savings for instance on the festive meals organized by mutual aid societies, a sign that reaffirming the strength of local solidarities was more important than husbanding assets for productive investments.[5] Distant networks formed part of such people's lives, but the means these provided were expected to serve ends woven into a dense fabric of long-established local relationships and values.

Eugen Weber portrays this world as one in which outside connections were both materially limited and culturally held in check, leaving it in many ways turned in upon itself. In much of France, roads were still poor and often in bad repair, limiting the kinds of vehicles that could use them. Traffic might be heavy but it was short-distance, directed to or from a nearby market or service; routes passed through

the need to rely on skills that workers brought with them compounded this dependency, because practical knowledge and training were still passed on inside families or communities that regarded them as a kind of patrimony, and hence the source of a right both to live at a certain level and to retain control over how work was done. Many early nineteenth-century conflicts between workers and employers focused on just these issues, with workers demanding the preservation of piece rates, called *tarifs,* calculated to support a certain expected level of life, while also retaining forms of workshop organization designed to assure continuity of employment inside families and communities. To be sure, *patrons* were sometimes the winners in these struggles, especially in large cities, but historians are increasingly aware that many features of the old world of work survived all the same.[9]

The impossible network

Nothing would be more important in transforming the basic features of this social landscape that the construction of railroads, and lively debates emerged over their likely benefits and costs as soon as news of the new technology began to spread. Quickly voices were heard that tied the country's future to realizing the potential much more rapid travel could unleash. A writer of 1832 insisted that investing in new industrial machines alone would never give France the means to catch up with England: what the nation chiefly needed was better transport. A few years later a reformer in Bordeaux argued similarly for measures that would "throw men, ideas, and capital into the whirlwind of rapid circulation. Put people's minds [*les intelligences*] into continual relation with each other from one end of the country to the other," and the whole of life would be transformed. A lawyer in the same city early in the 1840s compared the influence railroads would have to that of the compass and printing press, all things that "push people into contact with each other ... expand a society's sphere of activity ... Thinking, instead of remaining scattered and recumbent wherever it finds itself, which is to say sterile and inactive, sees its power grow infinitely."[10]

Despite these enthusiasms, actual construction was slow to begin. Businessmen who favored building lines often did so for narrow or selfish reasons (opposed on similar grounds by others), and their resources were only sufficient to cover small projects. More visionary figures, including some Saint-Simonians, hoped to get things going on a bigger scale by setting up cooperation between the state and high finance, thus drawing on people with large capital resources, such as the Rothschilds. But these proposals bred much conflict. The debate in part reflected the greater challenges that railroad building posed in France than in Britain, where the distances were shorter, but also the more fundamental transformation in the country's conditions that the new means promised. Against the expectation that bringing formerly isolated places into contact with each other would energize production and exchange, there grew up fears that the new means would upset the existing balance of social relations, either giving the state dangerous powers over society, or providing certain individuals with new means to dominate others. As François Caron puts it:

> In the imagination of contemporaries railroads quickly
> took on the dimensions of a monster with unlimited
> powers, capable of overturning fortunes and upsetting
> acquired position to the profit of some few. If this power
> fell into the hands of the administration, it could only
> increase its power immeasurably, to the detriment of
> individual liberty; if it fell into the hands of capitalists, it
> threatened to deliver the whole nation to the will of the
> money powers, to destroy the balance of fortunes.

The issue split French bourgeois opinion. What stood in the way of getting construction underway was not a lack of vision but "the real difficulties of the French case": first the practical problems created by the size of the challenge; and second a variety of fears that meeting it through strong action would strengthen either a dominating central power or selfish private interests.[11]

Onto these debates there was overlaid another, about where the lines should go. For some it was essential that Paris constitute the center of the network, in order to assure that it would both serve the needs of administration and strengthen efforts to overcome local particularisms. The Revolution had only begun the process of making the French all citizens of a single country, one *ponts et chaussées* official wrote in 1837; now it was necessary to set up the railroad network in a way that would allow the civilizing influence of Paris to radiate out to all the country's corners. Such a vision, whether the writer knew it or not, echoed the hopes for roads and canals voiced by his Old Regime predecessors. Like these earlier figures, those who took this tack in the nineteenth century also recognized the military importance of good connections between the capital and the country's borders (but the incompleteness of the attention given to having the lines serve this purpose would be demonstrated when war against Prussia came in 1870). On the other side were Saint-Simonians and others who saw railroads above all as implements for inserting France into worldwide networks of commerce and trade. Their ideal grid was dominated by lines tying the Channel port of Le Havre to the Mediterranean city Marseilles, and Nantes on the Atlantic to Strasbourg on the Rhine. But it was the first group that represented the decisive viewpoint of the government, first in the July Monarchy and then in the Second Empire, both regimes that cherished their continuity with the centralizing mission of the Bourbons and the Revolution.[12]

The 1840s saw the beginnings of construction on a sizable scale, financed both by state money and by an investment boom and speculative fever in the early part of the decade; but things turned sour as the crisis of the later 1840s led lenders to call in their funds, stopping the work and leaving many investors badly burned. The suspicion about railroads as an investment generated by this episode added to the existing tensions between the state and private entrepreneurs, slowing down building activity during the Second Republic (1848–52). In the end it was only Louis-Napoleon's *dirigisme* that was able to get things moving again, creating confidence and heightened activity by giving private companies long-term concessions to operate the lines, while insisting on the state's right to determine where they would go, and to oversee operations. I will come to the effects of his actions in a moment.

Paris and its bourgeoisie before 1850: the post-Revolutionary condition

First, however, we need to recognize some ways in which these general features of French life in the first half of the nineteenth century left their mark on Paris and its inhabitants in the same years. As the country's largest urban area and the place where many tensions and conflicts were most sharply felt, the capital appeared to many of its residents and observers (including Balzac, Baudelaire, and Marx) as the quintessential modern city, "the capital of the nineteenth century" as Walter Benjamin would later call it. So it was in some ways. And yet in others the city in the years before Napoleon III's reconstruction projects, like the country it dominated, remained close to what it had been a century before. Although much altered by the Revolution, it would acquire many characteristic features of modernity only after the mid century.

The city grew impressively after the end of the Revolutionary decade, from around half a million inhabitants in 1800 to twice that by the 1840s. A large part of the growth came from immigration, bringing people of all social classes into the city, at once putting some newcomers on a path to a better life while subjecting others to disappointment, frustration, and pain. Those who did well often obtained considerable wealth, and by 1847 the gap between the city's richest people and others (measured by the property listed in the official declarations required when a death was reported) was significantly wider than it had been a quarter-century before. Poorer immigrants, sometimes able to find work and sometimes not, often lived in squalid and unhealthy conditions, making them particularly susceptible to the scourges of cholera and tuberculosis; many observers linked such people to the rising crime rates that made the capital seem a dangerous place in these decades. These widening class differences certainly contributed to the passions unleashed in the revolutionary period that began in February of 1848, and on display with particular asperity and brutality in the "bloody June days" when army and militia forces put down a rebellion sparked by the abolition of the "national workshops" that had provided relief for the large numbers of unemployed workers (their proportion as high as 50 percent in some industries). Marx was not alone in seeing this as an exemplary moment of class conflict, and some more recent historians have found evidence that the largest proportion of participants in the uprising were workers in industries that were becoming "more modern," at least in the sense that their sectors of the economy had the highest proportion of male to female labor, and of employees to employers. All the same, the Parisian workforce in the 1840s was still overwhelmingly composed of traditional artisans and laborers, very few of them in factory-like conditions, albeit many (such as tailors) hurt by the increased discipline and the downward pressure on wages imposed by merchant entrepreneurs faced with heightened competition and attempting to organize larger workforces. Workers' responses to these challenges still drew heavily on Old Regime traditions of guild life and cooperation.[13]

To put these elements of Parisian existence in context, we need to consider the longer-term history of the city's population expansion. To those accustomed to thinking of the era in terms of gradually advancing industrialization, it is difficult not to read developments of the end of the century back into its early part, and to assume that urban growth was tied up with a modernizing economy. But Louis Chevalier's classic study of Parisian demographic development tells a different story. Looking at the social position of the immigrants, at the parts of the city they inhabited, the distribution of occupations in the individual *arrondissements* (administrative districts), and the degree to which these things changed over the century, Chevalier concluded that Parisian manufacture during the first half of the century was not directed primarily toward producing goods for export, but rather to supplying the needs of the city itself. Although some items were sold in distant markets, in particular the so-called *articles de Paris*, fine gloves, scarves, clothing, and so on, that used skilled urban labor, often female, what chiefly drew manufacturers and workers to Paris was the chance to be close to the capital's own consumers. For a brief time in the century's first years some merchant entrepreneurs made the city a place for modern cotton-spinning techniques, as well as hand looms to turn their thread into cloth, but the advantages of cheaper rent and labor elsewhere put an end to these projects by the time Napoleon fell. As in the eighteenth century, much of the power Paris had to attract new people depended on its role as the country's administrative capital; as the number of government employees expanded, they constituted a significant sector of the local consumer market that drew makers of consumption goods into the city.

Only from the 1850s did this situation begin to yield to a different one, first as the needs of railroad construction turned metal manufacturers toward making rails, engines, and other equipment for the new lines, and then, from the 1870s, as Paris followed the rest of France into greater involvement in the more integrated economic system that the completion of the railroad network and the new "second industrial revolution" industries were creating on the continent and beyond. At this time the suburbs grew into centers for major export industries, including bicycles and, later, automobiles. Until then, they too had chiefly hosted enterprises and workers devoted to supplying the needs of the Parisian market. The new phase in the city's economy was accompanied by a marked shift in the origins of its immigrants. Until the mid century they came primarily from nearby provinces, the Île de France, Normandy, and the Loire Valley. Afterwards many more began to arrive from farther way, the east, south, and southwest of the country (as well as from outside it): the insertion of France into the modern industrial economy was part of a more general transformation that included the tighter social and economic integration of the country's regions and provinces.[14]

Given this marked change in the city's demography and economy during the second half of the century, Chevalier ends by suggesting that the immigration that helped to double the population between 1800 and 1850 was largely continuous with a longstanding pattern of relations between urban and rural life. Pre-industrial cities regularly expanded and contracted as economic conditions changed, creating a shifting demand for labor and an up-and-down movement in wages. Paul Hohenberg and Lynn Lees even observe that early modern "European cities had almost a dual structure, a permanent cadre of inhabitants and a substantial floating group of recent immigrants, temporary residents, and transients." A sense of sharp class divisions, and evidence of resentment among the poor had often surfaced at times when this second group was present, and there is reason to view the early nineteenth-century growth in Parisian population at least partly as a continuation of this earlier model. Many observers at the time spoke of the poorer among its newly arrived residents in terms that could just as well have applied to earlier instances of immigration, seeing them as foreign and threatening elements, a barbarian "dangerous class" in need of oversight and discipline because of their lack of integration into city life.[15] It would be wrong to assimilate early nineteenth-century conditions wholly to older ones, but it was only the new phase of economic and social history ushered in by railroad construction on a large scale that brought the old model to an end.

Early nineteenth-century Paris was no longer the city Turgot and the *philosophes* had known, but apart from sheer size the things that made it different belonged more to the realm of politics and culture than to production and exchange. The Revolution did not modernize the French economy, but it surely altered political and social relations. Adeline Daumard makes this point in considering whether the divisions inside the Parisian bourgeosie still left room for its existence as a unified class. The whole formation was like a pyramid sliced into layers. At the summit was a narrow group of important officials, well-known professionals, and large-scale (mostly wholesale) merchants who constituted a kind of urban aristocracy (some with ties to the Old Regime one); from these heights the bourgeoisie sloped downwards through the merely "good bourgeois" with prosperous but smaller businesses or stable but less exalted positions in government and the professions, the "middle bourgeois" of solid shopkeepers, lower state officials, neighborhood notaries, lawyers, and doctors (who mainly acquired their positions through apprenticeship, not formal education), to the *bourgeoisie populaire* of corner grocers or craftsmen with at most a couple of employees, often struggling to maintain an independent position and fading off into the larger group of dependent artisans and workers beneath them. These divisions were criss-crossed by oppositions of interest and orientation, not to mention competition and jealousy. But what mainly distinguished the group's collective life from that of its ancestors in the eighteenth century, Daumard's picture suggests, was that the old system of fixed orders and legal privileges that constituted an alternative to bourgeois existence itself, drawing some bourgeois inside it and leaving others in its shadow, was no more. Earlier the bourgeois world that lived under the sign of motion, acting inside the fluid arena of the market, aspiring to social ascension, acting in ways that altered conditions for others, had been a subordinate pole in a field whose dominant one operated under the sign of stability and (in theory) unchanging order. With its demise the whole urban world shifted toward the pole of motion, exemplified by the departure of the Old Regime itself, "opening careers to talent," and the posing of a series of unanswered questions about what the future held. Whereas earlier commercial and professional people had looked to the monarchy as a source of honor and recognition, with the power to assign them a higher status, nineteenth-century bourgeois had to rely on the fruits of their own efforts and resources. Daumard concludes that these changes gave a new unity to the bourgeoisie, that their shared need to rely on themselves gave them a common soul, *une même âme.*[16]

It is an appealing metaphor, and in some ways an illuminating one, but we need to guard against letting it give us a false sense of either bourgeois modernity or unity. Many bourgeois retained values their ancestors had absorbed under the Old Regime, admiring aristocrats and aspiring to be like them, valuing stability over change and motion, and (as we shall see later on) looking with suspicion and scorn on those whose devotion to novelty and speculation threatened the order, balance, and moral steadiness they thought essential to social life. To many early nineteenth-century bourgeois, no less in Paris than outside, owning property itself still appeared more as a defense against change than a way of seeking it, a perspective that, as we shall see in a moment, only began to be generally altered by the reconstruction of the city undertaken by Napoleon III and Baron Haussmann from the 1850s. I noted in Chapter 3 that as the category of the bourgeoisie came to be employed in historical and political debates from the 1820s much confusion and uncertainty surrounded it, both in the contrasting images given by its supporters such as Thierry and Guizot and in the wavering understanding of whether bourgeois belonged to the past or the future developed by Saint-Simon. All these usages underline the degree to which the term "bourgeois" often had a rhetorical function much as did "middle class" at the same time in England, a situation that persisted during the 1840s. In a parliamentary debate of 1847 an anti-government speaker berated Guizot's resistance to widening the suffrage, on the grounds that the Revolution's abolition of legal privileges meant that the term bourgeois could no longer apply to a category separate from other citizens. But he provoked laughter a moment later when he looked around the room and went on: "I see here many bourgeois."[17] A satirical pamphlet of the time, the *Physiology of the Bourgeois*, played on these uncertainties. "My bourgeois is not yours, or your neighbor's," its author observed. To a soldier the term indicated a civilian, to a *grand seigneur* a well-dressed person who was "not *born*, even though he may be seventy or eighty years old." Workers used it for the boss, cab drivers for their fares, artists as a term of insult and abuse. "Properly so-called" a bourgeois was a person with a secure income and no debts, who lived comfortably, kept his feet warm, and carried a walking-stick.[18]

The term "class" was often applied to the bourgeoisie, but some observers rejected it, arguing that the group's permeability and the lack of clear barriers and boundaries between bourgeois and others made it at most "a condition," one which, as the *Journal des débats* wrote in 1847, could be acquired by hard work, prudence, and talent, and just as easily lost through laziness or vice. Daumard recognized a considerable degree of fluidity in the population she studied, since it included a significant number of newcomers; their origins were often rural but some rose from the ranks of artisans and workers, especially in such industries as construction, where many *patrons* began as *ouvriers*. J.-P. Chaline's study of the Rouen bourgeoisie shows that it too contained substantial numbers of self-made men in these years, particularly in the textile industry (although he notes that it often took two generations for members of worker families to become independent manufacturers). It was these features that the bourgeoisie's defenders had in mind when they cited its social prominence as a sign of the openness and basic equality of nineteenth-century society. From the outside, however, these opportunities appeared as far too narrow to validate such claims, and spokesmen for workers, such as Proudhon and Victor Considerant, had no doubt that the great majority of those born in poverty remained there, while those born to ease and wealth often reproduced the social position of their forebears. It could hardly have been otherwise, given that the proportion of the population even in Paris who could be called bourgeois on the basis of wealth, income, or occupation was, in Daumard's estimate, something around 15 percent.[19]

These observations about the world of early nineteenth-century bourgeois help us to focus better on the most prominent features of the portrait offered by one of its greatest students and harshest critics, Honoré de Balzac. As many in his time rightly saw, Balzac was often moved by hostility to bourgeois people, values, and aspirations; this was one reason why Marx found him so sympathetic and appealing. Engels declared that he had learned more about French bourgeois life from Balzac than from all the other writers he had read put together.[20] The stories and novels making up *La Comédie humaine* contain some of the classic portraits of bourgeois ambition, greed, determination, narrow-mindedness, and failure: Lisbeth Fisher, the spiteful cousin Bette of the novel named for her, Gobseck the usurer who appears in several stories, Goriot the newly rich pasta manufacturer ruined by his social ambitions for his daughters, Nucingen the shady banker and financier, Gaudissart the traveling salesman, César Birotteau the perfume merchant. Colorful and striking as these figures are, what needs to be remarked about them is that none were engaged in the kinds of activities most of us, inspired by Marx or not, associate with the bourgeoisie's role in making the world modern – setting up or running industrial plants, trying out new technologies, reaching for new markets. Whether in Paris or the provinces, the modern industrial and professional bourgeoisie is strikingly absent from Balzac's history of his times. Goriot was a pasta maker, but his wealth came from a rapid change of conditions during the Terror, when he was able to buy large quantities of flour cheaply and then sell it for ten times that cost. Nucingen was involved in house building in Paris but he made his money through fraud, not innovation or even clever speculation; he left no personal mark on the city. The great fortunes in Balzac's world are still aristocratic and the ambitions of people on the make are to rise into their world, not to participate in making a new one; these are the goals of the exemplary Balzacian provincials, Eugène de Rastignac of *Père Goriot* and other stories and Lucien Chardon (later de Rubempré) of *Lost Illusions* and *A Harlot High and Low* (*Splendeurs et misères des courtisanes*).

It was just such ambitions that tied Balzac himself to the people he portrayed so harshly, but also sometimes with sympathy. Coming to Paris from his native Tours as a student under the early Restoration, he quickly began to write, then abandoned his first tales and sketches in order to set up as a publisher. The business failed spectacularly, and one reason he worked so feverishly afterwards, producing his unending stream of stories and novels, was in order to pay off his debts. As he began to acquire both money and fame through his writing, he used his success to enter into some of the same precincts of the Parisian *beau monde* to which his characters aspired. Yet his achievements never erased from his mind the sense of injustice and oppression fostered by his early failure, and by his provincial's sense that Paris was both the great prize and the great abyss at the center of French life, the "glory and infamy" of the country, as one of his characters put it.

The power and the magnetic allure of bourgeois life as Balzac knew it was evident alongside its horrors in many of these famous stories, but the mix of qualities he saw in it was best revealed in a novel set outside Paris, although full of references and allusions to it, *The Search for the Absolute*. The title conveys perfectly what its author thought the human drama was most profoundly about, and could have been applied to many other of his stories, so rife with portrayals of people driven to great achievements and then to tragic failure by the force of some singular and Herculean passion. *Lost Illusions* (to many readers the most remarkable of the novels centered largely on Paris itself) names the repeated outcome of this pursuit, what is left in its aftermath: to Lucien Chardon forced to abandon the Paris he seemed at one moment to have conquered by literary talent; to "Honorine" (heroine of one of very few Balzac stories that might be read in a feminist spirit) after the collapse of her attempt to escape dependency and realize the dream of personal liberty; and to Frenhofer, the genius who destroys his paintings and dies after becoming aware that "The Unknown Masterpiece," the painting he believed his repeated reworkings had turned into an image of beauty at once so fully ideal and so palpably real that it lived and breathed, had become an indecipherable chaos.

In *The Search for the Absolute* this quest is undertaken by Balthazar Claes (his name enfolding Balzac as Honorine does Honoré), the descendant of an old bourgeois family in the northern French town of Douai. Claes becomes obsessed with a modern version of the alchemical dream of transmuting ordinary materials into gold, a passion mediated by his encounter with a Polish emigré in 1809, but rooted in his youthful stay in Paris just before the Revolution, where he had studied in the great chemist Lavoisier's laboratory. Seized with (or by) this passion Claes brings his family to the brink of ruin, selling off his picture collection, furniture, house, and most of his land in order to buy equipment and chemicals, before being rescued by his wife and daughter, who send him off to Brittany to serve as a tax collector while they adroitly and patiently reassemble the family's possessions. The qualities they display in doing so are not the heaven-storming aspirations that animate him, but the old virtues of steadiness, moderation, and the ability to find satisfaction inside a limited and imperfect world that marked the old bourgeoisie in which the family had its roots. The story pulses with the Swedenborgian spiritualism that infuses much of Balzac's writing (left open at the end is the mysterious and tantalizing possibility that, before he died, Claes may actually have succeeded in producing a nugget of gold in his laboratory), but it is also a clear allegory of contemporary life and politics. Critical turning points are coordinated with defining moments in the ascension and collapse of the Bonapartist empire, and Claes's wife is named Josephine; we are clearly invited to look through Balthazar into the life history of that other heroic searcher for the absolute who brought his country to near ruin in the same years. That Claes's obsession with chemical transformation had its roots in his stay in Paris (and in a laboratory devoted to identifying the elements of things and the effects of their combination) reminds us about the city's power to set provincials (whether from Douai or Corsica or Tours) on a path that leads at once to glory and to destruction.

What animates the Balzacian (and given Claes's social identity, we can add bourgeois) search for the absolute is not some anticipation of subsequent paths to a new modernity, but the kind of tie to Paris, and to the ambitions to gain power over the world that develop there, that had long drawn people to the city. All the great virtues and vices of Balzac's bourgeois figures revolve around this pole. Paris's ability to set such lives in motion did not begin in the nineteenth century, or with the Revolution. Indeed one would be hard put to think of a more striking case than that of Balzac's own father, one of eleven children of an illiterate (albeit not impoverished) peasant, and the only one who learned to read, who apprenticed himself to a notary in Albi, went to the capital in the 1760s, rose to be secretary to the royal council, and ended as a provincial administrator, having become very well-off. His marriage to a younger woman at once pleasure-loving and mystically inclined, the daughter of a prosperous Parisian grocer, was an unhappy alliance, with sad consequences for young Honoré, since his mother's search for amorous satisfactions elsewhere left him feeling abandoned in childhood (he first encountered spiritualist writings in her library).

This family history provided a major inspiration for what would become a central theme of the *Comédie humaine*, set out explicitly in the preface to the whole project published in 1842, namely the dire fates prepared for people drawn outside their original milieu by ambition and opportunity. Such individuals – Goriot and his daughters among them – end up weighed down by the difficulties of operating in a social world for which their birth and experience has not prepared them. One path into this wilderness was economic to be sure, as Goriot himself illustrates, but in Balzac's world the more powerful and meteoric trajectories were those traced by characters more plugged into the power sources of Paris itself, notably Lucien Chardon (or de Rubempré) and Eugène de Rastignac, both able to draw on aristocratic connections. Even Goriot's ascent depended on his connections to the Revolutionary state, as Bernard-François Balssa's (as he spelled his name) did to its predecessor. What made Balzac's France so full of splendors and pitfalls, a place where the search for absolutes and the illusions it breeds could constitute the recurring theme of the moral history of his time, was the effect on everyday life of politics and the disruptions it effected, not the country's economy. The bourgeois inhabitants of this world might be mean spirited and self-centered, drawn to projects that could be both self-destructive and dangerous to others, but like their real-world models they acted inside an economy little changed from before the Revolution, giving them a character still close to that of their Old Regime ancestors, as the Saint-Simonian Michel Chevalier insisted in 1837, when he depicted them as too mired in the past to take on the heroic features of the industrial *révelateur* to whom he looked to usher in a new age.[21]

Expanding the web

In the overall history of France, Europe, and bourgeois life in the nineteenth century, one crucial thing to which all these considerations point is the nature of the crisis that engulfed the continent in the 1840s, and that gave birth to the revolutionary struggles that began in 1848. It was this crisis that led Marx, as others have noted, to mistake the birth pangs of modern capitalism for its death throes; although in part brought on by English industrial overproduction, it was chiefly, as E. H. Labrousse put it, "a crisis of the old type," generated like many before chiefly by a series of harvest failures that drove up agricultural prices, sapped the demand for manufactured goods, pushed hungry people to cities in search of state-organized poor relief, and deprived political authorities of the legitimacy that came from ruling over a system that seemed to provide for people's basic needs. It was the last such juncture the continent would experience. Economic breakdowns would recur, to be sure, but not until the 1930s would Europe as a whole experience a crisis of such magnitude, when it would occur in a radically different context, its foundations laid down by the various post-1850 developments to which we give attention throughout this book.[22]

That the crisis of the 1840s turned out to be the last of its type can be attributed to a number of factors, among them the development of new chemical fertilizers that improved agricultural productivity and lessened the impact of weather conditions, and the beginning of a large-scale exodus from the crowded and impoverished countrysides where the traditional economy was rooted on the continent. Overall,

203 / Expanding the web

however, the largest catalyst for the change that now began was the resumption of railroad building that Napoleon III sponsored as part of his program of gaining support for his regime through fostering economic development, prosperity, and social peace. His formula of giving long-term concessions to operate new routes to companies willing to invest in building them, thereby assuring their profits (while preserving the state's right both to decide where the lines would go and to oversee operations) quickly drew capital from well-heeled bankers such as the Rothschilds and the Péreires, the latter also assembling funds from smaller investors through the new *Crédit Mobilier*, sponsored by the government for just this purpose. In the years before Napoleon III's fall in 1870 the government pursued a policy of consolidation among the private companies, thus increasing its control and preparing a still larger role for the state later on. Under the Third Republic the network would be completed by the building of many links to localities left out of the original plans. In addition, governments beginning in 1879 undertook a vigorous program of road construction, intended partly to improve the economic infrastructure, and partly to make it easier for politicians (now elected by universal male suffrage, with results to which we will come in a few moments) to reach voters at election time. It was thus that the old program of the *ponts et chaussées* officials to integrate the country with an effective transport network, making the whole territory a far more unified national space, was finally realized.[23] There has been much argument about the role of the state in French economic development, and it may never be possible to say just how important its activities were, compared with those of private individuals stimulated by the opportunities and pressures of the market. But Jean-Pierre Daviet's conclusion puts the situation neatly: "Everything happened as if the state ... prepared the conditions for the passage to a more sustained kind of economic growth."[24]

The importance of these accomplishments for the economy, and for much else, has been properly stressed by Eugen Weber. Economically the roads and railroads were at least as important as new machines in bringing industrial society into being because (as the contemporaries quoted above already understood) they "created a truly national market in which the wares that the machines turned out could be bought and sold."[25] This meant that investments previously avoided because they would have offered insufficient – or even negative – returns now became attractive. Added to the impetus given to construction and employment by the infrastructural projects themselves, the result was a major boost to growth, which helped to make the Second Empire and at least the early years of the Third Republic a time of prosperity for many people. Real wages for workers began a rise that continued for most of the rest of the century. Like other countries France became far more stable, quickly leaving behind the conditions that made the later 1840s so agitated and tense. Marx, who expected the crisis to return within a short period, waited through the 1850s with puzzlement, briefly regained his confidence with the renewed downturn of 1857, and again in 1866; but he spent these years working out his economic theory in such a way that it could encompass a long period of waiting before the expected demise of capitalism would take place. Whereas before 1848 he had repeatedly spoken about the way that underlying class conflicts were making themselves visible on the surface of society in the present, now he adopted a very different vocabulary, describing how both politics and economics created veils and screens, covering over and concealing the underlying forces whose eventual emergence he continued to believe would one day confirm his expectations and hopes.[26]

For France these changes did not mean only a spurt in economic growth but a reconfiguration of national life. The situation Bernard Lepetit described in his book on French cities up to the middle of the nineteenth century now came to an end: what had been a congeries of separate and only loosely linked economies, many of them producing and consuming most of the goods that sustained their inhabitants, now became a much more integrated national space in which a lessening of local distinctiveness in some regards coexisted with its preservation in others. Regional specializations were fostered by mutual exchange and trade, but many local styles in dress faded away (or turned into costumes reserved for special occasions), as people gained access to nationally distributed articles that were perhaps less colorful and evocative but more comfortable, often of higher quality, and giving people a sense – sometimes pressured to be sure – of participation in a wider world. There were surely many losers in this redrawing of the bounds of economic life, and some of what was lost doubtless deserves the nostalgia often directed toward it. But much was gained as well. Contemporaries referred to what the railroad brought as "an infusion of life," and Weber's remark about an Alpine village can serve to represent the way many situations changed: "The outside world, which until then had little bearing on their own life, now came in with a rush: skills like writing invoices and bills of lading, counting, and schooling in general acquired concrete meaning as occasions to use them multiplied."[27]

Remaking Paris and its bourgeois

No place was more strikingly transformed than Paris, where the web of connections that railway building spread in the country as a whole had a kind of counterpart in the reconstruction of the city under Napoleon III and his prefect, Baron Haussmann. Much has been written about this transformation, and we cannot enter much into the debates about its motives and purposes. These included staving off a recurrence of the kind of violence that erupted in June, 1848 (although it should be remembered that the chief lesson of the bloody days was that barricades could not withstand modern artillery even as things then stood), giving prestige to the regime, improving public health (always a problem in urban areas and now compounded by increased rates of immigration), and easing travel inside the city, including traffic between the railway stations that were portals to and from different parts of the country. Taking stock of the various reasons for the reconstruction, one recent French historian of urban life and development, Marcel Roncayolo, sees the rebuilding (not just in Paris but in other urban places as well) as inspired by a vision of the modern city as a single integrated space for interaction and exchange (a situation to which Paris had already been moving on a smaller scale, as we saw earlier, in the eighteenth century), one whose potential could only be realized by removing the barriers to movement accumulated over the centuries and opening up new channels for transporting people and things. The model displayed a certain harmony with the spirit of the stock exchange as a place where values could circulate from one person to another unimpeded, but industry as such played little part in the schemes. Jeanne Gaillard, who has made the most careful study of Paris in this period, sees things a bit differently, emphasizing the desire of Bonaparte and Haussmann to establish the regime's domination over the city, partly by clearing out the old center, the area around the Hôtel de Ville and the Rue de Rivoli where government and administrative offices were clustered but which was also the center of insurrection, and partly by creating new

streets that at once facilitated keeping order against possible insur-
rections and offered sites for ceremonial display of the Empire's regal
pretensions. Both Gaillard and Roncayolo recognize that the spirit of
the enterprise was liberal and *dirigiste* at the same time, a perhaps
paradoxical combination but one deeply rooted in French history and
politics, as we had occasion to note in regard to state policy in the
eighteenth century.[28]

When the plans became public they generated opposition in
a number of quarters, among them Parisian property owners, who
complained that the government's self-proclaimed power to seize
houses or lots in order to build new streets for reasons of "public
utility" trampled on their rights. Many of these opponents were soon
converted to the project, however, drawn in by a government decree
of 1858 that allowed those whose property was taken to put in a
claim of restitution for the parts of it that were not actually used by
the new roadways, especially once it became clear that the values
of parcels adjacent to the new avenues and boulevards would rise
dramatically. Their situation was well understood at the time by a
journalist named Edmond About, writing in a *Paris Guide* of 1867.
How was it possible, he asked, that a mere fraction of a property
valued for a certain amount before could be worth several times that
total once the debris had been cleared away? The answer was that the
new avenues and boulevards met the needs of modern city dwellers,
people impatient to "produce, exchange, enjoy, and be seen," and
who did not want to put up with the delays and obstacles created
by the streets and squares and stairways and turnings left over from
earlier phases of urban life. "A straight, broad, smooth street puts
two points a league apart from each other so to say in direct contact," and this kind of immediate communication was of great value
both to merchants in search of customers, and to idle people desirous
of going wherever pleasure calls them. "This explains the added value
that an apparently brutal destruction adds to demolished neighborhoods." Marcel Roncayolo remarks that About's article testifies to
the way the reconstruction effected a reversal of bourgeois values,
replacing the respect long accorded to property as an anchor of stability with a heightened appreciation of the virtues of movement and
fluidity.[29]

Jeanne Gaillard characterizes this overall reorientation of
Parisian life and especially the city's economy in terms of a shifting

balance from a traditional stance of "introversion" toward one of "extraversion." The old city had always been open to outside influences and connections, to be sure, but it was simultaneously shut up inside its walls like "the old bourgeoisie, frugal and turned in upon its family life and its [already acquired] riches." Gaillard is careful not to make this contrast absolute, for instance seeing the style of the residential buildings that still give the city so much of its character as a mix of aristocratic and modern urban features. But she describes the general reorientation of the economy in terms that fit well with Louis Chevalier's history of its population. Manufacturers in a number of industries now turned more toward external markets, including the makers of the luxury *articles de Paris* who had always produced for export (as well as for the aristocratically toned home consumption that inspired them in the first place), an example followed (mostly from the 1870s) by entrepreneurs in the new metallurgical and chemical industries that grew up in the suburbs.[30]

Gaillard documents these changes through a study of the business licenses (*patentes*) issued before and after the reconstruction made its impact. Between 1847 and 1860 it was the city's own custom that fed business expansion, and "no business could even remotely compare in its growth with the food industries. Paris made and sold first of all to nourish and lodge itself." After 1860 this came less and less to be true, as older kinds of manufacture turned increasingly to the export market, joined by new industries, and the city's share in national exports began a marked rise. To be sure, the new networks, both the roads and streets inside the city and the railroads outside it, did not simply impose these changes; it was individuals with an eye open to new opportunities who were the agents. But the tighter connections provided the ground where they could seize these chances to act. As in the countryside, industry was a beneficiary of such links before it began to create them on its own. What Gaillard called the city's "better insertion into the modern world" also now protected it from being subject to the kinds of economic fluctuations rooted in rural conditions that had brought it to a crisis point in the 1840s.[31] And it was from the Second Empire that the wealth of Parisians (followed at a distance by families in other French cities) prosperous enough to pay a tax on property left at their death began to shift from an earlier preponderance of real estate to a growing proportion of mobile holdings, including stocks and shares.[32]

One feature of the new Paris that Gaillard sees as exhibiting at once the older more introverted style of bourgeois life and its newer more extraverted manner is the appearance of the *grands magasins*, department stores of the kind that also sprang up in other European (and American) cities at the same time. Often located along the new boulevards, the stores drew in thrifty customers with lower prices, but they also used advertising and imaginative displays to entice buyers by associating goods with exotic places or vaguely invoked desires and pleasures. Not content with satisfying already-recognized needs, they announced a world, at once promising and problematic, in which consumption would become a need on its own. They belonged to Zola's Paris rather than Balzac's, the larger and more impersonal city where the metaphor of the machine was often invoked to describe a form of life some no longer felt to be on a recognizable human scale, but also the lighter, airier, more lively urban milieu that gave birth to impressionism. (Robert Herbert, in a study of the new painting on which we will draw later, notes that romantic depictions of urban space were often dark and somber, in contrast to the vivid, colorful atmosphere evoked by the impressionists.)

Among the new stores the still flourishing Left Bank emporium the Bon Marché stands out because it is the one for which we have the best information. The Bon Marché was the model for the place Zola described in his novel *The Ladies' Paradise* (*Au bonheur des dames*), but it is also the subject of an excellent social and cultural history. The novelist's account depicts a world fiercely divided between old-style *commerçants* loyally or obstinately devoted to their cloth or hats or umbrellas and the many-armed mutant beast methodically squeezing the life out of its puny competitors, but Zola also recognized the new stores as sources of previously unavailable energy and of a promise of abundance and well-being that the older-style shops could not provide, sites of a modern kind of urban adventure and even poetry, represented by the indefatigable, romantic, and seductive owner and manager, Octave Mouret, and by the book's heroine Denise Baudu, whose open-mouthed fascination with Mouret's place at the moment of her first arrival from the country forecasts the career she will make there.[33]

Mouret, however, bears little resemblance to the store's actual founders, Aristide and Marguerite Boucicaut. Coming from modest backgrounds and deeply rooted in the traditional *bourgeoisie populaire*, they firmly believed that their business preserved the values of their origins, despite its many innovations. In its publications – advertisements, catalogues, circulars, and agendas (day-books that encouraged customers to associate events in their lives with goings-on in the store) – the Bon Marché presented itself as an upholder of communal values, a defender of morality and virtue, and even as a great family, animated by a spirit of mutual regard and devoted to the proper formation of its members. Its paternalism was especially visible in the common life it created for its employees, who ate together (men and women in separate dining-rooms), enjoyed medical care provided by the firm, benefitted from a profit-sharing pension fund, participated in large numbers in a company savings bank paying 6 percent interest on deposits, and joined in cultural activities (the store was known for its regular concerts). The impetus for some of these policies may have come from Marguerite, an illegitimate daughter of peasants who came to Paris as a laundress and who retained a devout sense of moral and personal responsibility. Although there is little direct information about her participation in the store's day-to-day operation, its character as a kind of extended family was strongly highlighted in her will, which bequeathed a remarkable 13 million francs to the store's employees, "those who are my devoted collaborators, whatever rank they may occupy in this great House which my husband and I have, with them, brought to this present level of esteem and prosperity." These sentiments in part reflected her Catholic sensibility, but the store was no bastion of conservative opinion. Its rival the Grands Magasins du Louvre had close ties to the Bonapartist regime, but Boucicaut was closer to the left, contributing to a subscription for the Venetian patriot Daniel Manin in the 1860s and lending his delivery wagons to the Ligue Republicaine de Paris at the time of the Commune to evacuate people in Neuilly who were being attacked by the government in Versailles.[34]

The Bon Marché's historian Michael Miller is surely right to emphasize that the store wove together features of nineteenth-century bourgeois life often thought to be at odds: "The Bon Marché was a machine, but it was also a family; it was change but it was also tradition; and there was no clearcut distinction between one sphere and the other ... In Bon Marché imagery the family traditions of the French business community had not only survived, but had become transformed into the central ingredient of a mass bureaucratic market."

Such a portrait served the Boucicauts (and later their successors) as a defense against critics to be sure, but this does not mean that it was artificially constructed for such a purpose. It expressed the Boucicauts' own sense of who they were, and it clearly struck a chord with both customers and the wider public; its constancy "was symptomatic of the power that such an image held over the collective bourgeois mind," no less at the end of the century than before.[35]

We can clarify something about the modern mode of experience the new commerce fostered by taking a brief critical look at a notion put forward by Richard Sennett in his often-cited book *The Fall of Public Man*. In his view the new stores deprived buyers of the active involvement with sellers they had enjoyed earlier because they eliminated the bargaining that took place in small shops: by instituting marked and fixed prices, he maintains, the big stores imposed passivity on buyers, making them socially more flaccid and withdrawn. Inviting as such a suggestion may appear, Zola helps us to understand how much it leaves out, when he depicts women in search of goods as arming themselves with knowledge about various items and the different prices at which they were being offered around town, through advertisements and discussions with their friends. The new commerce did not make shoppers more passive, it replaced one kind of active involvement with another, shifting the ground where it operated. As with many other aspects of modern life, this ground was one where personal interactions increasingly took take place in conjunction with mediated exchanges involving wider networks of activity and information.

Politics in post-1850 France: teleocracy or republic

This same style of social existence would come to be the ground of modern politics in France just as in England, opening up the more abstract space that would be filled by nationally organized parties. But this outcome was slower to arrive there, and came about in ways strongly marked by the country's earlier history. In order for it to take place, provincial forms of life long marked by an "introverted" character much like the one Jeanne Gaillard describes for pre-Haussmann Paris would have to undergo a transformation toward "extroverted" ones in ways comparable to what she describes for the capital.

In the century after 1780, France passed through a number and variety of different regimes that finds no parallel in any other European country: the Old Regime monarchy, the constitutional kingdom of 1791, the First Republic of 1792, the Jacobin regime and the more moderate Directory that followed, the Napoleonic Empire of 1801, the restored Bourbon regime of 1815, the July Monarchy of 1830, the Second Republic of 1848, the Second Empire of 1852–70, the bloodily repressed Commune of 1871, before arriving at the Third Republic. Each constituted a separate model for the country and the state, so that in combination they provided a range of what Maurice Agulhon calls competing "legitimacies," that is, fundamental claims to organize national life and politics on a particular basis: as a monarchy ruled by a Bourbon, or Orleanist, or Bonapartist prince, as a revolutionary republic along lines given by the examples of 1792–94 or 1871, or a moderate one of the sort attempted between 1795 and 1798 and again between 1848 and 1851. Thus the issues at the center of French politics could not develop around the relatively simple question of who would be included inside an already settled political system that preoccupied the British: more fundamental divisions had to be faced at the same time.

At least as significant as their diversity is the point that each of these projected ways of establishing political life – with the exception of the last – bore features of the character we have described as "teleocratic." That is, each one, whether seeking the rule of a particular monarchical family thought to embody something essential about the nation, or the revolutionary tradition that aimed to impose a new form on it, sought to order politics by virtue of some quality or principle regarded as both more fundamental and more exalted than any that might either motivate the everyday interactions of citizens or subjects or emerge out of them; from such a perspective, any flow of political resources not in accord with whichever of these pre-established goals or values was enshrined as the state's directing rationale had to appear as illegitimate. There was, however, one state form that did not seek to give political life this sort of transcendent direction, but rather to establish the state as a field on which opposed principles and interests might interact and compete, but without any one casting out the others. This was the form that Agulhon calls "liberal republicanism," whose aim in constitutional terms (whatever the personal goals of particular individuals or groups who associated themselves with it) was simply to ground political life on the rule of law, putting this goal above "every claimed legitimacy, even of the popular sort."[36]

The persistence of these alternatives gave a special quality to liberalism in France. As a doctrine or political current liberalism had a certain independent existence, but the uncertainty about the basic form of the state meant that it was also subject to being drawn into one or another of the competing legitimacies, so that before 1870 liberal identities were often hybrid: there were liberal Legitimists (the name given to supporters of the Bourbons), liberal Orleanists, liberal Bonapartists, and liberal republicans (conservatives and even radicals were subject to the same pulls). All these species of liberals were on the scene in the 1870s, but the camp of liberal republicans came to assume a special kind of importance. Many people, bourgeois among them, hoped for some kind of monarchical restoration, but rivalry between the three candidate houses and their followers both ruled out cooperation between them and weakened the ability of any single one to impose itself. In this situation, liberals who had formerly espoused one or another monarchical alternative moved toward the republican camp, a shift exemplified by Adolphe Thiers. Thiers had been an Orleanist in his youth, albeit a pragmatic one who valued the liberal civic order he thought the family represented more than monarchy itself. He had accepted the Second Republic in 1848 once it was clear there was no alternative to it, and in a debate of 1850 gave voice to a phrase that would often be repeated: "the Republic ... is of all governments that which divides us least." He meant that it was a ground where none of the competing teleocratic legitimacies could squeeze out other alternatives. He still feared that a republic might provide the ground for populist claims that would lead to division and conflict, but the thorough suppression of the Commune in 1871 led him to believe that the state was unlikely to fall into the hands of radicals, making a republic, with its ability to accommodate the various competing factions, the best frame for orderly government; thus he moved, if not always steadily, toward supporting it.[37]

Thiers's evolution was highly personal, but in a general way it reflected developments that were nudging the country as a whole along the same path. To be sure, people strongly committed to traditional forms of society and the state were just for this reason deeply hostile to the republican project, and as its realization seemed more and more likely they would work to undermine or overthrow the regime – by inventing new styles of conservative politics, through the agency of a charismatic authoritarian figure in the Boulanger crisis of the end of the 1880s, and through nationalist and anti-Semitic campaigns in the Dreyfus Affair a decade later. On the other side workers' groups too would present their claims as socially and morally superior to the "neutral" liberal principle of the rule of law. But in the end enough people in all these camps would follow Thiers's lead and come to see the republic based simply on the rule of law as the best and most realistic framework within which to realize whatever they could of their diverse political goals. Only as they did, would modern parties emerge to occupy the political stage in France.

Bourgeois France and modern democracy

One precondition for this development was that liberalism had to clarify and in part alter its relationship to democracy. The issue confronted liberals everywhere, but it took on greater relief in France from the country's revolutionary history, which gave liberal politics a closer and yet more problematic relationship to popular action than elsewhere. In 1789 and later, as Agulhon observes, "the liberal revolution was able to triumph only thanks to its historical connection with an urban (and notably Parisian) *petit peuple* that was the bearer of broader social aspirations than was liberalism by itself."[38] In July of 1830 and February of 1848 the moment of closeness between liberal and popular forces was followed by one dominated by fear and shrinking back, since the same implicit collaboration that brought moderate liberals to power opened the way to violence and disorder, threatening the stability they sought. The challenge this pattern presented, and the way it was met, would have much to do with the manner in which the republic won out over the alternatives to it in the mid 1870s.

To see how this occurred, we need to recall that the memories and fears of revolutionary violence that helped push prominent French liberals to the right in the early part of the century contributed to the determination of those who established and dominated the "Bourgeois Monarchy" to set and keep the bar for voting very high (considerably above the level established by the English Parliamentary Reform of 1832). Significantly, these arrangements excluded not just workers or *le peuple*, but many people with a good claim to be considered bourgeois as well. The fact that people such as Guizot thought political stability required this exclusion is one reason why, in France as in Germany, the turn to universal male suffrage did not come about through gradual extension, as in England, but at the initiative of a politician who believed that elections on this basis, inside an essentially authoritarian regime, could be harvested for anti-liberal purposes. Once he abolished the Second Republic and made himself emperor in 1852, Louis-Napoleon gave the vote to all adult men, but until the 1860s elections were chiefly plebiscites, offering only a choice of "yes" or "no" on his person or policies; even after voters were allowed greater power, the government put much energy into manipulating the results. All the same, as a number of writers have pointed out, the Second Empire accustomed the country to voting, and to universal suffrage, so that when the regime fell in 1870 (at a moment of significant franchise extensions in both England and Germany), no politician was willing to take the risks involved in abolishing it.[39]

This did not mean that everyone, even among liberals, was ready to give free rein to electoral politics on such a basis. In the 1870s a number of prominent figures, among them Hippolyte Taine and Ernst Renan, proposed schemes aimed at limiting popular influence and power, either by having voters choose intermediate commissions or panels that would actually designate the members of governing bodies, or by establishing an upper chamber with legislative authority and a certain number of hereditary seats, on the English model. Some still trusted in the old-fashioned virtues of rural and small-town Frenchmen, but others (Renan among them) thought that the modernizing efforts and impact of the Bonapartist regime – railroad building, urban construction, industrial expansion, and the lessened influence of the Church and traditional elites – had led to a moral decline, based on the weakening of old communal ties and the spread of a more individualistic and self-centered ethos. Thus it was not only the longstanding worries that universal suffrage would give the propertyless power to seize the possessions of those better-off that prompted efforts to put restraints on voting, but also anxieties about the effects of modernizing social relations. It is in this light that the role played by Léon Gambetta in defeating the attempts at monarchist restoration and establishing the Republic on a clear republican basis takes on high significance.

The grandson of a poor Italian fisherman and son of a small grocer, Gambetta came to prominence through utilizing the French educational system as a pathway to social ascension, a classic pattern he shared with other Third Republic luminaries, including Alfred Dreyfus and Émile Durkheim. In 1860s Paris he became known as one of a number of young lawyers who emerged as republican opponents of the Empire. His electoral program as a candidate for the National Assembly from the working-class Parisian suburb of Belleville in 1868 involved anti-militarism, separation of Church and state, freedom of the press and association, and universal education. At the crucial moment of the attempt by conservatives led by Marshall McMahon to effect a monarchist restoration in May of 1877, it was Gambetta who animated the campaign that led to a republican victory and what became known as the "end of the notables," demonstrating the ability of national politicians to appeal over the heads of local luminaries to the mass of voters drawn more tightly into national life by newspapers, railroads, and the telegraph. Like Renan, Gambetta was highly aware of the effects of Bonaparte's policies on national and especially provincial life, but he reacted to them in precisely the opposite way. As François Furet put it, "Renan's regrets were Gambetta's optimism. The republican leader loved the new France which he sensed emerging from the progress of social wealth and enlightenment." It was this positive judgment that stood behind his declaration in a well-known speech that "I believe in the republican future of the provinces and the rural areas. All it takes is a little time and the wider spread of education."[40]

Gambetta's belief that developments already under way by the 1870s were creating a more solid basis for French democracy is supported by recent historians. Sudhir Hazareesingh has argued that the Second Empire saw the emergence of a new sense of citizenship, based on a widespread desire to draw people into national issues through the mediation of local ones, a vision shared in different ways by conservatives, liberals, and Bonapartists, but leading toward a level of involvement that pointed in a republican direction. Regular and more freely contested elections, especially in the 1860s (the government ceased interfering with organized local political groups in this decade), along with the better circulation of newspapers had a role in this transformation as well. Philip Nord has traced the efforts republicans expended in the same period to create support for democratic institutions by working within masonic, academic, religious, and commercial organizations, the building blocks of a new civil society.[41] These developments ran parallel to those that were creating a thickening tissue of economic relations, joining people in various regions together in an increasingly tightly knit web. It was to this more interconnected and thus less "introverted" France that Gambetta sought to appeal. In addition to the formerly more isolated rural population, his vision encompassed the petit-bourgeois and popular elements he famously called "new social strata" (*nouvelles couches sociales*); they were not a new section of French society, however, but an old one given new features by the changing world around them. Both groups had been put outside the *pays légal* by the liberal *doctrinaires* of the 1830s and 1840s, with their suffrage restrictions, and it was partly to reduce their influence that Taine and Renan conceived complex mechanisms of voting in the early 1870s.

Gambetta had emerged from these sections of society himself, and he based his case for their "republican future" on his confidence in the educative virtues of the structures and networks that were drawing them into national life. His France, as both his Marxist critics and his liberal defenders have noted, was in important ways a bourgeois France, but in a different sense than under the July Monarchy: instead of drawing a line between the well-off businesspeople and landowners who together formed the category of *notables* on the one hand, and those traditionally labeled *le peuple* on the other, it specifically sought to bring together large sections of both. Furet characterizes Gambetta's France as the bourgeois and petit-bourgeois France of 1789, but transformed by new conditions of work and education, so that the same meritocratic grounds on which Guizot and his friends had excluded large sections of the *pays réel* could be taken to warrant their inclusion instead. Because Gambetta's electoral campaign of May, 1877 could appeal to this transformed *peuple*, as a kind of substitute for the Parisian populace that had long been at once the support and the Achilles heel of earlier republican efforts, he was able to defeat the defenders of Old Regime social and political relations through electoral means, and without recourse to struggles likely to turn violent.[42]

Gambetta's vision of a changing France as providing support to a more democratic politics did not mean that divisions either inside the bourgeoisie or between it and other groups had been overcome; quite the contrary. The opposition between the competing groups of republicans labeled "opportunists" and "intransigents" defined a major cleft inside the politically active middle classes, one that had something to do with social difference, but just as much with individual temperament and regional conditions. Although many upper bourgeois and well-off businessmen could be found on the more moderate part of the political spectrum, in contrast to a certain number of visible figures whose more modest popular origins predisposed them to side with radicals, such cases were a minority. People at different levels of the middle class were found in all groups (as in other countries), and a recent study suggests that what chiefly allowed some deputies to vote in accord with their consciences while others were drawn into "opportunist" compromises was the greater stability of the former's electoral districts; in addition, loyalties to particular groups or factions were often determined by friendships, rivalries, and ambitions.[43] Little in the social origins of the opportunist luminary Jules Ferry and the "intransigent" leader Georges Clemenceau distinguished the two; both belonged to old provincial bourgeois families with established republican roots, and interestingly both sought to marry into the same clan, the well-known Scheurer-Kestners of Alsace, active in both textile and chemical production (and notable defenders of Dreyfus). Ferry succeeded, but Clemenceau was refused by Hortense Kestner, perhaps because she or her relatives recognized in him the unstable, dissatisfied, impatient temperament that would later make him known as a volatile politician, resistant to compromise and often responsible for the downfall of ministries. Religious divisions provided important fault lines inside the bourgeoisie too, both between Protestants and Catholics, and between believers and secularists; sometimes these divisions ran inside rather than between families, as was the case with the highly skeptical Jules Ferry, responsible for educational reforms that reduced the influence of the Church, and his devout sister, whose piety he always respected in private.[44] Given the persisting importance of these and other divisions, there is good reason to regard Gambetta's project of organizing the republic in a way that brought upper and lower bourgeois together as one manner of giving political unity to a group whose various other divisions it could not dissolve, an effort that recalls those of English liberals and that we will encounter in Germany too.

The advent of modern parties in France

Only once the Republic was established on this basis did nationally organized parties make their appearance in France. As in other places, groupings intended to represent the separate position and interests of workers exhibited a special affinity for the new form of organization, turning to it as they withdrew from the cooperation some of them had earlier maintained with liberal circles. In France, however, workers were slower both to call their organizations parties and to engage in electoral activity, since the earlier history of violent conflict and repression left them with a deeper estrangement from "bourgeois" forms of politics than elsewhere. Reluctance to participate in parliamentary activity also played a role in keeping French workers' organizations from effecting the tactical unity between different currents and factions their German and English counterparts accomplished; only in 1905, after some elements of the workers' movement had moved closer to parliamentary politics, but also under pressure from their German associates in the Second International, did a unified party emerge, its debt to international involvements displayed in its name, French Section of the Workers' International (SFIO).[45]

Behind this event lay a complex history, a major strand of which emerged with the founding of the first workers' organizations soon after the crisis of 1877. These were set up partly in response to Gambetta's failed attempt to draw workers into his liberal coalition, which he sought to do by invoking the common commitment to republicanism that had served as a sometime ground for such cooperation earlier, both before and after 1848. Gambetta held a series of meetings with working-class figures and hoped that the amnesty proclaimed in 1880 for people convicted of insurrection in the aftermath of the Commune would draw them to work with him, but the wounds from that conflict were still too raw, and workers did not take the proffered hand. Their refusal was stiffened in the following years by the difficult economic conditions of the 1880s, which sharpened conflicts between workers and employers, and also by the rapprochement with the Republic effected by many formerly monarchist businessmen, who rallied more from a desire for order than out of republican conviction, and who sought, often successfully, to enlist the government on their side in disputes, particularly by using force against strikers.[46]

It was in this atmosphere that a number of working-class organizations were founded, beginning with a "Federation of Socialist Workers" in 1879. The choice of "federation" over party expressed the sense that workers would not pursue their aims through parliamentary means, but unite in preparation for a more radical kind of struggle.

Over the next few years a number of other worker and socialist groupings would emerge, most of which also refused to call themselves parties, choosing "federation" or "alliance," and for the same reasons.[47]
An exception was the *Parti ouvrier* founded in 1880 by Marx's friend
Jules Guesde, which modeled itself on the German Social Democrats
and put up candidates in elections, with considerable success during
the 1890s. The Guesdiste Party became the first in France of any political persuasion to provide itself with a solid network of local, departmental, and national associations and agencies, here too modeled on
the German example, and putting in place procedures to assure control over both deputies and newspapers. But it remained closer to the
other workers' groupings in regarding this structure not as a vehicle
for winning elections, but as the basis of an "action party," preparing
itself for the revolutionary engagement that promised an end to representative government as then practiced.[48]

This is not to say that reformist currents did not emerge inside
French socialism. They were fostered both by a minority of moderate
workers and by left-leaning liberals, of whom the most eminent was
Jean Juarès, who showed that it was possible for a bourgeois republican with a strong belief in the continuity between liberal democracy
and socialism to obtain a central position in the movement. Juarès was
responsible for convincing many formerly intransigent figures that the
Dreyfus affair was no mere dispute between bourgeois factions and
that the defense of the Republic ought to be a working-class cause too,
since no other regime would provide conditions in which the movement could grow. Juarès became the leader of the unified Party in
1905, and remained its dominant figure until he was assassinated just
as World War I broke out. But the tension between his moderation
and the persisting radical alternative was demonstrated in 1899, when
Alexandre Millerand, like Jaurès coming from the ranks of bourgeois
radicals, became the first socialist to occupy a ministerial post, which
he accepted out of a similar sense that socialist advance required giving support to the Republic. Although he was able to add somewhat to
the regime's rather limited record of social reform, the fact that one of
the government ministers alongside whom he served had been involved
in the repression of the Commune provoked a passionate debate inside
the workers' movement, contributing to its continued division, and
his own later expulsion from the faction he had headed. By then the
old suspicion of parliamentary activity, rekindled by the Millerand

affair, had led the group to fuse with followers of the insurrection-ist Louis-Auguste Blanqui in 1901. It was this combined formation, renamed *Parti socialiste de France*, that merged, under pressure from the International, with Juarès's more moderate *Parti socialiste français* to form the "Unified Socialist Party" (SFIO) in 1905.

By this time other new-style political parties had begun to operate in France alongside and in competition with the socialists, but before considering them we need to take note of an inheritance from the French past that had to be eliminated before the Republic could become a ground on which organized political interaction could develop unhindered: until 1901 political organizations of the type pioneered by the socialists remained officially illegal. The prohibition went back to the Napoleonic Code that still regulated many aspects of public and private life; behind it stood the hostility to organizations that protected the partial and privileged interests of their members that inspired the Allarde and Le Chapellier laws of 1791 and 1793 abolishing Old Regime corporations, as well as a widespread fear of conspiracy and factionalism. More positive attitudes toward associ-ations, often as remedies for excessive individualism, were present in France to be sure, voiced for instance by the Saint-Simonians and even by Guizot in the early 1830s, but the government cracked down on them in 1834 after a series of uprisings in Paris and Lyons. The Second Empire kept these restraints on the books, although, as already noted, it ceased to interfere with local political associations (many of which sought to escape the law by presenting themselves as tempor-ary groupings that only existed at election times) during the 1860s. The republican liberals who gained control of the government after 1877 were in theory committed to freedom of association, and some of them attempted to do away with the old legislation at the time of the amnesty for Communards and the establishment of freedom of the press and other forms of public expression in 1881. But the attempt foundered because political associations were not the only ones against which the law operated; the other main category comprised the reli-gious orders of which many liberals were deeply suspicious, especially those that sought to set up schools where the doctrines and spirit of the Church remained alive and influential. Militant secularism was a major feature of the Third Republic, sometimes providing the kind of bridge between bourgeois and working-class moral attitudes afforded by Protestant Dissent in England. The Republic gave legal existence to unions in 1884, and to mutual aid societies four years later, but only in 1901 did freedom of association become the rule in France.

The law was passed under the government of "republican defense" set up at the height of the Dreyfus Affair, and headed by René Waldeck-Rousseau (in whose republicanism anti-clericalism was a key component), the one that made Millerand a minister, and which was supported by other moderate socialists. Now any organized group that registered itself as such could legally hold meetings, collect dues, and own property, save that religious orders were subjected to much more restrictive oversight, effectively barring them from operating schools. Proposals to restrict socialist organizations by outlawing groupings that sought to alter the constitution or that advocated the abolition of private property were advanced at the same time, but they were defeated in the Assembly.[49]

One thing that made this legislation necessary was that the earlier prohibition of associations had grown increasingly hollow, through the refusal of governments to enforce it. By 1901 there were over 45,000 associations of various kinds in the country, most of them theoretically illegal. At the time the law was passed, however, the major political grouping whose status was regularized by the legalization was the socialists, since other political currents had not moved so far in the reliance on organization as they. The reason for this slowness was not that liberals or conservatives were unaware of the expanding importance that organized parties were assuming in politics. Even before 1870 French figures displayed considerable interest in the American caucus system on which Joseph Chamberlain had modeled himself, and after that date much public attention was given to the new-style parties in both England and Germany. Various French groups took steps to follow their example and create national organizations, but none of them achieved any permanent results. It seems that two things stood in the way, one common to other countries and one more specific to France.

The first was that some of the habits and expectations of the older politics of notability still operated among both conservative and liberal politicians. Monarchist groups had long relied on webs of personal relations, drawing on private resources of a sort we will later see at work among German *Honoratioren*, and many of these survived; and Catholics continued to look to Church institutions to spread their views and mobilize support. Even Gambetta's relationship to his supporters had features of notable politics, in some ways resembling the "community of sentiment" John Vincent describes in regard to Gladstone. The *Union republicaine* he set up to give this relationship more solid form was closer to the mid-century Gladstonian Party than to the one that emerged once it took over Chamberlain's caucus; that it fell apart after Gambetta's death in 1882 was a sign of how closely it was tied to his person. Many political figures resisted more formal organization, fearing it would subject them to central discipline (just what the socialists did intend in regard to their parliamentary delegation and newspapers) and deprive them of their independence. Such attitudes helped to preserve divisions inside various camps, for instance between the opportunist *Association républicaine* and the radical *Féderation républicaine*.[50]

In addition, however, these views went together with a second barrier to party organization, namely the persistence of a longstanding conception of national politics that looked to public discussion and action not as a way for different interests and political ideas to compete and find some *modus vivendi*, but as a vehicle for forming the country as a whole in accord with some particular view of its essential being. Sara Maza points out that already at the end of the eighteenth century French figures insisted on the contrast between their country as seeking "the harmonious integration of various social groups into a transcendent whole," and the English model of "society as an arena in which opposing groups played out their conflicts, balanced interests, and reached compromises."[51] This notion of an ideal form of the nation, which one or another elite group would bring to realization, survived in the competing teleocratic "legitimacies" that still sought to provide alternatives to the Republic; later it would echo in Charles de Gaulle's appeal to "a certain idea of France."

All the same, a notion of politics more like the English one began to make its way from the 1870s, as the various ambitions to re-establish an ideal unity receded in face of a republican understanding of political life that, in Raymond Huard's words, "admits the permanent division of opinion into separate camps, distinct and often opposed to each other." This alteration corresponded both to the higher level of social and cultural differentiation brought about by modernizing trends, and to the expansion of the political public to include many excluded from it before, people whose participation could seldom be mediated by direct connections to notables, instead requiring the more abstract linkages constituted by impersonal organizations and mass-circulation papers. "The creation of the principal French parties between 1900 and 1905 was the culmination of this evolution."[52] The groups in question included, in addition to the Socialists, the *Parti radical*, consisting of leftist republicans often critical of the government, which gave itself a central organization in 1901, and an *Alliance démocratique*, peopled by more centrist republicans (who also called themselves "progressives") and founded in the same year. Groups to the right had still not freed themselves enough from their ancient loyalties to organize in a single grouping, acting instead through personal networks, the Church, or the activist "leagues" that mounted much of the anti-republican agitation in the Dreyfus Affair.

The conceptual shift described by Huard did not proceed in exact parallel with the organizational one, however. One reason was that socialism, among modern political currents the one whose need to draw in people with limited personal resources made it the most consonant with the new-style parties, resembled certain forms of conservatism in its rejection of the liberal republican vision of a state founded on the neutral rule of law. Nor could French liberals themselves quite live up to this standard, given the resistance many of them exhibited to extending the principle of free association to the religious orders. But they did extend it to the workers' parties. Whatever role either political calculation or sentiment may have played in the decision by Waldeck-Rousseau and his allies in 1901 to ignore the socialists' anti-liberal political rhetoric and anti-capitalist social visions and grant them legal status, the moment pointed toward a future in which socialist claims (their links to liberal principles increasingly acknowledged, despite protests from the far left) would take their place as one among other competing forces inside bourgeois politics, rather than as an alternative to it. The very conditions that made liberal republicanism the form within which modern French politics would develop, putting an end to the longstanding struggle of competing teleocratic legitimacies, also gave working-class parties a prominent place within the system.

7 ONE SPECIAL PATH: MODERN INDUSTRY, POLITICS, AND BOURGEOIS LIFE IN GERMANY

Of all European countries the one most strikingly transformed in the second half of the nineteenth century was Germany. A region hitherto devoid of both an integrated market that could foster and reward the development of productive resources, and of a national state able to draw on and give direction to the wealth they generated, suddenly acquired both. The results were especially momentous because the population and resources linked together by railroads and telegraphs were large in scale and because the state that emerged was subject to few of the constitutional restraints that elsewhere mitigated the pure pursuit of power. Supporters of the National Society founded in 1859 had hoped to give a more liberal quality to a united Germany by resting it on a foundation of expanded connections, both commercial and cultural, between its regions, overcoming the long-established fragmentation by multiplying the means through which individuals could independently become what Christoph Wieland had called "actual men of the nation," and thus increasing both their numbers and their influence. But the liberals' inability to bring about unification on this basis, and Bismarck's success in effecting it instead as part of his strategy to preserve the militaristic and authoritarian character of the Prussian state, demonstrated the dependency of *Bürger* politicians on the very monarchical authority whose character they had hoped to transform. Instead of yielding some of its power to social forces outside it, the Bismarckian Empire raised the traditional domination of the state over society to a higher level, keeping effective power in the hands of ministers and officials and severely limiting the influence of the organized national parties that in Germany as elsewhere now became a significant feature of public life. One result was that the social and political modernization that in France underpinned Gambetta's faith in the country's ability to manage its affairs through parliamentary give-and-take and without recourse to violence took very different forms in Germany, with results that would play a role in the country's later susceptibility to authoritarian appeals. *Pace* many eminent historians, there was indeed a German *Sonderweg*, a special path to and within modernity – just as there was an English and a French one too.[1]

Railroad building and economic transformation

As in France, the integration effected by railway networks provided the essential ground for economic modernization in Germany. Railroads by themselves did not create the modern industrial economy, but the new tracks and lines constituted its indispensable foundation, making possible the development of a national market that no previously available means of transport could bring to life. The sheer economic weight of railroad building in the period when modern industry was finding its footing is indicated by some figures: in 1870 almost half of the capital invested in joint-stock companies of all kinds in Germany belonged to railroads, making the aggregate worth of their shares roughly four times that of the stock-market value of mines and foundries, and forty times that of investment in machine-making firms. One thing that drew these funds was the shares' high rate of return, some of them paying yearly dividends of 18 or even 25 percent (although the average was much lower, around 6.25 percent). As Theodore Hamerow noted, "only government bonds could hold their own on the money market against rail shares."[2] One thing that made the activity these investments supported so valuable was the demand for all kinds of other products it generated, but this stimulus could be effective only because, as Knut Borchardt notes, the more rapid and economical connections between producers, consumers, and resources "meant that people who had never before been within reach of one another now entered into specific economic relationships. This is not merely incidental to the great advance of productivity in the nineteenth century. It can equally be described as one of its prerequisites."[3]

There were several reasons why the German railroad network advanced more rapidly than the French one, and why it took on a different shape, less rational in an a priori way but more broadly efficacious. Government action was important in getting building projects under way in both countries, but the plurality of German states meant that work was planned and undertaken simultaneously at a number of different points on the map, so that no single locale could claim to be the focus of all efforts. Several states had sought to foster economic growth in their territories by improving roads, canals, and harbor facilities in the immediate post-Napoleonic period, and railroads extended and magnified these efforts. Since there was no central government to impose a general plan, the role of states varied from place to place, some only aiding in capital formation, others building or running the lines themselves. The relative absence in most German territories of the kinds of tensions between government and citizens that turned French visions into a *réseau impossible* for a time also meant that building could get underway with less delay. By 1850 Germany had over 3,600 kilometers of track, while France possessed only half that number (at the end of the 1860s, however, the two totals would be nearly the same, just less than 11,000 kilometers). Some of the lines put in service in the 1840s were short but others were longer and more important, including one from Aachen in the west to Breslau (now Wroclaw) in the east, and one from Kiel in the north to Munich in the south (although political divisions meant that train changes were required along the way).

Private companies were responsible for most of the early building, but they were often aided by states, as illustrated by the Railway Fund established by Prussia in 1842; it purchased shares in companies, made loans, and guaranteed interest on some investments. In 1847 the state itself constructed a line in the Saar coalfield. Other German governments also built lines in the 1840s.[4] After 1848 Prussia turned more to direct government ownership, so that by 1860 about half the 5,700 kilometers of rail lines there were either owned or run by the state. In Germany as a whole at the same date there were some 4,600 kilometers owned and administered by private companies, 1,400 owned privately but managed by governments, and 5,200 kilometers of state-owned lines.[5] As the century went on, the economy, now stimulated by market integration and the new industries, picked up speed on its own, and the direct role of the state contracted. But the German states, like the French, retained their connection to those economic activities that were most directly concerned with their traditional aim of building up the unity of their territories, taking over general management of the railroads, even on some lines originally constructed by private companies. In the years before 1914 the Prussian state railway would be the largest employer in the world.[6]

Certainly the new network's effect on German life was rapid and remarkable. As David Blackbourn notes, the 1850s saw Germany's real breakthrough to industrialization, and at a pace that justifies the old term "industrial revolution" against the various doubts raised against it. In this transformation the railway was "at the center of everything," stimulating the production of metals, widening the circle of consumers, giving a boost to the chemical industry by creating a national market for clothing and thus for dyes to color it, "helping to spread the market culture into previously virgin land," and giving a new mobility to people of all kinds, beginning with the thousands of workers required to construct it. In industry itself, metals showed the most remarkable upswing: "The use of coke in iron smelting was virtually unknown in the 1830s, and in 1850 it still accounted for only 25 percent of iron output. By 1853, in just three years, the figure had risen to 63 percent." The famous Krupp metals firm employed 60 men in 1836, over 1,000 in 1858, 8,000 in 1865 and twice that number by 1873. Equally remarkable was the expansion of the building industry. "Over a million new buildings went up in Prussia alone during the years 1852–67, the fastest growth coming in factory plant and public buildings." There was a "mushroom-like appearance of new factories, gasworks, waterworks and railway workshops." Cities were reshaped as people drawn into them occupied new dwellings, for the first time built on a large scale for renting. Other forms of government action also contributed to this transformation. The Prussian government set up local chambers of commerce to encourage industry, partly financed by the state, and railroads made the stimulative effects of the *Zollverein* more important than before, with more states joining it from 1850.[7]

Many traditional patterns of life were disrupted and many immigrants to the expanding cities were thrown into confusion by the conditions they encountered there, but unprecedented quantities of energy and vitality were released at the same time. The conditions that had made the 1830s and 1840s decades of widespread anxiety, and suffering faded from view as industrial advance "broke the cycles of dearth and starvation, boosted output and demand, and provided employment for the underemployed of the Vormärz" (as the period before 1848 is known to German historians). Real wages began a rise that continued through most of the century, and when economic crises came in 1857 and 1873, they produced neither the widespread hunger and unemployment nor the revolutionary atmosphere of the 1840s. The overpopulation of the countryside that had been responsible for much of the crisis of *Pauperismus* that preoccupied observers now receded with remarkable speed, as immigration both to cities and to foreign lands, principally the United States, provided outlets. With rural labor no longer in oversupply the downward pressure on wages in country areas diminished at the same time that growing urban markets provided profitable outlets for rural goods of all kinds. The results were favorable both to small producers and to big landowners such as the Junkers, who were by no means turned into an economically declining class by the growth of industry. (To be sure, they pressed for tariff protection in the 1870s, as international competition in agriculture grew sharper, but so did industrialists.) The contrast with the rural world of a few years earlier was profound: "The countryside had never been so wealthy and stable."[8]

Bürgertum, state, and industry

As in every country, many individual and uncoordinated decisions and actions combined to produce this transformation, but it is impossible to escape the sense that the German case was marked by an unusually high degree of self-consciousness, a recognition that historical conditions required that the country remake itself both in order to keep up with its neighbors and rivals and to respond to its internal problems. Such awareness was by no means novel, since various German states had taken on a role as engines of economic, social, and cultural advance from the eighteenth century; even then, as Isabel Hull points out, the idea of a *bürgerliche Gesellschaft* was a future-oriented one. In the post-Napoleonic period the impact of the new industrial techniques in England led to public discussions about how and whether Germany should follow the British example, with some participants seeking ways to catch up (through tariff protections, for instance), while others were moved by a desire to avoid the negative consequences famously evident in Manchester.

This debate took a new turn in the 1840s, in the writings of a group of young and visionary businessmen whose most articulate spokesman was the well-known Cologne manufacturer, railroad builder, and banker Gustav Mevissen. Against those who preferred to see Germany expand manufacture on traditional lines the group argued that old-fashioned *Industrie* could not survive competition with the new kind of *Fabrikwesen*, and that only the latter could provide sufficient employment to sustain a growing population and provide the country with a stable and prosperous future; modern industry had to become the basis for a determined and thorough make over of the whole economy. Mevissen and his friends did not shrink from recognizing the negative effects of so sweeping a transformation: suffering and disruption were bound to accompany it. Just for this reason both officials and private people had to prepare to provide aid to those whose jobs or skills would be threatened. The group split over how large a directing role the state should be assigned, and how much distress could be avoided, with Mevissen himself (an intellectual as well as a businessman, and who later went on to a distinguished career in state service) resigned to a pessimistic assessment of the immediate future, for the sake of longer-term benefits.[9]

Mevissen's combination of visionary determination to foster industrialism with a hard-nosed acknowledgment that its damaging consequences could not be avoided deserves to be highlighted; it is difficult to think of a similar mix in either England, where change occurred largely on its own, or France, where the great champions of industrial advance, the Saint-Simonians, envisioned it as a remedy for the country's many and longstanding social antagonisms. Mevissen's views seem akin at once to the attitude of bureaucrats who thought effective modernization required guidance from some central point, and to the dialectical linkage of history's dark underside with its ability to realize human potential developed by both Hegel and Marx. The latter connection was not merely theoretical, since Mevissen was one of the founders of the liberal newspaper the *Rheinische Zeitung*, in which some of these ideas were put forward, and of which the young Marx became the editor for a time in 1842. Marx was then a radical Hegelian who looked to the state to "fulfill its concept" by directing society so as to defend the general interest and protect the poor against selfish individualism, a program akin to the ideas of Mevissen and his friends. In the event, the process by which Germany became industrialized would be more haphazard and less self-consciously directed than the Rhenish liberals envisioned, but their sense that it had to occur at a rapid rate, and that it would simultaneously disrupt many established patterns of life and resolve many of the problems that rendered the 1840s so dark, turned out to be very much on the mark.

Mevissen's career as both a businessman and a state official, alongside his ties to Hegel and Marx, should remind us that the kind of determined, even brutal realism he countenanced provided a not-always-remembered link between German bourgeois and the state that did much to shape their lives, after 1850 no less than before. Something of what tied them together can be illuminated by recalling that the idea of *Realpolitik* for which Bismarck provided the classic and most enduring realization actually made its entry into the political lexikon when a young liberal publicist, Ludwig August von Rochau, published a book about its "basic principles" in 1853. Asserting that "it is power alone which can rule," Rochau added that "the spoken and written word can accomplish nothing in the face of physical facts," which can only be altered by "other facts." This declaration reflected a widespread disillusionment with the idealistic hopes that inspired liberals in 1848, when for a moment it seemed that governments might remake themselves along the lines proposed by the representatives assembled in Frankfurt. But as other historians have noted, Rochau's views gave *Geist* a place in history alongside *Macht*. His manner of putting power at the core of politics included the recognition that no political program could succeed which did not accord with the *Zeitgeist*, a spirit still animated in the 1850s by principles that included "civic consciousness, the idea of freedom, national sentiment [and] the idea of equal human entitlements." Bismarck did not share von Rochau's commitment to all these values to be sure, but he was precisely trying to appeal to some of them when in a famous speech he sought to gain support for his program of strengthening the Prussian army by telling liberal nationalists that only "blood and iron" could realize the vision of unity they so cherished.[10]

That many middle-class liberals who had seen Bismarck as an enemy before 1871 became his supporters once the miracle of unification stood before their eyes was only one of many signs that large segments of the *Bürgertum* could not fail to acknowledge their closeness to, even dependency on state power. Such dependency was particularly evident in the case of the officials who constituted the kernel of the *Bildungsbürgertum*, for all the reasons noted in Chapter 4, and the *Wirtschaftsbürger* who assumed increasing prominence after 1850 inherited it in some degree by virtue of the role the state played in creating the conditions for industrial growth and innovation. One way in which they testified to it was through their often-remarked penchant for seeking and accepting official titles and honors. Although not unique to Germany, the phenomenon was far more extensive there, which is one reason why it has been a point of contention in debates about the so-called "feudalization" of the German bourgeoisie. Some historians have argued that accepting such honors testified to the desire of business people to turn their backs on their own identifies and inheritance, a penchant that reduced their ability to engage in the struggle against the aristocracy assigned to them by classic historical scenarios, both Marxist and liberal. But other scholars have offered good reasons to reject such a reading. Few *Bürger* received actual titles of nobility (Gustav Mevissen, late in his life was one exception), the most common distinction being "Commercial Councillor" (*Kommerzienrat*), a title that recalled no-longer functional bodies once set up to advise officials on business matters. What recent studies show is that the families who accepted the honor (it seems hardly ever to have been refused when offered) did not abandon business, but continued to be active, even in succeeding generations. The so-called "Buddenbrooks phenomenon," in which some offspring of business people abandoned commerce for cultural or aesthetic pursuits, affected some individuals, but few families as a whole (Thomas Mann had his own reasons for attributing it to his). Not only did most of them remain in mercantile occupations, they largely continued to socialize and to marry inside business circles too. Rather than providing any kind of escape from entrepreneurial life, the titles seem to have appeared to *Bürger* as aids in pursuing it, providing a sign of respect and recognition typical of the society they inhabited. All the same, as Karin Kaudelka-Hanisch, one of the critics of the "feudalization" thesis concludes, the importance of titles "indicates a peculiarity of the German bourgeoisie, namely its strongly marked statism ... Closeness to the state and bourgeois self-confidence seem to have gone together." To this it should be added that the peculiarly military nature of the German state literally left its marks on prominent members of the *Bürgertum* (at least those who attended universities) in the form of the dueling scars many of them bore from their student years (Max Weber, no less tough-minded than Mevissen, was one); the wounds were the price of membership in student fraternities whose aggressive and even brutal tone provided a vehicle for bourgeois to inherit the combative spirit embodied by Prussia, and which Bismarck represented so well. English observers, as Peter Gay colorfully shows, were shocked by the display of violence in German student life, even when they recognized that watching it in action put them in touch with aggressive feelings of their own for which their kind of gentlemanly education provided only sublimated outlets.[11]

One attraction of the titles was that they gave members of the *Wirtschaftsbürgertum* a sense of equal status with *Bildungsbürger*, whose claims to serve some general social interest that transcended mere self-seeking derived in part from their close relationship to the state that had long fostered their existence. Relations between the two groups were changing in a number of ways in the second half of the century. Jürgen Kocka points to the years between 1840 and 1870 as the period when *Wirtschaftsbürger* overcame the old sense of inferiority to official and professional groups, a change in part tied up with the former's increasing wealth and the more rapid growth in their income levels. Although the prestige of businessmen was sometimes tarnished by economic crisis and scandal, as at the moment when large numbers of new firms set up on shaky foundations in the euphoric atmosphere generated by the unification failed after 1873 (the so-called *Gründerkrise*), in the longer term it was heightened by the boost that Germany's rapid economic growth gave to the country's position in world affairs. The slogan of "industry for the fatherland" sometimes put forward in this period may have served as a justification as much as a motive, but at least some historians find evidence that pride in the transformation that made an economic powerhouse out of a country until then regarded as a sleepy backwater may have played a role in encouraging entrepreneurship. Clive Trebilcock thinks such feelings may have been particularly at work in those businessmen who formed the boards of the many cartels that ran important segments of German industry before 1914, a good number of them connected to banks.[12] Neither England, the country of early and spontaneous industrial progress, nor France, long accustomed to being the major political power on the continent, seems to have benefitted from a similar sense of new national purpose in their entrepreneurs (although competing with the

Germans did become a motive for promoting industrial and scientific advance in France after the defeat of 1870).

One dimension of state intervention in bourgeois life that played a significant role in Germany's industrial growth was the encouragement governments gave to both education and to the advancement of science. Although there is disagreement about just how much economic importance should be attributed to this orientation, it surely grew in significance as enterprises requiring increased scientific and technical competence – steel-making, industrial chemistry, electricity, optics, and precision instruments – assumed greater prominence from around 1880, especially in contrast with the more casual and informal approach to such things that prevailed in England. The interest governing authorities took in education and science had roots in the same competition between territorial states that encouraged the development of the class of officials who comprised the original core of the *Bildungsbürgertum*. In line with the notion that these *Beamte* were exemplars of the personal development that made individuals responsible and mature members of *bürgerliche Gesellschaft*, the universities provided them with an education based on the humanist classicism of Humboldt and Wolff. By the end of the Napoleonic Wars, this orientation was becoming a focus of inter-state rivalry, exemplified by the program of the Prussian minister of education Karl von Altenstein, who sought to make the University of Berlin a showplace for state support of intellect and culture by giving faculty positions to scholars with international reputations. He thus encouraged hiring people whose published work made them known outside Prussia and even Germany, in preference to candidates recommended by prominent local people, and he was instrumental in broadening this association between the state and *Wissenschaft* (the German term has a wider sense than its English counterpart science, referring to any organized body of knowledge) so that it spread from classical philology to the natural sciences.

Other states followed his lead. German science had by no means been backward during the eighteenth century, and a sense that scientists throughout the German lands formed a community was nurtured by publications devoted to chemistry and mathematics, which created widespread linkages not unlike those of the reading and patriotic societies considered in Chapter 4. These contacts expanded after 1815, and by the 1830s an association of scientists and physicians was holding meetings in various German cities, at first chiefly involving people who worked in practical fields such as medicine, but soon in areas of basic research and theory as well. A study of German physicists shows that none of those born around 1770 received specialized training in the subject, but that all of those born around 1800 did. These developments were given additional impetus by the spread of university research laboratories, of which the first was established by the chemist Justus Liebig at Giessen (in the state of Hesse) in 1825; it was based on the then novel idea that advanced students should conduct research under the direction of a professor. Liebig's innovation may have been facilitated by small size and relative flexibility of the University of Giessen, but his example was quickly taken up by people at larger and more famous places. By the time of the unification, the new state could boast a "costly and highly influential series of laboratories, seminars, and institutes."[13]

Both the development of industry and the general tone of bourgeois life in Germany were colored by these developments. The Bavarian entrepreneur Wilhelm Sattler, one of the central figures in Franz Bauer's highly informative study of "*Bürger* paths and *Bürger* worlds," was inspired to set up his first successful business, a plant to manufacture chemical dyes opened in 1814, by reading an article about how to make a bright green pigment that retained its quality in artificial light in a publication started by a professor at the University of Braunschweig. Bauer describes the journal, *Chemische Annalen*, as important both in furthering professional chemical research and in giving form to a "chemically interested public." Sattler did well with his dyes, using them for both paint and textiles, but he eventually gave up making them (turning to wallpaper, beet sugar, and pottery instead), perhaps because, as a person with no formal scientific education working at a time when businesses were still largely conducted within families (his wife, an artist, had an important role in his), he did not have enough technical knowledge to deal with the new processes of making dyes from coal tar that developed toward the middle of the century. But one of his correspondents, younger than he, was a chemist who had studied with Liebig and who turned precisely to these later ways of producing dyestuffs. Although he had no university education himself, Sattler had a number of friends and correspondents who were *Bildungsbürger*, among them lawyers and public officials, and the letters they exchanged give evidence both that he and they understood the different kinds of resources each group commanded, and that they were able to be of help to each other on this basis. Indeed, despite his lack of formal study Sattler was something of an intellectual himself. After serving in the Bavarian parliament during 1848, where he supported liberal reforms, unification, railroad-building and Jewish emancipation, he retired to devote himself to reading and writing, filling notebooks with discussions of science, literature, and philosophy (where he took a materialist and anti-religious stance close to that of contemporaries such as Ludwig Feuerbach).[14]

Later Sattler's descendants would intermarry with children of some of the people he knew through his political activities and his intellectual interests, forming a configuration of interlinked families whose members were involved at once in practical life and in science, art, and culture. Bauer traces these connections and their lineage into the early twentieth century, showing that the continuing connections both businessmen and scientists maintained with the humanistic *Bildung* originally associated with educating officials often remained an active element of their self-consciousness, providing an orientation that some of their children would more wholeheartedly take up by rejecting practical careers in favor of "higher" activities and values. To be sure, connections between business families and people who made careers in state administration or culture can be found in every country, but only in Germany did universities and the *Wissenschaftsideologie* they fostered infuse their values into such ties, giving to relationships like those between Sattler and his friends a quality distinct from the personal ties between sociologically similar people in other countries. One testimony to the special character these kinds of relations gave to German bourgeois life is suggested by what made the famous friendship between Engels and Marx typically, even uniquely, German: it was a bond between the *Wirtschaftsbürger* Engels, a person with no university degree whose highly developed interest in intellectual life shared much with the cases of Sattler and Mevissen, and a *Bildungsbürger* whose sense for the negative impact of contemporary economic advance went along with a belief in the universal historical and human significance of *bürgerliche Gesellschaft*.

A noteworthy figure who moved in some of the same circles as Sattler's descendants later in the century was Werner Siemens, the founder of the famous electrical company that still bears his name. Like Sattler, Siemens was a businessman who saw scientific advance as opening new paths for commercial activity; in his case, however, he sought the knowledge and training he needed not only in reports on university research, as Sattler did, but in another locus of the state's encouragement of science, namely the training in engineering provided by the Prussian army, and which led him to enlist in it in 1835. His later career drew at once on the technical skills he developed there (in 1846 he invented a telegraph whose receiving device could point to letters instead of just making clicks, saving operators the need to learn Morse code, and later he would patent an improvement to Alexander Graham Bell's telephone) and on government connections that stemmed from his military service. The company he founded with a partner in 1847 took off when it was hired to build the first telegraph line in Germany, connecting Berlin to Frankfurt to keep the Prussian government in touch with doings at the elected national assembly; official ties were of help too in the steps that rendered the business international, establishing it in Russia after building a line from Berlin to St. Petersburg, and then in London when the British hired it to establish a still longer connection between London and Calcutta.

Siemens's profile as a businessman was shaped by his combination of two seemingly contrasting features, one a traditional sense that business should remain a family affair, the other a penchant for bureaucratic organization. His desire to keep control in his family was responsible for a threat to the firm's future during the 1880s, when he rejected an overture from Emil Rathenau, the more venturesome founder of the German General Electric Company (AEG), to cooperate in manufacturing material to install electric lighting in Berlin; because the project would have required heavy borrowing from banks, Siemens feared it would give outsiders too much power over the enterprise. Fortunately for the firm his son Wilhelm did not share these scruples; taking over after Werner's retirement in 1890 he greatly expanded the company by moving into mass electric lighting and generating, and raised capital by selling shares. This expansion required a much larger organization (by 1912 the company would have some 12,000 office workers), but in this regard Werner Siemens had already laid the foundation by introducing a bureaucratized administrative structure whose form, as Jürgen Kocka points out, was modeled on that of the Prussian civil service. Although Werner still relied on family members and associates for the top positions in the company (his brothers headed the London and St. Petersburg offices), some of his middle managers were former government officials, and Kocka finds something of the spirit of discipline and pride typical of these *Beamte* operative in the firm even before Wilhelm gave it its new direction. One reason why further expansion does not seem to have sapped this spirit (despite the fact that, unlike government bureaucrats, the company's employees had no guarantee of permanent tenure and were subject to lay offs in bad times) is that the "first-class experts and administrators" it determinedly recruited from outside would only accept positions "if they were offered a high degree of autonomy." The result was an organizational structure marked by what Kocka calls "planned decentralization," giving the firm an efficient mix of flexibility and focused management that developed in other German electrical firms as well (and would later come to some American ones). The relative failure of contemporary British companies to evolve such an operating style has been cited by some historians as a contributing factor to the greater success of Germany in this field before 1914. Thus the history of Siemens points to some of the ways in which the preeminent position won by German industry at the end of the nineteenth century owed a debt to the special connection between *Bürger* of all kinds and the state.[15]

The Siemens story was not wholly a German one, however, and we need to take note of some of the ways it exemplifies the growing importance of distant and mediated connections in many spheres of late nineteenth-century life. The electric telegraph in whose early history the firm played so large a role was a crucial element in providing extended and thickened networks of communication, providing new opportunities and imposing new demands on businesses, banks, stock markets, political parties, diplomatic officials, police forces, spies, and of course newspapers. Telegraphy was closely linked to railroad transport, since telegraphic lines often followed the track routes, and one of their functions was to keep people along the grid informed about the movements of trains and their cargoes. The importance of this connection has been concisely summed up by a historian of telegraphy in America whose formula fits Europe too: the rapid transmission of data made it possible for railroads "to control efficiently and manage vast, complex flows of freight and passengers" and thus to integrate other large industries and markets; at the same time the experience of regular contact and interaction with distant places and conditions introduced people to "the new world of gigantic, impersonal, non-local institutions to which they had to accommodate as the century progressed."[16]

This description of the overall expansion of coordinated distant relations applies not only to industries and markets but also to activities in which information itself was the major object of exchange, and notably in learned, scientific, and technical professions among whose members were some of the "first-class experts and administrators" Siemens hired. It was in the period after 1850 that professions grew up in such new areas as chemistry, engineering and architecture; in the same decades the position of professionals in more traditional fields such as medicine and university teaching shifted from a long-standing dependence on connections to local structures of status and notability toward one in which personal standing derived from membership in national and even international bodies, devoted to developing and diffusing knowledge in some field and enhancing the lives and positions of those who made their careers within it. The activities of these organizations included setting standards for membership, sponsoring periodicals, encouraging correspondence between members, and holding regular meetings, as well as furthering the profession's reputation with the wider public, and lobbying governments in pursuit of its interests. German professional organizations differed somewhat from those in other countries, however, in that they seldom developed the independent capacity for self-regulation that characterized their counterparts elsewhere, since the state kept much of the power to decide about who could engage in particular activities in its own hands.[17]

What made these new grounds of professionalization so important for late nineteenth-century industry was not just that firms employed increasing numbers of engineers and scientists, but that the same structures and media of communication that supported and facilitated ongoing professional interchange also nurtured the expanding body of technical and scientific knowledge that fostered invention and innovation. The period before World War I was a great age of scientific and technological progress in part because researchers in widely scattered locations had more immediate and widespread access to each other's work. Joel Mokyr argues that the expansion of communication and interchange reduced the "access cost" of knowledge, enlarging the base on which new discoveries could be made at the same time that it gave people more regular and rapid entry to it:

An example is the simultaneity of many major inventions. The more a new technique depends on an epistemic base that is in the common domain and accessible to many inventors at low cost, the more likely it is that more than one inventor will hit upon it at about the same time ... it is hardly surprising that many of the inventions of the period were made independently by multiple inventors who beat one another to the patent office door sometimes by a matter of days.

Mokyr adds that the more complex organizations characteristic of such enterprises as Siemens derived not only from their sheer size, but also from the need to assemble and coordinate specialized information in quantities beyond what single individuals have the capacity to manage. "Given the limitations on how much each worker can know ... the total competence that the firm has to possess is chopped up into manageable bites and divided among the workers, and their actions are then coordinated by management."[18] These features of late nineteenth-century industrial culture were visible in many places, but the special relations between the state and *bürgerliche Gesellschaft* meant that Germans were particularly able to draw benefits from them. As we shall now see, however, these same relations carried a different set of implications for politics, both for the country in general, and for bourgeois in particular.

Parties, interest groups, and politics in the Second Reich

The era of modern nationally organized parties came to Germany as to other countries in the second half of the nineteenth century, but with a peculiar rhythm and shape. Organization proceeded at once more quickly and more slowly than in England and France: the Socialists established a modern structure with determination, and at a rhythm that easily outpaced their counterparts elsewhere, but no other major party moved at the same speed. The latter all started out as clusters of notables associated with parliamentary delegations, a form that survived until after World War I in the powerful Center Party for which large numbers of Catholics voted, especially in the south, and for a long time in the case of the liberals too. The latter moved toward more formal ties around the turn of the century but without creating a structure to rival that of the Socialists. This does not mean that Germany in the *fin-de-siècle* lacked national entities devoted to propaganda, influencing elections, and giving direction to government policy, but the chief groups set up to engage in these activities through local chapters tied into a central structure were not parties seeking parliamentary representation, they were interest groups (*Interessenverbände*), dedicated to protecting and furthering the concerns of particular and restricted parts of society. The conservatives in particular relied on one such group, the Agrarian League (*Bund der Landwirte*) to organize electoral support. This situation both reflected and intensified the political differences between Germany and her neighbors.

The chief reason for the different German pattern was that the Empire established in 1871 had the appearance of a parliamentary regime but not its substance. The national representative body, the Reichstag, was elected by universal male suffrage, and it had a certain part in passing legislation and influencing policy. But government ministers were not responsible to it, only to the emperor, who was also the king of Prussia, and only he could appoint and remove them. More powerful than the Reichstag (especially in regard to initiating legislation and putting it into effect) was a second representative body, the Bundesrat, whose members were chosen not by voters but by the governments of the individual states that made up the Empire. It was specifically intended as a brake on popular sovereignty. In addition many powers were left to the states, each of which elected its own assembly using a suffrage system of its own, none of them as democratic as the one in place for the Reichstag. Some of these arrangements distinguished between voters on the basis of status or function (giving special representation to clergy or landowners), but most famous was the Prussian one, which divided voters into three classes based on the taxes they paid, giving one-third of the delegates to the small number of very rich landowners and *Bürger* whose payments provided the top third of government revenues, an equal number to the larger but still limited group who provided the next third, and the remaining seats to the mass of voters, chiefly peasants and workers, who together contributed the rest. Since the constitution gave a dominant place to Prussia in both the Reichstag and the Bundesrat, the degree to which representative institutions could control policy, and with it the rationale for seeking to organize voters, was less than in England or France.

One might wonder why any moves toward organizing modern national parties were made at all in these conditions. One large reason was the example set by the social democrats, who achieved unity through merger of two separate organizations in 1875 and who saw common action of all kinds as a vehicle for achieving working-class solidarity and self-consciousness. By the 1890s the two wings that came to face each other inside the Party, revolutionary and reformist, each developed its own interpretation of this vision, the first (like their French comrades) seeing it as a preparation for revolutionary action, the second regarding the mix of unions, party committees, and social and cultural activities (including singing societies, lending libraries, theatrical projects, athletic clubs) as already containing the social relations of the future in embryo, so that (as the revisionist theorist Eduard Bernstein put it) preserving and expanding "the movement," not setting some end beyond it, was what mattered most. Fearing the power this organization might generate, the government seized an opportunity to outlaw the Party in 1878, giving it a pariah status that lasted until 1890 (socialist candidates could still run for office, but only under the cover of being independents); impediments were put in the way of other kinds of workers' associations too, leading many clubs and societies to hide their political aims. Once it was able to operate in the open again in the quarter-century before World War I, this complex constituted a kind of archipelago of diverse but interconnected groupings. The Party itself stood at the center, based on a well-articulated system of local units tied into a central structure of administration that allowed for sharing information and resources, organizing support, and providing encouragement and direction to the whole. By the time of the Reichstag election of 1893 this structure made it possible for the Social Democrats to garner more votes than any other party; a skewed way of drawing up electoral districts still kept them from having the largest number of seats, but in 1912 they became the largest Party by that measure too.[19]

The political power of the Social Democrats remained largely a matter of potential as long as the restrictions on representative government imposed by the Bismarckian constitution stayed in place, but it would become real enough once the Empire fell and Germany became a republic in 1918. Meanwhile the network's wide reach and the connections it provided to scattered and distant people and resources furnished individuals and groups with real and potential benefits that no merely local ties could provide. A certain number of people were able to make careers inside this structure, as clerks, officials, or journalists, and many more experienced it as providing resources for personal development – books, periodicals, social relations, participation in musical, dramatic, or athletic activities – they could obtain nowhere else, so much so that critics inside the movement feared that the life some workers led was making them "bourgeois." That these worries stemmed in part from worker participation in activities organized through intersecting chains of connection is a sign that what had long been chiefly a bourgeois form of existence was becoming part of the experience of people hitherto excluded from it. What Joel Mokyr says about knowledge and information in this period was true of other kinds of network ties too: as the webs became wider and thicker the "access cost" of such connections fell. Under the conditions that obtained before the second half of the nineteenth century participation in distant networks was generally open only to people who brought some species of personal assets to them, some store of wealth, or culture (literacy, knowledge about distant places), or social experience (family or business connections to people elsewhere). What marked the new forms of worker politics and culture was precisely that the more developed means available to establish mediated and distant connections meant that individuals required fewer personal assets in order to participate in them: little had to be asked of workers in order to join up. To be sure, the success of the Social Democrats in creating their thick mesh of associations owed much to a shared sense of class-based exclusion on the part of many workers, but it was also testimony to the special benefits that participation in relations at a distance now offered to people whose resources had not been sufficient to enter into them before.

Indeed the Social-Democratic organizations had some of their roots in earlier attempts by bourgeois liberals to accord such benefits to workers. In a way the whole archipelago of worker associations in place by 1914 was an extension of the culture of *Vereine* built up by bourgeois from the eighteenth century in support of *Aufklärung* and reform. Until late in the 1870s many German workers, like their English counterparts, gave support to liberal candidates, and cooperation across class lines was furthered by the efforts of middle-class liberals and democrats to aid in setting up and advancing workers' organizations – cooperatives, educational societies, and self-help groups. Out of these efforts there emerged in 1863 the League of German Workers' Associations (*Verband deutscher Arbeitervereine*), which aimed to coordinate the activities of workers' clubs and societies across the country, thereby extending the cooperation between workers and liberals. In 1869 leading figures in this League, notably Wilhelm Liebknecht and August Bebel, would be instrumental in founding the Social Democratic Workers' Party (dubbed the "Eisenach Party" after the city where it was set up), one of the two groups that merged to form the united Social Democrats in 1875. The other, called the General German Workers' Association (*Allgemeine deutsche Arbeiterverein*), contrasted with the *Verband* in that it sought a form of working-class activity that did not involve cooperation with liberals, but it still relied on *Bürger* leadership. Its founder was the colorful and eccentric figure Ferdinand Lassalle, whose mix of romantic panache and radical enthusiasm won him a following before his death in a duel in 1864, and who preferred cooperation with the Prussian state to efforts to curb its power (in 1863 he held a series of secret meetings with Bismarck, hoping to effect a kind of conservative-worker alliance over the heads of the liberals). Lassalle's call for workers to form independent organizations pointed toward the future, but in the conditions of the 1860s it produced only limited results, as Bebel later noted in his memoirs. Even after the Social Democrats began to set up their own organizations for education, leisure, and personal development beginning in the mid 1870s, liberal notions about the relationship between culture and self-improvement remained alive in them, and in some places middle-class people were notable among the participants.[20] Only in the 1880s and 1890s would the originally *Bürgerlich* vision of social and individual development through participation in such activities find effective embodiment in a specifically working-class organizational structure.

As this structure began to realize its political potential, its presence highlighted the failure of the liberals to establish a counterpart to it. This failure had many roots, one of which lay in the nature of earlier liberal politics. Just as English liberalism before the 1870s was not an organized movement but (in John Vincent's words) "a habit of cooperation and a community of sentiment," so was its German counterpart (as James Sheehan puts it) an "assemblage of convictions."[21] The liberal "party" of the 1860s was a loosely connected collection of notables (*Honoratioren*), and it retained this stamp even after unification, consisting of what Dieter Langewiesche describes as an aggregate of "influential persons, linked by a thick network of acquaintanceship, associations, and committees of all kinds, in communities, provinces and individual states." The political relations maintained by such people drew on personal, family or business connections that might reach back over generations, and that were sustained by resources of wealth and education sufficient to maintain them without the support of a formal framework. Leadership in some cities and regions easily passed from father to son.[22] By the 1890s the rise of the social democrats encouraged liberals to expand their efforts at organization, creating closer ties between local organizations and central administrative organs, and calling regular national party conventions; the number of local associations allied with the National Liberal Party grew from around 300 to over 2,000 by 1914. But Sheehan makes clear that these efforts bore only limited fruit. Liberal organizations remained dominated by the leaders of party factions, providing little role for "the full-time staff or the convention delegates," so that as late as 1907 one official complained that liberal organization only existed "for the most part on paper." The inability of both National Liberals and their cousins in the South German liberal *Volkspartei* "to attract the masses of new voters who came into the political system after 1890 was partly due to the failure of liberal organizations to provide these groups with satisfactory sources of information, cohesion, and direction."[23]

It is revealing to note, however, that those on the left side of the spectrum of liberal opinion and action were regularly more interested and more successful in establishing effective organizational ties than were their more moderate colleagues. In 1849 the democratic faction on the left of the Frankfurt Assembly created the *Centralmärzverein*, an organ that has been called "the first German political party with a modern character" because it sought to impose a central direction on the local associations tied in with it. By contrast the more moderate liberals set up only a less formal umbrella organization to share information.[24] The difference persisted in the period of unification, for instance in the enthusiasm shown by left-liberals such as Eugen Richter for a solid and organized base (which he succeeded in establishing to some degree for the Progressives he led) at a time when people to his right in the movement dragged their feet.[25] The divergence resembled the one that emerged in Britain when radicals such as Chamberlain set up their Caucus in the mid 1870s, as a kind of "machine" to organize electoral support on a basis that did not depend on the personal influence on which the Whig magnates had relied in times of a narrower suffrage, and which Gladstone, with his personal charisma, did not require.

One reason why organization made little progress in the liberal camp was the important place occupied within it by the *Bildungsbürgertum*. Although many rank-and-file members of the liberal *Nationalverein* in the 1860s were businessmen, the group's national leadership consisted almost entirely of *Bildungsbürger*, and this remained true of the movement as a whole up to 1914. Rooted in traditional humanistic studies and the sometimes elitist values they fostered, many such people were uncomfortable at the prospect of addressing or participating in big and perhaps unruly meetings, and some used the label "professional politician" as a term of abuse. In the 1860s and early 1870s, before large-scale organization really got off the ground, liberals formed associations intended to influence government action, notably the Social Policy Association (*Verein für Sozialpolitik*) of 1872, but by the end of the decade it had become less involved in public life and more devoted to academic discussion of social issues. The notion grew that educated people who spoke out on questions of the day should do so as experts, not as "party men." A number of people who declared their sympathy with liberal views and cast ballots for liberal candidates resisted involvement in organizations, preferring to see themselves as acting on the basis of "reason" or "good sense," not political loyalty. The novelist Theodor Fontane thought that his sharing views with the National Liberals and voting for them, while shunning concrete ties to the Party, made him "a typical National Liberal."[26]

Not all *Bildungsbürger* were liberals, however, which is one reason why the same social and cultural factors that slowed down the move toward formal organization in the liberal camp were also at work outside it. This was notably true of the Catholic Center Party with which Bismarck often cooperated after he put an end to the anti-church *Kulturkampf* that provided one ground for his temporary reconciliation with liberals before 1878; especially strong in the south, the Party would be part of the coalition with liberals and social democrats that established the Weimar Republic after the War. In the period before 1914 it was a Party practically without any defined organization, relying on the influence of local notables both religious and secular (many of them educated *Bürger*), and on a number of figures with national reputations who traveled about to address meetings and whose views were diffused in newspapers. The Center's electoral success (it had the largest percentage of votes in Reichstag elections between 1878, when it first outdistanced the liberals, and 1890, when it was overtaken by the Socialists, and remained the second largest party until 1914) rested on organization all the same, but in the form of the already-existing web of connections within and surrounding the Catholic Church rather than any specifically political structure. Catholic associations, orders, meetings, retreat and pilgrimage sites, and the ties established by the hierarchy itself were the vehicles by which the Party diffused information and called for support (much as did French Legitimists). As long as the Center could rely on this inherited scaffolding of convictions and loyalties, it did not seek to set up a separate structure that might have called this less formal one's persisting relevance into question.[27]

Catholics can be rightly described as an interest group, and the Center Party's reliance on the Church's panoply of organizations to firm up its support among voters resembled the way other parties employed *Interessenverbände* for similar ends. Of these the most prominent example was the already-mentioned *Bund der Landwirte* that worked on behalf of candidates of the *Deutschkonservative Partei*. Founded in 1876, the Conservative Party was the biggest vote-getter in elections of the 1880s and early 1890s, although its support fell off afterwards. Like the Center, it was a party almost wholly without any infrastructure (although it sometimes held conventions), but it employed different substitutes. One of these was the enormous influence big landowners were able to exercise over the mass of rural workers in Prussia, a mix of traditional dominance, monopolization of publicity organs, and tactics of encouragement and intimidation at election time some have described as quasi-terroristic; the other was the already-mentioned *Bund der Landwirte*. Founded in 1893, this Agrarian League had some 300,000 members, most of them small peasant proprietors and villagers, but it was organized and dominated by wealthy agrarians, and it hired journalists to mount propaganda campaigns in its papers. Its hostility to both socialism and urban capitalism made it a major vehicle for spreading anti-Semitic notions in the *fin-de-siècle*, a function that has led historians to recognize it as having had a significant role in developing the brew of racism and anti-modernism later brought to a boil by the Nazis (a point to which we will return in a moment). But in organizational terms it resembled other interest groups, including some looked to as sources of support by liberals, such as the Central Association of German Industrialists, founded in 1876, whose highly elaborated structure eventually drew power away from the manufacturers who set it up and toward its own permanent officials (some of whom had ties to the conservatives as well as to liberals). Another prominent interest-group in the years between 1909 and the War was the so-called *Hansabund*, which sought to defend the interests of modest consumers – shopkeepers, small traders, and white-collar workers in both industry and government – against heavy industrialists and large landowners who supported high tariffs. Other organizations too numerous to consider here grew up alongside these, representing the concerns of professional and occupational groups, regions, or people who shared cultural and leisure activities.[28]

In this way the *Interessenverbände* performed some of the functions exercised by party organs elsewhere, but two closely related things distinguished them from parties. First, they chiefly sought to gain influence not over legislators who had votes in the Reichstag, but over government ministers and officials who held the real reins of power; personal connections and lobbying were the chief means. Second, because the decisions they sought to affect were not reached in a parliamentary way, they did not have to involve themselves in the kinds of trade-offs and compromises that parliamentary life involves. They constituted a kind of second public sphere, both separate from and partly intertwined with the one where parties and the organs of opinion connected with them fostered debate about issues of the day. Like parties, the *Verbände* appealed to theory and ideology in support of the interests they represented, but without any prospect that the clash of principles they staged could have an impact on the form of national political life. Together the two spheres of parties and interest groups embodied the special kind of relationship between state and society Bismarck desired, and in large part established, namely one in which, as Thomas Nipperdey puts it, "the parties were reduced to merely social formations, in order to free the state from the burden of their pressures and thus assure the state's domination over society."[29] German politics did not provide an arena for resolving the struggle between "competing legitimacies" in the manner Maurice Agulhon describes for France; the Empire was constituted precisely so as to exclude the possibility that the independent interplay between various social forces could itself generate the regulating principles of their interaction, preventing any outcome that resembled the triumph of liberal republicanism in the Third Republic. Bismarck's politics were in their way anti-teleocratic, especially by virtue of his willingness to sacrifice traditionally legitimate authority to *Realpolitik*, but the primacy of state over society he sought to guarantee did not allow for the emergence of a political realm with the capacity to regulate itself autonomously. Such state primacy was not itself new; it had long found expression in the attempts by German governments to constitute *bürgerliche Gesellschaft* as an object of governmental action and remake it on this basis. In the conditions of the end of the century, however, the preservation of this relationship, especially in its Prussian version, precluded Germany from drawing the educative benefits from political integration that Gambetta identified for France.

One way to see how this contrast operated is by taking note of a development characteristic of the new historical moment that took form from around 1850, the crystallization of the social formation called the lower middle class – in German the *Kleinbürgertum*, in France the *petite bourgeoisie*, Hans-Ulrich Wehler has described its emergence in Germany with particular clarity and in terms that are at least partially applicable elsewhere. Situating the "birth-hour of the German lower-middle class" in the two decades after 1850, Wehler makes evident how closely its emergence as a distinct category was tied up with other post-1850 phenomena to which we have given emphasis here. Until the mid century the *Bürgertum* of German cities had consisted of a hierarchically ordered array of groups, each enjoying a particular measure of the privileges that conveyed the status of citizens or recognized inhabitants. That some individuals or groups, such as particular guilds, enjoyed greater wealth or honor than others, and were thus "bigger" than their neighbors was evident, but all owed their position to membership in the local and graduated order of *Stände*. The importance that belonging to such an overarching local community bore is evident in the arrangements set up in various cities (the example of Basel has recently been highlighted) which restricted the right of citizens engaged in long-distance trade to sell goods from elsewhere on local markets (outsiders had no such right in any case), thus protecting the position of smaller artisans and retailers from competition by richer and more powerful fellow-townspeople.[30] The power of local communities to define *Bürger* status was challenged by the notion of uniform *Staatsbürgertum* put forward by territorial states, but town life in general continued to revolve around the traditional order based on status differences. The opposition Mack Walker has examined between "hometown" loyalists and "movers and doers" already contained some of the later one, but such a distinction subordinated the contrast between different sorts of burghers to one between traditional ways of organizing town life and external threats to it.

After 1850, however, the simpler duality of "big" and "little" *Bürger* took on increasing salience, in response to three changes: the rapid industrialization encouraged by railroad construction, drawing a limited upper stratum of *Wirtschaftsbürger* into activities whose scale was increasingly out of proportion to those who remained chiefly involved in the local economy; the definitive abolition of guilds, ending the general association of economic life with a locally regulated order of privilege; and the replacement of the old and variegated forms of urban citizenship with a single definition of it provided by the newly unified state. It was in this context that the category of *Kleinbürger* emerged, replacing the differences that had once rested on people's position inside a graded order of privilege with one that reflected a more abstract and quantitative distinction. In actuality the term *Kleinbürgertum* (with which *Mittelstand* was more or less synonymous) referred to a heterogeneous group with many inner divisions, but widely diffused within it (and encouraged by those who sought to appeal to or lead it) was a sense of nostalgia for an older, more locally oriented and morally regulated life that had once been more characteristic of burghers as a whole.[31]

One sign that the distinction between big and little bourgeois owed much to differing degrees of involvement in distant relations is the emphasis observers at the time and since have placed on the orientation of lower-middle-class people toward local life. Friedrich Engels saw the contrast in just these terms when he wrote that "the petit bourgeois represents local interests, the bourgeois universal ones."[32] Recent scholars such as Geoffrey Crossick and Hans-Gerhard Haupt agree: "In most cases, the petit-bourgeois way of life was an introspective and family centered one that concentrated on their immediate world of family and neighborhood. From this came their characteristic suspicion of the outside world and the unknown which turned them against both the bureaucratic state and the forces of banking and high finance."[33] Many small and medium-sized retailers were famously hostile to the department stores that developed during the second half of the century, a phenomenon to which Zola gave sustained attention in *The Ladies' Paradise*. "The economic life of small enterprise remained bound within the perspective of the town itself, however much merchants tied them into wider economic relations," a phenomenon amplified by the propensity of such people to put their savings into buying neighborhood property (rather than bonds or shares), often buildings in which artisans or workers lived. They were thus tied up "with place, personality, and family, in a fashion far less marked amongst the more substantial bourgeoisie ... The material interests of property, credit and production were in this world bound up with moral and social relations that were often immediate and personal in character," and as the orientation of more prosperous bourgeois shifted increasingly toward more distant involvements, "so the local and personal dimensions of the petite bourgeoisie became more distinctive."[34]

This is not the only way in which the new conditions of the second half of the century gave new salience to the divide between upper and lower bourgeois, however. The post-1850 transformation also brought forth a different and more specifically modern kind of lower middle class, typically employed as civil servants or as administrators in large firms, and often referred to in Germany as a *neue Mittelstand*. An expanding lower civil service had been an important source of employment and a vehicle of social mobility for modest middle class families from early in the nineteenth century, but such opportunities expanded markedly after 1850. Private firms such as Siemens and public enterprises such as the Prussian state railway (by 1900, as we saw, the world's largest single employer), both contributed to this development; the numbers of teachers, postal workers, accountants and secretaries, and administrators of insurance and welfare schemes expanded everywhere, doubling in France between 1850 and 1914 (where most were employed by the central government, in contrast to Britain, where local government employees made up a higher proportion of a similarly expanding total), while the proportion of blue-collar to white-collar workers in the overall German economy dropped from over 10 to 1 in 1872 to only 3.5 to 1 in 1912.[35] In his pioneering social history of Friedrich Engels's native city, Barmen, Wolfgang Köllman showed that the percentage of middle-level clerks in private and public employment in the city mushroomed from 2.5 percent to around 11 percent of the population between 1861 and 1907, while the percentage of small and medium-sized entrepreneurs and employers (below the level of large-scale manufacturers and merchants who constituted the narrow elite at the top of the urban pyramid, whose numbers remained stable) more than doubled.[36] By the end of the century, in other words, there were two lower-middle classes, one the descendant of the earlier locally based order and one created by the expansion and thickening of public and private networks and the transformations it brought. There was, however, much coming and going between them, as many children of the first sought careers in the second, despite the aversion to large organizations and bureaucratic ways they or their relatives often voiced.

Like other sections of society the people who made up these groups were drawn into large-scale organizations and the forms of public life they helped to define. In Germany, as Geoff Eley pointed out some time ago, they joined a variety of different kinds of groups, including unions, professional, patriotic, and cultural associations. Some of these were explicitly political, on the left ones organized by socialists who sought to classify white-collar employees as workers and thus potential Party members, and on the right others associated with nationalist and agrarian interests whose anti-modernist and anti-socialist sentiments accorded with either the nostalgia for an earlier time or the sense of imperiled independence numbers of lower bourgeois felt. That both orientations were present is testimony to the falsity of the claim sometimes made that the category was uniformly rightist and anti-modernist, but this view of it does indicate one direction toward which some of its components could and sometimes did lean. Because this potential existed, the actual choices between democratically colored and authoritarian-tinged stances particular *petits bourgeois* or *Kleinbürger* made often depended on the kinds of connections between their immediate situations and national politics available to them, and these were broadly different in France and in Germany. When Gambetta based his strategy for establishing a stable democratic regime in France on a faith in the "republican future" of what he called the *nouvelles couches sociales* (strata that, as noted earlier consisted chiefly of lower bourgeois and *peuple* reshaped by the tighter integration of national life), a major support for his belief was an expectation that a parliamentary regime would provide an ongoing political education to citizens who had known only crisis politics before. Where parties could exercise real power, and defend the interests of their members and voters by way of the cooperation and compromise essential to parliamentary interchange, people whose ambivalence toward modern institutions opened them up to a variety of political appeals could learn to listen to ones that affirmed the value of constitutional self-government; where representative institutions were weak and interests sought protection outside them, people were more likely to be moved by demagogic invocations of some prior, often mythical order. In Germany, as Eley puts it, these choices were shaped "at the points of friction between the political parties and the pressure groups, the real mass organizations of Wilhelmine Germany," and by the time of the War they were already issuing in the kinds of "strident denunciations of parliamentary forms" on which fascist orators would later expand. To be sure such denunciations were part of French politics too, but as Robert Paxton has recently argued, they came into a political system whose institutions and traditions had by then shown their ability to offer many modest people, rural and urban, both protection and some degree of participation; the failure of anti-parliamentary agitation there suggests that "fascist interlopers cannot easily break into a political system that is functioning tolerably well." Much water would flow under many bridges before the situation these words describe would have to be confronted, but the political systems within which the challenges of the 1920s and 1930s would have to be met still bore many marks of the differing relations between state and society within which modern organized politics had emerged in France and Germany half a century before.[37]

Bourgeois politics: national weakness and local strength

In Germany, as elsewhere, the decades that saw the advent of both modern industry and nationally organized parties affected bourgeois in complex ways, bringing many *Bürger* large benefits in the economic realm, but presenting them with difficult challenges in politics. As in England, liberals in Germany experienced the end of the century as a period of crisis and decline, marked by the waning electoral fortunes of the liberal parties. The decline was not total: in terms of sheer numbers support for liberals of various stripes held up pretty well, keeping pace with the country's rapid demographic growth. Between 1874 and

1912 the liberal vote tally grew by 53%, nearly matching the 58% expansion of the population. But the overall number of voters swelled by 135% in the same period, so that the percentage share of liberal supporters contracted sharply. One seemingly positive sign was the breadth of the liberals' appeal: they were the only major political force to enjoy significant support in both urban and rural areas, as well as both large cities and small towns. The Social Democratic vote by contrast came almost wholly from big cities, mirroring in reverse the overwhelming concentration of conservative support in rural areas.[38] Liberal breadth was not necessarily a sign of strength, however, especially in an age when the anxieties generated by rapid social change drew many people toward the organized interest groups who promised more focused strategies of engagement or defense. Electoral statistics suggest that the other face of liberalism's diffuse appeal was unreliability: voters who favored liberals in some elections shifted to the conservatives or socialists in others, according to the issues at stake.[39]

Closely tied up with this weakness were the manifold divisions inside the broad middle classes that constituted liberalism's chief base. In addition to the ambivalent relations between *Bildungsbürger* and *Wirtschaftsbürger*, there were splits between large and small bourgeois, free-traders and protectionists, people attached to competing local interests, as well as the religious divide that made many middle-class Catholics see the liberals as enemies. As time went by some liberals who thought their weakness owed much to these uncertainties recommended that the party reconceive its mission in class terms, becoming explicitly the champion of the *Bürgertum*. The most famous of these was the great sociologist Max Weber, whose frustration with the weakness of his fellow liberals and *Bürger* led him to advocate that they mount a consistent campaign against their class enemies, the big Junker landowners (that Weber did not see the working class as a foe in the same way is an important point to which we will return). Such a course, he hoped, would both cement middle-class unity and weaken the conservative alliance of tariff-prone industrialists and agrarians that helped the government to resist reforms. Weber's proposal had something of the harsh spirit of *Realpolitik* operative in various reaches of German politics, and it made a certain sense, not only in the Marxist perspective on which it was partly modeled, but also because liberalism had become more bourgeois under the Empire, as the leftward shift of workers and the rightward turn of both peasants and

254 / One special path

some sections of the *Kleinbürgertum* left the liberals with a higher proportion of upper-middle-class followers. But such a strategy, however
hard-headed Weber believed it to be, appeared as unrealistic to other
liberals. As one prominent Party figure, Arthur Hobrecht, remarked:

> We are not the representatives of a class or a stratum; it is
> just an oratorical expression, which is perhaps sometimes
> useful, that we are the true representatives of the edu-
> cated *Mittelstand* – I myself have never been able to think
> anything like that. The so-called middle classes are too
> indefinite and diverse a substance on which to build a firm
> foundation, and the German *Bürgertum* is too German to
> be especially unified or concise.

Ernst Basserman had a similar view, seeing the liberals' base as too
varied and socially indefinite for the Party "to take the lead in any
class-based movement."[40] This ambivalent attitude toward class politics gave German liberals a certain common ground with their English
counterparts, but the Germans could not appeal to the trinity of "liberty, Parliament, and progress" that gave Gladstone's party an aura of
operating above mere interest. On the contrary, the German situation
we have outlined was one in which pursuing "interest" sometimes
seemed preferable to operating in the untrustworthy realm of party
politics.

These dilemmas help to account for the attraction German liberals exhibited for strategies that seemed highly practical but worked
out badly for them. One was participation in the *Kulturkampf*, the
high-blown name given to Bismarck's attempt in the early 1870s to
reduce the power of the Catholic Church. Bismarck's reasons for
mounting the campaign were very different from the liberal motives
for cooperating in it: for him it was a way to continue the struggle
against the pro-Austrian forces he had defeated on the battlefield, but
which retained influence inside predominately Catholic states such as
Bavaria; for them it seemed to offer a chance to attack a chief source
of resistance to modernism and progress, while providing a cause
around which to rally and enhancing their position in the new state.
But Bismarck's turn to a new course at the end of the 1870s, allying
himself with conservative forces including some of his former foes in
the south, and putting socialists in the place of Catholics as designated

enemies of the Empire, lowered the curtain on earlier hopes for a regime in which parliamentary life and public debate might become real forces, instead highlighting the very dependency on state power the liberals had hoped to reduce.[41]

A second failed strategy took that dependency as a premise, namely "liberal imperialism." A number of prominent liberals, Max Weber chief among them, gave their support to imperial expansion and competition with France and England (who had been in the game much earlier than Germany), hoping thereby to further liberal goals at home. Struggling against other powers on the wider field of the world, Weber and others believed, would energize the nation, presenting it with a goal above and beyond narrow private interests, and unifying it on behalf of a program that relied on the advance of industry and the powers it brought forth. Some liberal imperialists hoped that the economic benefits of imperial ventures would raise income levels in society as a whole, thus increasing the satisfaction of workers and their involvement in national life, and weakening the appeal of the socialist left. Others, such as Weber's associate Friedrich Naumann, hoped that these results would open the way to social reforms and expand the ability of progressive liberals to cooperate with unions and other worker organizations.[42] It was a heady and unstable mix of visions and hopes, never wholly disentangled from a sometimes desperate sense of liberal and middle-class weakness. The positive role assigned to state power led, not surprisingly, to alliances with forces on the right, as in the short-lived "Bülow Block" of 1907, but the dreams of left-liberals like Naumann that the policy might promote closer relations with the social democrats remained unfulfilled, as visions of national grandeur proved unable to draw many workers away from the socialist fold.

Naumann's hopes that liberal imperialism might help forge ties between progressive bourgeois and workers shines a light on a particularly significant division in middle-class politics, namely the range of opposing attitudes on the "social question." All through the nineteenth century some liberals placed their hopes in the broad (and often vague) category designated as the *Volk*, while others distrusted or feared it, especially as its urban working-class component stood out more. In the early part of the century, liberals such as Hermann Schulze-Delitzsch favored and sponsored cooperative societies and educational associations for workers, and their efforts, as noted earlier, were partly responsible for establishing one of the two organizations that fused to form the Social Democratic Party in 1875. Other liberals, such as Max Hirsch and Lujo Brentano, sought to further union organization. Such stances among liberals preserved earlier notions about the continuity between *Bürger* and *Volk* that had inspired the vision of a broadly inclusive *bürgerliche Gesellschaft* free of sharp social divisions; just for that reason they were vulnerable to being called into question in a period when rapid economic change and recurring crises made class relations tense and febrile. As early as 1849–50 anxiety about worker radicalism led some liberals to draw back from the demands for reform they had voiced in the spring of 1848, even to the extent of preferring a victory by harsh reactionaries.[43] Similar expressions of distance from workers were voiced later by prominent National Liberals, perhaps most bluntly by the Prussian historian Heinrich von Treitschke, who defended social inequality as both necessary and beneficial, and rejected universal suffrage in the 1870s (although he had favored it earlier). It was liberal skeptics critical of social and political intervention aimed at improving the condition of workers who tartly dubbed the largely professorial Social Policy Association "tenured socialists" (*Kathedersozialisten*), and one of them went so far as to deny, in 1872, "that a 'social question' or even a 'housing question' actually exists." The instability of liberal attitudes to social reform measures was heightened in a curious way by Bismarck's decision to sponsor a wide range of social insurance programs in the 1880s. Moderate National Liberals supported these measures, but some to their left who might have been expected to approve them recoiled, weighing their social benefits as less than their potential to justify authoritarianism. Most liberals opposed Bismarck's law outlawing the social democrats when he proposed it in 1878 (the Progressive leader Eugen Richter called it a confession of bankruptcy for *bürgerliche Gesellschaft*), and some continued to condemn it, but in the face of growing socialist strength, many voted in favor when it came up for renewal.[44]

It was in part fear of socialist advances that led liberals throughout the country to persist in defending the unequal voting systems that still survived for many regional and urban assemblies. Unaltered by the constitution that established democratic suffrage for the national *Reichstag*, these arrangements left as much as half the male population (and to be sure all women) disenfranchised in some local elections, giving greater weight to those who paid higher taxes or granting clergy or landowners special status. Bourgeois liberals were able to reject calls to alter these arrangements in many towns and cities because constitutions surviving from earlier eras still gave those in control of the governing councils power over suffrage qualifications; they justified their resistance on the grounds that local communities were concrete associations of taxpayers, not abstract bodies of citizens. Reduced to a minor force in national politics, bourgeois possessed governing authority in many cities.

If their behavior in regard to suffrage questions suggested that urban liberals were moved by a fairly narrow conception of self-interest, however, the ways they used their local power tell a different story. To be sure, there were expedient reasons as well as principled ones for improving town centers, building new streets and sewers, creating municipal waterworks, improving public health and popular education, establishing savings banks, and expanding poor relief. All the same, the energy and resources that liberal mayors and councils in many places devoted to such projects testify to how far their social vision stood from the unstinting allegiance to *laisser-faire* too often attributed to them. Town and city governments sometimes took over management of gasworks and electrical supplies (although there were cases where fears about the cost stood in the way), establishing a kind of municipal socialism similar to what their British counterparts were setting up in the same period. In both places, carrying out such activities involved overcoming the resistance some propertied citizens put up against paying the taxes to finance them. But Dieter Langewiesche sees in the German programs a stronger link to old urban traditions of communal commitment to the common good than in the English ones, a difference rooted in the greater autonomy possessed by many pre-modern German towns (by contrast a place such as Manchester had no independent institutions of government before the nineteenth century). The survival of that independence was not always a blessing to residents, as the example of Hamburg in 1892 shows: alone of cities on the continent the great port suffered a murderous outbreak of cholera in that year, in good part because its ruling circles' insistence on preserving what remained of their independence from nearby Prussia led them to turn their backs on the new discoveries about the disease's causes made in Prussian laboratories.[45] All the same, Langewiesche seems on firm ground in maintaining (and the transformation of

Hamburg's local government during the later 1890s confirms it) that these urban projects give evidence "that the old tradition of the commune as a *bürgerliche* protection society, with authority to limit the free economic movement of individuals for the good of all, had never been wholly displaced by the liberal economic idea of *laissez-faire*." Liberal opposition to government regulation of economic activity on the national plane was compatible with readiness to subordinate market freedom to communal solidarity on the local level when economic transformation put people's well-being in danger. Many liberals appear to have been aware of the duality this introduced into their position, and willing to accept it.[46] In some cities, in addition, close cooperation developed between liberals and social democrats, notably in Munich, where common opposition to clerical conservatives in the Catholic Center Party led at once to electoral alliances and to extensive arrangements for conciliation between employers and workers when disputes broke out.[47]

To some degree the power German bourgeois held in towns and cities made up for the weakness they could not overcome on the national level. But it was a very old kind of *Bürger* power, rooted in the pre-modern past and invested in measures that – for ill or good – preserved something of its character. Whether *fin-de-siècle Bürger* were aware of it or not, the limited degree of political control they were able to exercise was made possible by the Empire's preservation of the old German localism for which its pre-modern predecessor had served as the incubator.

German new liberalism and the problem of hegemony

One prism through which to examine the ways German bourgeois politics at once resembled and differed from its counterparts elsewhere is provided by the liberal left. As in England, so in Germany there appeared a "new liberalism," taking various forms, but in general seeking to reknit its ties to popular and working-class organizations. An early exemplar was the "Young Liberal" faction that surfaced in the Rhineland in 1898, espousing an anti-clerical program and seeking an end to liberal cooperation with the Right, a platform that soon broadened to include suffrage reform (short of full democratization, however) and other planks intended to support cooperation with the social democrats. The growing prominence of reformist and revision-ist currents among the socialists at the same time (Eduard Bernstein's *Evolutionary Socialism* was published in 1898) helped to identify con-tinuities between the two movements. Although never a major force on the national level, the *Jungliberalen* did establish a network of more than sixty local organizations, with around 10,000 members. When the "Bulow Block" joining liberals to conservatives collapsed in 1908–09, the new vitality of the liberal left helped to nurture hopes that a "Grand Block" of liberals and social democrats might replace it, dubbed by Weber's friend Naumann "from Basserman [the National Liberal leader] to Bebel [the Social Democrat]." Only in the tradition-ally liberal state of Baden (where it had actually begun some years earlier, putting through reforms of taxation and education) did this formation acquire any concrete importance, but the vision that inspired it also found expression in Naumann's persisting and well-publicized attempts to create ties with the Socialists, whom he regarded as "the proletarian wing of liberalism."

A similar spirit animated the left liberal *Nationalverein für das liberale Deutschland*, whose founding statement in 1907 declared that "being liberal means recognizing the right to economic organization, the full freedom of association for members of both sexes, and the equality of employees and employers," and called for "the extension of social legislation and its expansion to include fur-ther circles of the population." A pamphlet issued by the same group in 1910, with the title "What is Liberal?" insisted that the term could not be applied to existing German society because wealth was distributed in such a way that "two-thirds to three-fourths of the German population" had too little income either to satisfy basic needs or to sustain personal and moral development. All the same, the hopes for closer relations between liberals and socialists (them-selves deeply embroiled in debates about their relations to liberal ideas and practices) were stymied by various obstacles, notably the continuing rejection by most liberals of a fully democratic suf-frage in city and regional elections, and a suspicion of middle-class attempts to gain influence over workers on the part of working-class activists.[48]

Both the rhetoric and the dilemmas of German new liberalism point to the ground it shared with its British counterpart, but only the latter was able to make a significant impact on government policy before the War. German new liberals never had a chance to give direction to a major party, much less to make their ideas the basis for significant reforms of the kind Lloyd George and Asquith enacted in 1909. This did not mean that Germany lagged behind England in social policy; on the contrary one of the important models for the "People's Budget" lay in Bismarck's social insurance programs of the 1880s. That these measures came from an autocratic government in the German case and from organized social forces in the English one speaks volumes about the persisting power of longstanding differences: we saw earlier that a similar contrast was already visible in the two countries' social and political styles in the eighteenth century.[49]

The contrasting fates of the new liberalism in England and Germany, and the ways they reflect larger similarities and differences in the two countries' histories, highlight some of the central issues in the reinterpretation of the relations between modernity and bourgeois life we are pursuing here. Germany was the exemplary case of the rapid and transformative economic restructuring that came to Europe as a whole in the half-century before 1914. The shift in the relative positions of *Bildungsbürger* and *Wirtschaftsbürger* that accompanied it was one expression of this change; another was the legal reform embodied in a new civil code (the *bürgerliches Gesetzbuch*) at the end of the 1890s, and which established uniform provisions in regard to contracts, inheritance, and family relations in the Reich as a whole. It was a self-consciously modern measure, removing some traditional distinctions between landed property and other kinds, and reinforcing the right of individuals to own and dispose of their possessions; overall the new lawbook breathed a spirit that various commentators have described as individualistic and bourgeois.[50] Despite the striking and rapid nature of the country's transformation, however, Germany remained the place where bourgeois political power was weakest, unable to find even the limited effectiveness on a national scale it achieved in England (where the Liberal Party was losing its footing by 1914) or France (where persisting divisions of all kinds inside the bourgeoisie helped keep the regime from developing a stable tenor, setting the stage for anti-republican forces to gain prominence in the Boulanger crisis and the Dreyfus Affair).

Historians still loyal to traditional stories that put the rise of classes and their struggles for predominance at the center of historical development have regarded this configuration as a puzzle. Of the various ways they have sought to solve it one has relied on the notion of "hegemony" elaborated by the Italian Marxist theorist Antonio Gramsci. As Eric Hobsbawm put it, "the bourgeoisie was evidently not a ruling class in the sense in which the old-style landowner was, whose position gave him, *de jure* or *de facto*, the effective state power over the inhabitants of his territory"; instead a bourgeois had to operate "within a functioning framework of state power and administration which was not his own." What gave the bourgeoisie its grip on society all the same was hegemony, a subtle and indirect mode of domination rooted in control over many everyday interactions and organs of opinion, the arenas of civil society in which values, attitudes, and expectations are formed; by this means a class that did not rule directly was able to shape people's thinking and action by infusing them with a particular sense of how the world worked and how best to operate within it. Thus nineteenth-century bourgeois were able to attach leading strings to their various class enemies, in particular turning workers toward the parliamentary activity that gave them a false sense of power inside a social frame still bourgeois. (Gramsci hoped to see this deception dissipated as workers and activists developed the implications of Lenin's return to *The Communist Manifesto*'s original revolutionary vision, on which basis they would create their own hegemonic culture.)[51]

A somewhat different solution to the puzzle of how bourgeois forms of life were able to triumph in the absence of effective political power has been proposed by Geoff Eley and David Blackbourn, who argue (in a no-longer recent but still-influential book) that the Bismarckian regime provided for an unusual but effective triumph of bourgeois interests and values. They arrive at this conclusion by a complex, even tortuous argument. First, given that only France offers an example of what might be considered a revolutionary transfer of power from aristocracy to bourgeoisie, they purport to abandon the search for historical patterns operative everywhere in favor of an approach that considers each national story in its own terms: the kind of direct transfer of power supposed to have taken place in the French Revolution may have been possible and historically fitting nowhere else. Despite this, the two historians have no doubt that successive historical formations are all regimes of class power, and that every national story needs to be told in terms of it. Therefore they conclude that, since the Second Reich provided "the conditions of bourgeois predominance in society," that is, a ground on which both capitalism and the civil order of *bürgerliche Gesellschaft* could develop, the Bismarckian state should be regarded as a special kind of vehicle for bourgeois ascendency, "Germany's distinctive form of the bourgeois revolution."[52]

Although this account differs somewhat from the Gramscian one, the reasons for rejecting both are closely related. It may well be the case that in some general sense bourgeois culture exercises influence, even of a regrettable kind, over what people outside the middle classes think and do, but what makes this influence deserve the name of hegemony in Gramsci's sense can only be that it impedes the effective expression of the different and higher stage of consciousness and social being that it was the destiny of the working class to usher in. However attractive it may seem, such a reading suffers from a circular logic: only if the future form of life it theorizes can be shown to be gestating inside the world that keeps it from being born can the notion that it suffers repression make sense, but until that future arrives we have no ground for knowing it to be real. Believing it to be so requires a leap of faith that seemed reasonable to many people in the years following the Russian Revolution, and again in the 1960s, but it is bound to appear much less so in the aftermath of 1989–91, not to mention 2001. The Great Recession that began in 2007 has not revived it, despite the new doubts about capitalism's stability and future it has generated. Eley and Blackbourn put themselves at a certain distance from Gramsci, but they base their thinking on a similar belief in the progression of historical stages that brings successive social classes to power; otherwise they would not vitiate their own claim to recognize that no single historical path can be found in every country by attributing some particular "form of the bourgeois revolution" to each national story.

In the German case there are many reasons to reject the notion that the Bismarckian state should be seen as a vehicle of bourgeois power. Not only does such a view put out of account Bismarck's own sense that his whole political project revolved around an effort – highly successful in all the ways we have seen – to curb whatever power bourgeois liberals had, it ignores the special kind of relationship between state and society the Bismarckian constitution established, and that was rooted in the earlier history of relations between

German rulers and *bürgerliche Gesellschaft*. David Blackbourn himself recognizes this in a later writing. Taking note of the changes in tariff policy Bismarck used as part of his rightward shift at the end of the 1870s, he acknowledges that the Prussian Chancellor did not become the tool of the big industrialists who demanded protection for their goods: in order to safeguard consumers the tariffs were set lower than the representatives of heavy industry wished, and "any special privileges enjoyed by heavy industry have to be set against the larger context of government support for the industrial economy as a whole. This was the old idea of the state as representative of the 'general interest,' now cast in a more modern idiom. State and bureaucracy aimed to stand above and harmonize the conflicting interests, not to make concessions to any one group that would jeopardize that goal."[53] The creation of standardized law codes that extended uniform citizenship rights and protected property had long been part of this project.

In the perspective proposed here the questions to which "hegemony" and "national modalities of bourgeois revolution" are answers simply do not arise. We never need to ask how it comes about that bourgeois gain power under modern conditions, because both the power they possess and the limits to which it remains subject are inherent in the development of modernity from the start. Modernity unfolds as networks of means grow more extensive and thicker, drawing everyday social relations into distant connections and generating new forms of power, economic, political, and cultural; these alter life for society as a whole but they are distributed among individuals and groups in accord with their various capacities for directing or drawing on the resources that flow within them. As participants in such networks bourgeois of many stripes enjoy advantages over other categories of people, because their occupations – business, public administration, developing and diffusing knowledge and skills that are based on it – involve participation in networks more or less extended in space that provide experience of the mediations social action increasingly requires. If "hegemony" means the spread of values and attitudes originally identified with the middle classes to others, it has one main root in this overall fit between bourgeois life and modernity. But the actual effect of this correspondence differs according to the nature of particular networks and their degree of development, as the special benefits workers' associations derived from late nineteenth-century party organization testify. The same spreading involvement of society as a whole in distant relations that gave rise to new sources of bourgeois power simultaneously provided those who were not bourgeois with materials and energies to contest and limit it.

Part II

Calculations and lifeworlds

8 TIME, MONEY, CAPITAL

Time and money form a dyad often invoked in connection with both bourgeois life and modernity. To be sure, neither belongs exclusively to any social formation or historical moment, taking on different forms and playing different roles in particular periods and places. We will see in this chapter that ways of measuring time and the forms taken on by money both developed in tandem with other topics being considered there, taking a marked and significant turn after the middle of the nineteenth century as a consequence of the deepening impact of distant relations in practically every realm of life. In order to make the importance of this turning still clearer the current chapter looks at parallels between money's history and that of banking and finance, and concludes by considering the historical trajectory that has been attributed to one particular form of money, the one Marx sought to analyze in *Capital*.

Widening webs and the ordering of time

Whether it merits being called "natural" or not, the way of measuring time in Europe before the later Middle Ages (and in most other parts of the world) was less abstract than the one we know today, since it allowed the length of hours to fluctuate in accord with the longer or shorter period of daylight between sunrise and sunset. On sundials, for instance, each hour represented a given proportion of the total (a tenth or twelfth in most cases) regardless of the season. By contrast, modern "clock time" establishes days and hours of constant length, all divided into standard minutes and seconds, maintaining these regularities regardless of variations in daylight. Until fairly recently a number of historians attributed the turn to the more modern way of reckoning hours to merchants, concerned to use their own time and that of their employees in a disciplined and efficient way, in contrast to rural people whose lives were regulated by seasonal changes, and the Church, whose schedule of prayers and rituals made reference to the rhythms of the solar day. But closer attention, notably by the German historian Gerhard Dohrn-van Rossum, has revealed a different pattern.

Among the first seekers of mechanisms that could measure hours and minutes of equal length were astronomers and astrologers, wishing to calculate the movements of stars and planets; but technical advances were tied more closely with the use of clocks that could strike bells in monasteries and churches. Religious orders employed these at least from the thirteenth century as wake-up calls, sending monks to work and prayer on a schedule not governed by the vagaries of the sun; it was here that escapement mechanisms were devised that, by dint of much trial and error, allowed for more regular measurement of time itself. Churches found such improvements attractive not for precision's sake, but because mechanical clocks that could be counted on to perform some action on a regular schedule could become a vehicle for announcing services and attracting worshipers. Set up in towers, the clocks controlled complex displays: at stated hours a procession of figures, monks or the three Magi or the Virgin Mary and saints, would emerge and traverse some visible space, sometimes accompanied by animals and noises, or by skeletons as a *memento mori*. (Similar shows are recorded in classical sources, and they were produced, mostly using water-clocks, in the Islamic world as well.) Such extravaganzas were used, as officials acknowledged, "to lure people into church, to astound them, and thus to strengthen the authority of the Church." Some of them can still be seen in various towns and cities today.[1]

Set-ups of this sort spread rapidly from place to place beginning in the mid fourteenth century, especially in cities. Merchants as such, however, played no special role in diffusing them, nor did the Church or princely governments resist it. Prestige and a fascination for technical wonders often provided reasons for investing in such mechanisms, but the chief motive for regularizing the hour seems to have been administrative efficiency, and in particular the need to coordinate activities. Territorial rulers promoted the use of clocks in various parts of their domains for a variety of festive, admonitory, or practical reasons, for instance to designate the specific hour at which some event had occurred – a crime, a birth, a contract – or was to take place. Administrative ambitions, whether realized or not, were evident in the purpose announced for the still visible Paris Palace Clock (Horloge du Palais) not far from Notre Dame, in a fourteenth-century document: "to promote the orderly running of the court [*parlamenti curia*] and the orderly life of the citizens." Eighteenth-century German cameralist writers similarly declared that the accurate "division of time" was a way to coordinate "the great variety of businesses and the ordering of work and leisure." Independent towns seem to have regarded clocks as instruments for encouraging councils and administrators to deal efficiently with the increasing quantity and range of matters they had to take up as population grew. None of these arrangements, however, either required or created pressure for places at a distance from each other to coordinate their chronometiric practices with others. Sundials remained in common use and many people still thought of the division of the day into parts as referring to the period of sunlight.[2]

What brought this complex state of affairs with its many local variations to a definitive end was the post-1850 transformation of transport and communication, which rapidly created a need to coordinate time measurement for people in widely dispersed locations; it had long been understood that mechanical clocks could provide this synchronicity, but only rail travel overcame the resistance of custom and local independence. In order for people to plan journeys involving connections between lines, operators and travelers in separate locations had to be able to know the time at every place in the system. Some kind of universal reference point provided the obvious solution, and as early as 1847 the time at the royal observatory in Greenwich (Greenwich Mean Time, formerly used chiefly as an aid in marine navigation) was adopted by all the railway companies in Great Britain, creating a standard "railroad time." People who were not traveling did not need to use it, however, and local times were maintained (often at the insistence of town or village residents) for other purposes for some decades afterwards. Only in 1880, as the extension of the railroad network to many localities unconnected to it before brought the decline in the industrial and cultural regionalisms whose mid nineteenth-century importance was noted in Chapter 5, did GMT became the official time throughout Britain. By then a similar system had already been adopted in the United States (in 1874), followed by France in 1891 (which first declared Paris time to be universal throughout the country, adopting GMT as a reference point only in 1911), and by Germany in 1893 (where the Greenwich meridian was used as a benchmark right away). Only with these developments did hours become of equal length everywhere and throughout the year, putting an end to the practice of having the length of hours and the time at particular locations vary with the duration of daylight and thus with season and longitude.

This is not quite the whole story, however, and filling it in highlights the important point that it was the rising importance of distant connections, not technology as such, that belongs at its center. Well before the advent of railroads the expansion of government postal services led a number of states to impose the partial adoption of standard times in their territories. The Habsburgs, famous for their success in accumulating territories by marriage and other alliances, became pioneers in setting up rapid and centrally administered courier services from late in the sixteenth century. The system was intended to meet the needs of government and administration; what led officials to make the couriers available for private communications was the recognition that payments made by merchants could help to finance the operation. It was rulers and their aides who valued and sought ever-more rapid communication, since decisions were awaited on important matters (especially having to do with warfare) from a prince or other official who might be traveling between territories; by contrast the chief concern of early modern merchants seems to have been with reliability rather than speed, since most goods could not move quickly anyway. Sending official messages at a faster pace was the chief motive for instituting the system of "stages" or "posts," in order to overcome the effects of fatigue on horses. As linkages between different routes became important (their numbers augmented by agreements between governments), it became still more imperative to maintain predictable schedules, since missing a connection might delay delivery until the next departure days or a week later. Such concerns mounted during the eighteenth century, as governments sought to establish greater unity in their territories and eliminate internal barriers to trade and movement; both Enlightenment culture and the emergence of "public opinion" owed much to these efforts (in which governments still remained central, as we have seen), as did the culture of letter writing (to which we will come later).

All these developments created pressures to coordinate time-measurements at diverse places along postal routes; governments did not demand that towns or cities give up their local divisions of the day, but some insisted that they establish at least one clock, usually at the post office, set to a standard time for the whole system (a goal aided by the spread of pendulum drives that greatly increased accuracy), so as to assure the least delay between couriers. By early in the nineteenth century the Prussian state was insisting that church-tower clocks be set to this standard as well. Given the depth of the transformation brought by train travel, Dohrn-van Rossum may be too quick to conclude from this that, "Already before the beginning of the age of the railroad, the 'time of transport' had rendered the 'time of the cities' obsolete." Here as in the other topics we will consider in this chapter, things took on a recognizably "modern" shape only in the last decades of the nineteenth century. But even the possibility of such a conclusion highlights the point that involvement in distant connections was at least as important in bringing about the modern transformation of time measurement as were new forms of technology as such.[3]

Money and the social order: from private to public

Whatever else bourgeois life is about, it is surely about money, even if not solely in the ways most people ordinarily suppose. Our approach in this book takes Simmel's analysis of money and the social relations it fosters as its starting point, but so far we have had little to say about money itself. And yet the history of money has much to tell us about the modernity that was taking shape during the nineteenth century. Simmel himself provides a revealing point from which to approach this history. In its developed modern form, he maintained, money is a public institution: the claims it makes on us, and we on it, derive from our shared position as members of a given social and political order. The assurance that money can always be exchanged for some other good of equal value is an implicit promise made to each individual by the whole community of people who accept and use a certain currency, so that every monetary transaction between individuals ties them to the community as a whole. The confidence people place in money is an expression of a more fundamental trust in the social order as an integrated entity, in its ability to sustain and regulate the relations with others through which we fulfill our needs and desires. Seen in this light, money is not just an instrument of exchange, but a form of socialization, "one of those relations whose presence transforms a sum of individuals into a social group, because 'society' is identical with the sum of those relations." If having money gives us a sense of personal safety, the reason is not just that in it we possess something of "hard" value, but because our confidence in it is also a trust in the social order that sustains us as individuals. Conversely, fear that our money may not retain its value is anxiety about the continuing stability of that order; at moments of economic crisis (the Great Recession that began in 2007 is fresh in memory at this writing) even people whose own economic position may not be directly affected often experience anxiety and fear. These alternatives, together with the inequalities of wealth that money relations highlight, generate dissatisfaction and hostility toward money alongside this trust, but the latter feelings are further testimony to the involvement of all individuals in the social whole that money relations sustain. It is for these reasons that modern people have come to expect that money will be established and regulated by the state: "Money is less truly money to the degree that it is not guaranteed by the highest sociological sphere, in practice by its central organ."[4]

Although Simmel's characterization of money as a form of sociability may seem surprising, given the anti-social power it can clearly possess (and of which he was acutely aware), his association between money and public authority is likely to appear obvious or commonsensical to people whose experience of money has been formed in the West since late in the nineteenth century. But money has not always possessed such a clear public character; not only has its value often rested on something more concrete, it has also been guaranteed in more private ways. Taking this into account brings us back to a point made in Chapter 1 about the media that regulate access to networks of means, namely that they are at once abstract and concrete, and that money is the paradigmatic examplar of this duality. Today we accept both paper notes, which are mere promises by some authority to guarantee their value, and metallic coins, survivals from an era when most or all money took the form of some actual material good. The paper currency is abstract money (although it too must take a concrete form), the metallic coins are concrete (although they too represent abstract values), containing a quantity of (say) gold, silver, or copper taken to be more or less equivalent to the value stamped on them. There is no need here to recount the long history of other materials that have served as money, animal, vegetable, and mineral, but it is necessary to recognize that such money forms need not (although they sometimes do) have the public character Simmel remarked. Private ones have often served where no such public authority could guarantee them, as well as in situations where people have lacked the confidence in government, and even in society as a whole, that Simmel saw as essential. In such situations, people have preferred to rely on material objects of value, or on persons they take to be more trustworthy than officials and rulers.

Such preferences have been very common historically, and they persisted well into the age usually considered modern. Medieval coinages, bearing the likeness or seal of some king or prince who authorized them, were public in a sense, since it was expected that they would be accepted throughout some territory, and the right to coin money was quickly established as a prerogative of sovereignty. But pre-modern rulers were never so clearly public persons as modern ones are expected to be; heredity bound princely authority to the body, and even to its most "private" parts, royal governments evolved out of arrangements to manage the king's household, and our very word "state" developed from the phrase *status regis*, the king's personal status or condition (a confusion of what we think of as public and private spheres that is still preserved in the French usage of the word *état* to mean both a political entity and an occupation). Whether medieval or early modern people trusted a particular coinage or not depended very much on what they knew about the personal qualities of a given ruler, since they were well aware that governments could enrich themselves by debasing coins with cheaper metals, thus increasing the amount of money in circulation and appropriating the increment to themselves. In addition, coins could be and often were counterfeited or clipped by people willing to risk prosecution, and the many uncertainties about them meant that they commonly circulated below their stated value.

The private character of paper money was even more marked, albeit for different reasons. Before the mid nineteenth century, most paper currency took the form of either bills or banknotes. Bills could be of various kinds, but all of them involved a claim for payment;

people quickly realized that if the obligation a bill declared could be put off for some period of time, then it could be transferred from the original creditor to some other individual who would accept it, and who could pass it on in turn. Annotated in accepted ways (with marks or signatures), bills could be used to pay debts or make loans; they thus functioned as money, although they often circulated at a discount. One particular kind of bill came to have special importance as currency, namely the "bill of exchange." Such bills took the form of requests or orders issued by some person and addressed to a second one, to pay a certain amount to a third (a situation better named by the French term *"lettre d'échange"*); they were rather like modern checks, save that they were drawn by one individual on another rather than on a bank. Like modern checks, however, they often rested on some kind of actual or assumed pre-existing obligation to the writer on the part of the person to whom they were addressed, and they were commonly accepted by people who knew, or thought they knew (or were willing to take a chance) that the person on whom they were drawn was likely to honor the request. Eventually, however, the responsibility to pay came back to the person who issued the bill (by requesting the second party to pay it), except that if a bill of exchange was "accepted" (rather than merely "noted") by the person on whom it was drawn, in recognition of some liability to the person who drew it up (as between regular trading partners), then the responsibility passed to him or her. Bills of exchange seem first to have arisen in international trade sometime late in the fourteenth century, but came to be employed at closer range later on. They could be used as financial instruments for a wide variety of purposes, as payment for goods, as means for transferring credit or settling debts, and, since they were drawn up so that payment was due on a certain date, as loans (with interest open or hidden). Their actual value in circulation varied widely (we will see some examples of this below), depending on what a person to whom they were offered knew about the original issuer and or the endorser, and how soon the bill fell due and could be presented for payment.

Banknotes worked similarly. They were receipts for deposits (whether of specie or some other value accepted by the bank), and could also be passed from one person to another, sometimes requiring a personal endorsement, sometimes simply payable to the bearer. Their value fluctuated too, especially since many were issued by very small banks about whose condition the people to whom they were offered might know very little, especially outside the locales where they originated.

Compared to the money used in developed countries today these practices are likely to seem confusingly complex. They were also ingenious, however, and it is hardly surprising that something like them grew up in situations where most transactions were local, and where few authorities could be trusted even to guarantee the value of a currency inside a narrow territory, much less be able to vouch for it at a distance. The actual values of notes and bills, as opposed to their nominal ones, reflected some knowledge, or lack of knowledge, about the issuers, who were almost always private persons or entities. As money, they were far from what Simmel would later theorize as its true form. There were no national banks even of a quasi-public character able to issue notes before the late seventeenth century (a Swedish bank may have been the first to do so, around 1660, but it soon abandoned the practice; the Massachusetts Bay Colony was also a pioneer issuer of public money, and we will come to the Bank of England in a moment); even after such institutions began to function, the notes they provided were usually issued either in irregular amounts, reflecting the value of deposits, or in sums too large to be usable for everyday transactions. Moreover, it took much time before such currency effectively replaced the traditional kinds issued by some known nearby entity, or based on some personal relationship. This can be illustrated in the histories of the three countries we are focusing on here, albeit in somewhat different ways.

England was the country where paper money assumed a regular public or at least quasi-public character earliest, a development closely tied up with the establishment of Parliamentary control over state finances. Before 1688 the two chief forms of money were the royal coinage and notes issued by private banks, especially those operated by London goldsmiths, who gave out the paper in return for deposits, and used the resources they gained to make profitable loans to the king. This system collapsed in the 1670s when the Stuarts defaulted on their debt (the "Stop of the Exchequer"), ruining many goldsmith bankers and undermining confidence in their notes. The Bank of England, established in 1694, provided a different and in the end famously successful new system of government finance, whereby private investors could own shares in a permanently funded national debt, its use and administration overseen by Parliament. We have already taken note of the important role the Bank played in giving England a solid fiscal system, in stark contrast to the French one; we will come in a moment to its role as a lender. From the start, however, it was also a creator of money, issuing its first notes in the year it was founded. These were able to command much greater confidence than the gold-smiths' paper so sorely tried twenty years earlier, but they were far from being a national currency. Their quasi-public character was sig-naled by Parliament's setting the death penalty for counterfeiting them (which gave them a status akin to the royal coinage), but they were not legal tender, that is no one was required to accept them as payment for debts, and many other banks (mostly small and private, since restric-tions were placed on the creation of other joint-stock banks) continued to issue notes that also served as money. Bills of all kinds functioned as currency too, and as economic activity expanded in the eighteenth century so did the quantity of paper money in circulation, surpassing the quantity of specie for the first time.[5]

The resulting situation was both ridden with problems and chaotic, however. Bank of England notes, issued on partly printed paper that left details to be completed by a clerk, were often for odd amounts, although by the mid eighteenth century regular denomina-tions as low as £20 (still a large sum at the time) were available. By the end of the 1700s valuations as low as £1 were in circulation. But the notes were treated with considerable suspicion by many people, partly from memories of the South Sea Bubble crisis that reached its high point in 1720 (when a private company sought to take over a large part of the national debt from the Bank, causing a flurry of speculation and a sharp rise in its shares, followed by a disastrous collapse), and partly because extra borrowing in wartime led to inflation and a fall in the notes' values. Radical critics in search of remedies for poverty often focused on the country's financial system as especially damaging to the poor, and decried paper money as a tool of speculation and cor-ruption. These attitudes helped to preserve a preference for both local currency and metallic coins.

Neither served very well however. Coins were in short supply, especially as business expanded; one expedient to which people turned was private coinage, which (modern readers may be surprised to learn) was not illegal so long as it did not copy the designs of the official mint. Both James Watt's partner Matthew Boulton and John Wilkinson (the eighteenth-century "iron king") issued coins with their own symbols stamped on them. Some manufacturers (most of whom bought raw materials and sold products largely by way of bills of exchange) had no coin or paper currency with which to pay their workers; at least one went into retail trade in order to acquire money for this purpose, and others set up "truck" systems because they made it possible to pay workers in "shop notes" when no other form of money was available (the abuses of the "truck" system have often been noted, but recent writers suggest it was partly justified by the shortage of currency). As one historian concluded: "So many manufacturers were forced to adopt such measures that the first decade of the nineteenth century witnessed the heyday of the private token coin. When this stage was reached the government had almost completely lost control over the metallic currency of the Kingdom."[6]

Its control over paper currency was not much better, weakened in part by the preference people retained, particularly in some regions, for non-governmental issues. Notes from local banks appealed to many because their issuers were known to nearby people; many of these were also active as merchants or lawyers, and most were untainted by speculation in national funds or war finance. But such currency was often subject to being discounted outside the place where it was issued (as was true of private coinages). In addition, as long as Bank of England notes were not officially designated as legal tender, leaving people free to refuse them as payment, local banks faced with difficulty of some kind were moved to exchange the ones they held for gold, thus drawing reserves from the Bank, and putting downward pressure on the value of its paper.

Persisting economic difficulties in the 1820s and 1830s produced much public discussion of these problems, and a growing desire for a more stable and predictable currency. The result was, as one recent historian of money notes, to move dominant sectors of the public to agree that banknotes had to be recognized as "real money" in the same way as specie, and that some central authority had to take responsibility for their stability. Parliament undertook to do this in a series of acts. When the Bank's charter was renewed in 1833 its notes were declared to be legal tender throughout England and Wales (Scotland had its own Bank), ending the motive for local banks to drain away its reserves in a crisis. A comprehensive banking act in 1844 stabilized the value of the Bank's notes by establishing a "gold standard": the volume of paper money allowed to circulate was set in proportion to the reserves of gold bullion and government securities held by the Bank. The same act also set strict limits on the power of other banks within 65 miles of London to issue circulating notes, thus giving the Bank major control over paper currency. At the same time the Bank was now charged with adjusting the amount of money in circulation by raising or lowering the rate at which it would discount bills, thus contracting or expanding the supply. By later in the century it would use this power to set interest rates and stabilize the value of the pound in international trade. In the terms of contemporary debate, this marked the triumph of the "banking school" over the "currency school," since representatives of the latter had argued that banks should not attempt to control the circulation of money, on the grounds that currency was created by the transactions that engendered notes and bills, making the money supply grow or contract in response to business conditions themselves. In Simmel's terms to which we referred earlier, the victory of the "banking school" marked the point at which the monetary system came to rest on an understanding that money in a developed commercial society involved not just relations between private individuals, but their common relation to society as a whole: money was recognized as essentially a public and social function, its stability guaranteed by the state.[7]

One writer who drew the consequences of this step a bit later was the noted political commentator Walter Bagehot, in his book *Lombard Street* (the name given to the London money market) of 1873. Bagehot argued against the still widely held notion that the Bank ought to hold tightly to its monetary reserve in times of economic difficulty, lest the country's store of real wealth (the gold) be swallowed up in some whirlpool of commercial turbulence. The real wealth of the country was not in the Bank's vaults, Bagehot insisted, but in the exchanges that produced goods and services on a national level. The Bank's central function was to foster these in good times and bad; in moments when slowdowns in economic activity threatened valuable enterprises with collapse this meant making sure that funds were available to tide them over. Far from tightening credit at such moments, it should be eased, so that worthy but squeezed business people could borrow and thus survive. Even though a national bank looks like "a kind of ultimate treasury, where the last shilling of the country is deposited and kept," so that to lend it at moments of danger seemed palpably wrong, in fact this "ultimate banking reserve

... is not kept out of show, but for certain essential purposes, and one of those purposes is the meeting of a demand for cash caused by an alarm within the country." Bagehot did not quite say so, but his point was that an older idea of money tied up with its association with specie made people imagine the nation on the model of a private person who needed to hold on to his or her inheritance in order to survive, whereas what made money a source of wealth in a modern economy was its ability to serve as the medium by which commercial exchanges between large numbers of anonymous people take place. Bagehot saw the need to revise people's understanding of money as exactly parallel to the way he urged them to think differently about the state. In his more famous treatise on *The English Constitution* of 1867 he urged the public to look on state action not as "an imposed tyranny from without," but as "our own action ... as the consummated result of our own organised wishes."[8] Similarly, the Bank's role in a crisis was to serve as an organized support for the nation as a community of economic interaction.

In practice, however, private bills of exchange remained an important form of currency, and in fact a growing one in England until around 1880, and in some respects for considerably longer. London's importance as a money market rested on the presence there of many firms that specialized in raising funds, settling debts and transferring money through discounting bills of exchange. Their operations stretched around the world, and in international commerce their importance lasted well into the twentieth century (in different forms it still survives today). Domestically, however, their role (and with it that of the bills they issued) receded beginning in the mid 1860s, following the egregious collapse of some major houses (notably the firm of Overend and Gurney) during the commercial crisis of 1866 (an event that also resulted in restricting the supply of capital for British industry, as noted above). The eventual decline in the use of bills of exchange had other causes as well, ones tied up with the large-scale developments in economic and social relations ushered in by the completion of the railroad network. The faster transport and communication gave merchants quicker access to both materials and customers, allowing them to expand production and fill orders more quickly when demand rose, thus eliminating the need to keep large stocks of unsold goods in reserve to meet fluctuations in the market. Bills of exchange provided much of the credit required to keep up these inventories; as the pressure to maintain them declined, so did the need for the bills. At the same time the centralization of banking, with major London houses establishing regional branches, made it easier to use checks for payment, and bank finance, usually in the form of overdrafts, for credit. In this way banking operations, regulated centrally as part of the recognition of the public nature of money, increasingly replaced the privately generated currency of bills.[9] The move to the conception of money as a public function was part of the continuing transformation by which distant and abstractly mediated kinds of relations entered into people's lives at points where local and personal ones had predominated before.

Similar movements from private to public forms of money took place in France and Germany. In eighteenth-century France when people spoke about a sufficient or insufficient supply of money to effect commercial transactions, they often had in mind the quantity of bills of exchange available to be used for payment. Other forms of currency were often in very short supply.[10] The importance of such bills had not diminished by the middle of the nineteenth century, as Balzac testified in his great novel *Lost Illusions*. There he gave the still common use of bills in the publishing industry a prominent role in the final stages of Lucien Chardon's fall from the glittering heights he seemed to have achieved in Paris. "Then, as today [Balzac was writing around 1840 about a story set some two decades earlier], works were bought from authors in bills drawn to fall due in six, nine or twelve months' time – a payment based on the nature of the sale which publishers settle among themselves by means of even longer-termed values. The publishers paid the paper-manufacturers and the printers in the same currency." These practices allowed publishers (whose ways Balzac knew well, having been one himself) to operate speculatively and without having to assemble much capital of their own, or to subject their operations to oversight by banks concerned about the solvency of borrowers. In the story, Lucien (who had made a name for himself in journalism) receives the 5,000 franc payment for his historical novel in bills drawn up by the two partners who agree to publish it. When he and a friend run around Paris trying to exchange them for specie, however, they discover that their face value cannot be realized. The first broker to whom they turn offers them 3,000 francs, a hefty discount, but he is willing to go even that high only because he knows that the partners who issued the bills have debts they need to cover quickly, so that he will be able to pressure them into taking the bills back at their face value in exchange for the rights to two recently issued books with good future prospects but slow current sales. Hurt and believing he can do better (but knowing that the offer will not be renewed), Lucien refuses. A second broker at first says he will take the bills for 1,500 francs, but closely examining the dates (and knowing that Lucien himself has fallen into debt), he too makes the proposal conditional on the publisher giving him rights over the sale of some promising books. In the end nobody will take the bills, Lucien having rejected the proposal of letting his actor mistress ask a former lover who is a rich businessmen to exchange them for cash, knowing what the merchant would want from Coralie in return. Many things are bought with coin in Balzac's Paris, to be sure, but on the scale where well-off people live, cash appears as a privilege of those wealthy enough to stash it away. Without quite saying that discounted notes and bills cannot fulfill the function people expect money to serve because no public authority has found a way to guarantee their value, Balzac pictures this "money" as subject to the same kinds of corrupt manipulation as are – in his perhaps exaggeratedly jaundiced view – ideals, reputations, political principles, and personal destinies.[11]

Minus the novelistic coloration and the moral condemnation, the world of money and credit in Paris bears many of the same features in Jeanne Gaillard's illuminating account of the city in the Second Empire. Although checks and notes of the *Banque de France* (to which we will come in a moment) were available in principle, Paris business people seem to have made little use of them through the 1850s. Most transactions were settled with commercial notes or bills of exchange, and banks, usually reluctant to lend to firms, mostly confined themselves to giving credit in exchange for discounting these forms of currency. Evidence from other parts of the country testifies to the continuing predominance of the same practices there. Even in the midst of the big real estate speculations of the Haussmann years, Gaillard uncovers an "artisanal mentality" in credit matters, corresponding to the still "artisanal structure of Paris business." A number of banks operated almost as societies of mutual credit, preferring to endorse chiefly the notes and bills of their own shareholders. And because most people paid their suppliers with post-dated notes that the latter then used to pay their own debts, the predominance of these instruments as currency created a chain-like structure that threatened all the links

with collapse when one of them broke. After 1860, as the city's economy began to be more integrated into more distant relations, new credit
facilities and new modes of payment became more common, but it was
a long time before they substantially replaced the older methods.[12]

The persistence of privately generated forms of money in France
had much to do with the suspicion many people harbored toward the
state as a provider of currency. A major source of this mistrust was
the disastrous history of the *assignats*, paper certificates issued during
the Revolution, and designed to represent the value of the confiscated
church (and later *emigré*) lands that became *biens nationaux*. Printed
in quantities that greatly exceeded the value of the nationalized properties, they quickly lost value, ruining many people who held them.
Coming on top of the state's sordid history of financial manipulation
and debt repudiation during the *ancien régime*, the fiasco of the *assignats* left many distrustful of state currency. When Napoleon founded
the *Banque de France* in 1800, hoping it would help to revive economic
activity after the disruptions of the Revolution, he set it up as a partly
private, partly public institution, officially the property of its shareholders, and partially run by a council consisting of the 200 largest of
them, but overseen by state officials. The *Banque de France* was given
an exclusive right to issue banknotes, but only for Paris; elsewhere note
issue was in the hands of local, and more fully private banks. The local
banknotes were trusted in their regions by those who knew something
about the issuers, but elsewhere they could circulate only at a discount,
if at all. These arrangements make evident the quasi-public, quasi-
private status of money in the early nineteenth century. In this regard
the French case was much like the English, but it needs to be noted that
the French Bank was the product of an attempt by a distant and often
mistrusted state to intervene in the country's economic life, whereas
the English one had been founded by subjects or citizens in search of
a way to regularize, and profit from, the finance of a state over which
they were able to exercise considerable control.

Politics, alongside suspicion of the state as an issuer of currency,
marked the history of the *Banque de France* and its money well into
the nineteenth century. At the start no limit was placed on the amount
of currency the Bank could put in circulation, but it was obliged to
exchange its notes for silver or gold on demand, an arrangement that
increased confidence in the paper, but that was bound to create trouble
at moments of economic stringency. The crunch came in 1848. Faced

with a deep economic crisis, the provisional government had no choice but to suspend the bank's obligation to exchange its notes for specie. At the same time, in response to the failure of large numbers of provincial note-issuing banks, the government extended the *Banque de France*'s monopoly on emitting currency to the whole country. To prevent people from refusing the Bank's paper, its notes were given what was called *cours forcé*, requiring people to take them for payment. The return of economic stability allowed the government to abrogate the *cours forcé* in 1850, but the Bank's monopoly on note issue was maintained, and this situation led to a great expansion in the quantity of notes it put into circulation. The reviving economy provided a favorable environment for such changes, and this seems to have been the moment when people at least in some parts of the country began to look with more favor on the state-backed currency. Money of any sort had been in short supply in many parts of the country earlier, and François Caron writes that before 1860 "large areas of France were still deserts as far as money was concerned." The improvement that had already begun by that date is suggested by Maxime du Camp's comment that before the 1848 revolution no one in the southern city of Vichy was willing to accept banknotes, whereas by the mid 1860s no one refused them. Their usefulness was still limited to large transactions, however, because the smallest denomination, although progressively reduced from 250 francs, fell only to 50 in these years. Many transactions were settled by a system somewhere between traditional bills and modern checks, operated by discount bureaus (*comptoirs d'escompte*) whose number expanded from the 1850s. But suspicion of paper money preserved the country's preference for specie. In 1873 60 percent of the money in circulation was still metallic, large numbers of new coins, especially gold ones, having been minted under the Empire.[13]

The French monetary system remained an uncertain mix of quasi-private and quasi-public forms for longer than the English, but the shift toward practices that presumed the public function of money took a big step forward when the Bank's notes were made legal tender in August of 1870 (just as the Second Empire was about to fall). That this could be described as *cours légal* rather than the *cours forcé* of 1848 was a sign of the changes underway, especially given the fact that convertibility of the notes for specie was not re-established until 1877. By this date France had a public money uniform throughout the country (albeit still of limited everyday use) and resting on a metallic reserve. In contrast to the English situation, however, the French Bank was allowed to let the proportion between its reserves and the volume of notes in circulation fluctuate, relying on the assumption that the holders of paper money would never all demand to exchange their notes for precious metals at the same time. The value of the bank's issue was guaranteed by a mix of metallic and non-metallic reserves, the latter consisting primarily of state bonds and some private bills (the latter requiring three recognized signatures as security). Observers saw the chief function of the Bank as precisely to transmute all such obligations into recognized currency with a guaranteed value; as one of them put it, the purpose of discounting commercial paper was to transform "a promise to pay at a future date (*à terme*) into a promise to pay to the bearer on demand (*à vue et au porteur*)."[14]

Although the slower and bumpier evolution of the French monetary system reflected the country's lesser level of economic integration and development compared with Britain, the French arrangements with their greater state role provided certain advantages by late in the nineteenth century. During the 1850s the *Banque de France* began to establish provincial branches on a large scale, so that by 1900 it had offices in over 400 towns, all modeled on the central bureau in Paris, and tightly controlled by it. This made national banking a larger presence in French life than across the Channel (where the Bank of England had fewer than a dozen local branches), in contrast to the less-developed state of commercial banking there, a situation some historians have blamed for its laggard industrialization. After 1870, however, the official Bank became more involved in economic development, targeting lending to sectors its directors regarded as in need of help or encouragement. These contrasts became more salient as English banking came under greater control by the big London commercial banks that participated in the City's money market, giving them, as noted in Chapter 5, a reduced role in industrial development just at the moment when the new technologies and bigger firms of the period generated a need of greater quantities of capital. The contrast illustrates how the passage from private to public forms of money in each country was marked at once by the particular role the state played in national life and by the character and rhythm of each country's economic development.[15]

Certainly this was true in Germany, where the history of money in the nineteenth century took a decisive turn with the unification. Until then the country had two separate currency systems, one based on Gulden in the south, the other on Taler in the north. Both relied primarily on coin, although convertible paper money was also in circulation (non-convertible paper was generally outlawed). For much of the first half of the century exchanges between the currencies issued by the various states were vexingly complex, since bank issues were not always accepted outside their own regions, and the proportion of precious metal required in coins differed from place to place. A series of reforms beginning in the 1830s established more uniform standards, making exchanges between the two currency regions easier, but only the unification replaced this monetary Old Regime with an integrated one, based on a new unit, the Mark, largely regulated by the *Reichsbank* established in 1875 as a successor to the Prussian state bank. The circulation of notes issued by other banks was now frozen, so that the *Reichsbank* became the sole issuer of public paper money.

The proportion of metal currency compared to other forms, which had remained at more than half the total circulation until around 1860, began to fall after that date, and declined rapidly from the mid 1870s, as economic activity expanded much faster than the supply of coin. The Bank's notes now made up a significant proportion of the money supply. But their quantity was limited, by the strict proportion legislated between the volume that could be issued and the Bank's reserves, consisting of both metal and highly trusted paper instruments. As a result, the largest part of the money in use still consisted of commercial paper and notes deposited in banks, rather than any fully public currency. The ability of people to utilize these obligations as money was greatly eased by a system of endorsements (a "Giro" system) through bureaus rather like the French *comptoirs d'escompte*, but centrally run by the Bank, and which allowed those who deposited a small sum as guarantee to send and receive payments between branches. The transfers effected through this network grew at around 8 percent per year between 1873 and 1913, creating ever-closer relations between the central Bank and the world of private money transactions, adding significantly to the money supply, and quickening its tempo of circulation. The result was still far from the uniformity we take for granted today, but like England in the 1830s and 1840s, and France after 1850, Germany was clearly in motion from a system of local and in some ways privately generated currency to one that recognized money as a public function on a national scale.[16]

Banking and finance: persons and institutions

The rhythm of development of these monetary systems had a revealing counterpart in the history of bank financing, both of state activity and commercial development. Here too the nineteenth century witnessed an evolution from a situation largely dominated by private and personal relationships to one where activities and transactions increasingly took place in a wider public arena. The pattern has been recognized by a number of historians, and concisely described by Ron Chernow as *The Death of the Banker: The Decline and Fall of the Great Financial Dynasties and the Triumph of the Small Investor*. Chernow's formula, like the book whose title it provides, concentrates largely on America, but much of his account fits European developments too. He notes that what allowed bankers such as the Rothschilds, who began almost as servants of the princes in whose employ they were able to accumulate their great wealth, to become figures of great power and importance in their own right during much of the nineteenth century, was that only the webs of personal connections they controlled could provide means sufficient to mount armies and assemble the capital for large industrial projects. They lost their central position as wider, thicker, and more impersonal networks developed, linking firms in search of funds to a scattered legion of middling individuals with savings to invest, and as more democratically organized states (even if still dominated by elite individuals and groups) increasingly relied on taxpayers rather than financiers to pay for wars and other projects. As Louis Bergeron puts it, the big bankers at the beginning of the century operated in "a circle of people they knew – family, relations, friends, colleagues, meetings in circles and so on." But the changes the century brought, "railroads, urbanization, the revolution in marine transport, the new scale of mining and metallurgical industries, colonial enterprises ... made a different organization of credit necessary, a mobilization of savings in depth, reaching out to different social strata," drawing in more ordinary people whose participation constituted "an infinitely more modest kind of capitalism" (although closely tied to the larger-scale and more ambitious kind). Where bankers had previously moved in a world of personal relations, they now worked with a much larger number of anonymous clients; investors who once relied on insiders to place funds began to learn about investment opportunities through more public sources of information (newspapers, advertising), and "the use made of funds in bank accounts became a matter of distant and global strategies."[17]

The story of the most famous nineteenth-century bankers, the Rothschilds, illustrates these broad developments very well. The Rothschild bank was a private family bank, operating with its own capital; it neither accepted deposits from other people nor sold shares to the public. That the family could become so prominent and serve as a symbol of money's power in modern life while operating in this way is a sign of the particular and still-limited ways in which both state and private finance was carried on in the early nineteenth century. When James Rothschild, son of Meyer Amschel, arrived in Paris from Frankfurt in 1812, the family was already involved in a number of activities, including currency exchange, commodity trading, and private loans, but the chief source of its wealth was handling the finances of princes and governments. In Frankfurt they had served as agent for the Landgrave of Hesse, who like other rulers at the time preferred sources of income that offered little opening for his subjects to meddle in state business, in his case hiring out soldiers and collecting an excise tax on salt. In Paris the Rothschilds would expand their connections to government finance, becoming part of the so-called *Haute Banque* of houses – a number of them also immigrants to France, including both other Jews and Swiss Protestants – engaged chiefly in lending to the state. To this business the Rothschilds introduced an important innovation, based on the family's network of branches in London, Vienna, Frankfurt, and Naples. Like others, when the Rothschilds made loans to states, they parceled them out in amounts small enough to be sold (at a profit to be sure) to other investors. Having their branches in a number of cities allowed them to issue the bonds simultaneously in all of them, denominating them in local currencies. The people to whom they sold them were regular and well-off associates who formed a limited circle of connections; there was as yet no general and open offering of such securities. All the same as Niall Ferguson observes, the Rothschild system marked the first creation of "a truly international bond market." Operating in this way gave them the advantage that helped them outdistance their competitors, leading Heinrich Heine to write that they represented a new power: "Money is the god of our time, and Rothschild is his prophet."[18]

From the start, then, the wealth of the Rothschilds derived from mobilizing and concentrating scattered but relatively large-scale resources in ways that drew previously untapped power from them. Other prominent family banks operated in somewhat similar ways. The Barings, for instance, who were still chiefly petty bill discounters when the first family members arrived in England from Germany in the mid eighteenth century, achieved their wealth by virtue of personal ties they were able to form with British political figures. These connections allowed them to make highly profitable loans to finance British participation in the French Revolutionary and Napoleonic wars, becoming more important even than the Rothschilds in English government finance. They also did very well by financing Jefferson's Louisiana Purchase (together with their close associate the Hope Bank of Amsterdam). This project provided them with the contacts that allowed them to become the chief support of the French state in the difficult years following Napoleon's defeat. In 1817 their loan allowed the restored Bourbon government to pay the war indemnity imposed by the Vienna settlement; to raise the money they sold bonds to people in their orbit of connections, much as the Rothschilds did. A new loan in the following year put the Barings Bank in danger, however, when bad harvests created difficulties in financial markets. What saved them was that a number of prominent European diplomats had taken shares in the loan, and through their influence its terms were renegotiated and payment put off for a year. An air of corruption surrounded these proceedings, and they were much criticized at the time, but as Philip Ziegler points out, "Certainly the consequences would have been dire for France and Europe if Barings had been forced to default at this crucial moment." It was at this time that the Duc de Richelieu was reported to have called the Barings Bank the "sixth great power."[19]

For their part the Rothschilds, despite their innovations, were determined to keep the power their growing riches gave them inside the family, holding their operations private and even regularly marrying their cousins so as to keep outsiders at bay. When they invested in commercial operations, such as railroads beginning in the 1840s, it was their own by then immense funds they offered up. The various branches cooperated in these and other activities, adding to the available resources, exploiting the differences in currency exchange rates between cities, and coming to each other's aid at critical moments (such as in 1848, a catastrophe for the Vienna branch). Their ability to function in this way depended on having a means of rapid communication between cities, namely (quaint as it may now sound) carrier pigeons, whose advantages they recognized before others did. By 1850 the family was well-enough off that it could hew to generally conservative strategies, relying on steady returns on its vast capital to keep it in prosperity. Partly for this reason, they remained attached to their original forms of doing business into the second half of the century (and to the private character of their enterprise even longer), making them appear in many ways anachronistic and in decline (although the bank, its wealth, and the aura of its name, survives still).

One element in this situation was their suspicion of the telegraph, whose use in commercial affairs became possible at the end of the 1840s. The Rothschilds adopted telegraphy to be sure, but they often complained about it, both because it allowed for what appeared to them as suspect business practices, and because it imposed a new and more demanding rhythm. Doubtless some of their unhappiness can be chalked up to displeasure at being outdone by hungrier and more adventurous competitors, but their reactions testify to the changes under way all the same. In April, 1851, James Rothschild wrote to a relative that "yesterday a great many German scoundrels sold [French] railway shares in London with the telegraph," and went on to complain that certain people sent a dispatch "every day at 12 ... even for trivial deals, and realize [their profit] before the [B]ourse closes the same day." James was famous for putting in long hours at his desk, but all the same he complained about the way the pressures of keeping up with telegraphic information made people "work much more." Some years later, while on a vacation, he moaned that "One has too much to think about when bathing, which is not good." Even in the next generation the family continued to complain about the telegraph, and to conduct business with longhand letters in a kind of nostalgic protest.[20]

The other growing practice the Rothschilds deplored was raising money in more public ways, both by selling shares in investment banks, and by offering government bonds directly to the public. Much has been written about the rivalries between the Rothschilds and the joint-stock banks set up in the 1850s by other families such as the Péreires and the Foulds, and most historians today believe that the contrast was as much one of personal style mixed with some competition and jealousy as of basic principle. All the same, the practices of the new banks exemplify an expansion of the circle of investors that corresponded to wider changes in European economies after 1850. The two chief examples of this under the Second Empire were Fould's *Crédit Foncier*, set up in 1852 to raise capital for property development by selling mortgage bonds, and the Péreires's *Crédit Mobilier*, established the next year as a vehicle to funnel the savings of small investors, some of them burned in the speculative crisis of the previous decade, into railway development (as well as some associated industries). James Rothschild criticized the first because its interest rates were too high, and also because it was regarded with suspicion in the countryside; in fact it served mostly to finance urban property development, often of a speculative sort. The second operated by selling short-term bonds to the public, using the proceeds to invest in whatever enterprises its directors chose. Like the Rothschilds' mode of operation, this one still assumed that only bankers had enough knowledge to invest directly in business, and that share prices were too high to allow ordinary people to participate by themselves, but it was already some way along the road toward the more extended and anonymous later style of banking described by Louis Bergeron. It was just this that James Rothschild lamented, complaining that the directors of the Péreire bank would be "anonymous" and "irresponsible," and could easily misuse their control over other people's money. This may have been easy enough to say for someone able to operate almost entirely with his own funds, and may have reflected jealousy about the Péreire bank's great success in the early boom of railway construction during the 1850s when its bonds reached great heights on the market, but James's refusal to come to its aid when a financial crisis brought its collapse in 1867 may have reflected a genuine distaste for speculative investments on the part of somebody whose firm no longer needed to risk them.[21]

One reason to believe that James took such views seriously is that suspicions about rapid industrial development based on easy credit were widely voiced in France during the reign of the second Bonaparte, and particularly in the circles of the *Banque de France*, of which the Rothschilds were big shareholders and after 1855 directors. The Bank's historian, Alain Plessis, believes that its higher circles still shared the hostility toward *arrivistes* expressed in 1840 by Adolphe Thiers (despite his being something of a *parvenu* himself). In Thiers's view, easy credit encouraged incompetent and unscrupulous people to set up enterprises whose aggressive practices, such as flooding the market with cheap goods, endangered long-established and worthier ones, as well as the economy as a whole. In 1852 a member of the Bank's governing body proclaimed that it should not encourage "speculation," since the more of it there was, the more "nobody wants to remain in his own sphere. Everybody wants to try his luck and make his fortune in a day." As Plessis puts it, people who thought in this way, and they dominated the inner circles of the Bank, possessed "an ancient and aristocratic conception of society."[22] Such attitudes fit well with those of contemporary French manufacturers and observers such as Auguste Mimerel noted in earlier chapters, and in many ways they retained a powerful presence in French life for a long time. But the practices represented by the Péreires and deplored by James Rothschild (whatever his reasons) were gaining ground, reflecting the more extended and more deeply inserted networks of economic relations that were transforming French and European life.

A similar development is visible in government finance, the field in which the Rothschilds had made their fortune, and in which they still remained very active. Both the pressures to bypass their private wealth and power and the difficulties of doing so were illustrated in 1854, when Napoleon III offered bonds directly to the public to finance French participation in the Crimean War. A banker who cooperated with him, and who had been involved in a joint-stock bank for railroads, Jules Mirès, claimed at the time that such a practice "liberated the French government from a tyranny incompatible with the dignity of a dynasty born of universal suffrage," but Bonaparte was unable to raise enough money, so that he was forced to turn to the Rothschilds like it or not. (They would be crucial to financing Bismarck's wars in the 1860s too.) Before the fall of the Empire however all these practices were making evident that the conditions in which the Rothschilds had been able to achieve their remarkable position were passing. In 1866 the well-known journalist Émile de Girardin wrote that "the great [private] banking houses have lost their influence. They can still, when the political and monetary circumstances do not go against them (which is becoming rare) determine the great [financial] movements, but ... from now on the universal suffrage of speculation will prevail over the influence of this or that banker." As Niall Ferguson remarks at this point, the era of the great independent bankers was coming to

realize from selling industrial products that exceeds what the capitalist must pay out for the material and labor that go into the process. Surplus value is the source of capitalist profit and of the funds available for reinvestment: capitalism could not exist without it, much less expand and develop. The term does not appear in classical economics, whose theorists were interested simply in the distribution of revenue between the factors of production, that is the proportion that went to wages, to rent, and to profit, and the reasons for shifts in it. They did, however, develop the basic notion that the value of goods depends in the end on the labor required to produce them, and they recognized that an important source of profit and rent was that human labor is able to produce more than people require merely to subsist and reproduce themselves. Marx developed this recognition into a theory that revealed capital's power to extract more value from production, and in particular from the labor of workers, than capitalists expended to employ it. This analysis gave Marx's economic theory its sharp critical edge, by showing how capitalists exploited a hidden relationship that allowed them to pay workers less than their labor was actually worth. To do so seemed impossible from the perspective of classical economic theory, since it was premised on the belief that all commodities were exchanged in the market at prices that, however much they might fluctuate in the short term, were in the end controlled by the value of the labor required to produce them. How then could one commodity, labor, be regularly sold below its true value? The theory of surplus value was an answer to this question, explaining how capitalists managed to receive more value from their workers' labor than they paid in wages.

Marx was justifiably proud of the solution he provided to this mystery, but his understanding of it owed a debt to a figure to whom he was close for a time, but of whom he later became a harsh critic, the French socialist and anarchist Pierre-Joseph Proudhon. He too had a theory of surplus value, and we need to consider it for a moment in order to bring Marx's into clearer focus. Like Marx, Proudhon saw capitalist profit as rooted in a difference between what employers paid workers and the value the latter's labor actually produced. This difference, he believed, arose because the product workers could create when brought together in a group, whether a work gang or a factory, exceeded the sum of the individual values each of them could produce if working alone. When an employer pays each worker individually for the value of his day's labor, he pays nothing for "the enormous collective force" generated by their combination. And yet society relies on the product of this collective force for much of what allows it to subsist and flourish, as well as for projects that are more ornamental. Proudhon noted: "Two hundred grenadiers set up the Luxor obelisk [in Paris in 1836] in the space of a few hours. Does anyone suppose that one man could have managed it in two hundred days? Yet in the capitalist's reckoning the wages would have been the same. Now, cultivating a wilderness, building a house, or running a factory is like setting up an obelisk or moving a mountain."[26] The system that allows employers to pay individual workers as if their labor were isolated and not part of the collective that is able to produce such wonders assures both that capitalists grow rich and that workers remain in poverty.

The social and legal order that licensed the capitalist to regard the whole product of the laborers' efforts as his property assured the continuation of this injustice, and it was this order that Proudhon had in his sights when he famously declared that "property is theft." Despite its apparent generality, this slogan only genuinely applied to the property acquired by those who bought the product of collective labor; in other regards Proudhon was not an enemy of property, and his famous *boutade* made him sound much more radical than he was. His way of assuring that workers would receive the full value of their labor did not involve a revolutionary expropriation of property owners, but a new system of direct exchanges between groups of producers. Properly organized, these "mutualist" exchanges would allow all the workers who contributed to the overall value of a given product or quantity of them to receive a fair share of what each one's labor was really worth. (Proudhon's focus on such exchanges made his thinking akin to the Abbé Sieyès's analysis of the economy as a series of mutual representations of each other's labor by workers of various kinds that we discussed above.) In this way work, like politics, would be democratized, that is liberated from control by outside authorities (the state and the legal order it imposed), making way for a regulative principle that derived from the productive process itself. In the terminology we have adopted here, Proudhon's mutualist exchanges were a way to make the network of economic relations "autonomous," that is, organized according to principles that arose out of the proper understanding of the interactions on which it rested; so regulated they would no longer serve social ends imposed from outside.

Proudhon's notion that the social value of labor depended on its aggregation, the assemblage of workers and their energies at a single point, also informed his understanding of factory production. In his eyes the factory system was significant because it gave a new form and impetus to collective labor; machines were at best accessories to it. When Proudhon discussed Adam Smith's theory of the division of labor as the basis of factory organization, he insisted that "the division of labor is synonymous with multiplying the number of workers. The division of labor and the collective force, or cooperative action, are two correlative facets of the same law."[27] Whatever one may think of the solution Proudhon offered for capitalist injustice, his image of how work was organized corresponded better to the actual condition of work and manufacturing in his time than have many subsequent accounts. Not only was labor in groups or gangs still of central importance in the economy before 1850, even in England, as Raphael Samuel's studies cited above make clear, but factory work took its place inside a system still dominated by traditional methods, just what Richard Price highlighted by calling it an "economy of manufacture." One reason Proudhon's analysis could make a strong appeal in France during his lifetime and after (he died in 1865) was that these traditional methods were still dominant there. But the obverse of this virtue was that his thinking offered little guidance for understanding how production relations might be transformed by modern industry. That machinery driven by non-human power sources might produce a product still greater than the sum of the efforts of workers who labored without it, and thus raise more complex issues of distribution, was a possibility of little concern to Proudhon's theory.

It was of much greater concern to Marx, but in ways that left him closer to Proudhon than is usually recognized. Despite the strong connection Marx made between the proletariat as a source of historical transformation and the development of the factory system, his understanding of value and surplus value was no less grounded in pre-industrial relations fundamentally independent of machine industry than was his French rival's. Indeed he believed that modern factory production would prove to be incompatible with capitalism, and this conviction, combined with the limited experience of advanced industrial techniques available to him in the 1840s and 1850s meant that his theory of capitalism had its own way of remaining closely tied to pre-modern conditions of production.

Well aware that Proudhon had preceded him in arguing that a hidden aspect of capitalist production relations allowed employers to derive more value from their workers than they paid for (the manuscripts later published as the *Grundrisse*, containing the first working-out of what would be *Capital*'s basic theories, began with a critique of one of Proudhon's followers), Marx sought a different and deeper way to grasp the relationship. He found the answer not in the aggregation of workers, but in the nature of labor as a commodity; by focusing on it, moreover, he believed he could uncover the seeds of capitalism's demise in the fundamental relations that made the system work. Capitalism's insistence on providing people with use values (things that fulfill needs) only by way of exchange values (goods bought and sold in the market) was its fatal flaw, one that would eventually make it unable to fulfill needs and sustain life, so that it must eventually collapse. Adam Smith (and others before him) recognized that goods are valuable to us both because of what we can do with them (write with a pencil, wear a coat) and because they can be exchanged for others, so that we do not have to produce everything we need by ourselves. This distinction made the social division of labor possible. But Marx began by tracing the distinction between the use-value and the exchange-value of goods back to a more basic one between concrete and abstract labor. The labor that made a particular product have a specific use was the concrete labor that marked it as the work of a tailor or a miner or a writer, each of which produced an object of a certain sort, endowed with a specific utility. But the labor that made any product exchangeable with any other was abstract labor, the active effort that every form of human toil has in common with every other. It was this second kind of labor that gave any commodity a certain quantity of exchange value, and which allowed it to be traded against others in proportion to the relative amounts of labor embodied in each. Looked at globally, any society (that is, any group of people engaged in mutual exchanges) produced at once a quantity of goods based on concrete labor and a quantity of exchange values based on abstract labor; the use value of particular goods to different individuals might differ with their situation and preferences, but the exchange value of goods in the market depended on the quantity of abstract labor they embodied. In practice many subsidiary factors entered in: if different kinds of labor required differing quantities of training and preparation, then this affected the valuation in each case; raw materials, together with tools and implements of labor, also transferred to every commodity some proportion of the value that went into their production (I will return to this point in a moment). For these reasons (and others that must be left aside here) market prices were never exactly equivalent to values, but ultimately the latter grew out of and depended on the former, prices were regulated by the relative proportion of the total abstract labor produced in society that particular goods contained.[28]

Marx used this analysis to understand many things about capitalism. To capitalists use-values mattered only to the degree that they were the bearers of exchange values, since only the latter produced money income and profit. If for whatever reason conditions made it impossible to realize exchange value by selling goods (for instance if too many things had been turned out in the hope of raising profits and incomes, causing a glut and a crisis), the whole complex system would come to a halt, with painful consequences all round. But Marx's analysis of use-values and exchange-values, and of concrete and abstract labor, had its most important application in connection with the commodity that made capitalism function as a system, namely labor itself.

As a commodity labor appeared in the same dual guise as every other, that is as the bearer of both exchange value and use value. Its exchange value depended on the same calculus as every other good, namely the amount of labor necessary to reproduce it under given conditions; in other words workers would be paid for their labor at a rate that allowed them to support and reproduce themselves (in the manner and at the level assumed or expected in a particular time and place). But labor had a use value too, albeit of a particular kind. Its use value to the person who purchased it was its ability to produce goods in a system where they were offered for exchange. It was thus simultaneously concrete labor, the labor of particular workers that issued in ribbons or shirts, and abstract labor or labor-power, the labor of abstract "hands" who individually and together produced the values that were exchanged in the market. Although the bargain between worker and capitalist involved both kinds of labor, it was the first, concrete kind that mattered most to the worker, since it was labor as a spinner or weaver, miner or tailor, that he or she offered for sale, and that allowed him or her to survive. But it was the second, abstract kind that mattered most to the capitalist, and that he bought, because it was the abstract labor-power all goods embodied that made them exchangeable against others.

In addition, crucially, this abstract labor had a higher value than the concrete labor that mattered to the worker. The reason went back to the condition recognized by classical economists, namely that human labor is capable of producing more goods than human beings need in order to survive; thus workers could add more value to the products they manufactured than their own subsistence required. They would be paid what their labor was worth to them, that is what their survival required under given conditions. But the value the capitalist received was that of their "labor-power," that is, the amount it contributed to the expanding mass of values on the basis of which goods circulated in the market. As long as society produced more goods than it required for the mere survival of its members, the value of the labor-power set to work in it was bound to be greater than the sum of the individual values of the concrete labor for which workers were paid. The difference was surplus value, and except in certain cases where some particular group of workers produced at a level well below the social average, every instance of labor power bought in this fashion yielded a certain quantity of it. It was this surplus value that allowed capitalism as a system to work.

This analysis involved many complications which we can only briefly mention here. From one point of view what allowed capitalists to extract more value from workers than they paid them for was that the working day was long in the nineteenth century, sometimes twelve or fourteen hours in England before the legislation of 1847 that reduced it to ten (the higher figures often obtained until much later on the continent). This meant that workers were forced to toil for more hours than would have been required to produce the value of goods necessary for their subsistence, and in one sense it was out of the extra working hours that capitalist profits arose. Marx discussed this situation at length in *Capital*. But in another and deeper sense it was not the length of the working day itself but the nature of the production process, the hidden difference between the value of concrete labor and the value of abstract labor-power that really marked the labor market as the engine of capitalism as a system. The analysis of the work day was only a way of making the mysterious transaction at the center of capitalism concrete and visible. From the perspective that highlighted the length of the working day, it appeared that in order for workers to receive the full value of their labor power, only reforms, such as those already begun in England in the 1840s, were required. But such measures would still not put an end to capitalism as a system; wages might rise and hours be reduced, but workers would still be employed by capitalists, who would retain the advantage that flowed to them from the distinction between concrete and abstract labor. Only a transformation that did away with treating labor as a commodity could abolish this difference and remove workers from the inferior position that prevented them from rightfully receiving the full value of their labor.

The similarity between Marx's understanding of surplus value and Proudhon's should not be over-stressed. Proudhon's vision of the power of aggregated labor was just that, a visual representation of concrete groups of workers combining their labor at a given point; it gave no way to understand how capitalists might profit from employing workers in scattered situations, such as in the putting-out system. Marx's more theoretically sophisticated approach could do this, and of the two only his issued in a quantifiable analysis of the connections between prices and revenues in the market. Whether that analysis could successfully show how actual prices were set and profits arose is a different question, but the debates about it indicate that Marxian economics can at least make claims to account for the chief phenomena of modern economies, whereas it would be very difficult to argue that Proudhon's could do so. All the same, what Marx's theory shared with Proudhon's was the view that the source of surplus value lay in the difference between the sum of the individual values produced by the concrete labor of individual workers and the quantity of value produced by labor as a social aggregate. At this stage in the analysis, machines and the modern factory system have no more place in Marx's theory than in his rival's. Both traced the production of surplus value and of capitalist profits to a situation in which only workers and capitalists, not machines, were involved.

Marx of course understood that as the mechanization to which industrialists were turning proceeded it would transform productive life and with it social relations, but his conviction that this transformation would bring the end of capitalism encouraged him to give a peculiar slant to his analysis. Starting from the classical notion that labor was the source of all value, he regarded tools and machines as able to contribute value to the final product only in very limited ways, by transferring the value already congealed in them to the products. This they did over the period of their usefulness, so that a machine worth, say, £100 (Marx used the English currency of the day in his writings) would only add that amount to the value of all the goods to which it contributed over the period of its productive life. Machines were incapable of adding any new value to the product, and raw materials operated in the production process in the same way. Only living workers, creating the labor power that flowed through markets in the form of exchange value, could add new value, and thus contribute to profits. Marx therefore referred to the capital invested in machines, plant, and raw materials as "constant capital," because its value persisted unchanged as it passed into new products, whereas the capital devoted to paying workers was "variable capital," because its value expanded inside the production process it set in motion. The proportion between "constant capital" and "variable capital" he called "the organic composition of capital," the relation by which it acted as the animating agent of capitalist production. But since surplus value could arise only from the employment of the variable capital invested in living labor, it followed that the conditions for the production of surplus value and thus of profit grew narrower as the proportion of investment in constant capital, that is of machines and materials, rose relative to the value of the labor employed. And since the movement of modern industry was toward ever-larger investments in machines and plants, the historical tendency was for the quantity of surplus value, and with it the rate of return on capitalist investment, to fall as industry progressed. Marx referred to this crucial element of is theory as "the law of the falling rate of profit." Eventually the operation of this law would so deeply undermine the conditions of capitalist production that the system would collapse.

Like others of Marx's discussions, this one was subject to various complications. Marx understood that machinery allowed factories to turn out a much greater mass of goods than a given number of workers could produce without it, and that machines driven by nonhuman power sources raised the productivity of workers. Since this meant that capitalists would be able to bring more goods to market as industry developed and the organic composition of capital rose, there were clearly tendencies in capitalist development that went counter to the analysis that predicted a progressive decline in the rate of profit as capitalist industry advanced. Marx was much concerned about the relationship between these contradictory tendencies. When he first formulated the law of the falling rate of profit, in the manuscripts of the late 1850s that were later published as the *Grundrisse*, he saw many of its difficulties right away, but he remained convinced that his analysis grasped something essential about the historical tendency of capitalists development. Despite the complications, he asked himself, "is there not after all something correct in these figures? Does not absolute new value decrease despite an increase in the relative [i.e., in the quantity of goods produced], as soon as relatively more material and instrument than labor is introduced into the component parts of capital?" Here Marx's answer was still positive, and he saw his analysis of the falling rate of profit as the lynchpin of his economic theory, referring to it as "in every respect the most important law of political economy." But, as I argued a number of years ago in a much more detailed account of Marx's theory, his conviction on this score did not always remain so strong. His original doubts festered, the question continued to trouble him to the end of his life, and his inability to find a definitive demonstration of the principle that defined the historical limitations of capitalism as a productive system was an important factor in his never finishing his great work on economics.[29]

What matters most about this in our present context is not Marx's problems in finishing his book, but the place that the law of the falling rate of profit assigned to machine industry. Not only was machinery absent from the original analysis of surplus value, Marx actually regarded the advance of mechanization as incompatible with the historical survival of capitalism as a system. His account of what would eventually establish a limit to capitalist production assumed that capitalist profits in the age of machine industry were ultimately just as dependent on the proportion of living labor employed in factories as in the period when the latter were simply aggregations of workers. This should not be taken to mean that such a perspective was somehow inescapable for people whose mental framework was formed before the mid century. Engels, for instance, had many doubts about the law of the falling rate of profit, as he made evident in the editing he did for the unfinished second and third volumes of *Capital* he published after Marx's death, rearranging sections within Marx's chapters so as to highlight the presence of "counteracting influences" and even "internal contradictions" of the law. Engels recognized that the revolution in transport effected by railroads meant that industrialists could bring goods to market more quickly and reinvest the capital realized by sales at shorter intervals; this meant that the rate of turn-over on capital would rise and with it the effective rate of profit per year. In addition, he noted that some advances in factory technology recommended themselves to capitalists because they cheapened the cost of investment in machines and plant rather than saving labor, making the notion that the organic composition of capital necessar-ily rose as industry progressed far less certain than Marx thought. Together with modern industry's ability to raise labor productivity, these features greatly clouded the vision of capitalism's future Marx sought to preserve in his book.[30] It is well known that in his later life (he survived Marx by a dozen years) Engels became more sympathetic to reformist versions of socialism than the two friends had been earl-ier, and the spread of such ideas in the working-class movement itself reminds us that the conditions of political thinking and action in the latter part of the nineteenth century differed in significant ways from those of the "hungry forties" in which *The Communist Manifesto* had been written and Marx began his analysis of economics.

Marx was far from blind to the changes coming about in the years when he struggled to complete his book. As modern industry developed an ability to produce a much expanded quantity of goods, it evolved economic relations no longer limited by the conditions of pro-duction that obtained earlier. The powers unleashed by modern indus-try were so great that "[t]he *theft of alien labor time, on which the present wealth is based*, appears as a miserable foundation in the face of this new one, created by large-scale industry itself." But the ben-efits of this change could not be reaped within capitalism, because the new form of wealth creation was in principle incompatible with it: "As soon as labor in the direct form has ceased to be the great well-spring of wealth, labor time ceases and must cease to be its measure, and hence exchange value [must cease to be the measure] of use value."[31] This meant that by giving birth to modern industry capitalism pre-pared its own demise, bringing forth a system of production that did away with its very presupposition, the status of goods as commodities. Capital had not only an "organic composition" but a vital destiny, its eventual collapse prefigured by its fatal subordination of use-value to exchange-value.

It is just this sense of historical closure that we escape by expanding Simmel's notion of money as a social tool into an ana-lysis that focuses on the development of networks of means and the ongoing liberation of human energies they make possible. The results of this emancipation are by no means all positive; on the contrary the problems faced by a form of life increasingly grounded in distant relations and the abstractions they require have grown more dangerous and threatening since Marx's day. The open-ended perspective proposed here leaves us without any prospect of a passage to a higher order that might promise to resolve them. But there is little reason to put our faith in a solution rooted, like the theory of surplus value, in pre-modern conditions and relationships.

9 MEN AND WOMEN

Among the aspects of modernity whose relationship to bourgeois life have often been debated, none are more significant than the linked topics of relations between men and women, and the moral codes and attitudes that regulate them. In this chapter and the next I will try to show that the evolution of gender relations and the historical place of what is often called "Victorian" morality evolved in parallel between the middle of the eighteenth century and the end of the nineteenth: each began by entering a phase that gave a sharper and more defined quality or shape to attitudes and relationships that existed previously but that had been treated more informally and flexibly, and each ended by exhibiting a marked relaxation of the rigidities introduced in that initial moment. A major reason for this parallel was that both were similarly affected by the expansion and thickening of networks of means, and the two stages correspond, if somewhat imprecisely, to the successive moments in the development of modernity we have sought to distinguish in previous chapters. One reason the correspondence was imperfect was that impulses which only began to find significant realization in the second phase were already at work in the first, their push toward gender equality and moral flexibility having been introduced alongside forces that pressed in the opposite direction. This makes the story we try to tell in these two chapters complex; it is also necessarily incomplete, because the depth of the moral alteration whose prospects began to emerge toward the end of the nineteenth century only became widely visible after the middle of the twentieth, at which point it would prove far deeper than most people before 1914 were in any position to expect. But certain main lines of its later unfolding were becoming visible before the War. Tying the subject of this chapter to the one considered in the next is the institution that serves as the hinge at once between private and public life, and between male–female relations and morality, namely the family.

Separate spheres and relations at a distance

The feminist scholarship that blossomed in the second half of the twentieth century directed a powerful new light on gender relations in general and in particular on the "separate spheres" to which men and women were assigned and the contrasting public and private roles each were expected to play. A popular German publication of 1848 succinctly described the core division: "while the woman in the main lays the foundations for the ties that bind the family, the man is the link with the external world."[1] Numerous consequences followed from this distinction, among them limiting female education to subjects deemed relevant to the role girls would later fill as wives and mothers, excluding women from voting, restricting their freedom of movement in public, and imposing strict standards of modesty on the behavior and speech of "respectable" females. In practice a certain number of women escaped from the narrow bounds the schema projected, some by subtly evading or actively contesting them, others by finding ways to make an impact on public life as writers, moral reformers, or participants in business (sometimes visible, sometimes behind the scenes); recent historians have recognized the permeability of the enclosures by speaking of "connecting spheres." Even among those who themselves broke free in this way, however, there were many who accepted the assumption that women as a whole were destined to fundamentally different lives than men; the exceptions still left the rule more or less intact. The question is: what was "bourgeois" about these assumptions and distinctions and what is their relationship to the evolution of bourgeois life?

Although a number of historians have associated the establishment of a clear separation of spheres with the coming of bourgeois social and cultural relations, most of the elements of the system were clearly in place well before the late eighteenth century. Consider the schematic recipe for "A Godly Forme of Householde Gouernment" provided by two Puritan writers in 1614:

Husband	Wife
Get goods	Gather them together and save them
Travel, seek a living	Keep the House
Get Money and Provisions	Do not vainly spend it
Deal with many men	Talk with few
Be 'entertaining'	Be solitary and withdrawn
Be skilfull in talk	Boast of silence
Be a giver	Be a saver
Apparel yourself as you may	Apparel yourself as it becomes you
Dispatch all things outdoors	Oversee and give order within.[2]

The list seems to assume a family supported by some kind of middle-class occupation: the husband is not a manual laborer and female work is not explicitly mentioned, although the writers may have included some form of it in the "oversee and give order" of the last line. Divisions very close to the one it describes were evident where women's work was assumed to be a part of family life, however. Feminine work was often arduous (although it usually did not include the heavy labor in field and forest assigned to men in rural settings), but the kinds of "Godly" expectations that assigned contact with the wider world to men were one reason why households were dominated by them.

That the arrangements crystallized as separate spheres had long been in place has often been recognized. As a historian of France notes,

The Romans venerated the woman who lived chastely and served the hearth. Medieval didactic treatises such as *The Goodman of Paris* (c. 1393) exhorted women to cultivate the home as a shelter (for both men and women) from the turbulence and strife of the outside world. The seventeenth century French writer, Pierre Le Moyne, although quite prepared to concede women's moral equality with men and their equal aptitude for learning, repudiated the call for the extension of women's public education on the grounds that "I respect too much the boundaries that separate us."[3]

Writing about Britain, Amanda Vickery throws a bracing bath of cold water on the notion developed by a certain species of feminism that earlier times represented a kind of "golden age" of work and public activity for women. Female participation in business and commerce appears to have waxed and waned with levels of prosperity in periods well before the nineteenth century; comments or complaints about women withdrawing from productive activity or losing opportunities to engage in it were rife in the 1600s too. The only important female occupation lost as traditional manufacturing gave way to modern industry was domestic production of textiles, a system in which the (male) "putting-out" merchants who organized it most often dealt with male heads of households, even where wives and daughters spun the thread. Metalworking, furniture building, shoe- or barrel-making hardly ever involved families in the same way; nor did women travel as commercial agents buying and selling goods. The chief occupations of women in the seventeenth century were already those where they would cluster in the nineteenth, namely "the so-called feminine trades: petty retail, food and drink, textiles. One would search long and hard for significant numbers of female goldsmiths, blacksmiths, curriers and so on at any point in British history." The point holds for other countries: women contributed importantly to the economy, but in spheres that were specifically theirs; they stepped outside these limits when wives took over the businesses of deceased husbands (as they continued to do in the nineteenth century), but if they remarried, as many did, the headship reverted to a male. Guild offices and town councils (not to mention representative assemblies and administrative employments) were almost exclusively the preserve of men. As Vickery concludes, given that "separate spheres of gender power" have existed in many times and places (and in some degree persist), we should not appeal to them "to explain social and political developments in a particular century, least of all [as some historians have] to account for Victorian class formation."[4]

None of this means, however, that nothing altered in gender relations at the end of the eighteenth century. Both the general nature of the changes and the reasons for them are suggested by a recent study focusing not on bourgeois strata but on agricultural and rural life in Germany. Its author, Marion Gray, makes clear that male domination had been presupposed and recommended by a long line of writers from the sixteenth century to the nineteenth: at every moment men were described as "masters," "sovereigns," and "kings" in their households, ruling over children and women. The division of tasks was largely stable too, with men chiefly responsible for the fields, women for "household, kitchen, garden, and dairy." Together the gendered spheres made up a universe of family production, an economy devoted as much to its own subsistence as to producing and selling a surplus. It was close to what Aristotle had called an *oikos*, a productive household, ruled over by men but in which women's work constituted a substantial and necessary part. Germans called it the *ganze Haus*.[5]

As the nineteenth century approached, this form of productive and family life began to retreat to the social margins; the reason was not that women lost their employments, but that those reserved for men were drawn into an evolving system of production in which the household as a whole did not participate. The new regime was based on an increased orientation toward market farming (stimulated by population expansion and urban growth), and with it the attempt to increase output; in Germany this goal was encouraged and nurtured by state governments, whose officials recommended improved tools and techniques, better fertilizers, rational organization of the land, and an end to such barriers to human effort and ambition as serfdom. "As the ideal of increased yields gained predominance over older systems based on morals and tradition," the ancient model of a "hierarchical estate with interdependent components" gave way to one in which the male undertaking of growing crops that could be sold in the market gained a new and more powerful kind of predominance over the activities assigned to women.[6]

Such an evolution gave the traditional division between male and female spheres, and even the longstanding principle of male dominance in the household, a new basis. The spheres had always been separate but the distance between them now widened. In this instance the widening took place among people who can be called bourgeois only if we stretch the term to include anyone drawn into market relationships. But a similar change took place in urban and middle-class contexts too, in both cases brought about by the shifting relationship between work and the expanding and thickening web of activities outside the family. Margaret Hunt notes its presence in eighteenth-century England:

> As the flow of both trade and information extended its
> reach, women traders and the neighborhood networks

that formed their economic base became, in cultural terms at least, more marginal. The growing prestige of larger networks ... spelled a corresponding loss of local systems, which often were small scale, retail, based on oral transaction, and not coincidentally, populated heavily by women, the lower reaches of the middling and artisanal classes, and the laboring classes.

Theodore Koditschek describes a similar shift still proceeding half a century later: "the supremacy of men, which had hitherto rested on their patriarchal authority within the family, was now coming to depend in a more structured and less personal sense on the precedence that their sphere of capitalist production and market relations obtained over the female sphere of domestic consumption."[7] Economic change was not the only contributor to widening the distance between traditionally separate spheres; in Germany new forms of state employment, as we saw above drawing people out of local relations into more broadly territorial ones contributed too. More than one historian has noted that the earliest instances of the pattern whereby women's work consisted solely in household management were found chiefly among the families of state officials and professionals (although some long-distance merchants resembled them), where cooking, sewing, and cleaning comprised most of what wives and daughters did to sustain a family's material life.[8]

The family as resource and network

Focusing on the kinds of changes just noted gives an incomplete picture of what was happening to relations between women and men from around 1750; we will come in a moment to a development that pushed in a very different direction, namely Enlightened criticism of traditional gender relations. Although well known and debated, this critique had little practical impact, and we need first to recognize some of the circumstances that blunted its effect. Many of these lay in the central importance that family membership still played in individuals' lives.

In the eighteenth and nineteenth centuries, as before and since, families provided all kinds of benefits to their members, launching them into the world and sometimes sheltering them from its dangers and affronts; in contrast to the world we know today, however, family membership then served as an indispensable vehicle for practical survival and advancement. The terms in which Sarah Hanley describes the worldly importance of family relations for seventeenth-century French lawyers and bureaucrats need only be slightly altered to apply to conditions two centuries later: if family membership no longer "provided the only means of human survival through networks of influence (marriage alliances, inheritance practices, patronage, and apprentice systems)," it remained a chief one. What was "the most pressing business of early modern times" was still an imperative under more developed conditions, namely "the maintenance and extension of family networks, which were agencies of both social reproduction and economic production."[9] This was true not only for most nineteenth-century bourgeois but for many peasants and artisans as well.

There were, to be sure, differences between the ways early modern families served as vehicles for the worldly well-being of their members and those coming to be more prominent around 1800; the main shift has been pinpointed by David Sabean. Whereas social position had long depended chiefly on some kind of patrimony that passed vertically down a line of descendants, by late in the eighteenth century, and in a wide variety of social and geographical locations, it was coming to hinge more on people's ability to mobilize and draw on resources distributed horizontally through society. Where people had once sought "to inherit, maintain, and pass on an estate, a monopoly, or a craft," they now looked for ways to "manage the flow of property and resources," creating concentrations of property or talent that gave greater power to carry out projects or influence those who had such power. Marriage strategies aimed at "the creation of dense transfer points coordinating interests, activities, and values along horizontal rather than vertical tracks."[10] But families remained crucial vehicles for this kind of coordination.

One reason they did was what Jürgen Kocka calls "the low degree of institutionalization in the occupational and commercial realm" and Sven Beckert (in a study of New York City bourgeois) "a world of underdeveloped communication facilities and weak impersonal institutions." As commerce expanded but in a situation where banks of a modern sort were not yet on the scene, family members provided a main source for capital, and before the age when advanced education became an important qualification for managing large-scale firms based on increasingly complex technologies, they served as a chief supply of partners and associates too.[11] Thus the networks of influence Sarah Hanley pointed to in the seventeenth century had important counterparts in the nineteenth. Webs of family connections provided people with resources for gaining access to the more extended and powerful networks of means through which distant resources could be coordinated and directed toward particular goals. In some cases families were themselves networks of means, since they were assemblages of capital, talent, and information, but it was as vehicles for inserting themselves or their members into outside economic, political, or cultural linkages that they aided individuals in developing their talents or fulfilling their aims and ambitions. Kocka notes that certain families built up these kinds of connection by way of systematic cross-marriages between sons and daughters, producing at once intricate personal ties and loose but often highly useful structures of connection between firms, "which at the time could be neither put together nor maintained in any other way." Such bonds were often local to begin with, but as commerce expanded so did they, linking people in various cities or regions who had reasons to seek ongoing association with each other.[12]

Given the ancient and persisting expectation that men would be the heads of families and that many of them would work outside them, families could only play these roles if women devoted themselves especially to them, and the need for such female contributions was a chief reason why nineteenth-century people regarded the existence of a separate female sphere as crucial to personal and social well-being. Children were recognized as the building-blocks of ties between families, and the need to have them available provided one motive for keeping families large, generating pressure to keep women's biological role as mothers at the center of their social identity. As both physical links between families expected to be headed by men and vehicles for continuity between generations, women also played a large role in animating the personal relations through which family alliances were established, conducting correspondence and setting up visits and meetings. The need for women to perform these functions would diminish as time went on and individuals were able to pursue their goals and ambitions by way of resources provided by public facilities: institutionalized sources of credit, expanded primary and secondary schooling,

advanced professional training in university settings, publicly available information about career possibilities. As reliance on families for
survival and advancement diminished, so would the need for women
to devote themselves to strengthening the ties between them.[13]

Two recently published collections of French family letters
testify both to the crucial importance of family relations to individual
well-being during the nineteenth century and to the role women were
called on to play in maintaining them. One involved a constellation of
relatives that had been built up in just the fashion Kocka describes, so
that the couple at the center of the web were distant cousins who bore
the same last name before their marriage, and who had multiple blood
ties to other family members. This made it easier for them (especially
the wife and mother, the chief writer and recipient of the letters) to
maintain the weave of relations, keeping up correspondence with both
immediate and more distant relatives. Earlier the family's chief occupation had involved raising and selling horses in Anjou, but from the
mid century it was increasingly drawn into urban life, some members
in Paris, others in provincial cities, and into the expanding world of
professions. The need to operate in unfamiliar situations was one reason for keeping the network solid and active, since it provided personal
support that individual members could not yet find in the milieux into
which they were moving. The generation that followed would need
this kind of sustenance less, as its members established other kinds of
connections, to professional colleagues and their families, and more
generally to the extra-familial networks to which they gained access in
cities. Until late in the nineteenth century, however, individuals relied
on the links maintained through family ties for both material support
and for useful information on a wide variety of subjects – where to
obtain clothes, household supplies, servants (one cousin being able to
recommend candidates from among the large supply of unemployed
young women in his part of rural Poitou, and who were thought to
be good prospects because they were uncorrupted by city life), how
best to deal with illnesses of various kinds, where to seek marriage
partners. "Thanks to the network one knows where to go for a cure,
for a trip, for a vacation; one knows what to buy, to whom to turn for
the smallest service." It was a largely down-to-earth correspondence,
with little room for exchanges of intimacies, but people found much
psychic support in it all the same, and felt adrift if their letters went
unanswered; the mother at the center "insured a continual flow of gifts

and aid at a distance, and at home a climate of well-being and warmth such that being deprived of it was felt as a painful separation."[14]

A second, slightly earlier French correspondence has been studied and partly published by a descendant of the family, a clan of some significance here because one of its members was Edmond Goblot, author of an often-cited study, *La barrière et le niveau*, its title referring to the *baccalauréat* exam that still stands as the chief hurdle middle-class French students have to surmount in order to put themselves at the same level as their fellow bourgeois. Goblot, as noted earlier, coined the term "style of life," applying it to the complex of cultural and social practices and behaviors that gave the diverse members of the French middle classes a common identity. His father Arsène, the son of a peasant, married the sister of a school friend, thereby entering into an extended and multiply connected Norman clan called Dubois, many of whose male members had lower or mid level positions in the civil service, while some of the women, including Arsène's wife Augustine before their marriage, ran a boarding-school for girls. It was a solid bourgeois family of the kind not rich enough to qualify for the vote under the July Monarchy. With their help the elder Goblot extended his rather rudimentary education and eventually achieved a good post in the Departmental administration of Maine-et-Loire, where his salary was sufficient to pay back money he had earlier borrowed from his brother-in-law in a failed attempt to set up a business venture. The Dubois–Goblot correspondence shows the family members providing many of the same kinds of help to each other as the Angevin one considered a moment ago, but with much effort going into achieving the education and diplomas necessary for the kinds of careers most of them sought. Both families saw the material and moral solidarity the members afforded each other as especially important in view of the political and religious divisions within French society and the tension they often bred. Having moved to a new city to take up his administrative post, Arsène and his wife held back from establishing social relations there, for fear of being regarded as favorable to one or another of the existing rival coteries. One of their sons later bewailed the painful isolation this brought them, writing that it would have been better to remain in Normandy, even in an inferior position, since there the Dubois connections would have given them a recognized status. "Here we are isolated individuals; people who have a family that is known in the region, even if it isn't unblemished, have resources and receive consideration that we, numerous and all without any stain, do not have."[15] In such a world, it was difficult to imagine how people could live without the support of families, or without the roles that women played in making it effective.

There was a further reason why the notion that women were destined by nature to occupy a separate sphere seemed unquestionable to many people (even in some degree to feminists) through much of the nineteenth century, namely the sheer weight of biological reproduction in their lives. Given both the absence of effective contraception and the importance of children in family strategies, married women until late in the nineteenth century were fated to give a large portion of their lives to motherhood. In parts of Germany for which statistics can be cited, the average number of children born in educated middle-class households was 6.8, which meant that long years of women's lives were taken up with the duties of motherhood; one historian estimates that the Berlin cultural polymath Bettina von Arnim spent between thirty and forty years looking after children. The examples cited by Leonore Davidoff and Catherine Hall show that, among the English middle-class groups they studied, the period during which a woman bore children could often extend to between thirteen and sixteen years, during which time it was not uncommon for her to give birth to as many as eleven babies. In such circumstances, periods of pregnancy and nursing followed quickly on each other, often with very little respite between them. French families may have been slightly smaller, but motherhood was a large and inescapable part of female destiny there too; the protagonist of one Balzac story declared that "a woman without children is a monstrosity. We are made solely to be mothers." The onus of bearing and rearing children was so great that some historians have not hesitated to see the large size of families as something of a male plot to ensure wifely subordination. Ute Frevert believes that the burdens imposed by the maternal role, "tight-fitting and impossible to cast off," could have been lightened by more responsible use of contraception. Perhaps, but as Frevert herself admits in regard to the later Weimar period, preventing pregnancy long remained a very uncertain thing, even among those who knew about available methods. Neither sponges or pessaries nor condoms (made chiefly out of animal skins before rubber became available after the mid century) were reliable.[16]

One reason families made only limited efforts to prevent conception was that having more children made up for the painfully high rate of deaths in infancy and childhood, as great as 50 percent in the population as a whole; the numbers were no doubt smaller among those able to afford room, air, and hygiene, but there are many examples of middle-class families whose losses reached this scale. Of the seven children born to Jenny and Karl Marx in London, one died at birth, two after slightly more than a year, and a fourth at nine.[17] These numbers should serve to remind us that people in the nineteenth century had many fewer defenses against mortality and disease than we have become accustomed to since. As David Newsome observes, they "lived very much closer to pain, disaster and death than the generations that followed them," and were highly aware of the precariousness of their lives.[18] One phenomenon this helps to understand, in the face of the disappointment expressed about it by some historians, is the continuing homage women who themselves had public lives as writers or reformers paid to the general principle of separate spheres, reducing their availability as models of emancipation: in the conditions they knew it was difficult to imagine a world in which biological differences did not translate directly into social ones for the vast majority.[19]

Assertiveness and instability in the gender system

Despite all these grounds for assigning a distinct set of roles and tasks to women, there is much reason to regard the gender system as already unstable and showing signs of weakness even in the period when it seemed most firmly established. The very idealization accorded to women as wives and mothers created a tension with their subordination to men, helping to fuel demands for equality. Noting that many nineteenth-century feminist critics of separate spheres drew on "the conventional assumptions and discourses of domesticity," Richard Price describes the Victorian years when the ideology of separate spheres appeared most powerful and uncontested as simultaneously the moment when its underlying instability was becoming uncontainable. The suffragist Millicent Fawcett argued that public life could be much improved if "women's special experiences as women" could "be brought to bear on legislation"; far from making women more like men the result would be that "the truly womanly qualities in them will grow in strength and power."[20] Although Michelle Perrot does not stress the role played by the special virtues attributed to women in calling the system itself into question, she too notes that the moment when the distinctions were most insistently asserted in France, under the Second Empire in the 1860s, was also the point at which public contestations began to mount, producing a clamorous debate about the need for female education.[21]

Domestic ideology's assignment of such special qualities to women was not the only reason for its instability, however. Another was that heightened emphasis on the idea that natural differences between women and men justified assigning separate roles to each was itself in part a response to liberal and Enlightened criticism of traditional assumptions about inequality between the sexes. This connection has been most clearly recognized by Lynn Hunt. In 1790 the Marquis de Condorcet wrote that without equality between the sexes there could be no universal claim to human rights: "Either no individual of the human race has true rights, or all of them have the same ones; and he who votes against the rights of another, whatever his religion, his color, or his sex, has from that moment abjured his own rights." That the Revolution failed to give reality to such ideas has been regarded by some critics as a sign that liberalism and the Enlightenment mounted no serious challenge to traditional gender relations. Taking issue with these views, Hunt argues that the new grounds for gender division that now began to be asserted were themselves evidence that older and often unexamined premises were losing their force. Late eighteenth-century society (in good part for the reasons we have just given) was in no condition to put such views as Condorcet's into practice, or to countenance the upheavals that attempts to do so would have brought, so that defenders of male superiority easily had the upper hand. But they could no longer maintain it just as before. Far from merely confirming the traditional proscription of women from public life, "liberal political theory made the exclusion of women much more problematic. It made the exclusion of women into an issue." Domestic ideology was a response to this new situation, emerging "because political and cultural leaders felt the need to justify ... the continuing exclusion of women from politics." Looked at in this light, explicit arguments for female difference provided a replacement for the presuppositions about female inferiority that were implicit in traditional family relations. But assigning women to the private world of home and family on this basis only delayed the confrontation between this conventional subordination and the implications of the liberal principles that under-mined it.[22]

We can see the tensions this produced at work in an influ-ential German defense of gender inequality, Karl Theodor Welcker's article on "Relations Between the Sexes" (*Geschlechtsverhältnisse*) in the widely read *Staatslexikon* he edited together with Karl R. W. von Rotteck. In an often-cited essay, Karin Hausen notes that until late in the eighteenth century, German writers related differences between women and men primarily to each one's position in the family, taking the roles assumed there more or less for granted. In the nineteenth century, by contrast, writers such as Welcker provided elaborate justi-fications for gender roles, based on natural differences of temperament and character between the sexes. His description of the "stronger, bolder, freer" man as the natural founder, nurturer, and protector of the family, driven out into the world by the need to give scope to his creative powers, in contrast to the "weaker, more dependent and more timid" woman who accepted his protection inside the domestic space that was natural to her, provided a stronger justification for the sep-arate positions assigned to men and women than earlier writers felt a need to offer. In recognizing this as a new departure, however, Hausen does not note that Welcker was pushed to it by a troubled sense that the widely supported rejection of inherited privileges in his time and the dismantling of Old Regime despotisms seemed to imply a basic equality between the sexes. Enlightenment criticism led people to rec-ognize that the "voice of Nature is not readily decipherable," especially since "custom, prejudice and the interests of the stronger party here, as always where despotic and aristocratic relationships were involved, have corrupted the judgment even of the best enquirers." But he did not see how society could subsist without recognizing different roles for the two sexes, hence he sought to delve deeper into their natural bases, and to determine what social consequences did and did not fol-low from them. Both the larger role of men outside the family and their superiority inside it were justified by the natural contrast between strength and weakness, adventuresomeness and timidity, but the total exclusion of women from public life was not: what they shared with men gave them the right to take an interest in current debates, write for publication, and form benevolent societies. Reserved to men how-ever was direct participation in making political decisions (*politische Willensbildung*). Welcker distanced himself from those conservatives who gave no recognition to women's rights, even as he rejected radical claims that made them equal to men's. Since this left most of the traditional gender system in place, his discussion made little practical difference, but it testified to a recognition that the position of women in society could no longer simply be assumed; it had become a matter of public debate, and reasons needed to be offered for it.[23]

That debate was already in progress, and other writers, as Welcker well knew, had taken the liberal principles he espoused in directions that argued for much greater equality. One of these was the late eighteenth-century Prussian official and publicist Theodor von Hippel, who moved from being a defender of traditional gender roles to a supporter of women's rights during the 1790s. His shift seems to have come about partly in response to the French Revolution's demonstration that human institutions were more malleable than many believed, and that rational criticism could provide a path toward reconstructing them (Kant, whom Hippel knew well in Königsberg, believed that showing people's capacity to alter their form of life constituted the Revolution's greatest contribution to human progress), and partly through reading other Enlightened advocates of female rights, notably Condorcet. In the later editions of his book *On Marriage* and in a treatise *On the Civic Improvement of Women*, Hippel argued that biological differences between the sexes (whose importance he never denied) did not account for what many took to be the different capacities each exhibited; instead men had benefitted from their participation in civil society, whose challenges and opportunities expanded their understanding and powers of judgment, while "the soul of the woman shrank more and more into the limits of her household." If women were given the rights to live independent lives and to participate in public activities, their apparent inferiority would disappear – although they might still invest their abilities in characteristically female activities, such as poetry. Hippel's views had no practical effect in Germany, but they were widely known, and his giving expression to them had just the effect Lynn Hunt notes for liberal thinking in France, rendering the exclusion of women problematic, so that new grounds needed to be found by those who sought to justify it.[24]

That views such as Condorcet's and Hippel's were responsible for some of the tensions that marked the gender system, even as men's involvements in more powerful networks outside the family were giving them increased power and making women more dependent on them, is suggested also by the close relationship that can be documented between early feminism and liberalism. One sign of this kinship is that a high proportion of women who became active in early feminist movements came from liberal families, and had fathers, brothers, or husbands who promoted liberal causes. In the United States over half the women whose biographies were examined in a study of feminist origins came from families whose male members were active in anti-slavery or social reform societies. "In France, most feminists were married to, or were the daughters or sisters of republican politicians. In Germany, the left-wing liberals provided the family background of many feminist leaders, while in Hungary the most prominent feminists were generally the wives of nationalist politicians and thus presumably came themselves from nationalist backgrounds. An upbringing in a politically active liberal family would give such women not only an interest in and knowledge of politics, but also a belief in the right of the individual to freedom and self-determination."[25] To be sure, the feminists whose first exposure to politics came from discussions in their liberal families or participation in liberal organizations often found that their attempts to extend claims for individual autonomy to themselves and their sisters were not well received by their male relatives and associates. It was not a full openness of liberals to female emancipation that made liberal milieux a breeding ground for feminist activism, but the tension that developed there between the universality of the ideas advanced and the limited scope given them in actual life. But this is just the point: liberal notions were important in nurturing feminism precisely because they brought principles that implied equal rights to personal development and public participation up against the barriers still posed to them by existing conditions of social life and the attitudes they fostered.[26]

Intellectually, the connection is well illustrated by a comment of Jeanne Deroin, who moved to explicitly feminist activism after beginning as a supporter of the Saint-Simonians. She wrote in 1848:

> The reign of brute force has ended; that of morality
> and intelligence has just begun. The motives that led
> our fathers to exclude women from all participation
> in the governance of the State are no longer valid.
> When every question was decided by the sword, it was
> natural to believe that women – who could not take

part in combat – should not be seated in the assembly of warriors. In those days it was a question of destroying and conquering by the sword; today it is a question of building and of organizing. Women should be called on to take part in the great task of social regeneration that is under way. Why should our country be deprived of the services of its daughters?[27]

That conservatives understood this connection between liberal principles and challenges to existing relations between the sexes no less than did liberals is illustrated by the case of Balzac, whose most touching story of rebellion against social constraints makes the female protagonist for whom it is named, "Honorine," an avatar of liberal self-assertion too. Having unthinkingly accepted marriage at a young age to the aristocratic son of her guardian, Honorine suddenly flees from her husband with the first man who stirs her senses. Deserted by her lover when she becomes pregnant, and left alone by the death of her baby, she seeks to establish an independent life as a maker of artificial flowers, convinced that she has won her right to "freedom" through her devotion to "work." Balzac associates these terms with the liberal bourgeoisie who invoked them against inherited forms of domination by carefully establishing the chronology of the story so that it coincides with the coming of the 1830 revolution and the July Monarchy (Honorine's husband was an official under the Restoration). The author also makes clear in how negative a light his conservative and monarchist views cast Honorine's claims to have won her independence through devotion to productive labor, turning her belief in her own success into a childish fantasy by having it rest on the intricately orchestrated behind-the-scenes support of her husband, who never ceases to love her and want her back (his attempt to accomplish this leads to tragedy for both). Balzac was no friend of either feminism or liberalism; just for this reason he understood that the same modern ideas that challenged traditional forms of authority also undermined the assumed position of women.

Balzac's "Honorine" points to another source of instability in the gender system, namely that, despite what ideology called for, numbers of nineteenth-century middle-class women were active in business. In certain occupations, men sought out wives who could serve as partners, either to sell feminine products to customers, or to oversee production that involved typically female tasks such as sewing. This was the case with the French merchant and manufacturer of fashionable apparel Romain Lhopiteau, who, once he was well enough established to consider marrying, looked for a wife who could "share the work of the enterprise (*maison*) with me." He had no trouble finding someone who fit the bill. A lace merchant with whom he did business suggested the daughter of some associates; the practical purpose of the union did not prevent the young man (not yet thirty) from being smitten with her at once, finding her "adorable," "graceful," and "vivacious." Nor was she at all averse to the kind of life he proposed; "endowed with a lively intelligence, and a strong, precise mind," she also brought a dowry that added to the common capital. The marriage, concluded in 1857, was happy but short, since the young woman took sick and died six years later, despite elaborate (and Lhopiteau makes clear, expensive) efforts to save her. Her illness and death were partly responsible for the business falling into difficulties in the 1860s (increased competition and a shifting market contributed too), so that when the widower looked again for a wife who would take over the commercial role played by his first one he had to settle for an orphan with a reputation for intelligence and energy but no dowry. Despite their joint efforts the house was caught in a credit squeeze and went bankrupt; faced with the need to work hard to restore their position and reputation the couple lived frugally, but (at least as he tells the story) happily. The new wife's kindness to the children of the first one gained her the affection of her husband's former in-laws, and the birth of a daughter to the new couple, was "I assure you welcomed with joy ... and heartily celebrated," despite their narrow circumstances. In this part of their life the second Mme Lhopiteau became an independent entrepreneur, opening a shop to sell lace and lingerie, while Lhopiteau became a wine merchant, as well as taking a part in the business his wife had begun.[28]

The expectations about gender roles operative in this story were not universally shared in the middle classes, but nor were they truly exceptional. David Sabean provides an extensive catalogue of women active in business, largely, but not entirely, at a higher social level than Lhopiteau. "The well-known cases of Bertha Krupp, Sara Warburg, and Charlotte Oppenheim are good examples but there are many lesser-known ones ... According to Wolfgang Zorn, it was quite normal for widows in Swabia to take over the functions of their husbands, but it was not always just a matter of stepping into the breach because the role of wives in entrepreneurial activity was, as he notes, frequently important." (I noted the case of Wilhelm Sattler above.) Moreover, "the kind of family negotiating and network building that such women were used to doing, coupled with ownership or usufructuary rights over property, gave them a solid foundation for entering the world of trade and commerce."[29] Mme Boucicaut, the wife of the founder of the pioneering French department store the Bon Marché, played a role in giving the business the paternalistic cast that defined it; her fictionalized portrait as Mme Hédouin in Zola's novel *Pot Bouille* shows her running the business after her husband's death, while losing neither her respected position in society nor her attractiveness to men as a result. Certain examples of women who did not work have become nearly canonical in the historical literature, among them Bonnie Smith's colorful account of the shift from women active in business in northern French textile towns during the first half of the nineteenth century to their development of a separate world centered around household, child-rearing, and good works in the second half. But Smith makes clear that women in this later situation generated a strong sense of their own social place and power, and we must remember that the kind of evolution she describes was by no means a new one in the nineteenth century, since Amanda Vickery shows that similar movements toward greater domesticity for women had occurred at several points in earlier periods, in response to expanding prosperity and the opportunity it provided for women to live less careworn lives (a chance seized by many men too, when they could afford it).[30] Certain of the limits set to women's lives by nineteenth-century conditions and practices were ones that few people had the courage or means to transgress, but the very decades when new defenses sere offered for them were ones when the gender system's inner fragility began to show through.

Toward autonomy

During the third quarter of the nineteenth century many things combined to counter the sharper division between sex roles that set in after 1750 and to open up new paths and spaces for women. The first, and surely not the least important, was the establishment of organized feminist associations. Until they appeared, feminist activism had been largely a matter of individuals writing or acting on their own, although some of them worked within organizations in which male–female relations became an issue in connection with some other chief focus, such as the French Saint-Simonians or the English followers of Robert Owen. This situation began to change in England during the 1850s, when a group of feminists (quaintly referred to as "the ladies of Langham Place") established regular meetings explicitly devoted to women's issues and put out a paper, but the tempo of change picked up both there and on the continent in the next decade, with the founding of the German *Allgemeine deutsche Frauenverein* in 1865, the French *Société pour la revendication des droits de la femme*, in 1866, and the English National Society for Women's Suffrage in 1867. We cannot pause over the history of feminist activism save to note that the movement entered a new and more advanced phase of development in the 1890s, marked by a rapid expansion of the local and national associations, the appearance of many new periodicals, and the convening of a series of international congresses (some in connection with world's fairs or expositions).[31] In the rhythm of its birth and development, organized feminism took shape in connection with the same extension and thickening of networks of communication and action as did modern political parties and pressure groups.

Especially in the later period socialist and working-class figures put forward their own notions of how to improve the lives of women, but the earlier connection between feminism and liberalism continued to be central to the movement. A strong source of inspiration was John Stuart Mill's *The Subjection of Women*, which appeared in 1869. Behind it stood Mill's relationship with his long-time friend and eventual wife Harriet Taylor, whose own essay on "The Enfranchisement of Women" (written in 1851, partly in response to the American feminist convention held at Seneca Falls, New York, two years earlier) already made many of the arguments her husband would more fully develop after her death in 1858. Drawing on ideas that were much discussed in the Unitarian and Utilitarian circles where the Mills met, both writings mounted a direct attack on the notion of separate spheres, arguing that by excluding women from participation in the wider worlds of society and politics the existing system of gender relations blocked them from developing their intellectual and moral capacities, depriving society of the contributions half of its members could make to its well-being and improvement. The Mills expressly denied the often-repeated claim that women whose lives centered on home and family were able to develop qualities and virtues that provided a salutary influence on men, making them more polite, less selfish, or more morally responsible. On the contrary, the weakness imposed on women gave them a morally damaging taste for subtle forms of domination, teaching them to seek power in personal relations through deception, pretense, and artifice. Given the potent influence of circumstances on human development, the authors insisted, no one in the nineteenth century had a sufficient basis for speaking about what were presumed to be natural differences between the sexes: only if men and women were both allowed to develop their talents and abilities without artificial restraints could any valid inquiry into the influence of biological differences on socially relevant qualities begin.[32] Harriet Taylor's essay remained relatively unknown after its appearance in *The Westminster Review*, but Mill's book made a deep and wide impact; published just at the moment when feminist organizations were beginning to spring up in many places it was immediately translated into many languages, guiding the thinking of advocates for women's rights everywhere, and quickly becoming (as Richard Evans dubs it) "the feminist Bible."[33]

One reason why the campaigns to change opinion mounted by feminist organizations were able to have an impact was that some of the conditions that had long justified the tight association between women and family life were receding. One crucial development was the fall in the birthrate and in family size that became evident from around 1860. The scope of the reduction varied from place to place, but overall the average number of births in middle-class families shrank by almost 50 percent over the century, and the proportion of families with fewer than three children more or less doubled. Reasons for the drop appear to have been many and they are difficult to disentangle; condoms (now able to be made of rubber) and diaphragms were clearly in use among middle-class people by the 1860s, and increasingly so from the 1880s; knowledge about them was spread even by conservative attempts to forestall it, as in the prosecution of Charles Bradlaugh and Annie Besant for publishing a birth-control manual in 1877.[34] But social factors were also at work, as evidenced by the motivations that led professional families to reduce their numbers of children. In Britain the phenomenon began to be evident from the 1850s, but picked up speed after 1880, and F. M. L. Thompson argues persuasively that the need to provide education for children in these sectors of society had much to do with this rhythm. The first phase set in as the political reforms of the 1830s and 1840s closed off traditional paths to government jobs through influence and "corruption," creating uncertainty and raising the cost of preparing sons for positions. The second corresponded to the general expansion in education that took place all over Europe after 1870, involving not just young people aiming at professional careers but also those who sought the technical training required for managerial positions in the new sectors of industry. The primacy of professional groups in family limitation is equally evident in Germany, where in addition research shows that the birth rate fell faster among "free" professionals such as lawyers or doctors, and "independent" academics without regular appointments than among those in state employment (professors were officially civil servants), who could expect greater occupational security. City-dwellers also reduced family size well before rural people. Jews, who could not be civil servants before 1867, and few of whom became such afterwards, but who clustered in "free" professions and urban activities, show an especially marked and precocious tendency to smaller families. In the rest of the population the fall was slower in business circles, although it gathered speed as technical education took on greater importance. In every country the turn to smaller families was also fostered by the diminishing need for households to produce goods required for their members' lives. This development had been progressing throughout the century (and in some places earlier), as manufactured clothing and other consumer items became more available, and at prices that allowed them to compete with things produced at home, but it reached a higher stage in the more urbanized fin-de-siècle. As Ute Frevert observes, "the productive energies of entire bevvies of daughters – let alone unmarried sisters, cousins and sisters-in-law – were now superfluous."[35] The fall in family size, like the diminished dependence of individuals on family connections for survival and advancement, was thus a corollary of the evolution that spread modern bourgeois networks and frames of action through society as a whole in the decades before 1914.

As these changes in family life progressed, they were accompanied by a remarkable expansion of educational opportunities for girls and women. Calls for such expansion were often put forth before 1850, but little was done to implement them before the 1880s. In

England a small and gradual expansion in girls' schools took place in the 1860s, but as F. M. L. Thompson notes "it was not until the 1880s and 1890s that there was anything like a rush of foundations of girls' high schools and boarding schools." John Tosh finds in this period an increasing willingness on the part of middle-class fathers to spend money on educating their daughters, partly out of concern that those who did not marry would be unable to support themselves.[36] On the continent secondary education was largely in the hands of the state (as it began to be in Britain after 1870), which meant that the rhythm of change depended in part on politics; because the republican politicians who came to power in France at the end of the 1870s were eager to reduce the influence of the Church over female education, new schools for girls were established earlier there than in Germany. Under the Old Regime religious orders provided nearly the whole of the available education for girls; their *pensions* disappeared with the dissolution of the orders under the Revolution, but returned in hardly altered form afterwards. The instruction they offered was strictly limited to subjects expected to prepare pupils for their later roles as wives and mothers, consisting of reading, writing, sewing, and such "adornments" as music and dancing; the curriculum in schools run by laypeople (such as the one set up by the Dubois family into which Edmond Goblot's father married) largely copied the model.

Under the July Monarchy (as during the Enlightenment and even occasionally before) liberal reformers argued that female intelligence was not inferior to male and that girls deserved a more serious education in order to develop it; a periodical devoted to the subject was established in 1845. Things remained mostly at the level of discussion, however, until Napoleon III, in one of his attempts to gain liberal support near the end of his regime, appointed Victor Duruy as Minister of Public Instruction. Duruy proposed setting up state-run secondary schools for girls, and his supporter Jules Simon, later an important Third Republic politician, gave a much-noticed speech on the subject in 1867, saying that young women, with their special qualities of intelligence, tact, and sensitivity, ought not to remain as "decked-up idols." But his alternative was to make them "useful and charming companions in study for us," and his vision of female education remained focused on marriage and family life, with no intention of preparing young women for independent careers. He retained the strong sense of difference between male and female nature common among people of both sexes, and in any case the Bonapartist regime fell before Duruy was able to act on these ideas.[37]

It was in 1880, following Gambetta's triumph over the monarchists and clericals, that the Third Republic made a significant move in this direction, setting up state-run secondary schools for girls. The law was named for a young follower of Jules Ferry, Camille Sée (male, despite what his name may suggest), and its aims were still narrow. Ferry, like Jules Simon, was above all concerned to remove girls from a priestly education he blamed for creating a moral and intellectual abyss between husbands and wives; republican solidarity and the contentment of men were his motives more than the emancipation of women. But the Act's effect soon outran these intentions. Although the curriculum of the new schools did not contain the mathematics and classical languages that prepared students for university entrance, subjects deemed too "abstract" for girls, it did envisage female teachers for the new *collèges* and *lycées des filles* (hitherto advanced instruction in girls' schools had mostly been given by men), thus expanding opportunities for women in one area, and requiring a new teacher-training institute to prepare them. It was established at Sèvres (and headed by a woman) in 1881. There is considerable evidence that pressures were then mounting to bring instruction for girls closer to that given to boys, and thus to prepare them for the *baccalauréat* and the further education and careers to which it gave access. The demands seem to have come largely from bourgeois families of a modest sort, concerned (like their English counterparts mentioned above) to provide a career path for female children for whom marriage could not be expected to guarantee survival and security.[38]

Testimony that such attitudes were spreading in France comes from the new edition of a highly popular book of advice on choosing an occupation, Édouard Charton's *Guide pour le choix d'un état ou Dictionnaire des professions*, published in 1880. Its earlier versions in 1842 and 1851 assumed the book's audience to be almost wholly masculine; the only female occupation mentioned was teaching. By contrast the much-expanded book of 1880 contained a whole section devoted to *professions des femmes* with an extensive discussion both of particular female occupations (including accounting, commerce, and medicine) and of the whole question of women's work. Charton was traditional enough (almost no nineteenth-century people of either sex were not) to begin by saying that a woman has "a natural profession, fitting to her powers and faculties, that of manager of her household and educator of her children," but he rejected those who sought to confine them to it; many women needed to work for pay, whether to supplement a husband's income, provide for her own sustenance before marriage or in widowhood or if she remained single, or to help meet the needs of relatives. "We add that this obligation is not always an evil; valiantly and ably fulfilled it becomes an opportunity for merit, a source of inner satisfaction, a genuine dignity and a basis for the esteem and respect of all. If the independence of those women favored by fortune becomes an escape from every serious obligation, a cause of idleness and uselessness, it is an evil, not a good. What is considered as a privilege becomes a ground of inferiority, of loss." Charton's views were in accord with the large increase in the number of young women who attained lycée degrees, tripling to 13,000 between 1885 and 1890; five years later there were over 800 women (still a small number to be sure, but not to be ignored) registered in university faculties. Ferry and Sée probably did not anticipate such a result, but once the anti-clerical animus of the republican politicians got mixed in with the desire of families to assure some kind of stable future for their daughters, the wider aims of the feminist movement began to find an opening. Their power of fulfillment came less from acceptance by male politicians than from their pertinence to the conditions of existence inside a more fully modernized form of bourgeois life.[39]

The absence of a similar political impetus for expanding female education in Germany was a chief reason why things went more slowly there. Both the left-liberal Progressives around Friedrich Naumann and the social democrats supported the educational objectives of the expanding feminist organizations, but neither had sufficient clout in national politics to make their backing effective. Secondary education was available to girls whose families could afford it, in various kinds of Mädchen- or Töchterschule (as well as from private tutors), but the curricula were much like that in French pensions, giving students the materials to provide their later husbands with what one fed-up reformer called "a pretty domesticity." All the same some women succeeded in providing themselves with a good educational foundation, and clamored for admission to universities. Some went to Switzerland, where women could study medicine as early as the 1870s (a point noted by Édouard Charton). From the mid 1890s several German states (led, as in many such instances, by Baden) made it possible for girls who had spent sufficient time in schools to take the *Abitur* examination that was the German counterpart to the *baccalauréat*, and thus in principle have the right to attend universities. At first they were only accepted as "guests," but by 1900 they could register as regular students in the chief Baden university, Heidelberg, a right accorded in Berlin only in 1908. Meanwhile, the traditional *Töchterschule* began to be supplemented with *Lyceen, Oberlyceen,* and *Gymnasien* for girls. At the outbreak of the War women constituted around 6 percent of students in German universities.[40]

The rate of progress was slow, but Gunilla Budde thinks it was sufficient by the end of the century to encourage increasing numbers of young women to reject their longstanding exclusion from the putatively universal principles of autonomy and responsibility that were expected to orient the lives of their brothers. The reduction in family size increased the chances that resources hitherto devoted chiefly to sons might support the education of daughters, and at least in some families (Dolores Augustine cites the Siemens as one example), the expectation spread that *Bildung* for women should prepare them to chart their own path in the world, partaking of the *bürgerliche* ethic of *Leistung* (achievement) previously reserved to men.[41]

Achievements and limits

The overall pattern underlying all these developments can be clarified by considering the argument of an insightful if too-optimistically titled book, Robert Max Jackson's *Destined for Equality: the Inevitable Rise of Women's Status*. At the deepest level, Jackson argues, the advance of women that has taken place since the middle of the nineteenth century rests on the unfolding of modern institutions and practices.

> Modern economic and political organization propelled this transformation by slowly dissociating social power from its allegiance to gender inequality. The power over economic resources, legal rights, the allocation of positions, legitimating values, and setting priorities, once present in families shifted into businesses and government organizations. In these organizations, profit, efficiency, political legitimacy, organizational stability,

competitiveness, and similar considerations mattered more
than male privileges vis-à-vis females.⁴²

As long as political authority and productive activity were
regulated by the same hierarchical (and in our terms teleocratic) principles that underlay rigid male dominance inside families, "family
role differentiation was directly embedded in economic and political
inequality": the public and private arenas each reinforced the gender
inequality practiced inside the other. But as abstract considerations of
utility and efficiency gained power outside the family, the continuity
between the two realms was disrupted; men found themselves operating outside their families according to principles that did not support
the power they still claimed within them; male supremacy was called
into question by the evolution of the public world that had earlier mirrored and confirmed it. Jackson has no illusions that men in general
supported either the principles or the policies that called their power
into question; quite the contrary they often fought them, moved either
by prejudice or by the satisfaction some found in domination. But
"their institutional interests repeatedly prompted them to take actions
incompatible with" their personal views or desires. A similar point of
view has been upheld by other writers, for instance by Jürgen Kocka in
debates with certain feminists who regard any society capable of realizing equality between men and women as "post-bourgeois."⁴³

A telling example is provided by Jackson's discussion of the
"Married Women's Property Laws" that, beginning in the mid nineteenth century in America and somewhat later in Europe, abolished
the centuries-old practice of giving husbands control over the real
property of their wives for as long as the marriage lasted. Two linked
considerations lay behind these changes. One was that the older
arrangements reflected the situation in which families were centers of
economic enterprise, making it desirable that all the resources available for operating the business be controlled by a single head – who,
in the light of traditional assumptions, could only be male. As business organizations grew larger and more anonymous, becoming corporations with limited liability, often run by professional managers,
the close link between family property and business grew looser,
diminishing the need for husbands to control their wives' capital.
Even where family wealth and business remained intertwined, however, other considerations worked in favor of leaving title to property

332 / Men and women

in the wife's hands. During the nineteenth century, as we have already noted, businesses increasingly came to rely on credit no longer chiefly provided by family members but by anonymous lending institutions. In difficult times, if a firm was threatened by collapse, all the property in the hands of its head was at risk. Leaving the wife legal control over her property thus became a shield against ruin, quite apart from recognizing the rights of women. As Jackson notes, "In the fifty years after the laws' passage, most litigation invoking the married women's property acts concerned debtor–creditor relations, not husband–wife disputes. The spokesmen for commerce had condemned the common-law doctrine that stripped wives of legal independence because it muddied the legal obligations for debt. Women's social status did not concern them." Thus the evolution of commerce and finance undermined the inherited grounds for giving husbands control over their wives' resources.[44]

Jackson recognizes all the same that the separation between male and female spheres grew wider before it narrowed. As modern forms of economic and social activity spread, men's traditional connection to the world outside the household provided families with their only link to them. "Women deferred to men and depended on husbands because they had no practical alternatives outside the family. By shouldering the burden of sole economic responsibility, men gained deference and superiority within their families. As the structures of economic and political inequality gradually disengaged from gender inequality, the structure of family role differentiation faced increasing pressures." It was "not the permanent, inherent needs of industrial society" that fostered the heightened separation of spheres, "but the transitional imbalance between the long-term egalitarian implications of modern society and the momentum that sustained gender inequality. The role-differentiated family – with an employed husband and a homemaker wife – was a transitory family form that bridged the transition between a family economy and a modern industrial economy."[45] Although Jackson's argument probably underplays the role of cultural change – of the instability introduced into the gender system by Enlightenment criticism – and he does not try to understand the difference between the two phases in terms of the changing impact of involvement in distant connections for which I have argued here, the overall pattern he describes fits fairly closely with the one I have tried to sketch out.

Much of the path he charts, however, still remained to be traversed at the end of the nineteenth century. One way to describe what had been accomplished is Göran Therborn's conclusion that despite the persistence of patriarchal relations and the prejudices that underpinned them, "the subjection of women had nevertheless ceased to be self-evident in Europe." This was a limited achievement to be sure but it was far from a trivial one, since female subordination long rested precisely on such self-evidence, and there are parts of the world even in the twenty-first century where it still does.[46] Many things kept the principles put forward by Condorcet, Hippel, and the Mills from being able to find realization, including the resistance to feminist demands by the large majority of men; of these some feared women as competitors, while some recoiled from the more complex and subtle challenges to a domination that may have compensated for a weakness they could not escape feeling in other parts of their lives. Were there space we would consider both the often silly but revealingly anxious satires of the "new woman" that appeared in newspapers and magazines, and the "crisis of masculinity" that a number of historians have discerned in the work of artists and writers such as Gustav Klimt and Otto Weininger, and in the anxious attention paid to such threatening figures as Salomé and Delilah.[47]

One mode of equality that was slow to be established was the right to vote, among the chief goals sought by nineteenth-century feminists the one it took longest to achieve. Typically it came in stages in Britain, conceded to women over thirty in 1918, at the moment when suffrage became fully universal for men, and to those in their twenties ten years later (in the USA the ratification of the nineteenth amendment in 1920 eliminated sex as a basis for the franchise); in Germany it came with equally characteristic suddenness, by virtue of the universal suffrage established in the Weimar constitution of 1918, at a moment when defeat in war gave power to left liberals and social democrats; in France the belief on the part of republicans that women were still deeply influenced by the church, and would vote accordingly, served as an impediment to sex-blind suffrage, or an excuse for not granting it, until just after World War II. However, those who see in this delay a testimony to the unchecked power of ancient prejudices in France often forget that by 1914 fifty Departmental or local councils had endorsed suffrage for women and that a measure in favor of it passed the Chamber of Deputies four times in the period between the wars, nearly succeeding in the more conservative Senate in 1925.[48]

Opposition to women's rights was not a cause that united all men, it divided them along many lines, sometimes in parallel with other issues, sometimes not.

The consciousness that fundamental change had occurred was widespread, and what it involved can be shown from a text that I hope provides a fitting conclusion to this chapter. It was from the pen of Camille Mauclair, a writer and critic well known at the time, who began as a radical symbolist (like others in his literary camp sympathetic to anarchism) but turned to a series of reform causes, at once social and aesthetic. In 1899 he published an article on "Women in the Eyes of Modern Painters" ("La Femme devant les peintres modernes"). Although focused on representations of women by artists, it took the change it found there as evidence of a larger shift in the way women appeared to men. Mauclair was fully aware of the way traditional male ways of looking at women turned them into objects of masculine desire and fantasy, as illustrated by the portraits painters had long made of them. In such images,

> Her happy face, radiating a virgin brightness, is present by virtue of its smile and the clarity of its eyes; it is devoid of any mental mystery, it waits, like a sheet of blank paper, for the man's feeling to inscribe his dream on it. It is a permanent spectacle, open to admiration like a landscape. And what our contemplation seeks to discover on it is itself, the motive of its attraction, why it is that we invest so many sentiments, upsets and spiritual anxieties in that countenance, natural, calm, proffered and impersonal.

In recent decades, however, painters' representations of women had begun to alter, giving them a different kind of presence, first in work such as Manet's famous *Olympia* and *Déjeuner sur l'herbe* and Degas's portraits of women in his own family, then in pictures by lesser artists as well. Here Mauclair found women who give evidence of an individuality, a power of expression, and a testimony to independent thoughtfulness that make us aspire to know, no less than with portraits of men, what links these surface features to the mental and psychic life that animates them. In place of the ideal of a placid beauty, "carnal, radiant, and animal," of the dressed-up and indifferent creature who reflects the "aroused desire of the painter and the man of the time," we see a being whose enduring magnetism is accompanied by a "psychological expression whose birth is within."

> She has broken through the barrier imposed by gallantry
> and tradition, that isolated her from life and confined her
> in a narrow domain, by respect as much as by belief in her
> mental incapacity. She takes part in moral life, she shares
> the cares and responsibilities of modern man, she adopts
> the same mental habits, she is acquiring an equivalent per-
> sonality, and her physiognomy gives evidence of it.

This "new woman ... thoughtful and active" will inspire a new painting, where she will be studied and depicted not by lovers but by equals.[49]

One reason to regard Mauclair's essay as significant is that it was not merely an expression of personal sentiment, but an account of a historical change in the way modern women projected their being, especially evident since the mid century. Without claiming that the differences between women's and men's social roles could ever be wholly effaced, Mauclair pointed to an already palpable shift in their public and private relations, and to the future of greater equality and mutual recognition it promised.

10 BOURGEOIS MORALS: FROM VICTORIANISM TO MODERN SEXUALITY

Few features of classic bourgeois life have been more remarked on and bewailed than its morality, often derided as rigid, puritanical, and hypocritical, especially in regard to sex. Nineteenth-century moralists made large demands on speech and behavior in the name of decency and decorum, often in strikingly inconsistent ways. Men were allowed satisfactions considered unthinkable for women; representations of unclothed bodies were taken for granted so long as they could be assigned to some distant or mythical realm, but moralistic viewers were shocked by Manet's ironic and playful contemporary nudes (in contrast to Mauclair's celebration of them), and even by the suggestion of a falling gown-strap on the bare shoulder of an elegant woman in a portrait by John Singer Sargent. We can defend bourgeois morality on the grounds that many human societies have imposed narrow and inflexible standards of propriety on dress, demeanor, and public expression, especially for women, and that hypocrisy has reared its head wherever ordinary flesh-and-blood humans have sought to exhibit strict moral and religious principles in their daily lives. Bourgeois themselves were the first to call attention to hypocrisy in their midst, condemning it in the name of transparency and truth. In addition, Peter Gay's detailed and colorful studies have shown that many nineteenth-century middle-class women and men lived far more open and varied moral lives than has commonly been supposed, often regarding sensual and erotic satisfactions as a highly desirable part of respectable existence. Even his account leaves many features of the traditional picture intact, however, and with them the need to make sense of the perplexing contours of modern bourgeois moral belief and behavior.[1]

I will attempt to meet this need here by showing some of the ways bourgeois morality evolved in parallel to the developing pattern of gender relations set out in the previous chapter. Just as a longstanding and well-established system of separate spheres acquired new dimensions and justifications from late in the eighteenth century, but through social and intellectual developments that challenged its stability and whose further unfolding would render divisions between the sexes more permeable, so in morality a regime often taken to be peculiar to the nineteenth century is much better understood as a tighter and more rigid assertion of long-established distinctions between permitted and forbidden things. This moral stiffening was based on premises and practices often advanced and supported in the name of liberation and autonomy, resulting in an unstable compound whose demanding and rigid claims on individuals bore the seeds of a breakdown that would foster radical departures from traditional standards and expectations. This trajectory in morals, like the one we traced out for gender relations, owed much to the deepening importance of distant ties and relations in every sphere of life, and in particular to its impact on families.

Classic moralism and its transformations

The peculiar mix of continuities and contrasts between traditional attitudes and those that gave a new tone to moral thinking and practice during the nineteenth century has been most clearly set out by Michael Mason. Focusing on Britain, Mason shows that moderns inherited what he calls a "classic moralism," grounded in religious and secular ideas that legitimated sexual activity only for the sake of reproduction and inside the family, consigning premarital sex or pleasure sought for itself to the dark realm of vice, alongside concubinage, adultery, prostitution, and divorce. By contrast with what emerged around 1800, however, this classic moralism was often far from puritanical. Bathed in an aura of unquestioned universal acceptance, it radiated a kind of common-sense worldly wisdom, recognizing the weakness that flesh is heir to, and thus the unavoidable gap between what morality might demand and the conduct most people could be expected to achieve. The indulgence classic moralists sometimes showed to human foibles and weaknesses went along with an often earthy and ribald style of speech about bodily and sexual matters. The more rigid moral system that came to be called "Victorian" did not wholly displace the older one; people could still read periodicals that took pleasure in lewd puns and that did not hesitate to satirize the extremes of prudish reformers (one article proposed to ban rolling pins and pokers because of their phallic shapes). Such instances recall the spicy and racy language of Chaucer, Boccaccio, and Rabelais, in a way classic moralists themselves. It was characteristic of such traditional moralism that it sought to regulate and restrict prostitution but not to stamp it out, in contrast to some self-consciously modern nineteenth-century reformers who believed the oldest profession could and should be eradicated.[2]

Although this venerable ethic survived into the nineteenth century, it never lost certain marks of its pre-modern origins. Its mix of moral stringency and indulgence accorded well with a widely shared view of the world that gave everything within it an assigned place in a hierarchical order stretching from pure divinity at the top to sheer materiality at the bottom; human nature, positioned in the middle, was at once and naturally drawn upward toward higher things and downward toward base ones. Lowly as the body might be, it had an allotted place in this architecture, and thus an inescapable role in the drama of preordained ends that gave meaning to the whole. The wide disparities in social position and well-being between ranks were justified on the ground that those at the top were both physically and mentally distinct from those below them. Because social divisions rooted in nature were passed between generations by procreation (and "blood"), bodily functions could assume a social and moral significance they would lose as they came to be seen as merely "private" matters. Thus it made sense for people of high degree to make a show of the activities that sustained their corporeal existence, going to bed, getting up, eating, and even sometimes voiding in public. Alain Corbin points out that pre-modern ideas about bodies depicted them as caught up in the physical order that governed the lives of plants and animals, responding to the phases of the moon and subject to astrological and magical influences. These views were reflected in taboos concerning such things as placentas, nail cuttings, and lost teeth, and in the widespread belief that it was wrong and dangerous to allow anything to "impede natural bodily functions; accordingly people were quite tolerant of belching, farting, sneezing, sweating, and physical manifestations of desire." The unbuttoned nature of classic moralist speech noted by Mason belongs to this same cultural universe, one quite distant from the Christian image of humans as needing to look above all to the welfare of their souls. But in a world where people were exposed to both ways of thinking some mixing of them was bound to take place, and it seems sensible to regard the simultaneously rigid and loose ethic and language of "classic moralism" as one example.[3]

It may not be possible even to list, much less to treat adequately, all the sources from which flowed the elements of a less forgiving moral orientation, but two important ones will structure the discussion that follows. The first may be called restrictive, and had to do with the relevance of behavioral restraint to well-being within particular social groups, and in particular the historical developments that led middle-class people to impose greater discipline on themselves and others. It was here that the role of family membership so important in structuring male–female relations made itself felt in morality. The second can be labeled enabling, and found expression in more positive views about human nature and its potentials, fostered first by the Enlightenment and then by the French Revolution. The expanding role of distant connections in everyday life was important to both.

The different degrees to which moral restraint was demanded within particular sections of society, and the ways these changed, had much to do with the ends served by family membership within each. As noted in the previous chapter, family was crucial to individuals at many social levels; save for those whose resources were too meager to sustain stable unions (to be sure, they were many), families served as vehicles for passing assets and status between generations and as points from which social alliances and connections were made. This was true no less of many early modern peasants and artisans than of aristocrats and bourgeois, but it is the latter pair that chiefly concerns us here.[4] In one regard it was nobles who attached the greatest value to family, because they had the most to inherit and the greatest reason to preserve the purity of their blood lines; in every country great nobles prided themselves on the eminence and honor attached to their lineages. All the same, a longstanding and broadly diffused view regarded bourgeois as the people most devoted to family life, in the sense that they invested larger quantities of both affect and energy in domestic relations. Portraits of bourgeois couples, in sixteenth-century German or Netherlands towns, and later in the seventeenth-century Dutch Republic, give off an air of mutual involvement and intimacy palpably different from the self-conscious display of eminence that characterizes images of aristocrats. In eighteenth-century Paris, novels and plays often presented domesticity as a specifically bourgeois trait. Even those with far-flung commercial connections were described as caught up in everyday domestic relations and preoccupied by their problems and concerns, in contrast to nobles whose lives took on a freer and more exalted air through their ties to court and king.[5]

The moral implications of this bourgeois domesticity were often noted. Husbands and wives were described as living a kind of obligatory common life, and as sentimentally devoted to marital fidelity, traits parodied and scorned by some aristocrats. Daniel Roche finds evidence for an "intensification of affective space" in the way bourgeois household interiors were arranged and inhabited. Moral seriousness was an aspect of the sturdy, unpretentious existence attributed to German *Bürger* by eighteenth-century writers, in contrast to the *galanterie* of French aristocrats and their local imitators. If Lawrence Stone is correct, such a family style was less confined to middle-class people in England, since country gentry and even some nobles all provide evidence for the spread of "companionate marriage" there during the eighteenth century, involving terms of endearment and expressions of affection between spouses, both in person and in letters. Patriarchy still reigned, but it was of a less insistent kind, capable of greater attention to the needs and rights of wives, and even of an expanded recognition about the place of sexual pleasure in marriages. That such attitudes and behavior were less class-specific in England than elsewhere accords with what we have seen in other connections.[6]

Where the differences were marked various reasons have been offered for them, and there may be some truth in the often-repeated idea that bourgeois acted differently from nobles because they were less confident of their position and more fearful of disapproval. But a broader and more illuminating perspective arises from a contrast delineated by Göran Therborn in his wide-ranging world history of family life. The difference to which he points does not rigidly distinguish bourgeois families from aristocratic ones, but it places practically all of the former on one side of a line that runs through the world of the second; it rests on whether or not families were organized to support some form of productive life. Producing goods for their own survival or for the market, conducting some kind of business, or supporting the professional work of a household head (almost always male, to be sure) was an important part of what many families did; their survival and in some cases advancement depended on it. Rural activities were little different from urban ones in this regard, and Therborn stresses this continuity by employing the general term "estate management" to describe the practices that aimed to preserve family resources for the sake of supporting some occupation or employment. Where overseeing such assets was important to family survival, it was incumbent on members not to squander them, and individuals' involvements with each other was reinforced by the understanding that each one's fate was tied up with that of the household enterprise, however sharply differentiated the roles assigned (especially to men and women) within it. Although such a "family economy" contrasts with the later "male-breadwinner – female homemaker model" often associated with the nineteenth-century idealization of domestic relations, the earlier form already made whatever work sustained the family the focus of its members' mutual reliance and dependence. Indeed, many early professional families (and some commercial ones) conformed to the later model, since in them too the role of the wife was largely limited to managing a household that both relied on and supported the husband's work. To be sure, this interplay of domestic and practical concerns was not always productive of affection and harmony, nor did it constitute any guarantee of behaving morally, since complaints and fears about adultery, concubinage, resort to prostitutes, and children who schemed to fulfill their amorous desires against the will of their parents were present in every social sphere. "Classic moralists" would not have been surprised by such anomalies.[7]

The case was very different, however, with families whose position rested not on some form of "estate management" but on attempts to obtain personal favor and material advantage through participation in courtly life. To the end of the eighteenth century, and later in some places, royal or princely patronage offered access to very large resources, in the form of offices, gifts, and favors, some of which could be used to cement connections with equals or with clients further down the social scale. Such opportunities were especially attractive to nobles who considered ordinary work beneath them or whose other resources had somehow become diminished, and rulers were happy to provide them in exchange for loyalty and support. Preserving familial position was an important condition for pursuing such benefits, but everyday cooperation between family members had little to do with it; far more important were certain personal qualities – attractiveness, charm, good manners, speaking well – rather than the moral discipline that aided in directing resources toward collective survival and advance. These courtly qualities could be conceived as civilizing and even moral, as Baldessare Castiglione's famous treatise *The Courtier* and its many imitators showed, and court life sometimes sought to follow these models; indeed Norbert Elias regarded it as a major source of the internalization of discipline and self-control he famously labeled "the civilizing process," rooted in forms of politeness and restraint adopted in order to show respect for superiors, and to dramatize each person's place inside the hierarchy topped by a prince or king. But the personal qualities that made for success in courts could also pass over into self-promotion, seductiveness, wiliness, and intrigue. Where they did, Therborn observes, aristocratic society "let go of many family norms in favor of general sexual libertinism."[8]

The phenomenon was particularly marked in France, where it received literary representation in Choderlos de Laclos's famous *Dangerous Liaisons* of 1782, a story of sexual exploitation, intricate machinations, and cold-hearted personal revenge; its portrayal of scheming and self-indulgent aristocrats resembled those in the many now-forgotten but then highly popular *libelles* that portrayed the frivolity and decadence of courtly life, and whose role in draining away the Old Regime's aura of legitimacy has been highlighted by Robert Darnton. Most German courts had a more reserved style, but aristocrats were the object of moral critique there too, as in England, where people whose position depended on patronage sometimes exhibited moral attitudes close to their French counterparts, a phenomenon well illustrated by Samuel Pepys in his famous diary. Aristocratic libertinism may also have been encouraged by the close connection between nobles and military life, and Roy Porter and Leslie Hall point to the increased militarization of the British aristocracy at the time of the Revolutionary and Napoleonic Wars as feeding an upsurge in upper-class profligacy in England in the years around 1800. The increase in state budgets at the same time also meant more opportunities for people (not only aristocrats) to enrich themselves through state contracts; in England this meant a heightened awareness about the power of the kings to use their control of patronage to influence Parliament, an important aspect of the "old corruption" much decried at the time, feeding the movement that issued in the Parliamentary Reform Bill of 1832.[9]

The contrast between the lax and even libertine tenor of courtly and military morality and the more restrained and serious tone of bourgeois existence deepened during the eighteenth century. Enlightenment culture's attack on corruption and on unjustified claims to authority and domination in public and private fostered a heightened emphasis on moral responsibility in society as a whole, but Margaret Hunt, in a study of eighteenth-century middle-class business and family life, has identified some special reasons why "middling" people were becoming especially concerned about the link between self-discipline and family enterprise. These reasons remind us that the other side of what was regarded as the particular attachment of bourgeois to family life was the same people's participation in markets and other activities tied to relations at a distance. Hunt sees the evolving connections between family, commerce, and behavior as underlying the pervasive concern to foster moral responsibility evident in such periodicals a Addison and Steele's *Spectator* (to which we can add the German "moral weeklies" inspired by them, of which the Hamburg paper *Der Patriot* was the first). In places such as London (as well as Hamburg and Bordeaux), commerce involved relations with distant markets and suppliers, but business was conducted by family firms for whom relatives provided the chief sources of partners, collaborators, and capital (regularly assembled through marriage connections). Conditions in the far-away places where the funds were employed were difficult to monitor and could change unexpectedly, bringing danger of failure and imposing sudden needs for additional credit. In later periods businesspeople in such a situation would turn to a bank or other impersonal lender, on whom some of the loss would fall should things go badly. Given the rarity of such institutions through much of the eighteenth-century (and even later in many places), merchants and traders turned to family and friends to meet these needs, and if things went wrong a whole cluster of relatives and associates felt the impact. Blame would then be laid on those most directly involved. As Hunt puts it:

> Seventeenth- and eighteenth-century traders were
> only dimly aware of what would today be considered

'impersonal' economic forces: when they took it upon
themselves to explain why failure occurred they persisted
in tracing the problem to immoral acts on the part of
parties to business transactions. Accordingly, there was a
strong tendency to believe that the solution to failure and
most other business ills lay in a general reformation of
social mores, essentially along what we are accustomed to
call Puritan lines, although in fact they were more urban
and commercial than uniquely Puritan.

As conditions for doing business grew more complex and less easy to
monitor, while commercial activity remained closely interwoven with
family life, people felt themselves caught up in "a tight, highly interdependent system in which individual immoral acts almost invariably
caused chain-reactions of economic disorder." In such situations, bad
behavior was deplored not so much for its sinfulness (although that
could be invoked too) as for the dangers it posed to families.[10]

Parallel to this heightened emphasis on moral behavior, and
for similar reasons, there developed a widespread attention to "character," seen as a kind of overall matrix or frame of personal being,
within which certain specific qualities or virtues could be supported.
Kant wrote extensively about character in works intended for ordinary people rather than philosophers, seeing it as a kind of everyday
approximation to the difficult ideal of acting on the universal and
abstract principles of the categorical imperative he set out in his formal moral theory (and to which I will return in a moment). For him it
had a place in both business and in the activities of state officials; to
others character was important precisely because it provided a foundation for stable and disciplined behavior in unpredictable situations,
facing up to the unfamiliar conditions of city life or regulating relations with distant clients or associates who did not share some particular set of communal values. "Character," as recent writers about
its use in eighteenth-century Scotland have noted, "was partly a tool
for designating the terms of interaction between strangers." Both P. S.
Atiyah and Thomas Haskell have called attention to the heightened
emphasis on strict personal responsibility such interaction fostered.
Atiyah has shown that English courts from late in the eighteenth century changed the standards for judging whether contracts were valid,
declaring any covenant freely entered into as binding on those who

made it, in contrast to longstanding practices that limited legally enforceable agreements to ones judged to be in accord with traditional standards of equity. Not communal practices or the justice system but personal discipline had to provide a shield for families against reckless and irresponsible actions by some of their members. This new jurisprudence was part of what made the period an "age of principles," in which people were held strictly to whatever promises they made, a recognition that behavior once governed by collective standards had instead to be regulated on an abstract basis within the relations individuals established with one another.[11]

Both the emphasis on the possibility of developing character and the importance assigned to principles were part of the third factor in fostering a more rigid and demanding morality, namely a heightened estimation of the human power to direct individual conduct and to alter the forms of society and politics. Two broad historical phenomena contributed to this revaluation, Enlightenment culture and the impact of the French Revolution. Important as was the first, there are reasons to believe that it remained palpably incomplete until given greater force by the second.

As prisms through which to refract both the claims made for human autonomy in the Enlightenment and their limits we look briefly at two representative eighteenth-century figures, Jean-Jacques Rousseau and Immanuel Kant. Both were part of the larger contemporary project to make human nature itself rather than tradition or revealed religion the ground of morality; but it is not always recognized how much both also set clear boundaries for what individuals could be expected to achieve in this realm. Rousseau is well known for his declared belief in the fundamental goodness of human nature, and in the virtuous quality of feeling and sentiment in particular. In his various writings he sought ways to realize human moral potential by returning people to these natural sources of goodness. At the same time, however, Rousseau often portrayed people as weak and easily corrupted, not just by society, but at a deeper level where the very impulses taken to be the source of moral formation operated. Rousseau's fears on this score were at work in making him an influential contributor to the incipient near-panic about masturbation that spread from the middle of the eighteenth century, and that I will consider in Chapter 12, in connection with the changing situation of culture in which it developed. In a more general way these anxieties were ways, but all of them (as Dieter Henrich has shown) ran up against the problem that the link between reason and action had to be woven out of some kind of feeling, the vehicle through which the mind could influence the body, and feeling was rooted in need and desire, motives that sought suspect or equivocal satisfactions and sometimes worked in devious ways, as Rousseau recognized in *Julie* (so did other eighteenth-century figures, such as Diderot, in their works). In the end Kant was driven to a surprising and in a way desperate solution, resting the power of reason to direct behavior on something that he had begun by regarding as incompatible with the Newtonian reason on which the Enlightenment's intellectual liberation was founded, namely that deep within the order of nature, there might operate not the impersonal cause-and-effect relations on which modern scientific understanding was based, but a purposeful teleology that would predispose the material side of human nature toward the goals set by reason. As he put it in the last of his three major treatises, the *Critique of Judgment*, "without the help of nature to fulfill a condition beyond our abilities, the realization of this goal would not be possible."[15]

In other words, only if the ability to act in accord with the categorical imperative was rooted outside human reason, in a divinely instituted natural order, could it be realized in conduct. Such a conclusion suggested a need for reliance on external power much like the role Rousseau assigned to Wolmar; we might well argue that it left humanity as Kant knew it hardly less dependent on outside aid than the traditional state of "tutelage" from which Enlightenment was supposed to liberate it. Kant continued to envision the development of a different configuration of human nature, but it receded into a far-off future.[16] Like Rousseau, Kant was too wedded to the idea of virtue itself to sanction any of the indulgences characteristic of "classic moralism," but his actual understanding of what individuals could accomplish on their own remained closer to the old and limited expectations than his formal theory hoped to establish.

Preserved in Enlightenment thinking, these limits to the human capacity to make reason "practical" were weakened or even overcome for people of a progressive temper by news of the overthrow of the Old Regime in France, and the era of revolutionary transformation it ushered in. Even though revolution failed to realize the exalted visions of its supporters and enthusiasts, it served as the great midwife of utopian imagination, dissolving the aura of stability that had long surrounded established ways of life and opening a window on radically new horizons, no less moral and personal than political. What Alexis de Tocqueville said of the atmosphere in Paris following the fall of the July Monarchy in February of 1848, that "it seemed as though the shock of the revolution had reduced society itself to dust, and as though a competition had been opened for the new form that was to be given to the edifice about to be erected in its place," may have been less literally true for other instances of upheaval, but it describes the boost revolutionary change gave to the moral imagination very well.[17] Kant recognized this when he greeted the 1789 Revolution with enthusiasm, locating its historical importance less in the immediate or future changes it might effect in its own country than in the sympathy the spectacle of transformation aroused in the hearts and minds of observers at a distance; their disinterested enthusiasm testified to the existence of a "moral disposition within the human race," an innate impulse to rise above circumstance and inclination and to submit conduct to the liberating rule of reason (Wordsworth described the atmosphere of those heady days in a similar way: "Bliss was it in that dawn to be alive, / But to be young was very heaven!").[18]

To be sure, the later stages of the Revolution generated new motives for pessimism in the eyes of many, but the power of the spectacle to demonstrate the capacity of human beings to make their own rules and free themselves from the grip of both custom and nature can be seen in the case of two figures who made a significant impact on moral thinking in the nineteenth century. One of these, the radical anarchist William Godwin, was predisposed to receive such a message, but the other, the dour parson Thomas Mathus who predicted that people would not be able to feed themselves as population expanded, was not. Between them they wove a tissue of moral attitudes that would be of great moment for Victorian morality.

For Godwin, whose *An Enquiry into the Principles of Political Justice* saw the light as revolutionary radicalism reached its pinnacle in 1793, the ability of the French to overthrow the monarchy was testimony that people had the ability to organize their lives without submitting themselves to outside authority. The revolutionaries demonstrated that humanity was acquiring an increasing sway over mere circumstances, rooted in the moral capacity individuals developed as the spread of knowledge and understanding gave new strength to the mind. These developments would render government unnecessary in both public and private life, and Godwin specifically applied this vision of the coming future to sex, arguing that desire and passion would lose their power over conduct as humanity progressed and people turned instead to higher kinds of satisfactions.

Godwin moderated his expectations somewhat in later years, but his vision of the human aptitude to control behavior and institute a more moral tenor of life acquired considerable power to influence people less radical than himself when Thomas Malthus introduced it into the second edition of his *Essay on Population*, in 1803. Malthus had originally written his book (in 1798) as a conservative and Christian rejection of Godwin's rationalist optimism, presenting his argument that the expansion of population would outrun any possible increase in the food supply as evidence that hopes for a rise in the quotient of worldly happiness were vain and deluding. Part of his pessimism arose from a dour but unblinking recognition about how powerful a force sex was in human life; at the core of the "principle of population" that ensured that the growth in numbers was bound to outstrip the food supply was simply sexual desire. Beginning with the second edition, however, Malthus markedly changed his emphasis (rendering his book incoherent in the eyes of many critics), maintaining now that the working classes in particular, who would be the ones to suffer most as scarcity mounted, could improve their situation by "moral restraint," that is, abstention from marriage and sex (contraception he saw as unacceptable from a Christian point of view and it was generally unreliable at the time in any case) so as to keep their family needs within the bounds of their resources. Despite their political differences, Godwin and Malthus were friends and corresponded for some years, and there is reason to think (though we cannot be certain) that the anarchist philosopher's encouragement helped move the parson to take this new direction. In any case, the latter's doing so marked a significant turning in moral attitudes, giving the sanction of respectable conservative opinion to a view about the human potential for improvement hitherto associated with radicals and revolutionaries. Malthus never went over to Godwin's kind of optimism about human nature, with its belief that the sex drive would lose its power as "higher" satisfactions became more available, but in one place he pictured sexual self-control as generating feelings of "romantick pride" and a "brighter, purer, steadier flame" of love inside marriage.

Other religious moralists, whether directly influenced by Malthus or not, displayed an even clearer turn to optimism about the capacity of people to alter their behavior and give a more moral tenor to life. One churchman wrote in a very Godwinian vein that chastity would become increasingly painless as people felt the influence of the right kind of reading and thinking, and another that society's growing "intellectual refinement ... withdraws men from the mere sensualities of life," adding that "wherever society is highly cultivated more men will be found living in voluntary celibacy." A third linked such hopes to the "universally admitted truth" (one at the center of Enlightenment thinking but hardly in accord with Christianity's core understanding of human nature) that "man is what the circumstances in which he is placed make him." These pronouncements are the signs that the other side of the more rigid moral demands nineteenth century people imposed on themselves was a considerably more optimistic view of their capacity to meet them than obtained in "classic moralism."[19]

The Victorian polyphony

The connection between the radical Godwin and the conservative Malthus embodies one among a number of perhaps paradoxical but revealing and even defining features of nineteenth-century moral belief and action, highlighted for England by Michael Mason, but present elsewhere too. Although there were political radicals who saw sexual enjoyment in a positive light, and conservatives who regarded it more darkly, overall there can be no simple equation of favorable attitudes toward sex with forward-looking perspectives and of negative judgments with backward-looking ones. Contrary to a widespread notion that suspicion of sexual enjoyment and the search for less physical satisfactions were elements in a conservative world-view that set itself against challenges to tradition and authority, many of the most exalted visions of a life free of sensual enjoyment were put forward by liberals and progressives; there was even something utopian about such anti-sensualism. On the other side, even some quite orthodox religious figures affirmed sexual pleasure as a divinely sanctioned dimension of life, giving explicit and even detailed descriptions of it. Anything but monotone, nineteenth-century sexuality was made up of a complex satire, then as before and since (in the words of Porter and Hall) "the great debunker and leveler, toppling the pretensions of the mighty and the 'moral.'" There was considerable talk about free love among English Owenites, and at least some in the movement seem to have promoted it (we will return to them later). Their attitudes shared much with the "rehabilitation of the flesh" called for by the French Saint-Simonians, a formula echoed by their "Young German" followers, Heine, Karl Gutzkow and others (including the young Engels), and Charles Fourier and his followers put a whole catalogue of passions at the center of their plan for social reorganization.[24] But the intertwining of pro- and anti-sensual attitudes found among religious figures appeared in a different way on the secular left, through the presence there of notions about the coming triumph of intellectual over sensual pleasures in just the way Godwin had theorized.

Among progressives who upheld such views were William Hazlitt, the critic who stuck to his positive judgment of the French Revolution well after his friends Wordsworth and Coleridge turned against it, and their utopian associate Robert Southey, who spoke about the "absurdity of supposing that a community which ... had obtained the highest state of attainable perfection, should yet be without the virtue of continence." Similar views were put forth by William Cobbett and even by Francis Place, and they found expression in the circles where John Stuart Mill and Harriet Taylor developed their ideas about equality between men and women. Taylor's daughter Helen probably expressed the Mills's views when she wrote (in a letter of 1870) that as time went on "I think it probable that this particular passion will become with men, as it already is with a large number of women, completely under the control of the reason." What had enabled women to effect this was that, for them, achieving "the gratification of this passion in its highest form," in a loving and permanent relationship, had long been "conditional upon their restraining it in its lowest": they had to develop self control in order to gain "the strongest love and admiration of men." Although "it has not yet been tried what the same conditions will do for men," Helen Taylor believed the example of women showed what the future would be like.[25] Such a consequence of equality between the sexes is not what many later reformers hoped from it, but that it could appear as one in nineteenth-century minds helps us to see the sometimes surprising connection to progressive aspirations anti-sensual ideas possessed at the time.

Although England seems to have been the chief home of such thinking (all Mason's examples come from there) it was not the only one. In France Auguste Comte (admittedly a person difficult to place along the standard left–right spectrum, but certainly one inspired by Enlightenment notions of progress, albeit combined with older visions of hierarchy) adhered to it. As with Godwin, Comte's belief in humanity's desensualized future was partly a projection of his own personality; at various moments in his troubled life he denied himself one or another sort of physical satisfaction, and believed people in the future would follow his example. As Frank Manuel notes, his writings are full of "hints ... that sensual gratification denied was transmutable into vast resources of spiritual power of an intellectual or emotional character." The future he envisioned was one in which the female virtues of feeling and sociability would achieve power over the sheer strength of masculine nature, affecting human physiology itself; there would arise a growing influence "of the nervous on the vascular system," to the point that the female seed would no longer require help from the male "stimulating fluid" in order to be awakened to life. The masculine role in reproduction could thus disappear, bringing a sharp decline in the power of selfish motives and passions, and preparing the triumph of altruistic and social feeling.[26] In a similar way the spiritualist feminist Céline Renooz wrote that as the influence of women grew they would turn sexuality away from the animality male domination imparted to it, so that "peace, calm, happiness" and a "slackening of sexual activity" would ensue.[27] These examples testify to the presence of a utopian anti-sensualism among French radicals and progressives quite comparable to what Mason finds in their English counterparts. As with gender and the system of separate spheres, Victorian morality became more controlling in good part through the operation of factors that simultaneously introduced perspectives of autonomy into it, producing an unstable complex of ideas and attitudes whose further development would lead in very different directions.

Male and female sexuality, and the "first night"

One of the things that marks the kind of anti-sensual visions given voice by intellectuals such as Godwin, the Mills, and Comte as utopian is the contrast between them and attitudes toward sex in the population at large. Popular understanding about sex both before and after 1800 owed much to widely circulated manuals based on medical writings, of which the two most prominent were Nicolas Venette's *Conjugal Love (Tableau de l'amour conjugale)* and the curiously titled *Aristotle's Masterpiece* (the unknown author was surely not the Greek philosopher); the first, published in 1668, was more popular in France and Germany, the second in England, where it first appeared in 1690. Both were straightforward and unembarrassed in their approach to sex and treated it in a primarily functional way, focusing on conception and generation rather than on either the pleasures or anxieties that could accompany sexual relations; part of the reason for this focus was to fend off the charge, early and often made, that the books had the hidden purpose of providing illicit knowledge and stimulation, but it also reflected the less sentimental and more matter-of-fact character of sexual discussion in the period before Enlightenment and romanticism fostered a heightened emphasis on feeling and happiness. Venette all the same spoke about the way sexual pleasure could be followed by disappointment, worried about whether women or men derived greater pleasure from the act ("theirs" lasts longer but "ours" is more intense), and warned parents not to ignore the powerful force of sexual attraction when seeking mates for their children. The pseudo-Aristotle offered advice on how to increase the likelihood of obtaining a male or female child by varying the position of intercourse or the time at which it took place, and reassured husbands both that the absence of blood on the first night was not proof against the bride's virginity and that a baby born seven months after a wedding had not necessarily been conceived before it.[28] Changing standards of decorum and reticence made an impact on this literature. A new edition of the pseudo-Aristotle published soon after 1700 was even more frank than the earlier ones, but a subsequent and final one early in the nineteenth century showed the influence of Evangelicalism by eliminating explicit references to organs and warning against sex with prostitutes, and Porter and Hall think that Venette's use of sometimes crude language made his work appeal less in the new atmosphere; a revision of the book intended to be more decorous appeared in France in 1863.[29]

All the same there is evidence that many people continued to regard sex as a physiological necessity, and a proper source of intense physical satisfaction inside marriage. According to the British medical journal *The Lancet*, chastity was a severe danger to health among women, and more popular writings listed not only hysteria but various other diseases among the possible consequences of suppressing the sex drive. (I will come to some often-remarked-on exceptions in a moment.) Although most people still held that marriage was the only proper place for satisfying it, at least for females, the illogic of such a restriction was recognized by some, for instance the radical William Thompson who waxed indignant (in 1825) that women and girls were allowed no other way than marriage to find the fulfillment everyone needed, while bachelors were permitted "the gratification of every sexual desire." Robert Nye notes that French medical treatises unhesitatingly assumed the existence of female desire and that failing to satisfy it could damage health. Peter Gay has highlighted a number of remarkable instances showing that people could be very direct both in expecting and describing sexual fulfillment in marriage, as well as some remarkable but probably untypical cases in which spouses from highly respectable families accepted and even encouraged a partner's extramarital affairs. Courtship letters were sometimes frank in giving vent to passion and physical longing, as were those exchanged between spouses separated by travel or business.[30] The widespread and ancient belief that women could only conceive if they experienced orgasm led even people who regarded sex primarily as an inescapable vehicle for having children to accept the rightness of taking pleasure in it; the same notion may have worked in the opposite direction, however, since it implied that preventing women from coming to climax could serve as a means of contraception. Popular medical advisers reminded readers that women "are made to love and to be loved," using the terms in ways that made clear their sexual reference; there were warnings about having too much sex, but also recommendations that intercourse be enjoyed with gusto.[31]

There can be no doubt all the same that men and women were very differently placed in regard to sexuality; the idealization of female purity and the attempt to keep knowledge about sex away from young girls had the effect of giving men far greater power in sexual matters. But one consequence of this imbalance was (as John Tosh notes) that the burden of regulating sexual relations and sexual feeling fell more on men too, bringing a range of fears to some, including both the inability to master sex drives and the shame of impotence. There was considerable commentary on these problems in both France and England in the mid century; one patient told a French doctor that impotence was "what all women regard as an insult and rarely pardon." It is in this context of anxiety that we need to place the often-quoted declaration of the English physician Dr. William Acton that "the majority of women … are not very much troubled with sexual feeling of any kind." This pronouncement, as Michael Mason insists,

> must be seen for what it is: a remark, in a chapter on "Impotence," from a book aimed at male readers. Its corollary is that "no nervous or feeble young man need, therefore, be deterred from marriage by any exaggerated notion of the duties required of him." … The famous words are not even consistent with Acton's implied or stated views on female sexuality elsewhere in *Functions and Disorders* [*of the Reproductive Organs* (1857)]: when he writes of the 'efficiency' of the penis, for example.

Mason adds that such a claim about feminine sexual response was "as far as I know, without a parallel in the sexual literature of the day" (and no one seems to have read more widely in it than he), which to the contrary contains many expressions of surprise in the face of female frigidity. A possible slowness of female response was signaled in the notion that women's desire had often to be awakened by experience and might otherwise remain dormant, but sex's importance to life was affirmed in the recognition that women's health, like men's, might be endangered by abstinence.[32] Too much influenced by Acton's words, some historians have read them into idealizations of motherhood or celebrations of female purity, giving a one-sided slant to discussions of nineteenth-century sexuality in general.

One topic that helps to illuminate these questions, and that became an increasing focus of public discussion by late in the nineteenth century, was the "problem of the first night," the initiation of presumably virginal women into sexual life at the moment of marriage. It seems clear that many sheltered young brides everywhere found the discovery of the reality of sex difficult and upsetting, even shocking and disorienting, and people worried about the effects of such an experience on family life. The issue was aired more in France than in England (or in Germany, where Ute Frevert reports some private letters about it, but no public discussion). The reasons for this may have had to do with testimony that suggests that unmarried eighteenth- and nineteenth-century English girls enjoyed significantly more freedom in their social relations and behavior than their French counterparts (a situation partly reversed with marriage, which gave the latter license to behave more freely in public but deprived the former of some of the liberty they had enjoyed before). In addition, foreign travelers in England sometimes thought people there especially enthusiastic about sexual fulfillment in marriage, and some evidence suggests that the French by contrast recommended a higher level of restraint, lest wives stirred by pleasure seek an erotic life of their own, lose their husband's respect, or recoil from the discovery of their own physicality. To the extent that such notions existed in France, they probably owed a good deal to the effects on French women of the prim and strait-laced education many girls still received in Catholic schools or secular ones that took over their prudish spirit.[33] But the anti-clerical reactions provoked by the Church's persisting power, as well as the survival of the old courtly appreciation of seductive charm are evident in the light-hearted and even comic tone that French discussions of the wedding night could take.

Of this the best example is a wildly popular book that appeared under the Second Empire, Gustave Droz's *Monsieur, Madame et Bébé*. The book went through 20 editions within a year of its appearance in 1866, a number that grew to 85 by 1876, 121 by 1884, and 215 by 1908; although translated into other languages it never found the same success elsewhere as at home. A chief feature of the book was an imagined account of the first night of a marriage; frank and cheerful but serious too, it considered the occasion from both the husband's and the wife's point of view, basing each on what was assumed to be men's and women's prior experience. After a long day of ceremony and leave-taking, the husband (a whiskered soldier, clearly older than his wife, as was often the case in nineteenth-century marriages) finds himself in the room where the couple are to spend the night; full of uncertainties he sees himself as up against "that instant of anguish and happiness when one has to play the most difficult of roles without any prior rehearsal," needing to apply whatever resources he has "to the task of making the rudest of realities acceptable without driving the dream away, to bite into the peach without wilting its skin, to defeat an adored enemy and make her cry out without making oneself hated." When, after many preliminaries, beginning with kissing the tips of her fingers, he undresses and slips into bed next to her, she recoils at his first, accidental touch, bumping against him and irritating an old leg injury. She pleads to be left alone to sleep, and he moves to a chair where he expects to spend the night. Only when, later, she sees him shivering there and invites him back do things get under way.

Inside each partner, meanwhile, a separate monologue unfolds. Does he know that her hesitations do not arise from reluctance to learn the lesson planned for her, but from fear that her teacher does not understand the need to go slowly, that he will "turn the pages of the book too quickly, neglecting the abc's"? Does she understand that he too is trembling, from fear that he will be a bad teacher, that his emotion will make him forget whatever he knows? Does she realize how dry is his throat and how shaky are his legs? How can she explain the feeling that her formerly cherished gossamer purity and virtue suddenly feels a bit heavy and thick, a winter garment out of season? Her heart says yes and no at once; fearing both that she will be understood and that she won't she clams up, keeping the storm of feelings inside herself. Afterwards she writes in her diary that marriage is like a swimming lesson that consists of throwing someone in deep water and praying. From one moment to the next everything changes, "what was forbidden is permitted, the code changes its face, even words take on meanings they never had before."[34]

Droz prefaces this story with a defense of treating marriage as a real event between actual people and not idealizing it: if people are to be happy in it they must acknowledge its physical side and value the pleasures it can bring. His advice to women is to accept the bodily play and contact, even the foolishness that desire provokes in their husbands. "He adores your virtues, is it so astonishing that he also cherishes their envelope? Your soul is beautiful to be sure, but your little body is not so bad either, and when one loves one loves everything at once." That women need to be told such things is the fault of the education imposed on them: "Your nature is not guided and cultivated but stifled and cut up, you are treated like those yew-trees in Versailles made to represent goblets and birds." If you want to be happy in your marriage, make yourself loved: "Don't be satisfied with being virtuous, be seductive, perfume your hair, cultivate illusion like a rare plant in a golden vase." To do so is "moral and healthy; the world is not a damp convent and marriage is not a tomb. And do you not see that it is the family whose cause we are defending, that we preach happiness in living, the joy of being together, that good joy that makes us better."[35]

Droz's book gives a very different sense of the place of sexuality inside marriage than some other contemporary accounts, for instance the joyless, stiff and disillusioned portrait of bourgeois family life we find in Zola's novel *Pot Bouille*. It is hard to know how to reconcile such diverse images, nor do we know what Droz's legions of readers actually took from his book. He seems to have expected that it would surprise and even shock some of them, but in many ways he was a figure of his time, and far from radical. He found it natural to describe sex as "the rudest of realities," and he assumed that a newly married man and woman will approach each other across a great divide that only careful guidance can prevent turning into an abyss. His criticism of female education seems to imply a need to change it, but he made no proposals in this regard (nor it seems would anyone in France or elsewhere in Europe advocate sex education for girls before the very last years of the nineteenth century).[36] His aim was to aid people in dealing with the sudden changes marriage brought, not to end the situation that made them loom up. Above all, Droz locates his positive evaluation of sexuality inside the family and presents his purpose as strengthening it. His insistence on this score may have been partly defensive, but much of his book was about relations between parents and children; a cartoon promoting it in *La Vie parisienne*, the somewhat saucy journal where his sketches first appeared, showed a man telling his wife that it was "A dangerous book: saying such pretty things about children gives one too much desire to have them." Some people may have found titillation in the text, but it was clearly aimed at respectable bourgeois; its success reminds us that there were many among them who shared or countenanced his anti-clericalism, and who found a free-wheeling sheet like *La Vie parisienne* at once to their taste and compatible with their sense of themselves as upstanding citizens. Beyond all the reasons why such people remained devoted to the family as an institution we have several times stressed, new ones emerged after the French defeat of 1870 led to fears of national decline. These worries were fed by the contrast between the rapid rate of population expansion in Germany and the sluggish French one, and during the Third Republic people were encouraged to see the procreative function of the family as a kind of patriotic duty. Both men and women (including those in feminist organizations) regarded producing children as a demonstration that the country was not falling into the debilitating "decadence" induced by modern life with its luxuries.[37]

All the same, the success of Droz's book should help us to rethink the nearly universal view among historians that the widespread discussion of the "first-night" and of the dangers he sought to help people avoid constitutes evidence for the period's especially repressive character. Despite what almost every writer on the subject assumes, there is little reason to think that the "problem of the first night" was an exclusively nineteenth-century or bourgeois one. The daughters of the seventeenth-century *noblesse de robe* families Sarah Hanley studied, kept on a short leash by parents intent on using them as counters in marriage alliances, or of early modern German guildsmen determined to preserve the family honor on which status in their communities depended, the young girls described by Bernard Mandeville early in the 1700s, encouraged by those around them to develop reticence and reserve in every way possible, were all unlikely to enter marriage with much more knowledge and understanding of sex than were comparable women in the nineteenth century, and it is hard to imagine that some did not undergo similar experiences on their wedding nights. Anne-Marie Sohn finds that many French peasants were no less anxious and ignorant about sexuality than were bourgeois (rural women seem especially to have been under the influence of priestly inspired prudishness), so that first-night experiences were often no better among them.[38] If fewer testimonies to this effect exist, a chief reason may be the lesser regard given to individual feeling and sentiment in rural and village settings and in general before the eighteenth century: the increasing public attention to the problem after 1800 was a largely bourgeois phenomenon and reflected the growing concern about personal feeling and happiness that Enlightenment and romanticism voiced and fostered. The first person to stir up public attention about the dangers to be avoided on the wedding night was Balzac, whose *Physiology of Marriage* (1830) warned men "never begin your marriage with a rape." Balzac, as we saw in his remarkable story "Honorine," was no advocate of feminine liberation, but he was deeply aware that the high valuation placed on inner feeling and personal freedom by the culture of his time made the success of marriages more beholden to individual sentiment and emotion, particularly that of women, than before. His warning found many echoes in literary accounts of first nights for the rest of the century, giving evidence that the abyss Droz sought to bridge over remained in place for many couples. But the very frequency of these stories testifies no less to the age's greater sensitivity to the dangers of emotional injury, and its heightened awareness of the need to base marriage on sympathy.[39] The idealization of women that contributed to picturing them as ethereal creatures strengthened the sense that wives ought to be defended against the danger of violence inherent in untutored male passion. Moreover, putting sexual relations in the more psychically oriented light Droz applied was part of a general shift away from the attitudes Alain Corbin noted in earlier times and more popular milieu, where bodies and feelings were thought to be driven by external forces like the magical and astrological powers that governed animals and plants, and which made it appear questionable or dangerous to interfere with bodily impulses rooted in an unchangeable order of nature. In the perspective Droz helped to diffuse, individuals themselves were recognized as the sources of their affects and emotions, and thus as responsible for regulating them. This was a momentous change in moral attitudes, deserving of more recognition than it has received.

The 1860s and challenges to anti-sensualism

The decade in which Droz's book appeared was one marked by palpable changes in sexual understanding and behavior. Alain Corbin points to the 1860s as the moment when sexuality of a modern sort first made its appearance in France, along with outcries by conservatives against the forms it was taking. To be sure he does not mean by "modern" the kinds of attitudes and behavior that radically transformed personal and social life from the sixties of the next century, although as we shall see certain anticipations of those changes would become visible soon after World War I, along with backlashes against them that prefigure similar later ones. The enormous success of Droz's book may be taken as one testimony to the shift (although Corbin does not refer to it), whose elements included closer relations between husbands and wives and heightened concern for women's sexual needs and desires, so that "shared pleasure replaced selfish assault." The power of sex began to be more frankly acknowledged outside marriage too. Both novelists and medical writers described a new and more direct style of flirtation, in which a possible sexual outcome was acknowledged, even in interactions that presumed a sense of distance at the start; an early medical observer of such meetings, Auguste Forel, said that they began with "mute conversations regarding the sexual appetite," pointed glances or seemingly innocent touching, possible harbingers of caresses, foreplay, and even orgasm in some situations. Railway cars were cited as places where such encounters took place, followed by the away-from-home locations they made available – spas, casinos, hotels, and sanitariums (the potential Thomas Mann would famously draw on later in *The Magic Mountain*).

One remarkable unpublished diary reveals the excitement and confusions experienced by a properly brought-up French girl not yet twenty, Mireille de Bondeli, allowed to visit a spa with some relatives. Pleased by her ability to draw the attention of men, she recorded impressions of the ones she met, and even made up a kind of typology of flirting, with categories applicable to several of them. With one she allowed herself to imagine marriage, but never seriously contemplated it, since she knew that his position was not sufficient to meet her family's expectations, and she lacked either the desire or the courage to consider thwarting them. The experience made her feel some envy toward girls who seemed less closely watched than she, but she took satisfaction in thinking that the whole experience helped her to grow up. Her record indicates that participants in such behavior were by no means ready to engage in premarital intercourse, and many were willing to accept their family's ideas about a suitable marriage when the time came. But the new style expressed an openness toward sexual attraction and physical enjoyment that seems related to the more eroticized style in marriage relations.[40]

Forel believed that the tension between this attitude and the restrictions within which it emerged led some to a perverse preference for flirting over more lasting connections, and even for "orgasm without intercourse." His interest in such forms of sexual behavior was, as Corbin observes, part of the wider attention to "abnormal" types of sexual activity and desire characteristic of the new *scientia sexualis* represented also by Richard von Kraft-Ebbing, Magnus Hirschfeld, Havelock Ellis, and Edward Carpenter, and which sought to raise awareness of sexual needs as part of social and marital relations. A few years before divorce was legalized in France in 1884 (to the horror of Catholics and conservatives), one sexologist recommended promoting female orgasm within marriage as a way to forestall adultery.[41]

Michael Mason points to the 1860s as marking a shift to greater sexual liberalism in England too. He finds evidence in a wide

variety of texts, some describing events as they happened, others looking back with some nostalgia on the tone of those years after the back-
lash they provoked had changed the atmosphere (which is not to say
that all its effects were reversed). Flirting much like the kind described
by Forel and Corbin was one thing people noticed, sometimes "carried
to a remarkable extreme, to a kind of simulacrum of courtship ('half-
engagement,' 'playing at lovers')." The term given to young women
who engaged in such behavior was "fast," signifying an uninhibited
way of talking to and acting toward young men that suggested intimacy with ones they might not know very well. Some observers at the
time saw such demeanor as a way for girls to advertise their availability
for marriage, but others viewed it as aping the behavior of courtesans
or prostitutes, with whom some girls may have thought themselves to
be in competition for male attention. One account describes a young
woman from a well-placed family who ended up in what Mason
describes as "a kind of limbo between sexually transgressive behavior
… and respectability." Given what we noted about the greater freedom
exhibited by unmarried girls in England there may have been more
continuity there between these ways of acting and earlier ones, but certain people at the time were shocked all the same. One critical observer saw the new behavior as a return to pre-Evangelical days after the
"moral oasis" of the earlier nineteenth century.[42]

British comments (that is, in respectable publications; shadier
ones and music-hall songs are another story) seem never to exhibit the
light-hearted tone of *Monsieur, Madame et Bébé*, and the contemporary English book that represented the changed atmosphere, affirming a
frank acceptance of sexuality and sparking considerable public debate,
was the far grayer but intensely passionate and serious *Elements of
Social Science*. Written by George Drysdale, radical scion of a prominent family, it was published anonymously (originally with a different
title) in 1854 or 1855, and sometimes attributed to his better-known
brother Charles. Although never as popular with the reading public
as Droz, it seems to have sold steadily at around 3,500 copies a year
between the 1860s and the end of the century. Whereas Droz's argument for sexual pleasure in marriage fits with the pro-natalist propaganda of the Third Republic, Drysdale's was an argument in favor
of contraception, to which he looked at once to provide a much freer
sexual life and as a means of population control. Drysdale was a neo-
Malthusian, convinced that the "principle of population" posed great

dangers to social well-being and happiness, and concerned especially (though not only) to improve working-class lives by at once allowing greater sexual satisfaction and reducing the burden children constituted for laborers' families. This stance made the book suspect to many on the left, who had long seen Malthusian doctrines as an attack on workers' morality and a strategy for reducing their numbers and influence, but it provided grounds for many progressives to develop a positive attitude toward sexual fulfillment.

The reasons Drysdale offered for his position were both physiological and social. The first involved what he called the "law of exercise": like other bodily organs, those connected to sex needed to be put to use, by intercourse, at least twice a week, no less for women than men, in order to keep them in good health. Nature has made the sex drive so powerful in order to impress upon us that well-being depends on obeying her commands; what we feel as passion and desire are the calls of a moral conscience that *"will give youth no peace* till they be obeyed and all obstacles to an honourable and disinterested outlet for the sexual desires surmounted." This pressure created not just a personal right to sexual satisfaction but a moral obligation to help others achieve it: we must all do our parts in providing society with a "sufficiency of love" adequate to general happiness. Such a message required that the contemporary elevation of the mind and its satisfactions above the body be replaced by a recognition that, as one of Drysdale's followers put it, "the sexual part of our nature ... is intimately connected with what they are pleased to call the higher parts ... the strength of it is a measure of the strength of the whole nature." Like such antisensualists as Godwin and Helen Taylor, Drysdale believed that the sex drive could wax and wane with historical circumstances; unlike them, however, he expected its power to rise over time as contemporary "spiritualist" culture lost its hold. Contraception made the practical affirmation of these views possible, providing a shield against the two great sources of contemporary misery: sexual abstinence and working-class poverty. [43]

Drysdale's views were anathema to many who encountered them, but his highly moralistic tone (and the quirky ring his language is bound to have for many today) marks him very much as a person of his time, underscoring the continuity he embodies between nineteenth-century efforts to restrict sexual expression and later attempts – no less evangelistic in their way – to promote happiness by way of it. Although both birth control and greater sexual freedom had found radical supporters earlier – Francis Place was an exemplar of the first, and some Owenites of the second – moralists found it easy to attack their positions. Drysdale gave a much more serious and respectable character to the same causes. Although anti-sensualism continued to draw supporters among progressives, indeed some vocal critics of Drysdale's book attacked it in that spirit, his text marks the appearance of a strongly favorable attitude toward sexual fulfillment and pleasure in the serious intellectual circles where (as with the Mills) the opposite had long been dominant. This was a crucial transformation, making Drysdale into a kind of switching-point where some of the same progressive impulses that earlier fed negative valuations of sex now began to flow in channels that nurtured affirmative ones. By the 1880s, the debate between defenders of the position represented in *The Elements of Social Science* and those who attacked it had created a changed and strongly polarized climate, in which increasingly insistent conservative forces became the chief advocates of anti-sensualism. In this way "the old working alliance between classic moralism and the progressive temper, which had given such unanimity to the sexual culture of England for decades, was ... broken." The new configuration was visible in the almost exact contemporaneity of two events: the Oscar Wilde trial (1895) and the appearance of Edward Carpenter's first defenses of homosexuality (1896), as well as in the remarkable mix of condemnation and applause that greeted the appearance of Richard Burton's uncensored but also intellectually serious translation of *The Arabian Nights* a decade before. The intensity of the debate between emboldened liberalizers and panicked conservatives provided the ground on which "Victorianism" now took on the meaning it retained for most of the twentieth century, as a synonym for strict, even panicked moral and cultural conservatism, an object of distaste and scorn to liberals and progressives, instead of as the "polyphonic" interweaving of multicolored strands that better describes it.[44]

In France comparable public (rather than strictly medical) expression of views about sexual need close to Drysdale's came only in 1907, when the young ex-anarchist and future prime minister Léon Blum published *Du marriage*. Like Drysdale, Blum argued that male and female sexual urges were indistinguishable, and that society both endangered its stability and loaded its members with painful burdens by refusing to recognize this truth. His argument was blunt and straightforward, but he ended, like Droz, with a defense of the family. In adolescence, sexual needs are so powerful and unruly that only having a series of partners can possibly satisfy them; unless both sexes are allowed such satisfactions at that stage they will not be ready for monogamous marriage when the time comes. To deny women this gratification is thus tantamount to pushing them toward adultery later on, hence the best way to promote domestic fidelity and stability was to give young women no less than men full freedom to satisfy their passions before they enter the married state.[45] Blum's text, like Drysdale's, had little or no impact on behavior, but the condemnations rained on it helped to polarize discussion, as *Elements of Social Science* did in England, making clear that in matters sexual, as in gender relations more generally, much that had long been taken for granted no longer could be.

That Blum's arguments remained in people's minds is shown by the place they occupied in a much-read and much-decried novel of 1922, Victor Margueritte's *La Garçonne* (it sold 150,000 copies in three months). The story of a young *bourgeoise* who rejects the marriage engineered by her family when she learns that her fiancé has a mistress he does not intend to abandon, and flees from her parents' house when she discovers how little bothered they are to know it, the novel pictures its heroine living the kind of independent and free life supposedly allowed only to young men. She takes a series of lovers, but also enjoys an entrepreneurial success as a decorator; in the end she marries a teacher of philosophy with whom she had discussed Blum's book just before her marriage was to have taken place. A reader today is likely to be struck as much by Monique Lerbier's idealism and eventual embrace of stability as by her sexual transgressions, which serve to produce just the respectable outcome Blum sought. But Margueritte was stripped of his membership in the *Légion d'honneur* for publishing the book, a sign of how determined, even panicky, high-minded reactions to the public expression of such views could still be.[46]

Meanwhile a vigorous debate on sexual morality, at once high-toned and allowing for the expression of quite radical views, developed in Germany in the decades before World War I. Here too conservative defenses of traditional attitudes and practices, given new intensity by fears about the power of changing conditions to undermine them, collided with assertions that modern individuals, both men and women, had the right to develop new codes of conduct that would acknowledge both their autonomy and their sexual needs. The most explicit claims for female independence in this regard were put forward in the last decade before the War in connection with the League for the Protection of Mothers (*Bund für Mutterschutz*) led by Helene Stöcker, but from the early 1890s a German Society for Ethical Culture became prominent as a forum for debate on these issues. Recognizing that the intense conflict between liberals and conservatives was creating both hostility and confusion, the Ethical Culture Society aimed "to provide a forum for the discussion of ethics and related issues, a forum in which the contest for public opinion could play itself out." Its founders and members were largely *Bildungsbürger*, and one of their goals was to provide linkages between popular discussions of morality and evolving academic understandings of biology psychology, and social relations. In the end their irenic aims were frustrated by the growing polarization of opinion, but their activities testified to a broadening sense that traditional moral notions could no longer provide the guidance they once had.[47]

Toward modern sexuality

It would be long before that sense acquired the ability to reorient behavior in society as a whole; for some groups it still has not. All the same the new ways of thinking and acting that lead Alain Corbin to date the beginnings of modern sexuality to the 1860s deserve to be highlighted; how should we account for them? The first answer must be that then, as in the much greater change in sexual attitudes and behavior that came a century later, a major factor was the appearance of new and more effective kinds of contraception. It was from the mid century that thin condoms and diaphragms (made possible by Charles Goodyear's success in vulcanizing rubber) began to be available, first in England, then in other countries. They quickly joined the array of sexual aids and remedies long offered for sale by apothecaries, hawkers, and quacks, and widely (if somewhat coyly) advertised in newspapers. Cost or lack of knowledge may have kept them from many people, left with the traditional resort to douches, *coitus interruptus*, and simple abstention, but knowledge and interest in the new techniques spread all the same, aided by some sensational prosecutions of those who either sold or wrote about them; in England the trial of

Charles Bradlaugh and Annie Besant for selling birth-control literature in 1877 was also an important moment in widening the audience
for Drysdale's book. Mason even argues, against other writers (and
against the importance of the social factors noted in Chapter 9), that
the new methods' greater reliability and ease of use was the chief factor in the reduction of family size that marked the second half of the
century. Peter Gay highlights the enthusiasm with which the improved
contraceptives were greeted, citing evidence that people in search of
expanded sexual pleasure without the danger of pregnancy sometimes
exaggerated their effectiveness. Abortion spread alongside contraception, supported by the introduction of antiseptic techniques that made
it much safer.

Improved methods of birth control had an impact on both
sexes, but especially on women, since the consequences of non-mari-
tal pregnancy and the fears they bred weighed much more heavily on
them. One revealing instance of such anxieties in the early nineteenth
century was the negative reaction on the part of Owenite women to
Owen's and some of his followers' advocacy of substitutes for traditional marriage, which some took as support for "free love." From
the start female members objected that weakening marriage ties and
responsibilities would expose them to dangers and penalties both economic and moral not faced by men. This was by no means the only
or the last instance of protest by women on the Left that the sexual
liberation promoted by their male comrades would redound badly on
them (similar points were made in the 1880s and even in the 1960s and
1970s), but as better contraception became available one of the main
traditional grounds for it narrowed. As Anne-Marie Sohn notes, "The
retreat of undesired pregnancies is without doubt the decisive factor
that allowed women to accept extra-marital sexuality."[48]

As in the 1960s too, the changing attitudes toward sex a century earlier were tied up with politics. The 1860s, as we saw earlier, was the decade when feminism, like other political causes, began
to be promoted by large-scale organizations. In Germany some more
liberal members of the Ethical Culture Society were middle-class figures close to the social democrats, and arguments for a thoroughgoing
transformation of male–female relations were put forward by one
of the Party's leaders, August Bebel. In France, as we saw earlier, it
was republican politicians who set up secondary schools for girls in
the 1870s and 1880s, partly in an effort to reduce clerical influence

and lessen the cultural gap between men and women; the "republican marriage" they envisioned was to rest on trust and sympathy between spouses and include enhanced sexual pleasure for both partners, and its advocates, as Alain Corbin notes, were "the very same people who worked with Camille Sée to open the doors of secondary schools to female students." Republicans were also responsible for the legislation that allowed French women to sue for divorce from 1884 (as English wives had been able to do since 1857), an opportunity numbers of them seized, and by the end of the century the laws that punished female adultery more harshly than male, inherited from Old Regime practice and enshrined in the Napoleonic Code, were no longer being enforced in French courts; lawyers began to propose that adultery be treated as a civil matter rather than a criminal offense.[49] The rigid restrictions on unaccompanied women going about in public began to soften up in the same years, in part because public spaces in rebuilt cities (of which Haussmann's Paris was exemplary but by no means alone) offered better-lighted and more acceptable settings, as did the new department stories that drew in bourgeois women as their chief clientèle.[50] It was in this atmosphere that, as Göran Therborn notes, by the end of the century "the adulterous woman had become a literary heroine," albeit often a tragic one: Emma Bovary, Anna Karennina, Effi Briest.[51]

Alongside birth control, politics, and urban reconstruction, freer sexual expression and behavior was fostered by the proliferation of new spaces for meeting that lay beyond the surveillance of relatives, neighbors, and other overseers of local and traditional standards. Auguste Forel, as noted earlier, viewed railway carriages as well as the spas and vacation spots they served as prime sites for the new kinds of flirting and sexual play he saw around him, and of which Mirelle de Bondeli's diary gives personal testimony. As means of transport expanded, the liberating impact that access to such non-local spaces could have on behavior broadened beyond urban bourgeois to include rural people too. Anne-Marie Sohn notes that the reserve characteristic of peasant milieu earlier "often reflected the near-total isolation of some hamlets more than virtue," and it weakened as this insularity diminished, especially in places whose proximity or connections to urban areas allowed conduct earlier more typical cities to spread beyond them. Mobile people such as traveling salesmen or seamstresses had long been known for greater sexual freedom than those permanently under the eye of neighbors and relatives, and young people had often found opportunities for sexual exploration in situations that took them away from their families, for instance as shepherds and cowherds who oversaw migrating flocks; now this kind of liberation from surveillance became more generalized and permanent. One form it took in rural areas was the spread of dances for young village people, their music made possible by the phonograph (from the 1880s), and attendance boosted by improved roads and rail travel. The increased mobility and expanded chances to meet people at a distance offered an escape from oversight by village elders, opening the way to "more daring and furtive liaisons."[52] Here as in other instances class difference mattered less in giving the tone to social relations than access to distant resources and experiences.

Parallel to these changes was the spread of new ways to speak about sex. Here as elsewhere, many often-repeated claims about the special prudery of "bourgeois" language turn out to be much exaggerated. No doubt the heightened emphasis on decorum and respectability evident from around 1800 brought new attempts to purge everyday language of sexual references, but it is clear by now that often-repeated stories about people covering piano legs out of embarrassment and referring to human ones only as "limbs" turn out to be myths, generated by satirical barbs directed against the often-criticized evangelical fringe, and then blown up into general descriptions; in addition, many euphemisms about such things as sexual functions, body parts, and prostitution had been around for much longer, as Peter Fryer showed some time ago.[53] Sohn's studies reveal that the kind of linguistic reticence often thought to be bourgeois was at least as characteristic not just of peasants but of many workers, who could not bring themselves to refer to sexual parts save as "ça" or "le." In the mid nineteenth century it was common for peasant women to refer to their husband's interest in sex as "your dirty stuff" (vos saletés), and rural people of both sexes displayed a powerful reluctance to speak about sex in front of children. Many of them also expended much more effort than has been thought to hide their sexual activities from their own offspring, and it even seems that the commonly asserted ability of peasant children to learn about sex from watching animals was at least partly mythical too; in court some young women told judges, surprised by their earnest declarations that they did not know how they had become pregnant, that they never made such a connection between animals and humans.[54]

During the nineteenth century, however, two other vocabularies, both rooted in the literary and learned world of cities, operated to transform the ways sex was spoken about, at least in France. The first was the romantic idiom that had its literary roots in the seventeenth century and became common in novels of the nineteenth, introducing such expressions as "possess," "enjoy," "give oneself to" (*se livrer*), and "make love" (*faire l'amour*). This parlance spread to small towns and rural areas as some people exposed to it in print or through being read to adopted it for the refinement or elegance it seemed to convey. It was falling out of favor by the 1880s and 1890s, however, (although some terms, such as *faire l'amour* retained their place), as a more matter-of-fact lexicon, influenced by the prestige of science, came into use in many places. This idiom reduced the marked regional variations long displayed by sexual language, and introduced slang terms (*sauter, baiser*) alongside the more formal *rapports* and *relations*, to which the adjective *sexuel* was now joined. New terms with uncertain spellings also appeared, *penis* or *penisse* replacing *membre*, and *vagin* or *vasin* taking over from the old *matrice* (which survived in some rural places); *testicules* and *clitoris* came into common use only in the twentieth century. Sohn observes that this new anatomical vocabulary was especially appreciated by women for its qualities of "exactitude, detachment and neutrality."

> Its spread, which owed much to the medicalization of
> society and, for women, to the upsurge in abortions,
> desacralized sex, brought it out of hiding, relieved it of sin
> and wiped away its old stain by breaking its ties to dirti-
> ness. By freeing up speech, it contributed to the liberation
> of conscience and over the next century allowed for an
> increasingly natural way of approaching sexual relations.

As with the differently toned transformation of sexual language that set in after the middle of the twentieth century, this one owed much to the emergence of more closely integrated communication networks and the media for diffusing ideas and information they made possible.[55] This connection made the liberalization of sexual attitudes part of the larger widening and thickening of such webs that also reduced the "access costs" for information of all kinds, quickening the rhythm of invention and providing support for new forms of political organization. The German Society for Ethical Culture's aim, noted a moment ago, to contribute to society's moral reformation by providing a forum for discussion in which all viewpoints could find expression, was one sign of the way this extension of networks undermined the claims of traditional teleocratic principles to regulate them, nurturing the autonomy of their participants.

The same increase in the importance of distant and abstract relations lay behind a development without which many people, especially bourgeois, could not have developed more liberal sexual attitudes, namely the still far from complete but growing displacement of the family from the dominant position it had long held in providing the assets individuals needed to survive and advance. Margaret Hunt pointed to the part family membership played in generating the early modern turn to a more "puritanical" morality when she identified it with a particular juncture in the history of middle-class life, characterized by a growing involvement of commercial people in distant activities and relations but at a time when assembling personal and material resources for business still depended on linkages between family members. The moment she identified stood somewhere between the two identified by Sarah Hanley, a first one in which individuals could seldom maintain, much less improve their position in society without drawing on means provided by connections, patronage, and marriage alliances to which kin and clan gave access, and the now-familiar situation in which impersonal institutions both public and private "underwrite the life chances of individuals," reducing their dependence on family patrimony.[56] In the intermediate juncture identified by Hunt, the Enlightenment and later Revolutionary vision of human beings as able to put the impress of their will on society and history worked to encourage belief that the more stringent requirements embodied in the notion of "character" could be met, producing the "age of principles" portrayed by P. S. Atiyah as well as what Michael Mason calls "progressive anti-sensualism." By the end of the nineteenth century the same developing modern emphasis on human autonomy was working in the opposite direction, extending the Enlightenment and romantic call to respect human feeling and foster happiness toward sexuality, nurturing the dawning awareness of individual and social responsibility in this domain given expression by Gustave Droz, George Drysdale, and Léon Blum, as well as by the movement to provide a serious study of sexuality and recognize its power in which Kraft-Ebbing, Edward Carpenter, Helene Stöcker, and Freud were all exemplary figures. In all these ways, the growing impact of involvement in distant relations that had contributed to making moral norms more rigid during the eighteenth and early nineteenth century now worked instead to make them more open and flexible. Behind the moral liberalization of the nineteenth century's end there stood the elaboration of a form of life shaped by all the expanding networks of means of modern social existence.

11 JEWS AS BOURGEOIS AND NETWORK PEOPLE

Communities, networks, and capitalism

Of all the phenomena that call attention to the relations between modernity, bourgeois life, and the growing importance of extended networks and distant connections, none is more momentous and few more revealing than the role played by Jews in European history. That Jews have a singular connection to bourgeois life (despite the fact that many of them have been too poor to take much part in it), and to modernity (despite Jewish preservation of ancient traditions), is evident from the positions, actual and imagined, that many of them acquired between the eighteenth century and the twentieth, by the enmity that came to be focused on them, and finally by the fate to which they were subjected by German National Socialism. The outcome of this story lies beyond the scope of this book, but we cannot avoid trying to make sense of the relationship between Jews, modernity, and bourgeois life.

Jews have lived in Europe from ancient times, but have often been made to feel unwelcome there, repeatedly becoming objects of suspicion, hostility, persecution, violence, expulsions, exclusion from many occupations, and confinement in ghettoes. The instability such an existence imposed gave added importance to the ties Jews in particular countries felt and maintained with those in others, giving Jewish life an early and continuing reliance on extended chains of connection, and a cosmopolitan character unlike that of any other comparable population (I will come back to this point in a moment).[1] These features of Jewish life, alongside differences in language, culture, belief, and the role attributed to them as deicides in Christian tradition, became motifs of the animosity directed against them, as rootless and detached from the rest of society, inhabiting a separate and private space of their own, and representing a form of life at odds with the one sanctioned by communal and religious authority. By the nineteenth century the most powerful briefs against Jews stressed what linked them to modernity's most disruptive powers and impulses: on the one hand the economic and cultural transformations that threatened traditional life and its values; on the other the leftist radicalism that projected a different but equally challenging mutation.

Both in reality and in the images attached to it, Jewish existence shared important ground with bourgeois life. Even after bourgeois ceased to signal their separateness from the world around them by walling themselves off inside towns and claiming some degree of independence from outside authority, they still drew wealth and power from the distant connections these enclosures had originally been designed to protect, acting in ways that could seem mysterious and suspect to others. The aura of a life organized around fluid and unstable money relations clung to both groups. These resemblances have often been recognized, sometimes with a mix of insight and myopia. In 1911 the prominent German economist and historian Werner Sombart became an early theorist of the link, in a book later translated as *The Jews and Modern Capitalism*. At the time he wrote it Sombart located himself on the left, close to Marx and his followers, while taking inspiration from Max Weber as well; later, during the crisis years of the 1920s and 1930s, he would move far to the right, supporting the National Socialists. The book portrays Jews as pioneers of capitalism on grounds that blended admiration and reproof, leading some readers to dislike it as too favorable to its subject and others to tax it for anti-Semitism, a mix that seems to foreshadow its author's later orientation from within his earlier one.

Stressing the Jews' geographic dispersal as the foundation of their special role, Sombart noted that Jewish trading families exiled from Inquisitorial Spain and Portugal established themselves elsewhere (notably in such relatively tolerant places as Amsterdam, Bordeaux, or Hamburg), bringing with them the knowledge and some of the connections they had acquired before. Eighteenth-century observers somewhat begrudgingly acknowledged the power and importance this afforded them; a writer in the London paper *The Spectator* in 1712 noted that

> they are so disseminated through all the trading Parts of the World, that they become the Instruments by which the most distant Nations converse with one another and by which mankind are knit together in a general correspondence. The are like the pegs and nails in a great building, which though they are but little valued in themselves, are absolutely necessary to keep the whole frame together.

The writer's sense that what particularly gave Jews their advantage was their ability to gather and exchange information was shared by others; for instance a French ambassador in the low countries who maintained that Jews devoted Sundays (when, unlike pious Christians, they could do ordinary work) to absorbing reports sent to them by correspondents and sharing these with their associates, making them ready to seize commercial opportunities on the fly when Monday came. Their special knowledge about suppliers and markets in a wide variety of places gave them a boost when goods had to be acquired quickly, for instance in order to participate in the profitable trade of provisioning armies.[2]

To these reasons for Jewish commercial precocity Sombart added some others. Taking a leaf from Weber's account of the contribution made to early capitalist development by the Calvinist ethic of unceasing work and self-discipline, Sombart noted (as had Weber) its similarity to the Jewish focus on a kind of holiness directed more toward sanctifying life in this world than achieving salvation in the next. Both ethics generated a search for rational, methodical kinds of behavior well-adapted to rein in unruly impulses (in particular sexual ones), and thus to impose order and structure on life, directing energy toward distant goals. In the case of the Jews, Sombart added, this ethic gained an extra dimension of economic efficacy by virtue of the separation they felt from the people around them, which justified reserving the strict probity called for by biblical morality to relations with relatives and associates, leaving a margin of impunity in their interactions with others (whom experience taught them to see, although Sombart gives the point little heed, as enemies or oppressors). Such a margin was closed to Christians, at least in principle, by the moral strictness, attachment to traditional methods, and spirit of communal solidarity imposed by guilds (whose power persisted in some places into the nineteenth century), but Jews were excluded from guilds, and thus freer to follow economic interest. Being barred from citizenship worked in the same direction, allowing them to do business with both sides in a conflict, or to switch rapidly from one to another.[3]

Whether or not one reads parts of Sombart's argument as providing fuel for anti-Semitic attitudes, there is much in it that needs to be taken seriously. The ties that Jews scattered throughout Europe (and beyond) maintained with each other were indeed the foundation for some striking successes. One recent historian attributes the important role Jews played in the Amsterdam stock exchange in the later seventeenth century to the circumstance that their "far-flung network of contacts" (even after its connections to Spanish American had been much reduced) surpassed "those of every other trading diaspora of the age in range and perhaps cohesion," and another notes that Jewish connections were strengthened by the tendency of governments in some countries to rely on their ability to transmit information for official purposes.[4] These relations provided roots for enterprises such as the Rothschild bank (whose operations we discussed in Chapter 8) by way of its predecessors the "court Jews" of the seventeenth and early eighteenth centuries (about whom I will have something to say in a moment).

The habits formed in connection with such relations, strengthened by the kind of worldly and rationalizing orientation Sombart noted, doubtless played some part in the remarkable rise in economic position achieved by Jews during the nineteenth century. Statistics tell the story, even if they do not provide the same kind of information in every place. In London the economic status of Jews rose markedly between 1850 and the early 1880s (when mass migration of poor Jews from Eastern Europe skewed the numbers downwards): at the earlier date around 30% of Jews in the capital had middle-class incomes, with a sixth of that number belonging to the upper echelons of finance and commerce, proportions higher than the general population but not hugely so; thirty years later 42% were solidly middle-class (having incomes between £200 and £1,000) and nearly 15% belonged to the business elite whose members enjoyed annual family incomes of over £1,000: this at a time when only 3% of all families in England and Wales had £700 or more a year and under 9% earned between

£160 and £700.[5] In Germany the proportion of Jewish families active in commerce or finance greatly exceeded that of the population as a whole, hovering around 50% in Prussia, Württemberg, and Bavaria in the 1850s and 1860s, when only 2% of non-Jews were so engaged. This occupational profile underlay the remarkable economic transformation of German Jewry between the end of the eighteenth century and the middle of the nineteenth. Around 1800 the aggregate was made up of a few wealthy and renowned families surrounded by a large number who barely scraped by on peddling, small-scale crafts, or worse pursuits; such traditional ghetto Jews were much less in evidence by 1848 when, as David Sorkin notes, a majority of Prussian Jews belonged to the middle class, nearly a third of them in its central or upper sections. In 1816, only 38% of Jews in Hamburg were well-off enough to pay taxes; by 1832 the number was 65%, rising to 93.2% in 1848. At the time of unification in 1871 over half of Jews in many cities were solidly bourgeois, a proportion that grew still larger in the following years.[6]

These developments testify to the remarkable rapport between Jewish life and bourgeois life; were there space here for individual case histories, it seems likely they would support Sombart's attempt to understand this accord at once in connection with Jews' diasporic habituation to distant relations and the exchanges they encouraged, and in the orientation toward worldly activity fostered by a religious ethic that emphasized sanctification rather than salvation. All the same, there is much that is problematic in any attempt to establish a close relationship between Jews and modern capitalism.

To begin with, the kind of link Weber made between religion and capitalism cannot so simply be shifted from Protestants to Jews. Weber regarded the Calvinist ethic as primarily relevant at an early stage in economic development (his examples were chiefly from the seventeenth century), when rationalization and expansion were hindered by a widely shared sense that work ought to cease once income was sufficient to maintain a customary level of well-being. It was in regard to this situation that Weber argued for the transformative power of the Puritan orientation toward continuous and methodical activity, building up an enterprise through honest work, and plowing the profits back into it as testimony to the self-denial that virtue required (and which believers might take as a sign of election to God's chosen). Whether or not we think him right that modern capitalism owed something to this

Puritan ethic, we need to remember that Weber did not attach the same degree of significance to it under developed modern conditions, when markets and industrial organization had advanced to a point where they imposed their discipline on individuals regardless of their personal orientations: "The Puritan wanted to work in a calling, we are forced to do so."[7] In modern times other and external factors did much of the motivational work religion had once accomplished.

Giving heed to this distinction helps to highlight two kinds of gaps between Jews and modern capitalism. First, Jews were of very little importance in the kinds of early enterprises Weber had in mind, which were ones located in traditional communities beginning a process of self-transformation. Where Jewish enterprise played an important historical role in the seventeenth century it took different forms, lending money to rulers to finance wars, supplying armies, organizing colonial trade, or taking advantage of international connections in order to import cheaply produced goods from one place into another. All these activities could be very profitable, but they belonged to a kind of enterprise that had long existed and had little to do with the rationalized and methodical species of capitalism on which Weber focused; they were often highly speculative, sometimes predatory and rapacious, and oriented toward sporadic and unpredictable opportunities rather than toward the steady, driven pursuit of profit for its own sake that Weber identified as modern. By the nineteenth century many Jews were as likely to behave in these more rationalized ways as others, and the success they achieved doubtless owed much to their doing so. But whether such behavior was important in giving birth to a modern capitalist spirit or not, by this later period even Weber thought it no longer significant, compared to the power of markets, modern means of transport and communication, and eventually machine technology. Jews were at best minor actors at the points where these factors made their impact, whether in the beginnings of the factory system in England in the years around 1800 (where none of the most prominent innovators were Jewish) or in the transformation of continental economies by railroad building half a century later (sometimes involving Jewish bankers but fostered by governments with their own reasons for encouraging better transport and over whose long-term policies Jews had little influence). As we saw earlier the methods that made the Rothschilds so powerful and remarkable relied on the same kinds of personal connections that made notables prominent in politics before around 1870; they grew less relevant with the spread of modern industry and modern communications, leading finance, like politics, to involve previously excluded sections of the population, drawing them in by way of thicker networks whose threads penetrated into hitherto unintegrated regions of society.

These considerations all suggest that, however important Jews have been in European history, their role in creating modern capitalism, especially in industry, was never so great as was supposed either by the anti-Semitic movements that grew up at the end of the nineteenth century or by work such as Sombart's that in some way reflected their concerns. To grasp the roles Jews played, and the shifting fortunes they encountered, we need to look in a different direction.

Jews and states: an equivocal partnership

In his illuminating account of early modern Jewish life, Jonathan Israel makes clear that Jewish prominence before the nineteenth century had less to do with economic innovation than with connections between Jews and states, and with the ways the projects pursued by rulers drew the two groups together. These links became powerful during the seventeenth century, when the needs of warfare (first in the Thirty Years War that ended in 1648, then in the wars of Louis XIV that began in the 1660s) made the Jewish advantage in assembling finance from widely scattered resources of great importance to governments. In the previous century the intense religious concerns unleashed by the Reformation had subjected Jews to expulsions from many territories in Germany (although they were sometimes protected by needy rulers), as they had been from Spain and Portugal at the time of the Christian victory over the Muslims; combined with the earlier expulsions from England and France these brought Jewish life in Europe to a low point. Seventeenth-century warfare, endemic and larger in scale, provided grounds for a recovery, as the benefits Jews were thought able to provide encouraged rulers to receive them back into places from which they had been banished before. It was a fragile comeback, since the privileges granted were sometimes rescinded under the pressure of popular anti-Semitism that rulers could or would not resist, as occurred in Habsburg Vienna in 1669. But such reverses were often temporary, and elsewhere the gains held. Jews were allowed back into England from the 1650s; in France a liberal policy favored by *politiques* opposed to religious warfare was rescinded by Louis XIV after 1680, but even then the Jewish presence in the country was tolerated. In northern Germany both Prussia and Hannover provided havens.

This was the era of famous "court Jews" whose services to governments in many ways anticipated the later role of the Rothschilds, notably Samuel Oppenheimer and Samson Wertheimer in Vienna, and Solomon de Medina in London (knighted for his services by William III). What made them valuable, as Israel notes, was "the wide, not to say pervasive, reach of the closely knit Sephardic-Ashkenazi financial network and its ability to raise large sums with great speed, often on mere trust, and to remit the money swiftly from one part of Europe to another." Much of the assistance this network provided took the form of loans, but in an age when money was overwhelmingly coin, it also dealt much in metal that could be minted, and this circumstance made the connections wealthy Jews maintained with their much more modest brethren an important element in their success.

> The entire system resembled a pyramid, the middle strata of which consisted of the metal dealers of Frankfurt, Hamburg, and Prague and the base of which was composed of thousands of poor Jewish pedlars who scoured the villages and towns of central Europe buying up old metal and coin which they fed into the major ghettoes.

In addition to money transactions, most of these people furnished supplies to armies, an activity for which the same web of connections offered similar support. As with those who have profited from connections with governments in many times and places, they sometimes engaged in practices that were on the edge of the law or outside it, including smuggling and bribery. Non-Jews behaved in the same ways, but public exposure was especially dangerous to Jews, since it provided an excuse for claiming that their wealth rested on the immorality that followed from their faithlessness, justifying governments in not repaying loans and ruining some who made them.[8]

That Jews were vulnerable in these ways is a reminder that there was a close connection between the services they were called on to provide and the equivocal relationship they maintained with the principles on which European society had long been founded. They were not alone in being bearers of such ambiguity, however; those same principles were being challenged from within mainstream society itself, and precisely by the state powers that turned to Jews for help. Jonathan Israel recognizes this clearly when he writes that "Absolute monarchy and mercantilism tended to protect and favour Jews only because both trends were themselves fundamentally at odds with many features of traditional Christian society."[9] The transformations states undertook rested on principles of legitimacy to be sure, but they often undercut existing hierarchies, attacked established privileges – such as tax exemptions, guild regulations, and communal independence – and sought to stimulate productive energies difficult to contain within inherited frames and limits. This relationship between Jews and states needs to be grasped in more general terms in order to clarify the position Jews occupied in relation to the spread of modern forms of organization and practice. What put states at odds with traditional principles of social organization was their obedience to a logic that developed out of their own existence, a "reason of state" (as early modern writers called it) whose principles substituted purely political aims or goals for the religious, social, or cultural ones expected to guide action in a society regulated by pre-ordained ends. In the terms we are developing here, states were agents for the substitution of autonomous principles for teleocratic ones; that they were such in ambivalent ways, reined in by the simultaneous loyalty of rulers and their agents to traditional values and commitments, and sensing a threat to their own existence in the further development of these principles (a danger realized in many moments of crisis from the end of the eighteenth century), does not lessen the importance of their role in this regard.

It is in these terms, rather than as part of the rise of capitalism, that the role of Jews in European modernization needs to be understood. Jews were far from alone in operating through distant networks of means in the early modern period, but their networks had the singular feature of being excluded in principle from regulation by the pre-ordained values that were expected to guide others (including states, despite their partial dedication to a logic of their own). To recognize this is not wholly to accept Sombart's view that Jews in general felt free to act immorally toward Christians (even if some of them did), but it points to a kernel of truth within it. Jews were no less committed to the notion that social relations should be governed by a transcendent moral code than their neighbors, and Jewish communities were equally organized in order to embody such a code. But it was a code that neither reflected nor had any purchase on society at large. Because it did not, the specifically Jewish networks through which Jews raised money for loans or mustered goods to sell in various markets were not organized or regulated so as to sustain the social, cultural, or political hierarchies to whose preservation Christian frames of action were in principle dedicated. Christian merchants or financiers whose activities threatened those structures could be called to account on grounds whose validity they could hardly contest without placing themselves outside society, but Jews already bore the freedom such outsider status conferred. It was this that made them harbingers of a form of life where action would break out of the teleocratic frames in which it was presumed to be inserted.

Rulers whose activities also served to undermine those frames may not have considered this implicit harmony as part of what made them turn to Jews, but it contributed to the difference between their attitude and that of their subjects. Jews found little sympathy in the population as a whole, which regularly erupted in anti-Semitic outbursts, as every history of Jewish life in Europe recognizes.[10] It is easy to see these flare-ups as evidence of popular irrationality or ignorance, and such qualities were surely involved in them. But so was a less reprehensible sense that a society whose organization and self-conception rested on a commitment to foreordained goals was morally endangered by a group in its midst able to gain wealth and power in ways that escaped regulation on those grounds. People whose well-being was tied up with provisions aimed at protecting local artisans and others from competition by cheaper goods produced elsewhere had special reasons for sharing this sense, giving them common ground with those drawn to anti-Semitism for different reasons, such as rabble-rousing popular preachers in search of a following. Israel notes that Jews in Germany and elsewhere acted as importers of foreign manufactures, and that complaints about them as "eroding local industry and crafts" by introducing lower-priced goods (still produced by traditional methods, to be sure) "by no means lacked force." The opposition between the interest rulers had in protecting Jews and the hostility to them felt by others was well understood by a participant in the English Restoration debate about whether to rescind the re-admission accorded them earlier by Cromwell. Their presence, he wrote, was "likely to increase trade, and the more they do that, the better it is for the Kingdom in general, though the worse for the English merchant."[11] In these conflicts open material interest was just as much involved as underlying principle, but the point is precisely that the two were deeply intertwined where the relationship of Jews to the rest of society was at issue. Writing about a later period, Fritz Stern considers that the publicity campaign mounted against Bismarck's Jewish banker Gerson Bleichröder after the Prussian victory of 1871 constituted an indirect attack on the Iron Chancellor himself; similarly, earlier outbursts against Jews were partly assaults against rulers and others whose relations with them implied a less than total loyalty to the principles presumed to regulate social activity as a whole, and to which many ordinary people looked for protection.[12]

This complex and tension-ridden quality of the relations between European society and Jews made itself felt in later history, first in the knotty and sometimes perplexing status of what came to be called "the Jewish question" in the period between the middle of the eighteenth century and the middle of the nineteenth, and then in the negative turn marked by the rise of organized anti-Semitism in the decades just before 1900. The era of Enlightenment and revolution saw the emergence of projects to free Jews from earlier restrictions, grant them citizenship rights, and provide them with better education (all parts of what was called Jewish Emancipation), but it started out by closing off many of the opportunities that favored their re-entry into European life in the seventeenth century. In a kind of reversal of the same pattern, the remarkable rise in the social and economic position of Jews during the nineteenth century to which we referred earlier was quickly followed by (and contributed to) a situation that exposed Jewish life to much greater dangers than ever before. Behind each turning in this evolution, as the rest of this chapter will seek to show, there stood the precocious orientation toward acting through distant relations that gave Jews much of their distinctive character.

What closed off the seventeenth-century opportunities whose importance we noted earlier was first of all the decline of warfare that followed the death of Louis XIV in 1715, ending the financial needs that had brought court Jews to prominence (although such figures remained important in certain places, notably Vienna). In addition, states whose rulers had once sought their fortunes in armed conflict now turned more toward developing the resources of their territories and populations. Recent scholars have shown that seventeenth-century "absolutist" regimes actually left more autonomy to towns and regions than the label implies; in such conditions Jews no less than others enjoyed considerable independence in governing their communities, especially in the Habsburg lands and in Poland. Eighteenth-century rulers, however, sought to tighten their own control and encourage the internal development of their states by standardizing laws, expanding bureaucratic activity, and stimulating internal trade and manufacture, all elements in the compound named in Germany by the term *bürgerliche Gesellschaft*. In order to stimulate native commerce and industry, the Prussian monarchy sought to exclude foreign goods, and since Jews had been among their chief importers earlier, the new policy had a negative impact not only on Jewish merchants but also on the poorer co-religionists they had employed as producers. Similar effects were felt in other places.

Nor did Enlightenment principles bring much benefit to Jews. Lessing and a few others advocated toleration and acceptance, but the secular spirit of many *philosophes* made them no less hostile to Jewish influence in cultural and intellectual matters than to churchly power; indeed some were more negative toward traditional Jewish ritual and practice because some features of it appeared as less restrained and thus more primitive and irrational than Christian ones, and Jewish belief could be attacked with impunity. Such an attitude contributed to the mutual attraction between a figure such as Voltaire, who, despite his reputation for tolerance, referred to Jews as fanatics and barbarians, and Frederick II of Prussia, an "enlightened" ruler but one who excluded Jews from many occupations, restricted where they could live, and grotesquely forced them to buy offensively shaped pottery from the royal porcelain factory.[13]

In sum, whereas a century earlier it had been precisely Jewish distinctiveness that underlay the recovery of Jewish life from the low point of the Reformation, now that very difference became a drawback. In the 1660s they could appear as important catalysts of English commercial expansion, but by 1750 internally generated development had progressed enough to acquire momentum of its own. To be sure, the role of London Jews in banking and finance remained significant, and once economic expansion began to transform the English North Jews would become active there too (some of them immigrants from Germany). But their role no longer distinguished them from non-Jews in the way it once had. Jonathan Israel, who (taking issue with earlier writers) regards the period after 1715 as bringing a marked and general decline in European Jewish life, finds the dying off of their earlier distinctiveness clearly expressed in the often-noted pronouncement of a speaker in the Assembly that accorded Jews citizenship in Revolutionary France: "Jews should be denied everything as a nation, but granted everything as individuals." As we will see in a moment, the abstract humanitarianism suggested by such a maxim was at best irregularly applied, but it remained as an important element in the era of "Jewish emancipation" – much heralded but never free of ambiguity – that now began. We can best deal with this era by taking up the situation of Jews in the three countries on which we focus here one at a time; the differences between them add substance to the comparisons developed above in Part I.

Britain and France: paths to inclusion and rejection

The process by which Jews became accepted as part of English life, like many other features of that country's history, was more gradual and less dramatic than in other places, and a number of factors combined to make England the most hospitable country to Jews (save for the Netherlands) by late in the eighteenth century. Friendly feelings had little to do with it; hostility to Jews was hardly less widespread than elsewhere, and the expulsion imposed on them at the end of the thirteenth century effectively lasted until the middle of the seventeenth. The loud outcries and resistance provoked by an attempt to regularize Jews as British subjects by Act of Parliament in 1753 forced the Bill's sponsors to give it up, but the fact that it was attempted showed that many individual Jews had become prominent and well-connected enough, especially in London financial circles, to make the attempt worth pursuing. Their rise had taken place under the informal regime set up by Cromwell and continued by later rulers, whereby existing prohibitions were simply not enforced; because the return of Jews was not based on formal legislation, there were no provisions governing them as a community, an important contrast with both France and the German states. They were not subjected to special taxes and most occupations were open to them, as was residence in any part of the country. In many ways the disabilities they faced were much like those of Catholics and Protestant Dissenters: what barred them from voting (in theory, although in fact some did vote), from serving in Parliament, attending Oxford and Cambridge, or being members of the bar was not any statute directed against them but the fact that as non-members of the Church of England they could not or would not swear the requisite religious oath.[14] The contrasts between this situation and the conditions under which Jews lived elsewhere provide an example of the far greater degree to which British institutions assigned rights to people as individuals rather than as members of some legally regulated sub-group; this difference was rooted in one we have noted before, namely that English national integration, aided by both geography and history, did not have to be premised on according special status to regions, communities or classes of people whose claims to a separate regime of privileges governments were not powerful enough to deny.

Britain's precocious modernization, the same features of its history that gave it a national market that encouraged early industrial innovation and an aristocracy prepared to participate in modern institutions more readily than its continental counterparts, provided an additional benefit of great moment to Jews. The rise of anti-Semitic political movements beginning in the 1870s and 1880s on the continent was fed by the sudden and disconcerting social and political disruptions brought by rapid industrialization and the political struggles we considered earlier. England had felt the power of industrial change to destabilize society and politics half a century before, but her earlier start made the impact of modern industry after 1870 less disruptive, as did the country's earlier urbanization, and the greater integrative power of her political institutions. At a time when organized anti-Semitism was rearing its head in the Dreyfus Affair and the rise of anti-Jewish parties in Germany and Austria, it made no significant impact on British politics.

This weakness too cannot be attributed to an absence of hostile feelings toward Jews, which found expression in numerous literary portraits (Fagin in Dickens's *Oliver Twist*, or Melmotte in Trollope's *The Way We Live Now*, to whom an aura of Jewishness clings whether he is actually one or not) and in private speech (such as some highly offensive letters – by later standards – of the liberal Macaulay). For many, the limited degree to which Jews could be part of the nation rested on the old notion that society had to be directed by transcendent moral goals and that only those who accepted them – in this case

Christians – could be full members. But this teleocratic view was challenged by one that conceived the political nation as the product of interchanges between those who interacted within it, an opposition that was clear in the debates that arose over whether Jews should be allowed to serve in Parliament after Lionel de Rothschild was elected from London in 1847. Conservatives who insisted that he could only take his seat if he swore an oath on the New Testament (by then Dissenters and Catholics, both able to take such an oath, were no longer excluded) supported their case by arguing that the role of representation was not to reflect the will of particular voters but rather to give political substance to the nation's essential character. Jews could live and work in the country, but not legislate for it, because they were outsiders to "our system," in which Christianity served as "the vital and essential and fundamental principle." In contrast, those who favored allowing Rothschild to enter the Commons while retaining his Jewish identity, and who finally prevailed in 1858, acted not only in the name of minority or individual rights (although these were certainly part of what they supported), but on behalf of a sense of the political nation as constituted not by a transcendent principle, but by its members in their actions and relations as citizens. They were seeking, as one historian notes, a shift in constitutional understanding, moving "not only towards an electorate of free-choosing individuals but also towards the electorate as constituting the nation."[15] A teleocratic constitution denied full participation for Jews, since they stood apart from its preordained ends; an autonomous one, deriving its principles from the interactions of those who lived under it, recognized all those who participated as members.

The relative ease with which Jews were accepted into English life, even in the face of persisting anti-Semitic feeling, combined with other features of society there to give a distinctively modern cast to Jewish existence. One reason for this was that the informal, voluntary nature of Jewish communities, in contrast to the official character these retained elsewhere, rendered internal discipline much weaker. As a recent historian notes, the general level of Jewish religious observance in England by the mid eighteenth century was "markedly lower" than elsewhere; dietary laws were widely ignored, and the limited number of businessmen who attended synagogue on Saturdays were said to rush off afterwards to do business at the stock exchange or in coffee houses. Such growing secularism was evident elsewhere to be sure (Jonathan Israel views it as part of the general decline in Jewish life during the Enlightenment), but two things distinguished it: first, the greater social acceptance of Jews, especially in upper-class circles, both in London and in country life; and second the circumstance that these developments occurred in general without benefit of the movement of Jewish Enlightenment, the *Haskalah*, through which figures such as Moses Mendelssohn sought to provide a coherent intellectual basis for moving Judaism closer to modern society and culture. The greater ease with which English Jews made their way into the society around them, and the less formal character of their own communities, meant that they "felt no need" for such explicit justifications. This pragmatism made them resemble the British non-Jews in whose midst they lived. The *Haskalah* drew the attention of some English Jews all the same, and it seems significant that once it did those influenced by it attacked traditional Jewish practice with particular boldness. Isaac Disraeli (father of the future prime minister) dubbed old-style rabbis "dictators of the human intellect."[16]

Similar features continued to characterize English Jewish life in the nineteenth century. The modernized religious practice of Reform Judaism never achieved the importance in Britain it did elsewhere (particularly in Germany); such congregations did appear, offering shorter, more restrained, and more accessible services. But those in Manchester and Bradford were founded by German immigrants, while the one in London (which arose out of a largely personal split inside the Sephardic synagogue) preserved features of the service abandoned by consistent advocates of Reform elsewhere, keeping Hebrew as the language of worship and retaining prayers for the return to Zion, and referring to Jews as "chosen." The reason for this contrast, Todd Endelman suggests, was that English Jews felt "no compelling need to alter the public face of Judaism." It may be that these retentions were in part encouraged by the devotion to ancient ritual and ceremony inside the established English Church, together with the impulse to return to tradition that fed the contemporary Oxford Movement, but a deeper ground was that English society, for all the reasons we have already stressed, made no clear demand that Jews refashion themselves in such ways. Full emancipation for Jews was resisted by some conservatives, but its enactment (the acceptance of Jews as MPs in 1858 marked the final stage) came without any demand that Jews prove their fitness by abandoning the features that distinguished them from others. As with the secularization of Jewish life evident a century earlier, Jews in the nineteenth century did not have to justify becoming more modern either to themselves or to others, because, like much else in England, to do so required a less explicit break with the past than elsewhere.[17]

The similarities and differences between this story and its French analogue are extremely instructive. By the mid nineteenth century Jewish life in France resembled its British counterpart in a number of ways, but its path to this condition was bumpier and more abrupt, and its later history much more difficult. In principle Old Regime Jews, like Protestants after the Revocation of the Edict of Nantes in 1685, were outsiders to France, enjoying no civil status; even their births were officially unrecognized since to record them was the province of the Church, which registered only infants who were baptized. But principle was seldom the last word in a regime ruled by privilege; in fact Jews had certain rights as members of communities, officially recognized by the king in return for fees and taxes. The nature of these rights differed from place to place. In Alsace and Lorraine, the largest region of French Jewish life before the end of the eighteenth century, Jews could not be citizens of towns, but their communities governed many aspects of existence for their members, led by rabbis and prominent lay figures. A few Jews in eastern French cities were well-off; most were modest pedlars and artisans. By contrast, the smaller number in both Avignon and in the region of Bordeaux, mostly Sephardi and considerably more prosperous, had citizen rights and duties on a nearly equal basis with Christians; when the Estates General was called in 1789 they participated in the elections for it (in contrast to their Ashkenazi cousins in Alsace and Lorraine). The few Jews who lived in Paris at this time had neither political rights in the city nor any organization of their own, remaining theoretically under the jurisdiction of the communities from which they had come to the capital. The law granting Jews citizenship in 1791 marked a greater change for these Parisians and for Jews in eastern France than for those in the south and west, but what tied it to political reforms all over Europe in the period was that it made all Jews citizens on the same basis, in accord with the general elimination of bodies intermediate between individuals and the state. In the case of Jews, however, a vestige of the old order returned in 1808, when Napoleon set up a Consistory charged with overseeing Jewish religious practice and assuring its compatibility with the duties of Jews as citizens. The Consistory's local sections were responsible to the central one in Paris, and it was part of the system through which the government oversaw all religious life in the country. Until 1831, Jewish practice was distinct in that rabbis were paid by the congregations they served, not by the state, which bore the salaries of priests and ministers, but after this date rabbis received state salaries too. Jewish men could enroll in universities, become lawyers, and hold public office. Thus Jews were now at once full citizens and members of an officially recognized minority.[18]

This new political status would be one chief basis for the transformation of French Jewish life; the other was the freedom of movement that now allowed Jews to live anywhere in the country (a provision restricted in 1808 but restored after Napoleon's fall), and that led to a rapid increase in the number who moved to the capital. In 1800 there were around 3,000 Jews in Paris; the number swelled to 8,000 in 1841, 25,000 in 1861, and over 40,000 by 1880; by then nearly a third of French Jews lived in Paris, at a time when the city contained less than 5 percent of the country's population as a whole. This mushrooming reflected a search for opportunities both economic and cultural that Jews were more ready to seize than many others, and it was well under way before the transformation of the city's economy brought by railroad building and urban reconstruction in the Second Empire. The Jewish influx was unusual in drawing its numbers from regions far from Paris even before the mid century, at a time when other immigration to the capital still came largely from the nearby regions that had long been its chief source. In addition, those who made the trip achieved greater upward mobility than did the Parisian population as a whole, so that by 1851 a smaller proportion of Jews belonged to the *peuple* than was true of the city as a whole, and a larger percentage were entering the liberal professions. Some faced discrimination to be sure, and opportunities in teaching suffered after the Falloux law (1851) gave Catholics more influence in education, but those affected in such ways could find other careers, in law or the press. Jewish success had more to do with the end of Old Regime restrictions on movement and on entry into careers than with economic or industrial change; the most eminent among wealthy businesspeople were not manufacturers but constituents of the *Haute Banque* such as the Rothschilds, Foulds, and Péreires, or merchants who served the state by provisioning armies. They provided the leaders of the Paris Consistory, alongside professionals and intellectuals such as Adolphe Crémieux, lawyer and later republican politician, who came to Paris from Nîmes in 1830, and the philosopher Adolphe Franck, born in the region of Nancy and (like Durkheim later) destined for a rabbinical career before turning to a secular one. Some of these prominent Jews, like their English cousins, had close relations with important government figures. A parallel movement to the one they effected in Paris took place in eastern French cities such as Strasbourg and Mulhouse, to which rural Jewish families ready to distance themselves from traditional communal life, but either unable or unwilling to try their luck in the capital, migrated or sent their sons, and with similar success. Alfred Dreyfus's family was one example, achieving eminence in the Mulhouse textile industry. But the Paris Jews, with their greater chance for national notability and their closeness to political power, became the dominant figures in nineteenth-century French Jewish life. This Jewish elite, as Michael Graetz writes, "in large measure stood for the modernity of an open Western society, with its opportunities for upward mobility and for economic and social integration."[19]

Not all French Jews were able to profit from these openings, however, and relations between the favored ones in Paris and their co-religionists elsewhere were sometimes strained. Facing both greater prejudice and more widespread poverty, some in the provinces complained that the Parisians failed to use their resources to come to their aid. This was not wholly true, since Parisians did set up initiatives to provide education and charity for their poorer co-religionists, especially in Alsace, but the results were limited, and certain cases, for instance involving provincial Jews accused of crimes, became flash points for tensions between the two groups. If the efforts the Parisians put forth for their Jewish fellow-citizens remained modest, however, some of them reached out more energetically on behalf of Jews at a greater distance, seeing the issue of Jewish well-being in broad global terms. In 1840 they participated actively in the defense of Jews in Damascus accused of killing a Christian in order to use his blood in the Passover ritual (the "blood libel" by then had a long history, dating from the Middle Ages). In 1860 they formed the *Alliance Israélite Universelle*, an international organization through which French and British Jews sought to aid their counterparts elsewhere (Germans did not participate, for reasons to which we will come in a moment).[20]

Secure in their position as citizens, and accepted as such by many around them (despite the persistence, as elsewhere, of anti-Semitic feelings and ideas), Jews in Paris and other cities became at once French and Jewish, "assimilated," as Phyllis Cohen Albert notes, in the sense of living publicly like those around them, but without seeking to efface the marks of their origin. They "adopted the French language, norms and values, and merged them with their own traditions. They did not rush to disappear into the general French society, or to divest themselves of their own associations." Becoming French was a spontaneous process (sometimes dubbed "acculturation" as opposed to assimilation) that seemingly involved little tension; as the influential philosopher Léon Brunschwig remarked: "My father was a rabbi and I am an assimilated professor, but I am not an assimlator at all; I never made the decision to be a Frenchman. I became one all alone and quite naturally." Such experiences give the lie to the myth that the country's Jacobin traditions required that Jewish citizens efface any marks that distinguished them outwardly from others, a notion fed by some rabbis and concerned laypeople who feared the decline of religious observance among people such as Brunschwig and sought to counter it.[21]

But this sense that French Jews could move easily between their two identities, combining or separating them in accord with different situations, was sorely challenged by the anti-Semitic agitation of the *fin-de-siècle* and the Dreyfus Affair that made it so prominent in public life. About the Affair itself we do not need to say much, but we should remember that what made it bulk so large in both French and Jewish history was less the well of anti-Semitic feeling on which Dreyfus's enemies drew (since it had never dried up) than the recognition by conservative enemies of the Third Republic that it could serve their aim of trying to discredit the regime. What set the stage for the Affair was first the visible improvement in the status and position of Jews since the early part of the century, and second that France was (as discussed in Chapter 6) the only country whose politics revolved around a public debate between what Maurice Agulhon calls competing "legitimacies," warring conceptions of how the nation should constitute itself. Anti-Jewish rhetoric was a vehicle for associating the republic with rootless cosmopolitanism, disloyalty to French traditions, and a litany of anti-modernist complaints that included excess individualism, rationalism, materialism, and immorality. Anti-Semitism was part of the search for symbols around which to rally political support, but it was real Jews who bore the brunt of its feverish and strident claims, making the comfortable harmony between being French and being Jewish felt by figures such as Crémieux or Brunschwig far more difficult to sustain.

One result was that anxious French Jews now began to aim for a more thoroughgoing kind of assimilation. A revealing dimension of the change was linguistic: until the 1890s the two terms *juif* and *israélite* were largely interchangeable. The first was the more common, although both were already used in the eighteenth century; after emancipation the prominent Alsatian manufacturer and political figure Berr Isaac Berr sought to give greater relief to the second because it had fewer links to traditional anti-Semitism. He used both words about himself, however, as did many other nineteenth-century Jews, employing them to refer to themselves as at once a religious, ethnic and cultural group; by contrast anti-Semitic literature strongly favored *juif*, finding it particularly suited to the biological understanding of racial differences that spread from the 1880s. In response, Jews began to call themselves *israélites*, hoping that the term would convey a mere difference in origin compatible with being like their fellow-citizens in other respects. The first to dwell on the distinction was Bernard Lazare, a writer, literary critic and philosophical anarchist who was one of the first public defenders of Dreyfus. His family (enriched by his father's innovative use of the Jacquard weaving loom in Toulouse) was assimilated much in the manner Phyllis Cohen Alpert describes, living like those around them while continuing to celebrate the principal Jewish holidays. But Lazare, troubled by the upsurge in anti-Jewish rhetoric promoted by anti-Republican nationalists (Édouard Drumont published his foetid polemic *La France juive* in 1886), called attention to the change by writing a history of anti-Semitism soon after he moved to Paris. Published just at the time of Dreyfus's first trial in 1894, the book encouraged members of the Captain's family to turn to him for aid, and he devoted much energy and time to the Dreyfusard cause.

Lazare was also moved to insist on the term *israélite* by his distaste for the East European Jews then arriving in large numbers in Paris (some fleeing pogroms), whose traditional ghetto dress and behavior contrasted with people like himself who had absorbed the country's values and culture. The newcomers, he thought, not unjustifiably drew the label *juifs* to themselves. Echoing anti-Semitic ideas long advanced in radical anti-capitalist circles (and voiced decades earlier by Marx), Lazare saw the new arrivals as partly responsible for anti-Jewish feeling because of their attachment to peddling, pawnbroking, and shady dealing. In response he advocated a more thoroughgoing assimilation, now necessary in order to make clear that people like him were not *juifs* but *israélites*. As the power of the anti-Semitism brought to the light by the Affair became more evident, however, Lazare began to see such changes as insufficient or bootless; growing pessimistic about the future of Jewish life in Europe he turned to Zionism, working for a time with Theodore Herzl before deciding that his own visionary anarchism was incompatible with Herzl's "bourgeois" liberalism. His campaign to alter the language French Jews used about themselves seems to have generated little following at the time, perhaps because it called attention to the very vulnerability of Jews in the *fin-de-siècle* he sought to counter, but many followed his recommendation later, once the Dreyfus agitation had passed.[22]

The new threats Jews faced at the end of the century derived from these specifically *fin-de siècle* conditions, but their broader historical significance can be illuminated by taking note of the parallel between the crisis that now loomed for French (and European) Jewry and the post-1715 constriction of Jewish life delineated by Jonathan Israel. In the eighteenth century some of the opportunities earlier opened up by rulers seeking the special services Jewish networks of finance and commerce could provide were closed off as governments turned to policies aimed at developing the internal resources of their territories and populations through administrative and economic integration, and as prospering commerce and markets fostered economic expansion in society at large. The negative consequences of these developments for Jews were largely reversed by the boost given to liberal principles by the Enlightenment and the French Revolution, and by the modernizing efforts states undertook in response to both, providing the different kinds of pathways for Jewish advance illustrated by the English and French histories we have just considered (and by the somewhat different German evolution to which we will come in a moment). Behind the new reversal of Jewish fortunes that set in after around 1870 lay developments similar to those that underlay the earlier one, but on a larger scale, as the extended and thickened networks of transport and communication on which both modern industry and modern political parties rested gave a tighter and closer character to the national integration that governments had sought to promote with less powerful implements in the eighteenth century. In this situation, as in the earlier one, the distinctiveness Jews derived from their early involvements in distant relationships turned from a strength to a debility. Just as the resources the Rothschilds had been able to generate through their web of chiefly personal connections began to be overtaken by the power of larger and more impersonal financial structures, fed by the diffusion of information and investment, so did the position a larger number of less renowned Jews had acquired before around 1870 become endangered as nationally organized forces took over the field of politics. That Jewish distinctiveness now turned again from an advantage to a handicap was a sign that its consequences for Jewish life were in good part determined by the place occupied in European society as a whole by the kinds of distant connections long associated especially, and reasonably, with Jews.[23] What this situation entailed becomes still clearer when we consider the somewhat different contours of the relations between Jews, modernity, and bourgeois life that developed in Germany.

Germany: *Bildung* as a vehicle of inclusion and separation

The peril to which the new situation exposed Jews would turn out to be grave indeed, taking on the murderous forms that would stain European history in the next half-century. It is beyond the scope and capacity of this book to seek out all the reasons why it should have been in Germany that this danger was so disastrously realized, but among them were ones connected to the history that gave bourgeois life in Germany its particular character, and Jews a special relationship to it. At the center of that history was the contrast between the taken-for-granted nature of national existence in England and France by the mid eighteenth century and the evident German necessity that the national unity desired on many grounds had to be deliberately constructed. State power would ultimately prove to be the engine for achieving it, and territorial rulers had been seeking to expand their sway in the face of German disunity for two centuries. But the role of states in moving the fragmented German lands toward integration was deeply tied up with the part played by *Bildung* in the same process, and it was here that the special connection between Jews and German bourgeois life was forged.

Early modern Jews and Germans had in common a sense of unity as a people or nation that drew each together across gaps of distance and political division. In both cases this pull toward unity was cultural in a broad sense, involving common elements of history, religion, and everyday life. To be sure, Germany was divided by faith as well as by politics, but the determining place of the Reformation in the country's history gave religion a special place in its life too, crystallizing the divisions that made localism itself a defining element of national identity. It was characteristic of German history that the earliest attempts to reconcile the actual disunity of the region with the underlying sense of commonality felt by many who lived in it were the literary and cultural ones focused around the notions of *Bildung*, *Aufklärung*, and *Kultur* that Moses Mendelssohn linked together in his answer to the question "What is Enlightenment?" and that played a central role in both official and private efforts to give a new and modern form to *bürgerliche Gesellschaft*.[24]

The social vision that found expression through this cluster of terms was one of rational, responsible citizens emancipated from the shackles of the past, and it was to have room for Jews as well as Christians. Jews had to take their place in it on a different basis, however, because they were seen as more deeply tainted by their earlier history, a perception that was partly religious and partly secular, the latter aspect focusing on the numerous and visible poor Jews engaged in morally questionable or socially unproductive occupations such as peddling, hawking, begging, pawn-brokering, or petty theft. If Jews were to become upstanding members of civil society, they had first to undergo a process of improvement, a *bürgerliche Verbesserung*. The term was widely used after its introduction by the Prussian jurist Christian Wilhelm von Dohm in a treatise of 1781, advocating government programs to educate and uplift Jews, and thus to prepare them for productive citizenship. As David Sorkin points out, the policy was part of the general attempt by states and their officials to raise the moral level of German life as a whole, and it was exemplary of the notion that the state could and should improve both individuals and social relations by intervening directly to guide behavior and conduct. "Jewish emancipation belonged to the current of events that made *Bildung* into a principle for the reorganization of the German states through an extension of natural rights and individual freedom." But whereas other Germans were thought to be worthy of the new universal citizenship simply by virtue of possessing the rationality that made *Bildung* possible, Jews had to earn their right to political inclusion by demonstrating their moral and cultural progress. One of the earliest emancipation edicts, promulgated in the liberal state Baden in 1809, granted Jews legal equality in principle but told them it could become fully realized "only when you ... exert yourselves to match it in your political and moral formation." The general result was that "for the state ... the Jews' admission to citizenship became synonymous with *Bildung*."[25]

The notion that Jews who still bore the marks of ghetto existence needed education and guidance in order to enter modern social and political life was common everywhere in the years around 1800, but in England and France responsibility for offering such aid was taken up by more advanced or better-off Jews themselves, who set up schools and offered financial assistance (not always so generous as some would have liked); in Germany it became a project of states. For the most part Jewish leaders greeted it with approval and worked together with state officials to implement it. The goal was not to put Jews at the forefront of modernization, and surely not to use them as agents of economic transformation, but to have them take their place inside *bürgerliche Gesellschaft* conceived of as a stable and hierarchically ordered structure of activities; the occupations into which poor Jews were expected to move included farming and skilled craftsmanship, seldom commerce or finance. Numbers of people took such paths in the early nineteenth century, making use of education offered in state schools to achieve a steady, moderate existence. But the story did not end there, for several reasons.

First, even education intended to offer a means for only limited social mobility provided tools that had wider potential; schools taught literacy, writing, and basic arithmetic, all skills that could be put to broader uses. Second, Jews had never been part of the guild world that sought to dedicate such resources to the preservation of traditional methods of production and shared local ways of living. Instead their social relations often involved them with kin or co-religionists beyond their own places of residence, giving them access to knowledge about distant materials, methods, markets, and sources of finance. Such knowledge in the hands of trained craftsmen with a certain ambition could provide a base from which to undertake innovations in production and seek increased income. Although there seem to be no data to suggest that Jews followed this path more regularly than others, examples of those who did are far from rare. Among the instances cited in a recent book is the Elsas family of Württemberg; still dependent on peddling in the early nineteenth century, their position was radically altered by two brothers who learned weaving in a school devoted to *Judenverbesserung*. Beginning from traditional handloom production, they grew wealthy in the 1860s by becoming the first in their town to introduce sophisticated mechanical weaving of many-colored fabrics. This turn seems to have been inspired by a visit to the Crystal Palace Exhibition of 1851 in London, an event that allowed a number of German Jews to link up with relatives or associates resident in England. Later the Elsas brothers set up a modern textile factory in the city of Canstatt. Such people contributed to the remarkable rise in Jewish status during the nineteenth century, as noted earlier; some of them shifted from artisanship or industry to commerce or finance, which continued to outpace manufacturing as Jewish occupations. Meanwhile, governments' hopes that Jews would take up farming and the kinds of craft-work traditionally subject to guild organization were never fulfilled: Jewish participation in such occupations remained well below those of the population as a whole. By sometime in the second half of the century the form of Jewish entry into *bürgerliche Gesellschaft* had "little by little become separated from the vision of the states" that originally promoted it, becoming "an independent Jewish project with an economic and social content that grew ever-more independent of its original ideological assumptions and political considerations."[26]

We take this observation from Simone Lässig, who argues in a stimulating and challenging study that what chiefly lay behind the attainment of bourgeois status by so high a proportion of German Jews during the nineteenth century was *Bildung*, at once the practical kind provided by states in their *Verbesserung* projects, and the wider mode of cultivation the term commonly designated. The line between the two meanings was especially permeable for a group that had long cultivated both practical and cultural ties to distant kin and associates. Lässig does not make culture the sole cause of Jewish advancement, but she gives strong reasons for revising the entrenched notion that practical success generally preceded acquiring it. Rather than a consequence of an economically propelled entry into bourgeois existence, *Bilding* for German Jews "has to count as a fundamental and permanent concomitant of this process," providing the first step up for many. Jews were not unique in using culture as a basis for social ascent, but in no other section of society did so many people at lower levels of the social scale take this path.[27]

At the same time, this importance of *Bildung* gave Jews a special relationship to modernizing Germany and to its *Bürgertum*. Education and cultivation were central features of middle-class life in every country, but nowhere else did they play the role in national integration they did in Germany. Their importance rested on the close relationship between state-sponsored modernization projects and the body of officials and administrators at the core of the *Bildungsbürgertum*, together with the widespread sense that the cultivation fostered and espoused by this group was an important means for the integration of the country and the moral improvement of its citizens. Jews thus appeared as a special case of the larger German link between modernity and cultivation, marked by a particular need to demonstrate their ability to effect the tie. How much the remarkable attraction that drew German Jews to *Bildung* owed to the pressure this put on them to display their intellectual and moral progress, and how much to the role of learning and discussion in traditional Jewish culture, is an issue we need not try to decide here. Whatever the reason, German Jews assumed a presence in higher education and in German cultural life more generally far in excess of their numbers in the population. Already in the first half of the nineteenth century the increase in Jewish students at universities far outpaced that of the overall population, their numbers growing two-and-a-half times compared to merely 20 percent overall, and the proportion of Jews in Gymnasien and universities was far above that of other Germans from the 1860s. The phenomenon has been especially remarked in Austria, and from the 1890s among women:

In 1910, 46 percent of the female students at Viennese Lyzeum and 30 percent of those enrolled in Gymnasien in Vienna came from Jewish families. At the University of Vienna, which first began accepting women in 1900, the proportion of Jewish women quickly rose to 68.3 percent, a figure which does not include those with no denominational affiliation who came predominantly from the liberal Jewish bourgeoisie. In 1919, with the opening of the University's School of Law to women, Jews made up 50 percent of the female students.

Since academic employment and state service long remained closed to Jews, and even more to women, scholars have been uncertain what use they made of this advanced education, especially in the earlier period; some think it was the prestige attached to degrees that led Jews to seek them, others suggest that some of the knowledge, and many of the social contacts they acquired could be useful in business.[28]

In less formal contexts too, Jews were notably active in the institutions through which German *Bürger* simultaneously sought cultivation and the development of life on a national scale. The role eighteenth-century reformers assigned to creating a national literary language as a means to move the country away from its traditional fragmentation helped inspire the projects nineteenth-century nationalists conceived to celebrate great literary figures, notably Goethe and Schiller, as instruments of national integration, and here too Jews took a special part. The founding of the *Nationalverein* in 1859 corresponded with the centennial of Schiller's birth, and many people active in the first were also much involved in festivities to mark the second. Leopold Sonneman, the Jewish editor of a prominent organ of south German democratic liberalism, the *Neue Frankfurter Zeitung*, viewed the Schiller celebrations as an "effort by the people to feel itself as a single nation," and in Dresden practically the whole of the Jewish community took part. The *Allgemeine Zeitung des Judentums*, the most-widely circulated Jewish paper (run by Ludwig Philippson), wrote that "Jewish youth turns for aid to Schiller, it learns to read, think, and feel through him."[29] Idealistic as such a pronouncement may seem, it suggests something of the importance that literary cultivation bore for Jews seeking to feel their way into German society and culture. David Sorkin notes that from late in the eighteenth century Jews had followed the example of their German neighbors in organizing much of their social and cultural life through voluntary associations, a number of which reoriented themselves from religious to more secular principles after 1800. In their way these societies too, like their Christian counterparts, aimed at *bürgerliche Verbesserung*, and their members sometimes pointed to their participation in them as evidence of civic and moral worth.[30] At the same time German Jews sought to become model bourgeois in their family life, displaying features of decorum, self-control, and respectability prized by their neighbors. Given that Jews were the most highly urbanized segment of German society it is not surprising that toward the end of the century they were early

404 / Jews as bourgeois and network people

exemplars of such modern practices as smaller families, later marriages, and provision of education for women.[31]

Recent historians, however, have called attention to certain
problematic features of these various Jewish ways of joining *bürgerliche Gesellschaft*. Jewish *Vereine* had many features in common with
others, but they never did away with the gap between Jews and other
Germans. Instead, as Sorkin shows, they created a kind of parallel
civic culture, closely resembling the majority but exclusively Jewish in
its membership. The barrier between the two seemed to grow more
permeable between around 1815 and 1870, as certain at-large organizations animated by Enlightened principles, notably a number of
urban Masonic lodges, opened themselves to Jewish members. But in
the latter part of the century the line grew more rigid again, as rising
public anti-Semitism led these organizations to return to exclusion-
ary policies toward Jews. The result was an increasing divide between
German and German-Jewish civic culture, bringing the paradox that
the organizations through which Jews hoped to effect their integration
into the larger society actually solidified their separation from it.

> The consequence was that German Jewry could not
> understand its own situation. Unable to live either the
> autonomous existence of its ancestors or to integrate
> fully into the majority bourgeois society, German Jewry
> had created a new sort of identity combining elements
> of both under the auspices of a secular cultural ideal. Its
> embourgeoisement under the conditions of incomplete
> emancipation and partial integration had not led to
> assimilation, but to the creation of a new sort of Jewish
> identity and a new form of community, yet it was a
> community invisible to itself, one which its participants
> could neither recognize nor acknowledge.

Well into the twentieth century the social relations of German
Jews, even those who took the additional step of becoming formally
Christians, remained largely involved in a specifically Jewish world
many of them took to be simply German. Thus the harmony Jews
felt between themselves and the German culture they absorbed kept
many from recognizing the peculiarity of their situation, which left
their otherness unreduced in the eyes of those around them, and the

dissonance between the two perceptions grew sharper as time went on.[32]

This half-integrated, half-excluded condition of German Jews, and the special place of *Bildung* in it, had more than a little to do with the rise of public anti-Semitism in the 1870s and 1880s. As in France, Jews in Germany came to be seen as symbols of a modernity that felt foreign and threatening to many of their neighbors, all the more because the near-brutal rapidity of the country's political and economic transformations subjected many to painful dislocations, and in both countries anti-Semitic forces made good use of the new forms of communication and political organization. However much industrial transformation came to appear as the dominant element of modernization during the third quarter of the nineteenth century, *Bildung* continued as a powerful symbol of modernity, partly because of the large place that educated officials and state employees retained in the country's life (as Jürgen Kocka and others have pointed out, it was only at this time that the industrial and commercial *Wirtschaftsbürgertum* began to overshadow *Bildungsbürger*), and partly because migrants to the exploding cities could attribute their difficulties to the cultural and moral contrasts between the world they had left and the one they now entered. That Jews had by then attained great prominence in urban professions, and notably in that powerful medium and symbol of city life, the newspaper press, put their developed connection to *Bildung* in greater relief, sharpening the sense of separation many ordinary Germans felt from them. In these conditions, as Simone Lässig suggests, *Bürgerlichkeit*, the Germanically inflected manner of being bourgeois, came to appear both to Jews and – although in a different way – "in the eyes of the 'others' as a *Jewish* norm of life." To those to whom *Bürgerlichkeit* remained in some way foreign, Thomas Nipperdey observes, Jews appeared as its "model students, and model students are not beloved."[33]

Various signs of insecurity in German-Jewish life were linked to these ambiguities. German Jews were more wary than others about making visible their connections to co-religionists elsewhere, for fear of contributing to their own separation. When English and French Jews organized a common defense against a charge of ritual murder in Damascus in 1840 (the "blood libel" had a history going back to the Middle Ages), and later in response to the formation of the *Alliance Israélite Universelle* in 1860, German-Jewish leaders refused to join them. Writing in the *Allgemeine Zeitung des Judentums*, Ludwig Philippson voiced his resistance to the "political articulation" of Jewish concerns, especially on the international level: "Even the proper name 'Alliance' must raise fear in the hearts of thousands of Christians who might be afraid of an organized secret power uniting the Jews all over the world." Earlier, a sense that they faced common situations and problems had linked French and German Jews; by the mid century the contrast between the civic equality that opened many opportunities to the first and the persisting uncertainties faced by the second fed a sense of estrangement between the two communities.[34] The greater pressure felt by the German Jews to present themselves as modern and cultured also underlay the much greater strength of the Reform movement in Germany than elsewhere. And significant numbers of middle-class German Jews responded to the discomfort they felt in their country of birth by moving to England during the nineteenth century (earlier it had been mostly poorer Jews who took this path); among those who contemplated such a move without making it was Sigmund Freud, who "never ceased to envy his two half-brothers in Manchester" after visiting them in 1875. English Jews of German origin exhibited the continuing need they felt to demonstrate their acceptability not just by dominating the small movement of Reform in Britain, but also by becoming Anglicans or Unitarians in markedly larger numbers than those born in the country; the latter, as noted above, experienced an easier compatibility between Jewish identity and participation in society at large.[35]

Finally, there was something abstract and impractical about the way German Jews pursued *Bildung*, making their devotion to it a source of the same ambiguous relationship to the larger society that David Sorkin identifies in their associations. However lofty the tone in which German officials and academics celebrated classical and humanistic *Kultur*, higher education possessed a supremely practical side for such people, providing entry into prestigious careers and the social status they conferred. Jews could make use of their education in a number of ways to be sure (in medicine, increasingly in law, in journalism and writing), but well into the twentieth century many impediments hindered their pursuit of careers in both state service and academic life (as Max Weber lamented in his famous 1919 lecture on "Science as a Vocation," the barriers to advancement encountered by his friend Simmel much in his mind), depriving them of the practical advantages *Bildung* conveyed on others.

That there was something airy and visionary about the German-Jewish mode of cultivation has been suggested in a different way by George Mosse, who views it as rooted in Enlightenment notions of rationality and individual self-development that grew less relevant and credible as economic and political change gave romantic notions that emphasized the power of passion and symbolic identification greater purchase in an age of nationalism and ideological rivalry. The Jewish commitment to a form of national identity "that no longer corresponded to the realities of German life" isolated Jews from the rest of society. Mosse's formulation of the problem has only limited validity, since many non-Jewish liberals and social democrats maintained humanitarian visions rooted in the eighteenth century without being marginalized in the same way, and also because, as Shulamit Volkov rightly notes, *Bildung* was never an exclusively rationalistic conception, making room for feeling and sensibility, and tied up from the start with aspirations for national unity to which Mosse's perspective gives too little weight. What kept Jews from becoming full members of the nation (in France as well as in Germany) had more to do with those who looked on them as outsiders than with their way of trying to enter in.[36]

But the more exclusively cultural quality of the Jewish investment in *Bildung* was part of the general weakness of their position, and Mosse's observations accord with other indications that Jews may have contributed to that weakness by looking to cosmopolitanism as a substitute for the increasing *fin-de-siècle* pressure to organize politics around ethnic and national identity. The most interesting instances come from Austria, but the kind of Jewish orientation they reveal was present elsewhere too. The Habsburg government found its inherited task of overseeing an ethnically and linguistically diverse empire increasingly difficult as nationalistic forces, their self-consciousness deepened and augmented by more effective communication and organization, demanded more autonomy; after 1918 defeat in war would complete the Empire's dissolution into its component parts. Jews were a kind of "odd-people-out" in this mix, their collective existence relying much less on forms of local autonomy than on the weave of distant connections we have tried to highlight; to them the Habsburg state appeared not as a barrier to their own national aspirations but as a shield against the dangers posed by other people's. In the age of liberalism and nationalism they became, as Hannah Arendt famously put it, the "state people." This did not prevent some Jewish *Bürger* from conceiving the same strong identification with German *Bildung* as their cousins to the north; in Prague, attachment to German language and culture gave Jews a bulwark against rising Czech national feeling, and in Vienna the young Freud was among a group of students drawn to German cultural nationalism in the 1870s and 1880s. The turn to anti-Semitism among nationalists soon revealed the dangers of such a position, reviving or reinforcing Jewish loyalty to the Habsburg regime for some, while opening a way toward Zionism for others. But such allegiances remained perfectly compatible with devotion to German literature, thought, or music, reinforced by virtue of the aspirations to universal humanism that ran powerfully through it. To intellectuals such as Stefan Zweig and Joseph Roth, German in culture but Habsburg loyalists in politics, one of the attractions of the Habsburg system was that it offered a way of "mediating between universal humanity and cultural particularity."[37]

For others, however, the same cosmopolitan impulses could issue in a more one-sided identification with "universality." Emblematic of this outcome was Karl Popper, the influential logician of science and liberal social thinker. Born in 1902 to parents who had converted to Christianity two years earlier, and who were typical of assimilated German-speaking Jews whose social life was predominately lived in the company of others like themselves, Popper became a strong enemy of every form of national and ethnic identity (and of religion), notably both the German and Zionist ones. Such attitudes had roots in older liberalism, but as Malachi Hacohen notes in his valuable studies of Popper, they were also supported by participation in cosmopolitan networks linking intellectuals and institutions over a wide area, of which the Vienna Circle of logical positivists largely inspired by Popper (although he did not share all their views) was exemplary. "Multinational networks of intellectual exchange gave tangible existence to Central European cosmopolitanism during the *fin-de-siècle* and interwar years. The Vienna Circle, for example, developed, during the interwar period, an organizational network in central Europe's urban centers: Vienna, Berlin, Prague, Warsaw, Budapest, Lwow, Bratislava." Jews made up the majority of participants in these linkages; and either because of this preponderance or from some sense that there was something peculiarly Jewish about such social relations, even some non-Jewish members of the Circle were widely thought to be Jewish, notably the philosopher Moritz Schlick. Much was accomplished through these structures, but as Hacohen notes, there was something disquietingly "thin and fragile" about them, all the more evident in an age of rising ethnic and national consciousness. "German was their *lingua franca*, and they critically appropriated German culture traditions. This limited their appeal to non-German intelligentsia, while making them anathema to German nationalists."[38]

Typical as this situation was of its time and place, it recalls the conditions in which other intellectual reformers, similarly reliant on distant networks and uncomfortable with the existing forms of local life, found themselves. In eighteenth-century Germany the advocates of *Aufklärung* were recognized as "the actual *men of the nation*, because their immediate circle of activity is all of Germany," but they were simultaneously described as subject to a peculiar loneliness (*Einsamkeit*), brought on by the thinness of the social fabric they were able to cultivate through their distant connections.[39] The condition Hacohen sees as exemplified in Central Europe by the Vienna Circle also merits comparison with the role assigned to transnational networks at much the same time by Émile Durkheim, like Popper a Jew whose in many ways thoroughgoing assimilation never succeeded in effacing the marks of his origin.

Durkheim was moved to value such cosmopolitan connections by a curious tension in his social and moral theory. Animated partly by his need to affirm both his Jewish roots and his French identity, Durkheim sought to locate the source of morality in the "collective consciousness" of society. Groups at various levels had to provide their members with strong moral direction, because as individuals people were driven by self-centered needs and impulses; only an entity that transcended their egotisms could bring firm moral principles into the world. But such a sociological grounding of morality posed a dilemma Durkheim did not overlook, namely that societies can be one-sided too, imparting a limited and self-interested perspective to their members, rather than furthering altruistic and universal goals. "If society is something universal in relation to the individual," he wrote in 1912, "it is none the less an individuality itself, which has its own personal physiognomy and idiosyncrasies; it is a particular subject and consequently particularizes whatever it thinks of." In his time, however, he thought he could see evidence that these narrowing impulses would come to be "progressively rooted out," thanks to the appearance of a "social life of a new sort," the "international life which has already resulted in universalizing religious beliefs," and that would go on to engender a universal human morality.[40] Durkheim's position was actually closer to that of people like Zweig and Roth than to Popper, since he felt a strong identification with France, as they did with Habsburg Austria, and he saw the universal forms of citizenship posited by its republican tradition as already implying the wider cosmopolitan universalism to come. All the same he never fully escaped the equivocations that his idealization of society created for him, since the cosmopolitan networks to which he appealed would prove no more able to generate a universal morality than were structures such as the Vienna Circle to provide people like Popper with a secure substitute for national allegiances.[41]

Cases such as these bring us back to the relationship between extended networks of means and the abstraction from concrete things and people that operating through them involves and fosters. Alongside the power that such forms of activity can generate there arise dangers and weaknesses, one of which is the temptation to think that people can live wholly or chiefly inside the network itself, no longer constrained by the conditions that obtain at the places from which they enter into it. It is a temptation to which those who operate mostly through cultural networks may be particularly exposed, since in more worldly situations the negative impact of ignoring immediate practical conditions is likely to have quicker and more tangible effects. Whether in general Jews have been more open to such a enticements than others is a question to which no answer may be possible, but the situations in which intellectuals of Jewish origin such as Durkheim and Popper had to operate may have encouraged them to attribute more potency to the cosmopolitan networks they valued than these actually possessed. Ironically, to do so mirrored the image of Jewish networks projected at the same time by those who misguidedly attributed overweening strength to them, a troubling and ultimately tragic parallel, all the more since by 1900 other and more powerful webs of communication and action had come to overshadow those to which Jews owed much of their special compatibility with modern bourgeois life.

Part III

A culture of means

12 PUBLIC PLACES, PRIVATE SPACES

The transformation of culture: an outline

The nineteenth century brought a heightened attention to "culture," both as a particular sphere of life and as a word with varied and disputed meanings. The term now began to take on its two chief modern senses, one referring to the domain of literature and the arts (originally in their "high" rather than "popular" modes, a distinction much weakened today), and the other to the anthropological sense of culture as a "way of life," what the English Victorian sociologist Edward Tylor called the "complex whole" of values and habits characteristic of some people or group in a given time and place. Many reasons can be cited to account for culture's new prominence. In a justly celebrated book Raymond Williams showed that "culture" became a point of reference for conservative critics of market society and modern industry in England, who portrayed them as reducing all human relations to what Thomas Carlyle called the "cash nexus," in contrast to an older, more organic form of life based on humane sentiments and a respect for higher values. The notion of culture also served to distinguish more developed societies from those regarded as closer to nature, and thus to justify the superiority Europeans asserted over peoples in other parts of the world. Tylor used the term in this way, locating particular peoples on a scale of historical development according to how far they had progressed in casting off their original barbarism. Expressed earlier by eighteenth-century writers, this evolutionary view had been challenged by Johann Gottfied Herder, who saw different peoples as possessing a particular spirit that infused all the dimensions of their lives, and argued against claims to hierarchical superiority. But views closer to Tylor's remained dominant, and Herder's alternative would only become widespread in anthropological circles after Bronsilaw Malinowski and Franz Boas gave it prominence in the twentieth century.[1]

In the chapters that make up Part III of this book I will argue that there was a third and no less important reason for the new prominence assumed by culture, one that lay in the evolution of networks of means and of the kinds of social relations their extension and thickening fostered. Main vehicles of cultural activity such as books and periodicals, museums, and concert venues all grew in number and scale and took on new forms as participants and locations were increasingly linked together by an expanding web of periodicals, correspondence, and travel. These developments made the sphere of culture more concrete and palpable by expanding the reach and presence of cultural objects, while simultaneously changing the relations between writers and readers, artists and viewers, and composers, performers and their publics, making the links between producers and consumers at once more visible and less immediate and personal.

At the same time, however, these changes altered the conditions under which readers, spectators, and listeners encountered cultural objects: the same developments that made these interactions more public on one level allowed them to become more private on another. People partook of cultural objects in situations less subject to control by traditional authorities; ways of experiencing literature, art, and music were thus liberated to become more individuated, open to forms of feeling and imagination whose intensity and range evaded the limits set by religion, convention, and social expectation. Such experiences could be of great moment to individuals for whom traditional values and assumptions no longer provided reliable guides to conduct and personal formation, but they simultaneously opened up prospects of ungovernability and danger, against which new kinds of shields had to be fashioned. These parallel transformations are the subject of this chapter.

As culture took on this simultaneously more objective and more subjective character, its history exhibited certain parallels to subjects we considered earlier. As in industry as a whole, it is possible to describe the development of modern forms of cultural production and distribution either in terms of a gradual expansion across the whole of the nineteenth century or as occurring in two distinct phases, with the break coming in the decades after 1850; here too the first perspective captures much but the second highlights important changes that the first tends to veil. Like industry, the forms of organization assumed by literature, art, and music after the mid century acquired a distinctly modern character they had not possessed before. This is a significant parallel, but equally important is one that links cultural development to the pattern we found in gender relations and morality. In both, growing involvement in distant connections at first gave a new kind of solidity and relief to distinctions that had once called less attention to themselves. This was true not just between culture and other spheres of life, but also between "high" and "popular" culture. As cultural networks expanded and thickened, it was elite forms of literature, art, and music that first drew new energy and substance from them, and that acquired an enlarged presence in everyday life.

Soon, however, as will be argued in Chapter 13, it became evident that the same developments also worked in exactly the opposite direction, undermining the very differentiation they made more prominent. Whereas the cultural producers chiefly favored before the mid century had been those who addressed themselves to an educated public, after that date the growth of literacy and leisure inside growing cities linked by modern transport and communication offered new opportunities to those who could find ways to address less educated audiences and consumers. Traditional genres of popular literature, music, and visual entertainment once largely confined to weakly linked local audiences were energized and transformed as they were drawn into more distant and mediated connections. Mass-market newspapers and books were the earliest and most striking examples, accompanied by an expanding world of music-hall performance. The availability of the audiences these forms of popular culture addressed was a chief inspiration for the innovations that turned already-existing visual entertainments common at fairgrounds and market-days into the first "moving pictures." Out of them would arise the modern cinema, the first cultural form rooted in popular entertainment to become also a medium of serious artistic ambition. All these developments contributed to making the boundaries between "high" and popular culture that had visibly hardened earlier grow softer and more permeable by the end of the century. Like the world of politics, the universe of culture that was emerging by the onset of World War I was far more diverse, more unwieldy, and in an important sense more democratic than had seemed possible half a century before.

The distinction between the two levels never disappeared, however, in part because popular cultural forms remained closer to everyday experience and language than did those that developed inside what Max Weber identified as the separate "aesthetic sphere." Within that sphere there arose visions and ambitions that crystallized as the modernist avant-garde. In Chapter 14 I will try to show that the avant-garde exhibited a different relationship to the society and culture in which it took form than many of its representatives and supporters wanted to believe: despite the conviction of vanguard artists and writers that their activities were opposed to bourgeois life and promised some alternative to it, the avant-garde drew much of its energy and many of its aspirations from the very features of modernity of which it declared itself the enemy, preserving them in forms supposed to supplant them.

Parallel histories and their outcomes: publishing

We can best make clear the new and palpably public form that culture began to take on as the Old Regime ended, and the new stage of its development that set in after around 1850, by considering the three main cases of publishing, painting, and music in turn, beginning with books and newspapers. The production of printed materials began a rapid expansion during the eighteenth century. In France the number of books published grew threefold between 1700 and 1770, newspapers went from three titles to several hundred, and a veritable explosion took place in the output of pamphlets. An equally remarkable growth took place in Germany: the number of books listed in the catalogue of the Leipzig book fair expanded ten times across the century (from 265 between 1721 and 1763, to 2,821 between 1763 and 1805), while the print run of copies per edition commonly doubled or quadrupled in the same period.[2] In Britain books and pamphlets had been part of both the long history of political agitation and the growth of consumption throughout the eighteenth century, but what a recent historian calls "the explosion of reading" only took place after 1774, in part as a result of a legal decision by the House of Lords ending a longstanding regime of copyright restriction that gave London print-ers and booksellers tight control over sales and prices. By the 1820s, as William St Clair concludes, the changes had produced a significant fall in the cost of books, leading to a "surge in reading" that "marked the start of a continuing self-sustaining expansion." Before the nine-teenth century was much advanced "virtually everyone read books, magazines, and newspapers on a regular basis."[3]

The expansion of print and readers was an important ground for the creation of the new power of "public opinion" whose presence was noted in earlier chapters, but especially on the continent it was still limited by low levels of general literacy, and it took place inside Old Regime forms of commerce even as it began to undermine them. In both Germany and France publishing was hampered by censorship that sought to prevent the spread of unwelcome opinions, and by both guild and government regulation aimed at preserving the corporate economy and the hierarchical principles it embodied. The restrictions could be circumvented by putting a false place of publication on title-pages, often Amsterdam for titles printed in France, and forbidden books produced in Switzerland were regularly smuggled across the border, but fears of trouble with the authorities and the still limited scope of the market led many booksellers to accept the limits the sys-tem imposed on them, especially since it sometimes also gave them exclusive rights over the titles for which they had obtained a *privilège du roi*. Even those who sympathized with Enlightened ideas sometimes shied away from trying to publish the texts that contained them, pre-ferring, as one said in 1770 "tranquility to risky benefits." Already, however, it was clear that the censorship could not prevail over the swelling network of producers and consumers; by the mid century many titles were allowed to appear without official approval, under a regime of "tacit permissions" that forecast the eventual collapse of the system.[4]

To this evolution the nineteenth century added a number of innovations. A crucial moment came in 1836, when Émile de Girardin (closely followed by a competitor, Armand Dutacq), revolutionized the newspaper industry by setting the subscription price of his new sheet, *La Presse* at half of what others charged, predicting that he could attract 10,000 subscribers, in contrast to the 1,000 or so served by his rivals; within six months he could boast of 20,000. It was not to larger subscription income that he chiefly looked, however, but to the expanded advertising revenues the enlarged readership would draw in: "the ads will pay for the paper," he announced, and they did. One reason for Girardin's success was his decision to draw in readers not just with news, but also by publishing novels, often by well known writers such as Eugène Sue and Balzac, in daily installments as *feuilletons* at the bottom of the first page. At a stroke *La Presse* gave form to a new reading public, at once political, literary, and commercial, and extending from the middle- and lower-middle classes to the upper tier of workers (the more politically conscious of whom, however, seem to have been drawn in greater numbers to Dutacq's rival paper, *Le Siècle*, which espoused more consistently leftist views).[5]

Books were not far behind newspapers in acquiring a larger and more material public profile. The "surge in reading" already visible in England, and that seems to justify the notion of a "mass reading public" there before 1840 (by which date W. H. Smith was already selling books, as the firm still does, in railroad stations) only seems to have come to France as the century advanced. A major innovation in this direction was supplied by Gervais Charpentier, the first publisher to market a unified "collection" of titles in a standard format, all displayed together and offered at the same moderate price, and intended to entice buyers to make purchases on the spot. As a business practice, this contrasted with the model inherited from the eighteenth century (and little altered by the expansion that occurred then), whereby books were commonly purchased singly by people from a seller known personally to them; prices were relatively high and the market assumed to be narrow. Book dealers (who were often the publishers) commonly had to wait a long time to recover their investment in a stock of volumes, and failure threatened those whose resources were tied up in unsold inventories when demand slowed. Charpentier sought to avoid this fate by moving to a system that promised a steady flow of sales and income based on a larger pool of consumers. In shifting from a one-on-one relationship between sellers and buyers to a more plural and impersonal one (some historians refer to it as "industrial"), using a collection of goods on display to draw in a variety of possible buyers, and calculating profits on the whole rather than item by item, he resembled contemporary and later innovations in retailing. By the time he died in 1871 he had more than 400 titles in his list, and attracted a number of imitators, both in France and abroad (the German Universal Bibliothek founded by Reclam in 1867 was one). For them as for him, issuing a collection in a standard format "gave a material form to the house's image in the eyes of the public," affording a new status to publishers as well as to books, and opening the way to a kind of brand loyalty. Like Girardin, and together with such rivals as the Lévy brothers Michel and Calmann and Louis Hachette, he was part of a shift in the relationship between cultural producers and the public, replacing direct and personal ties framed by corporate membership or official privilege with ones based on expanded connection to a broader and more anonymous body of readers.[6]

Charpentier's enterprise extended across the mid century divide and in its later phases it was able to take advantage of the new opportunities opened up by the coming of railroads and the closer market connections they made possible. Overall however these developments marked a new phase in publishing history. Only with them did a mass reading public begin to develop in France; prices for books fell by 48 percent between 1840 and 1870, and another 23 percent by 1914. Elisabeth Parinet refers to the results as a "second revolution of the book." Publicity for books now reached larger numbers of people; whereas the typical novel was printed in an edition of 1,000 copies in the first half of the century, Jules Verne's were appearing in runs of 30,000 by the 1870s; by 1904 1.6 million copies of his works had been sold. Many of the buyers were country people now served by small-town bookshops supplied by railroads, a system that wiped out the earlier traveling booksellers, the *colporteurs*. Their mainstays had been almanacs, religious tracts, and chivalric and heroic literature, sometimes read to others by the few literate people at sewing or work sessions (*veillés*). The trade came under pressure from government opposition during the Second Empire, based on justified fear that it spread anti-government ideas, but literacy and railroads were the chief reasons for its demise. By the end of the century not only Verne but Victor Hugo, Eugène Sue, and other writers popular in cities were being read in the country too, their success contributing to the new status of novels, which only now overtook drama and poetry as the most popular genres. In every country the new developments in printing and bookselling in the age of railroads included a broad expansion of lending libraries in cities and towns (they, too, effectively established earlier in England than elsewhere), important contributors

to the much enlarged and more visible public world of print in existence by the end of the century.[7]

Museums and painting

Both the structural features and the chronology of the transformation
of literature were matched in the visual arts by the emergence of public museums in the run-up to the nineteenth century and the development of a more systematically organized market for pictures in its
last three decades. Before around 1750, collections of art and precious
objects were predominately private locales, housed in the residences of
the rulers or nobles who owned them, and opened to view only for their
friends or guests. One reason for showing the works was to let aspiring artists see the great work of the past, but even then the display was
expected to serve as a kind of symbolic manifestation of the collector's
grandeur. To this end objects were arranged not with regard to their
style or subject, but as what historians have recognized as a "spectacle
of treasures." During the eighteenth century these aims came to be displaced by or, in some cases, joined with the Enlightenment enthusiasm
for providing public instruction. This was at least part of the motive
that led a British physician, Sir Hans Sloane, to will his large collection
of antiquities, manuscripts, and other objects to the nation when he
died in 1753, providing the nucleus of the British Museum that opened
its doors six years later. Similar aims inspired the Elector of Saxony to
make his trove of paintings publicly available in a renovated Dresden
stable in 1746, and the Habsburg emperor Joseph II when he moved his
to the Upper Belvedere Palace and opened it to viewers in 1770 (small
groups had been admitted to the Imperial Gallery earlier). The Uffizi in
Florence and the Vatican both became public museums in 1773.[8]

   These spaces all mixed together the traditional motive of displaying the virtues of an individual patron or ruler with the eighteenth-
century enthusiasm for enlightening the public (with a characteristic
variation in England, where it was Parliament rather than the uninter-
ested king that accepted Sloane's gift and sponsored the new institution). The two purposes were especially entangled in France, where
the royal collection in the Luxembourg Palace was opened for a few
hours on specified days beginning in 1750, and plans made to fit out
the Louvre as a museum in the following decades. Louis XVI may have

been motivated by competition with a display set up by his cousin the Duke of Orleans in the Palais Royal, and writers at the time hoped that what some saw as a decline in the quality of contemporary painting could be arrested by exposure to great works of the past, but above all the king and his minister hoped to impress "public opinion" with the monarchy's devotion to art and the nation, and to identify it with ideals of heroism, virtue, and public service illustrated in the "history paintings" that critics regarded as art's most exalted and instructive genre. The various difficulties confronting the state in the last decades of the Old Regime kept the project from fruition, however, so that it was the Revolutionary state that realized the monarchy's Louvre project, opening the museum to visitors in 1793.[9]

Here the public nature of the space made its contrast with earlier collections more evident. Like the king, the republic was determined to present itself as the defender of the nation's cultural heritage and the vehicle of its unity. The museum was looked to as a riposte to critics who portrayed the Revolution as destructive both of respect for past achievements and of stability in every sphere of life. In addition, activist artists and writers such as Jacques-Louis David took over and recast the pedagogical hopes traditionally vested in art, hoping to make painting serve as a vehicle for inculcating republican virtue and patriotism. By rejecting objects thought to be redolent of tyranny and oppression and providing a new perspective on those that could be made to serve the needs of a free people, they sought to enroll the Louvre in the Revolutionary project of "regeneration," the renewal of human nature through participation in public activities, ceremonies, and festivals.[10]

The new setting also put its stamp on the way the objects were displayed. During the eighteenth century the idea that exhibits should serve some educational purpose rather than merely show the magnificence of collectors led to two proposals for how pictures ought to be arranged. The first aimed to make the excellence of a particular artist or technique stand out by juxtaposing works that illustrated commonalities and contrasts. Such presentations were seen as especially useful to young artists, and providing them would remain an important goal of nineteenth-century museums. But the new Louvre adopted the second arrangement, one already tried out in the Luxembourg when it was opened on a limited basis in 1750, and intended to serve the needs of a larger public. Here paintings were displayed not in relation to virtues important to students or connoisseurs, but in order to show the historical evolution of national schools and the place of individual artists within them. The goal, as a government spokesman put it, was to replace a disorderly jumble with "a continuous and uninterrupted sequence revealing the progress of the arts and the degrees of perfection attained by various nations that have cultivated them." Grouping pictures in this way showed the history of art as a story of innovation and advance (an idea first given currency by the sixteenth-century artist and historian Giorgio Vasari), and it was regarded as encouraging an appreciation of both tradition and innovation, by showing at once how great artists of the past had drawn sustenance from their teachers and the independence they achieved from them. The cosmopolitan edge given to this schema by including a variety of national schools was sharpened by French pride in having brought works thought to be insufficiently appreciated in their own countries to Paris through the power of the Revolutionary armies, giving viewers there access to what one writer described as "everything that may empower the imagination."[11]

In these ways the emergence of museums resembled the transformation of publishing, reorganizing the realm of culture by replacing a set of still largely private and hierarchical connections between producers and patrons with a more generally available and explicitly public sphere of interaction. For much of the nineteenth century, however, earlier principles and assumptions still put their stamp on this sphere's operation. One instance was the persistence of the already-mentioned classifying schema that made "history painting" the highest type, on the grounds that depictions of heroism or public spirit were the best vehicles for inculcating virtue. Such a perspective maintained the ascendency of moral considerations in the realm of aesthetics; because it survived, attempts to undermine the hierarchy by asserting the equal dignity of scenes of everyday life (traditionally called "genre" paintings) became an important front in the struggle to free art from the weight of the past. No less important was the persisting sway exercised over public taste by official guidance, in the form of the salons and official art exhibitions that determined which artists and works would receive a stamp of higher approval. Salons were state institutions, but they were also central to the way the art market functioned: some of the works accepted were bought by governments, and those that were not had a much better chance to attract private buyers than ones that lacked this cachet. The salon system had already been a central element in the way the market for pictures functioned in the eighteenth century, and dealers were involved in setting up some of the early public exhibitions (this was the case in England too, where a group of art merchants was behind a series of exhibits of contemporary painting beginning in 1760), recognizing that works included in them would have a special appeal to purchasers.

As with print culture, the role played by patronage and official authority in regulating relations between visual artists and the public generated much criticism, expanding as the eighteenth century gave way to the nineteenth. A French critic of the 1780s wrote that

> Those who patronize artists, whether grandees or rich men, are entitled at the very least to have a say in the work they order. But however right and natural may be their determination to have their way, it has often thwarted the best will in the world and checked the impulses of genius ... The mischief can only be undone by leaving the artist a free hand in the execution of his work, in all its parts.

Friedrich Schiller insisted that "I write as a citizen of the world (*Weltbürger*), who serves no prince," and the painter Jacob Carstens expressed a kindred sentiment in a letter to a Prussian minister, adding that his having received a pension from the Berlin Academy did not make him "a lifelong bondman" of it. In early nineteenth-century German cities artists formed societies to set up exhibitions of their own where they could present their work directly to the public, bypassing the narrow circle of aristocratic patrons. One Berlin painter involved in them excused himself for delaying work on a royal commission, explaining that he had first to complete some smaller works for the *breitere Publikum*, on whose interest and orders he was dependent "since your Majesty alone neither can nor will always employ me." Private exhibition spaces similar to those organized by artists and dealers in England were advocated in France as an alternative or supplement to the official salons (for instance by the painter Théodore Rousseau) from the 1830s.[12] At roughly the same time a writer in the French journal *L'Artiste*, Alexandre de Saint-Cheron, welcomed signs that the regime of patronage both official and private was giving way to market relations, since it was through them that cultural producers could address themselves directly to the public. Doing so freed artists from personal dependency, Saint-Cheron maintained, allowing them

424 / Public places, private spaces

to develop their talents by speaking to and for society as a whole. Hence the artist who "expects to be paid only for his work and the free products of his genius" acquired a social position that was "more moral, more independent, and more able to favor the progress of art."[13] Attacks on the Salon system grew in the following years, fed by the burgeoning number of submissions and what seemed the arbitrary responses of juries to it. In 1855 Gustave Courbet, the most frank and outspoken artist of the time in his desire to present his work directly to viewers and be judged only by them, set up his own exhibition as a direct challenge to the one sponsored by Napoleon III's government, and the famous "Salon des refusés" took place in 1863.

The old habits had staying power, however. As late as 1874 the critic Théodore Duret advised Camille Pissarro against participating in the independent exhibition mounted by the impressionists on the grounds that only the Salon gave painters the recognition that led to success with dealers and the public, and in 1881 Renoir wrote to the impressionists' dealer Paul Durand-Ruel that he doubted there were more than fifteen art lovers in Paris "capable of liking a painting without Salon approval." By this time however, the art world was entering into a phase that corresponded to the "second revolution of the book" in publishing; of this development Durand-Ruel was one of the crucial agents, fashioning a system that would provide a new foundation for the aspiration to put the relations between artists and their audience on a basis free of traditional patronage relations.

Durand-Ruel was moved by both self-interest and a desire to promote the careers of the painters he favored. His father had dealt with the Barbizon School of the mid century, and by the time Paul took over the business in 1865 there was considerable evidence that money could be made by investing early in talented artists' careers; indeed a young and penniless Émile Zola, in the course of defending the still often despised Manet in 1867, declared that had he any money he would buy up "all his canvasses today. In fifty years they will be sold for fifteen or twenty times as much." In 1872 Durand-Ruel did just what Zola had imagined, paying Manet the considerable sum of 35,000 francs for all twenty-three of his available pictures, a practice he soon extended to what was still called the "Batignolles School" of Renoir, Monet, Degas, and the others, assuring their survival while preparing substantial profits for himself. His desire to secure both his own profits and make his artists understood and appreciated by potential buyers found visionary expression in his other important innovation, seeking to form public taste by publishing exhibition catalogues in which competent critics discussed the new work's innovations and value. As Armand Silvestre, author of the first catalogue in 1874 explained, the painters were submitting their work "directly to the public that makes reputations even when it seems only to submit to them, and which will not fail to turn away, someday, from those who are content to follow its taste, toward those who make an effort to guide it."[14]

The success of this project was noted throughout Europe, and by the 1880s and 1890s groups of artists in other countries were making similar efforts on their own, "seceding" from authorized venues to set up their own exhibitions, supported by dealers who enlisted critics to publicize and evaluate the work shown. In Vienna Gustav Klimt was a central figure in the Secession; in Berlin the movement was animated by the eminent dealer Paul Cassirer. The result was the creation of a public world of visual art, brought to existence not by officials who shaped it for the "higher" purposes of morality or the state, but by artists and their collaborators themselves (we will consider some of the aesthetic aims and consequences of these movements later on). There can hardly be a better example of a shift from teleocratic principles regulating relations inside a network on grounds established outside it to autonomous ones derived from the activities pursued inside the network itself. As in other instances, a transformation rooted in the eighteenth century found much fuller realization through the new conditions emerging after 1850.[15]

Music

The corresponding developments that gave a more tangible and public character to musical culture included a marked increase in the number of public concerts, an expansion in music publishing that made scores available to many more people and in standardized form, and the changed relationship between private musical spaces and public ones to which this growth in publishing contributed. These changes underlay a phenomenon Carl Dahlhaus identifies as critical to the new situation of music in the nineteenth century, namely the emerging sense of a stable past repertoire against which music of the present was compared and judged. All these developments clearly began before 1800 but picked up speed in the era of the Restoration, spurred on by the renown accorded to Haydn, Mozart, and Beethoven.[16] As with literature and art, the second half of the century would see a new and more fully developed stage in this process.

Like museums, public concerts (as opposed to private occasions in the homes of well-off patrons) were largely a creation of the eighteenth century, achieving prominence especially in England, where they often featured foreign luminaries such as Handel and Haydn. But their numbers mushroomed only later, increasing threefold in London between the mid 1830s and the late 1840s and fivefold in Paris in the same years. Both the growth and the novelty were greater in Paris, because the Old Regime state had regulated and largely monopolized music performances, alongside opera and dance, through the Académie Royale de Musique (although a few ephemeral semi-public subscription concert series started up in the 1770s), and suspicion of popular gatherings continued to impede them until around 1800. The most important innovation of the first half of the century came through action by the Restoration government in 1828, just as the atmosphere that would lead to the Revolution of 1830 was heating up, when the regime provided money for a Concert Society associated with the Paris Conservatory, thereby instituting what the *Journal des débats* called "a musical revolution." A slower growth was visible in Vienna, as in some smaller German cities where *Kenner* and *Liebhaber* organized public concerts, and in some capitals where princely theaters previously attended only by courtiers and guests were opened to the public, foreshadowing later moves toward forms of musical life that allowed for still broader participation.[17]

In this period, however, even public venues retained features rooted in private patronage. In Paris and London the most common kind of public concert was one dubbed a "benefit," meaning not (as the term does today) that it was held in aid of some outside cause, but that it was put on to support the musician who organized it; he (occasionally she, but mostly for singers) solicited colleagues to participate (as they did in return), using the occasion not chiefly to profit from ticket sales, but to put his name before potential patrons who could provide "more lucrative private concerts and teaching contracts," still the best source of income for most performers.[18] The "benefit" concert's mix of public and private orientations was present also in appearances by the great and wildly popular traveling virtuosos Niccolò Paganini and

Franz Liszt, which generated large sums from ticket sales, but (like the tours of such earlier figures as Mozart) were still organized by the musicians themselves, through contacts with local patrons and colleagues, sometimes supported by aides whose relations to the soloists resembled servants more than later managers. Frédéric Chopin's career was even closer to the earlier model, since he gave few public concerts, and "lived on his earnings as a teacher with an extensive practice among the wealthy, [and] by his performances at the private concerts of the rich"; the chief modern element in his case was that he also derived income from publishing his compositions. The often extravagant occasions when Liszt and Paganini appeared in public profited from the growing prestige of classical performance, but they also bore features of popular street and theater entertainment; at the same time some of Liszt's concerts were more like salon appearances, given to small groups and with much socializing between the pieces. A popular spirit also marked the informal "promenade concerts" held first in Vienna and Paris and then in London from the 1830s; they attracted a mixed middle-class and worker audience but proved unable to become regular or permanent. Perhaps the most modern musical enterprise of the 1830s was the Paris Opera, run as a commercial undertaking by a self-consciously bourgeois entrepreneur and talented publicist, Auguste Véron, who drew in a large public by providing star-quality singers and dancers. But he often had to scramble to meet their demands and his success relied in part on a royal subsidy.[19]

The more palpable public presence these phenomena imparted to musical life in the decades before 1850 was boosted by a remarkable expansion in publishing and distributing musical scores. Although music had long been available in printed form (usually from engraved plates), the press runs were small and the range of available pieces limited. The situation began to change from the mid eighteenth century as many of the publishing houses whose names remain familiar today were founded, especially in Germany, a development much aided by the development of new and more flexible forms of movable type (pioneered by Breitkopf in Leipzig), easing access to both present and past work. Much music still circulated in manuscript however, and some published pieces were dedicated to patrons whose role in musicians' careers remained crucial, even to so widely acclaimed a figure as Haydn. The much greater expansion of printed music during the nineteenth century rested partly on the growing body of professional musicians, but probably more on students and amateurs, the latter chiefly responsible for the large place that music now assumed in the lives of families. According to one report there were only a dozen music shops in London around 1750, but 150 by 1824; between the same dates catalogues of available pieces exploded from a few pages to several hundred, and by the 1820s the publisher Boosey (today Boosey and Hawkes) listed 10,000 pieces from foreign printing houses alone. In 1834 a multi-volume "Musical Library" made its appearance in London, the publisher explaining that it was intended "to afford the same aid in the progress of the musical art that literature has so undeniably received from the cheap publications of the day."[20] Teaching aids were one significant component of this output, along with collections of songs and instrumental pieces, especially for the pianos that found their way into more and more middle-class homes from late in the eighteenth century.

This growth in publishing supported private performances as well as public ones, but these took on a different relation to public concerts as the locales shifted from princely and aristocratic salons to middle-class homes. In both milieux performances were also social occasions where individuals and families could establish or develop connections, while simultaneously asserting claims to leadership in setting taste. For princes and aristocrats, however, public figures even in their private existence, musical occasions in their salons were self-contained; the notion that they might derive even some of their significance from reference to a less personalized musical world outside would seldom have been welcome to them. In bourgeois settings by contrast music played at home often had just such a reference, since those who engaged in it often saw it in relation to the expanding number of public concerts; symphonic reductions for solo or duo pianists were very popular, serving both as vehicles for learning about pieces people might not ever get to hear in a full version, or as preparation for listening to them if a nearby performance was in the offing. To be sure, music in middle-class settings served other purposes as well, particularly for young women, for whom being able to play the piano was seen as a help in finding a husband, allowing girls to exhibit themselves and their accomplishments in an acceptable way on social occasions (especially since piano-playing did not involve the kind of bodily display connected with string or wind instruments, more often taken up by boys and men). Some middle-class daughters saw wider possibilities in music, taking such (rare) examples as Clara Schumann as inspiration for imagining an independent career; as with writing, it was a hope that few could realize (save as teachers), and most bourgeois families were at best ambivalent toward it (as they were toward sons with similar ambitions), but the prospect left its mark. Both in its relationship to concert-going and in the expectations that it could provide advantages to daughters, middle-class musical life drew sustenance from the more visible public world of music in connection with which it developed, a world tied together and animated by discussion in journals and reviews. So important to musical life was the role played in it by "the central public medium of the bourgeoisie, the press," that Carl Dahlhaus concludes that modern musical culture "might even be defined as music culture under the conditions of 'bourgeois publicity.'"[21]

In music too, however, the decades just after 1850 marked a palpably new phase in the relations between cultural producers and their public. What William Weber characterizes as the "free-wheeling" manner of the 1830s and 1840s with the continued importance of patronage, private performances and "benefit concerts," now began to disappear into "firmer and less speculative structures." Performers and composers themselves ceased to be the main organizers of their own concerts, as professional managers and agents began to appear from the 1870s, spreading to many cities in the next decades, and creating stable relations between players and their audiences much like those that Durand-Ruel and his imitators did for painters. "By 1900 almost every concert program in London, Paris, Berlin or Vienna denoted the concert agency that had arranged it."[22] A parallel development was the establishment of stable and more professional orchestras; the 1850s saw the founding of such ensembles in a number of cities, including Vienna and New York; a good illustration of the differences they made is provided by the northern English industrial cities of Manchester, Birmingham, and Leeds. As Simon Gunn notes, a lively musical life existed in these places before the mid century but it was sporadic and unorganized. "The idea that music existed as an art in its own right, disassociated from religious or social ends, appears to have been held only by a minority of devotees"; in that period, as a Manchester paper later recalled, the hall where "Gentlemen's" concerts took place resembled "rather a fashionable lounge than a society for the enjoyment or cultivation of music."

Central to making this distinction clear was the arrival in Manchester of a figure who was at once a musician and a musical entrepreneur of a modern type, Charles (originally Karl) Hallé. Taking over the orchestra in 1849, he became not just its conductor but its proprietor, and it still bears his name. A passionate advocate of Beethoven and an important force in making his music known in England, especially outside of London, he began his Manchester career by firing most of the musicians on the roster and replacing them with better-trained and better paid ones. To support the expense of his improved orchestra he sought to maximize revenues by selling programs, instructional manuals and sheet music. But the aim was to assure the material health of the ensemble, not just to make profits, and was to this goal that the Hallé Society he set up with the aid of prominent local citizens was dedicated. All this made Hallé himself an object of the increasing veneration accorded conductors in this period (Mendelssohn had been an early object of this attention, but it now spread more generally), and which was one reason for the expanded attention given concert music in the press. Public commentary on music grew from the 1840s, with the appearance of the London-based *Musical Times* and the *Birmingham Musical Examiner,* but beginning in the 1860s all the Manchester papers had critics and during the next decade the *Guardian*'s morning edition published program notes for music to be performed in the evening. Concerts remained social occasions to be sure, with whole families arriving dressed to be seen on opening nights and ticket prices set at levels that assured the audience would be primarily middle-class; but the availability of seats for a shilling meant that some better-off artisans and workers could attend and accounts describe some of them as regular concert-goers. A similar evolution of musical life occurred in Birmingham and Leeds, but organized by the citizenry rather than any counterpart to Hallé. Clearly music never became wholly independent of other public and private purposes in these places (in Birmingham and Leeds some concert revenues were used to support charitable causes), but as Gunn notes the new organizational forms were "instrumental in carving out a public realm for art."[23]

These parallel evolutions of print, painting, and music were surely central to the much greater attention paid to the notion of culture in the nineteenth century, and in particular to a basic transformation of the word's meaning highlighted by Raymond Williams. Whereas culture and its equivalents in other languages through the eighteenth century referred chiefly to a process, the cultivation of the mind through education and exposure to the arts (modeled on the improvement of the earth in agriculture), the term now signified the objectified realm of objects and activities to which it still points today. The people who established this meaning in the nineteenth century were clearly aware of its connection to the more palpable and visible sphere whose rise we have been chronicling. When Matthew Arnold characterized culture as "the best that has been thought and said in the world," he added that its ability to give vitality to society was most clearly demonstrated in moments "when there is a *national* glow of life and thought" that permeates the whole: the benefits to be derived from the repository of culture depended on its diffusion and by implication on means being available to effect it.

By the end of the century Georg Simmel would recognize the public and material presence of intellectual and aesthetic objects as a characteristic feature of modern culture, noting that over time ideas and images came to be increasingly embodied in "objective" or "supra-individual forms: books, art, ideal concepts such as father-land, general culture, the manifestation of life in conceptual and aes-thetic images, the knowledge of a thousand interesting and significant things." Simmel, not unlike Arnold, valued the realm of culture for its contrasts with material life, emphasizing that one person's enjoyment of its contents did not deprive others of access to them.

> The more values are transposed into such objective forms, the more room there is in them, as in the house of God, for every soul. Perhaps the wilderness and embitterment of modern competition would be completely unbearable were it not accompanied by this growing objectification … [which] contributes to the noblest and most ennobling result in the historical process: to build a world that may be acquired without conflict and mutual repression, to possess values whose acquisition and enjoyment by one person does not exclude that of another, but opens the door a thousand times for him to acquire such values as well.[24]

We will see later that Simmel himself regarded this as a one-sidedly optimistic assessment, and we will need to consider what it left out; for now we note only his testimony that the strong awareness of culture as an objective realm by the end of the century depended on its acquiring the more public and palpable forms whose appearance and evolution I have sought to describe here.

Cultural autonomy and ungovernable private experience: literature and letters

This movement of cultural activities toward forms of organization and relations to their publics that were no longer shaped by patrons and authorities was accompanied by assertions of culture's autonomy, its capacity to make its own rules. To show that the phenomenon was general across the whole field of culture, we look first for a moment at art and music, before turning to its specific embodiment in literature and letters. As settings expanded where painting and sculpture could be viewed not as accompaniments to churchly or courtly rituals, or as tributes to princely or noble status, but in a manner that gave prominence to the objects for themselves, there developed an awareness of what M. H. Abrams has called "art as such." The notion was adumbrated in the seventeenth century, but it became more prominent in the eighteenth-century locales that encouraged comparison between works, and thus an attitude that asked how well each one fulfilled goals specific to creative activity, rather than some extra-aesthetic aim. Kant's *Critique of Judgment* of 1790 theorized the judgment of taste in just these terms: when we say that something is beautiful, he argued, we mean that its way of being what it is fulfills its own purpose, independently of its reference to anything outside.[25] Max Weber regarded Kant's formulation of aesthetic self-sufficiency as an exemplary instance of the overall "rationalization" of modern life that allowed different spheres of action and theory to develop independently of each other, free from the control formerly exercised by overarching religious ideas and institutions. In the terms we are proposing here this replaced teleocratic principles with autonomous ones. The social dimension of this independence was the development of an institutionalized "aesthetic sphere," a "historically unique network," as Richard Wolin describes it, composed of "artists and persons of taste, whose interactions are mediated by a new series of public institutions" – museums, galleries, libraries, and periodicals.[26]

In music a similar claim to autonomy took the form of an insistence that compositions were "works" in an emphatic sense, enclosed, self-regulating entities that derived special value from their inner coherence. The notion of musical pieces as works in this sense has become so common since the nineteenth century that Lydia Goehr has justifiably chided modern composers, critics, and historians for inappropriately imposing it on certain of their predecessors, for whom it mattered much less whether particular instruments or voices executed a given line, how a melody was ornamented, or whether a composer re-used material from one piece in another; often it was non-musical purposes that determined these choices. The change did not come all at once, since aspects of it were developed by Bach, Couperin, and other early eighteenth-century composers who still retained the older practices, but the idea received much stronger expression in the years around 1800, when E. T. A. Hoffmann insisted that "the genuine artist lives only for the work," and cares about nothing so much as being true to what gives it its special being.[27] A work in this sense was the exemplary product of the figure Kant called the "genius," the creative poet or artist whose special powers at once provided liberation from inherited and traditional rules and allowed such a person to generate and follow new ones. Genius was a universal quality, but it had always to be rooted in the individuality that distinguished one person from others, and only works whose essence lay in this individuality could be called products of genius. For this reason Kant refused to recognize scientists as geniuses, since even the great Newton gave expression to the way the world was rather than to his own nature; his achievement might equally have been effected by some other person. The composer who best exemplified this power to nineteenth-century listeners was Beethoven; we will come in a moment to the ways by which listeners sought to enter into the powers thought to be lodged in his music.

These notions encouraged a new exaltation of art and artists. Kant's belief that a genius, by following only laws generated out of his own being, came as close as any human being could to transcending the material cause-and-effect relations that keep the rest of us from realizing the moral freedom to which humanity is called, was amplified by romantics into a view that raised poets and painters above everyone else. The critic W. H. Wackenröder demanded that "galleries become 'temples' where, in silent humility and in heart-raising seclusion, one could take pleasure in marveling at the greatest artists as the highest of earthly beings."[28] Such views set the bar for giving artists their due very high, so that we should perhaps not be too harsh on ordinary people, bourgeois or not, who failed to come up to it. Artworks now acquired a new and specifically aesthetic aura, different from the one that Walter Benjamin associated with their earlier ritual functions and settings. This more specifically modern aura could only shine forth when works were removed from contexts where they served "higher" purposes into ones organized to recognize and promote aesthetic value itself.

This changed situation of culture presented both new opportunities and new problems to those who drew on it, and it is these that will occupy us for the rest of this chapter. Literature provides our first point of entry into them. One powerful eighteenth-century testimony to the autonomy claimed for writing and reading as against the authorities previously entrusted with regulating them was Denis Diderot's enthusiasm for the positive effects that the sentimental novels of Samuel Richardson, *Pamela* and *Clarissa*, could have on the development of their readers. When one of Richardson's characters behaves in a particular way, Diderot declared,

> one pictures him [or her], one puts oneself in his [or her]
> place or at his side (*on se met à sa place ou à ses côtés*),
> one fires up [*on se passionne*] for or against him: if he is
> virtuous, one unites oneself with his role, if he is evil, one
> draws away from him indignantly … Often have I said
> while reading him: 'I would willingly give my life to be
> like a certain personage, I would rather be dead than be
> that other one.'

In a remarkable essay, Jean Starobinski has pointed to the important moment in cultural history marked by this notion of "putting oneself in the place" of literary characters. Made explicit by Diderot but implicitly practiced by other readers, it asserted a new relationship between literature and moral self-formation, giving to secular and novelistic materials and the feelings they evoke a role in shaping personal being that had earlier been reserved to religious and didactic texts and precepts. Diderot gave expression to the Enlightenment concern to foster the moral autonomy of individuals, their capacity to regulate their behavior free of outside direction, and thus also to set the terms of their interaction with the objects and feelings that nurtured their moral formation.[29]

In fact, however, Diderot was not always so confident about these things as his effusive praise for Richardson's novels suggests; at other times he was anxious or suspicious about the ideas and feelings generated by individuals' interactions with real or fictional others. He titled one of his plays *Is he good? Is he wicked?* [*Est-il-bon? Est-il méchant?*], a question rendered unanswerable by the revelation that what draws the story's main character to help others is the pleasure he takes in making them beholden and thus subordinate to himself. As with the couple at the center of Rousseau's *Julie*, persons moved by feelings toward others they regard as virtuous may be exposed to an undertow that carries them in equivocal directions. If this is what humans are like then novels such as *Pamela* that picture the vulnerability of a young woman to the seductive wiles of more powerful men (even though the story is about her successful resistance) may stir up anything but virtuous feelings.

The dilemmas this created for the expanding realm of literary culture during the eighteenth and nineteenth centuries are nowhere clearer than in the relationship between the developments that made printed texts of all kinds so easily available and one of the most remarkable episodes in the history of moral and cultural anxiety, the widespread fear about masturbation that spread from the middle of the eighteenth century. As both Thomas Laqueur and Isabel Hull have shown in remarkable studies, the near-panic about masturbation that lasted into the twentieth century (and still affects people to some degree today) was a specifically modern phenomenon, arising and spreading during the eighteenth century (the most powerful alarm bell was rung by Samuel Tissot's book *L'Onanisme* in 1760), and largely independent of earlier religious and communal attempts to regulate sexual behavior. More important in our context, both these writers show that the worries about the harms people inflicted on themselves through "self-abuse" were intricately tied up with awareness about the growing importance of relations to distant people and objects in individual lives, and with the spread of printed materials as a vehicle of such relations.

One thing that made the mounting terror modern was that writers on the subject often associated masturbation with a quality regarded as a great virtue in Enlightenment culture, namely imagination, the very faculty that enabled readers like Diderot to "put themselves in the place" of others. Imagination allowed people to expand the range of their associations and achieve independence from the narrow limits of their lives, but since it was directed toward objects that had no physical presence, it opened the way to the danger Goethe once described as "slipping into the seductive allurements of uncontrolled fancy." Masturbation was regarded as so dangerous because it had just this quality, allowing a person who engaged in it to enjoy any real or fictional partner, expanding his or her range of pleasure and power, but in a way that required no actual social or material relationship, no dependence on either real people or the conditions of establishing actual ties with them. Such a way of orienting oneself toward others threatened individuals and society from late in the eighteenth century as never before, Laqueur argues, because old ways of anchoring life to a transcendent structure were losing their force in favor of a moral order that rested on whatever resources of reason and feeling humans could bring to bear on constructing it. Masturbation rose up as "the vice of individuation for a world in which the old ramparts against desire had crumbled," the exemplary evil of "an age that valued desire, pleasure, and privacy but was fundamentally worried about how, or if, society could mobilize them."[30] Both Hull and Laqueur demonstrate the place of distant relations, especially literary ones, in this complex; it is well-illustrated by a passage the former cites from a German comment of 1801 about modern newspapers: "The kind of happiness that many newspaper readers enjoy has only been available to Europeans in the past century. [It consists of] sailing on the wings of fantasy out of their small civil [bürgerliche] and domestic sphere and into the great theater, and there playing in their minds the roles of a main actor, a public speaker, a statesman, a legislator, a hero." The kinds of relations to others that made masturbation appear so dangerous entered into people's lives in just the same way, through printed materials, both texts and images.[31]

An important portion of these materials was composed of the growing body of writing about masturbation itself. The masturbation literature was part of the Enlightenment project of improving life through spreading information about dangers and remedies of all kinds, and in particular of the belief that social and moral betterment could be fostered by publicity and discussion. Writings intended to publicize the perils of masturbation resembled novels such as *Julie* and *Pamela* in that large parts of them consisted of letters, real or made-up, in this case from people who reported on their experiences or fears, on the practice's bad effects on their health, or on how some treatment (not uncommonly offered for sale by writers or editors) had helped them. Like novel readers (of whom Rousseau's admirers provide the most famous but by no means the only case), readers of books on masturbation wrote to the authors and communicated with each other through them. As Hull notes, such groups of readers and writers were part of the modern search for self-improvement by way of formal and informal exchanges, a practice exemplified by the literary and patriotic societies, masonic lodges, and coffee houses that were important vehicles of Enlightenment.[32]

By its resemblance to these other projects of self-improvement, however, the masturbation literature revealed how much all of them were threatened by the uncertainties about the use people made of the expanding stock of publicly available materials. Open discussion of masturbation was presented as a way of increasing understanding about it, and therefore warning people away from a supposed moral and physical danger, but as Laqueur makes clear it was immediately evident that such discussion could not escape being a vehicle for drawing attention to the very practices it aimed to curb. Just because masturbation was a private and secret activity, many people only came to know how widespread it was, and how powerfully it drew others despite the guilt it inspired in them, through the literature intended to condemn and combat it. People learned about masturbation in many ways of course, by themselves or through various others, but private reading played "an essential part in creating the secret vice."[33] In these ways the anxieties about masturbation made evident a central feature of modern moral culture that would mark it through the nineteenth century and beyond. The expanding public sphere provided the frame for an enlarged and unregulated realm of private experience, within which people could invest the objects made available to them with hopes or desires generated inside themselves. Although the reading public was still relatively limited during the eighteenth century, its growth already engendered worries of a kind that would be amplified as the audience for books and periodicals (and later film and radio) swelled in the nineteenth century. It was not possible to know either just who the audience would be, or what use people would make of the materials made available to them.

We should not leave this subject however without recognizing that the spaces for private experience the new cultural relations opened up also made room for developments regarded as less problematic. One illustration is the expansion of letter-writing. In a sense most letter-writing was always a private activity but it too took on new and publicly supported-forms during the nineteenth century. What is often regarded as the golden age of correspondence began earlier, in part because of the important role it played in keeping up contacts between family members separated by distance, as well as between friends and business associates. The volume of postal exchange was still limited before the middle of the nineteenth century, however by arrangements that kept rates high and put the burden of paying them on recipients of letters rather than senders; since the former could refuse to pay, some letters were never delivered and the common practice of basing charges on distance kept many people's exchanges within strict bounds. It was to remedy these defects that cheap postal services were established, with uniform rates for whole countries and payment by senders, who could remain anonymous once stamps and mailboxes came into use.

The benefits such changes were expected to bring were identified earlier, for instance by a French government circular of 1792, which described the postal service as nothing less than

> the tie that draws together and unites all people from one
> end of the earth to the other, letting them enjoy the free
> circulation of their ideas and feelings through active and
> reciprocal correspondence. It is thanks to this adroit cir-
> culation that progress and enlightenment of all kinds are
> extended and multiplied, that the benefits of genius spread
> among the nations, and that society can reap the fruits
> of all the precious kinds of knowledge that have such an
> essential influence on human happiness.

Effective attempts to realize these benefits only began with the English penny post of 1840; it was copied in other countries but slowly (partly from fear that radical groups could make use of it), and only in the *fin-de-siècle* did the habit of correspondence begin to spread to people below the level of the middle classes, aided by rising levels of literacy, together with the still cheaper medium of the postcard, introduced at the very end of the century and costing about half as much to send as a letter.[34]

Literature and letter-writing had closer ties through much of the nineteenth century than nowadays, in part because many novels, including Rousseau's and Richardson's, were epistolary, cast as a series of letters. This gave novels a close connection to another genre that has lost its prominence over time, namely collections of model letters to which people, especially those with little experience or practice, turned on occasions when they needed to write one. Recent scholars have shown that these collections were often read as quasi-novels. One reason this could be the case was that the sample letters often referred to critical moments in people's lives, relations with lovers, seeking jobs or favors, asking for advice about difficult or dramatic situations. Richardson himself was the author of one of the most widely read compilations, and the plot of *Pamela* was foreshadowed by some of his models. Letter-books also provided pictures of social relations inside groups of which readers had no direct experience, adding to the possibility for fantasy identifications they created. Such was the case at least in France, where scholars have contrasted the relatively modest position of the readership with the elegant settings often posited for the model letters; the situation may not have been quite the same for Richardson's readers, since his examples assumed a less exalted social level, but curiosity and fantasy could be fed there too. One French student of the genre attributes much of its lasting success to its ability to serve as a kind of early illustrated novel, a *"roman-photo avant la lettre."*[35]

Letters by themselves had a similar capacity to free people from some of the confines of their lives. One student of eighteenth-century correspondence, Marie-Claire Grassi, notes that letters offered people a freedom to examine and express feelings that ordinary social situations did not, and speaks of an "emancipation of the social space materialized by letters." What made this "social space" a site of affective liberation was that, like reading, it opened up a realm of relations beyond immediate and local ones, and people inhabited it in moments of privacy, free of oversight by parents, relatives, or other people with a stake in preserving traditional forms of restraint. (Just for this reason husbands in France long asserted a right to read the correspondence of their wives, a practice that was drawing much criticism at the end of the nineteenth century.) Influenced also by the cult of sensibility in

which Rousseau and Richardson were central figures, the social space
of letter writing became the site of a remarkable transformation in epistolary style, as such traditional formulas as "your humble and obedient
servant" declined in favor of direct expressions of feeling such as "*je
me jette dans vos bras*," "I throw myself into your arms," alongside an
increased use of the familiar *tu* in French, and a spreading affirmation
of the suffering produced by absence.[36] It may be that such practices
diminished somewhat in the nineteenth century as moral and social
anxieties gained more sway over behavior. Michelle Perrot believes
that "confidences were muted and intimacy was impossible" between
most corespondents.[37] This was far from universally the case, however;
the participants in the family exchanges considered in Chapter 9 made
clear that they felt bereft of important affective ties when the correspondence was disrupted, and the limits Perrot speaks about simply
dissolved in the open avowals of affection and even physical longing
exchanged between temporarily separated spouses highlighted by Peter
Gay in the work cited in Chapter 10. Sometimes very effusive language
crops up where we might not expect it, as for instance in Jules Ferry's
letters to his younger brother Charles. The Third Republic luminary
addressed his sibling as "*mon bon chéri*" and "my true other half,"
complained that "I've lived too long separated from your sweet face,
I'm only a shadow of myself when you aren't here to complete me,"
described himself as "like a widower" without news of his brother,
and asked Charles to tell him explicitly that he loved him.[38]

To be sure, not all readers approved of either the public exposure of intimate relations or the freer expression of feeling both novels
and letter-collections helped to foster. When Baudelaire's old friend
the writer Jules Barbey d'Aurevilly published the private correspondence between Eugénie de Guerin and her brother in 1864, the highly
personal nature of the exchanges and the effusive, quasi-novelistic language in which they were conducted produced not only a debate about
the propriety of publishing the texts, but also speculations that Barbey
had made at least some of them up.[39] The discussion highlighted both
the close relationship that had developed between fiction and letters,
and the conflict over how far private feelings ought to receive direct,
and especially public expression. Some people would likely have been
made uncomfortable by the kind of language Ferry used in addressing his brother, but its existence testifies that the space of feeling and
expression opened up by the expansion of letter-writing remained an

important site of personal affirmation and exploration in the nine-teenth century. Like other spheres of modern culture it took advantage of the new and unpoliced sites for private experience made available by the more public character of a realm into which mediated and distant relations were closely woven.

Autonomy and privacy in music

Nowhere is the relationship between the increasingly public nature of cultural forms and the deepening of private experience they fostered more clear and significant than in music, in many ways the central sphere of bourgeois culture. Basic to this connection was a change in the behavior of audiences advocated from late in the eighteenth cen-tury but that became dominant only toward the end of the nineteenth, the turn to listening in silence. Eighteenth-century music venues were hardly tranquil places. Until the end of the Old Regime, as James Johnson notes in his revealing study of *Listening in Paris*, musical occa-sions (most were operas rather than concerts) were chiefly social events, the scene of often noisy interplay and conversation between audience members, and of a kind of social theater that dramatized the deference accorded to the socially most prominent among them. Individuals vis-ited and moved about, making contacts with others who mattered to them, often listening only sporadically; when the time came to express a reaction to the performance, they took their cues about when and how much to applaud from some prince, noble, or other dignitary. Etiquette books warned people not to express themselves before some nearby "person of quality" had a chance to do so. These forms of behavior came under pressure from around 1770. The expectation of a clear hierarchy inside the audience was upset by the political tensions of the declining Old Regime and the competition between groups and factions for prestige or privilege they generated, reflected inside the hall by rival claims for preeminence in judgment, and the formation of hostile cliques. At the same time, the late eighteenth-century cult of sensibility and feeling fostered an emphasis on more inward styles of both making music and experiencing it. Christophe Willibald Gluck's operas were at once a mirror and a source of this turn, replacing the attempt to represent external objects through sound (as in Haydn's "Clock" or "Military" Symphonies) with techniques aimed at evoking inner moods and feelings. Critics associated the change with the rise of a new regulator of musical taste, no longer the preferences of the socially preeminent, but the same diffuse court of "public opinion" that was coming to be regarded as having jurisdiction over politics.[40]

These developments prepared the way for the change in concert behavior that would occur during the nineteenth century, but the shift could not occur so long as Old Regime social principles still reigned inside the halls. It would be hard to imagine the regime of silence becoming established in aristocratic settings, since there musicians never ceased to be regarded as in some degree the servants of their patrons, which meant that the latter's impulses or desires, not the players' preferences, set the tone. The weakening of these notions allowed two connected but separable groups to gain influence over the etiquette of listening, on the one hand composers, critics, and performers, and on the other audience members who acted toward others in changed ways. Both seem to have been involved in the early moves toward silence in Germany, where aristocratic forms of behavior had less influence on society as a whole than in France. An organization established in Frankfurt in 1808 and calling itself the Museum recommended silence at concerts, and in his *Kreisleriana* of 1814 E. T. A. Hoffmann denounced talking during performances. Johnson finds evidence of pressures in the same direction in France during the Restoration and the July Monarchy. Advocates of silence saw themselves as part-teachers, part-police, disciplining others on behalf of an order whose benefits the latter did not yet understand, and sometimes castigating them as "philistines," a term to which the adjective "bourgeois" was not uncommonly attached. John Ella, the founder (in 1845) of a "Musical Union" in London devoted to serious instrumental works, was described as "enforcing silence with an iron rod" at its concerts, a sign that mere encouragement was not enough. There is considerable evidence that the spread and eventual triumph of silent listening had much to do with the growing professionalization of orchestras after 1850, and that conductors were powerful voices on behalf of it, sometimes publicly chastising audience members who were insufficiently respectful. This was clearly the case in the United States, and in the northern English industrial cities whose musical life was noted earlier. There an important impetus toward listening in silence came from conductors and concert organizers such as Hallé. But soon there were reports of audience members themselves directing harsh disapproval toward those who disrupted listening or left concerts early, and Simon Gunn concludes that "by the 1860s it is clear that audiences were policing themselves."[41]

Why did they come to do so? Johnson suggests that for some bourgeois audience members, to impose silence on others was a way of confirming their own sense of position or identity by enforcing manners against "those who didn't measure up," while the ones who were ready to sit silently and take their cues from more confident neighbors may have been moved by fear of making a *faux pas* (a point argued by Richard Sennett). But Johnson also recognizes the spirit of a particularly bourgeois species of equality at work here, in contrast to the hierarchical social relations on display earlier: "Politeness was no respecter of persons; it was anonymous and rule-bound where mid eighteenth-century theater behavior had involved personality and imitation."[42] Silence was a regime that had to be enforced by the audience itself on itself as a collective body of listeners, putting it in the position of the Rousseauian assemblage of citizens, at once the sovereign source of law and the body of individuals subject to it (Rousseau too understood that in practice such a regime did not do away with all disparities in power or influence between the members). By putting an end to the situation in which behavior inside the hall was expected to dramatize the relations of social hierarchy and deference that reigned outside it, the practice of silent listening created an autonomous musical space freed of domination by extra-aesthetic powers or principles, much like the one public museums opened up for experiencing visual art or that Diderot saw in reading. Music itself provided the sole recognized object of listeners' attention, encouraging them to regard the pieces as "works," products of the creative power Kant associated with genius.

What audience members actually listened for or heard depended of course on who they were and what performers or pieces they confronted. As today, many were more drawn by virtuosity or display than by inner qualities of the music; performers such as Liszt and Paganini became objects of a cult of sheer skill. A second object of interest to many listeners was a narrative quality evident in much music of the eighteenth and nineteenth centuries; the form of many pieces told a kind of story, common to both religious and secular contexts. There was a political aspect to musical narrative throughout the century, especially in operas such as Rossini's *William Tell* (whose famous overture was often played alone), Halévy's *La Juive* (*The*

Jewess), Meyerbeer's *The Huguenots,* and Verdi's *Sicilian Vespers.*
Henry Raynor thinks that in 1830s France such works presented their
material "from the point of view of the new middle class and its monarchy," but we need to remember that the July regime was riven with
conflict, and that works lying somewhere between the two parties of
"movement" and "resistance" (both largely bourgeois) might have the
widest appeal (an expectation that inspired Girardin's self-consciously
neutral political stance in *La Presse*).

Whether listeners thought the music took a side in politics
or not, the relevance of some symphonic and operatic subjects was
another reason for giving concentrated attention to it. That even politically resonant compositions could refer to broader social and personal
experiences has been deftly recognized by Edward Rothstein:

> An orchestral work is often constructed as a narrative;
> roughly it tells an abstract story with themes as characters
> subject to elaborate novelistic adventures. And the stories are
> precisely those that resonated most strongly with the middle-
> class listeners who filled nineteenth-century concert halls.
> Using the tonal musical language, melodies, harmonies and
> textures were shaped into highly charged tales of solitary
> desire and communal enterprise, primal encounters and
> heroic efforts. These compositions are public accounts of a
> new form of social life coming into being, made palpable
> in the virtuosic labors of the orchestral ensemble ... [They]
> were effectively autobiographies of a public, mythic accounts
> of its origins and concerns.

Simon Gunn notes that in northern English writing about music "cho-
ral and symphonic works were conventionally represented as a narrative leading from uncertainty to struggle and ultimate triumph. Thus
at Manchester in 1876, Beethoven's *Moonlight Sonata* was reported to
depict a movement from 'gloom' and 'grief' to glory and the 'impetu-
ous outflow of feeling', while the great oratorios [of Handel, Bach, or
Mendelssohn] involved a biblical transition from trial to redemption."
This language suggests that for some listeners, perhaps especially
where, as in England, religious motifs served as inspiration or justification for secular achievement, musical narratives helped to effect the
transition. More broadly, people who listened in this way imagined

composers as story-tellers, to whose work one of Marx's favorite classical tags was appropriate: *de te fabula narratur*, "the tale is about you."[43]

For the most devoted and serious listeners, however, these aspects of music tended to be absorbed by the qualities of inner coherence and structure that were the signs of genius. What these individuals aimed to do was, as Dahlhaus puts it, "silently [to] retrace the act of composition in their minds," thus becoming aware at once of the mental processes by which the composer achieved unity in a composition and of their own parallel attempts to partake of them. "Structural hearing meant immersing oneself in the internal workings of a piece of music as though nothing else in the world existed." Perhaps the best description of this way of listening came from Wackenröder, who in music as in visual art saw the realm of culture as a kind of secular temple:

> When Joseph was at a grand concert he seated himself
> in a corner, without so much as glancing at the brilliant
> assembly of listeners, and listened with precisely the
> same reverence as if he were in church – just as still and
> motionless, his eyes cast down to the floor. Not the
> slightest sound escaped his notice, and his keen attention
> left him in the end quite limp and exhausted.

Such an image of how music ought to be experienced also had implications for the changing attitude toward how works were to be performed. The practice still common at the beginning of the nineteenth century that interspersed movements of one symphony or oratorio with parts of others, alternating vocal and instrumental pieces, fit very well with the attitude that made music an accompaniment to socializing or conversation. But it made following a single work from beginning to end impossible, and the expectation that hearing a work required such continuity was a powerful spur to presenting compositions whole. As Karl Philipp Moritz wrote as early as 1780, "the autonomous work is a self-sufficient entity," it had to exist in independence from others.[44]

As the case of Wackenröder's Joseph makes clear, however, such an experience of music was far from being merely intellectual. Few who spoke of music from late in the eighteenth century failed to emphasize its deeply emotional character. Often this connection of music to feeling retained the religious overtones it possessed in the time of Bach and earlier, but increasingly the kind of affect involved was secular and more frankly sensual, while what raised it to a higher level was its connection not to spirituality but to intellect. E. T. A. Hoffman wrote about Beethoven that his music "discloses to humanity an unknown domain, a world that has nothing in common with the outer world of the senses that surrounds it," but George Sand told Liszt that the same composer "gives birth to feelings and ideas ... makes you enter once again into the most intimate depths of the self; everything you have felt, experienced, your loves, your suffering, your dreams, all are revived by the breath of his genius and throw you into an infinite reverie." That intellectual and sensual experiences could be opposed was obvious then as now; just for this reason great value was attached to the ability of art in general and especially music to combine them. This was what Kant saw the genius as doing in making his personal, materially embodied way of being the source of rules that could impose a coherent shape on the products of imagination. Contemporary aesthetic theory gave a more general formulation to these notions, as Peter Gay notes: "To the romantics, aesthetic subjectivity consisted of two closely allied but distinct mental operations: the musical – or painterly or poetic – idea welling up from the unconscious, and the schooled introspection that allows the creator to criticize, revise, and refine his creation."[45]

It was this combination that underlay nineteenth-century listeners' sense that music could serve at once as a vehicle of individual development and of integration with others. A number of observers from late in the eighteenth century recognized that dethroning socially prominent people from their position as taste-setters, together with the emerging regime of silent listening, allowed for a much wider variety of individual reactions to the pieces heard, and this mix of singular experience and universal form, interwoven with the compound of feeling and intellect, was a major reason for the central a place music assumed in nineteenth-century culture. As Gunilla Budde puts it:

> Music was understood by the nineteenth-century concert public not primarily as a mirror of reality, but as an autonomous world with its own structures, themes, forms of order, and encodings, one that required a high level of knowledge and analytical understanding for an adequate

response, and which thereby fostered a communal and
unifying potential for achieving such a response. At
the same time, however, it provided room for freedom
of personal experience and elaboration, whereby the
subjectively variable "emotional chaos," subdued by the
formal laws of harmony and rhythm, was transformed
into an extensively individual version of "cosmic order."
More than any other genre of high culture, concerts and
operas made it possible to gather the feelings of individuals
at a single place and time together in a shared experience
of artistic pleasure.

If Budde is right, and her account is based on wide reading in memoirs,
letters, and commentary, then music provided a point of interchange at
once between feeling and intellect, and between individual and social
being. The sense that it did so, even if seldom explicitly articulated,
must have been one reason why nineteenth-century people attributed
such importance to it. Claims for the "sacred" or "religious" status of
secular music were persuasive in part because it was experienced as a
vehicle for both personal and social integration.[46]

　　This was a highly positive function, but behind it lay some
pervasive and powerful anxieties, whose connection to the exaltation of music deserves more notice than it has received. The sentiments aroused by music were deep and compelling, and it is clear that
many people recognized how close they lay to sexual feelings and
desires; music, as many noted, was the pure language of the passions.
Schopenhauer (writing in the era of the Restoration but expressing
views that would acquire widespread impact only after 1850) made this
dimension more explicit than did George Sand, and his ideas would
provide justification for the frank sexuality Richard Wagner wrote into
some of his works (above all *Tristan and Isolde*). Even some descriptions that attribute music's power to its intellectual qualities end up
lodging music closer to sexual experience than they may intend, as in
Wackenröder's description of Joseph left "quite limp and exhausted"
afterwards. Music's power to draw listeners "downward" toward sen-
suality as well as "upward" toward contemplation and understanding
had long been recognized, in the classical and Renaissance opposition
between "noble" (usually string) and "base" (often wind) music, and
echoes of this distinction appear in the nineteenth century, for instance

in Felix Mendelssohn's often expressed disdain (noted by John Toews) for the egotism of mere virtuosic display and his "mistrust of sensual, 'materialistic' music that produced titillation of he senses rather than elevation and discipline of the feelings." Peter Gay suggests that the possibility music might affect listeners in the first way was one reason for the appeal of silent listening: to demand silence of those with whom one shared a musical experience was not a snobbish disapproval of others who boorishly let their feelings hang out, but a protective reaction against the possibility of "a deeply regressive communion with one's [psychic and unconscious] past."[47]

We have only to add that listening was widely recognized as a highly individualistic act, one with a potential to cut individuals off from those around them and retreat into a personal universe of imagination – for "Joseph" this was the essential precondition for the intense experience he sought – to see that music was capable of inhabiting the same force field as an activity whose presence likewise bulked larger as the public for culture expanded, namely solitary sex. As noted a moment ago, Thomas Laqueur and Isabel Hull have both helped us to see the intense anxiety about masturbation that lasted well into the twentieth century as a specifically modern phenomenon, fed by fears that the same liberation from traditional restraints that allowed individuals to develop previously dormant powers and energies also brought grave personal and collective dangers. Access to distant resources both material and imaginative offered many openings for personal and social development, but society could exercise little control over the uses particular minds might make of them; fantasy and the passions it could feed might go wild, exposing susceptible people to a tempting and dangerous world of illusory satisfactions. The kind of consuming, highly individualistic, often deeply emotional and at least potentially solitary experience offered by music, detached from religion and externally grounded morality, resembled that of novel-reading, widely feared as encouraging the resort to fantasized and solitary sexual pleasure.

The connection was made nearly explicit, albeit in a subtle way, in Thomas Mann's description of the pleasure that the teenage Hanno, the last member of the Buddenbrook family (sickly, he would not survive into manhood), took in the piano playing whose power to absorb him was a sign of his inability to invest his vital energy in the practical ethic of worldly achievement exemplified by his forbears. Hanno delighted in the equivocal moments when harmonies were suspended between expectation and resolution, finding in them "the delight of sweet rapture … insistent, urgent longing," a sustained intimation of the happiness that "lasts only a moment." When he tells his friend Kai that when left alone he could not hold himself back from improvising, instead of practicing studies and sonatas as he should, descending into the realm of unfettered imagination and desire it opened up, Mann describes the sequel as follows:

> "I know what you're thinking when you improvise," Kai said. And then neither of them spoke.
> They were at a difficult age. Kai had turned beet-red and was staring at the ground, but without lowering his head. Hanno looked pale and very serious; he kept casting Kai enigmatic, sidelong glances.[48]

This, however, was music as it affected a "decadent" person, cut off from the social involvements that pulled it back from such abysses for others. For "Joseph," as for the larger class of listeners pointed to by Budde, music's potential to encourage a descent into insidious solitude was restrained by the collective settings where hearing and performing it usually took place, as well as by the high level of attention required to perceive the formal structure of a piece. For listeners able to experience music in this way – and both their numbers and their exemplary power were greater, proportionally, in the nineteenth century than today – the potentially unbridled reverie spoken about by George Sand and others could be reined in by the desire for rational understanding music also called forth. Modern culture offered individuals ways to expand their imaginative reach and develop potentials hemmed in by the bounds of everyday experience, but it simultaneously confronted people with the need to set limits to the potentially dangerous liberation it promised. As musical experience was reconstructed, it intimated a possible solution, a frame that brought passion within the compass of comprehension, and where a potentially anarchic individuality could be drawn back toward sociability. This was not the least of the reasons why it occupied so central a place in nineteenth-century culture.

13 BOURGEOIS AND OTHERS

Culture high and low

From the beginning the forms of cultural activity that found expression in the more public settings emerging at the end of the eighteenth century exhibited a characteristic set of tensions. Like cultural practices in practically every time and place, they aspired to broad, even universal, validity, treating the content they presented as capable of enhancing human life in general. It became apparent quickly that these assumptions would be undermined or frustrated by the social distinctions they sometimes sought to ignore. In the case of visual art the tension was already implicit in the ways public exhibits were set up during the late eighteenth century, but it became more salient and troubling when the Revolutionary Louvre opened in 1793.

Eighteenth-century public art spaces seldom offered unrestricted entry, and when they did the results often led the organizers to think again. The British Museum admitted only small groups and for a brief time, save for students and critics who were given privileged access on certain days. The Luxembourg gallery in the 1750s was in theory open to anyone, but publicity about it was directed to the higher ranks of society, those one writer described as "men of good sense ... and good faith" who possessed "sensibility and quality of mind." After Joseph II offered free access to his collection in the Upper Belvedere in 1770 he was met with sharp criticism from both artists and his own curators, who complained that a rowdy crowd interfered with giving serious attention to the works. When a Society of Arts set up the first public show of contemporary painting in London in 1760 the art dealers who ran it offered free and open admission, but the next year they decided to impose a fee, explaining that without one the room was "crowded and incommoded by the intrusion of great numbers whose stations and education made them no proper judges of statuary or painting and who were made idle and tumultuous by the opportunity of a show."[1]

These difficulties surfaced more distressingly at the remodeled Louvre, since the nation as a whole was held to be the owner of the works put on display. Foreign visitors were troubled by the presence of "the lowest classes of the community," to which administrators quickly responded by publishing regulations for proper behavior and setting up safeguards against theft. It rapidly became evident that many of the visitors had little notion of what they were seeing, apart from a show of power and grandeur like that projected in earlier private or princely collections. When some classical statues seized from emigré nobles were exhibited in 1795, with labels listing their former owners, viewers mistakenly thought the names were those of the people portrayed, to the distress of curators who had assumed that the public would recognize a Greek bust by its look and know its subjects were not modern. The incomprehension manifested by many visitors quickly became a subject of mockery, as in Honoré Daumier's cartoon showing one viewer of a frieze telling another that "those Egyptians weren't very good-looking."[2]

As the first major museum aimed at a broad audience, the Revolutionary Louvre made evident a set of problems and tensions that have remained alive ever since. What was the aim, and what would be the effects, of displaying art objects with little connection to most people's experiences and tastes to a diverse and fractured public, the ancient works rooted in an unfamiliar form of life, and the modern ones originally produced to please a narrow circle of well-off and highly placed patrons? Similar questions would resound not just in museums but also in exhibitions of new art, where they would be deepened as modern painters and sculptors produced work that did not hide and sometimes self-consciously insisted on the distance artists felt between themselves and their assumed audience. Historians and critics have often answered these questions in terms of class differences, some even arguing that a chief function, even purpose of such public displays of art has been to make social distinctions evident and even to solidify them. Many readers have been drawn to Pierre Bourdieu's argument that a chief role of public culture has been to justify and perpetuate class hierarchies, by highlighting the contrast between the sense of satisfaction and validation such sites provide to those whose upbringing, education, and access to leisure allow them to feel at home in them, and the indifference, confusion, embarrassment, and sense of inferiority they not uncommonly engender in those who lack such assets.[3]

I will come back to Bourdieu's views in a moment, but first it should be noted that the kinds of contrasting reactions found in the Louvre during the 1790s have also been documented in many later settings. These have included some provided by middle-class figures with a clear political commitment to advancing lower-class well-being, and who believed in the capacity of audiences with little formal education to understand and benefit from high-quality art. One such case is provided by the exhibitions of paintings mounted in poverty-stricken East London during the 1880s and 1890s by Henrietta and Samuel Barnett, in connection with their pioneering settlement house, Toynbee Hall, established in 1884. The Barnetts, who supported the workers in the famous 1889 Dock Strike, were determined not to impose middle-class ideas on the local people who came to view their shows, an intention supported by their conviction (however naive or misguided it may appear today) that workers were capable of "purer" reactions than middle-class viewers, by virtue of being less exposed to the materialism that corrupted modern life. All the same, they found it necessary to provide Oxbridge-educated guides to explain the pictures, as well as explicit catalog descriptions. A number of workers were deeply moved by what they saw, especially the religious images (Samuel Barnett was an Anglican curate), but they often reacted in unexpected or distant ways. At least one compared a domestic scene to a poster advertising tea, some found the moralistic optimism that certain paintings sought to convey irrelevant to the difficulties poor people faced, and others lamented that seeing such beautiful things only made their spare and limited lives seem more tawdry.[4]

Historians and critics have recognized culture as an agent in both highlighting and consolidating class divisions in the history of music too. A particularly striking account of the social relations involved in the development of art music and its audiences is the one

Lawrence Levine has provided for the United States. There, as in Europe, musical life by the end of the nineteenth century was increasingly characterized by silent listening and the performance of symphonies or concertos in their entirety, in contrast to an earlier situation where a buzz of social interaction accompanied programs made up of songs or movements taken from various works, providing a variety that kept audience attention alive without demanding sustained concentration. In Levine's account this earlier regime was popular and democratic, giving a mixed audience freedom to enjoy the music and express itself in spontaneous ways (much the same was true of drama, especially for performances of Shakespeare, whose plays were often presented to diverse and sometimes happily rowdy audiences); by contrast the later one embodied the program of an increasingly self-conscious elite, determined to impose its standards on cultural life by damping down forms of expression out of harmony with their vision of culture as a quasi-sacred realm. In part Levine sees this shift as a response to new threats to social order, some of them from tensions between workers and employers in new and larger workplaces and others, in the American case, generated by the burgeoning numbers of new immigrants – Irish, Italians, Jews, and East Europeans, all strange and suspect in the eyes of entrenched Protestant Americans. In part too the new cultural regime was an attempt to counter what many saw as the rampant materialism of the "Gilded Age." Levine is careful not to portray the campaign for what was increasingly identified as "high" (and even "highbrow"), "true," or "legitimate" culture as a mere disguised attempt to impose social order, since cultural advocates were first and genuinely devoted to elevating life and expanding people's horizons. But if shoring up order was not the hidden purpose of these changes, order was "one of culture's salutary by-products." Turning away from the earlier situations where "audiences that cut across the social and economic spectrum enjoy[ed] an expressive culture which blended together mixed elements of what we would today call high, low, and folk culture," the new order instituted a strict separation between the artistic heights and the vast terrain beneath them, putting in place a hierarchy that would prevail until late in the twentieth century.[5]

Levine's account cannot be transferred directly to Europe, because there pre-nineteenth-century cultural life was organized in accord with an older and more deeply rooted hierarchy, whose presence gave a different shape and significance to the kinds of developments on which he focuses. In the private aristocratic spaces where most concerts took place until late in the eighteenth century, the musicians had roles analogous to those of servants; public concerts and operas were free of the earnest atmosphere introduced by the regime of silence, but the social relations on display were anything but democratic, and (as we saw above) deference was regularly paid to nobles and court figures. Against this background the changes introduced during the nineteenth century emerge as anti-hierarchical in both intention and effect. All the same, there is no doubt that the new and more public forms of culture chiefly benefitted sites and practices that appealed primarily to interested bourgeois and aristocrats; this was true no less of intellectually ambitious newspapers and books than of museums and concert halls; popular enjoyments and activities both rural and urban remained largely within the bounds where they had long operated. In addition, the claims for the quasi-sacred nature of visual art, music, and poetry put forward by romantic writers such as Wackenröder (as by Wordsworth and Coleridge) applied to high culture rather than popular forms (despite the high valuation given to them on other grounds by Herder and romantic writers); thus they too sharpened the boundary between cultural levels, much in the way Levine describes for late nineteenth-century America.

In other words, the increasing differentiation of cultural levels and its social implications were an important part of the history of cultural development in the nineteenth century in Europe as across the Atlantic, but this was never the whole story. Other impulses were at work even in the United States, where Thomas Bender and Joseph Horowitz have provided accounts of late nineteenth-century cultural life that show the boundaries between levels as much more permeable, and interactions between them more dynamic and fertile, than Levine's account allows. Looking at New York, rather than the narrower and more staid world of Boston that supplies much of Levine's material, they present the world of operas and orchestras as providing "a battleground over aesthetics" rather than a site for the triumph of any single cultural attitude. A mixed audience of natives and immigrants including artisans as well as middle-class families flocked to concerts where music by a wide range of European composers was performed. Anton Seidl, the conductor whose passion for Wagner put him near the center of New York musical life at the end of the century, acted on his conviction that he could interest widely diverse audiences in classical music, asking potential contributors to support the "grand and glorious mission" of providing free concerts of "*good* music" for ordinary people in parks and other sites of leisure (including the new popular amusement center Coney Island). Given a chance, such audiences would come not only to understand and appreciate quality fare, but even to see that it met an important need they might not otherwise have recognized in themselves. His attitude was widely shared among European working-class advocates, and partly inspired the program of the German Social Democratic Party to spread culture among its members.[6]

The forms of cultural capital

To see how these various possibilities worked themselves out over the course of the nineteenth century, we need first to consider some of the ways culture figures in the lives of people with differing social characteristics and experiences. A useful point of entry is provided by the notion Pierre Bourdieu introduced on behalf of his argument that modern culture works chiefly to make evident and justify class distinctions, "cultural capital." For him the term refers to the stock of attitudes, expectations, and ways of relating to things and people (Bourdieu names such a complex a "habitus") that bourgeois and other elite members of society acquire in the natural course of growing up in families where leisure and culture are part of everyday life. Those whose experience furnishes them with such capital possess a sense of ease and entitlement toward cultural goods that is bound to contrast with the feelings of distance, discomfort, even intimidation produced in less-favored people when they are confronted with socially valued objects and ideas for which their lives, and circumstances provide little or no preparation. Bourgeois may not consciously regard culture as a realm where their superiority to workers and country people finds confirmation, some of them may even see it as a potential vehicle for lessening social differences; but in settings such as art museums and symphony concerts most of them are all the same bound to act in ways that dramatize their distinction from others.[7]

That such differentials in inherited cultural resources exist and produce effects of the kind Bourdieu described is surely correct;

evidence for them jumps into view in any modern society. But Bourdieu was not the first person to call attention to such effects of culture, and others have done so in ways that help to see cultural capital in a more rounded and less one-dimensional light. One of his predecessors was Simmel, who in some moods could sound much like Bourdieu. In one place he called the "apparent equality" of access to cultural products a "sheer mockery," since like other goods in a society based on money relations the freedom to aspire to them was undercut by "the fact that only those already privileged in some way or another have the possibility of acquiring them." Just because education and its benefits seemed more accessible than wealth and power, nothing made "those in inferior positions ... feel so deprived and helpless, as the advantage of education." Worse, the benefits available to those who already possess cultural advantages grow greater the more they draw on them, since by doing so they accumulate more resources on which to nurture themselves, much in the way that the benefits individuals receive from passive investments grow as these returns are ploughed back in, enlarging the pool from which future gains will flow.[8]

We saw earlier, however, that Simmel simultaneously recognized a different and contrasting dimension to the relations between individuals and culture. Over time, intellectual and artistic contents come to be increasingly embodied in "objective" or "supra-individual" forms, giving birth to a kind of shared treasury of ideas, information, and knowledge, one that differs from the accumulation of material objects in that if one person consumes such goods he or she does not remove them from the stock available to others: "The more values are transposed into such objective forms, the more room there is in them, as in the house of God, for every soul."[9] Here Simmel points to the existence of cultural capital in a sense different from Bourdieu's, as the accumulation of an expanding treasure of intellectual and artistic resources much like the ones that the sponsors of the Revolutionary Louvre or of late nineteenth-century concert life sought to make as widely available as possible. Economists today have restated Simmel's point, naming the kinds of products from which people can benefit without excluding others from them "nonrival goods," meaning ones "whose consumption by one person" does not make them "less available for consumption by another." Once a novel, a piece of music, or a painting has been added to the stock from which a given human group (or the whole of humanity) can draw, it remains there whether you or I appropriate it for our purposes or not. To be sure, restrictions can be and often have been put on access to such goods through copyright laws and admission charges, but the situation this creates is not equivalent to the one whereby my inhabiting a desirable house or consuming a particularly fine dish or an excellent glass of wine prevents you from doing the same.[10]

For this reason, the analogy between "cultural capital" and money capital can never be more than partial. Simmel's other description of the general accessibility of cultural materials as a "sheer mockery" is not without its point, but it is far too harsh, greatly underestimating the way that expanding education has in fact made intellectual and artistic resources available to people whose inheritance provides them with few of them. Among the best evidence for this point is Jonathan Rose's remarkable history of British working-class intellectual life, rooted in a tradition of self-education that extends back into the sixteenth century, and that was given powerful new impetus first by the late eighteenth-century reduction in the price of books and by the "explosion of reading" noted in the previous chapter, and then by the spread of mass education after 1870. Taking issue with earlier writers, Rose finds much evidence that despite the limitations of the new "Board Schools" set up under the Education Act, working-class and lower-middle class students found both pleasure and nurture in the instruction they received there. Nor did literacy serve as an instrument for imposing middle-class ideas and values on the poor, who proved capable of using the literary and cultural resources made available to them to contest upper-class views about their inability to cultivate their minds, and to develop their own sense of singularity and self-worth.[11]

No less important, if "cultural capital" means the residue of experience and upbringing that gives people specific intellectual and aesthetic capacities, then it does not exist only in the singular, but takes different forms in different groups and settings. Just this point was made by an early twentieth-century British author who was also a coal miner, B. L. Coombes, in response to Virginia Woolf's contention that capital in the usual financial sense was a necessity for a writer, since to lack it was to be in want of the independence that made sustained creative work possible. Coombes replied that "a writer's capital" was not to be found in a bank account but in "all his experiences; his environment; his knowledge of human life and how people live and aspire, love and desire, hate and die." A working-class writer possessed a particular species of such capital, which derived from "living amongst the people of our kind" and knowing about the world from their point of view. Only by drawing on that capital could such a person function as a writer; to abandon it was to lose the chance to be one.[12]

All these perspectives, Bourdieu's, Simmel's, Jonathan Rose's and Coombes's, will provide illumination when we come, in the later part of this chapter, to the new forms of popular culture that arose in the second half of the nineteenth century. Before turning to these developments, however, we need to open up one more point of view on the mix of similarity and difference in the responses of bourgeois and non-bourgeois to culture in general, and especially to the new forms it was taking as the Old Regime ended. This standpoint comes from the subtle but revealing topic of the relations between social experience and language.

Class, language, and the uses of education

A number of writers have called attention to the differing communicative styles and attitudes toward language exhibited by particular social groups, and specifically to certain distinct features of bourgeois usage. Adeline Daumard notes that bourgeois speech, both in the nineteenth century and earlier, differed from that of other social groups in its greater concern for "clarity, precision, [and] grammatical correctness," adding that "one spoke or wrote not to distinguish oneself or follow fashions, but to express oneself as clearly as possible, in order to be understood by all ones interlocutors." Daumard's judgment may be insufficiently critical, but the type of linguistic practice to which she points contrasted with the more casual style of both popular speech and of various slang idioms – among them those evolved by individuals in a particular craft or employment, those employed by groups of young people, and by denizens of salons, artists' studios, or underworlds – all of which generally assumed a narrower and more predictable audience than did commerce, administration, or writing for the public.[13] Bourgeois usage also contrasted with aristocratic forms of expression, as Angelika Linke has pointed out. Aristocratic social relations often took place by way of gestures and other non-verbal actions, suited to acknowledging and articulating hierarchies: bodily postures, bows, and other modes of reverence (in French a common meaning of *reverence* is a bow). One reason dance was an art form particularly favored at princely courts was its ability to dramatize such relations, and the prominence of dancing-masters as instructors in proper behavior owed much to the model such modes of expression provided. Middle-class people participated in these usages too, but less so as the spread of communicative networks during the eighteenth century led them to value verbal discourse more. Linke finds that bourgeois speech in Germany (where part of the program of those who promoted Enlightenment was creating a literary language able to be understood throughout the still-fragmented country) exhibited features much like those Daumard describes for France, and that in these conditions verbal equivalents for some socially significant actions replaced performing them: people began to say "I kiss your hand" instead of actually doing it.

Linke offers several explanations for these changes, some cultural and some social. The Enlightenment goal that Kant called "maturity" was tied up with gaining some degree of rational control over oneself and one's surroundings, a capacity developed through discursive interchange and exercised through being able to speak in ways that could persuade others. Having power over words became a means to develop social and political standing that people did not otherwise possess. Linguistic change was also encouraged (as Simmel already recognized) by the increase in "the variety of communicative situations in which complex forms of speech had to be employed," as specialization advanced in both government agencies and business enterprises. In addition, geographical and social mobility put people into shifting and unfamiliar environments. The need for a kind of linguistic competence able to support such moves gave priority to forms of speech based on general rules of correctness, rather than on practices that signified membership in particular groups.[14]

Aristocratic resistance to such changes, based on an inherited preference for casual and truncated forms, was particularly salient in England, where the lesser importance of court culture reduced the role of gestural expression, while elite involvement in a mode of rural life infused with market relations fostered a kind of cursory directness. The offhand style extended to writing as well as speech, as George Eliot testified in a passage of *Middlemarch* set around 1832: "At that time the opinion existed that it was beneath a gentleman to write legibly, or with a hand in the least suitable to a clerk. Fred [Vincy] wrote the lines demanded in a hand as gentlemanly as that of any viscount or bishop of the day: the vowels were all alike and the consonants only distinguishable as turning up or down." At the moment to which this passage referred a campaign for correct grammar was in full swing, supported by books and periodicals. Among its chief targets were "vulgar" contractions such as "ain't," saying "me and him" where "he and I" is called for, unnecessary repetitions, omitted pronouns, and sentences that stopped short of the conclusions they seemed to imply. Some supporters of the drive took it very far, for instance opposing "don't" even when the subject "I" makes it grammatically correct, in order to forestall its use with he or she; such rigidity provided some justification for those who resisted "correctness" as stiff and intrusive (we saw earlier that some contemporaries protested against Evangelical purity in speech for similar reasons). But other supporters of older practices held to them more from a certain aristocratic revulsion toward any behavior that might mark one as a "clerk," preferring what some of Anthony Trollope's upper-crust characters regarded as "free and easy habits of speech." As late as 1907 one such author defended "ain't" as part of what one historian of language calls "a rearguard action for upper-class colloquial speech, and against the by now considerable forces of grammatical correctness."[15]

Some years ago Basil Bernstein provoked much controversy by his attempt to theorize what differentiates middle-class speech from that of other social groups, particularly the working class, in terms of the contrast between "restricted" and "elaborated" linguistic codes. Based on recorded interviews and conversations, Bernstein distinguished speakers whose vocabulary and syntactical patterns are largely predictable because they repeatedly follow models commonly used inside some defined group or community, from others whose practices are less easy to foretell or anticipate because they are individualized appropriations of a wider range of lexical possibilities. Speech that tends to the first set of alternatives conforms to some "restricted" code (ritualized speech would be the extreme example, never varying), while usage closer to the second is regulated by an "elaborated" norm or practice. Which style particular individuals or groups adopt will depend on the kinds of social situations they inhabit. "A restricted code is generated by a form of social relationship based upon a range of closely shared identifications self-consciously held by the members. An elaborated code is generated by a form of social relations which does not necessarily presuppose such shared, self-consciously held identifications, with the consequence that much less is taken for granted." Users of an elaborated code recognize each other as socially and culturally similar no less easily than do those who employ some restricted one, but the practices associated with the first reflect a more varied and shifting field of interaction, leading to a discourse that aspires more to general communicability than to identification with a self-consciously differentiated community. Bernstein's understanding of how elaborated codes arise is close to the account both Daumard and Linke give of what characterizes bourgeois speech, shaped by implicit or explicit orientation to a broad and sometimes anonymous public, in contrast both to aristocratic practices and to the slang of age or occupational groups, studios, or salons. The novelist George Meredith noted qualities similar to the latter in locally based rural speech in *The Ordeal of Richard Feverel*, giving a more negative twist to what Bernstein observed: "Their ideas sem to have a special relationship in the peculiarity of stopping where they have begun."[16]

What made Bernstein's argument so controversial was his attempt to describe working-class speech in general as following restricted codes, and to explain the relatively poor performance of working-class children in school as a consequence of their living in conditions that predisposed them to the narrow intellectual horizons to which such speech corresponded. Although his aim was to deny that this limited success was due to lesser intelligence, and thus to encourage educational practices that might make up for the difference, his characterization of workers and their culture still provoked pained and angry objections. Some of these were surely justified, since there is much evidence that working-class people were (and are) fully able to shift between contexts and the usages expected in them, and thus to participate in the conditions that foster elaborated codes. Testimony to this was provided by a careful observer of the London poor in the years around 1900: "A woman entirely alters her phraseology according to whether she is speaking to a child, to her husband, to a neighbor or an employer, and the difference is still more marked among men. In certain districts when men are speaking to one another even upon such general topics as the weather their language is almost unintelligible to a stranger, but they can if they choose make themselves readily understood by him."[17] The ability of non-bourgeois to use language whose vocabulary and syntax reach beyond the conditions Bernstein associates with restricted codes, and to draw intellectual sustenance from mental worlds distant from their own, is shown also by the rich tradition of working-class self-cultivation already noted.[18]

All the same, Bernstein's distinction has much relevance to cultural history, even if we need to guard against viewing workers' language and thinking in the narrow terms it may suggest. Some of the reasons for its relevance as well as evidence for its effects during the nineteenth century are provided by careful and insightful studies of working-class and rural culture by David Vincent for England and by Deborah Reed-Danahay for France. Both are concerned to understand the disappointment bred by reformers' hopes that the cultural differences between classes would be effaced by the expansion of public schooling and the consequent spread of education and literacy, fostered by the English Education Act of 1870 and the Third Republic's enlarged system of primary education. Instead, working-class culture remained in many ways just as separate from its bourgeois counterpart as before. Vincent, in an analysis driven by sympathy and identification with non-elite people and their experience, offers two chief reasons for this outcome in the English case, both of which apply largely to the French one as well. First, working-class and village communities retained their ties to a deeply rooted and robust oral culture, through which everyday skills and habits were handed down, and which imparted still-useful folk- and home-based knowledge. The therapeutic value of traditional lore about health and medicine (herbal remedies, for instance) was not superseded by scientific advances until well into the twentieth century. And second, the content of formal education was much less useful to those destined for working-class or peasant occupations than it was for those who would take up middle-class ones, a difference magnified by the limited opportunities that existed for social mobility.

In giving a central place to these two considerations, Vincent (like other recent students, including Jonathan Rose) calls into question earlier views that portrayed literacy as an instrument for imposing middle-class ideas and values on the poor: popular culture was an active and constructive response to the conditions in which it developed. But the schools where literacy was taught had an uncomfortable relationship to lower-class life. Vincent notes that whereas only one or two individuals in a typical community were able to show young people how to thatch a roof or shoe a horse, many adults knew enough to teach a "child its letters, yet reading and writing became the only skills which had to be acquired in a specialized building from a specialized teacher." Such learning had a similarly inorganic relationship to many who were exposed to it in France, where the Third Republic's educational system (although never so hostile to local cultures and languages as has sometimes been claimed) offered much that students and their families regarded as largely irrelevant to the everyday lives most urban and rural workers would face as adults. Individuals and groups welcomed book learning as a tool, using it where it was helpful (French peasants evinced a robust interest in literacy and arithmetic as aids in managing farms and other occupations, and English school-age children were taken to silent movies to read the titles to their unlettered parents), and they quickly learned to "make sophisticated shifts between written and oral forms in order to advance or defend their interests." But they never succeeded in fusing the two cultural worlds, both because the educational system that brought exposure to the first "rendered the tools of literacy both strange to handle and difficult to employ for any but the most mundane tasks," and because literate adult workers continued to inhabit "a limited field of practices and a subordinate system of meanings ... The children who spent more and more of their lives in school were denied the opportunity of connecting their basic training to higher forms of learning or to most of the problems they would face beyond the classroom." The continuity middle-class youngsters enjoyed between school and the work-life that awaited them deepened as education came to be a vehicle of preparation for professional tasks, government employment, or more highly organized forms of business; some in addition were exposed to elements of a literate and sophisticated culture inside their homes that was close to the one they encountered in classrooms. But for those below them "home and school, school and work remained widely separated forms of learning and activity, and over time it became more rather than less difficult to integrate practical and abstract work knowledge, sensational and 'classic' literature, oral and written history, botanic and 'scientific' medicine."[19]

Vincent's conclusions provide reasons for giving heed to Bernstein's application of the distinction between restricted and elaborated codes to the differences between middle-class and working-class language and culture, at least insofar as we do not allow it to become rigid or exclusive. The contrast Bernstein describes is not merely linguistic, it distinguishes two cultural styles, two ways by which forms of symbolic expression organize and communicate experience and the expectations it breeds. Only after recognizing the existence of many exceptions can this contrast of cultural styles be mapped on to class differences, but it takes on another level of significance in the perspective on modernity we are seeking to develop here. Whether in regard to popular or aristocratic language, a restricted code that ties a particular idiom to a bounded community is an example of the kind of regulative principle we have called ordained or teleocratic, one that directs the exchanges between individuals connected through some shared medium of interaction toward an outcome established in advance. By contrast an elaborated code is an instance of an autonomous principle, one that arises out of the developing exchanges and interactions themselves, and that aims to facilitate and extend those exchanges and their products. In the case of language as in others, the two alternatives become increasingly evident as formerly local or separated groups become more involved in networks that link their members to outside and often distant people and circumstances, presenting them with the choice between submitting their behavior to general and abstract standards that might challenge features of a group's existing identity, and resisting such changes in order to maintain communal ties and the principles and practices that underlie them. It is a contrast that has continued to find many expressions in the world of the twenty-first century; we shall now see that it also illuminates the relations between the largely elite forms of culture discussed in Chapter 12 and the "popular" ones that emerged at the end of the nineteenth century.

Networks and the new popular culture

As networks of communication expanded and grew thicker at the end of the nineteenth century, people and activities outside the middle classes were increasingly drawn into cultural forms infused with distant ties and connections. The more closely integrated and organized world that provided a foundation for modern industry and for modern political parties also opened up new spaces of leisure and entertainment, bringing into being novel and modern forms of information, amusement, and self-expression. Their emergence and expansion

would radically alter the cultural landscape, and in particular the relations between "high" and "popular" culture. At the start this alteration
may be described as mainly quantitative, as new energies flowed into
popular forms of leisure and expression and gave them greater prominence; but the change would come to be qualitative as well, replacing
the long-assumed hierarchical relations between cultural levels with
more shifting and uncertain mix of interacting components. In the
process the very meaning of culture would change, as longstanding
connotations of refinement and cultivation receded in favor of a loose
and multi-layered realm of representation and reflection, its various
components free from regulation by any common and ordained goal.

A good starting point for approaching these changes is provided
by the spread of popular literature and the rise of mass-circulation
newspapers, two phenomena that were linked together by common
bodies of writers and readers. Books and pamphlets aimed at people
with limited education had long existed, to be sure, their chief genres consisting of practical tools such as almanacs, devotional tracts,
and manuals, and popular novels, some based on chivalric themes and
some romantic in a more everyday sense. The latter in particular had
expanded from late in the eighteenth century, begetting much criticism
about their ability to inflame undisciplined imaginations and corrupt
morals, but the public for such work still remained small; some of the
outcry against such literature seems to have been inspired by male fears
about its effects on women.[20] The broad expansion of literacy after
the mid nineteenth century created a much enlarged popular reading
public, one part increasingly concentrated in cities, another in rural
areas now made more accessible through railroads. Serious literature
was a part of what this new public consumed, both classics such as
Shakespeare or Goethe and modern works by writers like Victor Hugo
or Jules Verne, but a larger part of the diet consisted of books written especially to appeal to the new audience. Often published serially
in newspapers or pulp magazines, these texts were the products of a
newly prominent breed of authors, some of whom (along with their
publishers) reaped huge profits from their work. The writers displayed
a variety of social origins, some having unsuccessfully sought careers
at a higher literary level before finding their niche in detective and
adventure stories, others taking to fiction writing for fun and profit, or
coming to it from daily journalism and retaining much of its spirit in
their books. Many, such as the French feminist Jeanne Lapauze, who

tied earlier ones to the traditions of elite culture, selling individual copies at a *sou* instead of by subscription, putting a humorous column on the front page, publishing only popular novels as *feuilletons*, and reporting news in the style of detective or adventure stories. A prominent, even defining, feature of the new journalism was the central place it gave to what was called the *fait divers*, a term applied to reports on everyday occurrences, curious (sometimes invented) happenings, human interest stories, and reports on crime and violence. One reason Millaud turned to such material was to avoid paying the tax levied on papers that dealt with politics (the levy would be eliminated in 1881), but he also seems to have had an intuition that he could appeal to a large and expanding audience by way of it. Crime stories were particularly effective in building up circulation, which jumped at moments when especially sensational or shocking events (such as the brutal murder of an entire family by an Alsatian immigrant, Jean-Baptiste Troppmann, in 1869) could be exploited. Other dominant *fin-de-siècle* papers, notably *Le Petit Parisien* and *Le Matin* began with ambitions to be more serious than Millaud, but in the end all took on some of the features that made the *Petit Journal* so successful.[24]

A similar evolution was visible a bit later in Berlin, where the first highly successful counterpart to the *Petit Journal* was August Scherl's *Lokal Anzeiger*, started in 1883 and aimed especially at newcomers to the city, providing them with much practical information alongside *feuilletons* of a racy sort. Leopold Ullstein's *Berliner Morgenpost* served similar functions and became the city's largest paper after it was founded a few years afterwards. All adopted sensationalistic styles similar to their French cousins (even publications linked to the social democrats did the same); in both places readers sought out papers for the information contained in advertisements (for activities and entertainments as well as goods) no less than in news columns, and papers sought to attract readers by calling attention to themselves, often through stunt-like competitions (such as challenging readers to spy out the journalist sent out to report on them) with prizes, so that the aura of mass publicity infused their whole existence. By World War I some three out of four French people were reading a newspaper every day. In Germany the number seems to have been closer to one in two, but people spoke of a *Lesewut*, an addiction to reading the papers.[25]

The large degree of attention the new publications gave to local happenings and conditions set them off from their predecessors. Earlier papers had devoted far less space to such things. News sheets had their origins in letters and reports that provided information on distant events and conditions, political, economic, or cultural; there was little need for them to report on local doings because most readers had direct or word-of-mouth access to the ones that mattered to them. When Hegel described reading the daily newspaper as a kind of counterpart to the morning prayer, orienting moderns such as himself toward the actual world much as religious rituals put medieval people in touch with a divine beyond, the reports he had in mind came from capital cities and distant correspondents, still the main content of journalism in the 1820s and 1830s.[26] As cities grew, papers began to include local news and features, but reported it in a restrained style modeled on their treatments of distant happenings. This was true of the French *Gazette des tribunaux*, founded in 1825 as a paper for lawyers; it attracted a large readership interested in the many stories of private life and public scandal that unfolded in courtrooms, but its tone remained calm and restrained.[27] The same was the case for Alexandre Privat d'Anglemont's very popular accounts of the "unknown occupations" – *métiers inconnus* – hidden in the shadowy reaches of Paris (published in the daily *Le Siècle* beginning in 1852); similarly, the scenes sought out by mid century *flâneurs* in their urban wanderings might harbor mysteries but the accounts they gave seldom ran to the lurid. The new papers made a clear departure from these precedents, not only giving much greater emphasis to local doings, but writing about foreign events in a manner modeled on adventure stories or other popular reading, a practice aided by the growing interest in extra-European exploration and conquest, its locations made exotic by distance and cultural difference, features the papers pumped up through this kind of reporting.[28]

The new journalism's mix of local and distant involvements extended much further. The papers relied on telegraphs for news and modern transport for distribution, and touted their pride at the speed with which they could get news to the public, often in "extra" editions, distributed with the aid of tramways (later trucks). These features of the papers reflected the deeper embeddedness of the cities they served in distant relations of all kinds, their economies tied up with national and world markets ("extroverted" rather than "introverted," in the terms Jeanne Gaillard used about Paris), their politics shaped by national and (especially for socialists) international connections, their burgeoning size creating urban spaces too large to be grasped (or navigated) in an older, more immediate way, and inhabited by large numbers of first-generation immigrants whose unfamiliarity with the world around them both gave it the air of mystery that sensationalistic writing exploited, and created a need for the information about local goings-on the papers provided. An editorial in *Le Petit Parisien* in 1893 stressed the papers' role in linking immediate and local experience to the distant places that increasingly impinged on it: "To read one's newspaper is to live the universal life, the life of the whole capital, of the entire city, of all France, of all the nations ... It is the newspaper that establishes this sublime communion of souls across distances." Some of the Paris papers moved their offices to the new boulevards where traffic flowed between neighborhoods and sections of the city, and where much of the faster-paced life fostered by Haussmann's rebuilding found its place, a development one observer regarded as "inevitable ... Where better than the boulevard to feel the pulse of the city?"[29] The new journalism drew on and gave expression to many of the same qualities of modern urban experience as did the impressionist painting we will consider in Chapter 14, notably the mix of physical closeness and psychic distance in personal relations Simmel described as typical of modern urban life, but in a style much more unbuttoned than in Manet's "The Railway" or Caillebotte's "Man at the Window." The potential for fantasy projection such experiences and relations created was responsible for much of the excitement (as well as anxiety) that urban experience generated, the property Peter Fritzsche evokes when he observes that "turn-of-the-century Berliners ... encountered the city as a place of previously unimagined possibility," and that a (female) newspaper editor looked back on from the 1920s, recalling that "I felt that I was sitting right in the navel of the world, life streamed by in thousands of photos, hundreds of people, in the voices of the entire globe."[30]

Thus papers, like the novels and magazines with which they shared writers and readers, helped to form a new kind of popular culture, at once altered and invigorated by its participation in expanding and thickening communicative networks. What would later be called "mediatization," encountering the world through vehicles set up to represent it, came to be part of cultural experience for individuals and groups whose relations with others and with ideas had hitherto taken place in more immediate and bounded ways. This gave a certain more commonly middle-class cast to popular experience, as socialist activists recognized when they expressed fears that workers in particular were being drawn away from their supposedly authentic existence and consciousness, made "bourgeois" through access not just to consumer goods but to the messages, entertainments, and leisure activities increasingly available to them.[31] The kind of entry-point to the world provided by mass-circulation papers with their focus on *faits divers* differed from that of more literate and reflective organs much in the way the popular novels studied by Anne-Marie Thiesse contrasted with traditional literature; the books and papers spoke directly to people in accents they knew, in restricted codes rather than an elaborated one. They specifically renounced the effort to challenge people's sense of what their experience and their relations with others might be. If some readers hungry for a diet of *faits divers* came close to the editor quoted above in feeling that they stood in "the navel of the world," their relationship to the network from which the messages flowed was more passive, and the content they received palpably different. Popular culture was acquiring new heft and strength from its ties to the sort of distant connections that high culture had largely monopolized before, altering the relations between them; but the orientations toward experience each fostered remained largely distinct.

Both movies and music provide illustrations of these processes and relationships. Moving pictures had their chief roots in popular cultural forms, some in the country and town fairs where entertainments included devices of various kinds able to pass a quickly shifting series of printed images before one or more viewers, creating the illusion of motion, and in dioramas or panoramas that (from the 1820s) produced comparable experiences for a larger audience by changing the light or angle in which spectators viewed a wall-size landscape or other scene inside an enclosure built for the purpose. Photography allowed similar effects to be produced by passing light through a series of plates or films, and in the 1890s both Louis Lumière and Thomas Edison contrived devices able to make and project images that conveyed the illusion of movement, opening the way to modern filmmaking (the near-simultaneity of their inventions illustrates the effects of what Joel Mokyr calls the "reduced access costs" for information brought about by thickened webs of communication). By 1900 large crowds were attending such showings, drawn in more by the pleasure of the illusion than for any particular content; before 1910 fairs and variety shows remained common venues, and the subjects were chiefly those of the popular entertainments just mentioned, often having to do with travel or everyday life (the arrival of a train, a bride at the end of her wedding day), and employing trick effects.

As makers began to offer longer sequences with more complicated subjects (marking the shift from what movie historians call the "cinema of attractions" to the modern narrative film) the popular origins of the genre remained an important element in the ways middle-class viewers reacted to it. Peter Jelavich has shown that educated Germans, especially *Bildungsbürger* formed on a diet of traditional culture, worried about whether they should allow themselves to be entertained by such fare as wild west films; in contrast, André Gide welcomed Charlie Chaplin with the journal entry that "it is so good to be able not to despise what the crowd admires." Gide's comment points to the important role that cinema would play in drawing French intellectuals into the romance with popular culture they have kept up ever since, a phenomenon less visible among their German counterparts, who (on the left as well as the right, a point to which I will come in a moment) displayed a greater fear that movies, like other forms of popular entertainment, would corrupt public and private taste. Even the French had to focus much of their enthusiasm for popular cinema on some supposedly more innocent past, however, partly in order to deal with longstanding alarms about immorality and the corrupting effect of "mechanical" procedures on culture of all kinds.[32]

Despite these anxieties, the early history of cinema is in good part a story about the way a form rooted in popular entertainment came to occupy a large place in high culture and the lives of people devoted to it, illustrating the similarities the two levels were acquiring as popular forms came to be organized in ways previously more characteristic of elite ones. An important moment in this transformation came with the building of large and often luxurious movie houses beginning in the years just before World War I (the Gaumont Palace, opened in Paris in 1911, was the first and most illustrious French example), an innovation that relied on the improving technology of photography and projection (and after 1927 on the introduction of recorded and coordinated sound) and that was accompanied by the shift to a system of distributing films to houses by rental instead of purchase, encouraging more rapid and regular program changes. The new locales also introduced a sliding scale of ticket prices corresponding to different seating sections, at once preserving class distinctions and providing for the simultaneous participation of elite and popular strata in a single cultural activity, a phenomenon that would mark such later instances as radio and television too. The striking expansion this produced led the Austrian novelist Robert Musil to observe after the War that the churches over the centuries "had not succeeded in creating as dense a network as cinema has done in thirty years," an achievement that rested on the reconciliation of the elite public with what a French historian describes as "a spectacle hitherto too-much tied to the fried-potato-oil smell of outdoor fairs and the sweat and tobacco odors of the music-halls." The two milieux never wholly fused, however, and by the 1920s people (at least in Paris) were speaking not about a single movie-going public but a number of different ones. These did not correspond neatly with social classes, but doubtless most of those who were drawn to the clubs and reviews making exalted claims for film as high culture that spread after the War (the first "Society of Art Cinema" had been founded in 1908) were mostly educated bourgeois, carrying on a discourse to which the majority of viewers remained indifferent. Thus there could arise the contrast between the *cinéma du quartier* and the *quartier du cinéma* that Anne-Marie Thiesse educes as symbolic of broader divisions within modern culture.[33]

A comparable evolution can be discerned in music. In Paris the roots of what would be modern popular musical culture in the years between the wars lay in the expansion of musical cafés (*café concerts*) under the Second Empire and the music halls that began to supplant them under the Third Republic. Both owed their prominence to urban expansion and the less inhibited style of leisure for which the rebuilt city of light was becoming famous (encouraged by the new boulevards and by the Empire's abolition of theater privileges in 1867). Tied up with earlier locales known chiefly for dancing, they bore names such as the Eldorado, the Folies Bergères, and the Reine Blanche, the last renamed the Moulin Rouge in 1888. The entertainment in the *café concerts* has been well described as a "mix of traditional song and fairground spectacle," alternating music with short dramatic pieces or street-performer routines. Music halls extended the mix of genres to include circus acts, side-show staples (dwarfs, "ugliest," fattest, or thinnest people, etc.) and troops of "girls" (in English), what one writer has called "a mosaic of borrowings from all the arts of show-manship." But increasingly they featured reviews with orchestras, dan-cing, songs – racy, saucy, sometimes political or taking a satirical view of contemporary events and personalities – and headed by performers whose reputation was cultivated by advertising. The music halls and their performers inspired some of the great classics of poster art, and figures such as Degas and Toulouse-Lautrec included them in work intended as something more than publicity.

Although each of the venues was an independent enterprise (there was some consolidation after the War), they quickly began to develop networks of outside connections that brought them wider attention and influence. One strand in this web was selling scores and texts for popular numbers from the reviews; the publisher François Salabert began to specialize in the genre during the 1880s, doing very well from a number of best-selling songs and collections and creat-ing an audience for current Parisian music outside the city. This, in turn, helped give popular singers a wider exposure, allowing some of them to become the first real pop stars, beginning with the *chanteuse* Thérésa, already well known enough in the mid 1860s to command an income equal to the top dancers at the Paris Opera; in 1885 she made a highly successful European tour. By then Yvette Guibert (born in 1865) was launching a career that would make her still more fam-ous, given extra cachet from the famous images of her by Toulouse-Lautrec and Cheret. In the same years imitators of the Parisian music halls sprung up in several provincial French cities; by 1900 there were "Eldorados" in Nice, Lyon, Poitiers and Albi, and Folies Bergères in Lyon, Le Havre, Rouen, and Brest, joined by still more before 1914; the same songs seem to have been part of the programs everywhere. As early as the 80s a maker of cough drops was using images of music-hall stars to advertise his product. The international prestige of the music-halls and their performers was at its height in the years between the wars, but firm foundations had been laid before 1914.[34]

Despite their connections with popular forms of entertain-ment, however, the music halls were far from being strictly lower-class locales. The well-known ones listed above often set admission prices at levels that excluded most workers and their families, who sought recreation instead in neighborhood hangouts or in the suburbs. This does not mean that working-class leisure went untouched by the changes occurring in other social milieux. At least in some places workers able to afford the admissions prices (in the Paris suburbs new industries such as machine building and automobiles paid relatively well) quickly became enthusiasts for movies, music halls, and even theaters; traditional genres such as gymnastics, singing, and animal training remained popular, but even for them "marketplaces and fairs were replaced by glamorous showcases; crowds became audiences."[35] The same can be said with even more emphasis about places like the Moulin Rouge and the Folies Bergères whose clientèle, as we know from the famous images by Manet, Toulouse-Lautrec, and Picasso, was in good part bourgeois; even before 1900 the patrons included many foreign and provincial tourists.

That both broadly middle-class audiences and serious artists were drawn to such places calls for several observations. The first is the obvious point that not all bourgeois were drawn to high culture; many were happy to seek communion through music and public performances that did not require the kind of attention associated with listening to Beethoven or Wagner. More than one observer thought the rapidly shifting components of music hall entertainment were necessary in order to hold the interest of a diverse audience. In addition, however, the features of such performances that drew Degas, Manet, or Toulouse-Lautrec to such locales were ones that had long attracted their fellows to non-elite locales and practices: Baudelaire's exemplary "Painter of Modern Life" had been a popular illustrator, Constantin Guys; Courbet found inspiration for the direct and unidealized style he called realism in popular prints and drawings; many composers incorporated elements of folk music into their works; and numerous literary figures from Balzac to Alexander Döblin and after were fascinated by the color and vitality of popular argot. To modernists in search of paths of escape from traditional limits and new sources of cultural energy, these alternative forms offered resources of much importance; in taking them up, artists of all kinds undermined from within the very separation between high and popular forms of representation and expression that other features of cultural evolution were rendering more rigid.

The complex mix that could result from such configurations of cultural elements by late in the century is well illustrated by the artistic cabarets that sprang up in Montmartre from the 1880s, the Chat Noir and its imitators. The Chat Noir's founders Émile Goudeau and Rodolphe Salis had been inspired to establish their venue by earlier Latin Quarter cafés intended to provide exposure and publicity for young poets, writers, and illustrators. Like these earlier ventures, the Chat Noir published a paper dedicated in part to calling attention to the artists and performers who appeared there, seeking to make a direct appeal to the public in a manner that had much in common with the strategies by which picture dealers such as Durand-Ruel were attempting to give a new kind of organization to the relations between visual artists and their audience. Some of the figures who appeared at the Chat Noir had or gained considerable stature (Maurice Rollinat, who had close ties to Rodin, presented Baudelaire's poetry and Erik Satie played piano there for a time), but others belonged more to the world of mostly forgotten popular writers we described above, and the general atmosphere was one that blurred the lines between high culture and things often thought to be incompatible with it. The mix of genres, recalling that of the music halls, and the fact that books and prints were for sale alongside drink (in a neighborhood where other pleasures, some suspect or illicit, were available too), helped encourage the comparison sometimes made between the cabarets and the increasingly prominent department stores. Like these, the Chat Noir and its imitators advertised throughout France, seeking to add tourists (even some who came to Paris in part for religious reasons) to their clientèle.[36]

The popular and commercial side of what made the cabarets so successful at the end of the century is well illustrated by the career of Aristide Bruant, the celebrated *chansonnier*, today known mostly through the striking lithograph Toulouse-Lautrec did as an advertising poster for him. Bruant got his start at the Chat Noir before setting up his own establishment, Le Mirliton, in 1885 (the name means a toy pipe) in the premises vacated by the first one's move to a larger space. His enormously successful appearances, along with published editions of his songs (sold throughout the country and advertised in his newspaper, also called *Le Mirliton*), took popular and working-class life as their subject, evoking the districts where workers lived, the poverty and suffering they endured, the experience of being out of work and "in the street" (*Dans la rue* was the title of his most famous collection). Bruant's forceful, colorful, often slangy language (he published a dictionary of *argot*), along with his sympathy for his subjects, gave a seemingly radical edge to his work; the songs were sometimes sung in anarchist meetings, and he greeted patrons in his café with ritualized insults and hard stares. But even more than

Courbet, he came to value such a style as a way of gaining notoriety, and thus a following. By the end he was defending property, patriotism, and right-wing causes. As a friend who was a former police officer wrote in a pamphlet about him, "The characteristic of Bruant's particular success is that he has known how to make himself the idol of the poor and at the same time gain the acceptance of the others, the highly placed people and those he calls *les fins-de-siècle*. He has on his side both the oppressors and the oppressed." His connection to the Chat Noir and his broad-based following show how the larger audience available by the end of the century, and the new techniques being developed to appeal to it, created a potential to redraw the boundaries between levels of culture.[37]

The same factors produced somewhat similar results as commercially viable sound recordings came on the scene from the late 1890s. Edison's gramophone became commercially available in the 1880s, like moving pictures appealing at first more for its novelty than for any particular content, and often to be found in the same kinds of places. In Europe the most important early pioneers of recorded music were the Pathé brothers who also played a role in the history of cinema; fascinated by their first encounter with one of Edison's machines they bought one to exhibit at fairs and in the bistro that was their original business, before beginning to make models of their own. From this they moved on to selling recorded cylinders and later discs; soon they were offering a catalogue that ranged from popular performers such as Bruant (modern remakes of his recorded performances can still be heard and bought) to eminent high cultural figures likely to have a wide appeal, including Caruso. From early on, therefore, classical music was closely associated with its popular counterpart in regard to efforts to add distant audiences to local ones through recordings; because the economic logic was the same for both, the distinction between the levels lost some of its prior relevance. In order for reproduction to become part of the new economy of culture the technical problems of how to reproduce sound had first to be solved, but one of the things that made facing up to them worthwhile was that a body of performers existed who could be expected to appeal to diverse audiences in widely separated places. This in turn rested on the expansion of musical culture we considered earlier, consisting in the establishment of stable orchestras, large-scale public concerts, and the aid given to traveling virtuosos by impresarios and agents. It was the reputations performers were able to acquire through these networks of communication that made investment in making their recordings available by entrepreneurs such as the Pathé brothers worthwhile. As these networks continued to develop, and as new technical innovations and improvements (radio, later long-playing records) came on the scene, the multiplication of listening opportunities would come to be at the very center of the relations between music and its audience. Already in the period between the wars there were composers (Maurice Ravel chief among them) and conductors (notably Alfred Cortot and Pierre Monteux) who saw records as an important element in the future of serious music and worked to produce a repertoire that would make it widely available.

As with cinema so in music the barrier between cultural levels was at once weakened and strengthened by these developments. The Pathé brothers included both popular and art music in their catalogue, but the audiences for the two were never identical (to be sure they were and have remained overlapping), and the divisions between them were heightened by the simultaneous expansion of both. Like culturally ambitious film, art music spawned its own organizations and periodicals, but with the difference that perception and commentary became more individualized and fragmented than with movie-going, because recordings could be played in private, and different versions of the same work compared. This possibility spurred the appearance of record collectors for serious music even before World War I, a phenomenon that spread to jazz as it acquired a large following during the 1920s. The letters columns of specialized periodicals created spaces where people with a strong interest in some kind of music, but no official credentials for speaking about it, could participate in written exchanges about styles, pieces, and performers, producing an active public discourse on music. The individuation of musical taste that began with the changing behavior of audiences from around 1800 now acquired new dimensions, but in a situation that replaced the relatively rare and therefore particularly intense kind of encounters called up by Wackenröder with ones that could be more quotidian and diffused, based on the larger and more stable public presence of both classical and popular forms from the last decades of the century. Ludovic Tournès highlights the "polycentricity" of these reactions, and the "multiplicity of norms of appreciation" that emerged out of them, features that gave a not always recognized quality of flexibility and independent choice to the cultural world brought to life by the spread of modern means of communication. Far from an undifferentiated mass, the expanding audience for cultural products included individuals and groups able to seize on new means for dialogue with cultural producers and with each other, bringing to light a variety of different ways to respond and relate to cultural objects and messages, and on a smaller scale foreshadowing similar phenomena that would emerge later on, in the Internet.[38]

To be sure, these anticipations of later developments were still strictly limited. As with separate gender spheres and moral puritanism, the more rigid separation between cultural levels long retained much force; in all three cases the 1960s brought far deeper disruptions than seemed possible earlier. But the motion toward dissolving these rigidities, and with them many of the far older oppositions on which they were based, had clearly begun, fostered by the continuing extension and deepening of the same networks that had earlier served to render traditional distinctions more strict. Even the special role that young people and cultural forms intended especially for them would play in the later period was clearly adumbrated earlier. In 1908 the first French comic-strip paper, *L'Épatant* began publication (originally as a supplement to the *Petit Journal*); one of its readers would be a young Jean-Paul Sartre (born in 1905), much to the dismay of his staid grandfather. Thumbing its nose at classical culture and the values conveyed by formal education, the paper (in Jean-Yves Mollier's words) "appealed to young people to constitute themselves as a distinct category, with its own codes and tastes, taking pleasure in seeing fictional characters subvert the rules of the social game." The paper's distance from traditional culture helped make way for an association between its subversive spirit and that of the bands of young "Apaches" whose criminal but colorful behavior attracted much attention in the press at the time; the resulting sense of connection between popular cultural forms and alternatives to existing social life would be one that certain of the paper's young middle-class readers would carry with them later.[39]

The two phases of widening and then narrowing of the distance between elite and popular culture were in part chronologically separate, but partly overlapping too, since "high" culture took on the more organized forms (permanent professional symphony orchestras and agents, new-style picture dealers) that made its separate existence seem so firmly established just in the years when less exalted kinds of cultural expression were beginning to acquire this new presence and energy. One result of the growth of popular literature, the mass press, and cinema was greatly to enlarge the body of people employed in various cultural occupations. David Blackbourn reports that by early in the twentieth century as many as 100,000 Germans "supported themselves from writing, music, the theater, and related activities, not including white collar occupations like box-office staff." Overall, he notes, the result of these changes was a general blurring of "the formal distinctions between various kinds of culture."[40]

The confusion contributed to making the decades just before and after World War I a moment of especially sharp conflict over how to respond to newly prominent means of popular expression and what they portended. The acrimony was heightened in Germany by the enactment of the so-called Heinze Law in 1900. Sponsored by Catholics and political rightists, the bill restricted the distribution not just of "obscene" pictures, texts, or theater productions, but of anything deemed "capable of giving offense through gross injury of feelings of shame or morality." Threatening those convicted with imprisonment, the legislation produced widespread protests and a confusing set of alliances. Some anti-modernist but secular *Bildungsbürger* joined with Catholics to support controls over expression in the name of morality, while many social democrats, whose fears about the power of "capitalist trash" to corrupt workers drew them closer to conservatives than to liberals, were moved by opposition to censorship to join with the latter in the "Goethe League" founded to protest and combat the Law. The debates revealed that the powers attributed to the new forms of expression and communication led people of all stripes to project either intense fears or outsize hopes onto them. On the one side were predictions of the end of civilization, made by people whose image of popular culture shared much with those who saw it as robbing the working-class of its revolutionary vocation. On the other were what today can only seem exaggerated expectations that print and the movies (later radio) could serve to diffuse education and traditional culture among those untouched by it hitherto, alongside utopian visions of the same media as tools for the production of revolutionary consciousness (views worked out in various ways by such figures as Berthold Brecht and Walter Benjamin). Until the outbreak of World War II and even beyond similar fears and hopes were expressed in France, some of them entering for a time into state policies, although (except during the Occupation) restriction and censorship never reached the same level as in Germany.[41]

Overall, there is much reason to agree with a recent German historian that the heightened presence and profile of popular culture brought forth an exaggerated sense of its potency on all sides, creating false expectations that large-scale media could be used to direct popular opinion, taste, or behavior along one or another desired or feared track. In the years between the Wars these views contributed to the theories about the power of the "culture industry" to defuse working-class radicalism developed by members of the Frankfurt School, and later to opposite visions of popular culture as a vehicle of radical liberation, given expression in a vocabulary developed by post-structuralists. What both sorts of theorists failed to recognize was precisely the "polycentricity" and multiplicity of reactions evident in regard to both music and film by the 1920s, and that recalls the earlier impossibility of directing or knowing in advance what uses readers would make of newly available printed materials.[42] No doubt there were and remain many passive consumers of what various media bring to them, but they occupy one place on a broad spectrum of responses. Others navigate the world of popular culture in ways closer to the paths Michel de Certeau portrayed people taking as they make their way through cities, finding unpredictable routes, turning the goods offered to new uses, injecting their own meanings into the scenes and images they find around them. The more the world of popular culture expands the less we know what directions it will take or what ways people will find to make some novel use of its contents.[43]

14 BOURGEOIS LIFE AND THE AVANT-GARDE

Fluidity, energy, and the promise of transformation

The opposition between cultural innovation and the bourgeoisie has become so ingrained in accounts of modernity and its history that the argument of this chapter may well surprise some readers. It is that beneath all the declarations of mutual hostility between artists and writers on the one hand and bourgeois life on the other, there lay a series of deep and revealing interconnections, and that the substance of these ties provided much of the ground on which the modernist avant-garde would mount its challenges to established forms of life and culture in the years before and just after World War I. The energies on which vanguard movements and figures sought to draw were ones generated by society at large, particularly in the selfsame commercial spheres from which aesthetic rebels sometimes felt most distant, and the pattern by which successive innovations in culture rose up to push aside their predecessors was intricately interwoven with what Joseph Schumpeter called the "creative destruction" that characterized typical bourgeois activities.

Although he did not live to encounter the figures and movements who constituted the avant-garde in the *fin-de-siècle*, Marx was well aware of these connections. In *The Communist Manifesto* he and Engels credited the bourgeoisie with revealing that humanity possessed previously unrecognized powers. "The bourgeoisie has been the first to show what man's activity can bring about. It has accomplished wonders far surpassing Egyptian pyramids, Roman aqueducts, and Gothic cathedrals; it has conducted expeditions that put in the shade all former Exoduses of nations and crusades." The economy was the sphere in which these forces were rooted, but the impact of their unleashing was felt in every corner of life, most notably in the realm of consciousness and culture. In order to survive and carry on in the world it was creating, the bourgeoisie had constantly to be "revolutionizing the means of production"; these repeated upheavals deprived things as they were of the stability that hitherto veiled the human capacity to alter them, revealing the true nature of social relations and their future. "All fixed, fast-frozen relations, with their train of ancient and venerable prejudices and opinions, are swept away, all new-formed ones become antiquated before they can ossify. All that is solid melts into air, all that is holy is profaned, and man is at last compelled to face, with sober senses, his real conditions of life and his relations with his kind."[1] The notion that bourgeois activity bore this power to uncover hitherto unrecognized truths underlay Marx's belief that his theory of revolutionary social transformation was "scientific," that is, based on actual observation of the developing conditions of modern life, in contrast to the "utopian" socialisms merely dreamt up by thinkers in the past.

Marx's pronouncement has often been noticed, but two things about it have not. One is that he was by no means the first person to regard radical fluidity as a defining quality of modern life, and that some of his predecessors were not moved to recognize it by any commitment to revolutionary change; we will look at some of them in a moment. The other is that by the end of the nineteenth century appeals to such fluidity were seldom voiced in Marx's realm of socialist activism, where the development of large-scale organizations fostered a vision of social transformation predicated on stable structures rather than on their dissolution (on this Lenin and Bernstein agreed); they had migrated to the modernist avant-garde, where finding ways to release deep and often hidden human powers to remake consciousness and through it life itself had become a central goal. Some of the figures who pursued this aim were leftists and revolutionaries, Louis Aragon for instance, but others such as Marcel Duchamp were not. One clear thread tied this avant-garde project to Marx's formulation regardless of politics, however, namely that it shared his recognition that the bourgeois life it aimed to overcome was itself a major source

of the energies it sought to employ against it. What defined the transformed state of existence that vanguard practices hoped to usher in
was precisely the fluidity to which Marx appealed, and this fluidity
arose at the very heart of bourgeois modernity, in the kinds of relations to everyday objects and experiences that modern networks of
consumption and communication fostered.

Of Marx's predecessors in recognizing unremitting fluidity as
an essential feature of *bürgerliche Gesellschaft* the most immediate
was Hegel, who identified civil society (in his *Philosophy of Right*)
with "flux, danger, and destruction." These qualities he associated
with the natural linkage between commerce and the ever-restless sea,
which as "the greatest means of communication ... creates commercial
connections between various countries," bringing cultural ties too.[2]
Still earlier the eighteenth-century Scottish writer Adam Ferguson, in
his *Essay on the History of Civil Society*, cited the activities of people
in countries with developed commercial relations as testimony to the
human capacity for repeated change and innovation. Arguing against
Rousseau that human beings had no original "natural" state, and that
whatever mode of existence they created for themselves was natural to
them, he attributed to humanity in general (in his language "man") a
creative power comparable to that of artists: "He is in some measure
the artificer of his own frame, as well as of his fortune, and is destined,
from the first age of his being, to invent and contrive."[3] Human creativity was of a particularly restless kind, because human satisfactions
were passing and momentary, giving rise to ever-new desires: "the
object of sanguine expectation, when obtained, no longer continues
to occupy the mind: A new passion succeeds, and the imagination,
as before, is intent on a distant felicity." Civil society thus revealed
human beings to be creatures who found pleasure more in activity
than in its products, leading them ever onward to new endeavors.
The last point in particular was one Ferguson shared with his friend
Adam Smith, who noted that people were moved to work and engage
in activities that improved both social life and culture by the desire to
acquire objects and positions whose presence in other people's lives
they saw as a means of increasing happiness. Experience shows that
having such things – houses, furniture, clothing, social status – seldom
succeeds in making us content, but we continue to desire them all the
same, and to expend our energies on attempts to come by them. "It is
well that nature imposes upon us in this manner. It is this deception

which rouses and keeps in continual motion the industry of mankind ... which first prompted them to cultivate the ground, to build houses, to found cities and commonwealths, and to invent and improve all the sciences and arts."[4]

Late nineteenth- and early twentieth-century vanguard visions of aesthetic and social transformation preserved these appeals to fluidity and the constant release of creative energy, but they did so in a more determined and insistent way. In 1922 the surrealist theorist and publicist André Breton, in a comment that marks in a way the end-point of the history I will try to trace in this chapter, hailed Marcel Duchamp for showing the way "to liberate modern consciousness from that terrible fixation mania" that had kept it from achieving the liberation it sought. Duchamp by then had (or seemed to have) abandoned the traditional artist's vocation of making special kinds of objects in favor of what he called "readymades," ordinary articles of everyday use supposed to be encountered at unpredictable moments – a bicycle wheel, a bottle drying-rack, a urinal – and given the status of art by the act of creative imagination that chose them. The artist of "readymades" no longer pursued the traditional aim of producing beautiful or interesting things, he merely designated objects in the world as "works." Liberated from the daily grind of the studio and the obligation to pursue goals defined in advance, he was able to give free rein to his creative energies whenever they bubbled up, dedicating himself to a life of chance encounters. So free was Duchamp that he could happily let the toss of a coin decide whether to go on a long journey or stay put. What made this move so exemplary in Breton's eyes was that it put an end to the self-defeating search for new styles and programs in which vanguard schools had engaged for half a century, a way of being modern that repeatedly raised up some new limit to creative imagination in the very act of seeking to unshackle it. Duchamp (who cherished his found objects in part because they had no stylistic features in common) showed that it was possible to take an axe to "the famous intellectual crab-apple tree which in half a century has borne the fruits called symbolism, cubism, futurism, dadaism." Freed of the obsession with art's products Duchamp provided a way of being an artist that empowered the creative imagination to overflow into the world around it, drawing all things into its sphere. Breton would seek to fashion surrealism on this model when he wrote its Manifesto in 1924, dedicating himself and his friends to the simultaneous destabilization of art and of life.[5]

Behind Breton's vision lay a history of claims by successive aesthetic movements to represent the true nature of modern existence, beginning with romanticism (which Victor Hugo defended for its harmony with modern experience in the 1820s) and including realism and impressionism as well as the later schools Breton listed. He recognized their serial appearance as itself a testimony to the constant change at the heart of modern culture, and yet at the same time to its proclivity for investing the flow of energy it generated in defined and therefore limited embodiments. What the rest of this chapter seeks to show is not that Hegel's or Ferguson's or Marx's pronouncements about the relations between modern life and fluidity were somehow picked up by the avant-garde in the *fin-de-siècle*, but rather that the conditions to which the earlier writers were responding also shaped the visions of the later ones. By the middle of the nineteenth century these conditions had come to include the new situation of culture itself that I sought to elucidate in Chapter 12, whereby the more public and tangible forms in which cultural activities were carried on were simultaneously the frames within which ungovernable private experiences could unfold, allowing people to follow where fancy and imagination led them. The desires called forth by commodities and the feelings given free rein by private encounters with literature or music were two sides of the imaginative life generated by modernity, and they flowed in and out of each other. But their potential was judged differently from diverse points of view.

Already in the eighteenth century Smith's understanding that people were drawn to objects by the imagined satisfactions they seem to promise was being applied to quite ordinary commodities, for instance by Wedgwood when he named pottery designs for aristocrats or royals and by shopkeepers who set up alluring window displays in town streets and squares. Such phenomena are part of what leads Colin Campbell to propose that modern consumption has ever since been driven by a "romantic ethic": when things are displayed, advertised, or seen in the possession of others, we project onto them some of the idealized pleasure generated in fantasy and day-dreaming. A buyer is drawn to some good because he or she believes it "can supply experiences which [s]he has not so far encountered in reality."[6] This connection between consumption and fantasy grew more widespread and intense during the nineteenth century, especially as department stores spread after 1850, with their attempts to appeal to growing numbers of potential buyers through an ever-wider set of techniques: creating an "image" of the stores through posters, distributing illustrated calendars and agendas, sponsoring concerts and other on-site activities, and creating displays whose colorful juxtaposition of different articles encouraged buyers to imagine a range and depth of gratification beyond what individual items might promise. Store owners doubtless hoped that such techniques would overcome customer resistance to spending money; certainly this was an aim of Gustave Mouret, Zola's fictionalized hero in *The Ladies' Paradise* (based loosely on Aristide Boucicaut, the founder of the *Bon Marché*), and some shoppers could not resist buying or even stealing things they could not afford.

In her remarkable book *Dream Worlds*, devoted to debates about consumption and its place in modern life, Rosalind Williams showed that the fantasies generated around consumption goods played a part in shaping the projects conceived by modernist movements. One example was the proto-symbolist protagonist of Joris-Karl Huysmanns' widely remarked 1884 novel *Against Nature (À Rebours)*, Des Esseintes, who surrounds himself with carefully chosen objects calculated to turn the world he inhabits into a mirror of his mental interior and thus a site where the desires generated by his powerful imagination find no material barriers to their fulfillment. Des Esseintes suffers defeat in the end, finding that his attempt to live only with material objects that sustain his aesthetic sense leaves him without the minimum physical nurture necessary to support his life, so that he has to return to the ordinary world in order to survive. But his project would echo in later ones, as Breton testified when he wrote about Picasso that the artist's aim in picturing things as he did was "to render the exterior object adequate to his desire," and thus to turn the world with its capacity to impede satisfaction into a vehicle of it. We shall look more closely at the diverse ways by which vanguard artists pursued this aim in a moment.[7]

Art as life: bohemia

First, however, we need to recognize the existence of a region of nineteenth-century experience that both dramatized these exchanges between bourgeois life and artistic creativity and made them the stuff of everyday existence, the simultaneously real and fictional realm of bohemia. Although one can find the term "bohemia" used in something like the sense it still bears today in the eighteenth century, the idea and the mode of life it represents only became objects of widespread pubic attention in the 1830s and 1840s, and first of all in France. To understand bohemia's cultural significance, we need to see that its prominence drew on two seemingly conflicting developments. The first was the heightened emphasis placed on what separated art and literature from ordinary social occupations; the second was a changed notion of what it meant to be an artist or poet, expanding the category in ways that attached these labels to a wider range of people than commonly bore them before. The emphasis on artists as separate kinds of beings was tied up with the exaltation of creative activity connected with the notion of "art as such," and to which Wackenröder gave voice when he exalted artists as "the highest of earthly beings." Such a description might be expected to narrow the boundaries of those to whom the label of artist could apply. By early in the nineteenth century, however, the close association between artistic identity and inner feeling promoted by romanticism, combined with the Revolutionary program of "careers open to talents," was issuing in a broadening of the category of artists, extending it to include all those whose belief in the special quality of their imaginative and emotional life set them apart from others.

A classic instance was the image of the poet defended by Alfred de Vigny in the preface to his 1835 play *Chatterton*, the drama of a neglected and suffering English writer who ended his life in suicide. Vigny specifically distinguished the kind of poet Chatterton represented from the "great writer." Whereas the latter (Victor Hugo, for example) had no trouble finding favor with the public, poets such as Chatterton lived in the shadows and might never demonstrate the reality of their vocations. The title of poet rightfully belonged to them all the same, because their deeply felt passion for dreams and the imagination made them unfit for ordinary occupations, impelling them to live in accord with a pure devotion to their ideal. So important were they in the human economy that society ought to support even those among them whose achievements would never validate their ambitions: "What gives us the right to snuff out the acorn by saying that it won't be an oak?"

Vigny's notion was part of a general romantic critique of the modern failure to give creative people their due that often took the bourgeoisie as a particular object of enmity, but so broad an extension of artistic identity could not help but weaken the very border between poets or painters and bourgeois it was intended to defend. Such weakening was at the center of the much more skeptical eye cast on people like the ones Vigny championed by a young writer who would have a long albeit never much-celebrated career in French literary circles and emerge as a supporter of the Commune of 1871, Félix Pyat. Writing just a year earlier than Vigny, Pyat found both significance and amusement in observing that nowadays little or nothing restrained people from claiming to be artists, visual or literary: "One is an artist the way one used to be a property-owner, it's the distinguishing mark of those people who don't have any." Drawn by the aura of a Hugo, young men who could do no more than touch his hand sought to live out this "artistism," refusing to take on ordinary work. The trouble was that those among them who lacked real originality would end up isolated from the life around them, "alien and bizarre," using their false sense of themselves as a justification for not becoming contributing members of society. They were, Pyat concluded, proposing a metaphor that would long echo in cultural history, "the bohemians of today."[8]

Pyat's word was *bohémiens* and translating it as "bohemians" is pushing things a bit. At the moment he used it, the term referred chiefly to gypsies (to call them Roma, as we are now asked to do does not convey the etymological link with the region that is now the Czech Republic where they were wrongly thought to originate; the English equivalent rests on a similarly mistaken notion that they stemmed from Egypt), and by extension to marginal street people who had been objects of interest and suspicion in Paris since the late Middle Ages. By applying the label to those afflicted with "artistism," Pyat attributed to them a comparable position on the margins of society, to which they belonged in some way but did not fully join. The people he had in mind were mostly young bourgeois, many of them students, including a good number of provincials. As such they were illustrative of a recognized bourgeois devotion to mobility, giving them a connection to those to whom the term *bohémiens* originally applied that was developed in a revealing way by a writer for the *Magasin pittoresque* in 1851. Because modern conditions made social relations more organized and rigid, he observed, the carefree, fluid gypsy lifestyle was threatened. At the same time, however, modernity provided a kind of replacement for nomadic wandering by drawing far-off peoples into closer relations:

modern travel and communication increased people's knowledge of foreign places and conditions and expanded their horizons. The result would be that things it had once been possible only to imagine would come to be objects of actual experience; fantasy, having once been the special realm of poets, would take on "a social character. The gypsies of the old civilization will have become the messengers of the new."[9] Thus would the ability of modern networks to establish closer relations between people at a distance bring aspects of experience once confined to the margins into society's center. Bohemian "artistism" testified to bourgeois life's role as both the death and the resurrection of gypsy existence.

An additional tie linked bourgeois mobility to what Pyat dubbed "artistism," namely that novelists and painters were among the most visible and striking examples of the "self-made man." Claims to have risen wholly by one's own efforts were entered on behalf of businessmen, soldiers, physicians, and publishers, but there was hardly a more striking success story than that of the family Balzac. The novelist's father (as we saw above), the son of poor peasants and the only one among eleven siblings who learned to read, went off to Paris where he rose by his own efforts to a high position in the royal administration. Honoré was born into the considerable comfort this ascension made possible, but also into a family rendered tense and unhappy by the mismatch between his father and the romantic and mystical grocer's daughter the elder Balzac married. From these origins their son emerged just as driven to make his own way as were any of the characters he created, determinedly and even obsessively devoting himself to writing partly in order to pay the debts he incurred through the collapse of the publishing venture he hoped would make him rich in the 1820s. Victor Hugo and Eugène Sue came from more comfortable and established backgrounds, but their fame made them seem self-made all the same; this was one reason Pyat gave Hugo a central role in his sketch. The self-consciously rural Courbet represented the same phenomenon among painters.

By the time Pyat used the term "bohemian" to refer to young bourgeois who imagined themselves as leading a life unimpeded by ordinary social obligations, the idea had been partly anticipated. Balzac in one story wrote of bohemia as the domain of talented young men not yet able to assume the social roles that awaited them, and George Sand portrayed an artist who labeled his freedom from ordinary social

attachments bohemian. None of these instances gained much resonance, however. The term began to acquire its lasting popularity and
notoriety toward the end of the 1840s, when Henri Murger published
the tales and sketches he would use as the basis for a highly successful play in 1849, and that he collected as *Scenes of Bohemian Life* in
1851. (The play and stories provided the characters and situations later
dramatized in Giacomo Puccini's more famous opera.) It was Murger
who put bohemia on the map of modern culture, portraying it as an
abode of artists while simultaneously highlighting the presence in it of
many people who were not. In his hands the figure of the bohemian
artist became a touchstone for a broader, and – as we will see in a
moment – chiefly bourgeois, identity.[10]

In the preface to his collected *Scenes of Bohemian Life* Murger
defined bohemia as the temporary habitation of young artists not yet
able to support themselves with their work, "all those who, driven
by an unstinting sense of calling, enter into art with no other means
of existence than art itself." It was to this group that he assigned the
Rodolphe and Marcel of the tales, the fictionalized versions of himself and his one-time apartment-mate Jules Fleury, later known under
the name Champfleury. But he went on to describe two other camps
whose presence was no less characteristic of the territory. On the one
side were a group he called the "unknown bohemians," those who
would never emerge from apprenticeship to become recognized artists,
either because they were too infused with a stoic ethic of purity to take
any of the practical steps that success required, or because what really
drew them to live among poor painters and writers was an indomitable
rebellion against ordinary life. On the other wing were the "amateurs,"
young bourgeois whose comfortable family position saved them from
any pressing need to live in poverty but who chose bohemia for the
sake of the adventure, freedom, and solidarity with other young people
it offered. (At least some of them were involved in what Erik Erikson
would later call a psychic "moratorium," a period of putting off troubling decisions about personal identity.) Although Murger made the real
future artists out to be the central figures, the other two groups played
a larger role in his bohemia than that claim presumed. He sometimes
scorned the "unknown bohemians" as "ridiculous martyrs," warning
against the dangers of "remaining too long in bohemia," but he had
been close to people like them (for instance to Joseph and Leopold
Desbrosses, a would-be painter and sculptor with whom he joined

in a group who called themselves the "Water-Drinkers" in the early 1840s), and some of his most engaging and touching portraits were modeled on these onetime friends. At the same time he was friendly and sympathetic, both in real life and in his writing, toward some of the amateurs whose status as future artists was most questionable: Charles Barbara, called Barbemuche in the stories, who supplemented the support he received from his wealthy family with tutoring and an occasional newspaper piece, and Alexandre Schanne, the Schaunard of the tales, who later abandoned bohemia to take over his father's toy business.

What especially made the presence of these two groups significant in the bohemia Murger depicted was that the stories revolved more around a set of issues dramatized by their lives than around questions of moment to early nineteenth-century artistic practice. One looks in vain in *Scenes of Bohemian Life* for any discussion of pressing aesthetic issues of the day: romantic versus classic, nature versus artifice, sublimity versus beauty, color versus line. What recur instead are a series of moral and social polarities: wealth versus poverty, enjoyment versus work, indulgence versus duty, communal obligation versus the individual focus on the self. Murger's bohemians are all in some way at odds with the bourgeois life around them, but for contrasting reasons. Sometimes what alienates them are the harsh and constricting limits society places on individuals, inhibiting their development and their pleasures through the imperatives of the market or the demands of moral conformity; but others draw apart from the same world because its potential enjoyments threaten to weaken and corrupt their devotion to some high calling. What turns the first away from bourgeois life is its rigidity and inflexibility, while the second fear the opposite, the debilitating temptations and satisfactions it offers. This dialectic creates a complex moral structure in Murger's tales whose presence contemporaries often recognized, but seldom with sympathy. As one wrote, "Contempt for the goods of this world has been, ever since Seneca, a philosophic and honorable sentiment – but on condition that one has authentic contempt for them and gives them up, and doesn't dream about them night and day and shed tears over their absence like a lover crying over his mistress."

There may have been (and continue to be) hypocrisy in bohemia, but the existence of what seem to be contradictory moral attitudes needs to be understood in other ways, the first being that it corresponded to the differing origins and attitudes of the "unknown" and "amateur" bohemians. Socially the first came chiefly from families of what was then called the *bourgeoisie populaire*, sometimes on the border with artisans or workers (the Desbrosses brothers were sons of a cabdriver, and Murger's father was a tailor who also served as concierge in a largely bourgeois building), while the second had more solid, even comfortable, backgrounds, as the examples of Barbara and Schanne testify. There are good reasons for young people of the first sort in search of an independent career to live frugally, since if they fall into debt they have few resources for getting out of it. Abstention is a logical and prudent strategy for them, whereas giving in to the material temptations of a great capital threatens the future they imagine for themselves. By contrast people at the same age from upper bourgeois backgrounds can expect more support from their families (provided their parents do not reject them for leading what they see as immoral lives, as some in Murger's time and since have done). Unlike their less favored companions, they are likely to have known material comforts and pleasures in childhood, so that to renounce them for a time may still leave them with a persisting sense of entitlement. Rather than a sign of hypocrisy, the simultaneous rejection of money and fascination for it and what it can obtain reflects the presence in Murger's bohemia of two distinct moral attitudes, with connections to different levels of bourgeois existence. The two stances were not mutually exclusive however; some people in Murger's world combined or shifted between them, most notably Murger himself. This moral double-sidedness gave his bohemia a broader correspondence to the bourgeois life that was its counterpart, since both work and enjoyment, production and consumption are central to it. The two sides may sometimes stand in tension with each other, but (as noted earlier in regard to the conditions that encouraged early industrial innovation in England) the desire for goods was one motive drawing people to expend more effort on the activities necessary to obtain them. One way bohemia and bourgeois life mirrored each other was in their simultaneous devotion to both.

What allowed this complex moral structure to occupy its important place at the center of Murger's bohemia was his instinctive highlighting of the enlarged sense of the "artist" developed earlier by Vigny and Pyat. Himself a person who felt called to the artistic life, but whose limited talent extended only to writing what Champleury called "slices of his own life," Murger found in bohemia both material and an environment through which to realize the literary aspirations he could fulfill nowhere else: he never wrote successfully about any other subject. No one embodied better than he the shift of creative imagination from work to life he summed up in the formula of bohemian existence, devoted as it was to adroit stratagems and clever expedients: "their everyday life is a work of genius." One virtue of this redefinition was that it could serve to recognize the kinship between artistic bohemia and the separate but neighboring realm of people who had or chose to live in comparable ways for different reasons, such as street performers, vagrants, eccentrics, people with non-standard sexual identities, even some petty criminals. It was to them that the extension of *bohémiens* beyond its original reference to gypsies had first applied, and a full census of the inhabitants of modern bohemia would have to include them, as Murger well knew. By virtue of redefining art as living the life, Murger made room for both. His readers, however, seldom belonged to this "other" bohemia; for them even the implied reference to vagrants or con men was part of what made the world he described of interest above all for the relations it bore to its bourgeois counterpart, which similarly claimed recognition as a realm of innovation and imagination (as well as of order and stability). Murger's claim that the true bohemians in his world were apprentice artists was not false, but it served, consciously or not, as a move in the strategy that made bohemia the common ground of people engaged in appropriating the life of art for some extra-aesthetic, more personal and social purpose: rebellion, moratorium, or dramatizing the ambivalence they felt toward their beckoning bourgeois destinies. It was bohemia's ability to serve as a real and symbolic reference point for all these projects, at once for rejecting bourgeois life and for finding an oblique way of entry into it, that put it on the map of modern culture. But it was the permeable boundary between bourgeois life and the life of art that Vigny made evident in spite of himself and that Pyat and Murger specifically confronted that made the space of bohemia so significant in modernity.

That it long retained this importance, and in terms close to Murger's, can be seen by attending for a moment to a much greater writer who both felt bohemia's attractions and feared its dangers, Thomas Mann. Mann, who frequented self-consciously bohemian circles in Munich where his mother (born in Brazil) brought him and his brother Heinrich from their native Lübeck after their father's death in 1891, recognized bohemia as a field for the shifting and permeable relations between artists and bourgeois, and like Murger saw the temptations of remaining there too long as a danger for an artist, writing at one point that what talent required was not "real hunger but hunger for the real." Putting a commitment to real life above devotion to imagination was a position to which he came only through much hesitation and struggle, however, or perhaps to which he was always coming, much in the way that Murger was forever leaving bohemia behind without ever getting free of it. Mann began his first novel *Buddenbrooks* (1901) from a perspective that made him identify with the figure of Hanno, the last of the family and the one whose intense devotion to music (as we saw earlier) was the sign of its having lost the capacity to act effectively in the world, a condition that might be seen as preparation for recognizing the "higher" (in Nietzsche's terms "aesthetic") understanding that reality was merely transitory, a fleeting appearance ever-destined to be replaced by other ones. But even in that book the ambivalence that drew him increasingly to the opposite position as time went on made itself felt, and it underlay his remarkable evocation of two simultaneous and opposed tendencies within the bourgeois life he portrayed, one to value appearance and role-playing in a way that drew bourgeois people toward a bohemian kind of "artistism," the other to attend to the ineluctable power of reality in the way of practical people.[11]

The chief vehicle of this dialectic in *Buddenbrooks* is the relationship between Thomas, later to be Hanno's father, and his younger brother Christian. The contrast between them appears in the novel's first scene, when the brothers, still schoolboys, return home; a visitor ("the town poet") notes the contrast between them, describing Thomas as "a serious, steady intellect; he'll have to go into commerce," whereas Christian, while "a lad of wit and brilliant gifts," appears "to go off in all directions." To this his father responds with a kind of affectionate exasperation: "He's a monkey," a description Christian straightaway confirms by giving a hilarious imitation of one of his teachers. He confuses his mental pictures with actual happenings in the world (once seeming to choke on an imaginary peach pit, already a sign of the psychically rooted weakness that will overcome his nephew Hanno). When, in response to a family conversation about business that he does not understand, Christian wishes "I were a businessman too," his brother gives back: "Right, you want to be something different every day." Indeed Christian never becomes a poet, or anything else, merely growing more preoccupied and unworldly as time goes on (the fate Pyat also predicted for those infected with "artistism"); later he attributes his weakness and illness to having nerves that are "too short on one side," leaving him unable to connect to the world. Thomas grows more critical of him over the years, but from early on he admits to having experienced a similar "preoccupation with one's self" at times too; this he struggles to overcome, so as to "sit ourselves down and accomplish something, just as our forefathers did" but with less and less success as time goes on, taking on something of his brother's concern for making things appear in a certain way as he loses his power to act effectively, so that he gives off signs of the family's fate before Hanno becomes its bearer.[12]

There is another dimension to this concern for show in Mann's work, namely overt attempts to create or "keep up" appearances, a phenomenon often associated with bourgeois life by its observers and critics. This theme takes on a sinister tonality in the person of Herr Grünlich, whose successful campaign to wed Tony, one of Thomas's and Christian's two sisters, is revealed to have been a stratagem on the part of an unscrupulous speculator to enlist the Buddenbrook family's name and resources to cover his debts and carry on his risky deals. His failure contributes to the family's decline, and highlights the dangers lurking in the bourgeois need to extend trust and confidence to associ-ates about whom it may be difficult to acquire reliable information, especially at a distance. In Grünlich's case Tony's father Johann made the usual inquiries about him, only to learn later that those to whom he turned were in on the scam, creditors of his prospective son-in-law who hoped the marriage would help them recoup their loans.[13] The problem of confidence between relative strangers (which as we saw earlier was an ingredient of the bourgeois emphasis on "char-acter"), and the masquerades undertaken in order to create it, drew much attention in the nineteenth-century. One notable instance was the American writer Herman Melville's novel *The Confidence Man*, whose title figure appears in a series of shifting disguises as he sells shares in nonexistent companies on a Mississippi River steamboat; a later example is Mann's own *Felix Krull, Confidence Man*, whose hero is at once a swindler and a symbol of the artist, about whom Mann wrote (calling up the Nietzschean notion that "reality" itself is an appearance): "He has learnt hoodwinking from the world and makes himself into an ideal, a stimulus to life, a power of seduction vis-à-vis the world ... and she falls into his trap."[14] The Buddenbrook family itself was seldom much concerned with strategies for keeping up appearances (for most of their history they did not have to be), but as Thomas's powers wane he worries more about the face he presents to the world, and Mann finds much that is theatrical in their life, at one point recounting how little Hanno (who like his uncle Christian is entranced by the theater), wandering through a room in the family's new house after others have left, "found a strange delight in roaming about as if this were a half-darkened stage after the curtain had fallen and he could peek behind the scenery."[15] The author of *Buddenbrooks* fully recognized the kinship in bourgeois life and in himself between the tendencies Thomas sought to embody and those that drew Christian toward bohemia.

Artists, markets, and the painting of bourgeois life

Murger's bohemia and Mann's world of burghers were not the only sites where the affinity between bourgeois life and the life of art was displayed; the sphere of productive and recognized artists exhibited it too. I noted in Chapter 12 that the shift from the various forms of personal and official patronage on which artists and writers had long relied toward market relations was – despite what has often been written – welcomed by many figures in modern culture. And, as we saw, the various Secession movements of the end of the nineteenth century all had close ties to art dealers and gallery owners, who were perfectly capable of using the impressionist idiom of independence and pure devotion to art as marketing slogans.[16]

The widely diffused view that a conservative public of viewers and buyers kept its finger in the dike of stability to hold back the disturbing flood of creative innovation describes some parts of the cultural landscape to be sure, but as Leo Steinberg pointed out some time ago, resistance to change came from within the ranks of practicing artists too, and not only backward-looking ones. Modern art, by moving constantly on from one form of expression to another, asks us "to discard visual habits which have been acquired in the contemplation of real masterpieces," giving birth to "a feeling that one's accumulated culture or experience is hopelessly devalued, leaving one exposed to spiritual destitution." Attending an exhibition in 1868, the romantic poet and novelist Théophile Gautier found that remembering how he and his generation had passed through the public's earlier condemnation of their work (including his own novel of 1835, shocking to many, *Mademoiselle de Maupin*) to a state of greater acceptance was not enough to prepare him for the new art then on view: being confronted with "Courbet, Manet, Monet, and *tutti quanti*" set him on edge. "One feels one's pulse in something of a panic, one puts one's hand on one's belly and on one's head to reassure oneself that one hasn't become stout or bald, incapable of understanding the courage and daring of youth," and he confessed himself uncertain "whether it is in fact possible to understand any art other than that with which one is contemporary, that is to say the art with which one shared one's twentieth birthday." The critic Jules Laforgue, defending the impressionists in 1883, admitted that the new painting was bound to bewilder and exasperate viewers whose perceptual armature had been formed around other styles; his expectation that they would accuse it of "willful eccentricity" was not far from the judgment that Zola, twenty years older than when he had defended Manet in 1867, provided in his novel *The Masterpiece* (*L'Oeuvre*), where a painter partly modeled on Manet and Cézanne, and on Balzac's Frenhofer, declined into isolation and derangement.[17]

That even artists identified with innovation found reasons to sympathize with those who resisted or rejected it adds a dimension of significance to the recent demonstration that between the two camps of progressive and academic art into which scholars have chiefly divided the modern cultural landscape there existed a vigorous and fertile middle ground, which Robert Jensen labels the *juste milieu*. The tag applies to such artists as Jules Bastien-Lepage, Carolus Duran, John Singer Sargent, James MacNeill Whistler, James Tissot, and others, whose widespread and continuing appeal Jensen attributes to their ability to combine "the semblance of modernity with the accessibility [and] the narrative and pictorial coherence of the academic tradition." Some of these figures, Sargent and Whistler for instance, were subjected to derision of the sort visited on the impressionists and members of later avant-garde movements, and much art-historical writing has put them in this company. But it was chiefly their interest in modern events and experiences, together with an occasional aesthetic provocation such as Whistler's early *White*

Girl, or a willingness to straddle moral boundaries as Sargent did in his *Portrait of Madame X* (to whose falling shoulder-strap and the scandal it provoked we alluded briefly in our discussion of morality) that inspired such judgments; engaged observers at the time roundly rejected them. Huysmans, in his early career a champion of the impressionists, insisted that an "unfathomable abyss" separated genuine members of the group such as Degas and Gustave Caillebotte from the likes of Bastien-Lepage; but Caillebotte, who was an important collector as well as an innovative painter, rejected even some candidates Degas was willing to accept as colleagues, such as Jean-François Raffaelli.[18] Just who ought to be assigned to which camp does not really concern us here; the point is that the line between tradition and innovation was uncertain and smudged even within what count as advanced artistic circles. This was particularly true within the group canonized as the impressionists, as Caillebotte's disagreement with Degas suggests; some of Monet's early pictures (for instance of gardens populated by beautifully clothed and comfortable figures) were both easy to read and affirmative in spirit, and (as Robert Herbert has pointed out) Renoir, whose lower-middle-class origins sometimes found expression in a style that emphasized the artisan-like materiality of paint, often depicted bourgeois scenes and especially the women in them with a longing rooted in his exclusion from their society, "as though he had his nose pressed to the window of the upper-class world," in contrast to the ironic distance the solidly bourgeois Manet put between himself and his subjects.[19]

Just how permeable was the line between aesthetic innovation and more conservative practice only becomes clear when we recognize that it sometimes ran inside the work of individual artists. This was eminently the case for Degas, as we can see by attending to a pair of pictures he made of a single subject. The two works are especially significant here because they illuminate at once the existence of these different possibilities inside impressionism, and the school's relationship to bourgeois existence. The pictures both depict the cotton-trading office in New Orleans of which Degas's uncle Michel Musson was a principal partner. Degas went there with his brother René in 1872 on a visit to relatives, especially his other brother Achille, who worked in the firm and who had married his widowed cousin, Musson's daughter (a common pattern among nineteenth-century bourgeois). One of the works, *Cotton Merchants in New Orleans*, is now in the Fogg

Museum at Harvard (Figure 1), the other, *Portraits in an Office (New Orleans)*, is in the Musée des Beaux Arts of Pau in southwestern France (Figure 2). Despite their common subject, the two pictures are strikingly different. Much of the space in the Fogg canvas (considerably smaller than the other) is taken up by a table covered in cotton, rendered in a way that makes it appear almost cloud-like; three disconnected figures appear in the upper half, one leaning into the table with his hands in the white substance, one at a small distance holding some, the third, just at one edge of the table, a mere profile emerging from behind a wall where hangs a partially visible print of a ship. The whole is "impressionistic" in a literal way (although the term was not yet in vogue in 1873); sketch-like and blurry in detail, it captures a moment more through the uncertain mood produced by its fuzzy surfaces and the unspecified relations of the figures than through any possible narrative of what is taking place. The other picture, now at Pau, although evidently of the same room (the print of the ship appears here too) makes a clear contrast. "In it," as Degas wrote in a letter, "there are about fifteen individuals more or less busy with a table covered with the precious material and two men, one half leaning and the other half sitting on it, the buyer and the broker, are discussing the sample." The scene is rendered in clear detail, with numerous identifiable figures. Degas's uncle Michel Musson sits in the foreground, examining a piece of cotton stretched between his hands (taken from a larger quantity on a chair to his right); his brother Achille leans against an interior window wall at the left edge, observing the goings-on, while René (who had earlier worked with Musson too) perches on a chair reading a newspaper just to the right of the picture's center. Other figures either look on or busy themselves with account or record books.[20]

Although Degas did the two pictures at nearly the same time, he saw them in different terms, characterizing the Fogg picture as "less complicated and more spontaneous, of a better art, where people are in summer dress, white walls, a sea of cotton on the tables." What likely made it "better" in his eyes was this simplicity and spontaneity, which kept it at a greater distance from the traditional academic ideals of "finish" and narrative coherence. Zola fleshed out the negative implications of such a standard for the Pau picture when he disapprovingly called it "bourgeois" after seeing it at the second impressionist exhibition in 1876. To Zola, Degas's best work was in his sketches: "As soon as he begins to polish a picture, his drawing grows weak and pitiable;

Illustration 1 Degas, *Cotton Merchants in New Orleans*

Illustration 2 Degas, *Portraits in an Office (New Orleans)*

the drawing in pictures like his *Portraits in an Office (New Orleans)* results in something between a marine painting and an engraving for an illustrated newspaper." Such a view (set down ten years before *L'Oeuvre*'s much more skeptical account of impressionist innovation), draws Degas toward the *juste milieu* painters with whom he sometimes had friendly relations: it was to Tissot in London that he wrote the descriptions of the New Orleans work quoted here. But the art critic and longtime friend of Degas, Edmond Duranty, found the work's subject matter and composition to be perfectly in accord with the aims of impressionism as he set them out in his book *The New Painting*:

> What we need are the special characteristics of the
> modern individual – in his clothing, in social situations, at
> home, or on the street ... It is the study of states of mind
> reflected by physiognomy and clothing, the observation
> of the relationships of a man to his apartment, or of
> the particular influence of his profession on him, of all
> the aspects of the environment in which he evolves and
> develops, as reflected in the gestures he makes ... The
> individual will be at a piano, examining a sample of
> cotton in an office, waiting in the wings for the moment
> to go on stage, or ironing on a trestle table.

All these were Degas's subjects, so that Duranty here presented him as what Baudelaire called a "painter of modern life," a title the poet had awarded precisely to a magazine illustrator, Contantin Guys, and which many observers attached to the impressionists, for reasons to which we will come in a moment. First, however, we need to ask what image of modern bourgeois life *Portraits in an Office* projected.[21]

Influential writers who have taken up this question emphasize the dissociated qualities of the scene. Robert Herbert quotes with approval Rudolf Arnheim's assessment that we are here confronted with "the atomization of society in an age of individualism ... No over-all constellation holds the crowd together, and hence there is no limit to the changes that may occur in the relationships between the participants." It is certainly true that very little direct interaction takes place between the people portrayed, all but two of whom (the buyer and broker at the table) seem to be preoccupied with some matter in which no one else participates. But this is in no way the whole story.

In the first place, relationships between the participants are far from indeterminate: we, like the painter, know that three of the figures belong to the same family (one of them married to his cousin). We recall that family relationships remained central to both business and personal life in this period, creating ties both cherished and bemoaned whose significance requires that we give less credence to the long-held image of bourgeois life as radically individualist; here the scene simply would not exist did it not rest on the triangle formed by the two Degas brothers and their uncle (cum father-in-law).

Second, all the participants bear some relationship to the enterprise of the Musson firm, which like others functioned precisely by giving unity to tasks that might appear to have no relation to each other. Herbert cites Simmel as a reference point for the abstract and indifferent nature of the social relations he finds in the picture: the centrality of money turned many interactions into matters of impersonal calculation.[22] True enough, but Simmel's analysis had another crucial side, in its focus on the ways that markets and other mediated relationships allow people to synthesize multiple distant ties and connections, creating long "chains of purposive action" through which individuals can gather and concentrate resources, pursuing and achieving personal and collective ends impossible without them. Such frames of action draw people together in ways different from traditional communities; some of their binding threads are less visible on the everyday surface because they stretch beyond local horizons and only come together inside people's heads; but they rest on concrete material relations all the same. *Portraits in an Office* makes numerous references to such linkages. The most obvious is the newspaper René reads at the scene's center, a nodal point in a web of information on both business and many other matters of interest to the scene's participants, and as good a symbol of the world to which such ties are central as one could wish. Less prominent but not to be missed is the image of a ship on the wall in the background, in its way a medium of the same kinds of links (Marilyn Brown thinks it may be a Confederate ship, and therefore a reference to the loyalty of the Musson family to the south in the Civil War, but even if this could be demonstrated the ship would still call up the firm's international connections, many of which were with northern English manufacturers and merchants). Then there are the many references to the firm's relations with its clients, the cotton growers for whom it largely served as an agent, some of whom were hundreds of miles from New Orleans: the records of transactions in the envelopes stacked on shelves at the rear, the record books to which the two figures on the picture's extreme right give attention, and the blue letter atop one of them. Finally, the picture stages a complex interplay of internal and external relations. The opening to a world outside highlighted by the newspaper is echoed in the window at the rear center, and reinforced by the wall of interior windows to its left. These elements of the scene were simply there, to be sure, but this does not prevent them from underlining the point that all the goings-on inside the office at once draw on, draw together, and animate its active connection to the complex movements of people, means, and products outside.

Although it may not be possible to draw up a balance sheet for the mix of dissociation and connection the picture calls up, there are good reasons for thinking that Degas himself did not think the first more significant than the second. Among them is his expressed hope to sell the canvas to some rich cotton manufacturer or merchant. His involvement in the commercial dimension of his work seems to have been deepened by living with his American relatives. Put off at first by finding himself in a place where business was the dominant subject of conversation, he yet admired his brother's ability to talk the talk (as Christian Buddenbrook did in regard to Thomas), ending up writing to Tissot that "Here I have acquired the taste for money, and once back I shall know how to earn some, I assure you." These words came at a moment when the Degas family finances were still strong and healthy, but they would cease to be so a year later, following the death of Edgar's banker father, leaving him with a much greater need to gain income on his own (and perhaps contributing to the sour mood he often displayed in his later life). The New Orleans letters suggest he already knew much about the market for pictures in England (where, as Diane Macleod has shown, there was a much livelier middle-class interest in contemporary art than has often been supposed), since they refer both to Durand-Ruel's London agent Deschamps, and to the Manchester picture dealer Thomas Agnew, who worked with collectors such as Henry Fairbairn and was important in assembling the "monster exhibition" of art treasures mounted there in 1857. Degas even named one Manchester manufacturer whom he knew to be a collector (although he misspelled his name, "Cottrell" for Cottrill) as a possible buyer of one or both of his New Orleans pictures, "for if a spinner ever wished to find his painter, he really ought to snap me up."

Illustration 3 Degas, *Portraits at the Stock Exchange*

The hoped-for sales did not come through, and it is perhaps possible that even a highly finished and easily readable canvas such as *Portraits in an Office* might have disturbed a potential buyer by reason of the dissociative qualities Herbert and Arnheim see in it; but it is just as likely that a person acquainted with the inside of a business office would recognize the ability of seemingly disparate activities to contribute to a coherent goal, as well as knowing how much business in the time rested on family relationships, even without being able to identify

507 / Artists, markets, and bourgeois life

the actual individuals in this one. Another of Degas's images of businessmen, *Portraits at the Stock Exchange* of 1879 (Illustration 3), provides what many might regard as an unflattering portrait of the investor Ernest May, listening over his shoulder as an associate whispers information to him, but May was a longtime friend and supporter of Degas, and bought the picture.[23]

One last aspect of the New Orleans canvasses needs to be noted. Although Degas may not have been explicitly aware of it, the scene given with such detail in *Portraits in an Office* depicted a mode of doing business that was about to disappear. Michel Musson and his partner were a firm of cotton factors, middlemen between growers and buyers. Mostly they worked one-on-one with the former, providing them with credit, purchasing supplies for them, and – the most speculative aspect of the business – buying the crops, often before they were harvested, and then selling them to brokers who in turn sent the material on to manufacturers such as the one Degas hoped might buy his picture (the Buddenbrook family business involved a similar relationship to rye growers in Germany). But the disruptions brought about by the American Civil War became the catalyst for the rise of a different system, in which individual factors such as the Musson firm yielded their importance to large-scale cotton exchanges operated by a multitude of agents. One reason for this shift was the demise of the old slavery-based plantation system, which led to an expansion of both sharecropping and of landowners who subdivided and rented out their holdings instead of farming them directly. The cotton exchanges served the needs of this larger number of smaller producers, who now sought credit not from factors but from the spreading number of banks, and operated in a market restructured by telegraphy and railroad shipping. The mid 1870s were the time of this transition (sped on by the disruptions in markets brought by the American Civil War and, in France, by the loss of Alsace to Germany in 1870), and in New Orleans some who had worked as factors, including Musson, were active in setting up and running the new exchange.[24] The move from the first to the second of these ways of doing business was part of the larger late nineteenth-century transformation in which forms of commerce and politics based on direct relationships between individuals gave way to more abstract and impersonal ones; the turn by Musson and his partners to the new cotton exchange was not unlike the absorption of traditional notables into modern political parties.

What is particularly significant about this transition here is that many features of impressionism as a recognizable school and style reflected it too, including both the way Durand-Ruel sought to organize the emerging and increasingly international market for new art, and characteristic qualities of the painting itself. That this was so has been especially and justly emphasized by Robert Herbert in the book to which we have already referred. Herbert highlights the close connection between the subjects and even the style of impressionist pictures and the transformation of Paris under the Second Empire. Not only do many impressionist streetscapes and urban scenes depict the new boulevards, squares, and parks opened up by the reconstruction (other favorite subjects were the suburban spaces of weekend leisure made accessible by railroads); the signal flooding of scenes with light and air and the new techniques developed to evoke it (such as painting on a white rather than a dark ground) reflect the change in urban atmosphere effected by the rebuilding, evident in the contrast between such images and the much darker urban scenes portrayed by romantic artists a few decades before.[25] Behind this mutation lay the shift Jeanne Gaillard describes from an urban lifestyle characterized by stability and "introversion" to one of mobility and "extraversion": many impressionist scenes call up a city of people in motion through the new streets, living their lives along the arteries that gave Paris a closer integration as a site for both business and pleasure, while simultaneously providing access to the railroad stations that gave it more rapid and effective access to the world outside.[26]

The resulting forms of experience became crucial elements of nineteenth-century modernism, and Herbert cites canvasses by several artists as exemplary of them. In Manet's *The Railway* of 1873 (Illustration 4), the title seems to refer only to a smoky presence in the background, visible through an iron fence; we find ourselves face to face with a young woman looking up from the book in her lap, seated next to a standing little girl who turns her back to us in order to look through the bars at the train yard. We appear to have interrupted the young woman's reading, forcing us "to recognize ourselves as that characteristic city dweller, the unknown passer-by ... It is the encounter of one stranger with others, one of those chance meetings that mark the modern city." Our inability to know how the two figures are related to each other (parent and child, sisters, caretaker and charge?) "reinforces the idea that we have simply happened upon them." Simmel recognized just this mixture of physical proximity and psychological distance as characteristic of

Illustration 4 Manet, *The Railway*

modern city life; one result might be a certain indifference and neutrality, but another was to allow individuals to invest others and the surroundings where they encountered them with imagined meanings that play a role in forming a sense of self. By making the railroad part of the scene and putting it in the title, Manet calls up the role it played in offering distant places as generators of both desire and imagination.[27]

The attempt to capture such moments, representative of what Baudelaire called "our more abstract modern life," inspired other paintings of the time, well illustrated by Gustave Caillebotte's *The Man at the Window* (Figure 5). Here a male figure inside an elegant apartment looks down into a square to observe a woman crossing it; rendered tiny by the effect of distance, she appears as "curiously vulnerable," her "fragile aloneness" heightening the scene's psychic import by enhancing her availability as a target of fantasy projection. The recognition that such experiences fed a specifically modern form of imagination, calling attention to the fluidity of both outer and inner experience, is evident in another railroad picture from the mid 1870s, Monet's *Gare St-Lazare* (Figure 6). Here we find ourselves inside the train shed, surrounded by recognizable objects (and human figures) that have all the same lost their clear outlines, partly through the effect of steam and partly from the patterns of sunlight and shadow. We do not know whether the engine to the left is leaving or entering the station, but the painter has provided (as Herbert notes) "a symmetrical, measured composition" that creates a kind of balance between the contained finitude of the scene and the way the many blurred objects and boundaries allow us to imagine things only implied or alluded to in it.[28] The near-reduction of a nameable and bounded prospect to a play of uncertain and suggestive shapes and colors goes beyond what we find in the smaller and more "impressionistic" of Degas's two cotton office pictures; it seems to point forward to Monet's own later images of water-lilies, to Cezanne's proto-cubist figures and landscapes, and more generally to the trajectory that would draw modernist painting toward the decomposition of objects and the turn to abstraction as a vehicle for rendering states of mind and feeling not susceptible to being directly depicted.

Toward the avant-garde

In the succession of movements that led from the mid century modernism of the impressionists to the revolutionary stance for which Breton

Illustration 5 Caillebotte, *Man at the Window*

called, the alternative he set up between an aesthetic that countenanced stability and one devoted to pure fluidity often made an explicit appearance. The two poles were self-consciously united by the poet whose fascination with the modern city as inspiration and subject gave

Illustration 6 Monet, *The Gare St-Lazare*

him close relations to the impressionists, Charles Baudelaire; but well before the century's end this mixture was being challenged by projects that pointed toward Breton's rejection of "all that is solid." Only a few years after Marx invoked this formula, Baudelaire defined the modern as "the ephemeral, the fugitive, the contingent." It was the task of "The Painter of Modern Life" to represent this mobility, but Baudelaire was never drawn to conceiving artistic expression in its terms alone. Beauty always had another component, "an eternal, invariable element" best expressed by "classical poets and artists," to whom he remained tied by virtue of his devotion to formal perfection and linguistic precision. Not for him the romantic aesthetic of spontaneity espoused by the bohemian likes of Murger, whose equation of art with the life lived in its name justified their refusal or inability to "submit themselves to any training. They do not know that genius (if indeed one can name the indefinable seed of the great man in this way) must, like the apprentice acrobat, risk breaking his bones a thousand times in private before dancing for the public; that imagination, in a word, is only the reward of daily practice." Baudelaire was all the same permanently drawn to the world of flux and instability he rejected in these places, praising the illustrator Guys for immersing himself in the ever-changing life of the city, for setting up house "in the heart of the multitude, amid the ebb and flow of movement, in the midst of the fugitive and the infinite," and at one point glorifying the bohemianism he derided at others, calling it "the cult of multiplied sensation."[29]

That these were contradictory positions was in no way lost on Baudelaire; they were the contradictions that modern life imposed on the artist who would be its observer and interpreter. Perhaps his best attempt to combine the two sides was an entry in his diary *My Heart Laid Bare*: "On the vaporization and centralization of the *Self* [*Moi*]. Everything is here." Being a modern artist required a twofold operation like the one through which water is distilled of its impurities, first heating up the ego to the point of evaporation, so that it expands into the world of objects and takes on their shape, then a cooling return that allows it to give stable expression to what it encountered in moments of self-loss. Baudelaire's attempts to be such an artist have much in common with the impressionist pictures we considered a moment ago. In both, the exploration of modernity and of the imaginative life for which it provided new spaces went hand in hand, so that modern art, as he put it, was "a suggestive magic containing at once the object and the subject, the world outside the artist and the artist himself." It was just this combination that many later modernists and vanguard artists would seek to dismantle, in order to give freer rein to imaginative energies by themselves, released from the constraints imposed by both material conditions and by the kind of continuing commitment to formal perfection Baudelaire maintained.[30]

The paradigmatic example of this more radical stance was the program of visionary poetics imagined by the young Arthur Rimbaud. Rimbaud saw Baudelaire as his principal predecessor, and nurtured his prodigious talent in part on the older poet's work, but he sought to free himself from the limits Baudelaire had imposed on imagination through what Rimbaud called his "small-minded (*mesquine*)" attachment to form. In a famous pair of letters written in the spring of 1871 (but published only on the eve of World War I), Rimbaud offered a tortured intensification of the Baudelairean-bohemian "cult of multiplied sensation," reporting that "I'm degrading myself as much as possible now. Why? I want to be a poet, and I am working to make myself a *seer* [*voyant*] ... To arrive at the unknown through the derangement of *all the senses*, that's the point." Elaborating his aim in the second letter he explained that "The poet makes himself a seer by a long, immense and methodical *disordering* of *all his senses*." The instruments of this *dérèglement* were "all the forms of love, suffering and madness" plus "all the poisons" (like Baudelaire he turned to alcohol and drugs to stoke his imaginative fires); the result was an "ineffable torture" that required deep faith and superhuman force to survive. What was merely personal turned to vapor at this temperature, overcome by universal powers and forces whose presence showed that (in a famous revolt against grammar) "je est un autre" – the "I" is other to itself.

The visionary who was to emerge from this tormenting baptism was no mere scribbler of verses; his vocation was to renew life. A new Promethean "thief of fire," the poet would give humanity access to visions and powers unknown before, revitalizing existence. Everything would grow new under the sun of his imagination – even love would be "re-invented." Whereas the great poets of antiquity had merely "given rhythm to action," the new poetry would be ahead of life, *en avant*, "truly *a multiplier of progress!*" In order to make it such the poet had to abandon the traditional concern for formal beauty or coherence: "If what he brings back has form, he gives it form, if it is formless, he gives it formlessness." Rimbaud's own poems were in no way formless, but the visionary program they sought to embody burdened their author with what he soon came to see as near-delusional faith in the reality of his metaphorical transformations. "I habituated myself to simple hallucination: I very sincerely saw a mosque where there was a factory, a school of drummers made up of angels, carriages on the roads of heaven," and "I ended up considering the disorder of my mind sacred." Facing the consequences of putting himself into such a state was one reason why Rimbaud gave up writing poetry while still in his twenties and fled Europe, passing briefly through Indonesia before ending up for some years in North Africa where he worked as a commercial agent dealing in coffee and weapons. Both his letters describing the poet-seer and his abandonment of poetry would later be celebrated by the surrealists as a foreshadowing of their still more programmatic attempt to replace the traditional image of the artist with one dedicated to releasing the powers once confined inside the aesthetic sphere, and thus to infuse life with utopian imagination. Rimbaud's project gave a new dimension to the formula for modern consciousness Marx had rooted in the bourgeois revelation of the potential previously hidden in human energy and activity: as "[a]ll that is solid melts into air" a new kind of knowledge of life and destiny emerges, but the "sober senses" Marx saw as taking in the result had given way to boundaryless intoxication. And the outcome pointed to dangers in the avant-garde faith in modern self-transcendence that many inspired by it have not been willing to admit.[31]

A strikingly similar progression from an artist dedicated at once to stability and to fluidity to one for whom the substance of aesthetic practice inhered in a radical and even violent commitment to the bursting of clear limits took place a generation later in Vienna, in the careers of Gustav Klimt and Oscar Kokoschka. Because Carl Schorske has given detailed and insightful accounts of both in his celebrated *Fin-de-Siècle Vienna*, a brief summary of their relationship can suffice here. Klimt's career began and ended with works whose devotion to clarity of outline shines forth, evoking a stability that his subjects still hoped their world preserved. He quickly made his reputation with a decorative canvas for the new Burgtheater that opened in 1888, a group portrait of the fashionable audience in attendance at the auditorium of the old one, showing nearly a hundred casually posed and easily recognizable figures, notables in Viennese politics, business, culture, and high society, and done in a style much like the one Jensen associates

Illustration 7 Klimt, *Auditorium of the "Altes Burgtheater"*

with the *juste milieu* (Illustration 7). His last works, the ones best known today, include luscious and yet highly stylized female images, some portraying upper-class women encased in elaborate dresses. There is an almost Byzantine strictness and formality to these pictures, but also a blurring of boundaries: in some, the mosaic-like construction of the dresses continues into the backgrounds of the paintings, causing figure and ground to merge into each other. This obscuring of outlines seems to confirm the stability of the central subjects, however, rather than threaten it (Illustration 8).

This identification with stability went into eclipse in the works that made Klimt a controversial figure in the years around 1900, the panels he produced as decorations for the new University of Vienna. Allegorical representations of the faculties of medicine, philosophy, and law, these pictures turned him from a favorite of the public to an object of widespread suspicion and hostility. Here all is flux and motion, qualities difficult to reconcile with academic claims to be the fount of

Illustration 8 Klimt, *Portrait of Adele Bloch-Bauer I*

stable, communicable knowledge. Schorske's evocative descriptions can hardly be surpassed. In the philosophy panel (Illustration 9), "the tangled bodies of suffering mankind drift slowly by, suspended aimless in a viscous void. Out of the cosmic murk ... a heavy, sleepy Sphinx looms all unseeing." "Medicine" was represented by a visually similar "phantasmagoria of half-dreaming humanity, sunk in instinctual semi-surrender, passive in the flow of fate ... lost in space."[32] One thing that lay behind these images (and others in Klimt's work we cannot pause to consider) was a fascination with the pessimistic, anti-rationalist philosophy of Arthur Schopenhauer, an interest Klimt shared with other Viennese in his time. Schopenhauer explained the repeated disappointment of human hopes in every realm – love and politics chief among them – by positing a cunning cosmic will that operated beneath the surface of events, an all-powerful but indifferent life force animated by

Illustration 9 Klimt, *Philosophy*

no other aim than its own survival, and which infused individuals with an illusory sense of their own independence in order to employ them as its vehicles, orchestrating the human drama of desire, aspiration, suffering, and death as the theater of its perpetuation. Sexuality was a central element in the will and its work, since it is the desiring body that bears the primal feelings and motions that give expression to life itself, and which join us to the cosmic All. Klimt's depiction of mostly nude bodies, mysteriously linked together and losing their clear outlines in a movement in which all participate but none can direct, called up the philosopher's dark vision. It was Schopenhauer who first inspired Nietzsche's belief – to which Thomas Mann always remained ambivalently drawn – that the artist who knew the stability of the world to be mere appearance possessed a deeper understanding than the rationalists who thought they could grasp items in the sunny clarity of logic, and Klimt's refusal to validate the professors' belief in the reliability of their knowledge was at least partly driven by a similar conviction. Even so he seems never to have wholly abandoned his sense that stability too had a place in art, since it finds expression in the mosaic geometries of his later portraits.[33]

Kokoschka's career would be marked by a turn away from this Baudelaire-like mix, and his case shared a number of features with Rimbaud's. At one point a protégé of Klimt, he aimed to give fuller and more direct expression to the hidden psychic and cosmic energies the former had portrayed in a more muted way, developing a style marked by rough, jagged forms of expression that called up a tense, conflicted, and potentially violent inner realm. The violence found realization in the work he produced in connection with a 1908 exhibition or *Kunstschau* directed by Klimt. Here Kokoschka's subjects were the destructive potential of adolescent sexuality, in a long and sometimes obscure illustrated poem, *The Dreaming Boys*, and the ravaging and fatal outcome of struggles for supremacy between the sexes, in a shockingly raw and blood-soaked play, *Murderer, the Hope of Women*. Later Kokoschka would pursue the search for the dissolving powers at work in the interior of individuals through a remarkable series of psychological portraits, in which the subjects seem to vibrate with a kind of galvanic force, an inner energy at once erotic and spiritual, and which supplied the artist with his vision at the same time that it gave life to his subjects. Stability is not wholly absent here, but it is pregnant with its own dissolution. In a double portrait of himself with

his lover Alma Mahler, Kokoschka pictured at once their union and
their separation: her calm restfulness contrasts with his rigid and tense
wakefulness, generating a complex force-field of attraction and repul-
sion that gave rise to the "Tempest" of their relations denoted in the
work's title, and carrying the couple toward what Peter Vergo seems
correct to regard as a kind of oblivion (Illustration 10).[34]

When André Breton called for the avant-garde to organize
itself around pure fluidity and thus cure itself of the "fixation mania"
that had impeded its efforts to release creative energy into the world,
he did not recognize his appeal as an echo of the moves that separated Rimbaud from Baudelaire and Kokoschka from Klimt, but both
sequences show that the impulses he sought to draw on and inten-
sify had long been at work. It would be wrong to claim too close a
connection between these recurring turns to fluidity by writers and
artists and the desires and impulses generated through relations with
everyday objects invoked at the beginning of this chapter, but the
link was palpably present in Klimt's milieu; he belonged to a group
within the Vienna Secession that sought to embellish and enrich life
by joining the "high" arts of painting and sculpture to craft products
including pottery, furniture, clothing, and books, thus creating living
spaces whose contents would infuse them with the qualities of imagination and fantasy of which art was the bearer. The *Kunstschau* of
1908 was a project of these artists, and the continuity its director's late
portraits established between elegant clothing and artful forms was
part of it. But the avant-garde work that most clearly made the connection between the world of commodities and the unquenchable desires
whose promise and threat to dissolve all stable boundaries radical art
sought to inherit was a French one, the surrealist Louis Aragon's *Paris
Peasant (Le Paysan de Paris)* of 1924.

Here most of the action takes place in an enclosed shopping
arcade, the *Passage de L'Opéra*, one of numerous such spaces opened
up in Paris during the first half of the nineteenth century. Aragon's
focus on them as peculiarly revelatory of modern life's potential for
self-transcendence would inspire Walter Benjamin to make them central to his more massive and theoretically ambitious attempt to portray nineteenth-century Paris as a repository of revolutionary promise.
The arcades had been important vehicles for expanding the consumer
goods market in the early nineteenth century, but their role was largely
usurped by the department stores that became prominent after 1850,

Illustration 10 Kokoschka, *The Tempest (Bride of the Wind)*

so that Aragon's locale was a remnant of a Paris receding into the past. Quaint, dark, and vulnerable, its days were numbered because the continuing reconstruction of the city along lines begun under Haussmann meant it was slated for imminent demolition. But that was just the point: not only was the *Passage* a transitional space, a symbol of urban life as a congeries of connections between separate and distant sites and things, it was itself proof of the instability and ephemerality of modern life. This made the arcade a peculiarly appropriate location for the dream-like experiences fostered by its shadowy, somewhat decayed, often mysterious, and suspect interior. Being inside it turns the writer into the urban equivalent of the gaping, astonished countryman overwhelmed at the mysterious powers lodged in the world.

Aragon (or his first-person narrator) first encounters the place's mysterious power in a shop selling umbrellas and canes, many extravagantly decorated, bearing animal heads with jewel-like eyes, "foliage, cats, women, hooked beaks, countless materials," the lot arranged in fan-like or crossed displays. Having spent an evening at a café table opposite the shop's window, swallowing drinks while waiting for a person who did not turn up, Aragon arises to leave just as the arcade's lights were being switched off (the place was gated up at night). In his tipsy and irritated state the darkened cane-and-umbrella shop suddenly becomes a phantasmagoric scene, bathed in an iridescent light and giving forth a sound like sea-shells; an ocean rolls in, with a swimmer who turns out to be a woman he had encountered some years earlier in another country. Then, as suddenly as it came, the vision fades away. Other establishments breed other ephemeral fantasies, so that by the end the *Passage* has become "a method of freeing myself of certain inhibitions, a means of obtaining access to a hitherto forbidden realm." Its true name rears up as on a fantasized street sign, "Passage de L'Opéra Onirique," "Arcade of the Opera of Dreams." For Aragon it provides a site from which to promote his own commodity, surrealism, a product put into circulation by enemies of order under "the anodyne pretext of literature," which "allows them to offer you at a rock-bottom bargain price this deadly ferment which it is high time to make generally available for consumption."

The exploration of the arcade concluded, he tells us that "the modern world is the one that weds itself to my ways of being": its constant undermining of permanence promises a great crisis that will leave no certainties standing, making contemporary life into "one moment of an eternal fall." Aragon proposed to construct a new mythology for this modernity, one whose tutelary divinities would be symbols of its peculiar powers of self-transcendence. Among them were gasoline pumps with their brashly colored "luminous, faceless heads," bearing mysterious dials with foreign and invented words, metallic counterparts to the stone ones "of Egypt or of cannibal tribes who adored only war. O Texaco motor oil, Eco, Shell, great inscriptions of human potentiality."[35] Aragon, it should be noted, saw himself as an enemy of bourgeois life; later he would be one of the few surrealists to remain inside the Communist Party after Breton and most of the others ended their brief flirtation with it. But like Marx he could not avoid the recognition that the transformative power of modernity to which he appealed was a product of the very bourgeois world for whose overcoming he worked, and that the energies that promised to turn it into a realm of pure fluidity had to be sought inside it.

Aesthetic autonomy and the temptation of modernity

The kinship between artists and bourgeois life visible beneath the hostility that often marked their surface relations, and that we have considered on the plane of ideas in this chapter, has been examined in a more sociological light by a recent German historian. The proclaimed opposition between artists and burghers, Dieter Hein observes, owed much to modernity's heightened segmentation of tasks; it was "a mirror image of the rapidly developing process of differentiation that took place both inside the *Bürgertum* and inside the realm of artists." Like professionals in law, medicine, or academic disciplines, artists and their close collaborators sought to organize and oversee their activities on their own, rendering themselves independent of the people and principles that had formerly claimed authority over them. This they did by constituting the realm of art and judgments about it as "a concern of professionals, artists, critics, museum directors, art-historians, gallery owners and patrons. Artists and bourgeois were much closer to each other in their professionalization than may appear from their conflicting claims about the meaning and position of art in society. Their distance from each other was like that which obtains for all occupations in the modern world of differentiated work."[36] Hein's description corresponds in a general way to the "aesthetic sphere" Max Weber regarded as one instance of the rationalization by which different forms of modern activity organize themselves according to their own standards and principles, and for which Kant already provided a theoretical basis in the 1790s, but it also applies in a more emphatic way to the organized system that emerged through the association between artists, dealers, and critics set up by Paul Durand-Ruel in the 1870s and the various Secession organizations of the 1890s that drew inspiration from him, followed by the sequence of vanguard movements Breton sought to supercede by drawing on Duchamp's example. Breton's taking Duchamp's turn to "readymades" as a liberation from the series of collective stylistic programs through which the avant-garde had developed points up an important difference between art and the other realms with which Hein compares it, namely the potential orientation toward pure individual autonomy it always bore, and of which Kant's theory of the genius and Duchamp's program of giving himself as an artist the right to name any object as his work were successive realizations. Duchamp's abolition of the boundary between objects that were "art" by virtue of meeting some specific set of aesthetic criteria and the much wider range of ordinary things of everyday use was another way of accomplishing the goal Breton also attributed to Picasso, namely "to render the exterior object adequate to his desire," just the project pursued earlier – and in a way that more clearly revealed its dangers – by Huysmans's hero Des Esseintes.[37]

This way of defining the realm of art belonged to a sequence whose overall trajectory we can plot in three historical moments. Its point of departure was the pre-modern assumption that art was to be judged by extra-aesthetic – ordained or teleocratic – standards, religious, moral, or social, shifting then to the successive forms of autonomy represented first by the notion of "art as such," where independent but shared and in principle objective aesthetic standards were employed to judge and place works, to end in the more radical Duchampian claim that art was whatever those individuals able to achieve recognition as artists declared it to be. Of these three moments, the second corresponded to the early extension and thickening of networks of means characteristic of the period before the middle of the nineteenth century; it brought the heightened public presence of culture represented by the rise of museums and public concerts and the networks of newspapers and periodicals that linked them to each other and to audiences, but in conjunction with the persistence of official salons and the hierarchy of genres that privileged "history painting," along with "benefit concerts" and traditional forms of musical patronage, all testimony to the long survival of old relations and assumptions. The third moment arrived in the railroad age, alongside the spread of modern industry and new-style political parties, whose more formal and articulated modes of organization found their artistic counterparts in Durand-Ruel's innovations and the Secession movements. All along this path the potential redefinition of the artist in modernity as living a certain kind of life rather than producing a distinct class of things was kept alive in bohemia, home to the kinship between artistic innovation and bourgeois life's inherent potential for fluid self-transcendence Murger evoked in his formula: "their everyday life is a work of genius." It was this potential that Duchamp realized by redefining the artist not as a maker of objects but as a happy inhabitant of the mobile modern world that Aragon equally embraced for its unstable, shifting connections and chance encounters. Putting the history of the avant-garde in this perspective locates it properly within the history of bourgeois life, and is a reminder that neither was able to bring about the utopian transformation its radical fluidity seemed to promise.

15 CONCLUSION

Spontaneity and structure

Marx and the avant-garde figures we have just considered were not wrong to see radical fluidity as a distinguishing feature of modernity. The dizzying pace of change that confronts twenty-first century people in so many realms fits the formula "all that is solid melts into air" very well. But what fuels the accelerating speed with which even newly created practices and expectations are left behind or cast aside is not any overall weakening in the structures within which individuals and groups act – markets, states, webs of communication – but on the contrary their increasing strength and power.[1] We might expect that larger and denser structures would impose a slower rhythm and inhibit the spontaneous actions of the individuals who act within them, and so they do sometimes. But structure and spontaneity may also coexist in a more positive relationship, each feeding off the other. The accounts I have given at various earlier moments point to some reasons why this is so, by providing particular instances of a phenomenon that it is now time to describe in general terms, since it helps to clarify and highlight some central elements of the picture I have been seeking to elaborate here.

As networks of means expand and thicken, they furnish those who have access to them with new resources, opening up opportunities to pursue individual goals and aims for which only various kinds of inherited assets provided sufficient support before. One reason these possibilities can arise is that the networks through which they develop are networks *of means*, that they link people together by way of tools and implements which are themselves vehicles of action. Their thickening extends opportunities to act in ways that have an impact beyond some immediate context to people from a wider range of geographical and social locations. The replacement of inherited resources with ones to which people gain access through distant and mediated connections has taken place in many regions of modern existence, stretching from the economy and politics to culture and morality. Recalling some of the specific instances of this general phenomenon now will allow us both to bring together and flesh out some central points of this book, and to suggest ways in which the lines of historical evolution we have sought to trace have continued into the present.

In economic life the central role played in individual destinies by wealth and social ties passed down within families has contracted as public and private enterprises have come to rely on impersonal institutions for financing and on formal and advanced education to train the specialized personnel they require. The declining significance of family resources has been only relative to be sure, leaving in place many inequalities based on birth and inheritance. But it has gradually brought an end to the situation Sarah Hanley described for the early modern period, many features of which persisted well into the nineteenth century, whereby "membership in a family provided the only means of human survival through networks of influence (marriage alliances, inheritance practices, patronage, and apprentice systems)," and people's "most pressing business" at various social levels "was the maintenance and extension of family networks, which were agencies of both social reproduction and economic production."[2] The lessening importance of family connections of these kinds made itself felt outside the economic sphere, providing an important basis for the developing shift toward a more liberal tone in the linked matters of gender relations and morality evident at the end of the nineteenth century. As people were able to draw more of the resources necessary for survival and advancement from participation in webs of relations that linked not families to other families but individuals to impersonal repositories of tangible and intangible assets, older restrictions that served to shield family continuity against the dangers posed by individuals acting on their own lost some of their rationale. They have continued to lose it since, partly through a gradual and continuous decline and partly through the impact of critical moments such as the 1920s and the

1960s, when particular circumstances weakened the still-considerable power of traditional forces and attitudes, adding impetus to the underlying tendencies toward individual emancipation.

A parallel diminution in the importance of personal resources took place in regard to politics, and in a similar rhythm. The decline of traditional modes of aristocratic dominance from late in the eighteenth century led not to specifically bourgeois forms of power but to the pre-eminence of what recent historians (following people in the time) have called notability. The *grands notables* of 1830s and 1840s France, the *Honoratioren* politics of mid nineteenth-century Germany, the liberal and conservative parties of early nineteenth-century Britain, were all examples of political situations that favored those who brought some set of personal, most often local, resources to them: wealth (often in land), connections, a longstanding family position in a town or region. Political parties in the mid century, even those of Gladstone and Disraeli, were, as Dieter Langewiesche says about Germany, aggregates of "influential persons, linked by a thick [but informal] network of acquaintanceship, associations, and committees of all kinds." The assets such people possessed never wholly lost their value to be sure, but their relative weight diminished as politics became more and more a matter of national parties contending for success in elections; the political power once possessed by loose associations of noteworthy people passed to more tightly knit organizations of mostly anonymous individuals. Notability did not disappear from politics, but it came to depend less on personal position than on party activity; new careers opened up in party administration and political journalism, often to people of modest backgrounds. As in the economy, the extension and thickening of networks widened the scope of opportunities for people with limited resources of their own, reducing the importance of inherited positions.

To be sure these parallel developments did not lead only to individual empowerment or emancipation. The growth of large-scale firms with complex organizations subjected their employees to elaborate, sometimes Byzantine rules that restricted action, and bureaucratized parties had similar effects in the political realm. Along with the pressures of everyday work, these structures contributed to the sense of enclosure Max Weber summarized in his powerful metaphor of the "iron cage," built up out of the unintended consequences of earlier efforts to give free rein to individual effort. Weber's famous figure conveys only part of the story, however; the overall picture in economic life, from the nineteenth century on into the twenty-first, is much better described by the pattern of alternating moments of stasis with ones of rapid movement and innovation analyzed by Charles Sabel and Maurice Zeitlin, and sometimes the latter persist for long stretches of time (think of Silicon Valley and its counterparts elsewhere). The grounds on which new enterprises can be founded and new ideas spring up are prepared by the widened availability of publicly available bank capital in the post-Rothschild age, and by the reduced "access costs" for information brought about by the expansion and thickening of communication networks, making possible the increase in simultaneous discoveries and innovations to which Joel Mokyr has called attention.[3]

A similar dialectic is evident in the political sphere. Weber himself noted the rising importance of what he famously called "charismatic leadership" as a response to the coming of bureaucratized politics, the heightened significance given to figures who possess some personal quality that legitimizes their power in the eyes of their followers, be it the sheer ability to accomplish what others are unable to, as in the case of Bismarck, or the capacity to embody some shared set of values, as with Gladstone or Gambetta. Such leaders impart new vitality, even a new mystique to the political sphere by restoring to it some of the personal energy and passion that large-scale party organization drains away. But Weber did not sufficiently emphasize how much modern charisma – already in the age of Gladstone, Disraeli, or Gambetta, but even more for later figures such as Churchill, Roosevelt, de Gaulle, and, alas, Mussolini and Hitler – relies for its power on modern networks of communication, first newspapers and railroads, then air travel, movies, radio, and for later figures television. The capacity of charismatic politicians to reinfuse politics with a sense of life and significance depends on the ability of these media to make such leaders' words, deeds, and images directly present to followers over great distances, giving a personal tone to the vast and otherwise machine-like web of connections that draws them together. All these phenomena testify to the ways that structures which provide distant and abstract connections serve no less to foment spontaneity than to check it.

The Internet in the history of networks

No modern instance better shows the way involvement in distant ties and relationships provides resources for autonomous and innovative activity than the worldwide linkage of computers and their operators that make up the Internet. This is not the place for a comprehensive discussion of the World Wide Web and its history, but commentary about it, whether popular or scholarly, often passes over the many features it shares with earlier networks of means. Thinking for a moment about these features will provide a long-term historical context for the Internet, as well as underscore the centrality and persistence of the connection between modernity and involvement in relations at a distance that I have sought to highlight in this book.

The first of these shared features is simply the palpable increase of power such ties and linkages generate for both individuals and society as a whole, a consequence widely recognized from late in the eighteenth century. A classic instance was Adam Smith's declaration that the level of productivity and thus the well-being of any given population depended on how far the division of labor had progressed, which in turn was determined by "the extent of the market," which is to say the degree to which people enter into exchanges with others at a distance. Smith included intellectual capacities along with material ones as potentials to which such ties could give realization: a particularly important species of the division of labor was that between physical and mental work, which gave birth to what he called "philosophers or men of speculation, whose trade is not to do any thing, but to observe every thing." Such people, he added, "are often capable of combining together the powers of the most distant and dissimilar objects."[4] In a similar spirit the Marquis de Condorcet described good roads as implements for making "something out of nothing," since they allowed a surplus of some commodity for which there was no demand in the region where it was produced to be moved rapidly to another, where its ability to meet a need gave it value it lacked at home. An article in one of the popular *Affiches* that published notices and advertisements in the same years declared that, in the progress of sciences and the arts since the days of the Greeks and Romans, "communication has done everything," adding that those regions of the world where lesser progress had been made owed their backwardness to "the small amount of communication they have with other peoples."[5] Other observers, however, thought that France suffered from such limitations itself; thus Arthur Young contrasted the energy generated in England by the rapidity with which information spread there with the more somnolent Bourbon kingdom, attributing this sleepiness to the isolation that kept some French regions from having regular contact with others. In 1832 a French writer warned that the country would not succeed in catching up with Britain simply by turning to more up-to-date machines: only better connections between people and regions would clear the ground for advancement. Putting forth a similar view a few years later, an observer in Bordeaux recommended measures that would "throw men, ideas, and capital into the whirlwind of rapid circulation. Put people's minds [*les intelligences*] into continual relation with each other from one end of the country to the other," and the whole of life would be transformed. His ideas were seconded by a lawyer in the same city early in the 1840s, who predicted that railroads would invigorate life much in the way the compass and printing press had, since the effect of such things was to "push people into contact with each other ... expand a society's sphere of activity ... Thinking, instead of remaining scattered and recumbent wherever it finds itself, which is to say sterile and inactive, sees its power grow infinitely."[6] Similar testimony to the currents of energy people felt flowing to them from such distant connections was voiced by the French newspaper writer of 1893 who said that "to read one's newspaper is to live the universal life, the life of the whole capital, of the entire city, of all France, of all the nations," as well as by the German editor looking back from the 1920s who "felt that I was sitting right in the navel of the world, life streamed by in thousands of photos, hundreds of people, in the voices of the entire globe."[7]

A second and much noted feature of the World Wide Web that was anticipated by earlier networks is its potential to introduce ungovernable and anarchic relations into what appear to be established institutions and practices. Among the phenomena of life on the Internet that exemplify this disruptive power have been musical file sharing, the emergence of free open-source software to rival products produced by traditional companies, the difficulty faced by journalistic sites in finding ways to profit from the valuable services they provide, and the meteoric rise (and fall) of such ventures as Friendster and Myspace. These and other anarchic challenges to position and authority have been met by worried and sometimes desperate attempts to create and impose new forms of stable organization.[8] Although few Internet users are aware of it, this pattern was foreshadowed by earlier networks of communication, first of all by the ones that sprang up around printing.

Print eventually became an instrument for producing standard and consistent versions of books and other texts, as well as for diffusing officially sanctioned forms of language and the works that embody them, but at the start the spread of printed texts had just the opposite effect, producing a situation of near-anarchy. Barely twenty years after Gutenberg first produced books printed with movable type an Italian scholar wrote to a friend that his hopes that the new invention would enrich the literate world by making previously unobtainable texts available to all those who desired to read them had been dashed because printers and publishers not only produced and diffused trash that would have been better forgotten; even "when they write something worthwhile they twist it and corrupt it to the point where it would be much better to do without such books." The early history of printing provided many illustrations of this plaint. The world of print was shot through with piracy, committed by printers and booksellers whose ease of access to literary markets encouraged them to produce unauthorized versions of texts of all kinds, including biblical translations, recently rediscovered classical works, sermon collections, scientific treatises, and contemporary literature. The versions they put out were often unreliable, badly proofread, with texts and images that did not conform to authors' or editors' intentions; the information given about place and date of publication was just as likely to be false as true, there being no mechanisms to verify or regulate it. This situation was not wholly unlike that in other trades, where shoddy goods were often produced when merchants eager to evade guild regulations put out work to people whose skills did not come up to craft standards; but books and pamphlets were more vulnerable to disorder because the core material used to produce the objects, the texts, did not have to be replaced like raw wool or ore as they were turned into cloth or metal. Supply costs were still less when the author's or editor's rights to compensation were simply ignored. Reflecting on the content of printed matter both in the eighteenth century and in our own time, Robert Darnton concludes that information is "always unstable."[9]

The histories of later media show that this anarchic potential of communications networks and the need to counter it was well understood by those who held power. This was notably true in regard to the telegraph, whose potentials and dangers were recognized even before the advent of electric telegraphy in the 1830s. In France an earlier system of sending messages semaphorically, spanning broad distances by virtue of a series of hilltop relay stations, was set up under the Revolution to furnish reports on battles. This "Chappe telegraph," named for its inventor, was expanded under Napoleon and remained important into the middle of the nineteenth century, providing rapid communication for journalists and financiers as well as officials, but always under the control of the state. That restraint was quickly extended to the Morse telegraph soon after the device became practicable, in 1837. What moved the state to assert its authority at that moment was a scandal involving attempts by private individuals to profit from price changes on the Paris Bourse by sending wire reports to agents at other exchanges in the country. When it was discovered that no law existed under which such actions could be prosecuted, one was quickly put in force, imposing punishment on "whoever transmits signals from one place to another without authorization, whether by telegraphic machines or any other means." Not only was the state to be the sole operator, but no one else would be allowed to send messages on its grid, for fear that conspirators or rebels would find ways to transmit coded communications to their allies. Only in 1850 was the (still limited) French network opened up to users outside the government, partly as a way to finance the system and partly out of pressure from commercial interests; even so the content of despatches was to be strictly overseen. In Prussia too the government controlled the construction and management of the lines, limiting their early use to administration and propaganda (beginning with the reports about doings in the Frankfurt Assembly sent to officials in Berlin over the wires in 1848).[10] Such arrangements, by restricting communication at a distance, paid tribute to the potential powers that rapid exchange of information was understood to bring.

The advent of telegraphy confronted people with a number of experiences and problems characteristic of newly powerful communication networks. One was a heightened sense of simultaneous proximity and distance, as instantaneous messages and reports arrived from far-flung and diverse places. The sudden awareness of the telegraph's capacity to transcend locality and abolish distance led people to exaggerate its power to transform life. Some compared it to God in its seeming ability to allow people to be in many scattered places at the same time, others to the nervous system as a vehicle for instantly transmitting perceptions to a center where they could be processed, and instructions to points where they were expected to be followed.

Much benefit was anticipated, for instance in bringing unity to fragmented countries, but it was quickly recognized that forces of discord such as political factions could draw strength from the telegraph too. Enthusiasts argued that illicit behavior, such as theft, elopement, and political subversion, could be brought under control by authorities able to broadcast information rapidly and widely, but their predictions were undermined as some of the objects of surveillance discovered ways to communicate by telegraph too, at least where government control was weak: in England some Chartists found ways to transmit plans and ideas to each other by wire in the 1840s. Diffusing information of all kinds was seen as a major benefit from the start, but very soon public recognition spread about the harm that could result from false or simply mistaken reports, as well as from misunderstandings about what the messages sent by faraway people with unfamiliar vocabularies actually meant.

All these factors contributed to establishing a large degree of governmental control over telegraph systems in practically every European country by around 1870. In France and Germany, as we saw, telegraphy was put under strict governmental management from the start; in England a similar result emerged when the Post Office took over the administration of lines and offices from three private companies in 1868, partly in response to complaints about the unreliability of their service. These situations did not put an end to anxieties about the ways dishonest or unscrupulous people could employ telegraphy, or its power to mislead or deceive the public; novelists such as Jules Verne, Alexandre Dumas, and Émile Zola all voiced such concerns, and an American observer in the mid 1860s feared that the private monopoly achieved by the Western Union Company would "fatally pollute the very foundation of public opinion." Politicians were not above turning this potential to their own ends, as in Bismarck's use of the "Ems Telegram" to provoke war with France in 1870 and the British Secret Service's circulation of an intercepted German communication (the "Zimmerman telegram") as part of the effort to bring the United States into World War I.[11]

Later media – the telephone, radio, television – would exhibit powers telegraphy lacked, and thereby fulfill more of the expectations it aroused, but no previous network could generate the rapid and ubiquitous impact of the Internet. The Web's powers are rooted to be sure in the remarkable technology it employs, in which computers widely available at relatively low cost and able to store and process enormous quantities of data replace earlier means of linking individuals to each other, allowing a far wider range of interactions both personal and public. All the same, it was crucial to the life and development of the Internet that the technology that made it possible came into a world where intellectual and cultural contents of all kinds were already and increasingly being embodied in a great mass of what Simmel called "objective" or "supra-individual" forms, constituting an ever-more-widely available accumulation of cultural capital. Drawing on some parts of this trove required considerable personal resources of education or experience, but others, as in the rapidly growing networks of popular culture, were much more widely open and accessible.

Those interested in the origins of the Internet have recently been reminded that the people usually regarded as its modern inventors had a visionary but largely forgotten early twentieth-century predecessor, the Belgian librarian Paul Otlet, who worked over many years to assemble a central body of references to all the world's available knowledge. Technologically his project remained far from what would emerge in the 1990s, especially since he could not imagine his grand repository save as a collection of index cards, each inscribed with some piece of information, and all filed in some central place. By the 1930s, however, he had worked out a plan to link the cards to the texts and images they identified by numeric symbols, and thus to make the catalogue an entry point to books, recordings, and even – although he assigned this part to the future – video clips. Access to this treasury of information was to be provided by a network (*réseau*) of "electric telescopes." Thus individuals scattered around the world would be able to search within the body of "objective culture" Simmel described, at once drawing nurture from it and contributing to its growth: "From his armchair, everyone will hear, see, participate, will even be able to applaud, give ovations, sing in the chorus, add his cries of participation to those of all the others."[12]

The Internet's relationship to this pre-existing treasury of information was evident both in the vision that inspired its early architects and in the ways it developed. The original impetus for creating the World Wide Web came from natural scientists looking for new ways (as the person with probably the best claim to be called the Web's inventor, Tim Berners-Lee, wrote in 1991) "to allow high-energy physicists to share data, news and documentation." What generated a widespread desire for extending and tightening such connections was the ongoing evolution of the networks of professional researchers and their implements created a hundred years before by the expansion of university departments and later private and government-sponsored laboratories, linked by periodicals, correspondence, and regular meetings.[13] This development engendered a felt need for ever-more-rapid connections as the reduced access costs of information and the expansion in the numbers of researchers accelerated the pace of new discoveries and the pressures to keep abreast of them. Although the need for ever-closer links was felt most strongly in natural science, members of other disciplines found significant benefits in such ties too, and Berners-Lee and his early colleagues spoke explicitly about making the kinds of connections they sought to establish available in other fields. Knowingly or not, their vision echoed such earlier ones as Paul Otlet's dream of providing universal access to the world's total repository of acquired knowledge through a network of "electric telescopes."[14]

People involved in business and commerce quickly recognized that their enterprises could be furthered and expanded by creating their own versions of the chains being constructed by scientists and researchers. One reason the Internet could serve them better than any previous way of diffusing information is that computers were not originally and continue to be not solely media of communication, but are simultaneously means and instruments of work, at the start higher-level calculators and typewriters. Both of these devices, it should be noted, entered into practical use in the last decades of the nineteenth century, as larger-scale enterprises linked to distant suppliers and markets sought ways to manage and exchange the larger bodies of information they employed. Early personal computers were used chiefly for one or both of these functions (both word- and data-processing spread rapidly in the mid 1980s, a few years before the first steps were taken toward the World Wide Web), and more advanced ones, linked to the Internet, have continued to be tools for accomplishing complex tasks – not just the management of text and data, but the further development of the machines' own capacities through writing new software. Software writers sometimes work independently of others much in the way of many mathematicians, theoretical scientists, historians, and philosophers, but one of the most significant developments in the Internet that testifies to its status as an instrument at once of work and of communication has been the emergence of cooperative sites for creating and developing "open-source" software, for which the basic codes are publicly available (not "proprietary") and participants build constantly on the work of others (the "Firefox" Internet browser is one striking example).

These features of the Internet show particularly well the way it exemplifies some of the chief characteristics of a network of means we noted at the start, and that were already evident in the early modern putting-out system and Republic of Letters: the linking up of tools and implements across distances and the creation of synergies between them, competition between products both material and intellectual fashioned at different places and in different circumstances, the challenges to local and established ideas and practices that arise through contact with distant alternatives, and the added motivation to employ otherwise dormant energies and capacities in productive ways. The last-listed element is particular evident on the Web not just in software development but also in the creation of cooperative repositories of information such as Wikipedia, where large numbers of individuals all devoting limited quantities of spare time to a common project combine to create an effective instrument out of otherwise diffuse and unfocused capacities; the only compensation most contributors receive is personal satisfaction or the expectation that the product will serve their own and others' needs. To be sure the same access to distant resources and benefits opens up possibilities for people to give misinformation, pursue selfish agendas, appropriate others' work or exploit them in some way, just as was the case in the early history of printing; but mechanisms to police or counter such activities have followed closely behind. Taken together these features constitute much of what Yochai Benkler has called "the wealth of networks," the expanding store of energies and resources that those who are joined together through them create and employ by way of their interactions.[15]

Recognizing that networks of means generate such a *sui generis* form of wealth and registering its contributions to the evolution at once of bourgeois life and of modernity have been central concerns of this book. Giving attention to continuities between the Internet and earlier networks may seem to shift our focus so much toward modernity that it leaves bourgeois life behind, but there are at least two significant ways in which the Internet can be understood as a bourgeois phenomenon. First, the practical activities the Internet chiefly serves and to which it imparts new energy are precisely the three that historians and others have long recognized as distinctively bourgeois, and that earlier networks of means affected in similar ways: business, public administration, and the professions (including to be sure a range of cultural ones). Each of the three has put its separate stamp on the evolution of social and individual life, but all have simultaneously served the common function noted at the start, namely providing the mediations through which individuals and groups establish operative relations with other people and with resources of all kinds at a distance, providing frames for the complex and extended "chains of purposive action" Simmel recognized as at work throughout modern existence. Because the Internet provides a universal frame for such mediation, it is a prototypical embodiment of the structural features of modernity on which we have focused here. Second, the cultural life fostered by the web of online communications bears two signal features that mark it as the descendent of the nineteenth-century sphere of culture that initially emerged as a chiefly bourgeois phenomenon: first, as we have already had occasion to note, it continues and extends the accumulation of intellectual and artistic resources in the "supra-individual" or "objective" forms Simmel recognized as constituting a kind of shared treasury of assets; and second, the Internet at once renews and heightens the public and palpable character of modern culture, its condition as a culture of means, and creates new spaces of unsupervisable private appropriation, allowing individuals and the groupings they form to access and employ its materials in unpredictable ways.

To be sure, many of the people whose lives are affected by the Internet cannot reasonably be labeled as bourgeois, at least not in the sense the term commonly bore before 1914. But the increasingly permeable boundary between bourgeois and non-bourgeois spheres of action and experience, and the ways in which bourgeois life itself has been transformed by the modernizing forces in good part generated out of it, have been central objects of this inquiry all along. Bourgeois have been key figures in establishing the mediated interactions at a distance that provide the framework of modernity, but the power to give concrete form to abstractions, of which money is the paradigmatic expression, is too basic a feature of humanity to have been confined to any single social group. Rulers seeking to link together localities with diverse features and formerly separate identities often pursued their goals by projecting a uniform grid of procedures and obligations over a broad territory, and in some contexts governments and officials engaged in such projects have been more important in making life bourgeois (and notably *bürgerlich*) than have bourgeois themselves. By the end of the nineteenth century a much larger range of social groups, some – such as workers and women – previously more restricted inside the local contexts most of them chiefly inhabited, were finding readier access to the resources provided by distant relations too.

One reason why bourgeois were hardly less transformed by these developments than others is that bourgeois life itself had long been largely shaped and molded by local attachments and conditions, and by the teleocratic principles that supported them, even when individual bourgeois were active in the more distant relations that generated alternatives to them. Town-based traditions and guild regulations governed activities and social relations in many places even into the nineteenth century, and the *notables* and *Honoratioren* who were so prominent at the mid century owed their status first of all to their positions in some locality or region. The extension and thickening of networks of means recast the way bourgeois inhabited their worlds no less than the ways others lived in theirs: it replaced the manifold and complex forms of civic privileges in German towns with uniform conditions of citizenship and crystallized the distinction between upper bourgeois and *Kleinbürger*; it turned Parisian property owners and manufacturers from an earlier "introverted" style to a more modern "extroverted" one and created the conditions whereby the *peuple* excluded from the *pays légal* of the "Bourgeois Monarchy" could become part of Gambetta's enlarged and republican bourgeois France; it underlay the shift from the private forms of money still dominant in the early nineteenth century to the public ones that were replacing them by its end and gave scope to Walter Bagehot's understanding that the function of a central bank was not to protect already acquired national wealth in the manner of a private person but assure the continuity of public exchanges, and it found expression in the increasing absorption of the local cultures that flourished in mid nineteenth-century English cities into national media emerging to prominence by the 1920s. These evolutions – and the list could easily be lengthened – were woven into the more general alteration described at the beginning of this chapter, whereby personal and social destinies came to depend less on local and inherited resources and connections, and more on distant and publicly available ones, giving new shapes to the economy, politics, and culture, and freeing up the new possibilities in gender relations and morality that began to find realization in the *fin-de-siècle*. It is by attending to this broad range of transformations, to the common grounds underlying them, and to the benefits and harms, hopes and illusions they fostered, that we can best understand the relationship between modernity and bourgeois life.

NOTES

1 Introduction: ends and means

1 On the decline of historical faith in the class narrative of the Revolution's origins, see William Doyle, "A Consensus and Its Collapse: Writings on Revolutionary Origins since 1939," in his *Origins of the French Revolution* (Oxford and New York, 1980; 2nd edn., 1988), 7–40. The first strong blast against the traditional view was Alfred Cobban, *The Social Interpretation of the French Revolution* (Oxford, 1964). Pierre Goubert, *The Ancien Régime: French Society 1600–1750*, trans. Steve Cox (New York, 1973), 247. The textbook referred to is R. R. Palmer, *A History of the Modern World* (New York, many editions, the later ones written in collaboration with Joel Colton). For 1830 see David Pinkney, *The French Revolution of 1830* (Princeton, 1972). I will return to the content of this and the following two paragraphs in Part I, where sources are cited.

2 Among historians who have recognized the limits of bourgeois power in the nineteenth century is Arno J. Mayer, *The Persistence of the Old Regime: Europe to The Great War* (New York, 1981). But Mayer, declaring himself to be a "lumper" rather than a "splitter," concludes from this that, since the middle classes did not rule, power must still have rested in the hands of old nobles. This is to fall into the error of *petitio principi* described above, assuming that some class must always dominate.

3 Georg Simmel, *The Philosophy of Money*, ed. David Frisby, trans. Tom Bottomore *et al.* (London and New York, 2nd enlarged edn., 1990). See especially the sections "The tool as intensified means," and "Money as the purest example of the tool," 209–11.

4 Among recent examples to capitalize on this see: Pierre Musso, ed., *Réseaux et societé* (Paris, 2003); Manuel Castells, *The Rise of Network Society* (Oxford and Malden, MA, 2000); Yochai Benkler, *The Wealth of Networks: How Social Production Transforms Markets and Freedom* (New Haven and London, 2006). I will return to Benkler's book in the Conclusion.

5 Mary Douglas and Baron Isherwood, *The World of Goods* (London and New York, 1979, 1996).

6 The connection being developed here between markets and states shares some ground with the general current of thinking employed by Mark Bevir and Frank Trentmann, "Markets in Historical Contexts: Ideas, Practices, and Governance," in their edited volume *Markets in Historical Contexts: Ideas and Politics in the Modern World* (Cambridge and New York, 2004), esp. 1–5. They use the term "governs" instead of "regulates," however, which seems to me open to a possible confusion between limits effected by impersonal conditions and ones that may involve the intentions of actors. All the same, networks impose restraints on those who operate by way of them, as the price of the benefits they bring, a point to which I will return in the discussion of bourgeois occupations below.

7 Identifying legitimacy as what Daniel Bell calls the "axial principle" of the political sphere is practically the only thing that the approach to the separate realms of bourgeois existence proposed here shares with the one he employs in "The Disjunction of Realms," his introduction to *The Cultural Contradictions of Capitalism* (New York, 1978; new edn., 1996), 11. The opposition he posits between the economy and what he calls "the culture" seems to me far too rigid and one-sided. I argued that the relationship between them is much closer and more complex in *Bohemian Paris: Culture, Politics, and the Boundaries of Bourgeois Life, 1830–1930* (New York, 1986; reprinted, Baltimore and London, 1999); see 391–92 for a comment on Bell's views. In addition, his understanding of the nature and claims of modern selfhood seems to me similarly one-sided. For a different account see my book *The Idea of the Self: Thought and Experience in Western Europe since the Seventeenth Century* (Cambridge, Eng., and New York, 2005).

8 Rousseau, *The Social Contract*, Book 1. Max Weber, "Politics as a Vocation," in *From Max Weber: Essays in Sociology*, ed. H. H. Gerth and C. Wright Mills (Oxford and New York, 1958), 78–79.

9 I have attempted to appreciate the ambiguities of this relationship in *Bohemian Paris*, cited just above (n. 7).

10 The shift was indicated by the description Bishop Sprat gave of the Royal Society of London in 1667. Its members, he said "have freely admitted men of different Religions, Countries, and professions of life," since their aim was not "to lay the Foundation of an *English, Scotch, Irish, Popish,* or *Protestant*

543   /   Notes to pages 19–26

Philosophy, but a Philosophy of *Mankind*." Quoted (from J. Robert
Oppenheimer's *Atom and Void* [Princeton, 1989]) by David A. Hollinger
in his introduction to *Science, Jews, and Secular Culture: Studies in Mid-
Twentieth-Century American Intellectual History* (Princeton, 1996), 14–15.

11 See Anne Goldgar, *Impolite Learning: Conduct and Community in the
Republic of Letters, 1680–1750,* (New Haven and London, 1995).

12 Letter 80; Penguin edn., trans. C. J. Betts (1973), 158.

13 Quoted by David Newsome, *The Victorain World Picture: Perceptions and
Introspections in an Age of Change* (New Brunswick, NJ, 1997), 73.

14 As readers of *The New York Times* were pithily reminded in 2006: "During
the Seventh Crusade, led by St. Louis, Yves le Breton reported how he once
encountered an old woman who wandered down the street with a dish full
of fire in her right hand and a bowl full of water in her left hand. Asked why
she carried the two bowls, she answered that with the fire she would burn
up Paradise until nothing remained of it, and with the water she would put
out the fires of Hell until nothing remained of them: "Because I want no one
to do good in order to receive the reward of Paradise, or from fear of Hell;
but solely out of love for God.'" Quoted by Slavoj Zizek, "Defenders of the
Faith," *New York Times*, Op.-Ed. page, March 12, 2006.

15 See Jerrold Seigel, *Marx's Fate: the Shape of a Life* (Princeton, 1978), ch. 7.

16 The original Marxist position is still broadly represented for instance by
David Blackbourn and Geoff Eley, *The Peculiarities of German History:
Bourgeois Society and Politics in the Nineteenth Century* (Oxford and
New York, 1984); in their view when states and administrators take the
lead in economic and institutional reform they serve "as a kind of surrogate
bourgeoisie" (176). Lenore O'Boyle regards the middle class as a plurality
of elements spread out between the aristocracy and the peasantry in "The
Middle Class in Western Europe, 1815–48," *American Historical Review* 71
(1966), 826–45, citing others who take similar views. For attempts to solve
the problem in the third, "cultural" way see Jürgen Kocka, "The European
Pattern and the German Case," ch. 1 of *Bourgeois Society in Nineteenth-
Century Europe*, ed. Kocka and Allan Mitchell (Oxford and Providence,
RI, 1993), Adeline Daumard, *La Bourgeoisie parisienne de 1815 à 1848*
(Paris, 1963), discussed in Chapter 6, and David Blackbourn, *History of
Germany, 1780–1918: the Long Nineteenth Century* (2nd edn., Malden,
MA, and Oxford, 2003), 161 (Blackbourn's views seem to have evolved since
the 1980s). The original theory of a "style of life" as giving unity to diverse
forms of bourgeois existence was Edmond Goblot, *La Barrière et le niveau:
étude sociologique de la bourgeoisie française* (Paris, 1925).

17 For a somewhat different critique of the attempt to find the unity of
bourgeois in a shared culture, especially as applied to Jürgen Kocka's and
his colleagues' approach to the German *Bürgertum*, see Jonathan Sperber,

"Bürger, Bürgertum, Bürgerlichkeit, Bürgerliche Gesellschaft: Studies of the German (Upper) Middle Class and Its Sociocultural World," *Journal of Modern History* 69 (June, 1997), 271–97.

18 From Maurizio Gribaudi's introduction to E. Beltrami, S. Cavallo, E. Gennuso, M. Gentile, G. Gribaudi, and M. Gribaudi, *Relazioni sociali e strategie individuali in ambiente urbano: Torino nel Novecento*, Ricerca Coordinata da G. Levi (Torino, 1981). For a similar perspective from a philosophical viewpoint see Bernard Williams, "Making Sense of Humanity," in *Making Sense of Humanity and Other Philosophical Papers* (Cambridge and New York, 1995), esp. 85–86. And from a sociological one, Raymond Boudon and François Bourricaud, "Individualisme," in *Dictionnaire critique de la sociologie* (Paris, 1982), esp. 287, as well as Bourdon's "Individualisme et holisme dans les sciences sociales," in *Sur l'individualisme*, ed. Pierre Birnbaum and Jean Leca (Paris, 1986).

19 Edoardo Grendi, "Repenser la micro-histoire?" in *Jeux d'échelles: la micro-analyse à l'expérience*, ed. Jacques Revel (Paris, 1996), 233–43, originally in *Quaderni storici* 86 (1994), 539–49. For a similar perspective, see Simona Cerutti, "La Construction des catégories sociales," in *Passés recomposés: champs et chantiers de l'histoire*, ed. Jean Boutier and Dominique Julia (Paris, 1995), 224–34, and her contribution to *Jeux d'échelles.*

20 *The Fable of the Bees: or, Private Vices, Publick Benefits*, by Bernard Mandeville, in two volumes, with a Commentary Critical, Historical, and Explanatory by F. B. Kaye, vol. II (Oxford, 1924), 353.

21 The claims made in a recent volume, *Urban Assemblages: How Actor Network Theory Changes Urban Studies*, ed. Ignacio Farias and Thomas Bender (New York, 2010), that Thomas P. Hughes's careful study of the construction of electric generating grids, *Networks of Power: Electrification in Western Society, 1880–1930* (Baltimore and London, 1983) supports the ideas of "ANT" deserve to be firmly rejected. Hughes's conclusion that "The style of each system was found to be based on entrepreneurial drive and decision, economic principles, legislative constraints or supports, institutional structures, historical contingencies, and geographical factors, both human and natural" fits what is said above in the text; to claim his work in support of a theory that denies the difference between human and non-human agency is somewhere between disingenuous and guileful. The chief inspiration for "action network theory" has been Bruno Latour, who bases his understanding of network relations on a theory of language as a network of signs that owes much to Jacques Derrida's ideas about speech and writing; see *Reassembling the Social: an Introduction to Actor-Network Theory* (Oxford, 2005). I have argued elsewhere that Derrida's attempt to portray human subjects as unable to exercise independent agency

because the linguistic practices through which they seek to establish stable relations with themselves and with the world impose their own structures on perception and expression rests on a misreading of Saussurean linguistics and cannot account for the actual ways people employ language and speech, and I believe that the same arguments point to the incoherence of Latour's thinking about non-linguistic relations. See *The Idea of the Self*, ch. 18.

22 Max Weber, "'Objectivity' in Social Science and Social Policy," in *The Methodology of the Social Sciences*, trans. and ed. Edward A. Shils and Henry A. Finch (New York, 1949), 49–112.

23 E. L. Jones, *The European Miracle: Environments, Economies, and Geopolitics in the History of Europe and Asia* (Cambridge and New York, 1981; 2nd edn., 1987). For a more recent and powerful restatement of this position see Joseph M. Bryant, "The West and the Rest Revisited: Debating Capitalist Origins, European Colonialism, and the Advent of Modernity," *Canadian Journal of Sociology* 31:4 (2006), 403–44, where much literature is cited. The views advanced by Dipesh Chakrabarty, *Provincializing Europe: Postcolonial Thought and Historical Difference* (Princeton, 2000), are quite distinct from those developed by Jane Burbank and Frederick Cooper, *Empires in World History: Power and the Politics of Difference* (Princeton, 2010), but both belong to the globalizing trend mentioned above; for notions close to Chakrabarty's see *After the Imperial Turn: Thinking With and Through the Nation*, ed. Antoinette Burton (Durham, NC, and London, 2003). I will have a word to say about some arguments advanced in the last work in Chapter 2.

2 Precocious integration: England

1 See, for instance, Lawrence Stone and Jeanne C. Fawtier Stone, *An Open Elite? England 1540–1880* (Oxford and New York, 1984), who quote Engels on 411 in order to insist that he got things the wrong way round.

2 Linda Colley, *Britons: Forging the Nation, 1707–1837* (New Haven and London, 1992), chapter 2. For views that make the age aristocratic, see J. C. D. Clark, *English Society, 1688–1832: Ideology, Social Practice, and Political Power During the Ancien Régime* (Cambridge and New York, 1985), and John Cannon, *Aristocratic Century: the Peerage of Eighteenth-Century England* (Cambridge and New York, 1984). Against this, Paul Langford, *Public Life and Propertied Englishmen, 1689–1798* (Oxford, 1991). Langford argues that aristocrats in the later eighteenth century adopted increasingly bourgeois values in their behavior, religion, and culture.

3 For the persisting aristocratic dominance see David Cannadine, *Lords and Landlords: the Aristocracy and the Towns, 1774–1967* (Leicester, 1980), ch. 1, esp. 26–36, for politics, and *passim* for the urban involvement of the elite; and for the later decline the same author's *The Decline and Fall of the British Aristocracy* (New York, 1990). For the fortunes, W. D. Rubinstein, "Wealth, Elites, and the Class Structure of Modern Britain," ch. 3 of his book *Elites and the Wealthy in Modern British History* (Brighton and New York, 1987), esp. 54. For the argument about industrial decline and values, Martin J. Wiener, *English Culture and the Decline of the Industrial Spirit, 1850–1980* (Cambridge and New York, 1981). For similar themes, Arno J. Mayer, *The Persistence of the Old Regime: Europe to the Great War* (New York, 1981), esp. ch. 2. For a fundamental critique of these notions see W. D. Rubinstein, *Capitalism, Culture, and Decline in Britain, 1750–1990* (London and New York, 1993).

4 For transport and the rivers in France and England see Rick Szostak, *The Role of Transportation in the Industrial Revolution: a Comparison of England and France* (Montreal, London, and Buffalo, 1991), esp. 55–88. Adam Smith understood most of the advantages geography gave to the development of the English economy; see *The Wealth of Nations* (Modern Library edn.), 393.

5 My understanding of the things noted in the second part of this paragraph owes much to my long association with the eminent medievalist Joseph R. Strayer, in whose courses I assisted as a young instructor. See his general history (with D. C. Munro), *The Middle Ages, 395–1500* (New York, 1959) and *The Medieval Origins of the Modern State* (Princeton, 1970). Also S. B. Chrimes, *English Constitutional History* (Oxford, 1965).

6 Jan de Vries, *European Urbanization, 1500–1800* (Cambridge, MA, 1984), 40.

7 There is much good information on the transport networks in Szostak, *The Role of Transportation in the Industrial Revolution*. For the London road connections, Roy Porter, *London: a Social History* (Cambridge, MA, 1994), 135.

8 Peter Clark and Paul Slack, *English Towns in Transition, 1500–1700* (Oxford and New York 1976), 119, 77–78. Also Porter, *London*, ch. 6, 133 for Defoe, and 138 for the figures on Newcastle coal. For London's effect on England's economic development see E. A. Wrigley, *Population and History* (New York, 1969), and more recently T. C. Barker, "Le Grand Avantage de la petite Angleterre," in *L'Économie française du XVIIIe au XXe siècle, Perspectives nationales et internationales (Mélanges offerts à François Crouzet)*, ed. Jean-Pierre Poussou (Paris, 2000), 477–99.

9 Smith is cited in Bernard Lepetit, *The Pre-industrial Urban System: France, 1740–1840*, trans. Godfrey Rogers (Cambridge and New York, 1994), 84.

10 Keith Wrightson, *Earthly Necessities: Economic Lives in Early Modern Britain* (New Haven, 2000), 231 and 213 (where Richard Grassby is quoted).

11 Joyce Oldham Appleby, *Economic Thought and Ideology in Seventeenth-Century England* (Princeton, 1978), 59–62.

12 Appleby, *Economic Thought and Ideology*, esp. ch. 9 (257 for the quotation).

13 Clark and Slack, *English Towns in Transition*, 108–09 on the general situation, and 79 on London merchant guilds.

14 See Christopher Friedrichs, "Capitalism, Mobility and Class Formation in the Early Modern German City," in *Towns in Societies: Essays in Economic History and Historical Sociology*, ed. Philip Abrams and E. A. Wrigley (Cambridge, London, and New York, 1978), 187–214. For the German story in a wider frame see the essays on individual towns collected in *Vom alten zum neuen Bürgertum: die mitteleuropäische Stadt im Umbruch, 1780–1820*, ed. Lother Gall (Munich, 1991). Gall's emphasis on the pressures growing up in various towns for economic liberalization seems justified, but the evidence provided by his students whose work is collected here shows clearly enough that only the French occupation led to effective reform.

15 Steven Laurence Kaplan, "Social Classification and Representation in the Corporate World of Eighteenth-Century France: Turgot's 'Carnival'" in *Work in France: Representations, Meaning, Organization, and Practice*, ed. Kaplan and Cynthia J. Koepp (Ithaca and London, 1986), 176–228; 194 for the quoted passage. For a broader perspective on guild history in France see James R. Farr, *Hands of Honor: Artisans and their World in Dijon, 1550–1650* (Ithaca and London, 1988), where the distinction between *villes libres* and *villes jurées* is explained on 16–17, and Farr's essay in *Cities and Social Change in Early Modern France*, ed. Philip Benedict (London, 1989). For useful essays on the history of guilds in various countries see *Das Ende der Zünfte: ein europäischer Vergleich*, ed. Hans-Gerhard Haupt (Göttingen, 2002). Unfortunately however, this volume is devoted chiefly to revising various old saws about guild history; it does not provide a comparative history of how the end of guild power arrived in different countries.

16 Neil McKendrick, John Brewer, J. H. Plumb, *The Birth of a Consumer Society: the Commercialization of Eighteenth-Century England* (London, 1982), ch. 1, *passim*. The quotation from N. Forster, *An Enquiry into the Present High Price of Possessions* (1767), is on 11; the excise statistics on 29, McKendrick's comment on 22–23. The quotation about milkmaids (by John Byng) is cited by Christopher Breward, *The Culture of Fashion: a New History of Fashionable Dress* (Manchester and New York, 1995), 129.

17 Robert C. Allen, *The British Industrial Revolution in Global Perspective* (Cambridge and New York, 2009); see 140 for a summary of Allen's views, 22 for his recognition that the factor prices on which he lays emphasis depended on "the commercial expansion of the early modern economy," 87ff. for the effect of London on the demand for fuel and the history of the decline in prices, and tables 4.2 and 4.3 for the statistics. Allen emphasizes the role of international commerce in London's expansion but he also recognizes its role as a wellspring of domestic consumption. The view I give above fits in general with the conclusions of the recent analysis of the whole issue of foreign and domestic markets in European industrial innovation developed in *A Deus Ex Machina Revisted: Atlantic Colonial Trade and European Economic Development*, ed. P. C. Emmer, O. Pétré-Grenouilleau, and J. V. Roitman (Leiden and Boston, 2006).

18 Samuel Lilley, "Technological Progress and the Industrial Revolution, 1700–1914," in *The Fontana Economic History of Europe*, vol. III: *the Industrial Revolution*, ed. Carlo Cipolla (London, 1976), 187–254.

19 See especially Joel Mokyr, *The Gifts of Athena: Historical Origins of the Knowledge Economy* (Princeton and London, 2002), who speaks of an "industrial enlightenment" that was particularly well developed in England. Also Jack A. Goldstone, "Efflorescence and Economic Growth in World History: Rethinking the 'Rise of the West' and the Industrial Revolution," *Journal of World History* 13:2 (2002), 323–89. The point is also made by David Landes in *The Unbound Prometheus*, 60–63. It may be that the continuities between "learned" and "practical" knowledge were less acknowledged or recognized in the countryside, where "gentlemen" credited themselves with a breadth of perspective not vouchsafed to ordinary farmers, but the separation seems to me exaggerated by James Livesey in "Improving justice: communitarian norms in the Great Transformation," ch. 2 of *Markets in Historical Contexts: Ideas and Politics in the Modern World*, ed. Mark Bevir and Frank Trentmann (Cambridge and New York, 2004). Livesey makes no distinction between French and British cultures in this regard, and seems to me to ignore his own evidence that the innovations in practice and knowledge brought about by "subaltern" figures were at the very least encouraged, if not spurred by their participation in distant relations that also brought them into contact with people more deeply inserted into them.

20 Jan de Vries, "The Industrial Revolution and the Industrious Revolution," *Journal of Economic History* 54.2 (1994), 249–70. McKendrick, 23. In his book developing further the ideas in his article, de Vries cites the work of Hans-Joachim Voth, *Time and Work in England, 1750–1830* (Oxford, 2001), showing that Londoners "increased their hours of annual labor by at least 40 percent in the period 1750–1830." *The Industrious Revolution:*

Consumer Behavior and the Household Economy, 1650 to the Present (Cambridge and New York, 2008), 91–92.

21 I take this to be the argument of Joel Mokyr, "Demand vs. Supply in the Industrial Revolution," *Journal of Economic History*, 1977, 981–1007. The importance of fossil fuels in raising productivity and income levels has been rightly emphasized by David Landes, *The Unbound Prometheus: Technological Change and Industrial Development in Western Europe from 1750 to the Present* (London and Cambridge, 1969).

22 See the figures in Landes, *The Unbound Prometheus*, 96, 104.

23 Landes, *The Unbound Prometheus*, 118–20. Asa Briggs, *Victorian Cities* (London and New York, 1965). Raphael Samuel, "Workshop of the World: Steam Power and Hand Technology in mid-Victorian Britain," *History Workshop Journal* 3 (Spring, 1977), 3–71. On retailing see the still useful work by James B. Jefferys, *Retail Trading in Britain, 1850–1950* (Cambridge, 1954). Jefferys has been criticized by later writers but mostly in details; see the literature cited in Gordon Boyce and Simon Ville, *The Development of Modern Business* (New York, 2002), 178–79.

24 Richard Price, *British Society, 1680–1880: Dynamism, Containment and Change* (Cambridge and New York, 1999),. For the debate about the relative importance of domestic and foreign markets and resources in the rise of European and especially British industry see *A Deus Ex Machina Revisted*, cited above.

25 Price, *British Society, 1680–1880*, 28–38. The point about the mix of factory production with older techniques is not new (see, e.g. Szostak, *The Role of Transportation*, esp. 9–28 and 137), but Price's notion that we should distinguish between an "economy of manufacture" and an "industrial economy" puts these developments in a different light. Jan de Vries points out that recent econometric studies show that actual economic growth, usually attributed to the new technologies, was much slower than earlier writers had assumed. *The Industrious Revolution: Consumer Behavior and the Household Economy, 1650 to the Present*, 7–8. For warehouses, Briggs, *Victorian Cities*, 106.

26 For a still useful summary see Peter Mathias's review of E. A. Wrigley and R. S. Schofield, *A Population History of England, 1514–1871* (London, 1981) in *Medical History* 28.4 (April, 1984), 214–15.

27 Price, *British Society, 1680–1880*, 24. Malthus quoted from the *First Essay on Population* (1798) by Gregory Claeys, *Machinery, Money and the Millennium: From Moral Economy to Socialism, 1815–1860* (Princeton, 1987), 20–21. Even Robert Owen, whose experience as a manufacturer gave him a precocious sense that machinery opened up a new prospect of "permanent abundance," still thought workers were bound to remain in poverty as long as middlemen retained their central role in the economic

system, since the income they extracted kept "productive workers" (a group that included masters) from receiving the full produce of their labor. See Claeys, *Machinery, Money and the Millennium*, 35–64.

28 John Brewer, *The Sinews of Power: War, Money and the English State, 1688–1783* (London and New York, 1988). Brewer acknowledges the importance of early centralization, and notes that the "system of provincial governance" was strong because it "relied for its implementation on local dignitaries." This amplified the "acceptance of the institutions of central government," so that "when king, lords and commons acted in unison, they were an overwhelming force … The lack of resistance is attributable to the universal (if tacit) consent to taxes obtained through the approval of Parliament and unchallenged by regional estates." 22.

29 Brewer, *The Sinews of Power*, 75–86.

30 *Ibid.*, 126–33.

31 Niall Ferguson, *The Cash Nexus: Money and Power in the Modern World, 1700–2000* (New York and London, 2001). This point is stressed in the thoughtful review of Ferguson's book by Alan Milward in *Times Literary Supplement* 20 (April, 2001), 14.

32 J. G. A. Pocock, "The Mobility of Property and the Rise of Eighteenth-Century Sociology," in *Virtue, Commerce, and History: Essays on Political Thought and History, Chiefly in the Eighteenth Century* (Cambridge and New York, 1985), 110.

33 Brewer, *The Sinews of Power*, 233, 243, 248.

34 See Brewer's chapter on "Commercialization and Politics," in *Birth of a Consumer Society*; 237–39 on the souvenirs; 260 on newspapers.

35 Peter Borsay, *The English Urban Renaissance: Culture and Society in the Provincial Town, 1660–1770* (Oxford, 1989), 286, 146, 270.

36 Dror Wahrman, "National Society, Communal Culture: an Argument about the Recent Historiography of Eighteenth-Century Britain," *Social History* 17 (1992), 43–72; Borsay, *The English Urban Renaissance*, 289, 300–01. Wahrman associates this alternative with a split between those who accepted patrician power based in London and those who opposed it, but such a division is questionable in light of the use the Wilksites made of the national press and the growing national market as anti-aristocratic instruments.

37 For the trade figures, see Colley, *Britons*, 68–69.

38 Antoinette Burton's Introduction to her edited volume, *After the Imperial Turn: Thinking with and through the Nation* (Durham, NC, and London, 2003), 5.

39 See Jack P. Greene, "Empire and Identity from the Glorious Revolution to the American Revolution," ch. 10 of *The Oxford History of the British Empire*, vol. II: *the Eighteenth Century*, ed. P. J. Marshall and Alaine Low (Oxford and New York, 1998).

40 See Jonathan Schneer, *London 1900: the Imperial Metropolis* (New Haven, 1999), 35 for one instance of such a conflict. Schneer cites most of the literature that stresses the impact of imperial experience on British identity and everyday life in the nineteenth century, nn. 17–20, and in general shares the views of these writers, but he also notes the presence of anti-imperial voices (chs. 7–9). For an interesting and balanced discussion of the tensions between imperial ambition and attempts to preserve commitment to the values thought to justify it in the first half of the nineteenth century, see John Clive, *Macaulay: the Shaping of the Historian* (London, 1973), 305–15. Half a century later J. R. Seeley emphasized the conflict of opinions about empire in the well–known series of lectures he gave on *The Expansion of England* (London, 1883); see esp. 293–94.

41 P. J. Marshall, "No fatal impact? The elusive history of imperial Britain," *Times Literary Supplement* (March 12, 1993), 10. For the importance of rivalry with France and Germany in the last quarter of the nineteenth century, see, for instance, Bernard Porter, *The Lion's Share: a Short History of British Imperialism, 1850–1995* (London and New York, 1976; 3rd edn., 1996), ch. 3.

3 Monarchical centralization, privilege, and conflict: France

1 For the last part of this paragraph, Jean-Pierre Daviet, *La Société industrielle en France, 1814–1914: Productions, échanges, répresentations* (Paris, 1997), 83–84. For the earlier part, Gérard Noiriel, *Les Ouvriers dan la société française: XIXe–XXe siècle* (Paris, 1986), 12–14.

2 Paul Butel, *L'Economie française au xviiie siècle* (Paris, 1993), 272–75.

3 *Ibid.*, and Robin Biggs, *Early Modern France, 1560–1715* (Oxford and New York, 1998), 66–71.

4 For physiocratic theory see A. R. J. Turgot's "Eloge de Vincent de Gournay" and other writings in A. R. J. Turgot, *Écrits économiques*, with a preface by Bernard Cazes (Paris, 1970). Also Butel, *L'Économie française,* 46–47.

5 For a focused and clear discussion of French agriculture, informed by recent work, see Gwynne Lewis, *France, 1715–1804: Power and the People* (Harlow, London, and New York, 2004), 62–66. On attempts to abolish guilds see Steven Laurence Kaplan, "Social Classification and Representation in the Corporate World of Eighteenth-Century France: Turgot's 'Carnival'" in *Work in France: Representations, Meaning, Organization, and Practice*, ed. Kaplan and Cynthia J. Koepp (Ithaca and London, 1986), 176–228.

6 François Caron, *Histoire des chemins de fer en France,* I: *1740–1883* (Paris, 1997), 50.

7 Caron, *Histoire des chemins de fer*, 13–21. Bernard Lepetit, *The Pre-industrial Urban System: France, 1740–1840*, trans. Godfrey Rogers (Cambridge and New York, 1994).

8 Szostak, *The Role of Transportation in the Industrial Revolution* (cited above in Chapter 2), 74–75.

9 Lewis, *France*, 95; the quotation is from Peter Jones.

10 For a summary of much literature, see Butel, *L'Économie française*, 61–67.

11 Butel, *L'Économie française*, 228–31.

12 Liana Vardi, *The Land and the Loom: Peasants and Profit in Northern France, 1680–1800* (London, 1993), 11; partly quoted in Lewis, 97; see also Lewis, 107 (where she is wrongly named Linda), and Vardi, 199ff. for the social consequences.

13 Butel, *L'Économie française*, 228–31 and 237–38.

14 *Ibid.*, 67.

15 For this and the preceding paragraph, John Bosher, *French Finances, 1770–1795: From Business to Bureaucracy* (Cambridge, 1970). The figures on the *ferme générale* are from Lewis, *France*, 13. For a more recent account of French administrative history see François Burdeau, *Histoire de l'administration française: du 18e au 20e siècle* (2nd edn., Paris, 1994). Bosher's account seems still to hold up for the Revolutionary period. On the later period Burdeau focuses mostly on the absence of social policy on the part of governments, thereby neglecting the important effect of government action on such things as railroad building. For a fine-grained study of the mix of continuity and change in the relations between state organs and local life, including tax-collecting, see Isser Woloch, *The New Regime: Transformations of the French Civic Order, 1789–1820s* (New York and London, 1994), esp. chs. 1 and 5.

16 Pierre Goubert, *The Ancien Régime: French Society 1600–1750*, trans. Steve Cox (New York, 1973), 241.

17 Guy Chaussinand-Nogaret, *The French Nobility in the Eighteenth Century: from Feudalism to Enlightenment*, trans. William Doyle (Cambridge and New York, 1985), 114–15. For the rest of this paragraph, Lewis, *France*, 104–05 (who also cites Chaussinand-Nogaret). For British uses of the term "capitalist" to refer to "fundholder" see Gregory Claeys, *Money, Machinery and the Millennium: from Moral Economy to Socialism, 1816–60* (Princeton, 1987), 29 and *passim*.

18 See Lewis, *France*, and Goubert, *Ancien Régime*, 238–52.

19 For bourgeois as a noble category see Joseph di Corcia, "*Bourg, Bourgeois, Bourgeois de Paris* from the Eleventh to the Eighteenth Century," *Journal of Modern History* 50 (1978), 207–33. On the nobility and capitalism, Chaussinand-Nogaret, *The French Nobility*, ch. 5.

20 For recent comments on this aspect of Old Regime society, see William M. Reddy, *The Navigation of Feeling* (Cambridge, 2001), 148. William H. Sewell, jr., *A Rhetoric of Bourgeois Revolution: the Abbé Sièyes and* What Is the Third Estate? (Durham, NC, and London, 1994), 64. I discuss this aspect of Old Regime life including some recent dissents from the view given above in the text, in *The Idea of the Self: Thought and Experience in Western Europe Since the Seventeenth Century* (Cambridge and New York, 2005), ch. 6. For evidence that bourgeois were treated more respectfully in French plays as the century went on, see Laurence Croq, "Les 'bourgeois de Paris' au XVIIIe siècle: identification d'une catégorie soicale polymorphe." Thèse de doctorat nouveau régime, Université de Paris I, Décembre, 1997 (there is a copy in the Bibliothèque Historique de la Ville de Paris).

21 Sarah Maza, *The Myth of the French Bourgeoisie: an Essay on the Social Imaginary, 1750–1850* (Cambridge, MA, and London, 2003), 39. Robert C. Darnton, "A Bourgeois Puts His World in Order: the City as Text," in *The Great Cat Massacre and Other Episodes in French Cultural History* (New York, 1984), 124, 126, 128. John Shovlin, "Emulation in Eighteenth-Century French Economic Thought," *Eighteenth-Century Studies* 36:2 (1993) 224–30. For the earlier history of such attitudes see Henry C. Clark, "Commerce, the Virtues, and the Public Sphere in Early Seventeenth-Century France," *French Historical Studies* 21:3 (1998), 415–40.

22 Mathieu Marraud, *De la Ville à l' état: la bourgeoisie parisienne, XVIIe–XVIIIe-siècle* (Paris, 2009). For the later situation see below Chapter 7.

23 David Garrioch, *The Formation of the Parisian Bourgeoisie, 1690–1830* (Cambridge, MA, 1996). The figures for office holders are on 213. Garrioch does not ask whether they mean quite what they appear to, but he suggests that some of those employed in 1795 may have been "Grub street writers who had made a precarious living in the pre-Revolutionary capital." Another vehicle for unity among Parisian bourgeois was provided by the monarchy's designating some of them as *bourgeois du roi* or *francs bourgeois*. Until late in the seventeenth century the privileged *bourgeois de Paris* were often regarded as indistinguishable from aristocrats, but this situation changed as Louis XIV, pressed by the need to increase tax revenues, began to attack some of their privileges. See Laurence Croq, "Les 'bourgeois de Paris' au XVIIIe siècle," 137–241 and conclusion; also his essay and Robert Descimon's in *Le Prince, la ville et le bourgeois, XIVe–XVIIIe siècles*, ed. L. Croq (Paris, 2004). These writings indicate that the old attachment to local *quartier* life still retained much of its force among Parisian bourgeois through the end of the eighteenth century and may have coexisted with the tendencies toward bourgeois unity rather than receding in the face of them.

24 Jürgen Habermas, *The Structural Transformation of the Public Sphere: an Inquiry into a Category of Bourgeois Society*, trans. Thomas Burger, with the assistance of Frederick Lawrence (Cambridge, MA, 1989; original German edn., 1962).

25 Keith Michael Baker, "Public Opinion as Political Invention," in *Inventing the French Revolution: Essays on French Political Culture in the Eighteenth Century* (Cambridge and New York, 1990), 171–72.

26 David A. Bell, *Lawyers and Citizens: the Making of a Political Elite in Old Regime France* (New York and Oxford, 1994), 12–13. It should be noted, however, that Habermas was well aware of the importance of governmental action in provoking individuals and groups outside it to constitute themselves as a "public" in opposition to its heightened claims. See *Structural Transformation*, 22–23.

27 Bell, *Lawyers*, 10–11.

28 Baker, "Public Opinion," 195–97.

29 Pierre Rosanvallon, "Political Rationalism and Democracy in France in the Eighteenth and Nineteenth Centuries," in *Philosophy and Social Criticism* 28:6 (2002), 687–701.

30 Sarah Maza, *Private Lives and Public Affairs: the Causes Célèbres of Prerevolutionary France* (Berkeley, Los Angeles, and London, 1993), 36, citing various statistical studies of publishing.

31 Colin Jones, "The Great Chain of Buying: Medical Advertisement, the Bourgeois Public Sphere, and the Origins of the French Revolution," *American Historical Review* (February, 1996), 13–40. See also Jack R. Censer, *The French Press in the Age of Enlightenment* (London and New York, 1994), 54–86.

32 Quoted by Gilles Feyel, "Négoce et presse provinciale en France au 18e siècle: méthodes et perspectives de recherches," in *Cultures et formations négociantes dans l'Europe moderne*, ed. Franco Angiolini and Daniel Roche (Paris, 1995), 448.

33 On the beginnings of the papers see Feyel, "Négoce et presse," 439–40; on censorship and the intendants, Jones, "The Great Chain," 26.

34 Quoted in Lewis, *France*, 103.

35 On French consumption in this period the fundamental works are those of Daniel Roche: *La Culture des apparences: une histoire du vêtement (xviie–xviiie siècle)* (Paris, 1989); *La France des lumières* (Paris, 1993), *Histoire des choses banales: naissance de la consommation, xviie–xixe siècle* (Paris, 1997). Also Cissie Fairchilds, "The Production and Marketing of Pupuluxe Goods in Eighteenth-Century Paris," in *Consumption and the World of Goods*, ed. John Brewer and Roy Porter (London, 1993); and Annik Pardailhé-Galabrun, *La Naissance de l'intime: 3000 foyers parisiens xviie–xviiie sècles* (Paris, 1988). Also Joan Thirsk, "Luxury Trades and

Consumerism," and Gillian Lewis, "Producers, Suppliers, and Consumers: Reflections on the Luxury Trades in Paris, c. 1500–c. 1800," both in *Luxury Trades and Consumerism in Ancien Régime Paris*, ed. Robert Fox and Anthony Turner (Aldesshot, Hampshire, and Brookfield, VT, 1998) 257–62 and 287–98. There is a good summary of recent literature on this subject in Maza, *Myth of the French Bourgeoisie*, 41–51. For the Montpellier chronicler, Darnton, "A Bourgeois Puts His World in Order," 134–35.

36 Roche, *Histoire des choses banales*, 232–34.

37 *Birth of a Consumer Society*, 43–45.

38 For Caen see Bernard Lepetit, *The Pre-industrial Urban System*, 130, citing the work of Jean-Claude Perrot. On Montpellier see Frederick M. Irvine, "From Renaissance City to Ancien Régime Capital: Montpellier, c. 1500–c. 1600," in Philip Benedict, ed., *Cities and Social Change in Early Modern France* (London, 1989), 105–33; and on Dijon, James R. Farr, "Consumers, Commerce, and the Craftsmen of Dijon: the Changing social and economic Structure of a Provincial Capital, 1450–1750," *Ibid.*, 134–73.

39 Lepeit, *The Pre-industrial Urban System*, ch. 10.

40 Lewis, *France*, 106. Roche, *La France des lumières*, 585.

41 For the best summary see Woloch, *The New Regime*, ch. 1.

42 Sewell, *A Rhetoric*, 40. For the cascade of disdain, see 63–64.

43 See Sara Maza's discussion of this writing in *The Myth of the French Bourgeosie*, 76ff.

44 On this topic see the concise and illuminating discussion by T. C. W. Blanning, *The French Revolution: aristocrats versus bourgeois?* (Atlantic Highlands, NJ, 1987), 41–46. Blanning also notes that the economic effects of the Revolution were far from favorable to modern industry. Lynn Hunt gives a certain twist to the image of the revolutionaries as bourgeois by noting a shift away from urban groups with established Old Regime positions to newer ones as the decade progressed (*Politics, Culture, and Class in the French Revolution* [Berkeley and Los Angeles, 1984], part II), but such generational or segmental shifts do not amount to a change from one class to another.

45 The point has been made by a number of writers. Maza gives a good summary in the pages cited just above.

46 Sewell, *A Rhetoric*, 76, citing Sieyès, *Écrits politiques*, 32.

47 Sewell, *A Rhetoric*, 78–79.

48 *Ibid.*, 102–04.

49 *Ibid.*, 93; 103–06.

50 Maza, *The Myth of the French Bourgeoisie*, 138–43.

51 *Ibid.*, 150–60, and Dietrich Gerhard, "Guizot, Augustin Thierry und die Rolle des Tiers État in der französischen Geshichte," *Historische Zeitschrift* 190 (1960), 290–310.

52 For Saint-Simon and his influence see Shirley Gruber, "The Revolution of
   1830 and the Expression 'Bourgeoisie,'" in *The Historical Journal* 11:3
   (1968), 462–71.
53 These general principles of Guizot's politics are well described by Douglas
   W. J. Johnson, *Guizot: aspects of French history, 1787–1874* (London,
   1963), ch. 2; see 57 for the quotation about French political rivalries and
   passions. For the expulsion and return of the aristocrats, see Patrick-Bernard
   Higonnet, "La Composition de la Chambre des Députés de 1827 à 1831,"
   Revue Historique 239 (1968), 351–79, and Patrick Higonnet and Trevor
   B. Higonnet, "Class, Corruption, and Politics in the French Chamber of
   Deputies, 1846–48," *French Historical Studies* 5 (1967), 204–24.
54 Pierre Rosanvallon, *Le Moment Guizot* (Paris, 1985), 65–72.
55 Rosanvallon, *Le Moment Guizot*, 44–51 (the quotation from Guizot
   is on 51).
56 *Ibid.*, 92–93. On centralization, see 61–63.

4   Localism, state-building, and *bürgerliche Gesellschaft*: Germany

1 David Blackbourn, *History of Germay, 1780–1918: the Long Nineteenth
   Century* (2nd edn., Malden, MA, and Oxford, 2003), 7–8. Hans-Ulrich Wehler,
   Deutsche Gesellschaftsgeschichte, I: *von Feudalismus des Alten Reiches bis zur
   defensiven Modernisierung der Reformära* (Munich, 1987), 48–50.
2 "Others make war; you, happy Austria, marry." On the politics of the
   Holy Roman Empire and its later consequences for German history, see the
   still valuable analysis by Geoffrey Barraclough, *The Origins of Modern
   Germany* (Oxford, 1957), esp. chs. 8 and 9 for the medieval situation and
   361–67 for the continuity with early modern German politics; and, more
   recently, Sheilagh Ogilvie, "The State in Germany: a Non-Prussian View,"
   in *Rethinking Leviathan: the Eighteenth-Century State in Britain and
   Germany*, ed. John Brewer and Eckhart Hellmuth (Oxford, 1999), 167–202.
3 Mack Walker, *German Home Towns: Community, State, and General
   Estate, 1648–1871* (Ithaca, NY, 1971, 2nd edn., 1998). Blackbourn, *History
   of Germany*, 10, 14. Outside powers were happy to aid the small states in
   preserving their independence, so as to prevent the formation of a serious
   rival in Germany. See Brendan Simms, "Political and Diplomatic Movements,
   1800–1820: Napoleon, National Uprising, Restoration," in *Germany, 1800–
   1870* (Oxford, 2004), 26–27.
4 Quoted in Thorsten Maentel, "Zwischen weltbürgerlichen Aufklärung und
   stadtbürgerlicher Emanzipation. Bürgerliche Geselligkeitskultur um 1800," in
   Bürgerkultur im 19. Jahrhundert. Bildung, Kunst und Lebenswelt, ed. Dieter
   Hein and Andreas Schulz (Munich, 1996), 142–43.

5 Thomas Ertman, "Explaining Variation in Early Modern State Structure: the Cases of England and the German Territorial States," in *Rethinking Leviathan: the Eighteenth-Century State in Britain and Germany*, ed. John Brewer and Eckhart Hellmuth (Oxford, 1999), 35.

6 Blackbourn, *History of Germany*, 15.

7 Ertman, "Explaining Variation," 42.

8 Hans-Ulrich Wehler, *Deutsche Gesellschaftsgeschichte*, I: *von Feudalismus des Alten Reiches bis zur defensiven Modernisierung der Reformära* (Munich, 1987), 211.

9 See Vivian R. Gruder, *The Royal Provincial Intendants: a Governing Elite in Eighteenth-Century France* (Ithaca, NY, 1968).

10 Isabel V. Hull, *Sexuality, State and Civil Society in Germany, 1700–1815* (Ithaca and London, 1996), 171.

11 Jennifer Jenkins, *Provincial Modernity: Local Culture and Liberal Politics in fin-de-siècle Hamburg* (Ithaca and London, 2003), 19–20. Andreas Schulz, "'...Tage des Wohllebens, wie sie noch nie gewesen...': Das Bremer Bürgertum in der Umbruchszeit 1789–1818," in *Vom alten zum neuer Bürgertum: Die mitteleuropäische Stadt im Umbruch, 1780–1820*, ed. Lother Gall (Munich, 1991), 26–27. Chapters on other cities in the same volume describe similar arrangements.

12 Much of this account relies on R. Steven Turner, "The *Bildungsbürgertum* and the Learned Professions in Prussia, 1770–1830: the Origins of a Class," *Histoire Sociale–Social History* XIII (1980), 105–35 (122 and 124 for the quoted passages), but I have not followed Turner's interpretation completely.

13 Anthony J. La Vopa, "Specialists against Specialization: Hellenism as Professional Ideology in German Classical Studies," in *German Professions, 1800–1950*, ed. Geoffrey Cocks and Konrad H. Jarausch (New York and Oxford, 1990), 32–34. Hull, *Sexuality, State and Civil Society*, 203.

14 On the officials as state dependents, see Hansjoachim Henning, *Das westdeutsche Bürgertum in der Epoche der Hochindustrialisierung, 1860–1914: Soziales Verhalten und Soziale Strukturen*, I: *Das Bildungsbürgertum in den Preussischen Westprovinzen* (Wiesbaden, 1972), 22–26. Kant noted the requirement of *Unabhängigkeit* for membership in the *Bürgertum*: James J. Sheehan, "Wie bürgerlich war der deutsche Liberalismus?" in *Liberalismus im 19. Jahrhundert: Deutschland im europäischen Vergleich. Dreissig Beiträge, Mit einem Vorwort von Jürgen Kocka*, ed. Dieter Langewiesche (Göttingen, 1988), 32.

15 For a clear and insightful description of the difference, see Jeffrey Freedman, *A Poisoned Chalice* (Princeton and Oxford, 2002), 88–91.

16 Wolfgang Ruppert, *Bürgerlicher Wandel: Studien zur Herausbildung einer nationalen deutschen Kultur im 18. Jahrhundert* (Frankfurt am Main

and New York, 1981), 43. Sheehan, "Wie bürgerlich war der deutsche Liberalismus?" 32.

17 See their introduction to *Rethinking Leviathan: the Eighteenth-Century State in Britain and Germany*, ed. John Brewer and Eckhart Hellmuth (Oxford, 1999), 17.

18 Quoted, from a magazine article of 1785, by Ruppert, *Bürgerlicher Wandel*, 101. On the promotion of a national language, *ibid.*, 35–37.

19 Sheehan, "Wie bürgerlich war der deutsche Liberalismus?" 33; Hull, *Sexuality, State and Civil Society*, 201–02 and *passim*. The phrase "communicative connection" is Ruppert's, referring to Kant and Moses Mendelssohn (*Bürgerlicher Wandel*, 149–50).

20 Étienne François, "Négoce et culture dans l'Allemagne du 18e siècle," in *Cultures et formations négociantes dans l'Europe moderne*, ed. Franco Angiolini and Daniel Roche (Paris, 1995), 29–48.

21 Quoted by Hull, *Sexuality, State and Civil Society*, 214.

22 Jennifer Jenkins, *Provincial Modernity*, 126–28. For an interesting account of the transformation from the earlier to the later notion of citizenship in a single town see Hans-Werner Hahn, "Von der 'Kultur der Bürger' zu 'bürgerlichen Kultur': Veränderungen in der Lebenswelt der Wetzlaurer Bürgertums zwischen 1700 und 1900," in *Armut, Liebe, Ehre: Studien zur historischen Kulturforschung*, ed. Richard van Dülmen (Frankfurt am Main, 1988), 144–85.

23 The most explicit analysis of this tension is Sheehan, "Wie bürgerlich war der deutsche Liberalismus?," cited above. The general themes of this paragraph are also well developed by Ruppert, Hull, and Jenkins.

24 Quoted in Sheehan, "Wie bürgerlich...," 34.

25 Stefan-Ludwig Hoffman, "Bürger zweier Welten? Juden und Freimaurer im 19. Jahrhundert," in *Juden, Bürger, Deutsche: Zur Geschichte von Vielfalt und Differenz, 1800–1933*, ed. Andreas Gotzmann, Rainer Liedtke, and Till van Rahden (Tübingen, 2001), 99, citing Lessing, *Ernst und Falk. Gespräche für Freimaurer...* ed. Ion Contiades (Frankfurt, 1968), 24–25. The passage is also quoted by Wehler, *Deutsche Gesellschaftsgeschichte*, I, 217.

26 See Sheehan, "Wie bürgerlich war der deutsche Liberalismus?" 31, and Ruppert, *Bürgerlicher Wandel*, 41.

27 For Herder's career, and for the impact that his experiences made on his theory of language and of the public, see Anthony J. La Vopa, "Herder's *Publikum*: Language, Print, and Sociability in Eighteenth-Century Germany," *Eighteenth-Century Studies* 29:1 (1996), 5–24.

28 Franklin Kopitzsch, *Grundzüge einer Sozialgeschichte der Aufklärung in Hamburg und Altona* (Hamburg, 1982), I, 142–44.

29 *Ibid.*, 135–37 for the traveler; 269–77 for *Der Patriot*.

30 Ruppert, *Bürgerlicher Wandel*, 122.

31 Kopitzsch, *Grundzüge*, 260–68 on the beginnings of the Enlightenment in Hamburg, and 280–85 on religion and the content of *Der Patriot*.

32 Chaussinand-Nogaret, *The French Nobility in the Eighteenth Century: from Feudalism to Enlightenment*, trans. William Doyle (Cambridge and New York, 1985), ch. 5. For Wahrman's work see above, Chapter 2.

33 Thomas Nipperdey, *Germany from Napoleon to Bismarck, 1800–1866*, trans. Daniel Nolan (Princeton, 1996; orig. edn., 1983), 1.

34 For developments in German cities before, during, and after the Napoleonic occupation, see the essays collected in *Vom alten zum neuer Bürgertum: Die mitteleuropäische Stadt im Umbruch, 1780–1820*, ed. Lother Gall (Munich, 1991). For a general discussion of Gall's work and that of his students in comparison with the "Bielefeld" school of Jürgen Kocka and others, see Jonathan Sperber, *"Bürger, Bürgertum, Bürgerlichkeit, Bürgerliche Gesellschaft*: Studies of the German (Upper) Middle Class and Its Sociocultural World," *Journal of Modern History* 69 (1997), 271–97.

35 David Blackbourn, *History of Germany, 1780–1918: the Long Nineteenth Century*, 54–65, 74–76.

36 Walker, *German Home Towns*, 123–38.

37 Blackbourn, *History of Germany*, 76–78 (although I am not certain he would quite share this conclusion).

38 *Ibid.*, 80–88.

39 James J. Sheehan, *German History, 1770–1866* (Oxford and New York, 1989), 503–04. Sheehan's conclusion reflects especially the research of Frank Tipton, "The National Consensus in German Economic History," *Central European History* 7 (1974), 195–224. For the regional character of German economic development see Tipton's still valuable book, *Regional Variations in the Economic Development of Germany during the Nineteenth Century* (Middletown, CT, 1976) and more generally Sidney Pollard, *Peaceful Conquest: the Industrialization of Europe, 1760–1970* (Oxford and New York, 1981).

40 F. D. Marquardt, *"Pauperismus* in Germany during the *Vormärz*," *Central European History* 11 (1969). Hegel, *Philosophy of Right*, trans. and with notes by T. M. Knox (Oxford and New York, 1952), paras. 241–45. For the Zwanziger and discussions of them, as well as the sense of the term *Fabrikant*, see Christina von Hodeberg, "Der Fluch des Geldsacks: Der Aufstieg des industriellen als Herausforderung bürgerlicher Werte," in *Der bürgerliche Wertehimmel: Innenansichten des 19. Jahrhunderts*, ed.

Manfred Hettling and Stefan-Ludwig Hoffman (Göttingen, 2000), 79–104. I admit I do not read the evidence quite as she does.

41 Manfred Hettling, "Bürgertum und Revolution 1848 – ein Widerspruch," in *Bürger in Gesellschaft der Neuzeit: Wirtschaft – Politik – Kultur*, ed. Hans-Jürgen Puhle (Göttingen, 1991), 210–22.

42 Pierre Ayçoberry, *Cologne entre Napoléon et Bismarck: la croissance d'une ville rhénane* (Paris, 1981), 119–21. Marx was not the only socialist who turned to the French term; for another example, Otto Lüning, see Wolfgang Hartwig, "Strukturmerkmale und Entwicklungstendenzen des Vereinswesens in Deutschland 1789–1848," in *Vereinswesen und bürgerliche Gesellschaft in Deutschland*, ed. Otto Dann (*Historische Zeitschrift Beihefte*, New Series, 9, Munich, 1984), 48.

43 On the influence of Württemberg politics and religion on Hegel's thinking see Lawrence W. Dickey, *Hegel: Religion, Economics and the Politics of Spirit, 1770–1807* (Cambridge and New York, 1987).

44 Hegel, *Philosophy of Right*, ed. Knox, para. 185, 123. On Ferguson and his relations to German thinkers, see Fania Oz-Salzberger, *Translating the Enlightenment: Scottish Civic Discourse in Eighteenth-Century Germany* (Oxford, 1995).

45 Para. 256, p. 154–55.

46 Paras. 190–92, p. 127.

47 See the note to para. 189, p. 268.

48 Para. 260, p. 161.

49 The quotes from the Preface are on 10–12. The comment about "vexation" as the typical modern mood is from Hegel's *Philosophy of Religion*, cited by Bernard Yack, *The Longing for Total Revolution: Philosophic Sources of Social Discontent from Rousseau to Marx and Nietzsche* (Princeton, 1986), 220. I discuss this aspect of Hegel's thinking more at length in *The Idea of the Self* (Cambridge and New York, 2005), ch. 12.

50 Preface to Hegel, *The Philosophy of Right*, 12.

51 W. H. Riehl, *Die Bürgerliche Gesellschaft* (1851; I cite the Stuttgart, 1861 edn.); for the passages referred to in this paragraph, see 247, 260. In quotations I have modernized Riehl's spelling of *Bürgerthum*. Blackbourn is among many modern writers who translate *bürgerlich* as bourgeois, *History of Germany*, 158.

52 *Ibid.*, 248–51, 257; 246 for the Revolution and "Seitdem drückt das Bürgertum den Universalismus des modernen gesellschaftlichen Lebens am entschiedensten aus. Viele nehmen Bürgertum und moderne Gesellschaft für gleichbedeutend."

53 *Ibid.*, 256, 245, 268.

54 See esp. 246–48.

55 He speaks about this in the introduction, 7–8.

56 For these parts of Riehl's argument, see both the introductory sections of his book, 5–11, and 322–36.

57 Gustav Freytag, *Debit and Credit*, trans. L. C. C. (New York, 1858; German edn., 1855; photographic repr., New York, 1990), 27, 125, 167. Peasants are altered by such relations in the novel too: "For five days of the week, the peasant had to cultivate his plot of ground, or to render feudal service to his landlord, and on Sunday his heart was divided between the worship of the Virgin, his family, and the public house; but the market-day led him beyond the narrow confines of his fields into the busy world." There he could feel his own shrewdness among strangers, "he greeted acquaintances whom else he would never have met; saw new things and strange people, and heard the news of other towns and districts." 372–73.

5 Modern industry, class, and party politics in nineteenth-century England

1 See the figures in B. R. Mitchell, *European Historical Statistics, 1750–1970* (Abridged edn., New York, 1978), 315–18, and William L. Langer, *The Unbound Prometheus: Technological Change and Industrial Development in Western Europe from 1750 to the Present* (Cambridge and New York, 1969), 194. There was a significant increase in Britain between 1848 and 1852, as shown by the maps reproduced in Samuel Lilley, "Technological Progress and the Industrial Revolution, 1700–1914," in *The Fontana Economic History of Europe*, III: *the Industrial Revolution*, ed. Carlo Cipolla (London, 1976), 208–09.

2 Lynn Hollen Lees, "Urban Networks," in *The Cambridge Urban History of Britain*, vol. III: *1840–1950* (Cambridge, 2000), 83. Richard Price, *British Society, 1680–1880: Dynamism, Containment and Change* (Cambridge and New York, 1999), 47–49. Langer, *The Unbound Prometheus*, 222–24.

3 Price, *British Society, 1680–1880*, 85.

4 Lilley, "Technological Progress," 211. For steam and water power and the importance of the turbine engine see Price, *British Society, 1680–1880*, 28–29.

5 Martin J. Wiener, *English Culture and the Decline of the Industrial Spirit, 1850–1980* (Cambridge and New York, 1981). For similar themes, Arno J. Mayer, *The Persistence of the Old Regime: Europe to the Great War* (New York, 1981), esp. ch. 2.

6 For the educational systems see Fritz Ringer, *Fields of Knowledge: French Academic Culture in Comparative Perspective, 1890–1920* (Cambridge and New York, 1992).

7 There is a detailed account in Glynn Davies, *A History of Money: From Ancient Times to the Present Day* (Cardiff, Wales, 2002), 285–93. See also Price, *British Society, 1680–1880*, 75–76, and Landes, *Unbound Prometheus*, 75.

8 For the material in this and the previous paragraph see Price, 78–87, and Davies, *A History of Money*, 340–64. For capital formation see the table in Walter Minchonton, "Patterns of Demand, 1750–1914," *The Fontana Economic History of Europe*, III, 84–85, reporting figures from Simon Kuznets, "Quantitative aspects of the economic growth of nations, VII: the share and structure of consumption," *Economic Development and Cultural Change*, X (1962), 72–3. Such numbers are far from perfectly reliable and figures for the rate of investment given by others are lower; however, the proportion between British and German rates is what matters here. For other dimensions of the relations between banking and industry in this period, see the still useful discussion in Langer, *The Unbound Prometheus*, 348–52.

9 Duncan Bell, "John Stuart Mill on Colonies," *Political Theory* 38:1 (2010), 55–56.

10 Penelope J. Corfield, "Class by Name and Number in Eighteenth-Century Britain," *History* 72 (1987), 38–61. Asa Briggs, "The Language of 'Class' in early 19th-Century England," in *Essays in Labour History in Memory of G. D. H. Cole*, ed. Briggs and John Saville (London, 1960); also in M. W. Flinn and T. C. Smout, eds., *Essays in Social History* (Oxford, 1974). For French usages similar to the ones Corfield notes in England, see Marie-France Piguet, *Classe: histoire du mot et genèse du concept des physiocrates aux historiens de la Restauration* (Lyon, 1996).

11 Dror Wahrman, *Imagining the Middle Class: the Political Representation of Class in Britain, c. 1740–1840* (Cambridge, 1995), ch. 7; the quotation from James Mackintosh's essay is on 247.

12 See the speech in Macaulay, *Selected Writings*, ed. John Clive and Thomas Pinney (Chicago and London, 1972), 172. Wahrman refers to it, 357, but does not quote the whole passage.

13 See Price, *British Society*, chs. 7 and 8.

14 In addition to Price, *British Society*, see David Cannadine, *Lords and Landlords: the Aristocracy and the Towns, 1774–1967* (Leicester, 1980), ch. 1, esp. 26–36, and Rohan McWilliam, *Popular Politics in Nineteenth-Century England* (London and New York, 1998), 44–46, where relevant literature is cited.

15 *Ibid.*, 272–74. On the electoral registration lists see M. Ostrogorski, *Democracy and the Organization of Political Parties*, vol. I: *England*, trans. Frederick Clarke, ed. Seymour Martin Lipset (Chicago, 1964; orig. edn., 1902), 75–77.

16 For examples of all these usages see Briggs, "The Language of Class," and Penelope Corfield, "Class by Name and Number." For the harmony of interests see Wahrman, 90ff.

17 "The landed interest alone has a right to be represented; as for the rabble who have nothing but personal property, what hold has the nation of

them?" Cited from a court case of 1793 by Ostrogorski, *Democracy and the Organization of Political Parties*, n. 5.

18 Briggs, *Victorian Cities* (London and New York, 1963, 1968), 88.

19 *Ibid.*, 122–23.

20 See *ibid.*, 120, 129; on divisions in London over the Corn Law and the League, see also David Kynaston, *The City of London*, vol. 1: *a World of Its Own, 1815–1890* (London, 1994), ch. 11 (and *ibid.*, 97 for the Reform Bill). Sidney Pollard, "Free Trade, Protectionism, and the World Economy," in Martin H. Geyer and Johannes Paulmann, eds., *The Mechanics of Internationalism: Culture, Society, and Politics from the 1840s to the First World War* (Oxford, London, and New York, 2001), 48.

21 Briggs, *Victorian Cities*, 123–24.

22 Leonore Davidoff and Catherine Hall, *Family Fortunes: Men and Women of the English Middle Class, 1780–1850* (Chicago and London, 1987), 110.

23 Theodore Koditschek, *Class Formation and Urban-Industrial Society: Bradford 1750–1850* (Cambridge and New York, 1990), 184–98.

24 *Ibid.*, 200, quoting from Edward Miall, *The British Churches in Relation to the British People* (London, 1849).

25 A notable example is the book by Davidoff and Hall, cited just above.

26 Thomas Walter Laqueur, *Religion and Respectability: Sunday Schools and Working-Class Culture, 1780–1850* (New Haven and London, 1976), 239.

27 See Barraclough, *An Introduction to Contemporary History* (Harmondsworth and Baltimore, 1964, 1967), 133–45.

28 For examples of this usage see James J. Sheehan, *German Liberalism in the Nineteenth Century* (Chicago and London, 1978), 15–16, for early nineteenth century instances, and 128–29 for its survival into the 1860s and 1870s.

29 E. J. Hobsbawm, *The Age of Empire, 1875–1914* (New York, 1987), 110.

30 Moira Donald, "Workers of the World Unite? Exploring the Enigma of the Second International," in Martin H. Geyer and Johannes Paulmann, eds., *The Mechanics of Internationalism* (Oxford, 2001), 188–89.

31 Sheehan, *German Liberalism*, 141–42.

32 Hobsbawm, *Age of Empire*, 94.

33 John Vincent, *The Formation of the Liberal Party, 1857–1868* (London, 1966), 257–58, and 77 for Gladstone and working-class voters. A similar analysis of Gladstone was offered much earlier by J. L. Hammond in *Gladstone and the Irish Nation*; see the discussion by Peter Clarke in *Liberals and Social Democrats* (Cambridge and New York, 1978), 278–80.

34 The growth and importance of these organizations is a story retold by many writers, but the original account by Ostrogorski in *Democracy and the Organization of Political Parties* remains a basic source, as Barraclough notes in *An Introduction to Contemporary History*.

35 See H. V. Emy, *Liberals, Radicals, and Social Politics, 1892–1914*
    (Cambridge, 1973), 285–87.
36 On the LRL see Margot C. Finn, *After Chartism: Class and Nation in
    English Radical Politics, 1848–1874* (Cambridge and New York, 1993), 265,
    and 132–33 for the Chartists after 1848.
37 See Briggs, *Victorian Cities*, 187–88.
38 G. R. Searle, *The Liberal Party: Triumph and Disintegration, 1886–1929*
    (London and New York, 1992), 37–38.
39 Simon Gunn, *The Public Culture of the Victorian Middle Class: Ritual and
    Authority and the English Industrial City, 1840–1914* (Manchester and
    New York, 2000), 24 for these quotes.
40 Among the many histories of the Liberal Party, I rely chiefly on Searle, *The
    Liberal Party*.
41 For these developments see Flinn, *After Chartism*.
42 D. S. Gadian, "Class Consciousness in Oldham and other North-West
    Industrial Towns, 1830–50," in R. J. Morris and Richard Rodger, eds., *The
    Victorian City: a Reader in British Urban History, 1820–1914* (London and
    New York, 1993), 251–52.
43 On "the two Hobs" there are excellent discussion in both Clarke, *Liberals
    and Social Democrats* and Emy, *Liberals, Radicals, and Social Politics*.
44 See David Powell, "The New Liberalism and the Rise of Labour," *The
    Historical Journal* 29 (1986), 369–93, who argues that a major tension
    between liberalism and workers in the years when the latter were gaining more
    independent power and organization was that the liberals were a governing
    party, and thus necessarily given to compromise and the balancing of interests,
    while Labour represented a sectional interest based on a suspicion of the
    capitalist state, which gave it a degree of freedom of action that the liberals did
    not have. Powell notes all the same that the traditional liberal opposition to
    class politics was an important element of this contrast; see esp. 388.

6   France and bourgeois France: from teleocracy to autonomy

1   Eugen Weber, *Peasants into Frenchmen: the Modernization of Rural France,
    1870–1914* (Stanford, 1976). Pierre Rosanvallon, *The Demands of Liberty:
    Civil Society in France since the Revolution*, trans. Arthur Goldhammer
    (Cambridge, MA, and London, 2007). Susan Carol Rogers, *Shaping
    Modern Times in Rural France: the Transformation and Reproduction of
    an Aveyronnais Community* (Princeton, 1991). Stéphane Gerson, *The Pride
    of Place: Local Memories and Political Culture in Nineteenth-Century
    France* (Ithaca, 2003). Gérard Noiriel, *Les Ouvriers dans la société française:
    XIXe–XXe siècle* (Paris, 1986).

2 Noiriel, *Les Ouvriers*, 33, 49.

3 For one example, see Claude Fohlen, *Une affaire de famille au XIXe siècle: Mequillet-Noblot* (Paris, 1955), 14.

4 Yves Lequin, *Les Ouvriers de la région Lyonnaise (1848–1914)* (Lyon, 1977). For a good account in English see Robert J. Bezucha, *The Lyons Uprising of 1834: Social and Political Conflict in the Early July Monarchy* (Cambridge, MA, 1974).

5 Eugen Weber, *Peasants into Frenchmen: the Modernization of Rural France, 1870–1914* (Stanford, 1976), 281; Noiriel, *Les Ouvriers*, 51.

6 Weber, *Peasants into Frenchmen*, 196, 233, 212ff.

7 Auguste Mimerel, *Du pauperisme et de ses rapports avec l'industrie en France et en Angleterre* (Lille, n.d.[1841]). Jean-Pierre Daviet, *La Société industrielle en France, 1814–1914: productions, échanges, répresentations* (Paris, 1997), 39–40, discusses this pamphlet, but he underplays Mimerel's emphasis on the English reliance on production for export. For some other examples of such sentiments see Yves Leclercq, *Le Réseau impossible: la résistance au système des grandes compagnies ferroviaires et la politique économique en France, 1820–52* (Geneva, 1987), 24.

8 Noiriel, *Les Ouvriers*, 69; 78–79.

9 Jean-Pierre Daviet, *La Société industrielle en France*, 123–32; Noiriel, *Les Ouvriers*, 58. For workers struggles over workplace control and *tarifs*, see Robert Bezucha, *The Lyons Uprising of 1834*, cited above, and William M. Reddy, *The Rise of Market Culture: the Textile Trade and French Society, 1700–1900* (Cambridge and New York, 1984). Jeff Horn emphasizes worker resistance to innovation as an important factor in slowing down industrial change in *The Path Not Taken: French Industrialization in the Age of Revolution, 1789–1830* (Cambridge, MA, and London, 2006).

10 All the texts are cited, with references, in Yves Leclercq, *Le Réseau impossible*, 13–17.

11 François Caron, *Histoire des chemins de fer en France*, I: *1740–1883* (Paris, 1997), 95–121; the quotation is on 113. Caron also draws on Leclercq, *Le Réseau impossible*.

12 *Ibid.*, 124–26.

13 For the thesis about the modern quality of workers, Charles Tilly and Lynn Lees, "The People of June, 1848," in *Revolution and Reaction, 1848 and the Second French Republic*, ed. Roger Price (London, 1975). For their traditional features, see Christopher H. Johnson, "Communism and the Working-Class before Marx: the Icarian Experience," *American Historical Review* 76 (1971), 642–89, and *Utopian Communism: Cabet and the Icarians, 1839–51* (Ithaca, NY, 1974). William Sewell, jr., *Work and Revolution in France: the Language of Labor from the Old Regime to 1848* (Cambridge and New York, 1980), combines both views, but

emphasizes the way workers in general preserved a corporate idiom from the Old Regime.

14 Louis Chevalier, *La Formation de la population parisienne au xixe siècle* (Paris, 1950). For cotton manufacturing in early nineteenth-century Paris, see David Pinckney, "Paris, Capitale du coton sous le Premier Empire," *Annales ESC* V (1950), 50–60.

15 Paul M. Hohenberg and Lynn Hollen Lees, *The Making of Urban Europe, 1000–1950* (Cambridge, MA, and London, 1985), 96. For the fears of the immigrants see Chevalier's other famous book, *Laboring Classes and Dangerous Classes in Paris During the First Half of the Nineteenth Century*, trans. Frank Jellinek (New York, 1973).

16 Adeline Daumard, *La Bourgeoisie parisienne de 1815 à 1848* (Paris, 1963), 647–50.

17 *Ibid.*, xi. The speaker was Garnier-Pages.

18 Henri Monnier, *Physiologie du bourgeois* (Paris, n.d. [1841?]). I argue in *Bohemian Paris: Culture, Politics and the Boundaries of Bourgeois Life* (New York, 1986; Baltimore, 1999) that the emerging figure of the bohemian in these years served in part to give more clarity to the image of the bourgeois.

19 Daumard, *La Bourgeoisie parisienne*, 220–46, and *passim*.

20 For Marx's literary interests in general, and for later socialist fascination with Balzac, see S. S. Prawer, *Karl Marx and World Literature* (Oxford, 1976), still the best survey of Marx's literary interests. But see also my account of their relations in *Marx's Fate: the Shape of a Life* (Princeton, 1978). Engels's letter about Balzac is cited in Peter Demetz, *Marx, Engels and the Poets* (Chicago, 1967), 173–74.

21 Michel Chevalier, *Religion Saint-Simonienne. Le bourgeois.–Le Revélateur* (Paris, 1834?), 3–4.

22 E. H. Labrousse, "1848, 1830, 1789: How Revolutions are Born," in François Crouzet, W. H. Challoner, and W. M. Stern, eds., *Essays in European Economic History* (New York, 1970).

23 Caron, *Histoire des chemins de fer*, 166–210; Weber, *Peasants into Frenchmen*, 207–10, and Daviet, *La Société industrielle en France*, 184. For resistance by local bourgeois to railroad building that required the intervention of the state, see also Louis Desgraves, Georges Dupeux *et al.*, *Bordeaux au XIXe siècle*, vol. VI of *Histoire de Bordeaux*, 8 vols., general editor Ch. Higounet (Bordeaux, 1969), 202.

24 Daviet, *La Société industrielle en France*, 182.

25 Weber, *Peasants into Frenchmen*, 221.

26 I have followed these events in Marx's career in *Marx's Fate*.

27 Weber, *Peasants into Frenchmen*, 207.

28 Marcel Roncayolo, "Logiques urbaines," in *La Ville de l'âge industriel: le cycle Hausmannien*, ed. Maurice Agulhon (Paris, 1983, paper edn., 1998),

vol. IV of *Histoire de la France urbaine*, sous la direction de Georges Duby, esp. 105; Jeanne Gaillard, *Paris, la ville (1852–1870)* (Paris, 1976; 1997 edn., ed. Florence Bourillon and Jean-Luc Pinol), 30–39.

29 Edmond About, "Dans les ruines," in *Paris Guide*, par les principaux écrivains et artistes de la France (Paris, 1867), 916–17. Roncayolo, "Logiques urbaines,"106–07.

30 Gaillard, *Paris, la ville*, 65–67. For an example of a *commerçant* whose business included ready-to-wear articles, hats, lingerie, and who increasingly sold his wares (including wine in the later part of his life) in England, see Romain Lhopiteau, *Soixante-deux Années de ma vie: recits intimes et commerciaux, 1828–90* (Paris, 1891). Lhopiteau fell foul of the difficulties in getting credit during the 1860s, as well as of the shifting winds of fashion, and had to declare bankruptcy at one point, but worked his way back to a measure of prosperity and respectability. I discuss what his memoir tells about gender relations later on.

31 Gaillard, *Paris, la ville*, 257–67, 429–30.

32 Adeline Daumard *et al.*, *Les Fortunes françaises au XIXe siècle* (Paris and The Hague, 1973), ch. 5.

33 Michael B. Miller, *The Bon Marché: Bourgeois Culture and the Department Store, 1869–1920* (Princeton and London, 1981). For the politics of the shopkeepers see Philip G. Nord, *Paris Shopkeepers and the Politics of Resentment* (Princeton, 1986).

34 On Mme Boucicaut see Miller, 46 and 127; on Boucicaut's politics see Gaillard, *Paris, la ville*, 413.

35 Miller, *The Bon Marché*, 226–27. For a similar persistence of older and more familial-based values and practices with more "extroverted" ones in French bourgeois of another city, Lille, see Jean-Pierre Hirsch, *Les deux rêves du Commerce: Entreprise et institution dans la region lilloise (1780–1860)* (Paris, 1991).

36 For the *légitimités* see Maurice Agulhon, *La République: l'élan fondateur et la grande blessure (1880–1932)* (2 vols; rev. and enlarged edn., Paris, 1990), I, 26.

37 On Thiers see J. P. T. Bury and R. P. Tombs, *Thiers, 1797–1877: a Political Life* (London, 1986). For the passages quoted see 123, 34; and for Thiers in the 1870s 197ff. I am grateful to Philip Nord for a conversation about Thiers.

38 *Ibid.*, 28.

39 For the importance of the Second Empire in this respect, see the works of Hazareesingh and Nord cited just below in note 41.

40 François Furet, *Revolutionary France, 1770–1880*, trans. Antonia Nevrill (Oxford and Cambridge, MA, 1992), 523–34.

41 Sudhir Hazareesingh, *From Subject to Citizen: the Second Empire and the Emergence of Modern French Democracy* (Princeton, 1998). Raymond Huard, *La Naissance du parti politique en France* (Paris, 1996). Philip G.

Nord, *The Republican Moment: Struggles for Democracy in Nineteenth-Century France* (Cambridge, MA, and London, 1995).

42 Furet, *Revolutionary France*, 525.

43 Agulhon, *La République*, I, 69–70.

44 For the two careers see *ibid.*, 53–59, and Jean-Michel Gaillard, *Jules Ferry* (Paris, 1989), 52–55.

45 I owe the suggestion in the first part of this sentence to Raymond Huard, *La Naissance du parti politique en France*, 205.

46 On them, see Jean Garrigues, *La République des hommes d'affaires, 1870–1900* (Paris, 1997); and Agulhon, *La République*, I, 51.

47 Huard, *La Naissance du parti politique en France*, 268.

48 *Ibid.*, 287.

49 For the history of legislation and much else on associations, see Carol E. Harrison, *The Bourgeois Citizen in Nineteenth-Century France: Gender, Sociability and the Uses of Emulation* (Oxford, 1999), ch. 2; also Huard, *La Naissance du parti politique en France*, 289–310, and Pierre Sorlin, *Waldeck-Rousseau* (Paris, 1966), 439–49. On the general hostility to intermediate bodies, see Lucien Jaume, *L'Individu effacé, ou le paradoxe du liberalisme français* (Paris, 1997). Also Jean-Claude Bardout, *L'Histoire étonnante de la loi 1901: le droit d'association en France avant et après Waldeck-Rousseau* (Paris, 2001).

50 See Huard, *La Naissance du parti politique en France*, 243.

51 Sara Maza, "Luxury, Morality, and Social Change: Why There Was No Middle-Class Consciousness in Prerevolutionary France," *Journal of Modern History* 69 (June, 1997), 228.

52 Huard, *La Naissance du parti politique en France*, 315; but I admit to going somewhat beyond him in this paragraph.

7 One special path: modern industry, politics, and bourgeois life in Germany

1 It may be that those who originally proposed the *Sonderweg* thesis were guilty, as Detlev Peukert puts it, of setting up "a 'normal' model of modernization against which individual non-normal 'deviations' can be measured" (Detlev J. K. Peukert, *The Weimar Republic: the Crisis of Classical Modernity*, trans. Richard Deveson [New York, 1992], xiii). But arguing as he and others do that because modern societies are often on the edge of crisis all have basically the same history simply inverts the model, blotting out the way that differing relations between the several spheres of life mark each case. The classic critique of the *Sonderweg* thesis as developed by Jürgen Kocka and Hans-Ulrich Wehler is David Blackbourn and Geoff Eley, *The Peculiarities of German History: Bourgeois Society and Politics in Nineteenth-Century Germany* (New York and Oxford, 1984). I take up some of their assertions at

the end of this chapter. A different kind of dissent was registered by Jonathan Sperber, "*Bürger, Bürgertum, Bürgerlichkeit, Bürgerliche Gesellschaft*: Studies of the German (Upper) Middle Class and its Sociocultural World," *Journal of Modern History*, 69 (June, 1997), 271–97. On the National Society see Theodore S. Hamerow, *The Social Foundations of German Unification, 1858–1871: Ideas and Institutions* (Princeton, 1969), and on the unification process, Otto Pflanze, *Bismarck and the Development of Germany*, 1: the *Period of Unification, 1815–71* (Princeton, 1963; reprinted 1990).

2 Hamerow, *The Social Foundations of German Unification*, 24.

3 Knut Borchardt, "Germany, 1700–1914," trans. George Hammerley, in *The Fontana Economic History of Europe*, vol. IV: the *Emergence of Industrial Societies*, ed. Carlo M. Cipolla (London and New York, 1973), 142–43.

4 W. O. Henderson, *The Industrial Revolution in Europe: Germany, France, Russia, 1815–1914* (Chicago, 1961), 19–20.

5 Hamerow, *The Social Foundations of German Unification*, 25–26.

6 David Blackbourn, *History of Germany, 1780–1918: the Long Nineteenth Century* (2nd edn., Malden, MA, and Oxford, 2003), 262.

7 Blackbourn, *History of Germany, 1780–1918*, 135–41. For a similar view see the chapter by Borchardt referred to just above.

8 *Ibid.*, 143–44, 148–49, 158–59.

9 See Rudolf Boch, "Von der 'begrenzten' zur forcierten Industrialisierung: zum Wandel ökonomischer Zielvorstellungen im rheinischen Wirtschaftsbürgertum 1815–1845," in *Bürger in Gesellschaft der Neuzeit: Wirtschaft – Politik – Kultur*, ed. Hans-Jürgen Puhle (Göttingen, 1991), 133–55. For similar discussions between Germans in Bavaria, see Franz J. Bauer, *Bürgerwege und Bürgerwelten: Familienbiographische Untersuchungen zum deutschen Bürgertum im 19. Jahrhundert* (Göttingen, 1991), 62–64.

10 On Rochau see James J. Sheehan, *German History, 1770–1866* (Oxford and New York, 1989), 853–54; Dieter Langewiesche, *Liberalismus in Deutschland* (Frankfurt am Main, 1986; translated into English by Christiane Bannerji as *Liberalism in Germany* [Princeton, 2000]), 70. On the "blood and iron" speech see Pflanze, *Bismarck and the Development of Germany*, 1, 180–84.

11 Karin Kaudelka-Hanisch, "The Titled Businessman: Prussian Commercial Councillors in the Rhineland and Westphalia during the Nineteenth Century," in David Blackbourn and Richard J. Evans, eds., *The German Bourgeiosie: Essays on the Social History of the German Middle Class from the late Eighteenth to the early Twentieth Century* (London and New York, 1991), 87–114, 107 for the quotation. See also Dolores L. Augustine, *Patricians and Parvenus: Wealth and High Society in Wilhelmine Germany* (Oxford and Providence, RI, 1994), ch. 1. Some German businessmen did seek nobility and hereditary titles, for instance the banker Gerson

Bleichröder. His behavior was often ridiculed by the more practical and prosaic Rothschilds, but Bleichrôder's acceptance of hereditary nobility from Bismarck did not lead him away from business either. Fritz Stern, *Gold and Iron: Bismarck, Bleichröder, and the Building of the German Empire* (New York, 1977), 168. On the duels as seen by an English visitor see Peter Gay, *The Cultivation of Hatred* (New York, 1993), 9–33.

12 Clive Trebilcock, *The Industrialization of the Continental Powers, 1780–1914* (London and New York, 1981). For a somewhat more skeptical view see Jürgen Kocka, "Entrepreneurship in a Latecomer Country: the German Case," in his book *Industrial Culture and Bourgeois Society: Business, Labor, and Bureaucracy in Modern Germany* (New York and Oxford, 1999), 70–102. There is a succinct and colorful account of the *Gründerkrise* and its effects in Gordon A. Craig, *Germany, 1866–1945* (New York and Oxford, 1980), 78–85.

13 For the material in this paragraph see R. Steven Turner, "The Growth of Professorial Research in Prussia, 1818 to 1848 – Causes and Context." *Historical Studies in the Physical Sciences*, 3 (1971), 137–82. On Liebig and his followers there is a fine concise account in Sheehan, *German History*, 808ff. On the associations see Everett Mendelsohn, "The Emergence of Science as a Profession in Nineteenth-Century Europe," in *The Management of Scientists*, ed. Karl Hill (Boston, 1963), 3–48.

14 Franz J. Bauer, *Bürgerwege und Bürgerwelten: Familienbiographische Untersuchungen zum deutschen Bürgertum im 19. Jahrhundert* (Göttingen, 1991). For the points emphasized here about Sattler's career see 28–32, 55–60, and for the general point suggested at the end of this paragraph, 280–84. I have not quite taken over all of Bauer's interpretations of these connections, however.

15 Kocka, "Family and Bureaucracy in German Industrial Management, 1850–1914: Siemens in Comparative Perspective," in *Industrial Culture and Bourgeois Society*, 27–50 (40–41 for the quoted phrases).

16 Menachem Blondheim, *News Over the Wires: the Telegraph and the Flow of Public Information in America* (Cambridge, MA, and London, 1994), 194–95, and Menachem Blondheim, "When Bad Things Happen to Good Technologies: Three Phases in the Diffusion and Perception of American Telegraphy," in *Technology, Pessmimism, and Postmodernism*, ed. Yaron Ezrahi *et al.* (Dordrecht, Boston, London, 1994), 85–86.

17 The literature on professions is of course enormous. For some of the points made in this paragraph see Konrad H. Jarausch, "German Professions in History and Theory," in *German Professions, 1800–1950*, ed. Geoffrey Cocks and Jarausch (New York and Oxford, 1990), 9–24; Claudia Huerkamp, "The Making of the Modern Medical Profession, 1800–1914: Prussian Doctors in the Nineteenth Century,"

in *ibid.*, 56–84; the essays by Kees Gispen and Jeffrey A. Johnson on engineers and chemists in the same volume; Charles McClelland, "Zur Professionalisierung der akademischen Berüfe in Deutschland," in *Bildungsbürgertum im 19. Jahrhundert*, I, ed. Werner Conze and Jürgen Kocka (Stuttgart, 1985), 233–47, and Ivan Waddington, "Medicine, the Market, and Professional Autonomy: Some Aspects of the Professionalization of Medicine," in the same volume, 388–416. For France, Toby Gelfand, "A 'Monarchical Profession' in the old Regime: Surgeons, Ordinary Practitioners, and Medical Professionalization in Eighteenth-Century France," in *Professions and the French State, 1700–1900*, ed. Gerald L. Geison (Philadelphia, 1984), 149–80, and Matthey Ramsey, "The Politics of Professional Monopoly in Nineteenth-Century Medicine: the French Model and its Rivals," in *ibid.*, 225–305.

18 Joel Mokyr, *The Gifts of Athena: Historical Origins of the Knowledge Economy* (Princeton and London, 2002), 101, 140.

19 See the electoral figures in Robert Hofman, *Geschichte der deutschen Parteien, von der Kaiserzeit bis zur Gegenwart* (Munich, 1993), 23. For the social-democratic movement and its organizations one can still rely on Vernon Lidtke, *The Alternative Culture. Socialist Labor in Imperial Germany* (New York and Oxford, 1985).

20 Sheehan, *German History*, 885–88, and *German Liberalism in the Nineteenth Century*, 93, and for the election statistics, 82–83, and Hofman, *Geschichte der deutschen Parteien*; Langewiesche, *Liberalismus*, 120; Karsten Rudolph, "On the Disappearance of a Political Party from German History: the Saxon people's Party, 1866–69," in *Saxony in German History: Culture, Society, and Politics, 1830–1933*, ed. James Retallack (Ann Arbor, 2000), 211. Thomas Adam, "How Proletarian Was Leipzig's Social Democratic Milieu?" in the same volume, 255–70.

21 James J. Sheehan, "Wie bürgerlich war der deutsche Liberalismus?" in Langewiesche's already-cited collection *Liberalismus im 19. Jahrhundert: Deutschland im europäischen Vergleich*, 37.

22 Langewiesche, *Liberalismus in Deutschland*, 58–59, 145.

23 Sheehan, *German Liberalism*, 231–33. See also 148–52 for the earlier history of the same matters, and Hofmann, *Geschichte der deutschen Parteien*, 30–53. John Boyer notes a similar ambivalence toward organization on the part of Austrian liberals: *Political Radicalism in Late Imperial Vienna: Origins of the Christian Social Movement, 1848–1897* (Chicago and London, 1981), 324–25, 369.

24 Langewiesche, *Liberalismus in Deutschland*, 59–60.

25 *Ibid.*, 206–07.

26 Langewiesche, *Liberalismus in Deutschland*, 153, 233–38.

27 Hofmann, *Geschichte der deutschen Parteien*, 107–08.

28 On the conservatives, Hofmann, *ibid.*, 92–94. For a general discussion of the *Verbände* see Thomas Nipperdey, "Interessenverbände und Parteien in Deutschland vor dem Ersten Weltkrieg," originally in *Politische Vierteljahrschrift*, I:2 (1961), reprinted in *Moderne deutsche Sozialgeschichte*, ed. Hans-Ulrich Wehler (Düsseldorf, 1981), 369–88. On the *Bund der Landwirte*, Hans-Jürgen Puhle, *Agrarische Interessenpolitik und Preussischer Konservatismus im Wilhelminischen Reich* (Hanover, 1967). On the Zentralverband deutscher Industriellen, see Hartmut Kaelble, *Industrielle Interessenpolitik in der Wilhelminischen Gesellschaft* (Berlin, 1968). There is an valuable review of the last two titles by J. C. G. Röhl in *Central European History*, vol. 1 (1968), 182–86.

29 Nipperdey, "Interessenverbände," 387.

30 Lionel Gossman, *Basel in the Age of Burckhardt: a Study in Unseasonable Ideas* (Chicago and London, 2000), 23–24.

31 Hans-Ulrich Wehler, "Die Geburtsstunde des deutschen Kleinbürgertums," in *Bürger in Gesellschaft der Neuzeit: Wirtschaft–Politik–Kultur*, ed. Hans-Jürgen Puhle (Göttingen, 1991), 199–209. Wehler specifically cites Walker as one of the few historians whose work identifies the roots of the distinction between *Bürger* and *Kleinbürger*.

32 Quoted in Geoffrey Crossick and Heinz-Gerhard Haupt, *The Petite Bourgeoisie in Europe, 1780–1914: Enterprise, Family, and Independence* (London and New York, 1995), 113.

33 Crossick and Haupt, 9. For the similar chronology in France, see Carol E. Harrison, *The Bourgeois Citizen in Nineteenth-Century France: Gender, Sociability and the Uses of Emulation* (Oxford, 1999).

34 Crossick and Haupt, 122–26 and *passim*. A pioneering discussion of the persistence of small enterprise is Charles Sabel and Jonathan Zeitlin, "Historical Alternatives to Mass Production: Politics, Markets and Technology in 19th-Century Industrialization," *Past and Present*, 108 (August, 1985), 133–76. On Paris shopkeepers see J. Le Yaouang, "Trajectoires sociales à Paris au XIXe siècle: le monde de la boutique," in *Bulletin du Centre Pierre Léon*, 4 (1993), 25–40, and for their relations with department stores and their politics, Philip G. Nord's important work, *Paris Shopkeepers and the Politics of Resentment* (Princeton, 1986).

35 David Blackbourn, *History of Germany, 1780–1918: the Long Nineteenth Century* (2nd edn., Malden, MA, and Oxford, 2003), 239, 245. Blackbourn also discusses the survival of small merchants and manufacturers, emphasizing the uncertainties many such people faced, 246–47. Theodore Zeldin, *France, 1848–1945*, vol. 1: *Ambition, Love and Politics* (Oxford, 1973), 114. For the earlier period, Eric Hobsbawm,

The Age of Revolution, 1789–1848 (London and Oxford, 1964; orig. edn., 1962), 226–33.

36 Wolfgang Köllman, *Sozialgeschichte der Stadt Barmen im 19ten Jahrhundert* (Tübingen, 1960), chart on 102–04. For a similar development see David F. Crew, *Town in the Ruhr: a Social History of Bochum, 1860–1914* (Cambridge and New York, 1979).

37 Geoff Eley, "The Wilhelmine Right: How It Changed," in *Society and Politics in Wilhelmine Germany*, ed. Richard J. Evans (London and New York, 1978), 125, 129. Robert O. Paxton, *The Anatomy of Fascism* (New York, 2004), 72–73. For a persuasive demonstration that lower-middle-class people could be drawn both to democratic and authoritarian forms of populist politics depending on the opportunities offered by forms of organization see Philip Nord, *Paris Shopkeepers* (cited above).

38 Langewiesche, *Liberalismus*, 133, 137–39.

39 As noted by Sheehan, *German Liberalism*, 246–47.

40 *Ibid.*, 251–52. Hobrecht is also quoted by Langewiesche, *Liberalismus*, 218. On Weber's politics the great work is Wolfgang J. Mommsen, *Max Weber and German Politics*, trans. Michael S. Steinberg (Chicago, 1984; orig. edn., Tübungen, 1974).

41 Langewiesche, *Liberalismus*, 182–85 (English edn., 202–05); Sheehan, *German Liberalism*, 134–37.

42 Mommsen, *Max Weber and German Politics*, *passim*; Langeiwesche, 219ff. (English edn., 237ff.).

43 See for instance the forthright admission of this by Gabriel Riesser in Langewiesche, *Liberalismus*, 64.

44 Langewiesche, *Liberalismus*, 115–18; Sheehan, 91ff., 152ff. and *passim*.

45 See Richard J. Evans's monumental study, *Death in Hamburg: Society and Politics in the Cholera Years, 1830–1910* (Oxford, 1987).

46 Langewiesche, *Liberalismus*, 200–11 (206 for the quoted passage); English edn., 218–28.

47 Karl Heinrich Pohl, "Power in the City: Liberalism and Local Politics in Dresden and Munich," in *Saxony in German History: Culture, Society, and Politics, 1830–1933*, ed. James Retallack (Ann Arbor, 2000), 289–308.

48 Langewiesche, *Liberalismus*, 224–27, English edn., 241–45; Sheehan, *German Liberalism*, 26–71. Langewiesche's assessment of the state of the party on the eve of the war is somewhat more positive than Sheehan's.

49 See Chapter 4.

50 See, for instance, David Blackbourn and Geoff Eley, *The Peculiarities of German History: Bourgeois Society and Politics in Nineteenth-Century Germany* (New York and Oxford, 1984), 193–94, where Otto von Gierke's judgment to this effect is cited with approval.

51 Hobsbawm, *The Age of Capital*, 274–75. See Antonio Gramsci, *Selections from the Prison Notebooks*, ed. and trans. Geofrey Nowell Smith and Quintin Hoare (London, 1971 and later edns.). There is a more complete English translation of the *Quaderni del carcere* in three vols., by Joseph A. Buttigieg (New York, 1991–2007).

52 Blackbourn and Eley, *The Peculiarities of German History*, 144.

53 Blackbourn, *History of Germany, 1780–1914*, 264. For a similar view see Fritz Stern, *Gold and Iron: Bismarck, Bleichröder, and the Building of the German Empire* (New York, 1977), 202.

8 Time, Money, Capital

1 Gerhard Dohrn-van Rossum, *History of the Hour: Clocks and Modern Temporal Orders*, trans. Thomas Dunlap, Chicago and London, 1996; orig. edn., 1992), 107–08.

2 *Ibid.*, ch. 5 esp. 156, and ch. 8, 245–51.

3 *Ibid.*, 346, and ch. 10.

4 For an insightful and convenient account of Simmel's thinking in this regard, see Laurence Scialom, "De 'Philosophie de L'Argent' à la compréhension de la cohesion d'une économie monetaire décentralisé: une esquisse," in *À Propos de 'Philosphie de l'argent' de Georg Simmel*, ed. Jean-Yves Grenier (Paris, 1993), 163–88. Somewhat similar ideas about money, in the face of the litany of complaints often made about it, were voiced by earlier writers. We noted Bernard Mandeville's view of money as "a thing more skillfully adapted to the whole Bent of our Nature, than any other of human Contrivance," in Chapter 1. Some decades later, the German poet and philosopher Novalis referred to the commercial exchanges made possible by money in a similar way, writing in his notebook that "The commercial spirit is the spirit of the world. It is the great spirit altogether." See Novalis's *Allgemeine Brouillon*, in *Novalis Werke*, ed. Gerhard Schulz (Munich, 1981), 495. The passage is discussed by Christoph Asendorf, *Batteries of Life*, trans. Don Reneau (Berkeley, 1993), 17–18.

5 Much of this account relies on Glynn Davies, *A History of Money: from Ancient Times to the Present Day* (Cardiff, Wales, 2002).

6 Quoted in Davies, *ibid.*, 294. For the radical critique of paper money see Gregory Claeys, *Machinery, Money and the Millennium: From Moral Economy to Socialism, 1815–1860* (Princeton, 1987), 25.

7 Davies, *A History of Money*, 305–16.

8 Walter Bagehot, *Lombard Street: a Description of the Money Market* (London, 1873; I cite the New York, 1910 edn.), 55. A somewhat similar understanding had already been put forward at the beginning of the nineteenth century

by Henry Thornton; see Forrest Capie, "Banking in Europe in the Nineteenth Century: the Role of the Central Bank," in *The State, the Financial System and Economic Modernization*, ed. Richard Sylla, Richard Tilly, and Gabriel Tortella (Cambridge and New York, 1999), 120–21.

9 Davies, 343–44. In addition, private banknotes continued to circulate as well. As Davies notes, "One of the purposes of the Bank Charter Act of 1844 had been to replace private banknotes with those of the Bank of England–though it was a long process which took nearly seventy years before the last note-issuing joint-stock bank, Fox, Fowler & Co., gave up issuing when absorbed by Lloyds in 1921, so enabling the Bank of England to increase its fiduciary issue to its eventual maximum under the 1844 Act, i.e. to £19 1/4 million" (376).

10 See Paul Butel and Jean-Pierre Pousssou, *La Vie quotidienne à Bordeaux au XVIIIe siècle* (Paris, 1980), 80.

11 Honoré de Balzac, *Lost Illusions*, trans. Herbert J. Hunt (Harmondsworth, Eng., and Baltimore, 1971); see 417 and ch. 35. For the dominance of such practices among early nineteenth-century French publishers, see Elisabeth Parinet, *Une Histoire de l'édition à l'époque contemporaine (xixe–xxe siècle)* (Paris, 2004), 27, and Frédéric Barbier and Catherine Bertho Lavenir, *Histoire des médias: de Diderot à Internet* (Paris, 1996), 68ff. For an example of the role of bills of exchange in bringing about an actual bankruptcy in the early 1830s see Jean-Baptiste Curmer, "Souvenirs d'un bourgeois de Rouen," in Jean-Pierre Chaline, ed., *Deux Bourgeois en leur temps: documents sur la société Rouennaise du XIXe siècle* (Rouen, 1977), 112, where Curmer describes the failure of his brother-in-law.

12 Jeanne Gaillard, *Paris, la ville (1852–1870)*, ed. Florence Bourillon and Jean-Luc Pinol (Paris, 1997), 272–76. That many businesses continued to operate in the old way is evident from the account in the autobiography of a *commerçant* who suffered bankruptcy as a result: Romain Lhopiteau, *Soixante-deux années de ma vie: recits intimes et commerciaux, 1828–90* (Paris, 1891). For similar practices in the Nord see Gaston Motte, *Les Motte: Étude de la descendance Motte-Clarisse, 1750–1950* (Roubaix, 1950), 68.

13 See Davies, *A History of Money*, 555–62, Alain Plessis, *La Banque de France et ses deux cents actionnaires sous le second empire* (Geneva, 1982), and François Caron, *An Economic History of Modern France*, trans. Barbara Bray (New York, 1979), 54–59. Eugen Weber finds that this situation persisted even longer in many parts of the French countryside: *Peasants into Frenchmen: the Modernization of Rural France, 1870–1914* (Stanford, 1976), 33–40.

14 Quoted in Plessis, *La Banque de France*, 31.

15 As Glynn Davies notes: "just when the banks in France, and even more so in Germany, were forging their close links with industry and strengthening the regional bases of their financial institutions, the British banks were loosening their ties with local industry, strictly avoiding becoming entangled in medium and long-term lending, and began centralizing financial flows and decision-making in London. Partly as a consequence the failure rate of the British banks declined–as did the growth rate of British industry together with Britain's long-held lead" in industrial finance. Davies, *A History of Money*, 562.

16 Richard Tilly, *Geld und Kredit in der Wirtschaftsgeschichte* (Suttgart, 2003), 86–99.

17 Ron Chernow, *The Death of the Banker: the Decline and Fall of the Great Financial Dynasties and the Triumph of the Small Investor* (New York, 1997). Louis Bergeron, *Les Rothschilds et les autres: la gloire des banquiers* (Paris, 1991), 95–96. For the story of a number of French banking families that gained great power in the nineteenth century but lost it later on, see René Sedillot, *Les Deux Cents Familles* (Paris, 1988).

18 Niall Ferguson, *The House of Rothschild: the World's Banker, 1849–1999* (New York and London, 1999), xxv. On Frankfurt as a center for government finance in Germany, see Bergeron, *Les Rothschilds et les autres*, 39–40.

19 Philip Ziegler, *The Sixth Great Power: a history of one of the greatest of all banking families, the House of Barings, 1762–1929* (New York, 1988), 85.

20 Ferguson, *The House of Rothschild*, 65.

21 *Ibid.*, 40–61.

22 Plessis, *La Banque de France*, 62–63, 256.

23 Ferguson, *The House of Rothschild*, 74, 159.

24 Ziegler, *The Sixth Great Power*, 199–202.

25 Chernow, *Death of the Banker*, 91.

26 *Selected Writings of Pierre-Joseph Proudhon*, ed. with an introduction by Stewart Edwards, trans. Elizabeth Fraser (New York, 1969), 42–43.

27 *Ibid.*, 45.

28 The summary of Marx's economic theory in these paragraphs is taken over from chs. 10 and 11 of my book, *Marx's Fate: the Shape of a Life* (Princeton, 1978), where all the texts are cited and analyzed at much greater length.

29 For the quotation in this paragraph and the context in which it appears, see *Marx's Fate*, 312.

30 On Engels's editing of the later parts of *Capital* and the complex relations between Marx's views on this topic and his friend's, see *ibid.*, 336–47.

31 Marx, *Grundrisse*, trans. Martin Nicolaus (London, 1873), 705. *Marx's Fate*, 315.

9 Men and women

1 Quoted from Meyer's *Grosse Conversations-Lexicon* by David Blackbourn, *History of Germany, 1780–1918: the Long Nineteenth Century* (2nd edn., Malden, MA, and Oxford, 2003), 162.

2 From John Dod and Robert Cleaver, *A Godly Forme of Householde Gouernment* (London, 1614), as reported in Kathleen M. Davis, "The Sacred Condition of Equality: How Original Were Puritan Doctrines of Marriage?" *Social History*, 5 (1977), 510, cited by Nancy Armstrong, *Desire and Domestic Fiction: a Political History of the Novel* (New York and London, 1987), 18–19.

3 James McMillan, *Housewife or Harlot: the Woman Question in France under the Third Republic* (New York, 1980), 9. For similar assumptions in the eighteenth century see Françoise Mayeur, *L'Éducation des filles en France au XIXe siècle* (Paris, 1979), 22–23.

4 Amanda Vickery, "Golden Age to Separate Spheres? A Review of the Categories and Chronology of English Women's History," *The Historical Journal*, 36 (1993), 383–414 (404–05 and 413 for the passages quoted above, save that the list of occupations is from the summary she gives in the introduction to her book, *The Gentleman's Daughter: Women's Lives in Georgian England* (New Haven and London, 1998), 4–5. The target of her critique was the (in many ways still valuable) work of Leonore Davidoff and Catherine Hall, *Family Fortunes: Men and Women of the English Middle Class, 1780–1850* (Chicago and London, 1987). There is a wide literature on female contributions to the economy, referred to by Angélique Janssens in the introduction to her edited volume, *The Rise and Decline of the Male Breadwinner Family?* (*International Review of Social History* Supplement, 5; Cambridge and New York, 1997), but Janssens somewhat confuses things by conflating the question of what women contributed quantitatively to incomes with the different issue of separate work spheres. For male power in guilds almost any history of the subject can be consulted (see those cited in the early chapters above), but there is overwhelming evidence for instance in Isabel V. Hull, *Sexuality, State and Civil Society in Germany, 1700–1815* (Ithaca and London, 1996).

5 Marion G. Gray, *Productive Men, Reproductive Women: The Agrarian Household and the Emergence of Separate Spheres during the German Enlightenment* (New York and Oxford, 2000). The kinds of relations Gray describes were even older, and deeply embedded in the early history of family life. As Raffaela Sarti notes, the word family originally meant the dependents of the family's head, typically the pater familias. "For a long time the etymological meaning of family as a group of servants extended its tentacles like an octopus to wives and children in the name of the dependency they

shared with the servants, thus impeding unity between spouses or between parents and children. So 'family 'often meant the wife, children and servants as a group distinct from the father, who was head of this group without being part of it." *Europe at Home: Family and Material Culture, 1500–1800*, trans. Alan Cameron (New Haven and London, 2002), 36. See also Otto Brunner, "Das 'ganze Haus' und die alteuropäische Gesellschaft," in *Neue Wege der Sozialgeschichte* (Göttingen, 1956).

6 Gray, 297–300. My way of drawing on Gray's work gives a somewhat different tone to these developments than he does, and as I will make clear in a moment I think the long-term implications of his argument are rather different from the ones he draws from it.

7 Margaret R. Hunt, *The Middling Sort: Commerce, Gender, and the Family in England, 1680–1780* (Berkeley and Los Angeles, 1996), 131. Theodore Koditschek, *Class Formation and Urban-Industrial Society: Bradford 1750–1850* (Cambridge and New York, 1990), 224.

8 Karin Hausen, "Family and Role-Division: the Polarisation of Sexual Stereotypes in the Nineteenth Century – an Aspect of the Dissociation of Work and Family Life," in *The German Family: Essays on the Social History of the Family in Nineteenth- and Twentieth-Century Germany*, ed. Richard J. Evans and W. R. Lee (London and Totowa, NJ, 1981), 68–69. Also Ute Frevert, *Women in German History: From Bourgeois Emancipation to Sexual Liberation*, trans. Stuart McKinnon-Evans (Material Word) in association with Terry Bond and Barbara Norden (Oxford and New York, 1989), esp. 32–33.

9 Sarah Hanley, "Family and State in Early Modern France: the Marriage Pact," in *Connecting Spheres: Women in the Western World, 1500 to the Present*, ed. Marilyn J. Boxer and Jean H. Quataert, with a foreword by Joan W. Scott (New York and Oxford, 1987), 54.

10 David Warren Sabean, *Kinship in Neckarhausen, 1700–1870* (Cambridge and New York 1998), 11, 414–15.

11 Jürgen Kocka, "Familie, Unternehmer, und Kapitalismus. An Beispielen aus der frühen Industrialisierung," in *Die Familie in der Geschichte*, ed Heinz Reif (Göttingen, 1982), 177–78. Sven Beckert, *The Monied Metropolis: New York City and the Consolodation of the American Bourgeoisie, 1850–96* (Cambridge and New York, 2001), 33.

12 Kocka, *ibid.*; Davidoff and Hall, *Family Fortunes*.

13 Hanley, "Family and State in Early Modern France," 54. She notes that the modern situation is "characterized politically by the separation of public (state) and private (individual) interests, and economically by sustained industrial growth, which supports large populations. Citizenship in a state

underwrites the life chances of individuals by guaranteeing basic social services (education, social security, welfare, etc.)."

14 Caroline Chotard-Lioret, "Correspondance en 1900, le plus public des actes privés, ou la manière de gérer un réseau de parenté," *Ethnologie française* XV (1985), 63–71.

15 Viviane Isambert-Jamati, *Solidarité fraternelle et réussite sociale: La Correspondance familiale des Dubois-Goblot, 1841–82* (Paris, 1995), 94 for the letter quoted.

16 Davidoff and Hall, 335–38. Frevert, *Women in German History*, 45, 187. Michelle Perrot and Anne Martin-Fugier, "The Actors," in *A History of Private Life*, IV: *From the Fires of Revolution to the Great War*, ed. Michelle Perrot, trans. Arthur Goldhammer (Cambridge, MA, and London, 1990), 196–201.

17 I gave an account of the Marx family in *Marx's Fate: the Shape of a Life* (Princeton, 1978), 279ff.

18 David Newsome, *The Victorian World Picture: Perceptions and Introspections in an Age of Change* (New Brunswick, 1997), 87.

19 The point is, I think, far too little appreciated by Davidoff and Hall in their account of women writers, *Family Fortunes*, 180–97. For other examples see Dagmar Herzog, "Liberalism, Religious Dissent, and Women's Rights: Louise Dittmar's Writings from the 1840s," in *In Search of a Liberal Germany*, ed. Jarausch and Jones, 55–85, and Frevert, *Women in German History*, 79, and 124–26 for the persistence among feminists of the view that motherhood had to remain a touchstone of their strategy even at the end of the century. Dittmar rejected the claim that the general principle of equality had to be tempered in accord with the natural differences between men and women, but her point was that the differences that existed were not relevant to either education or the need for individual independence, not that no differences existed. This point is not clearly recognized by Lynn Abrams, "Companionship and conflict: the negotiation of marriage relations in the nineteenth century," in *Gender Relations in German History: Power, Agency and Experience from the Sixteenth to the Twentieth Century* (Durham, NC, 1997), 103.

20 Richard Price, *British society, 1680–1880: Dynamism, Containment and Change* (Cambridge and New York, 1999), 192–214. Fawcett is quoted in Thomas Laqueur, *Making Sex: Body and Gender from the Greeks to Freud* (Cambridge, MA, and London, 1990), 197. Leonore Davidoff and Catherine Hall make a similar point in the book cited above.

21 See her comments in *Le Journal intime de Caroline B[rame]. Enquête de Michelle Perrot et Georges Ribeill* (Paris, 1985), 222, n.24: "c'est sans doute sous le Second Empire que la distinction des sphères et celle des rôles sexuels ont atteint son degré le plus fort. Mais elle commence à être contestée et c'est

ce qui fait l'apreté des discussions sur l'education des filles dans les années 1860 qui aboutissent à une véritable crise en 1867."

22 Lynn Hunt, *The Family Romance of the French Revolution* (Berkeley and Los Angeles, 1992), 43 (for the quotation from Condorcet) and 203.

23 Karin Hausen, "Family and Role-Division: the Polarisation of Sexual Stereotypes in the Nineteenth Century," cited above. Only the last quotation comes from her article, however (61); the others are from the text cited by Ute Frevert in her introduction to her edited volume, *Bürgerinnen und Bürger: Geschlechterverhältnisse im 19. Jahrhundert, Zwölf Beiträge, mit einem Vorwort von Jürgen Kocka* (Göttingen, 1988), 12.

24 On Hippel see Isabel V. Hull, *Sexuality, State and Civil Society in Germany*, where the passage quoted appears on 328. Hippel's works on this subject have been translated into English by Timothy F. Sellner: *On Marriage* (Detroit, 1994), and *On Improving the Status of Women (Über die bürgerliche Verbesserung der Weiber)* (Detroit, 1979). That the more complex and potentially more liberal relations between the sexes suggested here extended to other sections of German opinion has recently been argued by Brian Vick, "Liberalism, Nationalism, and Gender Dichotomy in Mid-Nineteenth Century Germany: the Contested Case of German Civil Law," *Journal of Modern History* 82 (2010), 546–84, where a large body of literature there is no space to list here is cited.

25 Richard J. Evans, *The Feminists: Women's Emancipation Movements in Europe, America and Australasia, 1840–1920* (London and New York, 1977), 33. For a particularly striking example see Susan Pedersen, *Eleanor Rathbone and the Politics of Conscience* (New Haven and London, 2004).

26 A very similar experience of liberal family values unrealized by action lies at the center of a persuasive explanation given for the formation of some later activists: Kenneth Kenniston, *Young Radicals* (New York, 1968).

27 Quoted in *Women, the Family, and Freedom: the Debate in Documents*, vol. II: *1750–1880*, ed. Susan Groag Bell and Karen M. Offen (Stanford, 1988), 247.

28 Romain Lhopiteau, *Soixante-deux années de ma vie: recits intimes et commerciaux, 1828–90* (Paris, 1891). Lhopiteau's story gives the lie to the commonly expressed notion that bourgeois marriages entered into with full respect for the practical and social constraints imposed by decorum and social standing were ordinarily loveless. For another example see Gustave-Emmanuel Roy, négociant, *Souvenirs: 1823–1906* (Nancy, 1906), esp. 83–89 on his courtship and marriage.

29 Sabean, *Kinship*, 507.

30 Bonnie G. Smith, *Ladies of the Leisure Class: the Bourgeoises of Northern France in the Nineteenth Century* (Princeton, 1981); Vickery, "Golden Age to Separate Spheres?" 405–07. These examples should be sufficient to

show how careless and exaggerated are the assertions of some writers that bourgeois status was incompatible with wives working for pay or profit, a notion put forward for instance by Anne Martin-Fugier in various writings, e.g. "Les repas dans l'horaire quotidien des ménages bourgeois à Paris au XIXe siècle," in *Le Temps de manger: alimentation, emploi du temps et rythmes sociaux*, ed. Maurice Aymard *et al.* (Paris, 1993), 227: "On est bourgeois au XIXe siècle à deux conditions: 1) La femme ne travaille pas pour gagner sa vie, ni à l'extérieur de la famille ni à l'intérieur..."

31 See Evans, *The Feminists*, cited above.

32 The texts are all printed in John Stuart Mill and Harriet Taylor Mill, *Essays on Sex Equality*, ed. Alice S. Rossi (Chicago and London, 1970). For the presence of these ideas among their friends see Rossi's introduction to this volume.

33 Evans, *The Feminists*, 18–19.

34 See Peter Gay, *Education of the Senses* (New York, 1984), 255–77, who emphasizes the new ground contraception opened up for making sexual pleasure a legitimate part of marriage. I will return to this question later on. Michael Mason, *The Making of Victorian Sexuality* (Oxford and New York, 1994), 62–64, and his companion volume, *The Making of Victorian Sexual Attitudes* (Oxford and New York, 1994), 179–88 and 195. J. A. Banks, *Prosperity and Parenthood: a Study of Family Planning Among the Victorian Middle Classes* (London, 1954).

35 F. M. L. Thompson, *The Rise of Respectable Society: a Social History of Victorian Britain* (Cambridge, MA, 1988), 64–66. Some evidence exists that lower-middle-class families were also early users of contraception in England, but Michael Mason notes that this may have been at least partly a continuation of pre-industrial attempts at family limitation, *Making of Victorian Sexuality*, 54–57. Frevert, *Women in German History*, 119. Marion A. Kaplan, *The Making of the Jewish Middle Class: Women, Family, and Identity in Imperial Germany* (New York and Oxford, 1991), 42–43; Gunilla-Frederike Budde, *Auf dem Weg ins Bürgerleben: Kindheit und Erziehung in deutschen und englischen Bürgerfamilien, 1840–1914* (Göttingen, 1994), 51–53; Karin Hausen, "'...eine Ulme für das schwanke Efeu.' Ehepaare im deutschen Bildungsbürgertum," in *Bürgerinnen und Bürger*, ed. Frevert (cited above), 97–98.

36 Thompson, *Rise of Respectable Society*, 65. John Tosh, *A Man's Place: Masculinity and the Middle-Class Home in Victorian England* (New Haven and London, 1999), 152. Eleanor Rathbone's father supported her desire to study at as university (she went to Oxford) even over the objections of her mother, a pattern visible in a number of other families: Pederson, *Eleanor Rathbone*, 36–39.

37 Françoise Mayeur, *L'Éducation des filles en France au XIXe siècle* (Paris, 1979); for Simon and Duruy, 114–15. For a liberal position that went

somewhat beyond Simon's but still drew back from full equality and left women in a separate sphere, see Louis Legrand, *Le mariage et les moeurs en France* (Paris, 1878). Legrand was a lawyer and republican deputy.

38 Mayeur, *L'Éducation des filles*, esp. 156–58. Debora L. Silverman, *Art Nouveau in Fin-de-Siècle France: Politics, Psychology, and Style* (Berkeley and Los Angeles, 1989), 65–66.

39 Edouard Charton, *Dictionnaire des Professions ou Guide pour le choix d'un état, indiquant les conditions de temps et d'argent pour parvenir à chaque profession, les études à suivre, les programmes des écoles spéciales, les examens à subir, les aptitudes et les facultés nécessaires pour réussir, les moyens d'établissement, les chances d'avancement et de succès, les devoirs,* 3rd edn., publiée avec le concours de Mm. Paul Laffitte et Jules Charton (Paris, 1880), 218–24. Cf. *Guide pour le choix d'un état ou Dictionnaire des professions*, 2nd edn. (Paris, 1851). For a similar recognition that women were entering into the professions, in particular medicine, see Paul Jacquemart, *Professions et métiers, Guide pratique à l'usage des familles et de la jeunesse pour le choix d'une carrière* (Paris, 1892) s.v. "Femmes médicins."

40 Frevert, *Women in German History*, 121–24. Augustine, *Patricians and Parvenus*, 118–19. Kaplan, *Making of the Jewish Middle Class*, 138–43. There is also an excellent general discussion in Gordon Craig, *Germany, 1866–1945* (New York and Oxford, 1980), 207–13. The future psychoanalyst Karen Horney attended the female Gymnaisum set up in Hamburg in 1900, after both her mother and brother worked on her father to gain his permission; see *The Adolescent Diaries of Karen Horney* (New York, 1980), 19. I am grateful to Samara Heifetz for this reference.

41 Budde, *Auf dem Weg ins Bürgertum*, 416–7; Augustine, *Patricians and Parvenus*, 122.

42 Robert Max Jackson, *Destined for Equality: the Inevitable Rise of Women's Status* (Cambridge, MA, and London, 1998), 3.

43 See the concluding essays by Jürgen Kocka and Ute Gerhard in *Bürgerinnen und Bürger: Geschlechterverhältnisse im 19. Jahrhundert*, 206–14.

44 Jackson, *Destined for Equality*, 31. The previous quotes are on 251 and 22. Similar considerations operated in England, alongside others. See Ursula Vogel, "Property Rights and the Status of Women in Germany and England," in Jürgen Kocka and Allan Mitchell, eds., *Bourgeois Society in Nineteenth-Century Europe* (Oxford and Providence, RI, 1993), 241–69. Vogel's overall views however are not in accord with the argument being made here. In every country the right of husbands over their wives' property was an inheritance from medieval law, a point Vogel recognizes for Germany as well as England but with too little acknowledgment of its

implications. Some developments that foreshadow the ones Jackson cites were already visible in eighteenth-century England. See Lawrence Stone, *The Family, Sex and Marriage in England, 1500–1800*, abridged edn. (London and New York, 1977), 221.

45 Jackson, *Destined for Equality*, 251–52.

46 Göran Therborn, *Between Sex and Power: Family in the World, 1900–2000* (London and New York, 2004), 27.

47 On the "crisis of masculinity," see Annelise Maugue, *L'Identité masculine en crise au tournant du siècle, 1871–1914* (Paris, 1987); Jacques Le Rider, *Modernity and Crises of Identity: Culture and Society in Fin-de-Siècle Vienna*, trans. Rosemary Morris (New York, 1993); and for an intelligent discussion of the whole question, Gerald N. Izenberg's introduction to his book, *Modernism and Masculinity: Mann, Wedekind, Kandinsky through World War I* (Chicago and London, 2000). For the range of opinions, mostly negative on the part of academics, expressed in a survey published in 1897, see Peter Gay, *The Bourgeois Experience: Victoria to Freud, I: the Education of the Senses* (New York, 1984), 221–25. For a skeptical view of the notion of a crisis of masculinity see the general account of gender relations in the Belle Epoque in James F. McMillan, *France and Women 1789–1914: Gender, Society and Politics* (London and New York, 2000; this book is a revision of Macmillan's earlier *Housewife or Harlot*, cited above), ch. 10. For the theme of a crisis in gender relations rather than masculinity see for instance Ann Taylor Allen, "Patriarchy and Its Discontents: the Debate on the Origins of the Family in the German-Speaking World, 1860–1930," in *Germany at the fin de siècle: culture, politics, and ideas*, ed. Suzanne Marchand and David Lindenfeld (Baton Rouge, LA, 2004), 81–101. On the "new woman" see Silverman, *Art Nouveau*, 66–74; Sally Ledger, *The New Woman: Fiction and Feminism at the fin de siècle* (Manchester and New York, 1997); Talia Schaffer, "'Nothing but Foolscap and Ink': Inventing the New Woman," in *The New Woman in Fiction and in Fact: Fin-de-Siècle Feminism*, ed. Angelique Richardson and Chris Willis (London, 2001), 39–52. For English cartoons about the "new woman" see Richardson's and Willis's introduction to the volume.

48 Patrick K. Bidelman, *Pariahs Stand Up! The Founding of the Liberal Feminist Movement in France, 1858–1889* (Westport, CT, and London, 1982), xx.

49 Camille Mauclair, "La Femme devant les peintres modernes, " *La Nouvelle revue*, N. S. vol. I, (15 November 1899), 190–213. The article is discussed by Debora Silverman in *Art Nouveau*, 69, but focusing on different passages from it. Silverman cites in addition an article with some similar notions, Marius-Ary Leblond, "Les Peintres de la femme nouvelle," *La Revue* (formerly *La Revue des revues*) xxxix (November 1, 1901), 275–90. I am

grateful to Tamar Garb for reminding me about Mauclair's essay at a time when I had forgotten about it.

10 Bourgeois morals: from Victorianism to modern sexuality

1 Peter Gay, *The Bourgeois Experience, Victoria to Freud,* vol. 1: *Education of the Senses* (New York and Oxford, 1984). See 420–21 for a particularly interesting point of entry to the general question. For the bourgeois sources of the obsession with hypocrisy and its dangers in nineteenth-century America, see Karen Haltunen, *Confidence Men and Painted Women: a Study of Middle-Class Culture in America, 1830–70* (New Haven and London, 1982). For a similar point about England see Michael Mason, *The Making of Victorian Sexuality* (Oxford and New York, 1994), 127, who discusses the relations between accusation of "cant" and actual behavior. I will return to this issue, and to the implications of Mason's studies of this subject, just below.
2 Michael Mason, *The Making of Victorian Sexual Attitudes* (Oxford and New York, 1994), 43–62. I have elaborated a bit on what he says, but in his spirit, I think. See also his companion volume, *The Making of Victorian Sexuality,* cited just above. I draw greatly on both books below, referring to them as, respectively, *Victorian Attitudes* and *Victorian Sexuality.*
3 Alain Corbin, "Backstage," in *A History of Private Life,* IV: *From the Fires of Revolution to the Great War,* ed. Michelle Perrot, trans. Arthur Goldhammer (Cambridge, MA, and London, 1990), 476–77.
4 See, for a general statement on this point Josef Ehmer, "Marriage," ch. 9 of *Family Life in the Long Nineteenth Century, 1789–1913,* vol. II of *The History of the European Family,* ed. David I. Kertzer and Marzio Barbagli (New Haven and London, 2002), 292–301, and the literature cited there.
5 Laurence Croq, "Les 'Bourgeois de Paris' au XVIIIe siècle: identification d'une catégorie sociale polymorphe." Thèse de doctorat nouveau régime, Université de Paris I, Décembre, 1997 (Copy in the Bibliothèque Historique de la Ville de Paris), 50–55.
6 Croq, "Bourgeois de Paris," 85–90. Norbert Elias, *The Civilizing Process,* trans. Edmund Jephcott (New York, 1982), vol. I, ch. 1, part I. Lawrence Stone, *The Family, Sex, and Marriage in England, 1500–1800* (abridged edn., New York, 1979), part IV. Various historians have pointed out that there were companionate marriages earlier as well, but Stone's evidence that the phenomenon was more diffused and had greater weight in the eighteenth century seems to me persuasive.
7 Göran Therborn, *Between Sex and Power: Family in the World, 1900–2000* (London and New York, 2004). On some of these conflicts, see Sarah Hanley, "Family and State in Early Modern France: the Marriage Pact," in

Connecting Spheres: Women in the Western World, 1500 to the Present, ed. Marilyn J. Boxer and Jean H. Quataert, with a foreword by Joan W. Scott (New York and Oxford, 1987).

8 Norbert Elias notes both aspects of aristocratic life; for the first see *The Civilizing Process*, trans. Edmund Jephcott (New York, 1982), for the second, the same author's *The Court Society* (New York, 1983), e.g. 129–30. Therborn, *Between Sex and Power*, 23.

9 *Les Liaisons dangereuses* has sometimes been thought to be a satirical attack on courtly *mores*, but Choderlos de Laclos was close to a number of high aristocratic figures, including the Duc d'Orléans, who read and admired the book, and it seems that only after the French Revolution was it seen in this way. On Pepys see Lawrence Stone's discussion of him in *The Family, Sex, and Marriage*, esp. 348–49, and for a broader account Claire Tomalin's fine biography, *Samuel Pepys: the Unequalled Self* (New York, 2002). For the general point about families or households as working units see also Ehmer, "Marriage," 297ff., who describes the shift to the "male-breadwinner–female homemaker model," 300. See also Stephanie Coontz, *Marriage, A History: How Love Conquered Marriage* (New York and London, 2005), 154–57. For the increase in aristocratic debauchery see Roy Porter and Lesley Hall, *The Facts of Life: the Creation of Sexual Knowledge in Britian, 1650–1950* (New Haven and London, 1995), 126.

10 Margaret R. Hunt, *The Middling Sort: Commerce, Gender, and the Family in England, 1680–1780* (Berkeley and Los Angeles, 1996), 37, 40. A page later she notes: "What came, rather later, to be called 'middle class values' initially emerged less from an urge to organize other people's labor more efficiently than as a result of common experiences with regard to credit and the mechanisms of commerce and investment."

11 P. S. Atiyah, *The Rise and Fall of Freedom of Contract* (Oxford and New York, 1979). Thomas L. Hakell, "Capitalism and the Humanitarian Sensibility," *American Historical Review* 90 (1985), 339–61 and 547–66. For Kant see his *Anthropology from a Pragmatic Point of View*, trans. Victor Lyle Dowdell (Carbondale, IL, 1978). The connection between character and relations between strangers is suggested in an as-yet unpublished introduction to a volume on sociability and character to be edited by Susan Manning and Thomas Ahnert. For the later history of character see Stefan Collini, "The Idea of 'Character' in Victorian Political Thought," *Transactions of the Royal Historical Society*, 5th series, 35 (1985), 29–51, where the connection between character and the need to prepare for action in unknown circumstances is stressed. In nineteenth-century London many firms kept "character books" in which they listed the features of people with whom they had dealings, indicating their degrees of trustworthiness. See David Kynaston, *The City of London*, vol. 1: a *World*

of Its Own, 1815–1890 (London, 1994), 8off. For the impact of this concern for character on child-rearing see Mary P. Ryan, *Cradle of the Middle Class: the Family in Oneida County, New York, 1790–1865* (Cambridge and New York, 1981).

12 See Claude Labrosse, *Lire au xviiie siècle. La Nouvelle Héloise et ses lecteurs* (Lyon, 1985); Robert C. Darnton, "Readers Respond to Rousseau: the Fabrication of Romantic Sensitivity," in *The Great Cat Massacre and Other Episodes in French Cultural History* (New York, 1984), and Jean M. Goulemot and Didier Masseau, "Naissance des lettres addressées à l'écrivain," in *Écrire à l'écrivain*, Textes réunis par José-luis Diaz, *Textuel*, 127 (February, 1994).

13 It is worth recalling, in connection with Göran Therborn's notion about the relationship between family history and middle-class morality developed above, that Goethe's hero Wilhelm Meister also becomes an estate manager, leaving behind his earlier attraction for a career in the theater. Like Julie and Saint-Preux, he comes to accept the practical basis of family survival as the determining ground for personal existence and moral choice.

14 Rousseau generalized this principle in the project he told about in his *Confessions* to make himself into the kind of person he was not but wished to be, which he named – it was to be a book title – *Sensory Morality or the Materialism of the Sage* (*La Morale sensitive ou le matérialisme du sage*). Since he, like others, was driven in unpredictable directions by things and events around him, he sought a solution through controlling all these circumstances. Thus he would be able always to direct his will in a virtuous and consistent direction. The plan was a kind of generalization of the way Wolmar managed Saint-Preux and Julie's feelings toward each other. Here, however, Rousseau himself is to be at once the manager of the scene and the object formed by it. Whether he realized how deeply self-contradictory the scheme was we do not know (he never wrote the book he contemplated about it), but Jean Starobinski is clearly correct that the scheme ignores "the fact that he deliberately created what he wants to experience as an independent force," which means that he was trying at once "to orchestrate the mystery and to be duped by it." To be sure he sometimes attributed the gulf between natural virtue and actual human behavior to the doleful influence of social relations, but on a deeper level he knew that human beings only existed inside society and that the contradictions they displayed there were part of what made them human from the start. See my discussion of Rousseau in *The Idea of the Self*, ch. 7, and Jean Starobinski, *Jean-Jacques Rousseau: Transparency and Obstruction*, trans. Arthur Goldhammer, with an introduction by Robert J. Morrissey (Chicago and London, 1988; orig. edn., 1971), 213–14.

15 *The Critique of Judgment*, trans. James Creed Meredith (Oxford, 1952) para. 88 (vol. ii, 124), but I have substituted the translation given in Veronique Zanetti, "Teleology and the Freedom of the Self," in *The Modern Subject: Conceptions of the Self in Classical German Philosophy*, ed. Karl Ameriks and Dieter Sturma (Albany, 1995), 53.

16 For a fuller elaboration and justification of this account of Kant, see ch. 9 of *The Idea of the Self*. The discussion there relies on a number of other writers, in particular Dieter Henrich, *The Unity of Reason: Essays on Kant's Philosophy*, ed. Richard L. Velkley (Cambridge, MA, and London, 1994), especially the essays "The Unity of Subjectivity" and "The Concept of Moral Insight"; Henry Allison, "Spontaneity and Autonomy in Kant's Conception of the Self," in *The Modern Subject*, ed. Ameriks and Sturma, 11–30; and John H. Zammito, *Kant, Herder, and the Birth of Anthropology* (Chicago and London, 2002). Kant introduced the same teleological principle appealed to in the *Critique of Judgment* into history in his well-known essay "Idea for a Universal History with a Cosmopolitan Intent," in *The Philosophy of Kant: Immanuel Kant's Moral and Political Writings*, ed. Carl J. Friedrich (New York, 1949).

17 *The Recollections of Alexis de Tocqueville*, trans. Alexander Teixeira de Mattos, ed. J. P. Mayer (London, 1948), 83.

18 Kant, "The Contest of Faculties," in *Kant's Political Writings*, trans. H.B. Nisbet, ed. Hans Reiss (Cambridge, 1970), 184–87.

19 For the relations between Godwin and Malthus and for these comments, see Mason, *Victorian Sexuality*, 262–74.

20 They give this title to ch. 6 of *The Facts of Life*. For a similar perspective on nineteenth-century American sexual culture see the remarkable study by Helen Lefkowitz Horowitz, *Rereading Sex: Battles over Sexual Knowledge and Suppression in Nineteenth-Century America* (New York, 2002). Painting a vivid and wide-ranging picture of alternative attitudes toward sex, she speaks of "competing conversations" and distinct "frameworks" within which very different ideas found expression.

21 See Mason, *Victorian Sexuality*, 20–32 and Porter and Hall, *The Facts of Life*, 126–27. Morality in the French working class both before and after the Revolution seems to have mixed strict appeals to discipline and restraint with much violent and ribald language and behavior; see William H. Sewell, jr., *Work and Revolution: the Language of Labor from the Old Regime to 1848* (Cambridge and New York, 1980), and Robert C. Darnton, "Workers Revolt: the Great Cat Massacre of the Rue Saint-Séverin," ch. 2 of *The Great Cat Massacre and Other Episodes in French Cultural History* (New York, 1984).

22 Françoise Barett-Ducrocq, *Love in the Time of Victoria: Sexuality, Class and Gender in Nineteenth-Century London*, trans. John Howe (London

and New York 1991), e.g. 24, 33. For similar views see Mason, *Victorian Sexuality*, 141–43.

23 Mason, *Victorian Sexuality*, 15–43; 19ff. for Kingsley.

24 Porter and Hall, *The Facts of Life*, 127. On the French groups see Frank E. Manuel, *The Prophets of Paris: Turgot, Condorcet, Saint-Simon, Fourier, and Comte* (Cambridge, MA, 1962; New York, 1965).

25 The letter is quoted by Alice S. Rossi in her introduction to John Stuart Mill and Harriet Taylor Mill, *Essays on Sex Equality* (Chicago and London, 1970), 50.

26 Manuel *The Prophets of Paris*, 289–93. *Auguste Comte and Positivism: the Essential Writings*, ed. Gertrude Lenzer (New York, 1975), 379.

27 James Smith Allen, *Poignant Relations: Three Modern French Women* (Baltimore and London, 2000), 147.

28 Porter and Hall, *The Facts of Life*, discuss both books and their circulation. For Venette's influence in France and the fears about it see Jean Flouret, *Nicolas Venette, médecin rochelais, 1633–1698* (La Rochelle, 1992), who gives 1668 as the date of the first edition. The earliest edition in the Bibliothèque Nationale catalogue is 1671. For Venette's influence in Germany see Isabel V. Hull, *Sexuality, State and Civil Society in Germany, 1700–1815* (Ithaca and London, 1996), 246. (She gives 1711 as the date of the earliest German version, but I have found a reference to a Leipzig edition of 1698 in a bookseller's catalogue. She rightly notes that some of its many editions were "knock-offs" by others.)

29 Porter and Hall, *The Facts of Life*, 128. Flouret, *Nicolas Venette*, 16–17.

30 Mason, *Victorian Sexuality*, 217. Robert A. Nye, *Masculinity and Male Codes of Honor in Modern France* (New York and Oxford, 1993), 69. Gay, *Education of the Senses*, esp. part I. John Tosh, *A Man's Place: Masculinity and the Middle-Class Home in Victorian England* (New Haven and London, 1999), 57–58.

31 Mason, *Victorian Sexuality*, 218–20; Alain Corbin notes that "vigorous intercourse was believed to increase the likelihood of successful conception" in France too, *Histoire de la vie privé*, IV, 591.

32 Nye *Masculinity*, 69. Mason, *Victorian Sexuality*, 195–96, 217–27.

33 Mason, *Victorian Sexuality*, 116–18. For an example of a French woman who felt liberated by the chance marriage gave her to go about by herself in public see *Mémoires de Madame Lafarge, née Marie Cappelle, écrits par elle-même* (Paris, 1867), 183–84. Anne Martin-Fugier, *La Bourgeoise: femme au temps de Paul Bourget* (Paris, 1983), 86–92.

34 Gustave Droz, *Monsieur, Madame, et Bébé* (Paris, 1884), 125–26, 131–33, 147–49. The information given about editions and translations comes from the online catalogues of the Bibliothèque Nationale, the New York Public Library and the British Library.

35 Droz, 96–102.

36 See Yvonne Knibiehler, "L'Éducation sexuelle des filles au XXe siècle," in *Le Temps des jeunes filles*, ed. Gabrielle Houbre (Paris, 1996), 139–60. A book published in 1885 and partly inspired by *Monsieur, Madame et Bébé*, did propose sex education as a defense against the dangers of the wedding night, but only for male students, not for young women. See Dr. Charles Montalban, [pseudonym of Charles Thomas-Caraman] *La Petite Bible des jeunes époux, suivie de considérations sur la possibilité d'avoir un Garçon ou une Fille, et de l'examen des doctrines, théories, fictions émises depuis Hippocrate jusqu'à la découverte de la loi de l'alternance des germes ou ovules* (Paris, 1885). In Germany the key figure was Helene Stöcker. See Gudrun Hammelmann, *Helene Stöcker, der "Bund für Mutterschütz," und "Die Neue Generation"* (Frankfurt am Main, 1998) and the works cited below, n. 47.

37 The cartoon in *La Vie parisienne* appeared in the issue of October 17, 1866. For the Third Republic see Robert A. Nye, *Masculinity and Male Codes of Honor in Modern France* (New York and Oxford, 1993), 81–82.

38 For the traditional view see for instance Laure Adler, *Secrets d'Alcove: Histoire du couple, 1830–1930* (Paris, 1983), ch. 2, and Denis Bertholet, *Le Bourgeois dans tous ses états: le roman familial de la Belle Epoque* (Paris, 1987). Both rely largely on literary accounts. Anne-Marie Sohn, *Du premier baiser à l'acove: la sexualité des Français au quotidien (1850–1950)* (Paris, 1996), 221–24.

39 Laure Adler in the book cited just above gives a number of examples of the genre, but in my view without sufficiently crediting nineteenth-century people for such concerns.

40 The diary was given to Denis Berthelot by Mireille de Bondeli's descendants; see *Le Bourgeois dans tous ses états*, 56–77. Betholet provides much interesting information on this subject, but I think his desire to see both incipient revolt and repressed sexual feeling in the text lead him astray.

41 Alain Corbin, "Backstage," 594–602.

42 Mason, *Victorian Sexuality*, 120–22, and *Victorian Attitudes*, ch. 4.

43 *Ibid.*, 212 for the quotation.

44 Mason, *Victorian Attitudes*, 189–213; the quotation is on 211. There is now a fine biography of Carpenter by Sheila Rowbotham, *Edward Carpenter: a Life of Liberty and Love* (London, 2009). For the reaction to Burton's translation of the *Thousand Nights and a Night* see the collection of press notices he assembled in the appendix to *Supplemental Nights*, vol. VII (London, 1887), 457–500. In 1883 Burton and some friends had succeeded in getting an English translation of the *Kama Sutra* published in London, but only by pretending it had been printed in Benares, and it received little attention.

45 Leon Blum, *Du mariage* (Paris, 1907).

46 For the discussion see section 4 of ch. 1 (46ff. of the Flammarion, 1978 edn.) of *La Garçonne*. For some indications of the polarization of discussion in France before World War I, see Corbin, "Backstage," 608–09. An organization called L'Union de l'action morale conducted various campaigns for decency in the 1890s, notably against publicity posters that employed suggestive images. See Christian-Marc Bosséno, "Le Répertoire du grand écran," in *La Culture de masse en France de la Belle Époque à aujourd'hui*, ed. Jean-Pierre Rioux and Jean-François Sirinelli (Paris, 2002), 157 and the literature he cites.

47 See Tracie Matysik, *Reforming the Moral Subject: Ethics and Sexuality in Central Europe, 1890–1930* (Ithaca and London, 2008), 21–22 on the Ethical Culture Society; and Kevin Repp, *Reformers, Critics, and the Paths of German Modernity: anti-politics and the Search for Alternatives* (Cambridge, MA, 2000), as well as Repp's essay "*Sexualkrise und Rasse*": Feminist Eugenics at the Fin de Siècle," in *Germany at the fin de siècle: culture, politics, and ideas*, ed. Suzanne Marchand and David Lindenfeld (Baton Rouge, LA, 2004), 102–26.

48 Gay, *Education of the Senses*, 256ff. Corbin, "Backstage," 600–01. Mason, *Victorian Attitudes*, 138–66, esp. 146ff., and 213ff. Sohn, *Du premier baiser*, 308–09.

49 *Histoire de la vie privée*, IV, 598, 605–8. Adler, *Secrets d'alcove*, 166.

50 For a comprehensive discussion of the increasing presence of women in the public spaces of later nineteenth-century cities see Richard Dennis, *Cities in Modernity: Representations and Productions of Metropolitan Space, 1840–1930* (Cambridge and New York, 2008), ch. 6. On Germany, where the phenomenon came a bit later than to France, see Peter Fritzsche, *Reading Berlin 1900* (Cambridge, MA, and London, 1996), 63–66.

51 Therborn, *Between Sex and Power*, 139.

52 Sohn, *Du premier baiser*, 37; 163–66; 174.

53 Peter Fryer, *Mrs Grundy: Studies in English Prudery* (London, 1963), see esp. 76–78, 83.

54 Sohn, *Du premier baiser*, 20, 153.

55 Sohn, *ibid.*, 23–37.

56 Hanley, "Family and State in Early Modern France," in *Connecting Spheres*, ed. Boxer and Quataert, 54. Hunt's work is discussed earlier in this chapter.

11 Jews as bourgeois and network people

1 For the spread of connections between Jews in various places during the era of Ghettoization, see Jonathan I. Israel, *European Jewry in the Age*

of Mercantilism, 1550–1750 (Oxford, 1985), 70–86; for the effect of this situation on many aspects of Jewish life, including marriage practices, see Marion A. Kaplan, *The Making of the Jewish Middle Class: Women, Family, and Identity in Imperial Germany* (New York and Oxford, 1991).

2 Werner Sombart, *The Jews and Modern Capitalism*, trans. M. Epstein, with an introduction by Bert F. Hoselitz (Glencoe, IL, 1951), 172–75.

3 *Ibid.*, 177, 181, 225–38.

4 Jonathan Israel, *Diasporas Within a Diaspora: Jews, Crypto-Jews and the World Maritime Empires, 1540–1740* (Leiden, Boston, and Cologne, 2002), 458. Evelyne Oliel-Grausz, "Networks and Communication in the Sephardi Diaspora: an Added Dimension to the Concept of Port Jews and Port Jewries," in *Jews and Port Cities 1590–1990: Commerce, Community, and Cosmopolitanism*, ed. David Cesarani and Gemma Romain (London and Portland, OR, 2006), 61–76. Other studies in the same volume also contribute information on this score.

5 Todd M. Endelman, *The Jews of Britain, 1656–2000* (Berkeley and Los Angeles, 2002), 92–93.

6 David Sorkin, *The Transformation of German Jewry, 1740–1840* (Oxford and New York, 1987), 109–10. Simone Lässig makes the transformation out to be somewhat slower but with the same results; see *Jüdische Wege ins Bürgertum: Kulturelles Kaptal und sozialer Aufstieg im 19. Jahrhundert* (Göttingen, 2004), 601.

7 Max Weber, *The Protestant Ethic and the Spirit of Capitalism*, trans. Talcott Parsons (New York, 1958), 181.

8 This and the previous paragraph rely on Israel, *European Jewry in the Age of Mercantilism*; 132 for the passages quoted.

9 Israel, *Diasporas Within a Diaspora*, 172.

10 In England, where government policy never turned against Jews after their readmission in the 1650s, anti-Jewish sentiments were still widespread; see Endelman, *The Jews of Britain*, 70–71.

11 Israel, *Diasporas Within a Diaspora*, 173, 160.

12 Fritz Stern, *Gold and Iron: Bismarck, Bleichröder, and the Building of the German Empire* (New York, 1977), 175.

13 For these developments see Israel, *Diasporas Within a Diaspora*, 247–49.

14 Endelman, *The Jews of Britain*, 74.

15 For these debates see David Feldman, *Englishmen and Jews: Social Relations and Political Culture, 1840–1914* (New Haven and London, 1994), ch. 1 (35 and 43 for the passages quoted). Feldman also provides a good account of anti-Semitic attitudes in Victorian England (ch. 4 and *passim*; see 76 for Macaulay's letter), and of the greater emphasis placed on them by recent historians critical of the too-rosy picture presented by earlier writers such as Cecil Roth.

16 Endelman, *The Jews of Britain*, 54–62. For a similar comparison between English and German Jewish relations to the countries they inhabited see David Sorkin's conclusion to *The Transformation of German Jewry*.

17 *Ibid.*, 115, 108–09.

18 Michael Graetz, *Les Juifs en France au XIXième siècle: de la révolution française à l'alliance israélite universelle*, trans. from the Hebrew by Salomon Malka (Paris, 1982), esp. 45. There is a useful mise au point available online: Jean-Marc Chouraqui, "Les Communautés juives face au processus de l'Émancipation", in *Rives nord-méditerranéennes*, Révolution et minorités religieuses, http://rives.revues.org/document407.html.

19 Graetz, *Les Juifs en France au XIXième siècle*, 64–78. Paula E. Hyman, "The Social Contexts of Assimilation: Village Jews and City Jews in Alsace," in *Assimilation and Community: the Jews in Nineteenth-Century Europe*, ed. Jonathan Frankel and Steven J. Zipperstein (Cambridge and New York, 1992), 110–29. There is a good general account of mid-nineteenth-century Jewish life in Paula E. Hyman, *The Jews of Modern France* (Berkeley and Los Angeles, 1998), ch. 4.

20 See Michael Graetz, "The History of an Estrangement between Two Jewish Communities: German and French Jewry during the Nineteenth Century," in *Toward Modernity: the European Jewish Model*, ed. Jacob Katz (New Brunswick, NJ, and Oxford, 1987), 159–69.

21 Phyllis Cohen Albert, "Israelite and Jew: How Did Nineteenth-century French Jews Understand Assimilation?" in *Assimilation and Community: the Jews in Nineteenth-Century Europe*, ed. Jonathan Frankel and Steven J. Zipperstein (Cambridge and New York, 1992), 88–109.

22 Albert discusses Lazare's place in this history in the article just cited. For his career, see Nelly Wilson, *Bernard Lazare: antisemitism and the problem of jewish identity in nineteenth-century France* (Cambridge and New York, 1978), and Jean-Denis Bredin, *Bernard Lazare* (Paris, 1992).

23 It is for this reason that I think Yuri Slezkine is wrong to equate Jews with modernity in his imaginative and thoughtful book *The Jewish Century* (Princeton, 2004). That Jews were able to play the special role they did in the Russian Revolution, a topic on which he provides valuable illumination, seems to me to tell more about the special conditions of Russian life than about modernity in general. Modernity is not a condition of pure fluidity ("Mercurian" in Slezkine's idiom), because it relies even more than earlier forms of life on large organized structures of interaction. To describe these structures as autonomous in the sense developed here is to recognize in them some of the features that Slezkine highlights, but without assimilating them to a "Mercurian" fluidity. We will return to these questions in the Conclusion to this book.

24 See above, Chapter 4.

25 Sorkin, *The Transformation of German Jewry*, 29–30.

26 Simone Lässig, *Jüdische Wege ins Bürgertum: Kulturelles Kapital und sozialer Aufstieg im 19. Jahrhundert* (Göttingen, 2004), 580–94. On the ties between German Jews and England in this period see Todd M. Endelman, "German Jews in Victorian England: a Study in Drift and Defection," in *Assimilation and Community*, 57–87.

27 Lässig, *Jüdische Wege ins Bürgertum*, 667. As she notes, the argument has been anticipated by others, notably David Sorkin in *The Transformation of German Jewry*; cf. 109. Lässig employs Pierre Bordieu's notion of "cultural capital" as an aid in understanding this phenomenon, although she notes that his general attribution of primacy to economic capital does not fit the situation she finds among her subjects. I both use and question Bordieu's notion in regard to various levels of culture in Chapter 13. It is worth noting at this point that if Jews did indeed make use of "cultural capital" for their entry into bourgeois society, it was at least partly of a negative sort, since one thing that oriented them away from traditional social relations was their exclusion from guild organizations and the values they imparted to German life. Bordieu's thinking offers little scope for recognizing the importance of such "negative" capital, that is the advantages that sometimes accrue from outsider status.

28 Lässig, *Jüdische Wege ins Bürgertum*, 596ff., citing Monika Richarz, *Der Eintritt der Juden in die akademischen Berufe* (Tübingen, 1974); also Lässig, *ibid.*, 618–19, where she emphasizes the importance of diffuse family ties in providing the conditions for upwardly mobile Jews to attend Gymnasien or universities away from their parental homes, often making important social contacts. For Austria, Helga Embacher, "Middle Class, Liberal, Intellectual, Female, and Jewish: the Expulsion of 'Female Rationality' from Austria," in *Women in Austria*, ed. Günter Bischof *et al.* (New Brunswick, NJ, and London, 1998), 6.

29 Erik Lindner, "Deutsche Juden und die bürgerich-nationale Festkultur: Die Schiller-und Fichtefeiern von 1859 und 1862," in *Juden, Bürger, Deutsche: Zur Geschichte von Vielfalt und Differenz, 1800–1933*, ed. Andreas Gotzmann, Rainer Liedtke and Till van Rahden (Tübingen, 2001), 171–91, 177–78 for the quotations. Lindner notes that Jews took much less part in the celebrations for Fichte (well known as an anti-Semite). In England too Jews participated together with their neighbors in the Schiller celebrations. See Todd Endelman's article in *Assimilation and Community*, cited above.

30 Sorkin, *The Transformation of German Jewry*, 118.

31 These features of family life are well documented by Marion Kaplan in *The Making of the Jewish Middle Class*.

32 Sorkin., 118–23. For more detail on the relations between Jews and the masonic lodges in Germany, see Ludwig Hoffmann, "Bürger zweier Welten? Jude und Freimaurer im 19ten Jahrhundert," in *Juden, Bürger, Deutsche,*

esp. 110ff. (although the basis on which Hoffmann accounts for the story he tells seems to me questionable). For an interesting account of twentieth-century Jewish life in this regard see the first part of Fritz Stern's memoir, *Five Germanies I Have Known* (New York, 2006).

33 Lässig, *Jüdische Wege ins Bürgertum*, 669.

34 Michael Graetz, "The History of an Estrangement," 159–69; 168 for the quotation from Philippson.

35 Todd M. Endelman, "German Jews in Victorian England: a study in drift and defection," in *Assimilation and Community*, 57–87.

36 George L. Mosse, *German Jews beyond Judaism* (Bloomington, IN, and Cincinnati, 1985), ch. 1 (18 for the sentence quoted). Shulamit Volkov, "The Ambivalence of *Bildung*: Jews and Other Germans," in *The German-Jewish Dialogue Reconsidered: a Symposium in Honor of George Mosse*, ed. Klaus L. Berghahn (New York, 1996).

37 Malachi Haim Hacohen, "Popper's Cosmopolitanism: Culture Clash and Jewish Identity," in *Rethinking Vienna 1900*, ed. Stephen Beller (New York, 2001), 173. On Jews in Prague see Gary B. Cohen, *The Politics of Ethnic Survival: Jews in Prague, 1861–1914* (Princeton, 1981). On Freud's circle of youthful nationalist friends see William J. McGrath, *Dionysian Art and Populist Politics in Austria* (New Haven, 1974). Hannah Arendt's views were developed in her classic book *The Origins of Totalitarianism* (New York, 1951; new edn., 1966), part I.

38 Hacohen, "Popper's Cosmopolitanism," 174. On Popper's family and his career see Hacohen's larger study, *Karl Popper – The Formative Years, 1902–1945: Politics and Philosophy in Interwar Vienna* (Cambridge and New York, 2000).

39 See above, Chapter 4.

40 Émile Durkheim, *The Elementary Forms of [the] Religious Life*, trans. James Ward Swain (New York and London, 1915; reprinted 1965), 493.

41 On Durkheim's intellectual difficulties in this regard see my discussion in *The Idea of the Self*, ch. 14.

12 Public places, private spaces

1 Raymond Williams, *Culture and Society, 1780–1950* (New York and London, 1958), part I. *Keywords: a Vocabulary of Culture and Society* (New York, 1976), 76–82. Brad Evans, in his book *Before Cultures: the Ethnographic Imagination in American Literature, 1865–1920* (Chicago and London, 2005), shows that the word culture, especially in the plural that seemed to be implied by many uses of it, was relatively absent from anthropological writing until nearly the time of World War I.

2 For France I take the figures assembled from various sources by Sara Maza, *Private Lives and Public Affairs: the Causes Célèbres of Prerevolutionary France* (Berkely, Los Angeles, and London, 1993), 36. For Germany see Wolfgang Ruppert, *Bürgerlicher Wandel: Studien zur Herausbildung einer nationalen deutschen Kultur im 18. Jahrhundert* (Frankfurt am Main and New York, 1981), 118.

3 William St Clair, *The Reading Nation in the Romantic Period* (Cambridge and New York, 2004), ch. 6 for the 1774 decision and its consequences, 13 for the quotes in the text. St Clair's observations suggest at various points that the early existence of a national market was an important contributor to the high incidence of reading in Britain; see 191, 199. He notes too that in England new works were more expensive than reprints of earlier literature and that the latter category was what most people read; see e.g. 202.

4 *Ibid.*, 35–37, 42–43. For a general discussion of piracy in the German book trade in the eighteenth century see Pamela E. Selwyn, *Everyday Life in the German Book Trade: Friedrich Nicolai as Bookseller and Publisher in the Age of Enlightenment* (University Park, PA, 2000), ch. 4. For the limited circulation of periodicals see David Blackbourn, *History of Germany, 1780–1918: the Long Nineteenth Century* (2nd edn., Malden, MA, and Oxford, 2003), 29–31. For a general discussion of the size of the German reading public see Helmiuth Kiesel and Pul Münch, *Gesellschaft und Literatur im 18. Jahrhundert* (Munich, 1977), 159–65.

5 The best overall source is still Maurice Reclus, *Émile de Girardin, le créateur de la presse moderne* (Paris, 1934); see 70–73 for most of these details. Girardin's strategy had been anticipated a few years earlier by Benjamin Day's *New York Sun*; see Paul Starr, *The Creation of the Media: Political Origins of Modern Communication* (New York, 2004), 131–32.

6 On Charpentier see Frédéric Barbier and Catherine Bertho-Lavenir, *Histoire des médias: de Diderot à Internet* (Paris, 1996), 81–82.

7 *Ibid.*, 82–83. Elisabeth Parinet, *Une historie de l'édition à l'époque contemporaine (xixe–xxe siècle)* (Paris, 2004). Martyn Lyons, *Le Triomphe du livre: une histoire sociologique de la lecture dans la France du xixe siècle*, traduit de l'anglais (Paris, 1987). I have not consulted the recently published English text: *Readers and Society in Nineteenth-Century France* (Basingstoke and New York, 2001)

8 Kenneth Hudson, *A Social History of the Museum: What the Visitors Thought* (Atlantic Highlands, NJ, 1974), 3–6.

9 Andrew McClellan, *Inventing the Louvre: Art, Politics, and the Origins of the Modern Museum in Eighteenth-Century Paris* (Cambridge and New York, 1994).

10 *Ibid.*, 91–99.

11 *Ibid.*, 135–49.

12 The French critic was the Comte de Caylus, a close friend of Watteau, quoted by Jean Starobinski, *The Invention of Liberty, 1700–89*, trans. Bernard C. Swift (New York, 1987), 57. For the German artists see Dieter Hein, "Bürgerliches Künstlertum. Zum Verhältnis von Künstlern und Bürgern auf dem Weg in der Moderne," in *Bürgerkultur im 19ten. Jahrhundert. Bildung, Kunst und Lebenswelt*, ed. Dieter Hein and Andreas Schulz (Munich, 1996) 104, 108. For the English societies and for Théodore Rousseau's agitation for similar groupings in Paris see Robert Jensen, *Marketing Modernism in Fin-de-Siècle Europe* (Princeton, 1994), 83–86.

13 I called attention to Saint-Cheron's position in *Bohemian Paris: Culture, Politics, and the Boundaries of Bourgeois Life* (New York, 1986; reprinted Baltimore, 1999), 14–15.

14 For Duret's and Renoir's comments and for Sylvestre, see *Bohemian Paris*, 306–07, where the sources are cited. I also discuss Courbet there. For the new activities of art dealers, especially Paul Durand-Ruel, see Harrison C. White and Cynthia A. White, *Canvasses and Careers: Institutional Change in the French Painting World* (New York, 1965; new edn., Chicago, 1993).

15 For the role of dealers in the "Secession" movements of the 1890s, see Robert Jensen, *Marketing Modernism in Fin-de-Siècle Europe* (Princeton, 1994).

16 Carl Dahlhaus, *Nineteenth-Century Music*, trans. J. Bradford Robinson (Berkeley and Los Angeles, 1989), 22–24. Dahlhaus emphasizes the role Beethoven's admirers played, after his death in 1827, in solidifying the idea of a core "classical" repertoire, but the notion was certainly given importance earlier; see Lydia Goehr, *The Imaginary Museum of Musical Works* (rev. edn., Oxford and New York, 2007), 245–46. See also Tim Blanning, *The Triumph of Music: the Rise of Composers, Musicians, and their Art* (Cambridge, MA, 2008), 111–14.

17 William Weber, *Music and the Middle Classes: the Social Structure of Concert Life in London, Paris, and Vienna* (London, 1975); see the table on 159. James Johnson, *Listening in Paris: a Cultural History* (Berkeley and Los Angeles, 1995), esp. ch. 11, "The Birth of Public Concerts," and 257 for the comment from the *Journal des débats*. Ute Daniel, "Vom fürstlichen Gast zum Konsumenten. Das Hoftheaterpublikum in Deutschland vom 18. zum 19. Jahrhundert," in *Le Concert et son public: mutations de la vie musicale en Europe de 1780 à 1914 (France, Allemagne, Angleterre)*, ed. Hans Erich Bödeker, Patrice Veit, Michael Werner Julia Kraus, Dominique Lassaigne, and Ingeborg Allihn (Paris, 2002), 347–86. Blanning notes a

spread of public concerts in eighteenth-century Germany and properly
locates it chiefly in the context of princely *Residenzstädte* and their often
aristocratic officials. *The Triumph of Music*, 85–89. For contemporary
observations on the importance of private musical settings in Germany
still in the 1840s, see the very interesting comments of the young Richard
Wagner, in *Wagner Writes from Paris: Stories, Essays, and Articles by the
Young Composer*, ed. and trans. Geoffrey Skelton and Robert Louis Jacobs
(New York, 1973).

18 McVeigh, "The Musician as concert promoter," in *Le Concert et son
public*, 76. "Benefits" were a common feature of theater productions
in the same period; some of them are described by Dickens in *Nicholas
Nickelby*.

19 On the promenade concerts see Weber, *Music and the Middle Classses*,
109ff. For Chopin see Dahlhaus, *Nineteenth-Century Music*, 63. On the
Paris Opera see Henry Raynor, *Music and Society Since 1815* (New York,
1976), 80–81. Weber provides a good account of the overall transition, but
I think he gives too much significance to the pleasure Liszt expressed in a
letter about the increase in "my originally tiny capital" brought by one of his
tours (132): he had no intention of investing the money to make more, and in
the more general sense he employed "capital" has little or nothing to do with
"capitalist enterprise."

20 For these numbers, Arthur Loesser, *Men, Women and Pianos: a Social
History* (New York, 1954), 251–52. For the development of printing see
the account in H. Edmund Poole and Donald W. Krummel, "Printing and
Publishing of Music," *The New Grove Dictionary of Music and Musicians*,
ed. Stanley Sadie (London and New York, 1980), xv, 243ff. The quotation
from the first volume of the Musical Library appears there, 247; it went on:
"before this work appeared, the exorbitant sums demanded for engraved
music amounted to a prohibition of its free circulation among the middle
classes; at a time too when the most enlightened statesmen saw distinctly
the policy of promoting the cultivation of the art in almost every class of
society." For the importance of Haydn in the development of publishing
at the end of the eighteenth century see Blanning, *The Triumph of Music*,
18–21.

21 Gunilla-Frederike Budde, *Auf dem Weg ins Bürgerleben: Kindheit und
Erziehung in deutschen und englischen Bürgerfamilien, 1840–1914*
(Göttingen, 1994), 136–42. Much of this material can also be found in her
article, "Musik in Bürgerhäusern," in *Le Concert et son public*, 427–58.
Dahlhaus, *Nineteenth-Century Music*, 49, 116–17. For information about
piano makers and the music collections see Loesser, *Men, Women, and
Pianos*. There is an interesting account of the Jewish "love affair with the

piano" in Marion A. Kaplan, *The Making of the Jewish Middle Class: Women, Family, and Identity in Imperial Germany* (New York and Oxford, 1991), 121–22.

22 For the early organization of concerts see Simon McVeigh, "The musician as concert-promoter in London, 1780–1850," in *Le Concert et son public*, 71–89, and William Weber, "The origin of the concert agent in the social structure of concert life," in the same volume, 134. Blanning gives a lively and interesting account of the concerts Johann Peter Salomon organized for Haydn in London, and the importance of this public exposure for Haydn's career, *The Triumph of Music*, 18–30, but Salomon's activities were mostly limited to London, he was only a partial precursor of the later impresarios. Johann Nepomuk Hummel organized his own concert tour in London in 1825. See Weber, "From the Self-Managing Musician to the Independent Concert Agent," in his edited volume *The Musician as Entrepreneur, 1700–1914: Managers, Charlatans and Idealists* (Bloomington and Indianapolis, 2004), 105–29; 109–10 for Hummel, and 117 for the quote.

23 Simon Gunn, *The Public Culture of the Victorian Middle Class: Ritual and Authority and the English Industrial City, 1840–1914* (Manchester and New York, 2000), 135–49. For reasons I will try to explain later on, I have not given this story the coloration Gunn does based on the perspective he shares with Pierre Bourdieu.

24 Georg Simmel, *The Philosophy of Money*, ed. David Frisby, trans. Tom Bottomore and David Frisby from a first draft by Kaethe Mengelberg, 2nd edn. (London and New York, 1990), 291.

25 M. H. Abrams, "Art as Such: the Sociology of Modern Aesthetics," in *Doing Things with Texts: Essays in Criticism and Critical Theory*, ed. Michael Fischer (New York and London, 1989), 113–34.

26 See Weber, "The Aesthetic Sphere," in "Religious Rejections of the World and their Directions," in *From Max Weber: Essays in Sociology*, trans. and ed. By H. H. Gerth and C. Wright Mills (New York, 1946), 340–43. Richard Wolin, *The Terms of Cultural Criticism: The Frankfurt School, Existentialism, Poststructuralism* (New York, 1992), 66.

27 Lydia Goehr, *The Imaginary Museum of Musical Works* (rev. edn., Oxford and New York, 2007), 1–2 on Hoffmann; for earlier eighteenth-century approaches to this notion see her references to Bach and Couperin, 28–29. Rossini was unhappy with the liberties taken by performers of his music, and Mendelssohn gave instructions to performers intended to bring out the unity of his works (240). See also Blanning, *The Triumph of Music*, 111–14.

28 Quoted by Detlef Hoffmann, "The German Art Museum and the History of the Nation," in *Museum Culture: Histories, Discourses, Spectacles*, ed. Daniel J. Sherman and Irit Rogoff (Minneapolis, 1994), 6.

29 Denis Diderot, "Eloge de Richardson," in *Oeuvres, IV: Esthétique–Théatre*, ed. Laurent Versini (Paris, 1996), 157–58. Jean Starobinski, "'Se mettre à la place': la mutation de la critique de l'âge classique à Diderot," *Cahiers Vilfredo Pareto* 38–39 (1976), 363–78.

30 Thomas W. Laqueur, *Solitary Sex: a Cultural History of Masturbation* (New York, 2003), 210. For the quotation from Goethe, see *Wilhelm Meister's Apprenticeship*, ed. and trans. Eric A. Blackall in cooperation with Victor Lange (New York, 1989), 248.

31 Isabel V. Hull, *Sexuality, State and Civil Society in Germany, 1700–1815* (Ithaca and London, 1996), 274.

32 *Ibid.*, 261–62. Laqueur makes this point too; see the reference just below. I discuss letters between readers and writers in *The Idea of the Self*, ch. 7. For other literature about it, see above, Chapter 10, n. 12.

33 Laqueur, *Solitary Sex*, 311–12. For a stronger emphasis on the importance of public discussion in creating the masturbation panic, and the ways in which it revealed anxieties on this score that would grow during the nineteenth century, see Roy Porter and Lesley Hall, *The Facts of Life: the Creation of Sexual Knowledge in Britain, 1650–1950* (New Haven and London, 1995), ch. 4.

34 The French circular is quoted in Barbier and Bertho-Lavenir, *Histoire des médias: de Diderot à Internet*, 122. On the whole history of postal relations see Yves Maxime Danan, *Histoire postale et libertés publiques: le droit de libre communication des idées et opinions par voie de correspondance* (Paris, 1965). A recent general account of the coming of the penny post and its effects is Catherine J. Golden, *Posting It: the Victorian Revolution in Letter Writing* (Gaineseville, FL, 2009). For the limited impact of the penny post outside the middle classes in England and the much greater importance of the post card, see David Vincent, *Literacy and Popular Culture: England 1750–1914* (Cambridge and New York, 1989), esp. 43ff. and 276. In France the number of letters exchanged in 1876 had not risen much from 1847 (the only dates with enough information to allow for comparison), but exploded before and during the world war. See Cécile Dauphin *et al.*, "L'Enquête postale de 1847," in *La Correspondance: les usages de la lettre au XIXe siècle*, ed. Roger Chartier (Paris, 1991), 57–60.

35 Cécile Dauphin, "Les Manuels épistolaires au xixe siècle," in *La Correspondance*, 238. For a similar point see also Roger Charter, "Des secrétaires pour le peuple?" in the same volume, 198–203.

36 Marie-Claire Grassi, "La Correspondance comme discours du privé au XVIIIè Siècle," in *L'Épistolarité à travers les siecles*, ed. Mireille Bossis and Charles A. Porter (Stuttgart, 1990), 180–83.

37 Michelle Perrot in *From the Fires of Revolution to the Great War: a History of Private Life*, IV, trans. Arthur Goldhammer (Cambridge, MA, 1990), 132. For an example of such a reticence see Marie Dolle-Ollier, "Les Silences

de la correspondance de Victor Segalen," in *Les Écritures de l'intime: la correspondance et le journal*, Actes du colloque de Brest, October 23–25, 1997, ed. Pierre-Jean Dufief (Paris, 2000), 139–48.

38 Cited in Jean-Michel Gaillard, *Jules Ferry* (Paris, 1989), 38–39. For similar examples of highly emotional language in letters between siblings and cousins see Christopher H. Johnson's articles, "Das Geschwister Archipel: Brüder-Schwester-Liebe und Klassenformation im Frankreich des 19. Jahrhunderts," *L'Homme. Zeitschift für feministische Geschichtswissenschaft* 13:1 (2002), 50–67; and "Kinship, Civil Society, and Power in Nineteenth-Century Vannes," unpublished paper.

39 Christine Planté "L'Intime comme valeur publique,"in *La Lettre à la croisée de l'individuel et du social*, ed. Mireille Bossis (Paris, 1994), esp. 87–89.

40 James Johnson, *Listening in Paris: a Cultural History* (Berkeley and Los Angeles, 1995), parts I and II.

41 For Ella, McVeigh, "Musician as Concert promoter," 83. Simon Gunn, *The Public Culture of the Victorian Middle Class*, 138–48; the quoted passage, 146. For the United States, Lawrence W. Levine, *Highbrow/Lowbrow: the Emergence of Cultural Hierarchy in America* (Cambridge, MA, and London, 1988), 186–95. I think, however, that Levine's description of conductors' intentions as "to render audiences docile" (189) understates the degree to which numbers of listeners themselves were part of the campaign, in America as well as in Europe, as Levine himself recognizes in other connections. I will return to the question of how this shift affected the relations between "popular" and "high" culture in Chapter 13.

42 Johnson, *Listening in Paris*, 228–29, 231–33.

43 Raynor, 74. Edward Rothstein, "Connections: Orchestras Still Preserve the Myths, but Who Cares Now?" in the *New York Times*, February 10, 2001. Gunn, *The Public Culture of the Victorian Middle Class,* 150.

44 Dahlhaus, *Nineteenth-Century Music*, 93, 51. Dahlhaus finds this attitude toward listening emerging in the 1790s, the decade in which Haydn wrote his final symphonies, in London. Like Gluck's operas they were praised for their ability to evoke and represent feeling and by early in the nineteenth century his compositions would be increasingly re-evaluated as "pure music," generated from their own internal elements. Important features of Haydn's work always marked it as generated by the relations between its own motivic elements, despite the external references it sometimes announced; see Pierre Barbaud, *Haydn*, trans. Kathrine Sorley Walker (New York and London, 1959). For his public re-evaluation in this direction, Johnson, *Listening in Paris*, 271. Peter Gay, *The Naked Heart* (New York, 1995), 15–19.

45 Gay, *The Naked Heart*, 26–28. Just how far we should recognize the presence of Beethoven's special personality, with its vulnerabilities, idiosyncrasies, and obsessions in his music has been a matter of debate. The best account I know that seeks to preserve the independence of Beethoven's creative power while still recognizing how closely it was tied to his peculiar individuality (much in the manner Kant had in mind) is Lewis Lockwood, *Beethoven: the Music and the Life* (New York and London, 2003), where the issue is explicitly discussed, 15–21. See also his discussion of Beethoven and Wackenröder, 172–73.

46 Budde, *Auf dem Weg ins Bürgerleben*, 142. For the individuality of responses recognized from late in the eighteenth century, see Johnson, *Listening*, 272–74. Gunn notes that in Manchester the inner and suggestive nature of music was given emphasis in concert programs, but that collective self-absorption was to take precedence over individual displays of emotion.

47 John Toews, *Becoming Historical: Cultural Reformation and Public Memory in Nineteenth-Century Berlin* (Cambridge and New York, 2004), 212. Gay, *The Naked Heart*, 23.

48 Thomas Mann, *Buddenbrooks. The Decline of a Family*, trans. John E. Woods (New York, 1993), 495, 716.

13 Bourgeois and others

1 Kenneth Hudson, *A Social History of the Museum: What the Visitors Thought* (Atlantic Highlands, NJ, 1974), 4, 15. Andrew McClellan, *Inventing the Louvre: Art, Politics, and the Origins of the Modern Museum in Eighteenth-Century Paris* (Cambridge and New York, 1994), 7–8.

2 McClellan, *Inventing the Louvre*, 9–12.

3 Pierre Bourdieu, *La Distinction: critique sociale du jugement* (Paris, 1979), trans. by Richard Nice as *Distinction: a Social Critique of the Judgment of Taste* (Cambridge, MA, 1984). Among those who have applied his views to the history of museums are Nick Prior, "Museums: Leisure between State and Distinction," in *Histories of Leisure*, ed. Rudy Koshar (Oxford and New York, 2002), 27–44, and Daniel J. Sherman, *Worthy Monuments: Art Museums and the Politics of Culture in Nineteenth-Century France* (Cambridge, MA, and London, 1989), although both offer materials that can be employed to support a different reading.

4 Seth Koven, "The Whitechapel Picture Exhibitions and the Politics of Seeing," in *Museum Culture: Histories, Discourses, Spectacles*, ed. Daniel J. Sherman and Irit Rogoff (Minneapolis, 1994), 22–46.

5 Lawrence W. Levine, *Highbrow/Lowbrow: the Emergence of Cultural Hierarchy in America* (Cambridge, MA, and London, 1988), 203–08 for the quoted passages.

6 Thomas Bender, *The Unfinished City: New York and the Metropolitan Idea* (New York, 2002), 97–99. Joseph Horowitz, *Wagner Nights: an American History* (Berkeley and Los Angeles, 1994), esp. 322–24, 210–11.

7 See Bourdieu, *La Distinction*, cited above, and the literature noted just above, n. 3.

8 Georg Simmel, *The Philosophy of Money*, ed. David Frisby, trans. Tom Bottomore and David Frisby from a first draft by Kaethe Mengelberg, 2nd edn. (London and New York, 1990), 439–40, 442. The translation they give, however, does not quite convey the German text, which reads: "Die scheinbare Gleichheit, mit der sich der Bildungsstoff jedem bietet, der ihn ergreifen will..." (*Philosophie des Geldes*, 2nd edn., Leipzig, 1907, 493).

9 *Ibid.* (English version), 291.

10 See the discussion of cultural goods in Yochai Benkler, *The Wealth of Networks: How Social Production Transforms Marekts and Freedom* (New Haven and London, 2006), 36–37. I will return to some of the issues that arise from this notion, and that Benkler treats, in the Conclusion.

11 Jonathan Rose, *The Intellectual Life of the British Working Classes* (New Haven and London, 2001).

12 Coombes is quoted by Christopher Hilliard, *To Exercise Our Talents: the Democratization of Writing in Britain* (Cambridge, MA, and London, 2006), 2.

13 Daumard, *Les Bourgeois et la bourgeoisie en France*, 33–34.

14 Angelika Linke, "Zum Sprachgebrauch des Bürgertums im 19. Jahrhundert. Überlegungen zur kultursemiotischen Funktion des Sprachverhaltens," in Rainer Wimmer, ed., *Das 19. Jahrhundert: Sprachgeschichtliche Würzeln des heutigen Deutsch* (Berlin and New York, 1991), 250–81; 255 for the quotation and the reference to Simmel.

15 K. C. Phillipps, *Language and Class in Victorian England* (London and New York, 1984), 67–70. The quotation from *Middlemarch* comes from ch. 56.

16 Basil Bernstein, *Class, Codes and Control*, vol. 1: *Theoretical Studies Towards a Sociology of Language* (London, 1971), 108. Meredith is quoted by Phillipps, *Language and Class in Victorian England*, 36–37, who applies the description to aristocrats as well.

17 The passage is quoted from M. E. Loane, *The Next Street but One* (London, 1907), ch. 1, by Phillipps, *Language and Class in Victorian England*, 81. Loane wrote a number of books about working-class life before World War I.

18 For Germany see Vernon Lidtke, *The Alternative Culture. Socialist Labor in Imperial Germany* (New York, 1985).

19 David Vincent, *Literacy and Popular Culture: England 1750–1914* (Cambridge and New York, 1989), 14–15, 273–74, 279. Deborah Reed-Danahay, *Education and Identity in Rural France* (Cambridge and New York, 1996). Phillipps notes (88) that in 1888 a report to the English Dialect Society said that children sent to the new schools set up by the Education Act of 1870 were learning correct grammar and pronunciation there and could use it at home but seldom did, reverting to the speech of their parents "at home and among [their] fellows." On the basis of the analysis he offers, Vincent comes to a conclusion about working-class intellectuals somewhat at odds with the one toward which Jonathan Rose works in the book cited just above: "The reciprocal relationships between individual and collective inquiry, between books and deprivation, and between literary and oral communication ensured that the working-class intellectual was unable to abstract himself completely from the lives of those with whom he lived and worked" (263). For a critique of the longstanding notion that the Third Republic's schools were hostile to popular culture and language, see Jean-François Chanet, *L'École républicaine et les petites patries*, Préface de Mona Ozouf (Paris, 1996).

20 A point developed in a too rigidly theoretical way but with much interesting information by Jochen Schulte-Sasse, "High/Low and Other Dichotomies," in *High and Low Cultures: German Attempts at Mediation*, ed. Reinhod Grimm and Jost Hermand (Madison, WI, 1994), 3–18.

21 There were, to be sure, popular novels and writers known for producing them earlier, but the subject matter was usually quite different, often involving upper-class characters and milieus; their appeal was more like that of the popular letter collections discussed in Chapter 12, and the audience was much narrower, given the lower level of literacy in society as a whole. For one interesting account, see Richard Switzer, *Étienne-Léon de Lamothe-Langon et le roman populaire Français de 1800 à 1830* (Toulouse, 1962).

22 Christopher Hilliard, *To Exercise our Talents: the Democratization of Writing in Britain* (Cambridge, MA and London, 2006), ch. 1. Some publishers had used readers earlier, but their numbers expanded in the *fin-de-siècle*: William St Clair, *The Reading Nation in the Romantic Period*, 160.

23 Anne-Marie Thiesse, *Le Roman du quotidien. Lecteurs et lectures populaires à la belle époque* (Paris, 1984).

24 Jean-Yves Mollier, "Le Parfum de la belle époque," in *La Culture de masse en France de la belle époque à aujourd'hui*, ed. Jean-Pierre Rioux and Jean-François Sirinelli (Paris, 2002), 72–115. Michael Beaussenat Palmer, *Des Petits Journaux aux grandes agences: naissance du journalisme*

moderne, 1863–1914 (Paris, 1983). *Le Fait divers*, catalogue of the exhibition held at the Musée national des arts et traditions populaires, November 19, 1982 to April 18, 1983, by Alain Monestier and Jacques Cheyronnaud (Paris, 1982). Edward Berenson, *The Trial of Madame Caillaux* (Berkeley and Los Angeles, 1992), ch. 6. Vanessa R. Schwartz, *Spectacular Realities: Early Mass Culture in Fin-de-Siècle Paris* (Berkeley and Los Angeles, 1998), ch. 1.

25 Peter Fritzsche, *Reading Berlin 1900* (Cambridge, MA, and London, 1996), esp. 59–86.

26 See Terry Pinkard, *Hegel: a Biography* (Cambridge and New York, 2001), 242. Fritzsche emphasizes this change, *Reading Berlin 1900*, 59.

27 As it promised in the prospectus published in the paper's first number, November 25, 1825, although the editors recognized the emotional kinship of its *reportage* with what readers sought in fiction.

28 For an insightful recent account of this interest see Edward Berenson, *Heroes of Empire: Five Charismatic Men and the Conquest of Africa* (Berkeley and Los Angeles, 2010).

29 Schwartz, *Spectacular Realities*, 26, 30.

30 Fritzsche, *Reading Berlin 1900*, 212.

31 See *ibid.*, 73, 130. That workers were in some sense "depoliticized" by such involvements may be true in a way, but we need to guard against preserving the questionable assumption that to be politicized must be the natural state or destiny of workers, rather than one among varied and diverse possibilities.

32 The best comprehensive history of the early French cinema is Richard Abel, *The Ciné goes to Town: French Cinema 1896–1914* (Berkeley and Los Angeles, 1994), see xiv–xv for the distinction between the two phases in early cinema history. Peter Jelavich, "'Darf ich mich hier amüsieren?' Bürgertum und früher Film," in *Der bürgerliche Wertehimmel*, ed. Manfred Hettling und Stefan-Ludwig Hoffman, (Göttingen, 2000), 282–303 (in English in *Germany at the fin de siècle: culture, politics, and ideas*, ed. Suzanne Marchand and David Lindenfeld (Baton Rouge, LA, 2004), 227–49. Christophe Prochasson, "De la culture des foules à la culture des masses," in *Choix culturels et memoire*, vol. III of *Histoire de la France*, ed. André Burguière and Jacques Revel (Paris, 1993; paper edn., 2000), 183–232, where Gide is quoted on 211. For relations between intellectuals and movies in Germany see Adelheid von Saldern, "Popular Culture: an Immense Challenge in the Weimar Republic," in *The Challenge of Modernity: German Social and Cultural Studies, 1890–1960*, trans. Bruce Little (Ann Arbor, 2002), 278–79.

33 Christian-Marc Bosséno, "Le Répertoire du grand écran: le cinéma 'par ailleurs'" in *La Culture de masse en France de la belle époque à*

aujourd'hui, ed. Jean-Pierre Rioux and Jean-François Sirinelli (Paris, 2002), 157–219, as well as the article of Jean-Yves Mollier already cited from the same volume. There is much more detail in Richard Abel's account cited in the previous note.

34 For a good summary see Ludovic Tournès, "Reproduire l'oeuvre: la nouvelle économie musicale," in *La Culture de masse en France*, 220–58. On the provincial music halls see Charles Rearick, *Pleasures of the Belle Epoque: Entertainments and Festivity in Turn-of-the-Century France* (New Haven and London, 1985), 94.

35 Lenard R. Berlanstein, *The Working People of Paris, 1871–1914* (Baltimore and London, 1984), 134.

36 This paragraph summarizes the account of the cabarets I give in *Bohemian Paris*, ch. 8.

37 This account of Bruant draws on the longer one in *Bohemian Paris*, 235–39, where more attention is paid to the strictly political side of his career.

38 Ludovic Tournès, "Reproduire l'oeuvre: la nouvelle économie musicale," in *La Culture de masse en France*, 220–58.

39 Mollier, "Le Parfum de la belle époque," 89–90.

40 David Blackbourn, *History of Germany*, 296–300.

41 In addition to Blackbourn, see Saldern, "Popular Culture," cited above. On the Heinze Law see Peter Jelavich, *Munich and Theatrical Modernism: Politics, Playwriting, and Performance* (Cambridge, MA, 1985), 141–42. For France see Philip Nord, *France's New Deal: from the Thirties to the Postwar Era* (Princeton and Oxford, 2010), ch. 4.

42 Saldern's conclusion, "Popular Culture," 295–97. But I think she is wrong on the basis of her own evidence to attribute confusion and uncertainty only or chiefly to bourgeois figures and circles: Benjamin was at least as deluded. For a similar and earlier caution about attributing too much power to popular culture from a figure who was an acute critic of it, see Richard Hoggart, *The Uses of Literacy* (London, 1957, and later edns.), 131, 250–51.

43 Michel de Certeau, *L'Invention du quotidien*, I: *arts de faire* (Paris, 1980), trans. by Stephen Rendall as *The Practice of Everyday Life* (Berkeley and Los Angeles, 1984).

14 Bourgeois life and the avant-garde

1 *Manifesto of the Communist Party*, in Marx and Engels, *Selected Works in One Volume* (New York, 1968), 38.

2 G. W. F. Hegel, *The Philosophy of Right*, trans. T. M. Knox (Oxford, 1952), para. 247, p. 151.

3 Adam Ferguson, *An Essay on the History of Civil Society*, 4th edn., London, 1773 [1st edn., 1767], 15, 12.

4 *Ibid.*, 67–68. Cf. also 81: Happiness "arises more from the pursuit, than from the attainment of any end whatever … it depends more on the degree in which our minds are properly employed, than it does on the circumstances in which we are destined to act, on the materials which are placed in our hands, or the tools with which we are furnished." Adam Smith *The Theory of Moral Sentiments*, ed. D. D. Raphael and A. L. Macfie (reprint of the Glasgow edn. of Smith's Works, Indianapolis, 1984), IV:i, 10; 183. The kinship with which W.H. Riehl's view of what modern society *bürgerlich* should also be noted.

5 Breton's appreciation of Duchamp can be found in *The Dada Painters and Poets*, ed. Robert Motherwell (New York, 1951), 209–11; there is an abridged version in *The Autobiography of Surrealism*, ed. Marcel Jean (New York, 1980), 84–86. I have substituted "crab-apple tree" for the "manchineel tree" of the original in the hope of making the meaning more evident.

6 Colin Campbell, *The Romantic Ethic and the Spirit of Modern Consumerism* (Oxford, 1987), 88–89.

7 Rosalind H. Williams, *Dream Worlds: Mass Consumption in Late Nineteenth-Century France* (Berkeley and Los Angeles, 1982). For Huysmans, see ch. 4. Breton's comment on Picasso is quoted by Mary Ann Caws, *André Breton* (New York, 1971), 46. This whole range of issues and the ties they create between the avant-garde and modern commerce is simply ignored by a recent book whose contrast with the perspective adopted here is indicated in its title, Walter L. Adamson's *Embattled Avant-Gardes: Modernism's Resistance to Commodity Culture in Europe* (Berkeley and Los Angeles, 2007). That particular vanguard figures felt alienated from "materialist" consumerism and from what Adamson calls "marketplace logic" is true enough, but artists' resistance to the commodification of their work, apart from being an old story (and one in which significant figures did not participate, as noted in Chapter 12), closes off access to the kinds of continuities between bourgeois activities and the creative impulses they helped let loose of which all the writers just discussed, including Marx, were powerfully aware.

8 This discussion of bohemia draws on and summarizes what I wrote in *Bohemian Paris: Culture, Politics, and the Boundaries of Bourgeois Life* (New York, 1986; reprinted Baltimore, 1999). For Vigny and Pyat see 15–18. For an eighteenth-century example see Anne-Gédéon Lafitte, *The Bohemians*, trans. Vivian Folkenflik, with an introduction by Robert Darnton (State College, PA, 2009).

9 *Magasin pittoresque* XVIII (1851), 893–94; cf. *Bohemian Paris*, 24–25.

10 The paragraphs that follow summarize my account of Murger in *Bohemian Paris*, Chapter 2, where sources are given for all the quotations.

11 Perhaps still the best account of these themes in Mann's life and work is T. J. Reed, *Thomas Mann and the Uses of Tradition* (Oxford, 1974, 2nd edn., 1998), where the quotation about hunger and the real appears on 102.

12 *Buddenbrooks*, trans. John E. Woods (New York, 1993), 10–11, 92, 258–59.

13 *Ibid.*, 219, 223.

14 Quoted in Reed, *Thomas Mann and the Uses of Tradition*, 112–13.

15 *Ibid.*, 526.

16 See Robert Jensen, *Marketing Modernism in Fin-de-Siècle Europe* (Princeton, 1994), chs. 2 and 6, discussed above in Chapter 12.

17 Leo Steinberg, "Contemporary Art and the Plight of Its Public," in *Other Criteria: Confrontations with Twentieth-Century Art* (New York, 1972), 3–16. Gautier's comment appeared in *Le Moniteur universel*, May 11, 1868, quoted in F. W. J. Hemmings, *Culture and Society in France, 1848–98* (New York, 1971), 177, and by Francis Haskell, "Enemies of Modern Art," *The New York Review of Books*, June 30, 1983, 19. Laforgue's comment appears in translation in Barbara Ehrlich White, ed., *Impressionism in Perspective* (Englewood Cliffs, NJ, 1978), 34. I discuss *L'Oeuvre* in *Bohemian Paris*, 303–05.

18 Robert Jensen, *Marketing Modernism in Fin-de-Siècle Europe* (Princeton, 1994), ch. 5; quotations on 139 and 149–50.

19 Robert L. Herbert, *Impressionism: Art, Leisure, and Parisian Society* (New Haven and London, 1988), 96–98 and *passim*.

20 My account of Degas's New Orleans pictures takes much information from Marilyn R. Brown's valuable study, *Degas and the Business of Art: a Cotton Office in New Orleans* (University Park, PA, 1994), although I disagree with many of its assertions. The letter quoted here appears on 17. There is a slightly different translation in the catalogue of the exhibit held at the Metropolitan Museum of Art in 1974–75, *Impressionism: a Centenary Exhibition*, ed. Anne Dayez, 99. There is also much information about the Degas family and the picture in Christopher Benfey, *Degas in New Orleans* (New York, 1997).

21 Zola's comment is quoted here from the Centenary Exhibition catalogue, 101–02; it appears also in Brown, 70, who also cites Duranty's comment, 77 (I have slightly altered the translation).

22 Herbert, 52–53.

23 Brown, *Degas and the Business of Art*, 16–17; Herbert, *Impressionism*, 56–57. On Agnew and Manchester interest in painting more generally, see Diane Sachko Macleod, *Art and the Victorian Middle Class: Money and the Making of Cultural Identity* (Cambridge, 1996). Peter Gay also discusses

these matters at length in *Pleasure Wars* (New York, 1998); see 75–90 on Manchester.

24 See Brown, 34–36, and Charles S. Aiken, *The Cotton Plantation South since the Civil War* (Baltimore, 2003). Brown emphasizes the difficulties of the Musson firm, which was liquidated in 1873, even proposing that René may be reading about is end in the paper. This is mere speculation, and imposes a narrowing perspective to boot, and her notion that the firm's difficulties had to do with the Panic of 1873 is questionable since the liquidation took place in March and the Panic only broke out in September. Because the new firm Musson formed took over the old one's debts, the old one was not bankrupt. All the same Musson may have had difficulty adjusting to the new conditions; that he never quite recovered the position he held earlier makes his history parallel to the one Mann ascribes to his fictional family at the same time in *Buddenbrooks*, but without the patina of "decadence" Mann attached to it.

25 Herbert, *Impressionism*, ch. 1.

26 See above, Chapter 6.

27 Herbert, *Impressionism*, 28–29.

28 *Ibid.*, 19–23 for Caillebotte; 24–27 for Monet. I do not know whether Herbert would accept the last sentence of this paragraph.

29 Baudelaire, "The Painter of Modern Life," in *Selected Writings on Art and Artists*, trans P. E. Charvet (Harmondsworth and Baltimore, 1972), 390–93. For his comments on Murger's bohemia see the preface to Leon Cladel's anti-bohemian novel *Les Martyrs ridicules* (1861), in Baudelaire *L'Art romantique*, ed. L. J. Austin (Paris, 1968), 354–55, 362. *Mon coeur mis à nu*, ed. Beatrice Dedier (Paris, 1972), 127. I discuss these features of Baudelaire's career in *Bohemian Paris*, ch. 4.

30 *Mon coeur mis à nu*, 45. Baudelaire, "L'Art philosophique," in *L'Art romantique* (Paris, 1925; part of the *Oeuvres complètes de Charles Baudelaire*, ed. Jacques Crepet, not the volume of the same title cited just above), 119.

31 The letters are conveniently available in Rimbaud, *Complete Works, Selected Letters*, trans. and ed. Wallace Fowlie (Chicago and London, 1966), 302–10. Rimbaud's comments on his state of mind can be found in *A Season in Hell [and] The Illuminations*, trans. Edith Rhodes Peschel (London and New York, 1973), 70, 80, 86. On this aspect of Rimbaud's career the comments of Yves Bonnefoy remain invaluable: *Rimbaud*, trans. Paul Schmidt (New York, 1973), esp. 43.

32 Carl E. Schorske, *Fin-de-siècle Vienna: Politics and Culture* (New York, 1980), 211–12, 227–28.

33 For the interest in Schopenhauer and Nietzsche in Vienna, see William J. McGrath, *Dionysian Art and Populist Politics in Austria* (New Haven, 1974). I discuss both thinkers in *The Idea of the Self* (Cambridge and

New York, 2005), ch. 16. Schorske's account of Klimt's career, for all its
illuminating insight, fails to recognize how much the aggression given vent
in these images was directed against the expanded and more professionalized
University as a representative of the "scientific" culture from which
Schopenhauer and Nietzsche also felt alienated, and not against bourgeois
life more generally, with parts of which he always retained close ties.

34 Schorske, *Fin-de-siècle Vienna*, 217, 222. Peter Vergo, *Art in Vienna,
1898–1918: Klimt, Kokoschka, Schiele and Their Contemporaries* (Ithaca,
NY, 1981), 198.

35 Louis Aragon, *Le Paysan de Paris* (Gallimard, 1953), 145 for the last
quotation, 135–36 for the other ones in this paragraph, 81–82 and 109–11
for the previous paragraph. There is an English translation by Simon Watson
Taylor, *Paris Peasant* (London, 1971, reissued Boston, 1994), some of whose
renderings I have used in the previous paragraph, but it is often unreliable.

36 Dieter Hein, "Bürgerliches Künstlertum. Zum Verhältnis von Kunstlern und
Bürgern auf dem Weg in die Moderne," in *Bürgerkultur im 19. Jahrhundert.
Bildung, Kunst und Lebenswelt*, ed. Hein and Andreas Schulz (Munich,
1996), 16–17.

37 For a much more extended analysis of Duchamp's career in these terms see
my book *The Private Worlds of Marcel Duchamp: Desire, Liberation and
the Self in Modern Culture* (Berkeley and Los Angeles, 1995).

15 Conclusion

1 That this is true of states, despite prophecies of their waning importance,
as well as markets and the Internet, has been persuasively argued by Saskia
Sassen, *Losing Control? Sovereignty in an Age of Globalization* (New
York, 1996) and *Territory, Authority, Rights: from Medieval to Global
Assemblages* (Princeton, 2006).

2 See above, Chapter 9.

3 Charles Sabel and Jonathan Zeitlin, "Historical Alternatives to
Mass Production: Politics, Markets and Technology in 19th-Century
Industrialization," *Past and Present*, 108 (August, 1985), 133–76. Joel
Mokyr, *The Gifts of Athena: Historical Origins of the Knowledge Economy*
(Princeton and London, 2002).

4 Adam Smith, *An Inquiry into the Nature and Causes of the Wealth of
Nations*, ch. 1.

5 Quoted by Gilles Feyel, "Négoce et presse provinciale en France au 18e
siècle: méthodes et perspectives de recherches," in *Cultures et formations
négociantes dans l'Europe moderne*, ed. Franco Angiolini and Daniel Roche
(Paris, 1995), 448.

6 All the texts are cited, with references, in Yves Leclercq, *Le Réseau impossible*, 13–17.

7 Both quoted above in Chapter 13.

8 For the economics of information, and its bearing on the Internet, see Yochai Benkler, *The Wealth of Networks: How Social Production Transforms Markets and Freedom* (New Haven and London, 2006), ch. 2. The observations about the Internet here owe much to Benkler. However, I am less sanguine about its potential for democratization of life as a whole than is he.

9 For these features of the early history of printing see Adrian Johns, *The Nature of the Book* (Chicago and London, 1998). Robert Darnton cites the letter of Franceso Guarnerio quoted in the text in *The Case for Books: Past, Present, and Future* (New York, 2009), xiv-xv, and discusses the situation of early modern printing and the instability of information in ch. 2 of the same book.

10 Catherine Bertho, "Le Télégraphe à la conquête du monde," in Catherine Bertho, ed., *Histoire des télécommunications en France* (Paris, 1984), 18–26.

11 In addition to the article cited in the previous note, this paragraph and the previous one are based on the following: Frédéric Barbier and Catherine Bertho-Lavenir, *Histoire des médias: de Diderot à Internet* (Pairs, 1996); Menachem Blondheim, *News Over the Wires: the Telegraph and the Flow of Public Information in America* (Cambridge, MA, and London, 1994); Menachem Blondheim, "When Bad Things Happen to Good Technologies: Three Phases in the Diffusion and Perception of American Telegraphy," in *Technology, Pessmimism, and Postmodernism*, ed. Yaron Ezrahi *et al.* (Dordrecht, Boston, London, 1994), 77–92; and Iwin Rhys Morus, "'The Nervous System of Britain': Space, Time, and the Electric Telegraph in the Victorian Age," *British Journal for the History of Science* 33 (2000), 455–75 (although I think Rhys Morus gives too much emphasis to the theme of discipline and too little to the increased agency nineteenth-century people found in telegraphy).

12 There is an excellent short summary account of Otlet's project in Alex Wright, "The Web that Time Forgot," *New York Times*, June 17, 2008, F 1–3. Wright relies on the informative but obtuse and difficult work of W. Boyd Rayward, *The Universe of Information: the Work of Paul Otlet for Documentation and International Organization* (Moscow, 1975).

13 As mentioned above in Chapter 7.

14 See the general history of the Internet in Wikipedia.

15 Yochai Benkler, *The Wealth of Networks*, cited above in n. 8.

INDEX